Classroom Assessment

What Teachers Need to Know

W. James Popham
Professor Emeritus
University of California, Los Angeles

6159

KH

Director and Publisher: Kevin M. Davis
Content Producer: Janelle Rogers
Development Editor: Curtis B. Vickers
Media Project Manager: Lauren Carlson
Portfolio Management Assistant: Maria Feliberty
Executive Field Marketing Manager: Krista Clark
Executive Product Marketing Manager: Christopher Barry
Operations Specialist: Carol Melville
Cover Designer: Carie Keller
Cover Image: Maskot/Shutterstock/Offset
Full Service Project Management: Thistle Hill Publishing Services, LLC
Composition: SPi Global
Text Font: 9.5/13 Palatino LT Pro

Library of Congress Cataloging-in-Publication Data
Names: Popham, W. James, author.
Title: Classroom assessment : what teachers need to know / W. James Popham,
    Professor Emeritus, University of California, Los Angeles.
Description: Ninth edition. | New York, NY : Pearson, [2020] | Includes
    bibliographical references and index.
Identifiers: LCCN 2019013736| ISBN 9780135569108 (pbk.) | ISBN 0135569109
    (pbk.)
Subjects: LCSH: Educational tests and measurements. | Examinations—Design
    and construction. | Examinations—Validity.
Classification: LCC LB3051 .P6142 2020 | DDC 371.26—dc23
LC record available at https://lccn.loc.gov/2019013736

4 2020

ISBN-13: 978-0-13-556910-8
ISBN-10:   0-13-556910-9

10/20/20

For Sarah:
Former Teacher, Former Principal,
Current Colleague, Current and Future Spouse

About the Author

W. JAMES POPHAM has spent the bulk of his educational career as a teacher. His first teaching assignment, for example, was in a small eastern Oregon high school where he taught English and social studies while serving as yearbook advisor, class sponsor, and unpaid tennis coach. The recompense meshed well with the quality of his coaching.

Most of Dr. Popham's teaching career took place at UCLA where, for nearly 30 years, he taught courses in instructional methods for prospective teachers as well as courses in evaluation and measurement for graduate students. At UCLA he won several distinguished teaching awards. In January 2000, he was recognized by *UCLA Today* as one of the university's top 20 professors of the twentieth century. (He notes that the twentieth century was a full-length century, unlike the current abbreviated one.) In 1992, he took early retirement from UCLA upon learning that emeritus professors received free parking.

Because at UCLA he was acutely aware of the perishability of professors who failed to publish, he spent his nonteaching hours affixing words to paper. The result: over 30 books, 200 journal articles, 50 research reports, and 175 papers presented before research societies. Although not noted in his official vita, while at UCLA he also authored 1,426 grocery lists.

His most recent books are *Transformative Assessment* (2008); *Instruction That Measures Up* (2009); *Transformative Assessment in Action* (2011); *Mastering Assessment* (2011, Pearson); *Unlearned Lessons* (2009, Harvard Education Press); *Everything School Leaders Need to Know About Assessment* (2010); and *Evaluating America's Teachers: Mission Possible?* (2013, Corwin). He encourages purchase of these books because he regards their semi-annual royalties as psychologically reassuring.

In 1968, Dr. Popham established IOX Assessment Associates, an R&D group that formerly created statewide student achievement tests for a dozen states. He has personally passed all of those tests, largely because of his unlimited access to the tests' answer keys.

Preface

Of Ancient Chinese Curses

Perhaps you have heard the ancient Chinese curse, *May you live in an interesting time!* Perhaps you haven't.

Well, I can definitely tell you where and when I first heard this curse—and how puzzled I was by its meaning. The year was 1961, and I was a rookie assistant professor at San Francisco State College. A campuswide speech was to be delivered by Robert Maynard Hutchins, an educational celebrity of that era. Hutchins was the founder of the Great Books Movement and had been the youngest-ever chancellor of the University of Chicago.

It was a simply marvelous speech—so fine, in fact, that I subsequently obtained an audiotape of the address and played it often in my classes. Hutchins opened his address with the following sentence: "Perhaps you have heard the ancient Chinese curse, '*May you live in an interesting time!*'"

As I indicated, upon hearing Hutchins's first sentence, I was immediately perplexed by the meaning of this "curse" that I'd never heard before. After all, if the time in which one lives is "interesting," this would seem to be a positive—not a negative. What's interesting is typically better than what's dull. But then, as Hutchins continued, he pointed out that an "interesting time" invariably involves *changes.* Indeed, the more profound the changes, the more "interesting" the time. And changes, at least for most of us, cause *discomfort.* We must accommodate to what's new. Routine, experience-honed approaches no longer work. New, "interesting" times simply bristle with uncertainty. Hutchins was warning his audience that education in the United States was entering an era of unprecedented change and,

as a consequence, U.S. educators should clearly regard themselves as consummately cursed.

Well, if you look at what's taking place these days in this nation's *educational assessment,* you'll quickly conclude that we are smack in the middle of what is, most certainly, another especially "interesting time." To illustrate, during the several years separating the publication of this ninth edition of *Classroom Assessment* from its immediately previous edition, we have witnessed several significant national changes that, almost certainly, will result in "interesting" alterations in the way much of the nation's classroom assessment takes place. On December 10, 2015, for instance, President Barack Obama signed into law the Every Student Succeeds Act (ESSA) as another federal reauthorization of the Elementary and Secondary Education Act of 1965. ESSA replaced the No Child Left Behind Act (NCLB) that had previously served as a reauthorization of 1965's ESEA. Both NCLB and ESSA contain provisions influencing how today's teachers are likely to use classroom assessments with their students. Granted, those federal laws only *influenced* how classroom testing is likely to take place. Federal education statutes such as ESSA typically impose regulations obliging *state* educational authorities to carry out certain sorts of requirements. Usually, these federally imposed constraints—or, sometimes, incentives—focus only on state-level actions, not on what happens in teachers' classrooms. And yet, more often than not, federal regulations for implementing an education statute lead to a state's adoption of programs or policies that soon arrive in the classroom.

As you will see, this is where the "interestingness" of today's classroom assessment situation becomes all too apparent. For starters, according to U.S. Department of Education press releases about ESSA, our current reauthorization of ESEA is seen as a far less "prescriptive" law than NCLB, the reauthorization replaced by ESSA. In other words, state authorities will have many more choices for carrying out the less restrictive requirements of ESSA than they had with NCLB. More choices, of course, mean more differences in how states attempt to comply with altered federal requirements. Ever since 1965, when ESEA was first enacted as what was essentially a civil rights law, some heavy-duty federal funds have been distributed annually to those states that carry out ESEA's stipulations. Not surprisingly, therefore, authorities in most states try to play the education game in accordance with federal rules so that their state can rake in its share of federal largesse.

And now, finally, we see that although NCLB laid out some pretty constraining obligations for states with respect to their state assessment programs, and monitored those state programs through state-specific review teams who appraised each state's assessment programs, the enactment of a less prescriptive ESSA will often lead to more changes, and more differences, in how a state's teachers are supposed to carry out their classroom assessment endeavors.

If Robert Maynard Hutchins (1899–1977) were still with us, his curse for today's teachers might well be *"May your classroom assessments be interesting!"* Whereas the federal testing regulations associated with NCLB were quite constraining—and offered few opportunities for state-sired innovations, our current incarnation of ESEA, namely, ESSA, encourages more diverse ways to measure students' status.

Teachers' bread-and-butter testing activities associated with classroom assessment—the activities not influenced by federal statutory shifts—remain relatively constant. And those main-line assessment decisions are the ones addressed in much of this oft-revised classroom assessment textbook—the one you'll soon read. A thorough review of the previous edition of the book has

taken place for purposes of updating. For example, since the publication of the eighth edition of *Classroom Assessment,* we have seen a substantial increase in the use of computer-*adaptive* testing. This topic, its advantages, and its drawbacks are considered in the new edition. Similar updating has been applied throughout.

Thus, if you are currently a teacher, or are preparing to become one, you will find in the ninth edition of *Classroom Assessment* a complete set of concepts and procedures that will enable you to do a solid job of testing your own students. But, during the last decade or two, we have seen a growing need for educators *and others* to become more knowledgeable about educational assessment itself. It is this advocacy that has led to the inclusion of exciting new features in this new edition of *Classroom Assessment.*

New to This Edition

- **Extensive discussion of the** *Standards for Educational and Psychological Testing* **and their impact on classroom assessment:** In mid-2014, three of our nation's organizations most concerned with educational measurement released a genuinely significant document—namely, the *Standards for Educational and Psychological Testing.* The standards (guidelines) included therein describe how education tests should be constructed, evaluated, and used. Because the standards in that publication are often relied on to resolve assessment-related courtroom litigation, the tenets set forth will have a profound impact on the way U.S. educational testing takes place in the coming years. The most important of these new standards have been incorporated into all relevant sections of this ninth edition of *Classroom Assessment.*

- **Keys for evaluating instructionally diagnostic testing:** Given today's pervasive pressure to boost students' test scores, a number of test publishers are hawking what they characterize as "diagnostic tests." To help teachers understand what's necessary for a diagnostic test to make a meaningful contribution to instruction, an important section on *instructionally diagnostic testing* will be found in Chapter 13. Readers who understand what's needed in a test that is truly diagnostic will be better able to choose among an ever-expanding array of supposedly diagnostic assessments now available commercially. Many of today's allegedly useful diagnostic tests should, regrettably, be sent to a shredder. The section on instructionally diagnostic tests will help readers evaluate the merits of commercial or locally developed "diagnostic" assessments.

- **Updated coverage of relevant legislation and policy changes, including the implications of the Every Student Succeeds Act (ESSA) on classroom teachers:** The ninth edition includes extensive coverage of the legislation and policy changes that affect the classroom teacher. Chief among these is the Every Student Succeeds Act (ESSA) passed in 2015.

- **Expanded treatment of technology and its implications for classroom assessment:** The ninth edition has responded to the rising popularity of computer-based tests, particularly computer-adaptive tests, by dedicating considerable coverage to their methods and their implications for classroom assessment.

- **Reliability, validity, and fairness in action:** Throughout the ninth edition, care has been taken to provide concrete examples of how assessment's so-called Big Three— reliability, validity, and fairness—come into play for classroom teachers in a variety of instructional settings.

- **Parent Talk:** Considerable attention is paid in this ninth edition to an important audience for teachers—namely, *parents*. Teachers often need to explain to parents such assessment-related topics as why a child scored a certain way on a standardized test or how a teacher's classroom exams are related to the grades a child receives. So, in every chapter, you'll find a feature titled *Parent Talk*. In these Parent Talk segments, a situation is described in which a teacher needs to explain something about assessment to parents. I next indicate what I would have said to the parents if I had been the teacher in that situation. What I hope readers will do, then, is decide how *they* would have responded had they been placed in this same situation. In fact, readers might even say *aloud* (in private, if they have any sense) what they'd tell parents. Teachers who can talk sensibly to parents about assessment-related concerns will find they're able to establish more effective rapport with parents. Such teachers will get along far better with parents than will teachers who convey to parents the idea that assessment is an exotic measurement mystery, well beyond the perceptive powers of mere parents.

- **MyLab Education:** One of the most visible changes in the ninth edition, and also one of the most significant, is the expansion of the digital learning and assessment resources embedded in the eText and the inclusion of MyLab Education in the text. MyLab Education is an online homework, tutorial, and assessment program designed to work with the text to engage learners and improve learning. Within its structured environment, learners see key concepts demonstrated through real classroom video footage, practice what they learn, test their understanding, and receive feedback to guide their learning and ensure their mastery of key learning outcomes. Designed to bring learners more directly into the world of K–12 classrooms and to help them see the real and powerful impact of classroom assessment concepts covered in this book, the online resources in MyLab Education include:

  Self-Checks. In each chapter, self-check quizzes help assess how well learners have mastered the content. The self-checks are made up of self-grading multiple-choice items that not only provide feedback on whether questions are answered correctly or incorrectly, but also provide rationales for both correct and incorrect answers.

Application Exercises. These exercises give learners opportunities to practice applying the content and strategies from the chapters. The questions in these exercises are usually constructed-response questions. Once learners provide their own answers to the questions, they receive feedback in the form of model answers written by experts.

Podcasts. In the podcasts, readers will learn about real events related to the key concepts in each of the 16 chapters in the book. These stories help awaken readers to the real-life consequences and power of assessment done well and done poorly.

- **Testing Takeaways:** To help promote assessment literacy, the ninth edition of *Classroom Assessment* has introduced a new feature called Testing Takeaways. Each Testing Takeaway is an easily digestible one-page explanation of a key assessment concept. These features are designed to be shared with parents, legislators, and any other person for whom assessment and assessment policy have bearing. An expanded discussion of the importance of Testing Takeaways and their application follows.

Promote Assessment Literacy: Share a Testing Takeaway

Because test results influence what happens not only in classrooms but also in state legislatures, it's increasingly important for educators, parents, students, and lawmakers to become more assessment literate. But what is this thing called "assessment literacy" that you're being urged to promote?

Assessment literacy consists of an individual's understanding of the fundamental assessment concepts and procedures deemed likely to influence educational decisions. Becoming assessment literate does not require someone to magically morph into a sophisticated testing wizard. Rather, an assessment-literate educator needs only to grasp a modest number of essential understandings—those that are apt to have a real-world impact on the education of real-world children.

To help promote assessment literacy, the ninth edition of *Classroom Assessment* has introduced a new feature, Testing Takeaways, which are a set of easily digestible explanations. Candidly, these new Testing Takeaways were not written for you, the reader, but instead are intended to be read by persons or groups with whom you decide such takeaways should be shared. By doing so, you are helping *others* acquire a few useful assessment insights that may, in time and with greater study, blossom into full-on assessment literacy.

There is a definite rationale for including this new feature in the ninth edition of *Classroom Assessment*. All of the Testing Takeaways are focused on an aspect of assessment literacy. The rationale supporting the inclusion of these new segments stems from a belief that increased assessment literacy—on the part of educators and other educational stakeholders—constitutes *the most cost-effective way* to improve our schools. Put simply, those who understand the basics of educational testing will make fewer mistakes than those who possess scant knowledge about educational assessment. Moreover, in contrast to other, patently effective but costly, school-improvement strategies (such as substantially raising teachers' salaries or reducing class sizes to permit more tailored per-student instruction), the *costs* necessary for promoting assessment literacy are truly trifling.

By the time you have finished reading this book, there'll be no doubt that you will, yourself, have become assessment literate. Unfortunately, not every educator will read this book. As the book's author, I am personally dismayed by this likelihood. In truth, my dismay is only *partially* due to the contemplation of the non-existent book royalties.

Yet, if we make the reasonable assumption that assessment-literate educators will make fewer test-related mistakes than educators who are not assessment literate, then we surely need to promote assessment literacy among the nation's educators. And not only among educators! Other groups who could benefit from a better understanding of the basics of educational testing include educational policymakers such as members of local or state school boards, parents of school-age children, citizens in general, and even students themselves. Obviously, it might be necessary to adjust certain assessment fundamentals to the concerns of different groups. Yet, most of the basic assessment understandings needed by teachers and school administrators will be useful to other stakeholders as well.

Thanks to Pearson, the publisher of the book you're about to read, in the following pages you will find a set of 16 *Testing Takeaways,* one per chapter, for which Pearson is relaxing copyright protection and authorizing their use *for increasing assessment literacy.* You have permission to make direct copies of each of these one-page Testing Takeaways (hereinafter abbreviated as TTs). A digitally shareable version is available from www.pearsonmylabandmastering.com.

Each TT has been written so that it represents a meaningful, self-contained chunk of assessment-related information pertinent to one of the ninth edition's 16 chapters. Sometimes a TT addresses the overall thrust of a chapter. In other cases, a TT describes an issue related to, but not identical to, a chapter's main message. Certain of the TTs will surely be of more interest to you than others. All TTs attempt to deal with a dollop of assessment-related content that's worth knowing—sometimes only by educators, sometimes by everyone.

The TTs are located at the very end of each chapter. Ideally, you will look them over so you can decide which of them you regard as worth sharing with others. They are not intended to summarize what's in a chapter, but rather to provide a roughly 400-word mini-essay related to the chapter. The TTs are supplied in the hope that you will use them to kindle an interest in assessment literacy on the part of others. This is why I say that the TTs were not really written for you.

If you are using this book in connection with a course focused on educational assessment, then your instructor may have some specific suggestions regarding the use of the TTs. (Because I have spent roughly half my life as a university professor, I urge you to be particularly deferential to your professor's preferences.) For example, instructors who support the promotion of assessment literacy may find it useful, collaboratively with their students, to discuss which TTs seem to be appropriate (or inappropriate) for different audiences.

However, if you happen to be reading the book on your own (yes, such an occurrence might actually take place!) or are using the book in connection with some sort of professional development activity, here are a few suggestions regarding how *you* might personally promote greater assessment literacy on the part of others by using the 16 TTs written for that specific purpose:

- *Send to a friend or colleague.* If you think coworkers or friends would be interested in (or benefit from) the focus of a given TT, you might fire it off as a digital or hard copy to those individuals. You'll probably need to supply a brief introduction so that recipients don't think they've been surreptitiously singled out as gravely needing remedial assessment information.

- *Relay to local news outlets.* Many community newspapers still deal with education-related issues of potential interest to their readers. Were the editors of such newspapers (or the program directors of local television stations) to receive a digital copy of a TT, along with an explanatory note from you, there might be sufficient interest to warrant occasional inclusion of certain TTs in their offerings.

- *Include in a school's parent newsletters.* Because many parents are understandably concerned about the ways educational assessments affect their children, if you find one or more of the TTs that you believe might be of interest to parents, you could send digital or hard copies home in parental newsletters. If, in a cover letter to parents, you could indicate a willingness to provide a list of parent-friendly introductions to educational testing, this would surely contribute to an expansion of assessment literacy among this significant set of educational stakeholders.

- *Initiate a professional development group dealing with assessment.* All teachers within a school could be provided with one or more of the TTs, along with an invitation to collaborate in some ongoing variant of professional development regarding educational assessment. If some participants in such a group had access to the book you are about to read, those educators could periodically supply assessment-relevant content to the group beyond what is found in the TTs themselves.

- *Feature a TT as a segment of regular faculty meetings.* Perhaps you are a teacher in a school where professional topics are treated during routine faculty meetings. If so, then by soliciting reactions to a list and brief descriptions of the available TTs, you might isolate sufficient interest in certain TTs to warrant future discussions of those topics during upcoming faculty meetings.

Other uses of the TTs, of course, are possible—and may be more effective than the suggestions proffered here. Nonetheless, because increased assessment literacy on the part of educators and other clienteles will surely provide more successful educations for our students, give the 16 TTs a serious look—thinking all the while about which groups might most benefit from reading particular TTs. If you can become a personal emissary promoting increased assessment literacy for one or more groups of potential interest, you'll be doing something commendable for kids.

Will This *Testing* Book Help You *Teach* Better?

Teachers these days who don't recognize that educational assessment impinges on their work are teachers in serious need of impingement therapy. Rarely, indeed, does a day go by in the Monday-through-Friday life of today's teachers when testing does not have an impact on one or more of their classroom decisions. It was not always this way.

Eons ago, I was a high school teacher in eastern Oregon. (It was so long ago that my friends contend Oregon must have been a territory rather than a state.) Way back then, we administered standardized achievement tests in our classes. However, students' scores on those tests made no difference in how we taught. Pressures to raise our students' scores on those achievement exams were nonexistent. We taught pretty much as we saw fit. But, of course, the world of education is different today—much different.

And even before those teaching days, when I was preparing to be a teacher, little attention was given to testing. In truth, the only time my professors actually dealt with educational tests was when, during an educational psychology class, we spent an entire week on the making and massaging of multiple-choice items. My fellow prospective teachers and I were not being prepared for educational assessment because, back then, educational assessment truly did not have an impact on teachers' decision making.

But today, educational tests certainly make a difference in what currently takes place in our classrooms. For openers, today's teachers find themselves directly in the crosshairs of some heavy-duty accountability artillery aimed at evaluating schools *and sometimes teachers* at least in part according to students' scores on accountability tests. A school's staff can be "restructured," or a school can be completely shut down, if its students don't perform well enough on externally administered accountability exams. Yes, teachers can be tossed. It is a scary time.

Fortunately, during the last two decades, growing numbers of educators have learned that the skillful use of classroom testing can make huge differences in how well students learn. Classroom assessment, if employed *formatively,* can dramatically increase the effectiveness of a teacher's *teaching.* And yet, sadly, we rarely see more than a token use of classroom assessments in the way that research clearly tells us will benefit students.

For both of those reasons, then, every experienced teacher and every teacher-in-training need to master the essentials of educational assessment. And that's why this book was first written and then revised so frequently. Its title, *Classroom Assessment: What Teachers Need to Know,* captures the book's intent. Readers won't be asked to learn any nice-to-know exotics about educational measurement. No, what's contained in this book is the stuff today's teachers *need to know* if they are truly going to be first-rate professionals.

Ancillary Materials

The following resources are available for instructors to download on www.pearsonhighered.com/educators. Instructors can enter the author or title of this book, select this particular edition of the book, and then click on the "Resources" tab to log in and download textbook supplements.

Instructor's Resource Manual with Test Bank (ISBN 0-13-556913-3)

The Instructor's Resource Manual includes suggestions for teaching a classroom assessment course using this text, additional learning activities, guidance on using MyLab Education, and a Test Bank.

PowerPoint Slides (ISBN 0-13-556893-5)

The PowerPoint slides include key concept summaries and other aids to enhance learning. They are designed to help students understand, organize, and remember core concepts and applications.

TestGen (ISBN 0-13-556919-2)

TestGen is a powerful test generator that you install on your computer and use in conjunction with the TestGen test bank file for your text. Assessments, including equations, graphs, and scientific notation, may be created for both print and online testing.

The tests can be downloaded in the following formats:

TestGen test bank file—MAC

TestGen test bank file—PC

Angel TestGen Conversion

Test Bank for Blackboard Learning System

Desire to Learn TestGen Conversion

Moodle TestGen Conversion

Sakai TestGen Conversion

Test Bank for Blackboard CE/Vista

Acknowledgments

To my colleagues who offered recommendations about how to improve this latest edition, I offer my sincere appreciation: Heidi Legg Burross, University of Arizona; Melanie DiLoreto, University of West Florida; Thomas J. Sheeran, Niagara University; and Maria D. Vasquez, Florida Atlantic University.

I am appreciative of the overall guidance in this project of Director and Publisher Kevin Davis, my very own Pearson Poohbah, whose executive preferences I obsequiously and instantly obeyed. He has been overseeing the periodic rebirth of this classroom assessment book for a good many years now, and doing a high-class job of it. I was simply delighted when he accepted my proposal to include this edition's new Testing Takeaways in an explicit attempt to promote increased assessment literacy among others. If we learn that a modest number of such limited waivers of copyright protection can broaden the reach of a book such as this, there is no reason why such a strategy might not be employed as well for content other than educational assessment. Kevin displayed genuine foresight in agreeing to try out this edition's copyright-relaxation outreach strategy.

When a textbook has been through the editorial re-birthing process as often as this one has, an author becomes particularly attentive to the caliber of the production team that transforms words on paper into a *bona fide* book. The following folks were atypically wonderful in creating this ninth edition, and they have my lasting gratitude: Janelle Rogers, Pearson Content Producer; Lauren Carlson, Pearson Media Producer; Krista Clark, Pearson Marketing Manager; and Andrea Archer and Angela Urquhart, Thistle Hill Publishing Services.

Finally, any writer will tell you that an editor can determine a book's quality and, depending on the editor, determine a writer's sanity. This ninth edition was my first opportunity to work with Curtis Vickers, who, as the designated editor for this edition, went through every word—ladling out his criticisms softly and occasionally granting praise when I chose the appropriate forms of pronouns to properly modify gerunds. He was always prompt and, most of all, immersed himself in my blather so he could suggest more beneficial blathering techniques. This new edition of *Classroom Assessment*, and I myself, are in his debt.

W. J. P.

Brief Contents

1 Why Do Teachers Need to Know About Assessment?   1

2 Deciding What to Assess   34

3 Reliability of Assessment   74

4 Validity   97

5 Fairness   127

6 Selected-Response Tests   154

7 Constructed-Response Tests   180

8 Performance Assessment   202

9 Portfolio Assessment   227

10 Affective Assessment   244

11 Improving Teacher-Developed Assessments   265

12 Formative Assessment   284

13 Making Sense Out of Standardized Test Scores   309

14 Appropriate and Inappropriate Test-Preparation Practices   341

15 The Evaluation of Instruction   356

16 Assessment-Based Grading   389

Glossary   411

Index   417

Contents

1 Why Do Teachers Need
to Know About Assessment?   1

Chief Chapter Outcome   1

Echoes of ESEA   2

   The *Standards for Educational and
Psychological Testing*   9

Assessment Versus Testing   10

Why Should Teachers Know About
Assessment? Yesteryear's Answers   14

   Determining Students' Current Status   14

   Monitoring Students' Progress   15

   Assigning Grades   17

   Determining One's Own Instructional
Effectiveness   18

Why Should Teachers Know About
Assessment? Today's Answers   19

   Influencing Public Perceptions of
Educational Effectiveness   19

   Helping Evaluate Teachers   20

   Clarifying Teachers' Instructional Intentions   22

What Do Classroom Teachers Really Need
to Know About Assessment?   24

   Creating Classroom Assessment Instruments   25

   Interpreting Standardized Test Results   26

   Instructionally Illuminating Assessment   28

Chapter Summary   31

References   32

A Testing Takeaway   33

2 Deciding What to Assess   34

Chief Chapter Outcome   34

What to Assess   34

   Decision-Driven Assessment   35

   The Role of Curricular Aims   36

   Cognitive, Affective, and Psychomotor
Assessment   41

Standards-Based Classroom Assessment   41

Norm-Referenced Versus Criterion-
Referenced Assessment   43

Selected Responses and Constructed Responses   46

A State's Official Curricular Aims   47

"Many a Slip . . ."   54

Science: Not to Be Left Behind   55

What's Assessed on Your State's
Accountability Test?   56

Other Exams You Should Know About   58

Assessment Blueprints   60

Collar a Colleague   61

A Collection of What-to-Assess Considerations   62

   Tests as Instructional Influencers   63

   Dividends of Assessment Illumination   65

   A Profusion of Item Types   66

What Do Classroom Teachers Really Need
to Know About What to Assess?   68

A Three-Chapter Preview   69

Chapter Summary   71

References   72

A Testing Takeaway   73

3 Reliability of Assessment   74

Chief Chapter Outcome   74

Test-Retest Reliability Evidence   80

Alternate-Form Reliability Evidence   82

Internal Consistency Reliability Evidence   84

   Three Coins in the Reliability/
Precision Fountain   87

The Standard Error of Measurement   88

What Do Classroom Teachers Really Need
to Know About Reliability/Precision?   91

Chapter Summary   93

References   95

Endnotes   95

A Testing Takeaway   96

4 Validity   97

Chief Chapter Outcome   **97**
A Quest for Defensible Interpretations   97
Validity Evidence   102
Validity Evidence Based on Test Content   105
    Developmental Care   107
    External Reviews   109
    Alignment   112
Validity Evidence Based on Response Processes   113
Validity Evidence Based on a Test's Internal
Structure   114
Validity Evidence Based on Relations
to Other Variables   115
    Test–Criterion Relationships   116
    Convergent and Discriminant Evidence   118
Sanctioned and Unsanctioned Labels for
Validity Evidence   120
The Relationship Between Reliability and
Validity   122
What Do Classroom Teachers Really Need
to Know About Validity?   122
Chapter Summary   **124**
References   **125**
A Testing Takeaway   **126**

5 Fairness   127

Chief Chapter Outcome   **127**
The Nature of Assessment Bias   128
    Offensiveness   129
    Unfair Penalization   130
Disparate Impact and Assessment Bias   131
Judgmental Approaches   133
    Bias Review Panels   134
    A Per-Item Absence-of-Bias Judgment   134
    An Overall Absence-of-Bias Judgment   135
Empirical Approaches   136
Bias Detection in the Classroom   136
Assessing Students with Disabilities and
English Language Learners   139
    Children with Disabilities and Federal Law   139
    English Language Learners   144

Is Fairness a *Bona Fide* Member of Educational
Testing's "Big Three"?   147
What Do Classroom Teachers Really Need
to Know About Fairness?   149
Chapter Summary   **151**
References   **152**
Endnote   **152**
A Testing Takeaway   **153**

6 Selected-Response Tests   154

Chief Chapter Outcome   **154**
Expanding Electronic Options   155
Ten (Divided by Two) Overall Item-Writing
Commandments   155
    Opaque Directions   156
    Ambiguous Statements   157
    Unintended Clues   157
    Complex Syntax   160
    Difficult Vocabulary   161
Binary-Choice Items   162
    Phrasing Items to Elicit Thoughtfulness   162
    Minimizing Negatives   163
    Avoiding Double-Concept Items   163
    Balancing Response Categories   163
    Maintaining Item-Length Similarity   164
Multiple Binary-Choice Items   164
    Separating Clusters   165
    Coordinating Items with Their Stem   165
Multiple-Choice Items   166
    Stem Stuffing   168
    Knocking Negatively Stated Stems   168
    Attending to Alternative Length   169
    Assigning Correct Answer Positions   169
    Dealing with "Of-the-Above"
    Alternatives   170
Matching Items   172
    Employing Homogeneous Entries   174
    Going for Relative Brevity   174
    Loading Up on Responses   174
    Ordering Responses   175
    Describing the Task for Students   175
    Same-Page Formatting   176

What Do Classroom Teachers Really Need
to Know About Selected-Response Tests? 176

Chapter Summary **177**

References **178**

A Testing Takeaway **179**

7 Constructed-Response Tests 180

Chief Chapter Outcome **180**

Short-Answer Items 181

Using Direct Questions Rather than
Incomplete Statements 182

Nurturing Concise Responses 183

Positioning Blanks 183

Limiting Blanks 183

Inducing Linear Equality 184

Essay Items: Development 184

Creating Essay Items 186

Communicating the Extensiveness
of Students' Responses Sought 187

Describing Students' Tasks 188

Providing Time-Limit and Item-Value
Guidance 188

Avoiding Optionality 189

Previewing Students' Responses 189

Essay Items: Scoring Students' Responses 190

Choosing an Analytic and/or Holistic
Scoring Approach 191

Devising a Tentative Scoring Key 193

Deciding Early About the Importance of
Mechanics 195

Scoring One Item at a Time 196

Striving for Anonymity 197

What Do Classroom Teachers Really Need
to Know About Constructed-Response
Tests? 198

Chapter Summary **199**

References **200**

A Testing Takeaway **201**

8 Performance Assessment 202

Chief Chapter Outcome **202**

What Is a Performance Test? 202

Identifying Suitable Tasks for Performance
Assessment 205

Inferences and Tasks 206

The Generalizability Dilemma 207

Factors to Consider When Evaluating
Performance-Test Tasks 209

Performance Tests and Teacher Time 210

The Role of Rubrics 210

Rubrics: The Wretched and the Rapturous 213

Task-Specific Rubrics 214

Hypergeneral Rubrics 215

Skill-Focused Rubrics 216

Ratings and Observations 219

Sources of Error in Scoring Student
Performances 220

Scoring-Instrument Flaws 221

Procedural Flaws 221

Teachers' Personal-Bias Errors 221

What Do Classroom Teachers Really Need
to Know About Performance Assessment? 223

Chapter Summary **224**

References **225**

A Testing Takeaway **226**

9 Portfolio Assessment 227

Chief Chapter Outcome **227**

Classroom Portfolio Assessment Versus
Large-Scale Portfolio Assessment 228

Classroom Applications 228

Who Is Evaluating Whom? 229

Large-Scale Applications 230

Key Ingredients in Classroom Portfolio
Assessment 231

Purposeful Portfolios 234

Work-Sample Selection 236

Appraising Portfolios 237

The Pros and Cons of Portfolio Assessment 237

What Do Classroom Teachers Really Need
to Know About Portfolio Assessment? 240

Chapter Summary **241**

References **242**

A Testing Takeaway **243**

10 Affective Assessment   244

Chief Chapter Outcome   244
Why Assess Affect?   244
  The Importance of Affect   245
  Spurring Affectively Focused Instruction   245
  Monitoring Students' Status   246
The Other Side of the Argument   247
Which Affective Variables Should Be
Assessed?   248
  A Closer Look at Affect   248
  Potential Attitudinal Targets   249
  Potential Interest Targets   249
  Potential Value Targets   250
How Should Affect Be Assessed in Classrooms?   251
Self-Report Assessment   252
  Likert Inventories   252
  Multifocus Affective Inventories   254
  Building a Multifocus Affective Inventory   254
  The Importance of Genuine Anonymity   257
  When to Assess Affect   258
What Kinds of Inferences Are at Stake in
Affective Assessment?   259
What Do Classroom Teachers Really Need
to Know About Affective Assessment?   261
Chapter Summary   262
References   263
A Testing Takeaway   264

11 Improving Teacher-Developed
      Assessments   265

Chief Chapter Outcome   265
Judgmentally Based Improvement Procedures   266
  Judging Your Own Assessment Instruments   266
  Collegial Judgments   268
  Student Judgments   269
Empirically Based Improvement Procedures   270
  Difficulty Indices   271
  Item-Discrimination Indices   272
  Distractor Analyses   277
Item Analysis for Criterion-Referenced
Measurement   277

What Do Classroom Teachers Really Need
to Know About Improving Their Assessments? 280
Chapter Summary   281
References   282
A Testing Takeaway   283

12 Formative Assessment   284

Chief Chapter Outcome   284
Assessment That Transforms Teaching   284
  What Is Formative Assessment?   285
  Is Formative Assessment the Same as
  "Assessment for Learning"?   288
  What Formative Assessment Isn't   289
Research Supporting Formative
Assessment   291
  The Black and Wiliam Research Review   292
Learning Progressions as Frameworks   294
  What Is a Learning Progression?   294
  Building a Learning Progression   297
  Formative Assessment: A Means-Ends
  Game   299
Why the Delay?   301
What Do Classroom Teachers Really Need
to Know About Formative Assessment?   303
Chapter Summary   305
References   306
A Testing Takeaway   308

13 Making Sense Out of
      Standardized Test Scores   309

Chief Chapter Outcome   309
Standardized Tests   310
Group-Focused Test Interpretation   312
Individual Student Test Interpretation   314
  Percentiles   314
  Grade-Equivalent Scores   316
  Scale Scores   320
  Contrasting Common Interpretive
  Options   323
  The Instructional Yield from Standardized
  Achievement Tests   325

Instructionally Diagnostic Tests   326

   What Is an Instructionally Diagnostic Test?   326

   How Good Is an Instructionally Diagnostic
Test?   328

The SAT and the ACT: Three-Letter,
High-Import Exams   332

   The SAT   332

   The ACT   334

   Predictive Accuracy—And Its Implications   336

What Do Classroom Teachers Really Need
to Know About Interpreting Standardized
Test Scores?   337

Chapter Summary   **338**

References   **339**

A Testing Takeaway   **340**

14 Appropriate and Inappropriate
    Test-Preparation Practices   341

Chief Chapter Outcome   **341**

High-Stakes Assessment Arrives   341

Assessment Results as Inference Illuminators   343

Two Evaluative Guidelines   344

Five Test-Preparation Practices   347

Applying the Two Guidelines   348

What About "Teaching to the Test"?   350

What Do Classroom Teachers Really Need
to Know About Test-Preparation Practices?   353

Chapter Summary   **353**

References   **354**

A Testing Takeaway   **355**

15 The Evaluation of Instruction 356

Chief Chapter Outcome   **356**

A Focus on Consequences   358

Classroom Assessment Evidence   361

   Pretests Versus Posttests   362

   The Split-and-Switch Design   363

   What to Assess   366

Evidence from External Accountability Tests   367

   Comparative Estimates of Progress: Student
Growth Percentiles   370

   Instructional Sensitivity   372

   The Genesis of Instructional Insensitivity 373

   Avoidance of Instructionally Insensitive
Items   379

   Determining Students' Progress: With
Value-Added Models   381

What's a Teacher to Do?   382

   Right Task, Wrong Tools   384

What Do Classroom Teachers Really Need
to Know About Assessment-Based Evaluation
of Teaching?   384

Chapter Summary   **386**

References   **387**

A Testing Takeaway   **388**

16 Assessment-Based Grading 389

Chief Chapter Outcome   **389**

The Purpose of Grading   389

   How Does Goal-Attainment Grading
Take Place?   392

Grade-Giving Specifics   396

   Evaluative Options   398

   What About Effort?   400

   What About Those Important Intangibles?   401

   Electronic Record Keeping   404

   Student-Involved Grading Conferences   404

   Grading's Inherent Imprecision   406

What Do Classroom Teachers Really Need
to Know About Assessment-Based Grading
of Students?   406

Chapter Summary   **408**

References   **409**

A Testing Takeaway   **410**

Glossary   411

Index   417

Chapter 1
Why Do Teachers Need to Know About Assessment?

 Chief Chapter Outcome

An understanding of why it is that four traditional and three recent reasons for educators to assess students should dispose teachers to learn more about the fundamentals of educational assessment

Teachers teach students. That hardly constitutes a breakthrough insight. Just as welders weld and plumbers plumb—teachers teach. That's why they're called teachers.

But what is a bit less obvious is that most teachers teach because they *like* to teach. Primary teachers like to teach younger children. High school teachers like to teach older children. Most high school teachers also like to teach about a particular subject. (Have you ever noticed how mathematics teachers' eyes get misty when they introduce their students to the raptures of the Pythagorean theorem?) Yes, most teachers love to teach. It is because they enjoy what they do that they waded through a medley of preservice teacher education courses, conquered the challenges of student teaching, and hopped the myriad hurdles of the certification process. Teachers overcame these obstacles in order to earn annual salaries that, particularly during the first few years, are laughably low. Yes, there's little doubt that teachers groove on teaching.

Although teachers like to *teach*, they rarely like to *test*. Yet here you are—beginning a book about testing. How can I, the author, ever entice you, the reader, to become interested in testing when your heart has already been given to teaching? The answer is really quite straightforward. Teachers who can test well will be better teachers. Effective testing will enhance a teacher's instructional effectiveness. Really!

If you're willing to suspend any preconceptions about testing while you're reading this book, particularly any negative ones, I'll make a pledge to you.

Learning Outcomes

1.1 Identify key legislation, discuss the history of assessment in the United States, and differentiate between testing and assessment.

1.2 Using the four traditional and three modern reasons for why teachers assess found in Chapter 1, identify and explain the rationale for the benefits of teachers as functional assessors.

If you tackle this text with even half the enthusiasm you might bring to a teaching assignment, I promise you'll discover how *testing will make you a much better teacher*. And, because I've been a teacher for more than 50 years, it's a promise I'll keep. Teachers should definitely not break promises to teachers. (Teachers' promises to administrators, on the other hand, should be regarded as eminently renegotiable.)

But before the book attempts to convince you, ever so subtly, that testing can be a boon to teaching, you need to get a fix on your own *current* views about educational testing. And, because this is a book about testing, what better way to help you explore those attitudes than to have you take a self-test that was devised just for readers of this book?

So, on the adjacent page (it's on the *right* from where you're currently reading!) you'll find a brief self-test similar to the ones you've surely encountered in many widely read magazines. I saw one such self-test in a health magazine recently. It was entitled "How Long Will You Live? A Self-Test." Frankly, I was afraid to try it. As one grows older, one gets more cautious.

But you have nothing to fear by taking the self-test that's been whipped up for you. To emphasize its brevity, it is entitled "A Terse Self-Test About Testing." It is an example of commonly used attitudinal inventories. Later, in Chapter 10, you'll learn more about attitudinal inventories. But for now, please take a crack at page 6's teensy self-test. The way to interpret your responses is given as a footnote at the bottom of the page.

Echoes of ESEA

Anyone who has completed even an introductory course in U.S. government knows that just as state laws can overturn the regulations enacted by local communities, federal laws can overturn state laws. When it comes to the art of overturning, federal folks clearly have the heftiest muscles. Interestingly, we often see those federal muscles flexed with respect to classroom assessment. The origins of the tests that we see used in today's classrooms can sometimes be traced directly to a state or a federal statute dealing with educational assessment. In the instance of classroom assessment, by far the most potent piece of test-influencing legislation bearing on such testing was the federal Elementary and Secondary Education Act (ESEA) of 1965.

Enacted more than a half-century ago, ESEA was a key component of President Lyndon B. Johnson's "Great Society." This precedent-setting law constituted what—at that time—was the federal government's most serious commitment to providing all the nation's K–12 youth with equal access to high-quality education. In contrast to previous federal spending on public education, ESEA's financial support to the nation's schools was downright gargantuan.

As set forth in the new law, unprecedented funds were doled out to states in support of instructional materials, professional development, resources to support educational programs, and the promotion of parental-involvement initiatives.

But because of the unprecedented magnitude of ESEA's federal funding for schools, key congressional leaders (including Robert F. Kennedy, who was then the junior U.S. senator from New York) insisted that the new legislation contain provisions intended to systematically evaluate whether these new federal dollars were being well spent. Formal educational evaluation was, in truth, birthed almost overnight by the passage of 1965's ESEA.

This potent federal statute has been reauthorized every 5–10 years since its enactment, and those reauthorizations have usually contained alterations, sometimes significant, to the law's key provisions. The various subsections of ESEA are designated as "titles." Title I, for example, established a program to distribute federal funding to districts and schools serving a high proportion of students from low-income families. Title I typically gets the most attention from policymakers because it accounts for roughly 80 percent of the total funding that's authorized under ESEA. Programs supported under Title I, at least at the outset, were intended to reduce the skill gaps in reading, writing, and mathematics between children from low-income households and children from the middle class. In general, this is still the case.

From a *classroom-assessment* perspective (and you will recall that classroom assessment is the focus of this book) what's significant about ESEA is that its many reauthorizations have sometimes led to changes in federal evaluation-related requirements that have a meaningful influence on the assessment practices recommended to states, districts, and schools. You will find several such changes embodied in the most recent incarnation of ESEA, and those modifications will be addressed as you saunter joyfully through this book's fun-filled pages.

The Every Student Succeeds Act (ESSA) was signed into law by President Barack Obama on December 10, 2015, and it succeeded the No Child Left Behind Act (NCLB) that was signed by President George W. Bush on January 8, 2002. If you have even modest calendrical and mathematical skills, you can see that, unlike the typical ESEA-reauthorization period of about 5 years, the reauthorization gap between NCLB and ESSA was more than 13 years.

Some observers suggest that the lengthy delay between the two authorizations was chiefly attributable to a markedly increasing polarization of the two major congressional parties. As was the case with the original ESEA, however, both NCLB and ESSA were passed by Congress with substantial bipartisan support. Whatever the cause for the uncommon delay in ESEA's most recent reauthorization, some of the alterations in the law are apt to have a direct impact on the kinds of directives about classroom testing issued to teachers by state and district education authorities.

ESSA's predecessor—NCLB—had attempted to reduce the growing achievement gap that left poor and minority students in failing schools, but it had also introduced a deliberately stringent accountability structure. As President Bush said during the law's signing ceremony (televised by C-Span), the law's fundamental premise is that "every child can learn, we expect every child to learn, and you must show us whether or not every child is learning." As you can infer, NCLB was laced with a strong *"show us"* orientation.

ESSA attempted to preserve the spirit of NCLB, yet it set out to remedy drawbacks that many critics believed stemmed from its "one size fits all" shortcomings. As he signed the act into law, President Obama asserted that NCLB was intended to promote high standards, close the achievement gap, and increase accountability. He regarded these as appropriate goals but he also believed that, in practice, the law failed to consider the distinctive needs of each community. NCLB, he observed in official press releases, had "led to too much testing during classroom time. It often forced schools and school districts into cookie-cutter reforms that didn't always produce the kinds of results that we wanted to see."

In looking back at the two most recent renditions of 1965's ESEA, then, we see that whereas NCLB and ESSA have fundamentally similar goals, ESSA attempts to provide greater flexibility, so that states and districts can particularize their programs for implementing chief provisions of the current successor to ESEA. The success of a given state in carrying out the provisions of ESSA's various titles, however, is supposed to be more closely controlled at the state level than at the federal level, as was the case in NCLB.

Before we depart from federal influence over the sorts of assessment provisions that have a tangible effect on a teacher's classroom testing procedures, it is important for you to recognize a few fundamentals about the ways in which legislatively enacted statutes can determine how teachers test their students. You see, once a federal bill (or, for that matter, a state bill) has been signed into law, a set of regulations is typically readied to guide the law's implementation. Typically, those regulations are drafted by the appropriate governmental agency (in the instance of a federal education-related statute, this would be the U.S. Department of Education) and then are made available in draft form, for a review period, so that those who wish to comment on the emerging regulations can do so. After the suggestions of commentators are taken into consideration, a final set of regulations is issued. These final regulations function as a way of operationalizing the law itself, which often contains segments that are somewhat ambiguous.

Because the nature of teachers' classroom assessments is often influenced by the way a state implements a law such as ESSA, the U.S. Department of Education calls on a special collection of *peer reviewers* who scrutinize a given state's assessment and accountability intentions regarding the implementation of ESSA. State officials, therefore, submit their state's plans for federal peer review and must often make identified changes in those plans before receiving peer-review approval. A federal peer-review panel of, say, a half-dozen assessment specialists, determines whether a state's accountability approach, including its state and local assessments, are sufficiently in accord with ESSA's stipulations. Failure to secure peer-review approval can result in withholding of federal funds, so peer-review approbation is typically sought with substantial zeal.

Classroom teachers who are uncertain about some of the ESSA-influenced issues to be addressed in the upcoming pages, therefore, will often find it helpful to seek the advice, first of district assessment specialists, and then of state-level authorities (such as the assessment personnel in a state department of education), about how best to carry out classroom assessment so that it meshes with state or federal regulations. Although the membership of a given state's peer-review panel is typically quite stable, changes in panelists can sometimes lead to subtle reinterpretations of ESSA. It is useful, therefore, for teachers to check periodically to see whether any significant alterations have been made in a given state's ESSA expectations.

COMMON STANDARDS = UNCOMMON RUCKUS

As a consequence of a collaborative effort by the National Governors Association (NGA) and the Council of Chief State School Officers (CCSSO), in 2009 we saw 48 states, 2 territories, and the District of Columbia initiate a project culminating in the creation of the *Common Core State Standards (CCSS)*. The English language arts (ELA) and mathematics learning outcomes embodied in the *CCSS* were intended, as a group, to represent a more challenging set of curricular expectations than were found at that time in many states' official instructional goals. As set forth in the *CCSS*, the key math and ELA content standards—that is, the sanctioned curricular targets at different grade levels—were identified.

In truth, the actual development of the *CCSS* was carried out in a less than totally transparent manner. This was because information about the nature of the content standards themselves—and the specific developmental procedures being used to identify those content standards—was not readily available to interested onlookers. Indeed, many complaints regarding the "covert" building of the *CCSS* were voiced by frustrated would-be observers of this important curriculum-building initiative.

Transparency notwithstanding, however, the resulting sets of math and ELA curricular targets were generally conceded to constitute high-quality collections of more demanding curricular goals than the official sets of intended learning outcomes then seen in some of the 50 states. Indeed, the high quality of the 2010-released *CCSS* surely contributed to their widespread adoption; by 2011, 45 states and the District of Columbia had signified acceptance of the new standards. In recognition that the ELA and mathematics curricular targets contained in the *CCSS* represented the essential features of what a state's schools should be promoting in its students, the emergence and pervasive adoption of these curricular goals constituted a landmark in the history of American schooling.

Let's look, ever so briefly, at what these curricular aims are—with a definite commitment to return in the next chapter for a closer look at the *CCSS*. In Chapter 2, you will see how the two sets of curricular aims identified in the *CCSS* are organized, as well as learn what some of the developers of those state standards were hoping to accomplish.

Let's be clear about what the two collections of ELA and math content standards are. They represent the curricular outcomes sought for the nation's students—that is, the knowledge and cognitive skills students are supposed to acquire in school. Because the reauthorized version of ESEA that was then in place (NCLB) had allowed each state to select its own curricular aims, its own tests to

A Terse Self-Test About Testing

Directions: For each of the statements below, use the following answer key to indicate how you react to the statement:

SA = *Strongly Agree*
A = *Agree*
U = *Uncertain*
D = *Disagree*
SD = *Strongly Disagree*

There are no right or wrong answers, so please answer frankly by circling the appropriate response for each statement.

1.	The chief reason why teachers should give classroom tests is to determine students' grades.	SA	A	U	D	SD
2.	Teachers should typically plan instruction that focuses on the skills or knowledge represented by a test.	SA	A	U	D	SD
3.	In their classroom tests, teachers should use only items that can be scored objectively.	SA	A	U	D	SD
4.	There are other legitimate indicators of a teacher's instructional effectiveness besides students' test scores.	SA	A	U	D	SD
5.	A teacher has no business measuring students' confidence in their ability to do schoolwork.	SA	A	U	D	SD
6.	Today's nationally standardized achievement tests should never be used to supply evidence about how well teachers are instructing children.	SA	A	U	D	SD
7.	Teachers rarely need to determine the reliability of their own classroom tests.	SA	A	U	D	SD
8.	It is impossible to judge the quality of students' written compositions with any meaningful accuracy.	SA	A	U	D	SD
9.	The enormous pressure to boost students' scores on important tests permits teachers to employ almost any sort of score-improvement preparation activities.	SA	A	U	D	SD
10.	Significant classroom tests should typically be built before a teacher plans instruction.	SA	A	U	D	SD

Self-Test Interpretation Guide: For statements 2, 4, 6, 7, and 10, use the following scoring key: SA = 5, A = 4, U = 3, D = 2, and SD = 1. For statements 1, 3, 5, 8, and 9, use the following scoring key: SA = 1, A = 2, U = 3, D = 4, and SD = 5. The highest possible total score is 50; the lowest possible total score is 10. The higher your total score, the more sensible is your view of educational testing. After finishing this book, you might wish to retake this terse self-test (without looking at your earlier answers, of course). If you come up with a postbook score that's substantially *lower* than your prebook score, then we should *both* be worried.

assess students' mastery of those aims, and its own cut-scores (that is, achievement standards) to signify students' mastery of those curricular aims, making sense out of the NCLB-spawned accountability picture in U.S. public schools was almost impossible. In an effort to rectify this chaotic situation, the NGA and CCSSO set out in late 2009 to provide a more suitable set of curricular targets for the nation's schools. The CCSSO is the organization of the state officials, elected or appointed, who head each state's public schools. The NGA performs a comparable function for the nation's governors.

On June 2, 2010, the CCSSO and NGA released the *CCSS* (National Governors Association, 2010). As noted earlier, many states soon accepted these standards—these "expectations for student knowledge and skills that high school graduates need to master to succeed in college and careers" (**www.corestandards.org/assets/ ccssi-introduction.pdf**). Given the long-standing reluctance of state education officials to abandon "local control" over important educational decisions such as curricular outcomes for students, the widespread adoption of the *CCSS* was genuinely astonishing. In essentially a single year, the CCSSO and NGA had crafted sets of national mathematics and ELA curricular aims defensible enough that all but a few states soon hopped aboard the *CCSS* Express.

The widespread and remarkably rapid adoption of the *CCSS* by so many states, however, did not take place merely because of the merits of a more carefully crafted set of challenging curricular targets. The role of nongovernmental organizations in nurturing such significant changes in U.S. education is now better understood. In the June 7, 2014, issue of the *Washington Post*, Lyndsey Layton reports that a major player in the adoption of the *CCSS* was the Bill and Melinda Gates Foundation. In an article entitled "How Bill Gates Pulled Off the Swift Common Core Revolution," Layton reveals that the Gates Foundation supplied more than $200 million not only for the actual development of the *CCSS* itself but also for building political support across the nation—often convincing state officials to make systematic and expensive changes in their curricular aspirations. Moreover, the foundation spread funds across the entire political spectrum, distributing dollars galore to the two major U.S. teachers' unions and such business groups as the U.S. Chamber of Commerce—organizations that have historically clashed but that soon became outspoken proponents of the Common Core. As Layton reports, within 2 years of the Gates Foundation's decision to support the Common Core, 45 states and the District of Columbia had fully endorsed the *CCSS*.

But the curricular aims embodied in the *CCSS* were destined to serve as much more than lofty statements of curricular intent that, like so many previously crafted sets of curricular aims, typically languished in rarely read reports. This is because, soon after the release of the *CCSS* in mid-2010, the federal government announced its intention to fund one or more consortia of states whose mission it would be to create assessments suitable for measuring students' mastery of the skills and knowledge embodied in the *CCSS*. Two such assessment consortia were selected by federal authorities (from competing bidders) and were funded with approximately $175 million each to create assessments that, by the 2014–15 school year, could be used to determine students' mastery of the *CCSS*. The two consortia were the *Partnership for the Assessment of Readiness for College and Careers (PARCC)* and the *Smarter Balanced Assessment Consortium (SBAC)*. Each of these consortia was initially composed of about 20 to 25 states, all of which agreed to promote students' mastery of the curricular goals represented by the *CCSS*.

It should be clear that the nature of the assessments devised by PARCC and SBAC would most likely have a considerable impact on America's public schools. Because the curricular aims being pursued by so many states would be identical, and the assessments used in those states would also be identical, comparisons among states' student performances could now be carried out in ways that heretofore had been impossible. The evaluative impact of such evidence, of course, was apt to be substantial.

As the assessments created by the two consortia became more widely understood, straightforward comparisons among states—the comparisons originally foreseen by proponents of the two assessment consortia—grew less likely to take place. Not only were the reporting categories and the cut-scores used by the two consortia dissimilar, but states were allowed unanticipated degrees of local determination in what was taught and what was tested. The original aspiration of the CCSSO and the NGA to install common curricular targets, mastery of which could be measured by essentially identical or statistically equivalent tests, was not to be.

In 2018, for example, although 35 states still regarded the *CCSS* as their official state curricular goals, many states had made minor changes in those curricular goals and, accordingly, described them by other labels). Eleven states had announced a major Common Core rewrite or replacement, four states never adopted *CCSS*, and one state adopted only ELA Common Core goals—not mathematics goals. As this version of *Classroom Assessment* was shipped off to the publisher in early 2019, the number of states and the District of Columbia using SBAC or PARRC assessments was 15—5 fewer than in 2016 or 2017.

Given that about a dozen states still use consortia-created assessments, what about the many other states? Where do their annual accountability tests come from? In many ways, we see state policymakers returning to the kinds of assessment operations they had in place before the arrival of the *CCSS* and the two sets of consortium assessments that, in league with the *CCSS*, were thought by some observers as likely to alter forever the nature of state-adopted curricula and annual assessments. During those pre-NCLB and pre-ESSA days, most states devised their own curricular targets in mathematics, ELA, and sometimes science. The chief determiners of those curricular aims were state-selected educators, K–12, and sometimes university content specialists. Then, to assess students' mastery of the state-selected curricula, most states publicly issued a request for proposals (RFP) so that independent vendors such as AIR, ETS, and Pearson Assessment could bid on developing and, if selected, administering a state's annual accountability tests. This appears to be the current direction of state-level annual testing. Even though we sometimes see small groups of states collaborating in such assessment ventures as a way of economizing (especially for tests covering particular content areas such as science, or for special student groups such as limited-English speakers), many states are essentially going it alone once more in the generation of annual accountability assessments.

The reason why teachers need to maintain at least a nodding familiarity with what's happening in their own state with respect to implementation of the ESEA reauthorization currently in place (in this instance, ESSA) is that the nature of those federally sired, often state-massaged decisions regarding the nature of state assessments can have a substantial impact on the way teachers should be building their own classroom assessments. For instance, if a state's annual ESSA account-ability tests in grades 3–8 feature a substantial emphasis on students' responding to at least a considerable number of constructed-response tests (such as short-answer or essay items), then most teachers in that state will understandably make sure that their own teacher-made classroom assessments also give students prac-tice in responding to such constructed-response items. Teachers who test their students exclusively with multiple-choice or binary-choice items are setting their students up for failure on the annual state tests. Yes, knowledge of federal or state assessment practices can sometimes make a whopping difference in the way teachers build their own classroom assessments. Moreover, the manner in which a state's officials decide to annually assess students' attainment of state-approved curricular targets often influences the way teachers in that state plan and imple-ment their own instructional activities.

The *Standards for Educational and Psychological Testing*

The *Standards for Educational and Psychological Testing* (2014), first published in 1966, contains a set of professionally approved expectations for the way educa-tional and psychological tests ought to be built and used. The *Standards* not only include a series of comments regarding the way that educational and psychologi-cal tests should be evaluated, but they also lay out a specific series of detailed "standards"—that is, mandates regarding what is appropriate in the nature and use of educational and psychological tests. This significant document is published by the American Educational Research Association (AERA) and is approved by that organization, as well as by the American Psychological Association (APA) and the National Council on Measurement in Education (NCME).

Because the *Standards* are often invoked during high-visibility courtroom contests involving educational tests, their influence on members of the educa-tional measurement community is considerable. Thus, for example, those who write textbooks about educational testing almost always try to make sure what they are recommending in those textbooks is in accord with the latest rendition of the AERA, APA, NCME *Standards*. Such authors, indeed, universally defer to the *Standards* when recommending how to play in educational testing's sandbox.

Periodically revised, the 1999 version of the *Standards* held sway for about one and a half decades, because until mid-2014 the 1999 *Standards* were essentially the only game in town. During that 1999–2014 period, a series of extraordinarily important applications of educational testing took place (for example, the role of students' test scores in educational accountability programs such as those fostered by NCLB and ESSA). Not surprisingly, then, the 1999 *Standards* were regarded by many educators as being somewhat out of date. So when, after a lengthy revision and review process, the 2014 edition of the *Standards* was published, great interest was predictably displayed by assessment specialists. To illustrate, if pivotal concepts regarding educational assessment were altered, or even if such concepts were more clearly explicated, these alterations and these clarified explications would, in a very few years, be incorporated into the guidelines governing not only what was being professionally recommended, but also what educators ought to be learning about educational testing.

The 2014 *Standards* do not introduce any dramatic reconceptualizations of the fundamental notions of educational testing that have guided educational measurement specialists since the 1999 version of the *Standards*. However, the new edition of this influential document both clarifies and tightens the interpretation of several key concepts in educational assessment. We will consider the most salient of those clarified "tightenings" in Chapters 3 and 4 on reliability and validity. The 2014 *Standards* did, however, more clearly emphasize the importance of assessment *fairness* than had earlier revisions. Thus, in the most recent *Standards* the three chief emphases for educational assessment are validity, reliability, and fairness.

Do classroom teachers need to become knowledgeable regarding all (or even most) of what's contained in the 2014 *Standards?* Surely not! We can let the educational measurement specialists of the world fuss with adhering to and interpreting content in the 2014 edition of the *Standards*. But it is a reasonable expectation that teachers at least realize that the ground rules of educational assessment did not arrive from outer space or from a Far Eastern measurement guru. No, these nuts-and-bolts guidelines about educational testing undergo a rigorous review, rewriting, and approval process every decade or two by committees of three national organizations most concerned with such testing. What teachers need to know, however, is that if they ever find themselves embroiled in any sort of test-related controversy, there exists an authoritative collection of definite dos and don'ts. It is called the *Standards for Educational and Psychological Testing* (2014) and it is available to all.

Assessment Versus Testing

So far, you have encountered several contrasts between teaching and testing, even though, when you glance at this book's cover, you find that it's supposed to be a book about assessment. If you're alert, you've already started to wonder, What's this author trying to pull off? Am I going to learn about *testing* or am I going to learn about *assessment?* Is *assessment* simply a more fashionable word for *testing?*

In short, what's the author up to? These are reasonable questions, and you will now be supplied with a set of compelling, confidence-engendering answers.

Almost everyone knows about the kinds of tests typically encountered in school. Most of today's adults, indeed, were on the receiving end of a hoard of teacher-dispensed tests during their own days in school. There were final exams, midterm exams, end-of-unit tests, pop quizzes, and even (in the interest of gender equity, of course) "mom quizzes." All those tests had one thing in common. They represented the teacher's attempt to get a fix on how much the teacher's students had learned. More accurately, such tests were employed to determine a student's status with respect to the knowledge or skills the teacher was attempting to promote. This is an altogether praiseworthy endeavor for teachers—to find out how much students know. If teachers are reasonably sure what their students currently know, they can more accurately tailor any future instructional activities to promote what their students truly need to learn.

The sorts of tests referred to in the preceding paragraph, such as the quizzes and examinations most of us took in school, have historically been paper-and-pencil instruments. When most of us were in school, the three most common forms of tests were essay tests, multiple-choice tests, and true-false tests. Until the past decade or so, those three kinds of tests were, by far, the most prevalent sorts of tests found in classrooms.

In recent years, however, educators have been urged to broaden their conception of testing so students' status is determined via a wider variety of measuring devices—a variety extending well beyond traditional paper-and-pencil tests. It is not merely for the sake of variety that teachers have been challenged to expand their repertoire of testing techniques. Rather, thoughtful educators have recognized that a number of important kinds of student learning are not measured most appropriately by traditional paper-and-pencil tests. If, for example, a teacher wants to determine how well students can function orally in a job interview, it's pretty clear that a written true-false test simply doesn't cut it.

Moreover, the widespread use of computers, along with all sorts of digitally based communication devices, has led to a dramatic upsurge in the use of computer-based testing. Later in the book, you will learn about not only computer-based assessments, but also computer-adaptive assessment. It almost seems that every new advance in computer capabilities is soon followed by a derivative computer-rooted version of educational testing. Although most classroom teachers will not be generating computer-controlled assessments for their own classroom use (because of the sophisticated programming demands of such test building), a teacher's students will occasionally be on the receiving end of large-scale computer-controlled standardized tests—often administered under a teacher's supervision. Accordingly, teachers should become at least reasonably conversant with the nature of these increasingly prevalent assessments. As you will learn later in this book, while there are wondrous things that can be accomplished when a test developer's inventiveness hooks up with computers' capabilities, computer-governed assessments can also be misused. It is not merely the presence of a high-powered computer that leads to appropriate assessment. Rather, assessment appropriateness depends on the specific way a computer is applied.

Thus, because many worthwhile learning outcomes are not best measured by paper-and-pencil tests, and because, when most people use the word *test* they automatically think of traditional paper-and-pencil tests, the term *assessment* has been increasingly adopted by many educators and measurement specialists. Assessment is a broader descriptor of the kinds of educational measuring teachers do—a descriptor that, while certainly including traditional paper-and-pencil tests, covers many more kinds of measurement procedures as well. Here is a working definition of **assessment** as it is used in an educational context:

> Educational assessment is a formal attempt to determine students' status with respect to educational variables of interest.

Lest you be put off by this fairly foreboding definition, let's briefly consider its chief elements. Note that the kind of assessment we're talking about is aimed at determining the status of students regarding "educational variables of interest." *Variables* are merely things that vary. (You probably figured this out all on your own!) In education, for example, we find that students vary in how much they know about a subject, how skilled they are in performing certain operations (such as long division), and how positive their attitudes are toward school. Those are the sorts of variables with which a teacher is typically concerned. Accordingly, they are the "variables of interest" that teachers typically measure. If the teacher's instructional focus is on the Industrial Revolution, then the teacher may wish to assess how much students know about the Industrial Revolution. In that case, the variable of interest would be the degree of students' knowledge regarding the Industrial Revolution. If the teacher is interested in how confident students are in their own written composition skills, then students' composition confidence would be a variable of interest. Educational assessment deals with such variables.

Our working definition also indicates that educational assessment constitutes a "formal" attempt to get a fix on students' status. (If you prefer, you could replace "formal" with "deliberate," "systematic," or "planned" because educational assessment is not a "seat of the pants" undertaking. Rather, it is a careful, purposive activity.) As human beings, we make all sorts of informal determinations regarding people's status. For example, we may conclude that the woman who cut into the supermarket line ahead of us is rude, or that the man who keeps stumbling as he climbs a set of stairs is clumsy. But these are informal status determinations. Teachers, too, make numerous informal judgments about their students. For instance, a teacher might conclude, on the basis of a student's glum demeanor during the first few moments of class, that the student is definitely grumpy. Such *informal* appraisals, although they may be quite useful to teachers, should not be regarded as educational assessment.

When I was a high school teacher, for example, I employed informal judgment to conclude that Raymond Gonty, one of the seniors in my U.S. government class, was not really interested in what I was teaching. I suspected this chiefly because Raymond usually slept during class. And I became more firmly convinced when he began arriving to class carrying a pillow!

The kind of educational assessment you'll be reading about in this book is formal—that is, it's a deliberate effort to determine a student's status regarding such variables as the student's knowledge, skills, or attitudes. The kind of educational assessment you'll be considering is more than a teacher's "impressions." Rather, you'll be learning about systematic ways to get an accurate fix on a student's status.

Assessment, therefore, is a broad and relatively nonrestrictive label for the kinds of testing and measuring teachers must do. It is a label to help remind educators that the measurement of students' status should include far more than paper-and-pencil instruments. Assessment embraces diverse kinds of tests and measurements. In the remaining pages, you'll find that, although the label *assessment* is used often, the terms **test** and **measurement** are sometimes used interchangeably with it. This does not represent any subtle nuances regarding the topic at hand—rather, it reflects an author simply getting tired of using the A-word.

Why Should Teachers Know About Assessment? Yesteryear's Answers

Let's indulge in a bit of time travel. Suppose you were magically transported back to the 1950s or 1960s. And, as long as we're in a let's-pretend mode, imagine you're a new teacher taking part in a fall orientation for first-year teachers in a large school district. The thematic topic of the particular session you're attending is "Why Should Teachers Know About Testing?" The session's lecturer, Professor Tess Tumm, is supplying the audience with a set of traditional answers to this thematic question based on how teachers actually can use classroom tests. Because you are a docile new teacher (remember, this is imaginary), you are compliantly taking notes to help guide you during the coming school year.

What's being suggested, as you've probably guessed, is that there are a number of fairly traditional answers to the question of why teachers should learn about assessment. Those answers have been around for several decades. There is also a set of more current answers to the question of why teachers should know about assessment. Let's give tradition its due and, initially, consider four time-honored answers to the question. Although these reasons for knowing about classroom assessment may have been around for a while, they're still compelling because they are rooted in the realities of what skilled teachers can do with classroom assessment. These four reasons may well have been the major points treated by Professor Tumm during our imaginary orientation session of yesteryear.

Determining Students' Current Status

One important reason why a teacher might assess students is to determine what they presently know and can do—for instance, what a group of students' current levels of knowledge are or what their current cognitive skills happen to be. If, for example, a teacher has been instructing students about a series of mathematical operations, there are moments during an instructional sequence when it would be useful for the teacher to know which of those operations have been mastered— and which haven't. Based on students' test performances, then, a teacher can decide which mathematical operations seem to need more instructional attention and which seem to need only a brief review.

There is one oft-encountered instance in which teachers can benefit considerably by using tests to determine students' current status, and it comes up many times during a school year. When teachers are trying to promote their students' attainment of knowledge or skills that are relatively *new* to the students, it is remarkably helpful to get a fix on what it is that students already know and can do.

For instance, if Jaime is already proficient in solving simultaneous equations, it's a waste of Jaime's time to make him plow through practice piles of such equations. In my youth, the following expression was sometimes used: "That's like carrying coal to Newcastle." It was used to disparage any scheme that reeked of redundancy. (One assumed that coal mining was a big deal in Newcastle.) Well, teachers who relentlessly keep instructing students in knowledge or skills that the students already possess are definitely carting coal to Newcastle. Assessment, if it is working the way it is supposed to work, allows teachers to identify students' current capabilities and, as a consequence, can help teachers avoid superfluous and wasteful instruction.

Thus, by measuring students' status, teachers can discern (1) where to put their instructional energies to ameliorate a student's shortcomings and (2) what already mastered skills or knowledge can be instructionally avoided. Such assessment is particularly useful for a teacher's planning if the assessment is carried out at the beginning of an instructional sequence. This kind of early diagnosis is often referred to as *preassessment* because it is assessment that takes place prior to the teacher's initiation of instruction.

Monitoring Students' Progress

A second, related answer to the question of why teachers should assess is that such assessments help teachers determine whether their students are making satisfactory progress. Sometimes, of course, it's easy for teachers to tell whether their students are progressing satisfactorily. I can still recall, with suitable embarrassment, the absolutely scintillating lesson I provided as a high school English teacher on the topic of modifying gerunds with possessives. It was a lesson designed for a full-class period, and I was confident that, at its conclusion, my students would not only understand the topic but also be able to explain to others why one of the following sentences contains an appropriate pronoun and one does not:

Improper
Pronoun   Gerund
↓   ↓

☹ **Sentence 1:** I really appreciate you sending the brownies.

Proper
Pronoun   Gerund
↓   ↓

☺ **Sentence 2:** I really appreciate your sending the brownies.

At the end of a bravura 40-minute lesson, replete with all sorts of real-life examples and a host of on-target practice activities, I was certain I had effectively taught students that because a gerund is a noun-form of a verb, any modifiers of such gerunds, including pronouns, must be possessive. And yet, at the end of the lesson, when I looked into my students' baffled faces, I realized that my optimism was unwarranted. After asking several students to explain to me the essence of what I'd been talking about, I quickly discerned that my lesson about gerund modifiers was not an award-winning effort. Most of my students couldn't distinguish between a gerund and a geranium.

Although teachers can occasionally discern informally, as I did, that their students aren't making satisfactory progress, more often than not we find teachers' believing their students are progressing quite well. (Note in the previous sentence that the modifier of the gerund *believing* is the possessive form of *teachers*. Yes, I'm still trying.) It's only human nature for teachers to believe they're teaching well and their students are learning well. But unless teachers systematically monitor students' progress via some type of assessment, there's too much chance that teachers will improperly conclude that progress is taking place when, in fact, it isn't.

A useful function of classroom assessment, therefore, is to determine whether students are moving satisfactorily toward the instructional outcomes the teacher is seeking to promote. If progress for all students is satisfactory, of course, then the teacher need make no instructional adjustments. If progress for most students is satisfactory but a few students are falling behind, then some separate doses of remedial assistance would seem to be in order. If progress for most students is inadequate, then the teacher should substantially modify whatever instructional approach is being used. Progress monitoring is a time-honored and altogether sensible use of classroom assessment.

A teacher also ought to monitor students' progress via classroom assessment because, more often than you'd think, the teacher can stop instructing on a certain topic well in advance of what the teacher had anticipated. Suppose, for instance, you're attempting to get your students to acquire a certain skill, and you've set aside 2 weeks to promote their mastery of that skill. If you monitor students' progress with an assessment after only a week, however, and discover your students have already mastered the skill, you should simply scrap your week 2 plans and smilingly move on to the next topic.

Another way of thinking about the monitoring of student progress is that it positions teachers to use the results of classroom tests as part of *formative assessment*—that is, the use of assessment-elicited evidence intended to improve unsuccessful yet still modifiable instruction. *Summative assessment*, in contrast, refers to the use of tests to make a final success/failure decision about a relatively unmodifiable set of instructional activities. In a review of research studies focused on the instructional payoffs of formatively oriented classroom assessment, two British investigators (Black and Wiliam, 1998) concluded that the use of progress-monitoring classroom assessments can promote striking gains in student learning on both teacher-made and external exams.

Based on the Black and Wiliam conclusions about the major instructional dividends of formatively oriented classroom assessment, members of Britain's Assessment Reform Group introduced the idea of classroom assessment *for* learning—in contrast to assessment *of*, learning. They describe this approach as follows:

> Assessment for learning is any assessment for which the first priority in its design and practice is to serve the purpose of promoting pupils' learning. It thus differs from assessment designed primarily to serve the purpose of accountability, or of ranking, or of certifying competence. (Black et al., 2002)

Stiggins and Chappuis (2016) have also pushed assessment for learning as the cornerstone of effective classroom measurement. Later, in Chapter 12, you will learn much more about the fundamentals of formative assessment.

Assigning Grades

If we were somehow able to carry out an instant nationwide survey of beginning teachers and asked them, "What is the most important function of classroom assessment?" The answer we'd get from many of the surveyed teachers is eminently predictable. They'd respond: *to give grades.*

That's certainly what I thought testing was all about when I taught in public schools. To be honest (confession, I am told, is good for the soul), the *only* reason I tested my students was to give them grades. I've talked to hundreds of teachers during the past few years, and I've been dismayed at how many of them continue to regard grade giving as testing's *dominant* function. A third reason, therefore, why teachers assess students is to assemble the evidence necessary to give their students grades. Most school systems are structured so that the end-of-course or end-of-year grades a student earns constitute the beginnings of a record of the student's personal accomplishments—a record destined to follow the student throughout life. Thus, it is imperative that teachers not assign grades capriciously. Whether we like it or not, students' grades are important.

The best way to assign grades properly is to collect evidence of a student's accomplishments so the teacher will have access to ample information before deciding whether to dish out an A, B, C, D, or F to a student. Some school systems employ less traditional grading systems—for example, the use of descriptive verbal reports that are relayed to parents. Yet, whatever the reporting system used, it is clear that the teacher's assessment activities can provide the evidence necessary to make sensible student-by-student appraisals. The more frequent and varied the evidence of student accomplishments, the more judiciously the teacher can assign to students the grades they deserve.

A corollary principle linked to "tests as grade determiners" is that some teachers also employ the prospect of upcoming tests to motivate their students. Because a student's grade is often dependent on the student's test performances, teachers frequently employ admonitions such as "Be sure to study this chapter carefully, because you have an important end-of-chapter exam coming up on Thursday!" Some teachers surely employ comments about impending tests as a motivational device.

In recent years, several thoughtful educators have proffered sensible guidance regarding how teachers ought to award grades to their students (for example, Guskey, 2015). A consensus of these writers' thinking—a consensus focused on "standards-based" grading—will be presented in Chapter 16 to wrap up this edition of *Classroom Assessment*.

Determining One's Own Instructional Effectiveness

A fourth and final reason why teachers have traditionally been told they should test students is that students' test performances can help teachers infer how effective their teaching has been. Suppose a teacher sets out to have students master a set of worthwhile skills and knowledge regarding Topic X during a 3-week instructional unit. Prior to instruction, a brief test indicated students knew almost nothing about Topic X, but after the unit was concluded, a more lengthy test revealed students had mastered most of the skills and knowledge addressed during the Topic X unit.

Because the comparison of students' pretest and posttest results indicated the teacher's students had acquired ample knowledge and skills regarding Topic X, the teacher had a convincing chunk of evidence that the instructional approach being used appears to be working. If the teacher's instruction seems to be promoting the desired outcomes, then it probably shouldn't be altered much.

On the other hand, let's say a teacher's Topic X pretest-to-posttest results for students suggest that students' progress has been minimal. Comparing results on the end-of-instruction posttest to students' performance on the preinstruction test reveals that students barely know more than they knew before the instruction commenced. Such trivial student growth should suggest that the teacher make adjustments in the instructional activities when teaching Topic X again next term or next year.

This does not imply that students' pretest-to-posttest results are the only way for teachers to tell whether they're flying or flopping instructionally, but students' end-of-instruction performances on assessment devices constitute a particularly compelling indication of whether teachers should retain, alter, or jettison their current instructional procedures.

In review, then, we've considered four fairly traditional answers to the question of why teachers should assess students. Here they are again:

Traditional Reasons Why Teachers Assess Students

- To determine students' status
- To monitor students' progress
- To assign grades to students
- To determine instructional effectiveness

You will notice that each of these four uses of educational assessment is directly related to *helping the teacher make a decision*. When a teacher assesses to determine students' status, the teacher uses test results to *decide* what instructional objectives to pursue. When a teacher assesses students' progress, the teacher uses test results to *decide* whether certain parts of the ongoing instructional program need to be altered. When a teacher assesses students to help assign grades, the teacher uses students' performances to *decide* which students get which grades. And, finally, when a teacher uses pretest-to-posttest assessment results to indicate how effective an instructional sequence has been, the teacher is trying to *decide* whether the instructional sequence needs to be overhauled. Teachers should never assess students without a clear understanding of what decision will be informed by the results of the assessment. Indeed. the chief function of educational assessment is to improve the quality of educational decision making.

Taken in concert, the four traditional reasons just described should incline teachers to assess up a storm in their classrooms. But these days, even more reasons can be given to explain why teachers need to know about assessment.

Why Should Teachers Know About Assessment? Today's Answers

In addition to the four traditional reasons why teachers need to know about assessment, there are three new reasons that should incline teachers to dive joyfully into the assessment pool. These three reasons, having emerged during the past decade or so, provide compelling support for the conclusion that today's teachers dare not be ignorant regarding educational assessment. Let's consider three new roles for educational assessment and see why these new functions of educational testing should inspire you to pump up your assessment knowledge and skills.

Influencing Public Perceptions of Educational Effectiveness

When I was a high school teacher a long while ago, teachers were occasionally asked to give nationally standardized achievement tests. But, to be honest, no one really paid much attention to the test results. My fellow teachers glanced at the test-score reports but were rarely influenced by them. The public was essentially oblivious to the testing process and altogether disinterested in the results, unless, of course, parents received a report that their child was performing below expectations. Testing took place in the 1950s and 1960s, but it was no big deal.

During the 1970s and 1980s, however, a modest journalistic wrinkle changed all that. Newspaper editors began to publish statewide educational test results on a district-by-district and even school-by-school basis. Citizens could see how their school or district stacked up to other schools or districts in the state. Districts and schools were *ranked* from top to bottom.

From a news perspective, the publishing of test results was a genuine coup. The test scores were inexpensive to obtain, and readers were really interested in the scores. Residents of low-ranked districts could complain; residents of high-ranked districts could crow. More important, because there are no other handy indices of educational effectiveness around, test results became the measuring stick by which citizens reached conclusions about how well their schools were doing. There are many reports of realtors trying to peddle homes to prospective buyers on the basis of their being located "in a school district with excellent test scores."

As matters stand, students' performances on a state's accountability tests are certain to influence the way that *all* teachers are evaluated—even if a particular teacher's own students never come within miles of an accountability test. Here's how this will happen.

Suppose you teach ninth-grade social studies, and your ninth-graders aren't required to take federally required accountability tests. Suppose you're a second-grade teacher, and your students aren't required to take any sort of accountability test. Suppose you're a high school teacher who teaches subjects and grade levels where no federal or state accountability tests are required. In all these "suppose" situations, *your* students won't be taking accountability exams. However, the public's perception of *your* personal effectiveness will most certainly be influenced by the scores of *your* school's students on any accountability tests that are required *and reported* for such schools. Let's be honest—do you want to be a teacher in a "failing" school? Do you want your students' parents to regard *you* as ineffective because you happen to do your teaching in what's thought to be a sub-par school?

The reality is that the performance of any school's students on federally stipulated accountability tests will reflect on every teacher in that school. If you teach in a school that's regarded as successful, then you will be seen as a member of an effective educational team. The opposite is also true. Unless federal accountability requirements are substantially softened, no public school teacher will be able to remain isolated from the impact of externally imposed accountability tests.

And, as will be pointed out later in the book, the nature of a school's success on high-stakes external assessments, such as federally required accountability tests, will (and, indeed, *should*) have an impact on the sorts of classroom assessments you personally choose to employ. Today's educators live in an era when public perceptions of schooling are more important than many educators might prefer. Yet, like it or not, that's the reality current teachers must face.

Helping Evaluate Teachers

Teaching skill is coming under increasing scrutiny these days. With the push for more rigorous evaluation of a classroom teacher's performance, we now see many teacher appraisal systems in which students' test performances constitute one key category of evidence being used to evaluate teachers. Sometimes, teachers are directed to assemble pretest and posttest data that can be used to infer how much learning by students was promoted by the teacher. And, of course, teachers whose students are *required* to take a state's annual accountability tests understand all too well that their students' scores on those tests will play a prominent role in teacher evaluation—that is, in the evaluation of *their* teaching.

Decision Time

Pressure from "Higher Ups"

Laura Lund has been teaching second-graders at Horace Mann Elementary School for the past 3 years. During that period, Laura has become increasingly convinced that "developmentally appropriate instruction" is what she wants in her classroom. Developmentally appropriate instruction takes place when the instructional activities for children are matched not only with the typical developmental level of children in that grade but also with the particular developmental level of each child. Because of her growing commitment to developmental appropriateness, and to its clear implications for individualized instruction, Laura's students now no longer receive, in unison, the same kinds of massed practice drills in reading and mathematics that Laura provided earlier in her career.

Having discovered what kinds of changes are taking place in Laura's second grade, however, the third-grade and fourth-grade teachers in her school have registered great concern over what they regard as less attention to academics, at least less attention of the traditional sort. Because state accountability tests are given to all third- and fourth-grade students each spring, Laura's colleagues are afraid their students will not perform well on those tests because they will not be skilled at the end of the second grade.

A year or so earlier, when Laura was teaching her second grade in a fairly traditional manner, it was widely recognized that most of her students went on to the third grade with a solid mastery of reading and mathematics. Now, however, the school's third- and fourth-grade teachers fear that "Horace Mann's accountability scores may plummet."

As Laura sees it, she must decide whether to (1) revert to her former instructional practices or (2) maintain her emphasis on developmentally appropriate instruction. In either case, she realizes that she must try to justify her action to her colleagues.

If you were Laura Lund, what would your decision be?

Although we will consider the topic of teacher evaluation far more thoroughly in Chapter 15, it should be noted at this point that a pair of federal initiatives have spurred much greater use of students' test scores in the appraisal of teachers. In 2009, the federal Race to the Top Program offered some serious financial grants to states that would be willing to install, among other reforms, teacher evaluation systems in which students' test performances played a prominent role. Two years later, in 2011, once again federal officials offered a flexibility program that allowed states to seek a waiver from the harsh penalties linked to the final days of the No Child Left Behind Act if they installed teacher evaluation programs in which students' test scores were regarded as a significant factor in evaluating the state's teachers.

Even though the education officials of most states signed up for one or both of those federal incentive programs and promised to implement systems for evaluating teachers (and principals) using programs featuring students' assessed growth, a good many states now seem to be treading water or scurrying away from the implementation of their once-promised educator evaluation programs. Nonetheless, in most of our states, descriptions of the current state-decreed teacher evaluation system call for use of students' *measured* growth as one key evaluative criterion.

As a practical matter, then, because educational assessments will be employed to collect evidence of students' learning, and because this evidence will be used to evaluate teachers, a teacher would have to be a downright dunce to dodge the acquisition of information about sensible and senseless ways to measure students' status.

However, as you will learn in later chapters, only certain kinds of educational assessments can properly carry out this sort of test-based task. Most of the tests proposed for this purpose are altogether inappropriate for such an evaluative assignment. Nonetheless, if judgments about teachers' quality are—because of well-intentioned legislative actions—to be based in part on students' assessment performances, then it is apparent that teachers need to learn about the kinds of tests that will support, or possibly distort, this evaluative endeavor.

Experienced teachers will be quick to tell you that the caliber of students' test performances is dramatically influenced by the caliber of the students being tested. It should be apparent that a teacher who is blessed with a flock of bright students will almost always get better test results than a teacher who must work with a less able group of students. And let's not forget about the quality of students' previous teachers. Wouldn't you rather be receiving a new group of students who had been effectively taught by Mrs. X than a group of students who had been ineffectively taught by Mrs. Y? Nonetheless, increasing numbers of statewide and districtwide teacher evaluation systems now call for teachers to assemble tangible evidence of student accomplishments based on external exams or teacher-made classroom assessments. It is clear, therefore, that today's teachers need to know enough about educational assessment to corral compelling evidence regarding their own students' growth. In Chapter 15 we will consider today's teacher evaluation strategies in more detail.

Clarifying Teachers' Instructional Intentions

For many years, educational tests were regarded as instructional afterthoughts. As soon as an instructional unit was over, the teacher got busy cranking out a test. Tests were rarely created before instruction was initiated. Instead, tests were devised *after* instruction to fulfill some of the traditional functions of educational assessment described earlier in the chapter—for example, the assignment of grades.

Today, however, many educational measuring instruments have become high-stakes tests. A **high-stakes test** is an assessment for which important consequences ride on the test's results. One example of an educational high-stakes test is a statewide test of basic skills that must be mastered before a student graduates. (Note that the important consequences are for the test taker.) Another example is the results of a districtwide achievement test that are publicized so local taxpayers' judgments about their schools' educational effectiveness are influenced by the test results. (Note that in this second case, the important consequences affect the educators who prepared the students, not the test takers themselves.)

A federally required accountability test falls into this second category of high-stakes tests. Because students' performances on these tests will so powerfully influence the way people regard a school staff's quality, such accountability tests will be genuinely high-stakes tests. You should know, however, there is nothing in ESSA that requires diploma denial or obliges students to be held back at grade level if they fail to perform well enough on a test. A *state's* decision, however, can transform a federal test into one that has an adverse impact on particular categories of students. Many people continue to be confused by this, because they assume that any federally mandated accountability test automatically requires diploma-denial or promotion-denial testing. It's just not so.

Insofar as important consequences are directly linked to assessment results, the content of such high-stakes tests tends to be emphasized instructionally by teachers. Because teachers want their students to perform well on high-stakes tests (for the students' own good and/or for the teacher's benefit), high-stakes tests tend to serve as the kind of curricular magnet seen in Figure 1.1.

On some educational grounds, teachers might prefer that tests did not influence instruction so directly, but the reality is that high-stakes assessment will almost certainly have an impact on classroom instructional practices. Because this curricular influence is sure to be present, it will be in teachers' and students' best interests if the nature of the upcoming assessment is well enough understood so that the teacher can organize the most effective, on-target instruction possible. (Later in the book, we will consider the deficits of teaching exclusively in terms of assessment targets.) In a sense, however, the more that teachers understand what the innards of a test are, the more effectively they can use this understanding to clarify what's to be sought instructionally.

Figure 1.1 The Curricular Impact of High-Stakes Tests

Even the low-stakes classroom tests routinely employed by teachers can help teachers clarify their instructional targets. Tests should obviously not be instructional afterthoughts. Rather, classroom assessment instruments should always be prepared *prior* to any instructional planning, in order for the teacher to better understand what is being sought of students and, therefore, what to incorporate in instructional activities. Assessment instruments prepared prior to instruction concretely exemplify a teacher's instructional intentions and, as a consequence, help clarify those intentions. Accordingly, clarified instructional intentions characteristically lead to more effective instructional decisions by the teacher. The better you understand where you're going, the more efficiently you can get there.

To reiterate, we've now looked at three reasons why today's teachers, unlike their counterparts of a few decades ago, need to be well informed about assessment. These reasons supplement, but do not replace, the traditional reasons why teachers assess students. Here are the three new reasons for teachers to be familiar with educational assessment:

Today's Reasons for Teachers to Know About Assessment

- Test results determine public perceptions of educational effectiveness.
- Students' assessment performances are often included as part of the teacher evaluation process.
- As clarifiers of instructional intentions, assessment devices help improve instructional quality.

These reasons are also linked to decisions. For instance, when citizens use test results to reach judgments about a school district's effectiveness, those judgments can play a major role in determining what level of taxpayer support will be provided in that district. There are also decisions on the line when students' test scores are used to evaluate teachers. Such decisions as whether the teacher should be granted tenure or receive merit-pay awards are illustrative of the kinds of decisions that can ride, at least in part, on the results of educational assessments. Finally, from the teacher's perspective, when tests serve as clarifiers of the teacher's instructional intentions, the teacher can make better decisions about how to put together instructional activities likely to help students attain the instructional outcomes represented by the assessment. With these three current roles of educational assessment, just as was true with the four more traditional roles of educational assessment, test results should contribute to educational *decisions*.

What Do Classroom Teachers Really Need to Know About Assessment?

Whether you are already a teacher or are preparing to become a teacher, you really do need to know about educational assessment. But the field of educational assessment contains reams of information. In fact, some educators devote their entire careers to assessment. Clearly, there's more to educational assessment than you probably need to know. What, then, should *classroom teachers* know about assessment?

The title of this book—*Classroom Assessment: What Teachers Need to Know*—suggests an answer. The key word in the title, at least for purposes of this discussion, is *need*. There are oodles of fascinating things about assessment. But to help your students learn, you really don't *need* to know a host of assessment esoterica. This book about educational assessment is deliberately focused on those things that you really *must know* in order to promote your students' learning most effectively. It is flat-out silly to clutter your skull with a galaxy of nice-to-know but nonessential knowledge about educational assessment. Such nice-to-know content often crowds out the need-to-know content. There is, after all, only so much skull-space available.

As a preview, let's consider briefly what you will have learned by the time you reach the book's index. (Because no research evidence supports any book's index as a teaching tool, if you haven't learned what's needed by the time you get to this book's index, it's likely to be too late.) It may be easier for you to get a handle on what you'll be reading if you realize you'll be covering topics dealing chiefly with

1. Constructing your own assessment instruments
2. Using assessment instruments constructed by others
3. Planning instruction based on instructionally illuminating assessments

Creating Classroom Assessment Instruments

Let's start with the kinds of classroom assessment devices you will personally need to create. The chief thing you will learn in this book is how to construct a wide variety of assessment instruments you can use as part of your day-to-day classroom instruction. You really do need to know how to determine what your students have learned—for example, whether they comprehend what they have read. You also really do need to know how to get a fix on your students' educationally relevant attitudes—such as how positively disposed your students are toward the subject(s) you're teaching. Thus, you are going to be learning how to create classroom assessment approaches to measure students' *achievement* (that is, the knowledge and/or skills students acquire) as well as students' *affect* (that is, the educationally relevant attitudes, interests, and values influenced by school).

As suggested earlier, the classroom assessment procedures you'll be learning about in the following pages will extend well beyond traditional paper-and-pencil testing instruments. You may even learn about a few assessment approaches with which you are currently unfamiliar.

In a related vein, you will also learn how to judge the quality of the assessment devices *you* create. And, at the same time, you will learn how to judge the quality of assessment devices created by others. Those "others" might be your own colleagues or, perhaps, the folks who devise large-scale assessment instruments such as districtwide or statewide tests. It may seem presumptuous to suggest that you, a classroom teacher (in practice or in preparation), could be judging the efforts of folks who create large-scale standardized educational tests. But you'll discover from this book that you will, indeed, possess the knowledge and skills necessary to distinguish between tawdry and terrific practices by those who create such large-scale educational tests. In particular, you can use your new knowledge to judge the quality of any accountability tests that may be used in your setting. Those tests are going to be so important that, if you are teaching in a state where accountability tests are educationally unsound, you definitely need to know it. What can you do if you discover that your state's high-stakes tests are inappropriate? Well, two action options come quickly to mind. For openers, you can learn enough about the shortcomings of the state's tests so that you are able to explain coherently to your students' parents why the high-stakes tests that your state has chosen are unsound. Second, and this may require some effort on your part, you can take get involved in educator organizations that are willing to help bring about the installation of more suitable educational assessments. You can do neither of these things, of course, if you have only a skimpy knowledge of what makes your state's tests tick—and how they really ought to be ticking.

It is also important for you to know enough about educational assessment so that you can assist your colleagues in evaluating an ever-increasing array of commercially developed educational tests. Educators have seen a spate of such tests developed in recent years. Some of these vendor-produced tests may be quite useful to teachers. Some of them, however, are seriously flawed—apparently cranked out merely to bring in a few bucks from desperate educators. There is no guarantee that a published test ought ever to have been published. Only an educator who possesses at least a small sack full of assessment sophistication will be able to tell whether a commercially created educational test is yummy or gummy.

Fundamentally, educational assessment rests on a foundation of common sense. Once you learn the technical vocabulary of assessment, you'll be able to identify departures from common-sense assessment practices, whether those departures are seen in your own tests, in the tests of a teacher down the hall, or in the tests created by district, state, or national assessment specialists. In short, after you finish this book, you really won't need to defer to any "measurement experts." You'll know enough to spot serious shortcomings in their efforts.

In Chapter 3, for example, you will learn about three criteria you can use to evaluate all educational tests. Those criteria apply with equal force to tests you might personally develop and to tests that are commercially developed. Once you get the hang of how to evaluate educational tests, you can apply this evaluative skill to any educational test you encounter.

Interpreting Standardized Test Results

Because your students will often be assessed with nationally developed or state-developed standardized tests, you will need to know how to interpret the results of such tests. In general, commercially developed educational tests focus either on (1) students' *achievement*, which, as noted earlier, deals with the knowledge

Assessment Literacy: Only for Grown-Ups?

Students' performances on tests can have an enormous impact not only on the students who take educational tests but also on the test taker's family. Teachers, too, are often affected by their students' test scores. To illustrate, today's teachers seem to be frequently buffeted by educational accountability tests whereon students' test scores can have an impact on teachers' tenure, assignment, and salaries. Clearly, educators at all levels, whether teachers or administrators, need to learn enough about educational tests to carry out their responsibilities successfully.

What those educators need, then, is a reasonable dose of **assessment literacy**. And here's a definition of it:

> Assessment literacy consists of an individual's understandings of the fundamental assessment concepts and procedures deemed likely to influence educational decisions.

Notice that this definition is focused on someone's understandings of educational measurement's *basic* concepts and procedures of educational assessment. What an assessment-literate person needs to understand is not esoteric and incomprehensible. Rather, most of it is just common sense applied to educational measurement. Describing assessment literacy a bit differently, it represents the main-line measurement procedures and concepts thought to make a difference in the decisions made about the students who take educational tests.

Well, if that's what assessment literacy is, who needs to have it? There's considerable pressure these days on teachers to become more assessment literate. You are currently reading a book that, unless the book's author has really let you down, ought to help you personally become more assessment literate. But what about educational

policymakers? And what about parents of school-age children? And, finally, *what about students themselves?* Don't all three of these groups need to beef up their understandings about the key assessment-related principles and processes that can influence students' lives?

Here's a little challenge for you. As you read this book, occasionally pause to think how you might relay to policymakers (such as school board members), parents (such as your own students' parents), and students (such as the ones you're teaching) the most essential things about the assessment-related concepts and procedures you're encountering. Remember, because test results these days can increasingly enhance or impair the decisions made about students, don't those students *at least* have the right to know what's going on behind the assessment curtain? A reasonable helping of assessment literacy is good for almost everyone!

It should be noted that, recently, increasing numbers of educational leaders have advocated the acquisition of **data literacy** by educators. Whereas assessment literacy is exclusively focused on understandings about the use of educational tests, the notion of data literacy typically also covers an educator's comprehension of a broader range of educational evidence, typically numerical in nature, regarding schools, districts, or states. To illustrate, students' attendance and tardiness are both variables of interest to educators—variables that can contribute to key decisions about educational programs—but such data are not captured by educational testing devices. Thus, the label "data literacy," because it can also include attention to scads of test results, is more inclusive than "assessment literacy." As a practical matter, however, both of those literacy genres are eminently worthy of advocacy.

and skills that students have acquired in school, or on (2) their *aptitude,* which is a term used to describe a student's academic *potential.* You should know, however, that the term *aptitude* is falling from grace these days. Several decades ago, people comfortably talked about "intelligence." Prospective teachers learned all about the *intelligence quotient* (IQ), which was a numerical way of indicating the degree to which a particular individual's intellectual abilities exceeded or fell short of conventional expectations for such individuals.

To calculate someone's IQ, you simply divided a student's *mental age* (based on how well a student's test score stacked up against a norm group's scores) by the student's *chronological age* (based on a nearby calendar). The result of this division was that student's IQ:

$$\frac{MA}{CA} = IQ$$

But "intelligence" has fallen out of favor with educators during the past few decades. The term *intelligence* conveys the notion that students possess an inborn, *intractable* potential over which schools have little influence. Yet the so-called intelligence tests, widely used until recently, often measured what students had learned at school or, more important, what students had learned at home. Thus, the term *aptitude* has been increasingly used rather than *intelligence* to convey a notion of a student's academic potential. But even the term *aptitude* tends to create the perception that there is some sort of innate cap on one's potential. Because of this perception, the commercial test makers who formerly created so-called intelligence tests, and then renamed them aptitude tests, are looking for a less negatively loaded descriptor. Interestingly, the tests themselves, although they've often be re-christened, haven't really changed all that much.

At any rate, you'll learn how to make sense out of the kinds of reports regarding student performance released by those who conduct large-scale assessments. You will need this knowledge not only to inform your own decisions about classroom instruction, but also to interpret students' test performances to parents who may demand answers to questions such as, "What does my son's standardized test performance at the 40th percentile really mean?" or "If my fifth-grade daughter earned a grade-equivalent score at the eighth-grade level on this year's standardized achievement test, why shouldn't she be promoted?" In short, you'll learn how to interpret students' performances on both **achievement tests** and **aptitude tests**. Moreover, given the relatively recent arrival of computer-administered and computer-adaptive educational tests, you'll find that parents are apt to be raising questions about such technologically abetted tests. Teachers need to be able to respond to such questions—preferably with the correct answers.

Instructionally Illuminating Assessment

Earlier, we suggested that because assessment devices exemplify a teacher's instructional intentions, those assessment instruments can clarify the teacher's instructional decision making. You'll learn more about how the link between

But What Does This Have to Do with Teaching?

This chapter contains over half a dozen reasons why teachers need to learn about assessment. Actually, there are seven reasons presented in the chapter, and that's one more reason than a half-dozen. (Notice how low-level the arithmetic in this book is going to be!)

But let's single out the *two* reasons why, *from an instructional perspective*, all teachers need to know about testing. The first of these reasons is the last of the seven reasons cited in the chapter—namely, the *instructional-planning payoffs* teachers can get from a clarified understanding of what they're trying to have their students accomplish. Because a properly constructed classroom test can truly exemplify what a teacher is trying to achieve, the resulting *clarity of intention* helps teachers make more astute decisions when they plan their instruction.

The second reason why all teachers should become more astute regarding assessment is also instructionally rooted. It's the second of the four traditional reasons considered in the chapter—namely, so teachers can *monitor students' progress*. If teachers use students' assessed levels of achievement to determine whether the current instructional plan is stellar or sickly, then teachers' adjustments in lessons can, if warranted, be more accurately made. Without the evidence yielded by classroom assessments, a teacher will often fail to spot instructional inadequacies. As the British investigators Black and Wiliam quite clearly reported, the instructional dividends from monitoring students' progress can be striking. Their views were based on solid research investigations, not wishful yearnings. And of course, any assertion delivered in a British accent simply reeks of credibility.

testing and teaching can prove beneficial to your students because you will be able to provide more on-target, effective instruction.

On the other hand, you'll also learn how some teachers inappropriately prepare their students for tests, particularly for high-stakes tests. You will learn about ways of judging whether a given test preparation practice is (1) in students' best interests from an educational perspective and (2) in educators' best interests from an ethical perspective. In short, you'll learn about the increasingly important relationship between instruction and assessment.

Later, you'll discover ways to build classroom assessments so that they'll have a decisively positive impact on how well you teach. *Tests*, if deliberately created with instruction in mind, *can boost your personal success as a teacher*. We'll dig into that topic in Chapter 12.

There's another important issue that should be brought to your attention—namely, the possibility (after you've finished the book) of your helping *parents* learn more about educational assessment. And why, you might ask, should a teacher be messing around trying to promote parental measurement moxie? It's a good question. And the answer is this: Parents who are *assessment literate* will be better able to *help you help their children learn* more successfully.

You see, most parents know little more about testing than what they can recall, often vaguely, from their own classroom days as students. But the nature of classroom testing has changed dramatically since that time. Not only are new approaches to assessment being used in classrooms, but students' test scores are also being used to judge the success of teachers' instructional efforts. You'll learn in Chapter 15 that, depending on the tests being used, this may be a dumb idea. If you and your students' parents truly understand the fundamentals of educational assessment, you can work together in many ways that will benefit your students. Assessment-literate parents can be a potent force to counter the serious misuses of educational tests we see so often today. And if you are teaching in a setting where officials have opted to use instructionally inappropriate accountability tests, you'll find that assessment-literate parents can be a potent political force that might, if you're lucky, help get more appropriate accountability tests installed.

There's another audience for assessment literacy that you should consider as you wend your way through this book. Please recognize that the lives of today's students are increasingly influenced by their performances on various kinds of educational tests. Why not, therefore, administer at least a dose of assessment literacy to students themselves? As you will see, most of the assessment concepts treated in this book are not particularly complicated. Indeed, the truly essential assessment understandings needed by students are well within the grasp of those students. Why not provide them with a bit of assessment literacy? They really need it!

Parent Talk

Mr. and Mrs. Smothers are attending a back-to-school night at a middle school where their daughter, Cathy, is a fifth-grader. After briefly leafing through Cathy's math portfolio and language arts portfolio, they get around to the real reason they've come to school. Mrs. Smothers, looking more than a little belligerent, says, "Cathy tells us she gets several teacher-made tests in class every week. All that testing can't be necessary. It obviously reduces the time you spend teaching her! Why is there so darn much testing in your class?"

If I were you, here's how I'd respond to Mrs. Smothers:

"I suppose it might seem to you that there's too much testing going on in my class, and I can understand your concern about testing time taking away from teaching time. But let me explain how the time my students spend doing classroom assessments really leads to much *better* use of instructional time.

"You see, the way I use classroom assessment is to make sure my instruction is on target and, most important, to make sure I don't waste the children's time. Last month, for instance, we started a new unit in social studies, and I gave students a short pretest to find out what they already knew. To my delight, I discovered that almost all of the students—including Cathy—knew well over half of what I had been planning to teach.

"Based on the pretest results, I was able to shorten the social studies unit substantially and spend the extra time giving students more practice on their skills in map interpretation. You probably saw some of the maps Cathy was interpreting as part of her homework assignments.

"Mr. and Mrs. Smothers, I want Cathy's time in class to be as well spent as possible. And to make sure of that, I use formal and informal classroom tests to be certain that I'm teaching her and her classmates what they really need to learn."

Now, how would you respond to Mrs. Smothers?

Chapter Summary

In this chapter, the emphasis was on why teachers really need to know about assessment. Early in the chapter, the assessment-related features of various reauthorizations of the Elementary and Secondary Education Act of 1965 were briefly described, because this oft-revised federal law's impact on most teachers' instructional and assessment decisions is becoming profound. *Educational assessment* was defined as a formal attempt to determine students' status with respect to educational variables of interest. Much of the chapter was devoted to considering why teachers must become knowledgeable regarding educational assessment. Based on teachers' classroom activities, four traditional reasons were given for why teachers assess: (1) to determine students' status, (2) to monitor students' progress, (3) to assign grades, and (4) to determine a teacher's own instructional effectiveness. Based on recent uses of educational assessment results, three more reasons

why teachers need to know about assessment were identified. Those more recent functions of educational tests are (1) to influence public perceptions of educational effectiveness, (2) to help evaluate teachers, and (3) to clarify teachers' instructional intentions. Regardless of the specific application of test results, however, it was emphasized that teachers should use the results of assessments *to make better decisions*. That's really the only excuse for taking up students' time with assessment.

The chapter identified three major outcomes to be attained by those reading the book—namely, they should become more knowledgeable about (1) how to construct and evaluate their own classroom tests, (2) how to interpret the results of standardized tests, and (3) how to teach students to master what's assessed in classroom and high-stakes tests. It was also suggested that an assessment-literate teacher should attempt to promote parents' and students' assessment literacy.

MyLab Education Self-Check 1.1

MyLab Education Self-Check 1.2

MyLab Education Application Exercise 1.1: Understanding Legislation

MyLab Education Application Exercise 1.2: Persuasive Writing

References

Andrade, H. (Ed.). (Winter 2009). "A special issue on classroom assessment," *Theory into Practice, 48*, no. 1.

Black, P. J., Harrison, C., Lee, C., Marshall, B., and Wiliam, D. (2002). Working inside the black box: Assessment for learning in the classroom. London, UK: King's College London School of Education.

Black, P., and Wiliam, D. (1998). "Inside the black box: Raising standards through classroom assessment," *Phi Delta Kappan 80*, no. 2 (October): 139–148.

Curwin, R. L. (2014). "Can assessments motivate?" *Educational Leadership, 72*, no. 1 (September): 38–41.

Goodwin, B. (2014). "Better tests don't guarantee better instruction," *Educational Leadership, 71*, no. 6 (March): 78–81.

Gotch, C. M., and French, B. F. (2014). "A systematic review of assessment literacy measures," *Educational Measurement: Issues and Practice, 33*, no. 2 (Summer): 14–18.

Guskey, T. R. (2015). *Challenging the conventions of grading and reporting.* Bloomington, IN: Solution Tree.

Hess, F. M. (2008/2009). "The new stupid," *Educational Leadership, 66*, no. 4 (December/January): 12–17.

Layton, L. (June 7, 2014). "How Bill Gates pulled off the swift Common Core revolution," *The Washington Post.*

National Governors Association Center for Best Practices and Council of Chief State School Officers. (2010). *Common Core State Standards for English Language Arts and Mathematics.* Washington, DC: Author.

Nichols, S. L., and Berliner, D. C. (2008). "Testing the joy out of learning," *Educational Leadership, 65*, no. 6 (March): 14–18.

Popham, W. J. (2009). *Unlearned lessons: Six stumbling blocks to our schools' success.* Cambridge, MA: Harvard Education Press.

Stiggins, R. J., and Chappuis, J. (2016). *An introduction to student-involved assessment FOR learning* (6th ed.). Boston: Pearson.

Wiliam, D. (2013). "Assessment: The bridge between teaching and learning," *Voices from the Middle, 21*, no. 2 (December): 15–20.

Assessment Literacy: What Is It, Who Needs It?*

W. James Popham, University of California, Los Angeles

It is becoming increasingly difficult these days to take part in any conversation about public education without someone's referring to *assessment literacy*—usually as a plea in support of it. But what is "assessment literacy"? And who ought to be assessment literate?

"Literacy," through the years, has referred to the ability to read and write. More recently, the term has come also to describe knowledge or competence in a specified area—such as one's "wine literacy." It is in this sense that most educators now conceive of assessment literacy, namely, a person's knowledge or competence regarding educational testing. What it is that different people need to know about educational testing, of course, varies from situation to situation. To illustrate, here's a definition of assessment literacy intended for teachers and other educators: *Assessment literacy consists of an individual's understanding of the fundamental assessment concepts and procedure deemed likely to influence educational decisions.*

As you can see, this educator-focused conception of assessment literacy addresses the *basics* of educational testing and, specifically, those fundamental concepts and procedures that are apt to have *an impact on educational decisions*. Thus, a teacher or administrator who wants to be assessment literate need not know as much about testing as an expert who specializes in measurement. Instead, educators merely need master a handful of assessment understandings—the understandings likely to impact educational decisions.

Other non-educator groups (for instance, school board members or parents of school-age children) typically need less knowledge about educational testing than those who are making daily decisions about students, because some of those decisions depend on students' test scores.

But *why* does anyone need to be assessment literate? The answer to this key question is that without the necessary knowledge regarding educational testing, *mistakes*—sometimes serious ones—are made regarding how to educate children. Examples of such mistakes, typically made by those who are *not* assessment literate, are listed as follows:

- *An Error of Commission*: A school board decides that an *ineffective* school serving students from affluent families is *successful* based on the wrong accountability test.

- *An Error of Omission*: Teachers in a middle school fail to use the formative-assessment process in their classrooms, despite its research-ratified record of success.

Because assessment-literate educators make fewer test-based errors of commission or omission than teachers who are less well-informed, please do what you can to promote the wider acquisition of assessment literacy among all education stakeholders. Indeed, increasing assessment literacy may be the most cost-effective way to improve our schools.

Chapter 2
Deciding What to Assess

Learning Outcomes

2.1 Identify key factors impacting teachers' decision-making when determining measurement targets for classroom assessments.

2.2 Identify key components of the Common Core State Standards when determining measurement targets for classroom assessments.

∨ Chief Chapter Outcome

An ability to identify, and understand the impact of, key factors that can help teachers determine the measurement targets for their classroom assessments

If classroom assessment does not help teachers do a better job of educating their students, then classroom assessment has no reason to exist. Consistent with that premise, this book about classroom assessment is really about teaching, not testing. That's because well-conceived classroom assessment will almost always lead to better taught students. So, before getting into some of the measurement concepts typically linked to educational testing, this chapter addresses an overridingly important *educational* question that each teacher must answer about classroom assessment. This crucial question, suitably highlighted in uppercase type, is

WHAT SHOULD A CLASSROOM TEACHER TRY TO ASSESS?

In this chapter you'll encounter a collection of factors that teachers should consider before deciding what sorts of things their classroom assessments should measure.

What to Assess

Far too many teachers simply stumble into an assessment pattern without giving serious consideration to why they're assessing what they're assessing. Many teachers, for example, test students in order to dispense grades in a manner that somehow reflects the levels of academic performances that students have displayed on those tests. Students who score well on the teacher's tests are given good grades; low-scoring students get the other kind. Traditionally, the need to dole out grades to students has been a key factor spurring teachers to assess their students. Other teachers, of course, also employ classroom tests as motivational tools—that is, to encourage students to "study harder."

Yet, as suggested in Chapter 1, there are a number of other significant reasons why teachers construct and use assessment instruments. For instance, results of classroom assessments may be employed to identify certain students' areas of deficiency so the teacher can more effectively target additional instruction at those content or skill areas where there's the greatest need. Another important function of classroom assessment is to help teachers, understand more clearly, *before* designing an instructional sequence, what their end-of-instruction targets really are. This clarification occurs because properly constructed assessment procedures can exemplify, and thereby illuminate, the nature of instructional targets for teachers.

Decision-Driven Assessment

Teachers use tests to get information about their students. Teachers typically make score-based interpretations about their students' status with respect to whatever curricular aims are being represented by the tests. Based on these interpretations, teachers then make decisions. Sometimes the decisions are as straightforward as whether to give Steve Smith an A or a B. Sometimes the decisions are more difficult, such as how to adjust an ongoing instructional unit based on students' performances on an along-the-way exam. But whatever the decisions are, classroom assessment should be unequivocally focused on the *action options* teachers have at their disposal. The information garnered from assessing students is then used to help a teacher make the specific decision that's at issue. Because the nature of the decision to be illuminated by the test results will usually influence the kind of assessment approach the teacher selects, it is important to clarify, *prior to the creation of a test*, just what decision or decisions will be influenced by students' test performances.

It may seem silly to you, or at least somewhat unnecessary, to identify *in advance* what decisions are linked to your classroom assessments, but it really does make a difference in determining what you should assess. For instance, suppose the key decision riding on a set of test results is how to structure a series of remedial instructional activities for those students who performed poorly during a teaching unit promoting a higher-order thinking skill. In this sort of situation, the teacher would definitely need specific diagnostic information about the "building-block" subskills or enabling knowledge each student did or didn't possess. Thus, it is not sufficient for a test merely to assess students' mastery of the overall skill being taught. There would also need to be a sufficient number of items assessing students' mastery of enabling knowledge or each building-block subskill. Based on the diagnostic data derived from the test, a sensible set of remedial instructional activities could then be designed for the low performers.

If, on the other hand, the decision linked to test results is a simple determination of whether the teacher's instruction was sufficiently effective, a pretest–posttest assessment of more global (and less diagnostic) outcomes would suffice. It's also appropriate, when judging the quality of a teacher's instruction, to assess students' *attitudes* relevant to what was being taught. We'll look into how you can measure your students' attitudes in Chapter 10.

In short, the decisions to be informed by assessment results should always influence the nature of the assessments themselves. Teachers should, therefore, routinely consider the decision(s) at issue prior to creating a classroom assessment device.

A fairly easy way to decide whether a test's results will really influence a classroom teacher's decision is to imagine that the test results turn out in two opposite ways—for example, a set of excellent student test performances versus a set of disappointing student test performances. If the teacher would be likely to make a *different* decision based on those disparate sets of performances, then the teacher truly has a test that can help inform decisions. If the teacher's decision would be pretty much the same no matter what the test results were, there's a strong likelihood that the assessment procedure will be more ritual than genuine help for the teacher.

The Role of Curricular Aims

Much classroom assessment takes place after an instructional sequence has been completed. There are exceptions, of course, such as the during-instruction monitoring of students' progress as part of the formative-assessment process (about which you'll learn lots more in Chapter 12). There's also the pretesting a teacher might use as part of a pretest–posttest evaluation of the teacher's instructional effectiveness. Yet many classroom tests are used at the close of instruction. And, because much classroom instruction is intended to help students achieve specified outcomes, it is quite reasonable to think that if, early on, teachers consider the outcomes they want their students to achieve, those teachers can more readily answer the what-to-assess question. What teachers should assess will, in most instances, stem directly from the intended consequences of instruction, because those hoped-for consequences will influence what the teacher will be teaching and, most likely, what the students will be learning.

Let's pause for just a moment to consider how best to label a teacher's instructional intentions. This might seem unnecessary to you because, after all, why should the way teachers label their instructional aspirations make any real difference? Aren't a teacher's instructional aspirations simply what a teacher hopes will happen to kids as a consequence of the teacher's instruction?

In recent years, the label "content standards" has emerged as the most fashionable descriptor for what in one locale might be called "learning outcomes" and, in another setting, "instructional goals." If you accept that reality as you rumble through this book, you might prefer to mentally slide in whatever synonym suits you. Regrettably, there is confusion among educators about how to describe the outcomes we hope students will achieve. If you are aware of this potential confusion, you can adroitly dodge it and move on to more important concerns. If you don't understand the nature of curriculum-label confusion, however, you are likely either to become confused yourself or, worse, add to the confusion.

Getting down to basics, ***curriculum*** consists of the sought-for *ends* of instruction—for example, changes in students' knowledge or skills that a teacher hopes students will experience as a result of what was taught. In contrast, ***instruction*** is the *means* teachers employ to promote students' achievement of the curricular ends being sought. Instruction, therefore, consists of the activities a teacher has students carry out in an attempt to accomplish one or more intended curricular outcomes. Simply put, *curriculum equals ends* and *instruction equals means*. Confusion arises when educators try to plaster diverse sorts of labels on the curricular ends they hope their students will accomplish.

No widespread consensus among educators exists regarding what to call the intended outcomes of instruction. During the past half-century, for example, we've seen curricular outcomes referred to as goals, objectives, outcomes, expectations, benchmarks, and content standards. In most instances, certain labels were supposed to apply to broader, more general curricular outcomes, while other labels were given to more specific, less general outcomes. What's important when carving out what you want your classroom assessments to measure is that you must understand precisely the meaning of whatever curricular labels are being used by colleagues in your school, district, or state. In most instances, whatever the curricular labels are, they are presented (often with examples) in some sort of official curricular document. Be sure you have a handle on what sorts of curricular descriptors are being used in your own corner of the world. You'll dodge much curricular chaos if you do. Most crucially, do *not* assume that you and your coworkers are using curricular labels in the same way. More often than not, you won't be. So, in passing, just do a dandy definition dance to see whether you are all dancing to the same tune.

More often than not in this book, the label ***curricular aim*** will be employed to characterize the desired outcomes of instruction. That phrase *curricular aim* has not been around for all that long and, therefore, has not had most of its meaning leeched from it. You'll sometimes encounter in the book such phrases as "educational objectives" or "instructional objectives" to describe curricular aims—just for a descriptive change of pace. But, as indicated, you need to find out what sorts of curricular labels are being used in the setting where you teach. Odds are that those labels will be different from the descriptors used here. That's okay, so long as you know what's going on—and can clarify terminology tangles when they transpire.

Consideration of your own curricular aims, then, is one action you can take to help get a fix on what you should assess. The more clearly you state those aims, the more useful they will be to you in answering the what-to-assess question.

In the 1960s and 1970s, there was widespread advocacy for *behavioral objectives*— that is, educational objectives stated in terms of the postinstruction behavior of learners. The push for behavioral objectives was fueled, at least in part, by a dissatisfaction with the traditional form of extremely general and ambiguous instructional objectives historically used by educators. Here is an example of such an overly general objective: "At the end of the course, students will understand the true function of our federal government." My favorite gunky instructional objective of that era was one I ran across in a state-level language arts syllabus: "The student will learn to relish literature." Thereafter, I kept on the lookout for an objective such as "The student will mayonnaise mathematics." I haven't encountered one—yet.

Still, in their attempt to move from unclear general objectives toward super-clear behavioral objectives, the proponents of behavioral objectives (and I was right in there proposing up a storm) made a serious mistake. We failed to realize if we encouraged teachers to use instructional objectives that were *too* specific, they would generate a profusion of small-scope behavioral objectives. The resulting piles of hyperspecific instructional objectives would so overwhelm teachers that they would end up paying attention to no objectives at all.

If you are currently a classroom teacher, *you already know* that you can't realistically keep track of whether your students are achieving hundreds of curricular aims. If you are preparing to be a classroom teacher, *you'll soon know* that

Decision Time
On-Demand Assessment

Dolly Davis is a fourth-grade teacher who has set up her social studies activities on a mastery learning basis. Students are allowed to work through most of their social studies assignments at their own speed. Much of the social studies program in Dolly's class is based on reading assignments, so students can move at their own pace. When students believe they are ready to demonstrate mastery of the social studies skills and knowledge that Dolly has described in written documents distributed early in the school year, students set up an oral assessment. Dolly then spends 10 to 15 minutes presenting a series of short-answer items that students must answer orally. So that students do not discover from previously assessed students what the items on the assessment are, Dolly selects items at random from a pool of nearly 50 items for each of the 4 major social studies assessments during the year.

Although most students seem to appreciate Dolly's willingness to let them be assessed when they're ready, several students have complained that they "got a harder test" than some of their classmates. The dissatisfied students have encouraged Dolly to retain her mastery learning model, but to assess all students at the same time.

Dolly is deciding whether to maintain her on-call oral assessments or revert to her former practice of using written examinations administered to the entire class at the same time.

If you were Dolly, what would your decision be?

dozens and dozens of curricular aims will overwhelm you. The trick in conceptualizing curricular aims that help rather than hinder is to frame those aims broadly enough so you can sensibly organize instruction around them, while making sure that the aims are still measurable. The degree of *measurability* is clearly a key in the way you should state your curricular aims. The broader the objective is, while remaining measurable, the more useful the objective will be, because you can be guided by an intellectually manageable set of curricular intentions. If you can conceptualize your curricular aims so that one broad, measurable aim subsumes a bevy of lesser, smaller-scope objectives, you'll have a curricular aim that will guide your instruction more effectively and, at the same time, will be a big help in deciding what to assess.

In language arts instruction, for example, when teachers set out to have their students become good writers, a curricular aim is often focused on students' ability to generate an original composition. That aim, although still measurable (by simply having students write an original essay), encompasses a number of smaller-scope aims (such as the students' ability to employ appropriate syntax, word choice, and proper spelling).

The concept of *measurability* is trickier than it first appears to be. Let's see why. A mere two paragraphs ago you were urged to frame your curricular aims broadly—so they subsumed more specific curricular intentions. However, you must also be sure your students' mastery of a curricular aim can be measured by a single, conceptually *unitary* assessment approach—not a fragmented flock of separate assessment tactics. Beginning teachers soon discover how difficult it is to arrive at instructional decisions based on a diverse array of dissimilar assessment tactics.

To illustrate, when teachers measure a student's ability to compose an original persuasive essay by asking the student to whip up such an essay (a writing sample) from scratch, those teachers can use the writing sample to get a fix on the student's punctuation skills, content mastery, spelling, and word usage—all at one time. A unitary assessment strategy has been employed that, in one fell swoop, captures students' mastery of lesser, contributory subskills and bodies of knowledge. The way to use students' writing samples to arrive at an inference about their composition prowess—and the separate subcomponents of that prowess—is an example of *unitary* measurability.

On the other hand, if the only way to measure a student's mastery of a curricular aim is by relying on a collection of substantively *different* assessment tactics, then unitary measurability is not present. To illustrate, suppose a teacher had formulated a curricular aim labeled "Geometry" that embraced (1) congruence, (2) similarity, (3) circles, (4) equations, and (5) geometric measurement. However, in order to determine students' mastery of the "Geometry" goal, five separate sets of items were constructed, each focused on one of the five separate subcomponents of the "Geometry" curricular aim. This conceptualization, as you can see, does not constitute unitary measurement of students' curricular-aim mastery. The five distinct subcomponents of the curricular aim have not been consolidated in such a way that a single assessment strategy can accurately reflect students' attainment of the five subcomponents. What we would have here is what might be characterized as "counterfeit coalescence." What teachers should try to identify is a modest number of high-import curricular aims that can be measured via a unitary assessment approach. A bevy of divergent, uncoalesced subtests clearly does not constitute unitary measurability.

Many educators these days use the concept of *grain size* to represent the breadth of a curricular aim. More specific curricular aims are considered "small-grain-size" instructional objectives, whereas more general curricular aims are regarded as "large-grain-size" instructional objectives. One useful way of distinguishing among curricular aims in terms of grain size is to estimate the amount of instructional time it will take for students to accomplish what's embodied in a particular curricular aim. If the curricular aim can be achieved by students in a short while, perhaps in a few days or even in one class session, then the aim is usually thought of as a small-grain-size outcome. If, on the other hand, a curricular aim seems likely to take weeks or months to accomplish, such an aim is regarded as a large-grain-size outcome.

Here are two examples of small-scope (small-grain-size) curricular aims in language arts:

- When presented with reading passages containing unfamiliar words, students can employ context clues to infer the unfamiliar words' meanings.
- The student will be able to write sentences in which verbs agree in number with relevant nouns and pronouns.

Now let's look at a broad-scope (large-grain-size) language arts curricular aim that subsumes these two small-scope objectives plus a number of similar small-scope objectives:

- After reading an age-appropriate nonfiction essay, the student will be able to compose two paragraphs, the first of which summarizes the essay's central message and the second of which describes the student's personal reaction to the essay's message.

Strive to come up with a half-dozen or so truly salient, broad yet measurable curricular aims for your own classroom. Too many small-scope, hyperspecific objectives will be of scant value to you because, if you're at all normal, you'll soon disregard an overwhelming array of overly specific curricular targets. On the other hand, a small number of intellectually manageable, broad yet measurable curricular aims will not only prove helpful to you instructionally but will also help you answer the what-to-assess question. Simply put, you need to create assessments to help you determine whether your students have, as you hoped, achieved your chief curricular aims. This means that when deciding what to measure in your classroom tests, you will frequently need *curricular courage*—that is, the courage to measure well what's most important.

Cognitive, Affective, and Psychomotor Assessment

In thinking about what to assess, classroom teachers can often be helped by considering potential assessment targets according to whether they are chiefly focused on cognitive, affective, or psychomotor targets. *Cognitive assessment* targets are those that deal with a student's intellectual operations—for instance, when the student displays acquired knowledge or demonstrates a thinking skill such as decision making or problem solving. *Affective assessment* targets are those that deal with a student's attitudes, interests, and values, such as the student's self-esteem, risk-taking tendencies, or attitudes toward learning. *Psychomotor assessment* targets are those focused on a student's large-muscle or small-muscle skills. Examples of psychomotor assessments include tests of a student's keyboarding skills in a computer class and tests of a student's prowess in shooting a basketball in gym class.

The distinction among cognitive, affective, and psychomotor educational outcomes was first introduced in 1956, when Benjamin Bloom and his colleagues (Bloom et al., 1956) proposed a classification system for educational objectives organized around those three categories. While recognizing that there are usually admixtures of all three domains of behavior in most things teachers ask students to do on tests, the 1956 *Taxonomy of Educational Objectives* made it clear there is typically a dominant kind of student behavior sought when teachers devise educational objectives for their students. For example, if a student is completing an essay examination in a social studies class, the student may be using a pencil to write (*psychomotor*) the essay and may be feeling remarkably confident (*affective*) about the emerging quality of the essay. But the chief domain of performance involved is *cognitive* because it is the student's intellectual analysis of the test's items and the student's intellectual organization of a response that mostly account for what the student's essay contains. Bloom's cognitive taxonomy included six levels of students' intellectual activity—ranging from the lowest level, *knowledge*, all the way up to the highest level, *evaluation* (1956).

Standards-Based Classroom Assessment

Whether you are an elementary teacher who has instructional responsibility for a number of subject areas, or a secondary teacher who has instructional responsibility for one or two subject areas, you should be concerned that your instruction and your assessments embody appropriate content. Fortunately, in the last decade or so, various national organizations have attempted to isolate the most important content to teach in their respective subject areas. These efforts to delineate content can prove quite helpful to teachers who are trying to "teach the right things." And they were a pivotal part of the 1990s *educational standards movement*.

First off, let's define what an educational *standard* actually is. Unfortunately, you'll find that different educators use the term all too loosely and often incorrectly. Actually, there are two types of educational standards you need to know about:

- A *content standard* describes the knowledge or skills that educators want students to learn. Such curricular aims are also referred to as "academic content standards."

- A *performance standard* identifies the desired level of proficiency at which educators want a content standard mastered. Such sought-for performance levels are also referred to as "academic achievement standards."

It should be apparent that although we might refer to both of the above as "standards," they are very different creatures. Just as cowboys in a western movie might loosely refer to "cattle," those cowpokes know that boy-cattle and girl-cattle perform decisively different functions. It's the same story today when educators utter the word *standards*. An academic content standard (a curricular aim) is patently different from an academic achievement standard (a performance level). To refer to them both as "standards" can cause a cattle-car full of confusion!

During the 1990s, standards were recommended by many organizations, led by the National Council of Teachers of Mathematics (NCTM), which in 1989 published *Curriculum and Evaluation Standards for School Mathematics* (1989). In that publication, NCTM made a major effort to reconceptualize what mathematics should be taught by identifying a set of important new content standards. Those content standards defined the chief curricular aim of mathematics education as the promotion of students' mathematical power—that is, students' ability to use mathematical thinking and understanding to solve problems and to communicate the results of those solutions mathematically.

Soon thereafter, other national subject-matter associations began to bring forth their own sets of content standards and, in some instances, performance standards as well. Most of them turned out to be very impressive. All of the standards documents represent the efforts of top-flight subject-area specialists who devoted a great deal of time to describing the knowledge and skills in a particular content area that students should learn.

It would be great if *you* could spend some time reviewing these standards documents to identify what you might be teaching (and, therefore, testing). But if you ever do engage in such a binge review of national content standards, try not to meekly succumb to the curricular preferences expressed in those standards collections. The reason for such a warning is straightforward. These standards documents were produced by subject-matter *specialists*. And subject-matter specialists, more often than not, simply adore their subject matters. Subject-matter specialists would like to see students master almost *everything* in their field.

Subject specialists often approach their standards-identification tasks not from the perspective of a busy classroom teacher, but from the perch of a content devotee. Content devotees and classroom teachers, just like steers and cows, are different members of the cattle crowd. If teachers tried to teach students to do *all* the things set forth in most standards documents, there'd be no time left for food, sleep, or movies! Content specialists, or so it would seem, have never bumped into the process of *prioritizing*. Establishing curricular priorities is far more challenging than one might think. Nonetheless, from an instructional point of view, it is far better for students to master *deeply* a subject's highest-priority content standards than to possess a spotty or superficial mastery of an expansive range of that subject's content.

Perhaps the safest curricular course of action for teachers, particularly novice teachers, is to *consult* the most recent national standards document(s) relevant to your own teaching responsibilities, and then see which of the content standards you have time to address instructionally. Without question, you'll get some wonderful ideas from the standards documents. But select your own content standards judiciously; don't try to stuff a whole wad of national standards into your students' skulls. That wad, more often than not, just won't fit.

Norm-Referenced Versus Criterion-Referenced Assessment

There are two rather distinctive, yet widely used, assessment strategies available to educators these days: *norm-referenced measurement* and *criterion-referenced measurement*. The most fundamental difference between these two approaches to educational assessment is in the nature of the interpretation that's employed to make sense out of students' test performances.

With **norm-referenced measurement**, educators interpret a student's performance in relation to the performances of students who have previously taken the same examination. This previous group of test takers is usually called the *norm group*. Thus, when educators try to make sense of a student's test score by "referencing" the score back to the norm group's performances, it is apparent why these sorts of interpretations are characterized as norm referenced.

To illustrate, when a teacher asserts that a student "scored at the 90th percentile on a scholastic aptitude test," the teacher means the student's test performance has exceeded the performance of 90 percent of students in the test's norm group. In education, norm-referenced interpretations are most frequently encountered when reporting students' results on academic aptitude tests, such as the SAT, or on widely used standardized achievement tests, such as the Iowa Tests of Basic Skills or the California Achievement Tests. In short, norm-referenced interpretations are *relative* interpretations of students' performances, because such interpretations focus on how a given student's performance stacks up in relation to the performances of other students—usually previous test takers.

In contrast, a ***criterion-referenced measurement*** is an *absolute* interpretation, because it hinges on the degree to which the criterion (for example, a curricular aim) that's represented by the test has actually been mastered by the student. For instance, instead of a norm-referenced interpretation such as "the student scored better than 85 percent of the students in the norm group," a criterion-referenced interpretation might be that "the student mastered 85 percent of the test's content and can be inferred, therefore, to have mastered 85 percent of the curricular aim's skills and/or knowledge represented by the test." Note that a criterion-referenced interpretation doesn't depend at all on how other students performed on the test. The focus is on whatever curricular aim (or educational variable) has been measured by the test.

As you can see, the meaningfulness of criterion-referenced interpretations is directly linked to the clarity with which an assessed curricular aim is explicated. Accurately described curricular aims can yield crisp, understandable criterion-referenced interpretations. Ambiguously defined curricular aims are certain to yield fuzzy criterion-referenced interpretations of scant utility.

Although many educators refer to "criterion-referenced tests" and "norm-referenced tests," there are, technically, no such creatures. Rather, there are criterion- and norm-referenced *interpretations* of students' test performances. For example, educators in a school district might have built a test to yield criterion-referenced interpretations, then used the test for several years and, in the process, gathered substantial data regarding the performances of district students. As a consequence, the district's educators could build normative tables permitting norm-referenced interpretations of the test that, although devised to provide criterion-referenced inferences, can still provide meaningful norm-referenced interpretations.

Because most of the assessment-influenced decisions faced by classroom teachers are benefited by those teachers' understanding of what it is students can and cannot do, not merely their relative standing in relationship to one another, classroom teachers will generally want to arrive at criterion-referenced rather than norm-referenced interpretations. A teacher's instructional choices, for example, are better serviced by evidence about particular students' skills and knowledge than by evidence about how those students compare with one another.

About the only instance in which classroom teachers will need to employ norm-referenced interpretations occurs in fixed-quota settings—that is, when there are insufficient slots for all of a teacher's students to be assigned to a given educational experience. For example, suppose there were five students to be chosen for a special outside-of-class enrichment program in mathematics, and the teacher had been directed by the school principal to choose the "best" mathematics students for the program. In such a situation, because *best* is, by definition, a relative descriptor, norm-referenced interpretations would be warranted. A teacher might build a test to spread students out according to their mathematics skills so that the top students could be identified. Barring those rare situations, however, most classroom teachers would be better off using tests yielding criterion-referenced interpretations. Criterion-referenced interpretations provide a far more lucid idea of what it is that students can and can't do. Teachers need such clarity if they're going to make solid instructional decisions.

Later, in Chapter 13, you'll be considering standardized achievement tests, assessment devices usually built to provide norm-referenced interpretations. At that time, the appropriate and inappropriate uses of test results from such assessment instruments will be identified. For most classroom assessment, however, the measurement strategy should almost always be criterion referenced rather than norm referenced.

Before saying farewell to the distinction between criterion-referenced and norm-referenced assessment strategies, let's highlight a confusion that first emerged about 50 years ago but seems to be bubbling up again in recent years.

When Robert Glaser (1963) first introduced the notion of criterion-referenced measurement more than five decades ago, there were actually two different meanings he provided for the term *criterion*. On the one hand, Glaser used it in a fairly traditional manner to represent a *level of performance*, such as one might employ when saying, "Let's get the quality of all trainees' performance up to a suitable criterion." In the 1960s, most people tended to use the word *criterion* in precisely that way—as a desired level of performance. On the other hand, in Glaser's article he also used "criterion" to represent a clearly defined criterion behavior such as a well-explicated cognitive skill or a tightly delineated body of knowledge. Well, in those early days, many educators who were beginning to learn about criterion-referenced testing were not sure which of those two very different notions to employ.

Yet, it soon became apparent that only the "criterion as defined behavior" notion really made much sense because, if the "criterion as level of performance" interpretation were adopted, then all of the existing education tests could instantly be designated as criterion referenced simply by choosing a desired performance level for those tests. Such an approach to assessment would be fundamentally no different from the traditional approaches to educational testing so widely used at the time. Glaser was looking for a new way of thinking about educational testing, not more of the same (1963). Thus, in the 1970s and 1980s, criterion-referenced testing was seen as a way of ascertaining a test taker's status with regard to one or more well-defined criterion behaviors. This interpretation was sensible.

Just during the last few years, however, many measurement specialists are once more touting the "criterion as level of performance" notion. This is a clear instance of regression toward confusion. It is not a suitable way to think about criterion-referenced assessment. Please be on guard so you can spot such flawed thinking when it crosses your path. Criterion-referenced measurement is built on an assessment strategy intended to determine a test taker's status with respect to a clearly defined set of criterion behaviors, typically well-defined skills or knowledge. These issues are treated elsewhere (Popham, 2014).

Selected Responses and Constructed Responses

Assuming a classroom teacher has come up with a reasonable answer to the what-to-assess question, an important point in determining how to assess it arises when the teacher must choose between assessment strategies that elicit *selected responses* and those that elicit *constructed responses* from students. If you think for a moment about the way educators assess students' educational status, you'll realize there are really only two kinds of responses students can make. Sometimes students *select* their responses from alternatives we present to them—for example, when we give students multiple-choice tests and students' responses must be selected from each item's available options. Other examples of selected-response assessment procedures are binary-choice items, such as those found in true–false tests where, for each item, students must select either a true or a false answer.

In contrast to selected-response tests, in constructed-response tests, students *construct* all sorts of responses. In an English class, for instance, students construct original essays. In a woodshop class, students construct coffee tables. In a speech class, students construct 5-minute oral speeches. In a drama class, students construct their responses while they present a one-act play. In a homemaking class, students construct soufflés and upside-down cakes. Constructed-response tests lead either to student *products,* such as the coffee tables and soufflés, or to *behaviors,* such as the speeches and the one-act plays. When the students' constructed responses take the form of a tangible product, classroom teachers have the luxury of judging the quality of the product at their leisure. For instance, after students create an original essay, the teacher can take this product home on the weekend and, while relaxing in the jacuzzi, either grade or immerse each essay.

When students' constructed responses are in the form of behaviors, however, such as when students are asked in a physical education class to run a mile in less than 12 minutes, the teacher must somehow make a record of the behavior—or else it disappears. The record might be created by the teacher's use of written summaries or be captured electronically via an audio or video recording. For example, when students in a speech class give a series of impromptu speeches, the teacher typically fills out some sort of evaluation form for each speech. Similarly, physical education teachers use their stopwatches to note how much time it takes for students to run a mile, and then note those elapsed times in a record book.

It was formerly thought that, although selected-response tests were difficult to create, they were easy to score. Similarly, it was once believed constructed-response tests were just the opposite—simple to create but tough to score. These days, however, educators have become more sophisticated about constructed-response tests and are employing many more types of constructed-response assessment procedures than essay tests and short-answer tests. It is generally conceded that both selected-response and constructed-response tests require taking considerable care when creating them. It is still true, however, that scoring selected-response tests is substantially easier than scoring constructed-response tests.

If, as a classroom teacher, you're choosing between these two assessment schemes, you need to focus on the nature of the score-based inference you wish to make from your students' responses. Some score-based inferences simply shriek out for selected-response assessment schemes. For instance, if you want to make inferences about how many historical facts your students know, a selected-response procedure will not only fill the bill, but will also be simple to score. Other score-based inferences you might wish to make really require students to display complex behaviors, not merely choose among options. If, for example, you want to make inferences about how well students can compose sonnets, then selected-response assessment schemes just won't cut it. To see whether students can create a sonnet, you need to have them construct sonnets. Reliance on a selected-response test in such a situation would be psychometrically silly. As usual, the *test-based inference* the teacher must make should guide the choice between selected-response and constructed-response assessment strategies. Nonetheless, if teachers plan to incorporate constructed-response items in their tests, they *must be sure to have sufficient time and energy available to score students' responses accurately.*

It is always possible, of course, for teachers to rely on both of these two assessment strategies in their classrooms. A given assessment, for instance, might represent a blend of both selected- and constructed-response approaches. As always, the assessment procedure should be employed to help the teacher get a fix on the students' status with respect to an otherwise unobservable variable in which the teacher is interested.

It should be noted that the distinction between selected-response and constructed-response test items is not meaningfully related to the previously drawn distinction between norm-referenced and criterion-referenced measurement. A test composed exclusively of selected-response items could lead to results destined for *either* norm-referenced or criterion-referenced interpretations. Similarly, a test consisting only of constructed-response items might legitimately lead to norm-referenced or criterion-referenced interpretations about test takers. The more comfortable a teacher is with various types of testing tactics, the more likely it is that the teacher will select the most appropriate assessment alternative to inform whatever decision is being informed by the results of a classroom test.

A State's Official Curricular Aims

A state's designated educational policymakers typically decide on the curriculum aims—that is, the content standards—to be promoted for the state's public school students. This is because education, not having been identified in the

Parent Talk

Suppose that Ms. Collins, a parent of one of your students, has cornered you after school and asked for a few minutes of your time. She wants to know what all the talk about "new, challenging standards" really means. She's read an article about educational standards in the local newspaper, and she wonders whether the "new" standards are really new. Her question to you is, "Why is there all this fuss about educational standards these days when it seems that teachers in this school are still teaching pretty much what they've always taught and testing what they've always tested?"

> If I were you, here's how I'd respond to Ms. Collins:

"I really understand your concern about educational standards, Ms. Collins. They've certainly been receiving plenty of attention from educators during recent years. But, regrettably, there's still a fair amount of confusion about standards, even among educators.

"Actually, there are two kinds of educational standards that you and I need to consider. A *content standard* simply identifies the skills and knowledge we want students to acquire in school. For example, your daughter has recently been improving her composition skills quite dramatically. She can now write narrative and persuasive essays that are quite wonderful. An example of a fairly general content standard would be '*Students' mastery of written communication skills.*'

"A *performance standard*, on the other hand, indicates *how well* a content standard should be mastered. In this school we score our students' essays on a four-point scale, and the school's teachers have agreed that a student should achieve at least a three in written communication to be considered satisfactory.

"What we now call *content standards*, we formerly described as goals, objectives, or outcomes. What we now call *performance standards*, we formerly described as passing levels or cut-scores. So some of the descriptive labels may be new, but the central idea of trying to teach children important skills and knowledge—this hasn't really changed very much.

"What is new, at least to me, is a much greater concern about the *defensibility* of our content and performance standards. All across the nation, educators are being urged to adopt more challenging standards—standards that demand more of our children. This has also been taking place in our own school. Thus, if you look more closely at what we're teaching and testing here, I think you'll see important differences in the kinds of skills and knowledge we're pursuing—and the levels of excellence we expect of our students."

> Now, how would you respond to Ms. Collins?

U.S. Constitution as a federal responsibility, has historically been regarded as a state obligation. Until the last decade or so, the usual way for a state to identify the curricular targets for its schools was to assemble groups of content-capable educators who, after substantial deliberation, identified the content standards to be promoted in the state's public schools. As might be expected, considerable agreement was seen between the official curricular aims of different states, but meaningful differences in curricular preferences were also observed. With the arrival of the *Common Core State Standards (CCSS)* in 2010, however, this changed rather dramatically. Many states have now accepted the mathematics and English language arts (ELA) curricular aims represented by the *CCSS*. Yet, because of the perception that the *CCSS* were being "pushed" on states by the federal government, substantial antipathy developed in many states toward what was often seen as a federal intrusion on states' curricular choices. Although, as was pointed out in Chapter 1, a number of states have still adopted the *CCSS* as their official state curricular goals, numerous states have renamed them—in part to discourage the perception that the state's official curricular aims were fashioned with the support of "the feds." As was true in earlier years when state-specific curricular aims were identified by each state, the adoption of the *CCSS*, or a differently labeled version of them, was usually accomplished by a state board of education or, in some instances, by a state legislature.

THE *COMMON CORE STATE STANDARDS*

As noted earlier, on June 2, 2010, the *CCSS* were released by the National Governors Association (NGA) and the Council of Chief State School Officers (CCSSO) (2010). In the next section of this chapter, an attempt will be made to provide a brief introductory picture of the *CCSS* in English language arts and mathematics. Yet, because these curricular aims have now been accepted (sometimes after being renamed) by many of the 50 states, it should be apparent that any teacher in a state where the *CCSS* curricular aims have been adopted (whatever they are called) should have much more than a nodding acquaintance with these curricular targets. Accordingly, educators are encouraged to consult either the CCSSO (http://www.ccsso.org) or the NGA (http://www.nga.org/cms/home.html) for a far more detailed depiction of what makes up the *CCSS*. Moreover, if you are a teacher in a state where some rendition of the *CCSS* has been adopted, it is likely that your state or district will have information available regarding the nature of these curricular aims. *Finally, if your state's curricular aims are not the* **CCSS** *themselves or based directly on those aims, you should consider simply skipping ahead in your reading to the treatment of science standards on page 55.*

When the previous edition of this book was published, the *CCSS* were at the height of their heyday. Almost all states had accepted them as their official state curricular aims, and it was thought that a pair of federally supported, consortium-based accountability tests would soon be in place to measure students' mastery of those nearly identical content standards. Accordingly, the previous edition of the book contained a considerably expanded treatment of the *CCSS* and urged readers to familiarize themselves with those curricular aims. But, to the surprise of many observers, the quest for widespread acceptance of an essentially identical set of curricular aims simply evaporated, and the availability of identical consortium-built accountability tests disappeared in the same way. As a consequence, what you'll find in this new edition of *Classroom Assessment* is a much abbreviated treatment of the *CCSS*. After all, if you are teaching in a state where a set of curricular targets *other* than the *CCSS* has been adopted, why do you need to pore over the intricacies of a set of curriculum targets at which your state's schools are not aiming?

Clearly, however, teachers must become comfortably conversant with *whatever* way their state has chosen to carve up its curricular goals. Moreover, if your state has chosen a set of assessments to measure students' mastery of the skills and knowledge embodied in those curricular aims, try to cozy up to descriptions of those state assessments. What's advocated at the state level can, and should, have an impact on what you teach and test. Even though it might be interesting to contrast your state's curricular aspirations with those of other states, what's imperative is that you understand what curricular targets *your* state's teachers are supposed to be pursuing and, of course, how students' mastery of those targets is going to be assessed.

Before presenting what will be, then, an abbreviated introduction to the chief features of the *CCSS*, a few stage-setting remarks regarding these curricular aims are in order. The *CCSS* did not arrive until June 2010, and in the early months thereafter many U.S. educators were not familiar with the nature of the *CCSS*. When many educators began to dig into the substance of the *CCSS*, they anticipated that these newly spawned curricular targets would be similar to the sets of state-specific content standards then seen throughout the nation. Those state-identified curricular aims had typically consisted of a list of content standards (that is, the sets of the knowledge and skills that students were supposed to master)—typically grouped under subject-area headings such as reading, writing, and mathematics. Beneath those subject headings, the content standards themselves usually were grouped under a set of general labels (sometimes called "strands") such as geometry, numeration, and algebra. Beneath those content standards, we usually found further particularization, such as the specific bodies of knowledge or skills a student should achieve in order to attain mastery of any content standard. These collections of state curricular aims were often too numerous, at least in the view of the educators who were required to promote students' mastery of them, but these state-specific aims—as typically formulated—were relatively easy to understand.

Regrettably, such was not the case with the *CCSS*. Several categorization strata have been employed to describe the curricular targets in the *CCSS*, and unfortunately, the labeling scheme employed for the ELA curricular targets is not the same as the labeling approach employed in mathematics. Thus, elementary teachers who are instructionally responsible for both English language arts and math are obliged to shift gears continually when seeking guidance from *CCSS* documents regarding appropriate curricular targets for those two content fields.

In the next few paragraphs, then, a particularly brief introduction to the organizational structure of the *CCSS* ELA and mathematics content standards will be provided. This "handshake" with the *CCSS* can be followed up with a much more meaningful "hug" by your spending time with the actual content of the *CCSS* (NGA and CCSSO, 2010). Let's begin with English language arts.

ENGLISH LANGUAGE ARTS *COMMON CORE STATE STANDARDS*
In an effort to identify K–12 standards to help ensure that all U.S. students would be college and career ready in *literacy* no later than the close of high school, those crafting the *CCSS* identified a set of curricular targets both in English Language Arts and in Literacy in History/Social Studies, Science, and Technical Subjects. As you review the complete array of these standards, your comprehension of them will usually be enhanced if you are aware of the several ways in which the ELA and literacy standards have been categorized in the *CCSS*. Let's consider those categorizations.

For openers, there's a fairly straightforward distinction between grades K–8 and grades 9–12. For grades K–8, the standards are set out on a grade-by-grade basis. At the secondary level, however, two grade bands are used to describe the standards for grades 9–10 and 11–12.

Then, at each K–8 grade level you will find sets of standards for *reading, writing, speaking and listening*, and *language*. For the reading outcomes, there's an important distinction drawn between standards based on students' reading of *literature* versus *informational text*. Architects of the *CCSS* reading standards wanted U.S. students to experience greater exposure to informational text than in years past. In grades K–5, in fact, the standards are broken out separately for literature and for informational texts. Ten "College and Career Readiness Anchor Standards" are presented under the following four general categories: (1) Key Ideas and Details, (2) Craft and Structure, (3) Integration of Knowledge and Ideas, and (4) Range of Reading and Level of Text Complexity.

In addition to the ELA reading standards, the *CCSS* also spell out anchor standards for writing, for speaking and listening skills, and for language. As was the case with reading, these curricular aims are broken out by separate grades in K–8, and then two grade ranges are used in grades 9–10 and 11–12.

Beyond the identification of ELA standards as described here, separate standards are also provided in the *CCSS* for literacy in grades 6–12 dealing with history/social studies, science, and technical subjects. Both reading and writing standards are given for students in three grade ranges: 6–8, 9–10, and 11–12. Authors of these grade 6–12 literacy standards in reading intend for instructional attention to those standards to be integrated along with instruction focused on the K–5 reading standards described earlier (NGA and CCSSO, 2010, p. 61).

The original publication by CCSSO and NGA (2010) not only contains substantial introductory material related to the *CCSS* but, in the case of the ELA standards, also presents a number of components intended to assist in the implementation of the standards. To illustrate, the *CCSS* authors strongly advocate that students become ever more able to engage in "close analysis" of increasingly complex textual materials. Accordingly, helpful illustrations of increasingly complex materials—both literary and informational text—are supplied (NGA and CCSSO, 2010, p. 32).

Given the several ways in which the designers of the *CCSS* attempt to organize the curricular aims embodied in their conceptualization of what students should learn, educators who wish to take full advantage of the *CCSS*—not only in ELA but also in mathematics—should become flat-out familiar with any *CCSS* segments in which they are interested. Thus, rather than being overwhelmed and/or confused by a set of seemingly off-putting curricular aims, educators can become knowledgeable about these influential collections of curriculum goals. If you're an educator in a state where the curricular aims are decisively different from the content standards found in the *CCSS*, of course, you have far less reason to cuddle up to the *CCSS* curricular aims.

MATHEMATICS *COMMON CORE STATE STANDARDS*

Let's look now at the *CCSS* for *mathematics*. The working group that identified the math standards divided those standards into two groups, the mathematical *practice* standards and the mathematical *content* standards. The content standards are identified for each grade level, kindergarten through grade 8, and also at high school. These mathematics curricular aims are categorized in three ways.

Standards define what students should understand and be able to do. Here is an example of a standard: "Use place value understanding to round whole numbers to the nearest 10 or 100."

Clusters represent groups of related standards. Here is an example of a cluster that includes the preceding standard: "Use place value understanding and properties of operations to perform multi-digit arithmetic."

Domains are larger groups of related standards. For example, the domain "Number and Operations in Base Ten" includes the preceding clusters of related standards.

To illustrate how this sort of categorization system works, let's take a quick look at one grade level and the numbers of domains, clusters, and standards identified for that particular grade. In the fourth grade, we find five domains, each of which contains one, two, or three clusters of standards. And each of these grade 4 clusters contains one to three standards. (Several of the standards have been broken down further into subdivisions reflecting two, three, or four different aspects of a student's understanding of a given standard.) In all, then, there are 28 grade 4 *CCSS* standards with, if one also considers the three "subdivided" standards, a grand total of 37 curricular targets in the *CCSS* mathematics standards.

Turning from the math *content* standards, let's look at the mathematical *practice* standards. The practice standards remain the same across the grades because they describe varieties of expertise that mathematics educators at all levels should seek to foster in their students. These practice standards are drawn from processes and proficiencies that have traditionally occupied important places in mathematics education. They are presented in Figure 2.1.

As the designers of the *CCSS* saw it, the Mathematical Practice standards describe ways in which those who engage in the discipline of mathematics should increasingly engage with the subject matter as they grow in mathematical expertise and maturity. It was the hope of those who crafted the *CCSS* mathematical standards that educators would make a serious effort to connect the Standards for Mathematical Practice to the Standards for Mathematical Content. Candidly, given the relatively few years that the *CCSS* math standards have been with us, there is still much work to be done in finding the most sensible ways to interrelate these two meaningfully different sets of expectations.

There is an important curriculum truth nicely revealed in the efforts of the *CCSS* architects to come up with the practice standards shown in Figure 2.1 and then urge educators to adroitly blend them with the *CCSS* mathematics content standards. This truth is that integrating different conceptualizations of standards is tough to do. For example, how does a fifth-grade teacher whomp up items to measure students' skill in solving elementary geometric problems while, at the same time, gauging students' ability to "reason abstractly and quantitatively" (Mathematical Practice Standard No. 2)? Whereas it is understandable that those who generated the mathematical standards would wish students to master key content and, at the same time, adopt sound mathematical practices, it is far easier to request such double-dipping than to implement it.

Turning to high school, the *CCSS* mathematics standards are listed as conceptual categories: (1) Number and Quantity, (2) Algebra, (3), Functions, (4) Modeling, (5) Geometry, and (6) Statistics and Probability. These six categories are believed to represent a coherent view of high school mathematics. To illustrate, a student's work with functions can cross a number of traditional course boundaries up through and including calculus.

Figure 2.1 *Common Core Standards* for Mathematical Practice

1. Make sense of problems and persevere in solving them.
2. Reason abstractly and quantitatively.
3. Construct viable arguments and critique the reasoning of others.
4. Model with mathematics.
5. Use appropriate tools strategically.
6. Attend to precision.
7. Look for and make use of structure.
8. Look for and express regularity in repeated reasoning.

Each of these *conceptual* categories is broken out at the high school level by the *CCSS* architects. For example, the geometry category is subdivided into (1) Congruence, (2) Similarity, Right Triangles, and Trigonometry, (3) Circles, (4) Expressing Geometric Properties with Equations, (5) Geometric Measurement and Dimension, and (6) Modeling with Geometry. And each of these subdivisions typically comprises several further subdivisions. Slight differences also exist for high school in the mathematical *practices* for the conceptual categories that, in elementary grades, had remained the same.

It should be apparent that the manner in which the *CCSS* mathematics standards are organized could easily become confusing. There are so many curricular targets—in different categories and at different levels—embraced by the math standards, that educators really do need to arrive at a "mentally manageable" way of representing the diverse mathematical outcomes being sought *for* students and expected *of* them.

"Many a Slip . . . "

The older I get, the fewer folks I find who are familiar with the maxims I've relied on most of my life. One of those sayings is, "There's many a slip twixt the cup and the lip!" Besides giving me an opportunity to use the word "twixt" (an option that doesn't come along very often), this maxim reminds us that as we raise our cups of hot cocoa toward our mouths or make any set of serious plans, numerous things can go wrong. Through the years, loads of laps have been scalded by errant, about-to-be-consumed drinks of one sort or another. Yet, this little-used adage still alerts us to the fact that well-conceived, headlong hopes often stumble en route to the finish line. And so it is with curricular aims such as those embodied in the *CCSS*.

For the most part, the *CCSS* curricular aims are equal to or better than the state curricular goals they are replacing—that is, the ones that were adopted by individual states during the last several decades. Indeed, a report was issued in late 2011 by the respected nonpartisan Center on Education Policy in Washington, DC, seemed to confirm such an estimate of *CCSS* quality. After surveying school districts in the 44 states where the *CCSS* had been officially adopted, this report concluded that almost 60 percent of officials in those districts agreed "that the new standards in math and English language arts are more rigorous than the ones they are replacing" (Center on Education Policy, 2011, p. 1). Moreover, many district-level officials recognize the merits of those curricular aims. Where, then, does "slip twixting" mar this happy picture? Here's an answer to that question: *Curricular aims—whether local, state, or national—are just words, and sometimes fairly meaningless words.* That's right, no matter how laudable the curricular aspirations embodied in the *CCSS* or similar goals are, if they are poorly assessed, then their positive impact will almost certainly be minimal.

Science: Not to Be Left Behind

At the same time that the *CCSS* was coming into being, and thereby exerting a serious influence on curricular thinking about English language arts and mathematics, another important content area was undergoing some major rethinking, as well—namely, science. This thinking culminated in the *Next Generation Science Standards* (*NGSS*). Teachers who have responsibility for the teaching of science, whether in elementary school or secondary school, are certain to be encountering curricular thought stemming directly from the conceptualization of science education that's contained in the *NGSS*.

The *NGSS* derived from a multistate effort to create a new set of curricular aims for science predicated on the belief that there are three distinct, yet equally important, dimensions to learning science: (1) disciplinary core ideas, (2) scientific and engineering practices, and (3) crosscutting concepts. These three dimensions are combined to form every content standard. Ideally, each dimension works with the other two to help students build a coherent understanding of science over time. These important science standards were developed by a consortium of 26 states, along with the National Science Teachers Association, the American Association for the Advancement of Science, the National Research Council, and Achieve, a nonprofit organization active in the generation of content standards in English and mathematics. Unlike the development procedures witnessed in the creation of the *CCSS*, a major effort was made so that interested parties could review the emerging versions of these new science standards. To illustrate, not only were science-specialist reviewers called on from the participating consortium states to help shape the draft science standards, but the public was also invited to review and react to the standards that were under development. The final version of the *NGSS was* released in April 2013.

Central to the *NGSS* are the previously mentioned three dimensions: disciplinary core ideas, scientific and engineering practices, and crosscutting concepts. Disciplinary core ideas consist of specific content and subject areas. The second dimension, scientific and engineering practices, is intended to foster students' mastery of specified content and subjects, but to do so via the methods employed by engineers and scientists. Finally, crosscutting concepts help students explore interrelationships among four domains of science—that is, physical science, life science, earth and space science, and engineering design. For example, when such concepts as "cause and effect" are made explicit for students, those concepts can help students develop a coherent and scientifically based view of the world surrounding them.

But, as we saw with respect to the *CCSS* in mathematics, melding different ways of describing curricular aspirations, as was done when math practices were to be amalgamated with math content, is no trivial challenge. Given that the developers of the *NGSS* were committed to creating a science curriculum wherein all three *NGSS* dimensions coalesce, of disciplinary core ideas, scientific and engineering practices, and crosscutting concepts, it is apparent that teachers charged with promoting their students' scientific mastery will need ample support in the way of instructional materials, assessment instruments, and guidance regarding how best to test and teach their students.

James Pellegrino, co-chair of the National Academy of Science committee tasked with developing assessments for *NGSS*, believes that a coherent science assessment system must include (1) large-scale assessments to audit student learning over time so as to evaluate the effectiveness of science education programs, (2) classroom assessments to help identify areas where students are making progress or struggling, as well as for assigning course grades, and (3) regularly collected information on the quality of classroom instruction to determine whether students have had an opportunity to learn what's being tested via both large-scale and classroom science assessments (Pellegrino, 2016, p. 1). Clearly, teachers who wish to promote in their classroom assessments the conceptualization of science embodied in the *NGSS* will need to devote some serious thinking, ideally with colleagues, to decide how best to implement this conceptually captivating but challenging way of thinking about how to teach science.

Early reports from teachers who have attempted to both teach and test their students' mastery of the *NGSS* indicate that the multidimensionality of those curricular aims presents an implementation obstacle to even the most ardent *NGSS* proponents. Remembering that the three basic dimensions to learning science are (1) disciplinary core ideas, (2) scientific and engineering practices, and (3) crosscutting concepts, many teachers who are not entirely comfortable with scientific content have difficulty arriving at coherent ways of blending instruction and, thereafter, measuring their students' attainment. So, if you embark on a personal attempt to fit those three basic dimensions together in your own teaching and testing, do not be surprised if substantial effort is required. Making the distinct dimensions mesh merrily with one another is flat-out tough to do.

What's Assessed on Your State's Accountability Test?

Teachers working with students who are on the receiving end of a state's annual accountability tests should, without question, take into consideration what is to be assessed each year on state accountability assessments. Results from such tests are typically administered in the spring, near the close of a school year, and the results can have a substantial impact on the evaluations awarded to schools, school districts, and teachers. Accordingly, when deciding what to measure in your own classroom tests, you would be foolish not to consider what's being assessed by such unarguably significant tests.

Because the education officials of each state must determine what sorts of accountability tests will be employed in their state, every teacher needs to find out for certain what's to be measured by state assessments in that teacher's state. Having done so, the teacher needs to determine whether his or her students, because of grade levels taught or subject matter taught, will be assessed each year regarding what the teacher was supposed to be teaching. Obviously, what's eligible for assessment on such high-stakes tests should have a major impact on what the teacher tries to teach and what the teacher tries to assess.

Even teachers whose students will be assessed only in later years should become conversant with what's to be measured in those assessments to come. For example, teachers of 1st-graders or 2nd-graders—whose students will not be tested each year—should surely consider what's to be tested in the third grade, when state-level accountability testing begins. Similarly, a 9th-grade English teacher whose students won't be taking an accountability test until the 10th or 11th grade should still look into what will be assessed in English language arts when accountability testing resumes.

Just a few years ago, many educators still clung to a belief that because of more widely accepted common curricular aims, such as those embraced in the *CCSS* and the *NGSS* (or in modest variations of those content standards), it might still be possible for a small set of accountability tests to measure various states' mastery of essentially identical curricular goals. Yet, in the words of the ancient Greek philosopher Heraclitus, who claimed that "change is the only constant in life," we seem to be in the midst of an era of all-out assessment flux. State education authorities are, with relatively few exceptions, going their own way. Although it seems likely that small groups of states may collaborate to develop mutually acceptable curricular goals and accountability assessments, the vision of an accountability testing system in which test results from nearly all states could be meaningfully contrasted seems as dead as the proverbial dodo.

For a variety of reasons, such as (1) cost considerations, (2) a public backlash against too much testing, and (3) the perception that the *Common Core State Standards* had been a federal rather than a state initiative, many states have withdrawn their acceptance of the *CCSS* altogether, only to adopt a set of state-determined curricular aims and state-commissioned assessments of how well the state's students have achieved those aims. Accordingly, what's to be assessed by important external tests will have an impact on a teacher's decisions about the content of classroom assessments—especially if the teacher's own students will be taking those assessments immediately or in later years. This doesn't mean that whatever is tested on a later, important test needs to be completely mirrored by a teacher's classroom tests. But some serious scrutiny of what's to be measured by any subsequent significant assessment is called for.

It is invariably expected that a state's accountability tests should be *aligned* with the state's official curricular aims. Let's look briefly at the term *alignment*. In the field of education, *alignment* is the only 9-letter word that seems to function as a 4-letter word. This is because many people play fairly fast and loose with a term that, by its nature, seems to evoke fast and loose play. **Alignment** is the degree to which there is a meaningful agreement between two or more of the following: curriculum, instruction, and assessment. What is generally called for, of course, is the agreement of a state's accountability tests with the state's content standards. To the extent that such alignment between curriculum and assessment has been achieved, a teacher would have to be a ninny not to recognize that it is sensible to also align her or his classroom curricula and assessments with whatever state content standards are to be assessed by the accountability tests in that teacher's state.

A major difficulty with the concept of alignment, unfortunately, is that it is decidedly *squishy*. What constitutes alignment in one educator's eyes may be seen as nonalignment by another educator. And there is often much self-interested "seeing alignment where none exists." So, whenever you hear someone touting the alignment among instruction and curriculum and assessment, try to dig a bit deeper so you can see whether the alignment being described is based on rigorous or relaxed ways of determining agreement levels. (An excellent guide to the determination of alignment has been provided by Cizek et al., 2018.)

But what do teachers do if they wish to align their classroom tests with important exams such as a state's annual accountability tests? This can be a quandary for most teachers, and it turns out to depend—almost totally—on the quality of the accountability exams. If your state's accountability exams are capable of accurately detecting instructional quality, then you'll probably want to make sure your classroom assessments mesh with what's assessed on those accountability tests. If your state's accountability tests, on the other hand, are *not* capable of accurately detecting instructional quality, then you may pay less heed to what's assessed by those statewide tests. If you continue reading until you arrive at this book's final chapter, you'll learn how to distinguish between state-level accountability tests that are grubby and those that glisten.

Other Exams You Should Know About

Although classroom teachers should be at least aware of key international assessments of students' learning, as well as the most prominent national assessment of students' achievements, rarely will the content of those examinations have a meaningful impact on what teachers attempt to assess with their own students. Nonetheless, to be totally unaware of such large-scale standardized educational tests would not be the mark of a knowledgeable educational professional. Accordingly, here is a quick summary of the best known of these exams.

The National Assessment of Educational Progress (NAEP) is a congressionally mandated project of the U.S. Department of Education. It assesses U.S. students' knowledge and skills in geography, reading, writing, mathematics, science, U.S. history, the arts, civics, and other academic subjects. Since 1969, NAEP has periodically surveyed the achievement of students at *ages* 9, 13, as well as 17 and, since the 1980s, in *grades* 4, 8, and 12. NAEP was originally intended to measure U.S. students' levels of academic achievement over time. Because NAEP scores, for several of its subject areas, are employed to rank states' performances, NAEP results typically generate considerable interest—especially for those states ranked high or low. Due to the sampling procedures used, NAEP scores, however, are not reported for individual students, schools, or districts—other than two dozen or so of the nation's largest school districts. Given the purposefully national orientation of NAEP, it is remarkably difficult for classroom teachers to derive practical instruction-related insights from what's assessed by the NAEP tests. Thus, although NEAP is widely regarded as "the gold standard" of educational testing because of the technical care with which its tests are developed, administered, and analyzed, its implications for classroom assessments are limited.

Turning from national to international assessments, one soon seems to be operating in an alphabet soup of testing labels. The oldest of three best-known international educational assessments is TIMSS (Trends in International Mathematics and Science Study), which was initially administered in 1995. TIMSS measures students of 10 and 14 years of age every 4 years, and, as its title implies, it assesses students' skills and knowledge in mathematics and science. TIMSS is managed by the International Association for the Evaluation of Educational Achievement (IEA).

In 2000 we first saw the administration of PISA (Programme for International Student Assessment), a project of the Organization for Economic Cooperation and Development (OECD). These examinations measure students at age 15 in reading, mathematics, science, and problem solving. They are administered every 3 years, and special emphasis is given to one of those 4 areas during each assessment.

Finally, IEA began offering another international exam in 2001 with the release of PIRLS (Progress in International Reading Literacy Study). PIRLS is administered to samples of 10-year-old students every 5 years, and it focuses on their abilities in reading.

Because NEAP is carried out by the U.S. federal government, the actual size of the national samples and the frequency with which different assessments are repeated depend substantially on governmental funding. For the three international studies, students from a meaningful number of nations take part. To illustrate, for PISA we often see about 70 nations participating, for TIMSS the number of nations approximates 60, and for PIRLS more than 50 countries typically take part. Reports from these assessments, as well as NAEP, are available from the usual Internet sources.

Because this second chapter is focused on a teacher's decisions regarding what to assess in the teacher's own classroom, are there any content determiners for a teacher's classroom tests lurking in these major exams and what they measure? Well, a substantial diversity of opinion exists with respect to what NAEP or the trio of international assessments offer in the way of curricular guidance or, for that matter, what their results tell us about the quality of schooling offered in the United States and, in the case of NAEP, in its various states. Yes, for every person who supports the importance of these prominent exams, there seems to be another who worries that the substantial differences among nations—and states—renders the rankings of nations—and states—according to students' results must be ladled out with so many cautions as to render the implications of those rankings largely meaningless. If you ever decide to probe these sorts of issues in greater depth yourself, you will discover that reaching a personal decision about the instructional or evaluative merits of NAEP, TIMSS, PISA, and PIRLS is far from easy.

Assessment Blueprints

A number of teachers find it helpful, especially when constructing major examinations, to develop what's called an *assessment blueprint* or a *test blueprint*. Such blueprints can vary dramatically in the level of rigor and specificity they embody. For the most part, these blueprints are two-way tables in which one dimension represents the curricular aims the teacher wants to assess, and the other dimension represents the levels of cognitive functioning being sought. For instance, the following example from a teacher's assessment blueprint illustrates how these organizational schemes work by dividing each curricular aim's items into knowledge (low-level recall of information) and cognitive levels higher than mere recall.

| | Number of Items | |
| | Cognitive Level | |
Curricular Aim	Knowledge	Above Knowledge
1	3	1
2	1	4
3	2	2
etc.	etc.	

Assessment blueprints can help teachers identify curricular aims that are not being measured with sufficient items or that lack sufficient items at an appropriate level of **cognitive demand**. As noted earlier in the chapter, the Bloom *Taxonomy of Educational Objectives* (Bloom et al., 1956) has been around for well over a half-century, and for about 50 years it was the *only* system used to contrast different levels of cognitive demand. As you can see in the previous illustration, sometimes Bloom's six levels of cognitive demand were scrunched into a smaller number—for instance, into a simple dichotomy between Bloom's lowest cognitive level (that is, memorized *knowledge*) and any cognitive demand above knowledge.

However, in 2002, Norman Webb of the University of Wisconsin provided educators with a procedure for gauging the alignment between a test's items and the curricular aims supposedly being measured by that test (Webb, 2002). A key component of Webb's alignment process was his proposed four **Depth of Knowledge** categories, which functioned as a cognitive-demand classification system similar to Bloom's. Because Webb's depth of knowledge (DOK) system is often used by today's educators not only in connection with assessment blueprints, but also when choosing among contending curricular aims, you should be familiar with its composition:

DOK Level	Title of Level
1	Recall and Reproduction
2	Skills and Concepts
3	Short-Term Strategic Thinking
4	Extended Thinking

As you can see, the DOK levels range from a lowest level of Recall and Reproduction, which is similar to Bloom's lowest levels of Knowledge and Comprehension, up to a highest level of Extended Thinking, which is akin to Bloom's highest levels of Synthesis and Evaluation (1956).

Clearly, if you are ever involved in making any sort of curricular choices among competing curricular aims or are attempting to create an assessment blueprint for your own tests or for those of your colleagues, you should become more knowledgeable about both the Bloom and the Webb frameworks for categorizing the cognitive demands reflected in different curricular goals. It is much tougher to get an accurate fix on the levels of cognitive challenge associated with diverse curricular aims than it first might appear.

Collar a Colleague

Too many classroom teachers carry out their professional chores in isolation. If you're trying to figure out what to assess in your own classroom, one straightforward scheme for tackling the task is to seek the counsel of a colleague, particularly one who teaches the same sort of class and/or grade level you teach.

Always keeping in mind that what you assess should be governed by the decisions to be influenced by your students' assessment results, simply solicit the advice of a respected colleague regarding what sorts of things you should be assessing in your class. If you're uncomfortable about making such a request, simply read (with feeling) the following scripted question: "If you were I, what would you assess?" I admit the phrasing of the question isn't exotic, but it will get the job done. What you're looking for is some sensible advice from a nonpartisan coworker. If you do choose to solicit the advice of one or more colleagues regarding what you plan to test, remember you are getting their *advice*. The final decision is yours.

If you've already devoted quite a lot of thought to the what-to-assess question, you might simply ask your colleague to review your early ideas so you can discern whether your planned assessment targets seem reasonable to another teacher. A second pair of eyes can frequently prove useful in deciding whether you've really staked out a defensible set of emphases for your planned classroom assessments.

A Collection of What-to-Assess Considerations

So far, eight factors have been identified for potential consideration by teachers who are trying to decide what to measure with their classroom tests. Teachers who consider all or most of these factors will generally come up with more defensible assessment targets for their classroom assessments than will teachers who do not take these factors into consideration. Accordingly, this chapter's chief intended outcome is that you will not only remember what these eight factors are but will also understand the probable impact of each of those factors on a teacher's choice regarding what to measure with classroom tests.

Presented next, then, are eight potential factors a teacher should consider when determining what to assess via classroom tests. You'll note that each consideration is now framed as a question to be answered, and brief labels have also been added to each factor in a transparent attempt to make the factors more readily memorable. This should help if you ever choose to employ them in constructing your own tests.

1. **Decision Focus:** Are clearly explicated decision options directly linked to a test's results?

2. **Number of Assessment Targets:** Is the number of proposed assessment targets for a test sufficiently small so that those targets represent an instructionally manageable number?

3. **Assessment Domain Emphasized:** Will the assessments to be built focus on the cognitive domain, the affective domain, or the psychomotor domain?

4. **Norm Referencing and/or Criterion Referencing:** Will the score-based inferences to be based on students' test performances be norm referenced, criterion referenced, or both?

5. **Selected-Response Mode Versus Constructed-Response Mode:** Can students' responses be selected responses, constructed responses, or both?

6. **Relevant Curricular Configurations:** Will students' performances on this classroom assessment contribute to students' mastery of your state's officially approved set of curricular aims, such as, for example, a set of consortium-chosen content standards?

7. **National Subject-Matter Organizations' Recommendations:** Are the knowledge, skills, and/or affect assessed by this classroom assessment consonant with the curricular recommendations of national subject-matter associations?

8. **Collegial Input:** If a knowledgeable colleague is available, has this educator reacted to the proposed assessment targets in a classroom test to be built?

Tests as Instructional Influencers

Historically, teachers have administered classroom tests at or near the close of an instructional sequence. And, of course, teachers would like their students to perform well on any end-of-instruction tests. If students are successful on end-of-instruction classroom tests, it usually means that they have learned well and, accordingly, teachers have taught well. More often than not, teachers' classroom tests have been constructed only *after* instruction is over or when instruction is nearing its conclusion (for instance, near the end of a semester, a school year, or a short-duration teaching unit). Obviously, classroom assessments devised *after* instruction is over will have little impact on what the teacher teaches. The teacher's instruction, or at least the majority of it, is a "done deal" by the time the test is constructed.

Classroom assessments, therefore, have typically had little impact on instructional planning. At least this was true until the era of **educational accountability** arrived in the 1970s and 1980s. During that period, legislators in most states enacted a string of laws requiring students to pass tests on basic skills in order to receive high school diplomas or, in some cases, to be advanced to higher grade levels. Thereupon, what educators have come to call "high-stakes" tests originated. That's because there were important consequences for the students who were required to take those tests.

There is another sense in which statewide tests became high-stakes tests. In schools where all, or almost all, students passed the tests, a school's teachers and administrators were applauded. But in schools where many students failed the tests, a school's teachers and administrators were blamed. The stakes associated with statewide testing were elevated even more in the 1980s, when newspapers began to publish annual statewide test scores of all districts and all schools in the state. Each school and district was *ranked* in relation to the state's other schools and districts. There were, of course, numerous winners as well as a comparable number of losers.

As noted in Chapter 1, what was being measured by the tests soon began to influence the nature of what was taught in classrooms. The phrase ***measurement-driven instruction*** became widely used during the eighties to mean an educational reform strategy in which it was hoped that the content of high-stakes tests would have a substantial and positive influence on the content of classroom instruction.

Because of this heightened attention to student performance on important statewide and districtwide tests, we also saw increased attention being given to the evidence of student success on teacher-made *classroom* tests. Many educational administrators and policymakers concluded that if students' performances on statewide tests reflected a school's educational effectiveness, then even at the classroom level, test results could indicate whether good teaching was taking place. Greater and greater emphasis was given to "evidence of effectiveness" in the form of improved student performance on whatever types of classroom tests were being employed. Increasingly, *evidence* of student learning—evidence in the form of student performance on classroom tests—is being used in personnel appraisals of teachers. In many settings, a teacher's competence is currently being assessed in terms of how well the teacher's students perform on the teacher's classroom tests. During the past several years, considerable pressure has been brought on educational leaders to make students' test scores a prominent factor when evaluating individual teachers. We'll look into recent developments regarding teacher evaluation in Chapter 15.

Given this ever-increasing administrative reliance on student test results as one indicator of a teacher's instructional effectiveness, it was only natural that many teachers tried to address instructionally whatever was to be tested. Tests had clearly begun to influence teaching. And it was increasingly recognized by teachers not only that the content of their tests *could* influence their teaching but also that the content of those tests *should* influence their teaching.

If testing should influence teaching, why not construct classroom assessments *prior to* instructional planning? In this way, any planned instructional sequence could mesh more effectively with the content of the test involved. Moreover, why not build classroom assessments with the instructional implications of those assessments deliberately in mind? In other words, why not build a classroom assessment not only before any instructional planning, but also in such a way that the assessment could beneficially inform the teacher's instructional planning? The contrast between a more traditional educational approach, in which instruction influences assessment, and the kind of assessment-influenced instruction being described here can be seen in Figure 2.2.

Figure 2.2 Traditional Instruction-Influenced Assessment Versus Assessment-Influenced Instruction, Both of Which Are Governed by Curricular Aims

In a traditional approach to instructional design, an approach in which instruction influences assessment, the teacher (1) is guided by the curriculum that's been adopted by the state and/or district, (2) plans instructional activities to promote the educational objectives set forth in that curriculum, and (3) assesses students. In an assessment-influenced approach to instructional design, also indicated in Figure 2.2, the teacher (1) starts with curricular aims, (2) then moves to create assessments based on those goals, and (3) only thereafter plans instructional activities intended to promote students' mastery of the knowledge, skills, and/or attitudes to be assessed. In both approaches, curriculum is the starting point. Curricular aims still govern the entire process. But the two contrasting approaches differ in the order in which instructional planning and assessment development occur.

Dividends of Assessment Illumination

Assessment-illuminated instruction rests on the assumption that, in many instances, what is to be assessed *will* influence the teacher's instructional decisions. Consequently, if the assessment can be planned prior to the teacher's instructional planning, the resulting clarity will help the teacher make more appropriate instructional choices.

When teachers develop their classroom assessments *before* making instructional plans, teachers are meaningfully *clarifying* the curricular aims being pursued. In other words, the assessment serves as the operational definition of whether a curricular aim has been achieved. Such clarity provides far more insight for teachers when, subsequently, they make their instructional plans.

It is important to remember that classroom assessments represent the knowledge and/or skills being promoted. Teachers should *never* teach toward the classroom test itself. Instead, they should teach toward the knowledge, skills, and/or attitudes sampled by the classroom test. As you will learn in Chapter 4 dealing with validity, the entire edifice of educational testing rests on our arriving at score-based inferences about what's lurking inside students' skulls. Teaching directly to a test's items can seriously muck up the accuracy of such inferences. Happily, when teachers construct classroom assessments prior to instructional decision making, they will have a markedly better understanding of what the instructional targets really are. And, of course, the more clearheaded teachers are about curricular *ends*, the more skillfully they can select suitable instructional *means* to accomplish those ends.

Increased clarity regarding the nature of the curricular aims being promoted yields all sorts of instructional-planning benefits. Here are a few of the most salient dividends you, as a teacher or a teacher-in-preparation, will receive:

- *More accurate learning progressions.* Because you'll know more clearly what the terminal results of an instructional sequence are supposed to be, you can better pinpoint the enabling knowledge or the subskills your students must acquire along their way to mastering what's being taught. (You'll learn more about "learning progressions" in Chapter 12).

- *More on-target practice activities.* Because you'll know better what kinds of end-of-instruction outcomes are being sought for your students, you can make sure to select guided-practice and independent-practice activities that are more accurately aligned with the target outcomes.

- *More lucid expositions.* Because you'll understand more clearly what's to be assessed at instruction's conclusion, during instruction you can provide clearer explanations to your students about the content involved and where the instructional activities are heading.

Instructional planning will benefit from early development of classroom assessments most fundamentally because you will, as a consequence of prior assessment construction, better understand what it is hoped that your students will be able to do when instruction has been concluded.

A Profusion of Item Types

Beyond the basic constructed-response versus selected-response distinction considered earlier, there are numerous types of items available for inclusion in classroom assessment procedures. Certain of these item types have been employed for many, many years. The essay test, for example, has probably been around since Socrates was strutting his instructional stuff. Multiple-choice tests have been with us for more than a century. True–false tests were probably used, at least in oral form, by prehistoric teachers who might have tossed such true–false toughies to their students as "True or False: Today's dinosaur was a leaf-munching *Apatosaurus* (or *Brontosaurus*) rather than a people-munching *Tyrannosaurus rex*."

During recent years, however, there have been some significant advances in educational measurement procedures so that, for example, some educational measurement specialists now advocate wider use of *portfolio assessment* and *performance assessment*. These significant item types must now be added to the menu of assessment alternatives open to today's classroom teacher. In coming chapters you'll be learning how to create classroom assessments using all of the major item types now available in the classroom teacher's assessment arsenal. And, of course, as each hour goes by, advances in technology enable teachers to rely on a number of sophisticated computer programs to provide online or other gyrations leading to computer-configured assessments. Fortunately, states and districts are substantially expanding the range of electronic options available to today's (and tomorrow's) teachers.

We're going to start off with the more traditional sorts of selected- and constructed-response items because, quite frankly, you're more likely to be familiar with those item types, and you'll have less difficulty in learning about how to crank out, for instance, a simply splendid short-answer test item. Thereafter, in separate chapters, we'll be considering portfolios and how they can be used for classroom assessment, as well as performance tests and how they can be employed. After that, we'll deal with the special kinds of items to use when you're trying to get a fix on students' affective status.

As a preview, then, in subsequent chapters you'll be encountering the following types of items that can be employed in classroom assessments:

- Binary-choice items (Chapter 6)
- Multiple binary-choice items (Chapter 6)
- Multiple-choice items (Chapter 6)
- Matching items (Chapter 6)
- Short-answer items (Chapter 7)
- Essay items (Chapter 7)
- Observational approaches (Chapter 8)
- Performance tests (Chapter 8)
- Portfolios (Chapter 9)
- Affective assessment procedures (Chapter 10)

Many of these types of items can be presented to test takers via computers, so we'll also be looking at how common this practice has become, particularly for large-scale educational exams.

As you can see, there are plenty of options open to classroom teachers when it comes to item types. When you're choosing among item types, select the one that best allows you to make the test-based inference in which you're interested and whatever decision is linked to it. Sometimes it won't make much difference which types of items you choose. In many instances, a batch of multiple-choice items is not vastly superior to a group of matching items. In other cases, however, there will be substantial differences in the suitability of differing item types. To make your own choice, simply ask yourself, Will my students' responses to this type of item allow me to reach a defensible inference contributing to the educational decision facing me?

But What Does This Have to Do with Teaching?

Most first-year teachers have only a foggy idea of what stuff they should be teaching. Oh, of course, there is often a state curriculum syllabus setting forth a seemingly endless array of knowledge and skills that students might possess. But, unfortunately, many teachers find such syllabi altogether overwhelming. So new teachers often gravitate toward whatever content is addressed in textbooks. And, when I was a first-year teacher, that's just what I did. Along with courses in high school English, speech, and U.S. government, I also had to teach a course in geography. Having never taken a college course in geography, and knowing barely more than the four major directions on a compass, I thanked heaven each night for the bright red geography textbook that allowed me to feign geographical competence. Had it not been for that comforting red textbook, I surely would have perished pedagogically before I learned the difference between the equator and a Mercator map.

It should be apparent to you that if teachers carry out a consummately classy instructional act, but focus on the wrong curricular content, this would be a genuine waste. Yet many beginning teachers don't devote sufficient thought to what they need to teach and, therefore, what they need to assess. And many seasoned teachers also can't provide a solid rationale for what they're teaching.

The impact of the federal accountability legislation on most teachers' instruction—and classroom assessment—has been considerable. That's why you really need to find out how *your* state carries out its accountability program. If your state's leaders have installed suitable accountability tests, you'll be in a good position to key off those tests and supply your students with equally sensible classroom tests and on-target instruction. If your state's accountability tests are inappropriate, however, you'll find yourself in the midst of an insoluble puzzle.

This chapter's focus on what to test and how to test it is intended to help you recognize that you should be *assessing* the most important skills, knowledge, and affect you want your students to acquire. And this recognition should help you realize that that is also what you should be *teaching*.

Unless, of course, you're using a red geography textbook. If so, forget everything you just read.

As we consider various types of items later, you'll become more conversant with the particulars of each item type, and thus more skilled in identifying their utility to you in your own classroom assessments.

What Do Classroom Teachers Really Need to Know About What to Assess?

What is the main message of this chapter for classroom teachers who must decide what to assess? The answer is rather straightforward. All you need to do is to think seriously about this issue. Any experienced teacher will, if pressed, confess that *instructional inertia* plays a key role in what usually goes on in the teacher's classroom. Classroom teachers find it far easier to engage in activities this year that they engaged in last year. simply because it takes less effort to employ "same-old same-old" instructional procedures than to install new ones. There's also *assessment inertia* inclining teachers to rely on whatever assessment schemes they've previously utilized. It's so much simpler to re-use or slightly massage last year's true–false exams than to whip up a brand-new performance test.

In recognition of these all-too-human tendencies to adopt the path of least resistance, it becomes more important to try to "get it right the first time." In other words, the more up-front thought teachers give to answering the what-to-assess question, the more likely they'll be able to dodge serious assessment errors that, because of temporal pressures, may plague them for years.

Because of the impact of federal accountability laws on you and your fellow teachers, you need to understand the nature of the tests your state's leaders have chosen to satisfy the state's accountability needs. You definitely need to find out whether the state's accountability tests are winners or losers. Those tests will have an enormous impact on what you try to teach, what you try to test, and how you try to teach it.

A Three-Chapter Preview

Because the next three chapters in the book are highly related, here's a little previewing of what you'll be encountering in those chapters. Later in the book, you'll learn all sorts of nifty ways to assess your students. Not only will you learn how to create a variety of traditional paper-and-pencil tests, such as the true–false and multiple-choice instruments, but you'll also discover how to generate many of the alternative forms of educational assessment that are receiving so much attention these days.

If you're evaluating a test—whether it's your own test, a test developed by another teacher, or a test distributed by a commercial test publisher—you will need some criteria to help you decide whether the test should be wildly applauded or, instead, sent scurrying to a paper shredder.

Judging educational tests, in fact, is fundamentally no different from evaluating brownies. If, for example, you are ever called on to serve as a judge in a brownie bake-off, you'll need some evaluative criteria to use when you assess the merits of the contending brownies. I realize your preferences may differ from mine, but if I were chief justice in a brownie-judging extravaganza, I would employ the three evaluative criteria presented in Table 2.1. If you are a brownie aficionado and prefer other evaluative criteria, I can overlook such preferences. You may, for example, adore nut-free and high-rise brownies. However, I have no personal interest in establishing a meaningful brownie-bond with you.

When we evaluate just about anything, we employ explicit or implicit evaluative criteria to reach a judgment about quality. And although there may

Table 2.1 Potential Criteria for Brownie Judging

Criterion	Optimal Status
Fudginess	Should brim with chocolate flavor—so much, indeed, as to be considered fundamentally fudgelike.
Chewiness	Must be so chewy as to approximate munching on a lump of fudge-flavored Silly Putty.
Acceptable Additives	Although sliced walnuts and extra chocolate chips are praiseworthy, raw shredded brussels sprouts are not.

be substantial disagreements among brownie devotees regarding the criteria to employ when appraising their favorite baked goods, there are far fewer disputes when it comes to judging the quality of educational assessment devices. In the next three chapters, we're going to look at the three widely accepted criteria that are used to evaluate educational assessment procedures. Two of these criteria have been around for a long while. The third is a relative newcomer, having figured in the evaluation of educational tests only during the last few decades.

Table 2.2 lists the three criteria we'll be considering in the next three chapters. The capsule description of each criterion presented in the table will let you know what's coming. After considering each of these three criteria in its very own chapter, you'll get some recommendations regarding what classroom teachers really need to know about the three criteria. In other words, you'll get some advice on whether you should establish an intimate relationship or merely a nodding acquaintance with each criterion.

Of all the things you will learn from reading this book, and there will be lots of them, the topics treated in the next three chapters are regarded by psychometricians (assessment specialists) as the most important. Chapters 3, 4, and 5 will familiarize you with the pivotal criteria by which assessment specialists tell whether educational assessment procedures are fabulous or feeble. But because this text is focused on classroom assessment, we'll be looking at the content of the next three chapters in relation to educational decisions that must be made by classroom teachers.

Table 2.2 A Preview of the Three Test-Evaluation Criteria to Be Considered in Chapters 3, 4, and 5

Criterion	Brief Description
Reliability	Reliability represents the *consistency* with which an assessment procedure measures whatever it's measuring.
Validity	Validity reflects the degree to which evidence and theory support the *accuracy* of interpretations of test scores for proposed uses of tests.
Fairness	Fairness signifies the degree to which assessments are free of elements that would *offend* or *unfairly penalize* particular groups of students on the basis of students' gender, ethnicity, and so on.

Chapter Summary

One major question guided the content of this chapter: What should a classroom teacher assess? It was contended that a teacher's conclusions must be primarily influenced by the decisions the teacher hopes to illuminate on the basis of assessment data gathered from students.

A teacher's curricular aims play a prominent role in the teacher's choice of assessment emphases. In particular, large-grain-size, measurable objectives were recommended as helpful vehicles for identifying potential assessment targets. The three domains of student outcomes contained in Bloom's *Taxonomies of Educational Objectives* were also suggested as a helpful framework to decide whether certain kinds of outcomes are being overemphasized in instruction or assessment (1956). A state's curricular aims, like nearly all intended curricular outcomes, will be clearly understood only when assessments to measure students' mastery of the aims have been created.

This chapter identified eight considerations for teachers to keep in mind when deciding what to assess: (1) decision focus, (2) number of assessment targets, (3) assessment domain emphasized, (4) norm-referenced versus criterion-referenced assessment, (5) selected-response versus constructed-response mode, (6) relevant curricular configurations, (7) national subject-matter organizations' recommendations, and (8) collegial input. Teachers who attend to all or most of these eight considerations will be more likely to arrive at defensible decisions about what to measure in their classroom assessments.

MyLab Education **Self-Check 2.1**

MyLab Education **Self-Check 2.2**

MyLab Education **Application Exercise 2.1: Eight Potential Factors**

References

Arffman, I. (2013). "Problems and issues in translating international educational achievement tests," *Educational Measurement: Issues and Practice, 32*, no. 2 (Summer): 2–14.

Bloom, B. S., et al. (1956). *Taxonomy of educational objectives: Handbook I: Cognitive domain.* New York: David McKay.

Center on Education Policy. (2011). *District officials view common state standards as more rigorous, expect new standards to improve learning.* Press Release, September 14. Washington, DC: Author.

Cizek, G. J., Kosh, A. E., and Toutkaushian, E.K., "Gathering and evaluating validity evidence: The generalized assessment alignment tool," *Journal of Educational Measurement, 55*, no. 4 (Winter): 477–512.

Davis-Becker, S. L., and Buckendahl, C. W. (2013). "A proposed framework for evaluating alignment studies," *Educational Measurement: Issues and Practice, 32*, no. 1 (Spring): 23–33.

Glaser, R. (1963). "Institutional technology and the measurement of learning outcomes: Some questions," *American Psychology, 18*, 519–521.

McMillan, J. H. (2013). *Classroom assessment: Principles and practice for effective standards-based instruction* (6th ed.). Boston: Pearson.

National Council of Teachers of Mathematics. (1989). *Curriculum and evaluation standards for school mathematics.* Reston, VA: The Council.

National Governors Association and the Council of Chief State School Officers. (2010). *The Common Core State Standards initiative.* Washington, DC: Author.

Pellegrino, J. W. (2016). *21st century science assessment: The future is now.* SRI Education White Paper. Menlo Park, CA: SRI International.

Pellegrino, J. W., Chudowsky, N., and Glaser, R. (Eds.). (2001). *Knowing what students know: The science and design of educational assessment.* National Research Council, Division of Behavioral and Social Sciences and Education, Center for Education, Board on Testing and Assessment. Washington, DC: National Academy Press.

Popham, W. J. (2014a). "Criterion-referenced measurement: Half a century wasted?" *Educational Leadership, 71*, no. 6 (March): 62–67.

Popham, W. J. (2014b). "The right test for the wrong reason," *Phi Delta Kappan, 96*, no. 1 (September): 46–52.

Rutkowski, D, Rutkowski, L., and Plucker, J. A. (2014). "Should individual schools participate in PISA?" *Phi Delta Kappan, 96*, no. 4 (December): 68–73.

Webb, N. L. (2002) *Alignment study in language arts, mathematics, science, and social studies of state standards and assessment for four states.* Washington, DC: Council of Chief State School Officers.

Zimba, J. (2011). *Priorities in the* Common Core State Standards' *standards for mathematical content.* Discussion Draft, March 31, 2011.

Deciding What's Worth Assessing: Prioritization Is the Key*

W. James Popham, University of California, Los Angeles

A key moment arrives during the development of any educational test, whether the test is a nationally standardized achievement exam or a classroom quiz in a U.S. history class, when a decision must be made about *what to assess*. Depending on how the "what to assess" question is answered, today's educators are often pressured to improve students' performances on educational tests that measure way too many assessment targets. Let's look at this harmful test-development mistake.

Because a chief function of educational tests is to collect evidence to help teachers arrive at accurate inferences about students' hidden knowledge and skills, and then to teach those students, evidence from educational tests must support accurate inferences about students' covert abilities. Thus, each cognitive skill or body of knowledge measured by an educational test must be represented by enough test items. For instructional purposes, it would make scant sense to use an achievement test intended to measure students' mastery of 25 different things with a 25-item test—one item per thing.

Moreover, because most educational tests are intended to satisfy one dominant purpose, the nature of a test's measurement mission is pivotal in determining how many items should measure what's being assessed. For example, if a test is supposed to *support instruction*, then each thing measured ought to be assessed by enough items (say, 5–10) to help teachers arrive at an accurate, *actionable interpretation* regarding each assessed skill or body of knowledge.

The chief obstacle to choosing appropriate content to be assessed is the absence in most curricular decision makers (including many teachers who build their own classroom tests) of *the courage to prioritize assessable content*. Yes, those deciding what a test will assess often identify too many curricular targets—too many to be taught well in the available instructional time, and too many to be measured well in the available testing time. Those determining what's to be measured simply "want it all"! Yet having too many assessment targets, which invariably translates into too many instructional targets, often leads to superficial levels of teaching in a valiant effort by teachers to "cover everything that's being assessed."

If you, personally, ever have an opportunity to offer reactions to proposed test content, be sure to urge decision makers to have the courage to prioritize. It is far better to teach students to master *deeply* a modest number of important, prioritized outcomes than to teach them to master too many unprioritized outcomes *superficially*.

Chapter 3
Reliability of Assessment

Learning Outcomes

3.1 Explain the basic conceptual and mathematic principles of reliability.

3.2 Identify and apply the kinds of reliability evidence needed for particular uses of educational assessments.

⌄ Chief Chapter Outcome

An understanding of commonly employed indicators of a test's reliability/precision that is sufficient to identify the types of reliability evidence already collected for a test and, if necessary, to select the kinds of reliability evidence needed for particular uses of educational assessments

Reliability is such a cherished commodity. We all want our automobiles, washing machines, and spouses to be reliable. The term *reliability* simply reeks of solid goodness. It conjures up visions of meat loaf, mashed potatoes, and a mother's love. Clearly, reliability is an attribute to be sought.

In the realm of educational assessment, reliability is also a desired attribute. We definitely want our educational assessments to be reliable. In matters related to measurement, however, reliability has a very restricted meaning. When you encounter the term *reliability* in any assessment context, you should draw a mental "equals sign" between *reliability* and *consistency*, because reliability refers to the consistency with which a test measures whatever it's measuring:

Reliability = Consistency

From a classroom teacher's perspective, there are two important ways the concept of reliability can rub up against your day-to-day activities. First, there's the possibility that your own classroom assessments might lack sufficient reliability to be doing a good job for you and your students. For example, suppose you are using your students' performances on a tough reading test you've developed to determine which students need an additional dose of reading instruction. If you discover that students who take the test early in the day consistently outscore students who take the test later in the day, it seems that your home-grown reading test is not measuring with consistency and that, therefore, you are likely to make at least some inaccurate decisions about which students should receive additional reading instruction. Later in this chapter you will learn about some straightforward ways of collecting reliability evidence regarding your teacher-made assessments.

Second, if your students are obliged to complete any sort of commercially published standardized tests, you're apt to find a parent or two who might want to discuss the adequacy of those tests. And reliability, as noted in the previous chapter's preview, such as for your state's accountability tests, is an evaluative criterion by which external standardized tests are judged. You may need to know enough about reliability's wrinkles so you'll be able to talk sensibly with parents about the way reliability is employed to judge the quality of standardized tests. To provide explanations for parents about the meaning or, more accurately, the *meanings* of assessment reliability, you'll need more than a superficial understanding of what's meant by reliability when it is routinely determined by publishers of commercial standardized tests.

As explained in Chapter 2, a particularly influential document in the field of educational assessment is the *Standards for Educational and Psychological Testing* (2014).[1] Commonly referred to simply as "the *Standards*," this important compilation of dos and don'ts regarding educational and psychological measurement was developed and distributed by the American Educational Research Association (AERA), the American Psychological Association (APA), and the National Council on Measurement in Education (NCME). The *Standards* provide the nuts and bolts of how educational tests should be created, evaluated, and used. Because the 2014 *Standards* constituted the first revision of this significant AERA-APA-NCME publication since 1999, assessment specialists everywhere are particularly attentive to its contents, and we can safely predict that most of those specialists attempt to adhere to its mandates. Let's consider, then, what the new *Standards* say about reliability.

Well, for openers, the architects of the *Standards* use a different label to describe what has historically been referred to as the "reliability" of tests. The authors of the new *Standards* point out that the term *reliability* has been used not only (1) to represent the *traditional reliability coefficients* so often employed through the years to describe a test's quality, but also to refer more generally to (2) the consistency of students' scores across replications of a testing procedure *regardless of the way such consistency is estimated or reported*.

In case you are unfamiliar with the meaning of the technical term *coefficient* as used in this context, that term typically refers to a *correlation coefficient*—that is, a numerical indicator of the relationship between the same persons' status on two variables, such as students' scores on two different tests. The symbol representing such a coefficient is r. If students score pretty much the same on the two tests, the resulting correlation coefficient will be strong and positive. If the individuals score high on one test and low on the other test, the resulting r will be negative. If there's a high reliability coefficient, this doesn't necessarily signify that students' scores on the two testing occasions are *identical*. Rather, a high r indicates that students' *relative* performances on the two testing occasions are quite similar. Correlation coefficients can range from a high of +1.00 to a low of –1.00. Thus, what a *reliability coefficient* really means is that a correlation coefficient has typically been computed for test takers' performances on two sets of variables—as you will soon see.

To illustrate, if the developers of a new achievement test report that when their test was administered to the same students on two occasions—for example, a month apart—the resulting test-retest correlation coefficient was .86, this would be an instance involving the sort of traditional reliability coefficient that measurement experts have used for roughly a full century. If, however, a test-development company creates a spanking new high school graduation test, and supplies evidence about what percentage of students' scores can consistently classify those test takers into "diploma awardees" and "diploma denials," this too constitutes a useful way of representing a test's consistency—but a way that's clearly not the same as reliance on a traditional reliability coefficient. A variety of different indices of classification consistency are often employed these days to supply test users with indications about the reliability with which a test classifies test takers. Don't be surprised, then, if you encounter an indicator of a test's reliability that's expressed in a manner quite different from oft-encountered reliability coefficients.

Architects of the 2014 *Standards* wanted to provide a link to traditional conceptions of measurement consistency (in which a single reliability coefficient typically indicated a test's consistency), but they wished to avoid the ambiguity of using the single label *reliability* to refer to a wide range of reliability indicators, such as measures of classification consistency. Accordingly, the 2014 *Standards* architects employ the term **reliability/precision** to denote the more general notion of score consistency across instances of the testing procedure. The label **reliability coefficient** is used to describe more conventionally used coefficients representing different forms of test takers' consistency.

The descriptor *reliability/precision*, then, describes not only traditional reliability coefficients but also various indicators of classification consistency and a number of less readily understandable statistical indices of assessment consistency. As the writers of the *Standards* make clear, the need for precision of measurement increases as the consequences in terms of test-based inferences and resultant decisions become more important.

Whether the label *reliability/precision* will become widely employed by those who work with educational tests remains to be seen. In this chapter, you will encounter descriptions of reliability in several contexts. Those contexts should make it clear whether the term applies to a quantitative indicator representing a traditional relationship between two sets of test scores—that is, a *reliability coefficient*—or, instead, refers to another way of representing a test's consistency of measurement—that is, a *reliability/precision* procedure.

What does a teacher really need to know about reliability or about reliability/ precision? Well, hold off for a bit on that question, for the answer may surprise you. But one thing you do need to recognize is that the fundamental notion of reliability is downright important for those whose professional lives bump up against educational tests in any meaningful manner. This overriding truth about the significance of assessment consistency is well represented in the very first, most basic expectation set forth in the 2014 *Standards*:

> Appropriate evidence of reliability/precision should be provided for the interpretation of each intended score use. (AERA, 2014, p. 42)

Based on this call for appropriate evidence supporting the reliability/precision of an educational test, the new *Standards* include fully 20 subordinate standards dealing with various aspects of reliability. Taken together, they spell out how the authors of the 2014 *Standards* believe the consistency of educational tests ought to be determined.

Please note, in the above snippet from the 2014 *Standards*, that *evidence* of reliability/precision is supposed to be supplied for *each intended score use*. What this signifies, of course, is that a test itself is not reliable or unreliable. Rather, because of the evidence that's available, we reach a judgment about the reliability regarding a test's use for Intended Use *A*, Intended Use *B*, and so on. Although many educators casually refer to the "reliability of a test," what's really represented in that phrase is the "reliability of a test for a specified use." In the next chapter (*spoiler alert!*) about validity, you will learn that tests are not valid or invalid but, rather, it is the validity of test-based interpretations that are up for grabs. Similarly, regarding the reliability of tests, a test's reliability revolves around the evidence supporting the consistency of scores for each and every intended test usage.

But how, you might ask, can a teacher's test be unreliable? That is, how can certain features of a teacher-made test result in a test's yielding inconsistent scores? This would be a good ask, and a few examples might help in responding to it. Let's say that the directions for a teacher-made tests are somewhat ambiguous and that, as a consequence, students arrive at several meanings of what they are being asked to do with the test's items. Result: *Inconsistency*. As another illustration, suppose that in the multiple-choice items a teacher has ginned up for her physics tests, many items seem to have not one but two correct answers. Students, of course, can choose only one option per item. Result: *Inconsistency*. And, as a final example, suppose that the teacher's test contains a flock of true–false items that are arguably *either* true or false. Students need to guess which is which for each item. Result: *Inconsistency*.

As you read further in this chapter, you will encounter some fairly technical notions about ways of calculating the reliability with which a test can capture test takers' performances. Try not to get so caught up in the techniques of collecting reliability evidence that you begin to believe the unreliability of an educational test is visited on that test by extraterrestrial forces. No, when someone put the test together, mistakes were made that allowed the test to yield inconsistent test takers' scores. Perhaps the evildoer was a classroom teacher, perhaps a psychometrician from a major testing firm. Whoever the culprit was, somebody messed up. What we have learned in the field of educational measurement, fortunately, are ways of spotting such mess-ups.

So, recognizing that we can estimate a test's consistency in a number of ways, and that the expression *reliability coefficient* refers to particular sorts of evidence that are traditionally served up when educational tests are scrutinized, let's look at the three traditional reliability coefficients presented in Table 3.1: *test-retest coefficients, alternate-form coefficients,* and *internal consistency coefficients.* Along the way, while describing how these three sorts of reliability coefficients are obtained, we will consider other approaches to be employed when describing a test's reliability/precision.

If you have only recently been tussling with different conceptions of assessments' consistency (such as in the last few paragraphs), an altogether reasonable question for you to ask about reliability coefficients is: How big must a reliability coefficient be? For instance, looking at the three sorts of reliability coefficients tersely described in Table 3.1, how high do those correlation coefficients need to be for us to regard a test as sufficiently reliable? Regrettably, the answer to this straightforward question is apt to be more murky than you might like.

For openers, if a correlation coefficient is involved, it needs to be positive rather than negative. If test developers from an educational measurement company were trying to measure how consistently their newly created history test does its measurement job regardless of when it is administered, they would typically ask a group of students to take the same test on two separate occasions. Thereupon a test-retest correlation could be computed for the test takers' two sets of scores. Clearly, the hope would be that students' scores on the two administrations would be decisively positive—that is, the scores would reveal substantial similarity in the way students performed on both of the two test administrations. Okay, the test's developers want a positive **test-retest reliability** coefficient to signify test-score stability. But how large does that coefficient need to be before the test's developers start clinking glasses during a champagne toast?

Well, get ready for an answer that's often to be encountered when judging the quality of educational tests. That's right: *It depends.* The size that a correlation coefficient needs to be before we regard a test as sufficiently reliable depends on the context in which a test is being used and, in particular, on the nature of the test-based decision that will be influenced by test takers' scores.

In general, the higher the stakes involved, the higher should be our expectations for our tests' reliability coefficients. For instance, let's suppose that a

Table 3.1 Three Types of Reliability Evidence

Type of Reliability Coefficient	Brief Description
Test-Retest	Consistency of results among different testing occasions
Alternate Form	Consistency of results among two or more different forms of a test
Internal Consistency	Consistency in the way an assessment instrument's items function

teacher is working in a state where the awarding of a high school diploma requires a student to perform above a specific cut-score on both a mathematics test and an English language arts test. Given the considerable importance of the decision that's riding on students' test performances, we should be demanding a much greater indication of test consistency than we would with, say, a teacher's exam covering a single-month unit on the topic of punctuation.

But because the contexts in which educational tests are used will vary so considerably, it is simply impossible to set forth a definitive table presenting minimally acceptable levels for certain kinds of reliability coefficients. Experience shows us that when teachers attempt to collect evidence for their own teacher-constructed tests, it is not uncommon to encounter a test-retest r of .60 plus or minus .10 and an alternate-form r reflecting about the same range. Accordingly, when deciding whether a test's reliability coefficients are sufficiently strong for the test's intended use, this decision boils down to *professional judgment* based on the correlation coefficients seen over the years in similar settings. Yes, we use historical precedent to help us arrive at realistic expectations for what's possible regarding reliability coefficients. For instance, with significant high-stakes examinations such as nationally standardized achievement tests that have been developed and revised many times at great cost, it is not uncommon for the test developers to report internal-consistency coefficients hovering slightly above or slightly below .90. However, for a district-made test requiring far fewer developmental dollars, the identical sorts of internal-consistency coefficients might be closer to .80 or .70.

In general, reliability coefficients representing test-retest or alternate-form consistency tend to be lower than internal consistency coefficients. However, in certain contexts—when a test has been developed in an effort to provide distinguishable subscores—we should expect internal consistency coefficients to be much lower, because the overall test is not attempting to measure a single, all-encompassing trait but, rather, a set of related subscales scores. As indicated earlier, *it depends*. The judgment about whether a test's reliability coefficients are sufficiently strong for a given use should hinge on what is a realistic expectation for such coefficients in such situations.

Similarly, when looking at reliability/precision more generally—for instance, when considering the consistency with which a set of test scores allow us to classify test takers' levels of proficiency accurately, once more we need to be guided by historical precedent. That is, based on the experience of others, what expectations about reliability/precision are realistic—irrespective of the quantitative indicator employed? For example, if we look back at recent percentages of identical classifications of students on district-developed end-of-course exams, and we find that these decision-consistency percentages almost always reach at least 80 percent (that is, 80 percent of the test takers are given the same classifications irrespective of the test form they completed), then as educators we ought to be wary if a new test yields evidence supporting only a 60 percent estimate of decision consistency.

Test-Retest Reliability Evidence

The first kind of reliability evidence we'll be looking at is called *test-retest.* This conception of reliability often comes to people's minds when someone asserts that reliability equals consistency. Formerly referred to in earlier versions of the *Standards* as "stability reliability," *test-retest evidence* refers to consistency of test results over time. We want our educational assessments of students to yield similar results even if the tests were administered on different occasions. For example, suppose you gave your students a midterm exam on Tuesday, but later in the afternoon a masked thief (1) snatched your briefcase containing the students' test papers, (2) jumped into a waiting armored personnel carrier, and (3) escaped to an adjacent state or nation. The next day, after describing to your students how their examinations had been purloined by a masked assailant, you ask them to retake the midterm exam. Because there have been no intervening events of significance, such as more instruction from you on the topics covered by the examination, you would expect your students' Wednesday examination scores to be somewhat similar to their Tuesday examination scores. And that's what the *test-retest coefficient* conception of test reliability refers to—evidence of consistency over time. If the Wednesday scores weren't rather similar to the Tuesday scores, then your midterm exam would be judged to provide little test-retest reliability.

To get a fix on how stable an assessment's results are over time, we usually test students on one occasion, wait a week or two, and then retest them with the same instrument. Because measurement specialists typically use the descriptors *stability reliability* and *test-retest reliability* interchangeably, you are hereby allowed to do the same thing. Simply choose which of the two labels you prefer. It is important, however, for no significant events that might alter students' performances on the second assessment occasion to have taken place between the two testing occasions. For instance, suppose the test you are administering assessed students' knowledge regarding World War II. If a widely viewed television mini-series about World War II is presented during the interval between the initial test and the retest, it is likely that the performances of the students who watched the mini-series will be higher on the second test because of their exposure to test-relevant information in the mini-series. Thus, for test-retest coefficients to be interpreted accurately, it is imperative that no significant performance-influencing events occur during the between-assessments interval.

One reliability/precision procedure for calculating the stability of students' performances on the same test administered on two assessment occasions is to determine the percentage of student classifications that were consistent over time. Such a ***classification-consistency*** approach to the determination of a test's reliability might be used, for instance, when a teacher is deciding which students should be exempted from further study about Topic X. To illustrate, let's say that the teacher establishes an 80 percent correct as the degree of proficiency required in order to exempt students from further Topic X study. Then, on a test-retest basis, the teacher would simply determine the percentage of students who were classified the same way on the two assessment occasions. The focus in such an approach would not be on the specific scores a student earned, but only on whether the *same classification* was made about the student on both occasions. Thus, if Jill Jones earned an 84 percent correct score on the first testing occasion and a 99 percent correct score on the second testing occasion, Jill would be exempted from further Topic X study in both cases, because she surpassed the 80 percent correct standard both times. The classifications for Jill would be consistent, so the teacher's decisions about Jill would also be consistent. However, if Harry Harvey received a score of 65 percent correct on the first testing occasion and a score of 82 percent correct on the second testing occasion, different classifications on the two occasions would lead to different decisions being made about Harry's need to keep plugging away at Topic X. To determine the

Decision Time
Quibbling over Quizzes

Wayne Wong's first-year teaching assignment is a group of 28 fifth-grade students in an inner-city elementary school. Because Wayne believes in the importance of frequent assessments as motivational devices for his students, he typically administers one or more surprise quizzes per week to his students. Admittedly, after the first month or so, very few of Wayne's fifth-graders are really "surprised" when Wayne whips out one of his unannounced quizzes. Students' scores on the quizzes are used by Wayne to compute each student's 6-weeks' grades.

Mrs. Halverson, the principal of Wayne's school, has visited his class on numerous occasions. Mrs. Halverson believes that it is her "special responsibility" to see that first-year teachers receive adequate instructional support.

Recently, Mrs. Halverson completed a master's degree from the local branch of the state university. As part of her coursework, she was required to take a class in "educational measurement." She earned an A. Because the professor for that course stressed the importance of "reliability as a crucial ingredient of solid educational tests," Mrs. Halverson has been pressing Wayne to compute some form of reliability evidence for his surprise quizzes. Wayne has been resisting her suggestion because, in his view, he administers so many quizzes that the computation of reliability indices for the quizzes would surely be a time-consuming pain. He believes that if he's forced to fuss with reliability estimates for each quiz, he'll give fewer quizzes. And because he thinks students' perception that they *may* be quizzed really stimulates them to be prepared, he is reluctant to reduce the number of quizzes he gives. Even after hearing Wayne's position, however, Principal Halverson seems unwilling to bend.

If you were Wayne Wong and were faced with this problem, what would your decision be?

Table 3.2 An Illustration of How Classification Consistency Is Determined in a Test-Retest Context

A. Percent of students identified as exempt from further study on both assessment occasions	=	42%
B. Percent of students identified as requiring further study on both assessment occasions	=	46%
C. Percent of students classified differently on the two occasions	=	12%
D. Percentage of the test's classification consistency (A + B)	=	88%

percentage of a test's classification consistency, you can simply make the kinds of calculations seen in Table 3.2.

Whether you use a correlational approach or a classification-consistency approach to the determination of a test's consistency over time, it is apparent that you'll need to test students twice in order to determine the test score's stability. If a test is yielding rather unstable results between two occasions, it's really difficult to put much confidence in that test's results. Just think about it—if you can't tell whether your students have really performed wonderfully or woefully on a test because their scores might vary depending on the day you test them, how can you proceed to make defensible test-based instructional decisions about those students?

Realistically, of course, why would a sane, nonsadistic classroom teacher administer identical tests to the same students on two different testing occasions? It's pretty tough to come up with a decent answer to that question. What's most important for teachers to realize is that there is always a meaningful level of *instability* between students' performances on two different testing occasions, *even when the very same test is used*. And this realization, of course, should disincline teachers to treat a student's test score as though it were a super-scientific, impeccably precise representation of the student's achievement level.

Alternate-Form Reliability Evidence

The second of our three kinds of reliability evidence for educational assessment instruments focuses on the consistency between two forms of a test—forms that are supposedly equivalent. *Alternate-form reliability evidence* deals with the question of whether two or more allegedly equivalent test forms do, in fact, yield equivalent scores.

In the classroom, teachers rarely have reason to generate two forms of an assessment instrument. Multiple forms of educational tests are more commonly encountered in high-stakes assessment situations, such as when high school students must pass graduation tests before receiving diplomas. In such settings, students who fail an examination when it is initially administered are usually given other opportunities to pass the examination. Clearly, to make the assessment process fair, the challenge of the assessment hurdle faced by individuals when they take the initial test must be the same as the challenge of the assessment hurdle faced by individuals when they take the make-up examination. Alternate-form reliability evidence bears on the comparability of two (or more) test forms.

Multiple test forms are apt to be found whenever educators fear that if the same test were simply reused, students who had access to subsequent administrations of the test would have an advantage because those later test takers would have learned about the test's contents, and thus have an edge over the first-time test takers. Typically, then, in a variety of high-stakes settings such as (1) those involving high school diploma tests or (2) the certification examinations governing entry to a profession, multiple test forms are employed in which substantial portions differ.

To collect alternate-form consistency evidence, procedural approaches are employed that are in many ways similar to those used for the determination of test-retest reliability evidence. First, the two test forms are administered to the same individuals. Ideally, there would be little or no delay between the administration of the two test forms. For example, suppose you were interested in determining the comparability of two forms of a district-developed language arts examination. Let's say you could round up 100 suitable students. Because the examination requires only 20 to 25 minutes to complete, you could administer both forms of the language arts test (Form A and Form B) to each of the 100 students during a single period. To eliminate the impact of the order in which the two forms were completed by students, you could ask 50 of the students to complete Form A and then Form B. The remaining students would be directed to take Form B and then Form A.

When you obtain each student's scores on the two forms, you could compute a correlation coefficient reflecting the relationship between students' performances on the two forms. As with test-retest reliability, the closer the alternate-form correlation coefficient is to a positive 1.0, the more agreement there is between students' relative scores on the two forms. Alternatively, you could use the kind of classification-consistency approach for the determination of alternate-form reliability/precision that was described earlier for stability. To illustrate, you could decide on a level of performance that would lead to different classifications for students, and then simply calculate the percentage of identically classified students on the basis of the two test forms. For instance, if a pass/fail cutoff score of 65 percent correct had been chosen, then you would simply add (1) the percent of students who passed both times (scored 65 percent or better) and (2) the percent of students who failed both times (scored 64 percent or lower). The addition of those two percentages yields a classification-consistency estimate of alternate-form reliability for the two test forms under consideration.

As you can see, although both species of reliability evidence we've considered thus far are related—in the sense that both deal with consistency—they represent very different conceptions of consistency evidence. Test-retest reliability evidence deals with consistency over time for a single examination. Alternate-form reliability evidence deals with the consistency inherent in two or more supposedly equivalent forms of the same examination.

Alternate-form reliability is not established by proclamation. Rather, evidence must be gathered regarding the between-form consistency of the test forms under scrutiny. Accordingly, if you're ever reviewing a commercially published or state-developed test that claims to have equivalent forms available, be sure you inspect the evidence supporting those claims of equivalence. Determine how the evidence of alternate-form comparability was gathered—that is, under what circumstances. Make sure that what's described makes sense to you.

Later in the book (Chapter 13), we'll consider a procedure known as *item response theory*. Whenever large numbers of students are tested, that approach can be employed to adjust students' scores on different forms of tests that are not equivalent in difficulty. For purposes of our current discussion, however, simply remember that evidence of alternate-form reliability is a special form of consistency evidence dealing with the comparability of the scores yielded by two or more test forms.

Internal Consistency Reliability Evidence

The final entrant in our reliability evidence sweepstakes is called **internal consistency reliability evidence**. It really is quite a different creature than stability and alternate-form reliability evidence. Internal consistency evidence does not focus on the consistency of students' scores on a test. Rather, internal consistency evidence deals with the extent to which the *items* in an educational assessment instrument are functioning in a consistent fashion.

Whereas evidence of stability and alternate-form reliability require two administrations of a test, internal consistency reliability can be computed on the basis of only a single test administration. It is for this reason, one suspects, that we tend to encounter internal consistency estimates of reliability far more frequently than we encounter its two reliability cousins. Yet, as you will see, internal consistency reliability evidence is quite different from stability and alternate-form reliability evidence.

Internal consistency reliability reflects the degree to which the items on a test are doing their measurement job in a consistent manner—that is, the degree to which the test's items are functioning *homogeneously*. Many educational tests are designed to measure a single variable, such as students' "reading achievement" or their "attitude toward school." If a test's items are all truly measuring a single variable, then each of the test's items ought to be doing fundamentally the same assessment job. To the extent that the test's items are tapping the same variable, of course, the responses to those items by students will tend to be quite similar. For example, if all the items in a 20-item test on problem solving do, in fact, measure a student's problem-solving ability, then students who are skilled problem solvers should get most of the test's items right, whereas unskilled problem solvers should miss most of the test's 20 items. The more homogeneous the responses yielded by a test's items, the higher will be the test's internal consistency evidence.

There are several different formulae around for computing a test's internal consistency.[2] Each formula is intended to yield a numerical estimate that reflects the extent to which the assessment procedure's items are functioning

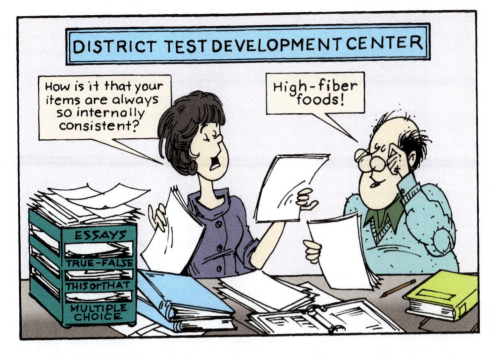

homogeneously. By the way, because internal consistency estimates of test-score reliability are focused on the homogeneity of the items on a test, not on any classifications of test takers (as we saw with stability and alternate-form reliability), decision-consistency approaches to reliability are not used in this instance.

Parent Talk

One of your strongest students, Raphael Hobbs, has recently received his scores on a nationally standardized achievement test used in your school district. Raphael's subtest percentile scores (in comparison to the test's norm group) were the following:

Subject	Percentile
Language Arts	85th
Mathematics	92nd
Science	91st
Social Studies	51st

Raphael's father, a retired U.S. Air Force colonel, has called for an after-school conference with you about the test results. He has used his home computer and the Internet to discover that the internal consistency reliabilities on all four subtests, as published in the test's technical manual, are higher than .93. When he telephoned you to set up the conference, he said he couldn't see how the four subtests could all be reliable when Raphael's score on the social studies subtest was so "out of whack" with the other three subtests. He wants you to explain how this could happen.

If I were you, here's how I'd respond to Colonel Hobbs:

"First off, Colonel Hobbs, I'm delighted that you've taken the time to look into the standardized test we're using in the district. Not many parents are willing to expend the energy to do so.

"I'd like to deal immediately with the issue you raised on the phone regarding the reliability of the four subtests, and then discuss Raphael's social studies result. You may already know some of what I'll be talking about because of your access to the Internet, but here goes.

"Assessment reliability refers to the *consistency* of measurement. But there are very different ways that test developers look at measurement consistency. The reliability estimates that are supplied for Raphael's standardized test, as you pointed out, are called internal consistency correlation coefficients. Those correlations tell us whether the items on a particular subtest are performing in the same way—that is, whether they seem to be measuring the same thing.

"The internal consistency reliability for all four subtests is quite good. But this kind of reliability evidence doesn't tell us anything about how Raphael would score if he took the test again or if he took a different form of the same test. We don't know, in other words, whether his performance would be stable across time or would be consistent across different test forms.

"What we do see in Raphael's case is a social studies performance that is decisively different from

his performance on the other three subtests. I've checked his grades for the past few years, and I've seen that his grades in social studies are routinely just as high as his other grades. So those grades do cast some doubt on the meaningfulness of his lower test performance in social studies.

"Whatever is measured on the social studies subtest seems, from my inspection of the actual items, to be measured by a set of homogeneous items. This doesn't mean, however, the content of the social studies subtest meshes with the social studies Raphael's been taught here in our district. To me, Colonel, I think it's less likely to be a case of measurement unreliability than it is to be a problem of content mismatch between what the standardized examination is testing and what we try to teach Raphael.

"I recommend that you, Mrs. Hobbs, and I carefully monitor Raphael's performance in social studies during the school year so that we can really see whether we're dealing with a learning problem or with an assessment not aligned to what we're teaching."

Now, how would you respond to Colonel Hobbs?

For tests containing items on which a student can be right or wrong, such as a multiple-choice item, the most commonly used internal consistency approaches are the *Kuder-Richardson* procedures (usually referred to as the K-R formulae). For tests containing items on which students can be given different numbers of points, such as essay items, the most common internal consistency coefficient is called Cronbach's *coefficient alpha* after its originator Lee J. Cronbach. Incidentally, if you want to impress your colleagues with your newfound and altogether exotic assessment vocabulary, you might want to know that test items scored right or wrong (such as true–false items) are called *dichotomous* items, and those that yield multiple scores (such as essay items) are called *polytomous* items. Sometime, try to work *polytomous* into a casual conversation around the watercooler. Its intimidation power is awesome.

Incidentally, other things being equal, the more items there are in an educational assessment device, the more reliability/precision it will tend to possess. To illustrate, if you set out to measure a student's mathematics achievement with a 100-item test dealing with various aspects of mathematics, you're apt to get a more precise fix on a student's mathematical prowess than you would if you asked students to solve only a single, lengthy mathematical word problem. The more times you ladle out samples from a pot of soup, the more accurate your estimate of what the soup's ingredients are will be. One ladleful might fool you. Twenty ladlesful will give you a much better idea of what's in the pot. In general, then, more items on educational assessment devices will yield higher reliability/precision estimates than will fewer items.

Three Coins in the Reliability/Precision Fountain

You've now seen that there are three different ways of conceptualizing the manner in which the consistency of a test's results are described. Consistency of measurement is a requisite for making much sense out of a test's results. If the test yields inconsistent results, how can teachers make sensible decisions based on what appears to be a capricious assessment procedure? Yet, as we have seen, reliability evidence comes in three flavors. It is up to you to make sure the reliability evidence supplied with a test is consonant with the use to which the test's results will be put—that is, the decision linked to the test's results. Although there is surely a relationship among the three kinds of reliability evidence we've been discussing, the following is also unarguably true:

Test-Retest Reliability Evidence	$\neq$	Alternate-Form Reliability Evidence	$\neq$	Internal Consistency Reliability Evidence

To illustrate, suppose you were a teacher in a school district where a high school diploma test had been developed by an assistant superintendent in collaboration with a committee of district teachers. The assistant superintendent has claimed the test's three different forms are essentially interchangeable because each form, when field-tested, yielded a Kuder-Richardson reliability coefficient of .88 or higher. "The three test forms," claimed the assistant superintendent at a recent school board meeting, "are reliable and, therefore, equivalent." You now know better.

If the assistant superintendent really wanted to know about between-form comparability, then the kind of reliability evidence needed would be alternate-form reliability, not internal consistency. (Incidentally, it is not recommended that you rise to your feet at the school board meeting to publicly repudiate an assistant superintendent's motley mastery of measurement reliability. You might, instead, send the assistant superintendent a copy of this text, designating the pages to be read. And send it anonymously.)

Yet, even those educators who know something about reliability and its importance will sometimes unthinkingly mush the three brands of reliability evidence together. They'll see a K-R reliability coefficient of .90 and assume not only that the test is internally consistent but also that it will produce stable results. That's not necessarily so.

The Standard Error of Measurement

Before bidding adieu to reliability and all its raptures, there's one other thing you need to know about consistency of measurement. So far, the kinds of reliability/ precision evidence and reliability coefficient evidence we've been considering deal with the reliability of a *group* of students' scores. For a few paragraphs, please turn your attention to the consistency with which we measure an *individual's* performance. The index used in educational assessment to describe the consistency of a particular person's performance(s) is referred to as the ***standard error of measurement (SEM)***. Often a test's standard error of measurement is identified as the test's SEM. The standard error of measurement is another indicator that writers of the 2014 *Standards* would classify as a reliability/precision procedure.

You should think of the standard error of measurement as a reflection of the consistency of an individual's scores that would emerge if a given assessment procedure were administered to that individual again, and again, and again. However, as a practical matter, it is impossible to re-administer the same test innumerable times to the same students; such students would revolt or, if exceedingly acquiescent, soon swoon from exhaustion. (Swooning, these days, is rarely encountered.) Accordingly, we need to *estimate* how much variability there would be if we were able to re-administer a given assessment procedure many times to the same individual. The standard error of measurement is much like the plus-or-minus "sampling errors" or "confidence intervals" so frequently given in the media these days for various sorts of opinion polls. We are told that "89 percent of telephone interviewees indicated that they would consider Brussels sprouts in brownies to be repugnant" (± 3 percent margin of error).

Other things being equal, the higher the reliability of a test, the smaller the standard error of measurement will be. For all commercially published tests, a technical manual is available that supplies the standard error of measurement for the test. Sometimes, when you have occasion to check out a test's standard error, you find it's much larger than you might have suspected. As is true of sampling errors for opinion polls, what you'd prefer to have is small, not large, standard errors of measurement.

In many realms of life, big is better. Most folks like big bank accounts, houses with ample square footage, and basketball players who tower over other folks. But with standard errors of measurement, the reverse is true. Smaller standard errors of measurements signify more accurate assessment.

It's important that you not think a test's standard error of measurement is computed by employing some type of measurement mysticism. Accordingly, the formula assessment folks use in order to obtain a standard error of measurement is presented here. If, however, you don't really care if the standard error of measurement was spawned on Mysticism Mountain, just skip the formula as well as the explanatory paragraph that follows it.

$$S_e = S_x \sqrt{1 - r_{xx}}$$

where S_e = standard error of measurement

S_x = standard deviation of the test scores

r_{xx} = reliability of the test

Take a look at the formula for just a moment (especially if you get a kick out of formula looking), and you'll see that the size of a particular test's standard error of measurement (s_e) depends on two factors. First, there's the standard deviation (s_x) of the test's scores—that is, how spread out those scores are. The greater the spread in scores, the higher the scores' standard deviation will be. Second, there's the coefficient representing the test's reliability (r_{xx}). Now, if you consider what's going on in this formula, you'll see that the *larger* the standard deviation (score spread), the larger the standard error of measurement. Similarly, the *smaller* the reliability coefficient, the larger the standard error of measurement. So, in general, a test will have a smaller standard error of measurement if the test's scores are not too widely spread out and if the test yields more reliable scores. A smaller standard error of measurement signifies that a student's score is more accurately reflective of the student's "true" performance level.[3]

The standard error of measurement is an important concept because it reminds teachers about the *imprecision* of the test scores an individual student receives. Novice teachers often ascribe unwarranted precision to a student's test results. I can remember all too vividly making this mistake myself when I began teaching. While getting ready for my first group of students, I saw as I inspected my students' records that one of my students, Sally Palmer, had taken a group intelligence test. (Such tests were popular in those days.) Sally had earned a score of 126. For the next year, I was absolutely convinced not merely that Sally was above average in her intellectual abilities. Rather, I was certain that her IQ was *exactly* 126. I was too ignorant about assessment to realize that there may have been a sizeable standard error of measurement associated with the intelligence test Sally had taken. Her "true" IQ score might have been substantially lower or markedly higher. I doubt that if Sally had retaken the same intelligence test 10 different times, she would ever have received another score of precisely 126. But, in my naivete, I blissfully assumed Sally's intellectual ability was dead-center 126. The standard error of measurement helps remind teachers that the scores earned by students on commercial *or* classroom tests are not so darned exact.

There's one place a typical teacher is apt to find standard errors of measurement useful, and it is directly linked to the way students' performances on a state's accountability tests are reported. Many states classify a student's performance in at least one of three levels: *basic, proficient*, or *advanced*. A student is given one of these three (or more) labels depending on the student's test scores. So, for instance, on a 60-item accountability test in mathematics, the following classification scheme might have been adopted:

Student's Mathematics Classification	Student's Mathematics Accountability Test Score
Advanced	54–60
Proficient	44–53
Basic	37–43
Below Basic	36 and below

Now, let's suppose one of your students has a score *near the cutoff* for one of this fictitious state's math classifications. To illustrate, suppose your student answered 53 of the 60 items correctly, and was therefore classified as a *proficient* student. Well, if the accountability test has a rather large standard error of measurement, you recognize it's quite likely your *proficient* student might really be an *advanced* student who, because of the test's inaccuracy, didn't earn the necessary extra point. This is the kind of information you can relay to both the student and the student's parents. But to do so, of course, you need to possess at least a rudimentary idea about where a standard error of measurement comes from and how it works.

The more students' scores you find at or near a particular cut-score, the more frequently there will be misclassifications. For example, using the previous table, the cut-score for an "Advanced" classification is 54—that is, a student must get a score of 54 or more to be designated "Advanced." Well, if there are relatively few students who earned that many points, there will be fewer who might be misclassified. However, for the cut-score between "Basic" and "Proficient," 44 points, there might be many more students earning scores of approximately 44 points, so the likelihood of misclassifications rises accordingly.

Although teachers who understand that a standard error of measurement can reveal how much confidence we can place in a student's test performance, and that this is a useful cautionary mechanism for users of test results, few teachers routinely rely on SEMs as they work with test results. Particularly for important tests employed to classify test takers, SEMs can even be tailored so that they allow test users to make more precise interpretations at or near classification cut-scores.

Here's how this process works: As you probably know already, in a given distribution of students' scores on a particular test, we will ordinarily find substantial differences in the number of students who earn certain sorts of scores. Usually, for example, there are more students who score toward the middle of what often turns out to be a "bell-shaped curve" than there are students who earn either very high or very low scores. Well, assume for the moment that five classification categories have been established for a state-administered achievement test, and that there are four cut-scores separating students' performances into the five groups.

Because it will be important to assign test takers to one of the five groups, not only is it possible to calculate an overall standard error for the entire array of students' test scores, but we can also compute SEMs around each of the four cut-scores established for the test. Yes, these are called "conditional standard errors of measurement," and conditional SEMs can vary considerably in size when calculated for cut-scores representing different areas of an overall distribution of test scores.

It seems unlikely that classroom teachers will ever want to compute standard errors for their own tests, and it is almost certain that they'll never wish to compute conditional SEMs for those tests. However, for particularly high-stakes tests, such as those affecting students' admission to universities or students' attainment of scholarship support, reliability/precision is even more important than usual. Teachers should recognize that it is possible to obtain both overall and conditional SEMs at the cut-score segments of a score distribution, and that access to this information can prove particularly helpful in estimating how near to—or far from—the closest cut-score a given student's performance is.

What Do Classroom Teachers Really Need to Know About Reliability/ Precision?

What do you, as a teacher or teacher in preparation, truly need to know about reliability/precision of educational tests? Do you, for example, need to gather data from your own classroom assessment procedures so you can actually calculate reliability coefficients for those assessments? If so, do you need to collect all three varieties of reliability evidence? My answers may surprise you. I think you need to know what reliability is, but I don't think you'll have much call to use it with your own tests—you won't, that is, unless certain of your tests are extraordinarily significant to the students. And I haven't run into classroom tests, even rocko-socko final examinations, that I would consider sufficiently significant to warrant your engaging in a reliability-evidence orgy. In general, if you construct your own classroom tests with care, those tests will be sufficiently reliable for the decisions you will base on the tests' results.

You need to know what reliability is because you may be called on to explain to parents the meaning of a student's important test scores, and you'll want to know how reliable are the scores yielded by those important tests. You need to know what a commercial test manual's authors are talking about and to be wary of those who secure one type of reliability evidence—for instance, a form of internal consistency evidence (because it's the easiest to obtain)—and then try to proclaim that this form of reliability evidence indicates the test's stability or the comparability of its multiple forms. In short, you need to be knowledgeable about the fundamental meaning of reliability, but I do not suggest that you make your own classroom tests pass any sort of reliability muster.

Reliability is a central concept in measurement. As you'll see in the next chapter, if an assessment procedure fails to yield consistent results, it is almost impossible to make any accurate inferences about what a student's score really means. Inconsistent measurement is, at least much of the time, almost certain to be inaccurate measurement. Thus, you should realize that as the stakes associated with an assessment procedure become higher, there will typically be more attention given to establishing that the assessment procedure is, indeed, able to produce reliable results. If you're evaluating an important test developed by others, and you see that only skimpy attention has been given to establishing reliability for the test, you should be critical of the test because evidence regarding an essential attribute of an educational test is missing.

You also ought to possess at least an intuitive understanding of what a standard error of measurement is. Such an understanding will come in handy when you're explaining to students, or their parents, how to make sense of a student's scores on such high-stakes external exams as your state's accountability tests. It's also somewhat useful, but not all that often, to know that for very important tests, conditional SEMs can be determined.

The other thing you should know about reliability evidence is that it comes in three brands—three kinds of evidence about a test's consistency that are *not interchangeable*. Don't let someone foist a set of internal consistency results on you and suggest that these results tell you anything of importance about test-retest evidence. Don't let anyone tell you that a stability reliability coefficient indicates anything about the equivalence of a test's multiple forms. Although the three types of reliability evidence are related, they really are fairly distinctive kinds of creatures, something along the lines of second or third cousins.

What is clear is that classroom teachers, as professionals in the field of education, need to understand that an important attribute of educational assessment procedures is reliability. The higher the stakes associated with a test's use, the more that educators should attend to the assessment procedure's reliability/precision. Reliability is such a key criterion by which psychometricians evaluate tests that you really ought to know what it is, even if you don't use it on a daily basis.

But What Does This Have to Do with Teaching?

Students' questions can sometimes get under a teacher's skin. For example, a student once asked me a question that, in time, forced me to completely rethink what I believed about reliability—at least insofar as it made a difference in a classroom teacher's behavior. "Why," the student asked, "is reliability *really* important for classroom teachers to know?"

The incident occurred during the early seventies. I can still recall where the student was sitting (the

back-right corner of an open-square desk arrangement). I had only recently begun teaching measurement courses at UCLA, and I was "going by the book"; in other words, I was following the course's textbook almost unthinkingly.

You see, as a graduate student myself, I had never taken any coursework dealing with testing. My doctoral studies dealt with curriculum and instruction, not measurement. I wanted to learn ways of instructing prospective teachers about how to whip up winning instructional plans and deliver them with panache to their students. But after graduate school, I soon began to recognize that what was *tested* on important tests invariably influenced what was *taught* by most teachers. I began to read all about educational measurement so I could teach the introductory measurement course in the UCLA Graduate School of Education. Frankly, I was somewhat intimidated by the psychometric shroud that testing experts sometimes employ to surround their playpen. Thus, as a beginner in the field of measurement, I rarely strayed from the "truths" contained in traditional measurement textbooks.

I can't recall my answer to that 1970s student, but I'm sure it must have been somewhat insipid. You see, I was merely mouthing a traditional view of reliability as a key attribute of good tests. In my own mind, at that moment, I really didn't have an answer to her *Why* question. But her question kept bothering me—actually it did so for several years. Then I finally rethought the realistic value of reliability as a concept for classroom teachers. As you'll see in this chapter's wrap-up, I now downplay reliability's importance for busy teachers. But I suspect I still

might be dishing out the same old psychometric party line about reliability—if it hadn't been for this one student's perceptive question. One of those psychometrically sanctioned truths was "reliability is a good thing." Accordingly, I was in the midst of a lecture extolling the virtues of reliability when this memorable student, a woman who was at the time teaching sixth-graders while also working on her master's degree, said, "I can't see any practical reason for teachers to know about reliability or to go to the trouble of computing all these reliability coefficients you've just described. Why should we?"

Teachers *do* need to make sure they evaluate their students' test performances with consistency, especially if students are supplying essay responses or other sorts of performances that can't be scored objectively. But as a general rule, classroom teachers need *not* devote their valuable time to reliability exotica. In reality, reliability has precious little to do with a classroom teacher's *teaching*. But this doesn't make key notions about reliability totally irrelevant to the concerns of classroom teachers. It's just that reliability is way, way less germane than how to whomp up a winning lesson plan for tomorrow's class!

The situation regarding your knowledge about reliability is somewhat analogous to a health professional's knowledge about blood pressure and how blood pressure affects health. Even though only a small proportion of health professionals work directly with patients' blood pressure on a day-by-day basis, there are few health professionals who don't know at least the fundamentals of how one's blood pressure can influence one's health.

You really need not devote any time to calculating the reliability of the scores generated by your own classroom tests, but you should have a general knowledge about what reliability is and why it's important. Besides, computing too many reliability coefficients for your own classroom tests might give you high blood pressure.

Chapter Summary

This chapter focused on the reliability/precision of educational assessment procedures. *Reliability* refers to the consistency with which a test measures whatever it's measuring—that is, the consistency of the test's scores for any intended use of those scores.

There are three distinct types of reliability evidence. *Test-retest reliability* refers to the consistency of students' scores over time. Such reliability is usually represented by a coefficient of correlation between students' scores on two occasions, but it can be indicated by the degree of classification consistency displayed for students on two measurement occasions. *Alternate-form reliability evidence* refers to the consistency of results between two or more forms of the same test. Alternate-form reliability evidence is usually represented by the correlation of students' scores on two different test forms, but it can also be reflected by classification consistency percentages. *Internal consistency* evidence reliability refers to the degree of homogeneity in an assessment procedure's items. Common indices of internal consistency are the Kuder-Richardson formulae and Cronbach's *coefficient alpha*. The three forms of reliability evidence should *not* be used interchangeably, but they should be sought if they are relevant to the educational purpose(s) to which an assessment procedure is being put—that is, to the kind(s) of educational decisions linked to the assessment's results.

The standard error of measurement supplies an indication of the consistency of an individual's score by estimating person-score consistency from evidence of group-score consistency. The standard error of measurement is interpreted in a manner similar to the plus-or-minus estimates of sampling error that are often provided with national opinion polls. Conditional SEMs can be computed for particular segments of a test's score scale—such as those scores near any key cut-scores. Classroom teachers are advised to become generally familiar with the key notions of reliability, but not to subject their own classroom tests to reliability analyses unless the tests are extraordinarily important.

MyLab Education Self-Check 3.1

MyLab Education Self-Check 3.2

MyLab Education Application Exercise 3.1: **Applying the SEM**

MyLab Education Application Exercise 3.2: **Reliability in Context**

References

American Educational Research Association. (2014). *Standards for educational and psychological testing*. Washington, DC: Author.

McMillan, J. H. (2013). *Classroom assessment: Principles and practice for effective standards-based instruction* (6th ed.). Boston: Pearson.

Miller, M. D., and Linn, R. (2012). *Measurement and assessment in teaching* (11th ed.). Columbus, OH: Pearson.

Endnotes

1. The Winter 2014 issue of *Educational Measurement: Issues and Practice* (Volume 33, No. 4) is devoted to the most recent *Standards*. It contains a marvelous collection of articles related to the nature of the *Standards* and their likely impact on educational practice. Those who are interested in the 2014 *Standards* are encouraged to consult this informative special issue.

2. Please note the use of the Latin plural for *formula*. Because I completed 2 years of Latin in high school and 3 years in college, I have vowed to use Latin at least once per month to make those 5 years seem less wasted. Any fool could have said *formulas*.

3. Because different kinds of reliability coefficients are used to reflect a test's consistency, the size of a test's standard error of measurement will depend on the *particular* reliability coefficient that's used when calculating a standard error of measurement.

Reliability: A Testing Necessity*

W. James Popham, University of California, Los Angeles

Reliability is one of those concepts that our society has always held in high esteem. Historically, people have yearned for reliability in their autos, their politicians, and their spouses. In educational testing, reliability is also an urgently sought commodity. That's because it describes the *consistency* with which a test measures whatever it measures. If evidence is not present to support a test's reliability, the likelihood of our accurately interpreting a students' test scores is diminished.

But unlike autos, politicians, and spouses, the evidence to support an educational test's reliability is collected in three distinctive ways:

- *Test-retest reliability evidence* describes the consistency between students' scores after they have completed the same test on two time-separated occasions.

- *Alternate-form reliability evidence* refers to the consistency of students' performances after completing two supposedly equivalent forms of the same test.

- *Internal consistency reliability evidence* tells us how similarly a test's items are functioning to measure what they're measuring.

What is important to understand about test reliability is that these three kinds of evidence represent fundamentally different ways of supporting the degree to which a test is measuring with consistency. Although related to one another, somewhat like second cousins, these three officially approved varieties of reliability evidence are *not* interchangeable.

To illustrate, suppose a school district's officials have purchased a commercially sold mathematics test to use "whenever a student's achievement level indicates that the student is ready." Different students, therefore, take the tests at different times during the school year. The test's publisher supports this use of the test's reliability by presenting positive evidence of the test's internal consistency.

But, as you can see, the consistency evidence in this example should focus on test-retest reliability. That's because the test must measure consistently *regardless of when students completed it* during the school year. The publisher's internal consistency reliability evidence describes the similarity in how a test's items function, not their test-retest consistency.

When a test fails to yield consistent test scores for the intended use of the test, it is unlikely that accurate—that is, *valid*—interpretations will be made based on a student's test performance. Evidence of the right kind of consistency *must* be at hand. Unlike in a court of law, where the accused is regarded as innocent until proven guilty, in educational measurement a test is seen as *guilty* until its reliability has been demonstrated—using the right kind of reliability evidence, of course.

Chapter 4
Validity

 ## Chief Chapter Outcome

A sufficiently deep understanding of assessment validity so that its essential nature can be explained, its establishment can be described, and the most appropriate kinds of validity evidence can be selected for specific uses of educational tests

4.1 Explain the basic conceptual principles of validity including common shortcomings of assessments with weak validity evidence.

4.2 Identify and differentiate between the four sources of validity evidenced in Chapter 4.

We'll be looking at *validity* in this chapter. Validity is, hands down, the most significant concept in assessment. In order to appreciate the reasons why validity is so all-fired important, however, one first needs to understand why educators carry out assessments in the first place. Thus, let's set the stage a bit for your consideration of validity by explaining why educators frequently find themselves obliged to mess around with measurement.

Before you eagerly plunge into this important chapter, you need a heads-up warning. This chapter on validity contains some fairly unusual concepts—that is, ideas you're not apt to see on Saturday night television or even encounter in the "Letters to the Editor" section of your local newspaper (if you still have one).

Don't be put off by these new concepts. When you've finished the chapter, having smilingly looked back on its entrancing content, you'll be better able to focus on the really necessary ideas about validity. These really necessary ideas, when all the hotsy-totsy terminology has been stripped away, are simply gussied-up applications of common sense. Thus, be patient and plug away at Chapter 4. When it's over, you'll be a better person for having done so. And you'll know oodles more about validity.

A Quest for Defensible Interpretations

As noted in Chapter 1, we assess students because we want to determine a student's status with respect to an educationally relevant variable. One kind of variable of relevance to teachers is a variable that can be altered as a consequence of instruction. How much students have learned about world history is one such variable. Another kind of educationally relevant variable is one that can influence the way a teacher decides to instruct students. Students' attitudes toward the study of whatever content the teacher is teaching are examples of this sort of variable.

The more knowledge teachers have about their students' status with respect to certain educationally relevant variables, the more likely they are to make defensible educational decisions regarding their students. To illustrate, if a middle school teacher knows that Lee Lacey is a weak reader and has truly negative attitudes toward reading, the teacher will probably decide *not* to send Lee scampering off to the school library to tackle an independent research project based on self-directed reading. Similarly, if a mathematics teacher discovers early in the school year that her students know much more about mathematics than she had previously suspected, the teacher is apt to decide that the class will tackle more advanced topics than originally planned. Teachers use the results of assessments to make decisions about students. But appropriate educational decisions depend on the *accuracy of educational assessment*. That's because, quite obviously, accurate assessments will improve the quality of decisions, whereas inaccurate assessments will do the opposite. And this is where validity rumbles onstage.

Teachers often need to know how well their students have mastered a *curricular aim*—for example, a skill or body of knowledge that students are supposed to learn. A curricular aim is also referred to these days as a *content standard*. To illustrate, if we set out to determine how well students can comprehend what they have read, it is obviously impractical to find out how well students can read *everything*. There's too much out there to read. Nonetheless, teachers would like to get an accurate fix on how well a particular student can handle the full collection of relevant reading tasks implied by a particular curricular aim. Because it is impossible to see how well students can perform with respect to the entire array of skills or knowledge embodied in a curricular aim, we must fall back on a *sampling* strategy. Thus, when we measure students, we try to sample their mastery of a curricular aim in a representative manner so that, based on students' performance on the sample (in a test), we can infer what their status is with respect to their mastery of the entire curricular aim. Figure 4.1 portrays this relationship graphically. Note that we start with a curricular aim. In Figure 4.1, that's the oval at the left. The left-hand oval represents, for illustration purposes, a curricular aim in reading consisting of a student's ability to comprehend the main ideas of written passages. The oval at the right in Figure 4.1 represents an educational assessment approach—in this instance a 10-item test—that we use to make an *inference* about a student. If you prefer, you can think of a test-based inference simply as an *interpretation* of what the test results signify. The interpretation concerns the student's status with respect to the entire curricular aim (the oval at the left). If this interpretation (inference) is accurate, then the resultant educational decisions are likely to be more defensible, because those decisions will be based on a correct estimate regarding the student's actual status.

The 2014 *Standards for Educational and Psychological Testing* (American Educational Research Association, 2014) don't beat around the bush when dealing

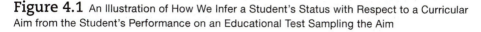

Figure 4.1 An Illustration of How We Infer a Student's Status with Respect to a Curricular Aim from the Student's Performance on an Educational Test Sampling the Aim

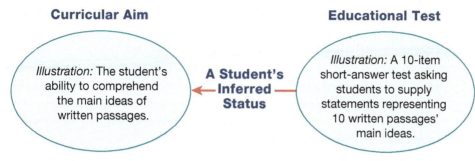

with the topic of assessment validity. Early on in their consideration of validity, for example, the authors of the *Standards* indicate that "validity is, therefore, the most fundamental consideration in developing and evaluating tests" (AERA, 2014, p. 11). But in the intervening years between publication of the 1999 *Standards* and the 2014 *Standards*, we have seen some disagreements among members of the educational measurement community about whether assessment validity should emphasize (1) the accuracy of *the test-based interpretation* regarding what a test taker knows or can do *or* (2) the *consequences of usage*—that is, the appropriateness of the uses of test-based interpretations. Indeed, some of those who stressed the importance of test-score usage introduced the concept of "consequential validity" to highlight the salience of looking at what action was taken because of test-based inference about test takers' status.

Happily, the 2014 *Standards* resolve this issue decisively by proclaiming that assessment validity involves accumulating relevant evidence to provide a sound scientific basis for "proposed uses of tests." In other words, those who set out to collect validity evidence should do so in relationship to specific intended uses of the test under consideration. If an educational test is employed to provide an interpretation about a test taker's status that's to be used in a particular way (such as, for instance, a student's grade-to-grade promotion), the accuracy of the interpretation must be supported *not in general* but, rather, for the specifically identified use. If another use of the test's results is proposed, such as to help evaluate a teacher's instructional effectiveness, then this different usage requires usage-specific evidence to support any interpretation of the test's results related to teachers' instructional skills.

The 2014 *Standards*, then, explicitly link the accuracy of score-based interpretations to the application of those interpretations for particular uses. There is no separate "consequential validity," because the usage consequences of a test's results are inherently derived from the accuracy of test-based interpretations *for a specific purpose*. Thus, clearly, for the very same test, evidence might reveal that for Usage X, the test's score-based interpretations were resoundingly valid, but for Usage Y, the test's score-based interpretations were insufficiently valid.

It is the *validity of a score-based interpretation* that's at issue when measurement folks deal with validity. Tests themselves do not possess validity. Educational tests are used so that educators can make interpretations about a student's status. If high scores lead to one kind of inference, low scores typically lead to an opposite inference. Moreover, because validity hinges on the accuracy of our inferences about students' status with respect to a curricular aim, it is flat-out inaccurate to talk about "the validity of a test." A well-constructed test, if used with the wrong group of students or if administered under unsuitable circumstances, can lead to a set of unsound and thoroughly invalid interpretations. Test-based interpretations may or may not be valid. It is the accuracy of the test-based *interpretation* with which teachers ought to be concerned.

In real life, however, you'll find a fair number of educators talking about the "validity of a test." Perhaps they really understand it's the validity of score-based inferences that is at issue, and they're simply using a shortcut descriptor. Sadly, it's more likely that they really don't know the focus of validity should be on test-based interpretations, not on tests themselves. *There is no such thing as "a valid test."* And, just to be evenhanded in our castigations, *there is no such thing as "an invalid test."*

Now that you know what's really at issue in the case of validity, if you ever hear a colleague talking about "a test's validity," you'll have to decide whether you should preserve that colleague's dignity by letting such psychometric short-comings go unchallenged. I suggest that, unless there are really critical decisions on the line—decisions that would have an important educational impact on students—you keep your insights regarding validation to yourself. (When I first truly comprehended what was going on with the validity of test-based interpretations, I shared this knowledge rather aggressively with several fellow teachers and, thereby, meaningfully miffed them. No one likes a psychometric smart ass.)

Decisions about how to marshal a persuasive validity argument, either for a test under development or for a test that's already in use, can often be abetted by developing a set of claims or propositions that support a proposed interpretation for a specified purpose of testing. Evidence is then collected to evaluate the soundness of those propositions. It is often useful, when generating the propositions for a validity argument, to consider rival hypotheses that may challenge the proposed interpretation. Two variations of such hypotheses hinge on whether a test measures less or more of the construct it purports to measure. Let's look at both of these rival hypotheses that can often, if undetected, meaningfully muck up a validity argument.

Content underrepresentation describes a shortcoming of a test that fails to capture important aspects of the construct being measured. For example, a test of students' reading comprehension that systematically fails to include certain kinds of reading passages, yet claims it is supplying an accurate overall estimate of a child's reading comprehension, embodies a content-underrepresentation mistake.

Construct-irrelevant variance is a test weakness in which test takers' scores are influenced by factors that are extraneous to the construct being assessed for a specific purpose. Using a reading example again, if a test included a flock of reading passages that were outlandishly too complicated or embarrassingly too simple, our interpretation of a student's score on such a reading test would surely be less valid than if the test's passages had meshed with the test takers' abilities. In some instances we have seen test developers creating mathematics tests for which the required reading load clearly undermines a test taker's mathematics prowess. Construct-irrelevant variance can cripple the validity (that is, accuracy) of the score-based interpretations we make for a test's avowed purpose.

There are some pretty fancy phrases used in the preceding paragraphs, and the idea of having to generate a compelling validity argument might seem altogether off-putting to you. But let's strip away the glossy lingo. Here's what's really involved when test developers (for their own tests) or test users (generally for someone else's tests) set out to whomp up a winning validity argument. In turn, we need to (1) spell out clearly the nature of our intended interpretation of test scores in relation to the particular use (that is, decision) to which those scores will be put; (2) come up with propositions that must be supported if those intended interpretations are going to be accurate; (3) collect as much relevant evidence as is practical bearing on those propositions; and (4) synthesize the whole works in a convincing validity argument showing that score-based interpretations are likely to be accurate. Sure, it is easier said than done. But now you can see that when the exotic nomenclature of psychometrics is expunged, the what needs to be done is really not all that intimidating.

Decision Time
Group-Influenced Grading

A junior high school English teacher, Cecilia Celina, has recently installed cooperative learning groups in all five of her classes. The groups are organized so that, although there are individual grades earned by students based on each student's specific accomplishments, there is also a group-based grade that is dependent on the average performance of a student's group. Cecilia decides that 60 percent of a student's grade will be based on the student's individual effort and 40 percent of the student's grade will be based on the collective efforts of the student's group. She uses this 60–40 split when she grades students' written examinations, as well as when she grades a group's oral presentation to the rest of the class.

Several of Cecilia's fellow teachers have been interested in her use of cooperative learning because they are considering employing such an approach in their own classes. One of those teachers, Fred Florie, is uncomfortable about Cecilia's 60–40 split of grading weights. Fred believes that Cecilia cannot arrive at a valid estimate of an individual student's accomplishment when 40 percent of the student's grade is based on the efforts of other students. Cecilia responds that this aggregated grading practice is one of the key features of cooperative learning, because it is the contribution of the group grade that motivates the students in a group to help each other learn. In most of her groups, for example, she finds that students willingly help other group members prepare for important examinations.

As she considers Fred's concerns, Cecilia concludes that he is most troubled about the validity of the inferences she makes about her students' achievements. In her mind, however, she separates an estimate of a student's accomplishments from the grade she gives a student.

Cecilia believes she has three decision options facing her. As she sees it, she can (1) leave matters as they are, (2) delete all group-based contributions to an individual student's grade, or (3) modify the 60–40 split.

If you were Cecilia, what would your decision be?

Validity Evidence

Teachers make scads of decisions, sometimes on a minute-by-minute basis. They decide whether to ask questions of their students and, if questions are to be asked, which student gets which question. Most of a teacher's *instructional* decisions are based to a large extent on the teacher's judgment about students' achievement levels. For instance, if a third-grade teacher concludes that most of her students are able to read independently, then the teacher may decide to use independent reading as a key element in a social studies lesson. The teacher's judgment about students' reading abilities is almost always based on evidence of some sort—gathered either formally or informally.

The major contribution of classroom assessment to a teacher's decision making is that it provides reasonably accurate evidence about students' status. Although teachers are often forced to make inferences about students' knowledge, skills, or attitudes on the basis of informal observations, such unsystematic observations sometimes lead teachers to make invalid estimates about a particular student's status. I'm not knocking teachers' informal observational skills, mind you, for I certainly relied on my own informal observations when I was in the classroom. Frequently, however, I was off the mark! More than once, I saw what I wanted to see by inferring that my students possessed knowledge and skills they really didn't have. Later, when students tackled a midterm or final exam, I often discovered that the conclusions I had drawn from my observation-based judgments were far too generous.

Classroom assessments, if they're truly going to help teachers make solid instructional decisions, should allow a teacher to arrive at valid interpretations about their students' status. But, more often than not, because a classroom assessment can be carefully structured, an assessment-based interpretation is going to be more valid than an on-the-fly interpretation made while the teacher is often focused on other concerns.

The only reason why teachers should assess their students is to make better educational decisions about those students. Thus, when you think about validity, remember it is not some abstruse measurement mystery, knowable only to those who've labored in the validity vineyards for eons. Rather, validity reflects the accuracy of the interpretations teachers make about what their students know and are able to do.

Even though there are different ways of determining whether test-based interpretations are apt to be valid, the overriding focus is on the *accuracy of an assessment-based interpretation*. It usually helps to think about validity as an overall evaluation of the degree to which a specific interpretation of a test's results is supported. People who develop important tests often try to build a **validity argument** in which they assemble evidence and analyses to show that their tests permit the interpretations being claimed.

As a teacher or a teacher in preparation, you may wonder why you need to devote any time at all to different kinds of validity evidence. Your puzzlement notwithstanding, it's really important that you understand at least the chief kinds of evidence bearing on the validity of a score-based inference. Here, we will pay close attention to the sort of validity evidence with which classroom teachers should be dominantly concerned.

In the last chapter, we saw that there are several kinds of reliability evidence that can be used to help us decide how consistently a test's scores measure what the test is measuring. There are also several kinds of evidence that can be used to help educators determine whether their score-based interpretations are valid for particular uses. Rarely will one set of evidence be so compelling that, all by itself, the evidence assures us our score-based interpretation is truly accurate for a specific purpose. More commonly, several different sets of validity evidence are needed for educators to be really comfortable about the test-based inferences they make. Putting it another way, in order to develop a powerful validity argument, it is often necessary to collect *varied* kinds of validity evidence.

When I was preparing to be a high school teacher, many years ago, my teacher education classmates and I were told that "validity refers to the degree to which a test measures what it purports to measure." (I really grooved on that definition because it gave me an opportunity to use the word *purport*. Prior to that time, I'd had few occasions to do so.) Although, by modern standards, that traditional definition of validity is pretty antiquated, it still contains a solid seed of truth. If a test *truly* measures what it sets out to measure, then it's likely that the inferences we make about students based on their test performances will be valid for the purpose at hand. Valid test-based interpretations will be made because we will typically interpret students' performances according to what the test's developers set out to measure—and did so with a specific use in mind.

In some instances we find educators making meaningful modifications in the sorts of assessments they use with children who have physical or cognitive disabilities. We'll look into this issue in the next chapter, particularly as it has been reshaped by federal assessment-related legislation. However, try to think about an assessment procedure in which a *reading* achievement test is to be read aloud to a blind child. Let's say that the child, having heard the test's reading passages and each multiple-choice option having been read aloud, scores very well. Does this permit us to make a valid inference that the blind child can *read*? No, even though a reading test is involved, a more valid interpretation is that the child can derive substantial meaning from read-aloud material. It's an important skill for visually impaired children, and it's a skill that ought to be nurtured. But it isn't *reading*. Validity resides in a test-based interpretation, not in the test itself. And the interpretation must always be rooted in a specified use that's intended.

Let's take a look, now, at the three most common kinds of evidence you are apt to encounter in determining whether the interpretation that's made from an educational assessment procedure is valid for a specific purpose. Having looked at the three varieties of validity evidence, you'll then get a recommendation regarding what classroom teachers *really* need to know about validity and what kinds of validity evidence, if any, teachers need to gather regarding their own tests. Table 4.1 previews the four sources of validity evidence we'll be considering in the remainder of the chapter.

Through the years, measurement specialists have carved up the validity pumpkin in sometimes meaningfully different ways. Going back even earlier than the 1999 *Standards*, it was sometimes recommended that we were dealing not with types of validity *evidence* but, rather, with different types of *validity itself*. Both the 1999 and the 2014 *Standards*, however, make it clear that when we refer to validity evidence, we are describing different types of evidence—not different types of validity.

The 2014 *Standards* make the point nicely when its authors say, "Validity is a unitary concept. *It is the degree to which all the accumulated evidence supports the intended interpretation of test scores for the proposed use*" (AERA, 2014 p. 14). I have taken the liberty of slathering a heap of emphasis on that truly important sentence by italicizing it. The italicizing was added because, if you grasp the meaning of this single sentence, you will have understood what's really meant by assessment validity.

In Table 4.1 you will find the four types of validity evidence identified in the new *Standards*. Two of those four kinds of evidence are used more frequently, so we will deal with those two categories of evidence more deeply in the remainder of this chapter. Please consider, then, the four sources of validity evidence identified in the new *Standards* and daintily described in Table 4.1.

Table 4.1 Four Sources of Validity Evidence

Basis of Validity Evidence	Brief Description
Test Content	The extent to which an assessment procedure adequately represents the content of the curricular aim(s) being measured
Response Processes	The degree to which the cognitive processes that test takers employ during a test support an interpretation for a specific test use
Internal Structure	The extent to which the internal organization of a test confirms an accurate assessment of the construct supposedly being measured
Relations to Other Variables	The degree to which an inferred construct is predictably correlated to measures of similar and dissimilar variables—including foreseen and unforeseen consequences

As you consider the four sources of validity evidence set forth in Table 4.1, each accompanied by its terse description, you will discover that in many settings, the most significant sources of validity evidence teachers need to be concerned about are the first and the fourth entries: validity evidence based on *test content* and validity evidence based on *relations to other variables*. On rare occasions, a teacher might bump into the remaining two sources of validity evidence—the kind based on *response processes* and those based on a test's *internal structure*—but such sorts of validity evidence aren't often encountered by most classroom teachers. Accordingly, we will take a serious look at two of the sources of validity evidence set forth in Table 4.1, and we will give only a demure sideways glance to the other two, less frequently encountered sources of validity evidence.

Validity Evidence Based on Test Content

Remembering that the more evidence of validity we have, the better we'll know how much confidence to place in score-based inferences for specific uses, let's look at the first source of validity evidence: *evidence based on test content*.

Formerly described as *content-related evidence of validity* (and described even earlier as *content validity*), **evidence of validity based on test content** refers to the adequacy with which the content of a test represents the content of the curricular aim(s) about which interpretations are to be made for specific uses. When the idea of content representatives was first dealt with by educational measurement folks many years ago, the focus was dominantly on achievement examinations, such as a test of students' knowledge of history. If educators thought that eighth-grade students ought to know 124 specific facts about history, then the more of those 124 facts that were represented in a test, the more evidence there was of content validity.

These days, however, the notion of *content* refers to much more than factual knowledge. The content of curricular aims in which teachers are interested can embrace knowledge (such as historical facts), skills (such as higher-order thinking competencies), or attitudes (such as students' dispositions toward the study of science). Content, therefore, should be conceived of broadly. When we determine the content representativeness of a test, the content in the curricular aims being sampled can consist of whatever is contained in those curricular aims. Remember, the curricular aims for most classroom tests consist of the skills and knowledge included in a teacher's intended outcomes for a certain instructional period.

During the past decade or so, the term *content standard* has become a common way to describe the skills and knowledge that educators want their students to learn. Almost all states currently have an officially approved set of content standards for each of the major subject areas taught in that state's public schools. Teachers, too, sometimes pursue additional content standards (or curricular aims) associated with the particular grade level or subjects they teach. Clearly, teachers need to familiarize themselves with whatever descriptive language is officially approved in their locale regarding what it is that students are supposed to learn.

But what is adequate representativeness of a set of content standards, and what isn't? Although this is clearly a situation in which more representativeness is better than less representativeness, let's illustrate varying levels with which a curricular aim can be represented by a test. Take a look at Figure 4.2, where you see an illustrative curricular aim (represented by the shaded rectangle) and the items from different tests (represented by the dots). As the test items coincide less adequately with the curricular aim, the weaker is the evidence of validity based on test content.

For example, in Illustration A of Figure 4.2, we see that the test's items effectively sample the full range of the curricular aim's content represented by the shaded rectangle. In Illustration B, however, note that some of the test's items don't even coincide with the curricular aim's content, and those items that *do* fall in the curricular aim don't cover it well. Even in Illustration C, where all the test's items measure content included in the curricular aim, the breadth of coverage for the curricular aim is insufficient.

Trying to put a bit of reality into those rectangles and dots, think about an Algebra I teacher who is trying to measure his students' mastery of a semester's worth of content by creating a truly comprehensive final examination. Based chiefly on students' performances on the final examination, he will assign grades that will influence whether his students can advance to Algebra II. Let's assume the content the teacher addressed instructionally in Algebra I—that is,

Figure 4.2 Varying Degrees to Which a Test's Items Represent the Curricular Aim about Which Score-Based Inferences Are to Be Made the algebraic skills and knowledge taught during the Algebra I course—is truly prerequisite to Algebra II. Then, if the curricular aims representing the Algebra I content are *not* satisfactorily represented by the teacher's final examination, the teacher's score-based interpretations about students' end-of-course algebraic capabilities and his resultant decisions about students' readiness for Algebra II are apt to be in error. If teachers' educational decisions hinge on students' status regarding the curricular aims' content, then those decisions are likely to be flawed if inferences about students' mastery of the curricular aims are based on a test that doesn't adequately represent those curricular aims' content.

How do educators go about gathering evidence of validity derivative from a test's content? Well, there are generally two approaches to follow. Let's consider each of them briefly.

Developmental Care

One way of trying to make sure a test's content adequately taps the content of a curricular aim (or a group of curricular aims) is to employ a set of test-development procedures carefully focused on ensuring that the curricular aim's content is properly reflected in the assessment procedure itself. The higher the stakes associated with the test's use, the more effort is typically devoted to making certain that the assessment procedure's content properly represents the content in the curricular aim(s) involved. For example, if a commercial test publisher were trying to develop an important new nationally standardized test measuring high school students' knowledge of chemistry, it is likely there would be much effort during the development process to make sure the appropriate sorts of skills and knowledge were being measured by the new test. Similarly, because of the significance of a state's accountability tests, substantial attention is typically given to the task of verifying that the test's content suitably represents the state's most important curricular aims.

Listed here, for example, are the kinds of activities that might be carried out during the test-development process for an important chemistry test to ensure the content covered by the new test properly represents "the content high school students ought to know about chemistry."

Possible Developmental Activities to Enhance a High-Stakes Chemistry Test's Content Representativeness

- A panel of national content experts, individually by mail, electronically via an Internet webinar, or during extended face-to-face sessions, recommends the knowledge and skills that should be measured by the new test.

- The proposed content of the new test is systematically contrasted with a list of topics derived from a careful analysis of the content included in the five leading textbooks used in the nation's high school chemistry classes.

- A group of high school chemistry teachers, each judged to be a "teacher of the year" in his or her own state, provides suggestions regarding the key topics (that is, knowledge and skills) to be measured by the new test.

- Several college professors, conceded to be international authorities regarding the teaching of chemistry, having independently reviewed the content suggestions of others for the new test, offer recommendations for additions, deletions, and modifications.

- State and national associations of secondary school chemistry teachers provide reviews of the proposed content to be measured by the new test.

With lower-stakes tests, such as the kind of quiz that a high school chemistry teacher might give after a one-week instructional unit, less elaborate content reviews are obviously warranted. Even classroom teachers, however, can be attentive to the content representativeness of their tests. For openers, teachers can *give deliberate consideration* to whether the content of their classroom tests reflects the instructional outcomes supposedly being measured by those tests. For instance, whatever the test is, a teacher can deliberately try to identify the nature of the curricular aim the test is supposed to represent. Remember, the test itself should not be the focus of the teacher's concern. Rather, the test should be regarded as simply a "stand in" for a curricular aim—that is, the set of skills and/or knowledge embraced by the teacher's instructional aspirations.

To illustrate, if a teacher of 10th-grade English wants to create a final examination for a one-semester course, the teacher should first try to identify all the important skills and knowledge to be taught during the semester. An outline of such content, or even a simple list of topics, will usually suffice. Then, after identifying the content of the curricular aims covering the English course's key content, the teacher can create an assessment instrument that attempts to represent the identified content properly.

As you can see, the important consideration here is that the teacher makes a careful effort to conceptualize the nature of a curricular aim and then tries to see whether the test being constructed actually contains content that is appropriately representative of the content in the curricular aim. Unfortunately, many teachers generate tests without any regard whatsoever for curricular aims. Rather than trying to figure out what knowledge, skills, or attitudes should be promoted instructionally, some teachers simply start churning out test items. Before long, a test is born—a test that, more often than not, does a pretty poor job of sampling the skills and knowledge about which the teacher should make inferences.

We have seen, then, that one way of supplying evidence of validity based on test content is to deliberately incorporate test-development activities that increase the likelihood of representative content coverage. Next, these procedures should be documented. It is this documentation, in fact, that constitutes an important form of evidence of validity for specific uses. The more important the test—that is, the more important its uses—the more important it is that test-development activities be documented. For most teachers' classroom assessments, no documentation is requisite.

External Reviews

A second approach to gathering evidence of validity based on test content involves the assembly of judges who rate the content appropriateness of a given test in relationship to the curricular aim(s) the test allegedly represents. For high-stakes tests, such as a state's accountability tests or a state-developed examination that must be passed before a student receives a high school diploma, these content reviews are typically quite systematic. For run-of-the-mill classroom tests, such external reviews are usually far more informal. For instance, when one teacher asks a colleague to scrutinize the content coverage of a midterm exam, that's a version of this second approach to reviewing a test's content. Clearly, the care with which external reviews of an assessment procedure's content are conducted depends on the consequences associated with students' performances. The more significant the consequences, the more elaborate the external content-review process. Let's look at a couple of examples to illustrate this point.

Suppose state department of education officials decide to construct a statewide assessment program in which all sixth-grade students who don't achieve a specified level of competence in language arts or mathematics must take part in state-designed, but locally delivered, after-school remediation programs. Once the items for the new assessment program are developed (and those items might be fairly traditional or quite innovative), a panel of 20 content reviewers for language arts and a panel of 20 content reviewers for mathematics then consider the test's items. Such reviewers, typically, are subject-matter experts who have considerable familiarity with the content involved.

Using the mathematics portion of the test for illustrative purposes, the 20 members of the Mathematics Content Review Panel might be asked to render a yes/no judgment for *each* of the test's items in response to a question such as the following. Please recognize that this sort of review task must definitely describe the test's intended use.

An Illustrative Item-Judgment Question for Content-Review Panelists

Does this item appropriately measure mathematics knowledge and/or skill(s) so significant to the student's further study that, if they are not mastered, the student should receive after-school remedial instruction?

Note that the illustrative question is a two-component question. Not only should the mathematical knowledge and/or skill involved, if unmastered, require after-school remedial instruction for the student, but also the item being judged must "appropriately measure" this knowledge and/or skill. In other words, the knowledge and/or skill must be sufficiently important to warrant remedial instruction on the part of the students, *and* the knowledge and/or skill must be properly measured by the item. If the content of an item is important, *and* if the content of the item is also properly measured, the content-review panelists should supply a *yes* judgment for the item. If either an item's content is not significant, or the content is badly measured by the item, then the content-review panelists should supply a *no* judgment for the item.

By calculating the percentage of panelists who rate each item positively, an index of content-related evidence of validity can be obtained for each item. To illustrate the process, suppose we had a five-item subtest whose five items received the following positive per-item ratings from a content-review panel: Item One, 72 percent; Item Two, 92 percent; Item Three, 88 percent; Item Four, 98 percent; and Item Five, 100 percent. The average positive per-item ratings for the entire test, then, would be 90 percent. The higher the average per-item ratings provided by a test's content reviewers, the stronger the content-related evidence of validity. This first kind of item-by-item judgment from reviewers represents an attempt to isolate (and eliminate) items whose content is insufficiently related to the curricular aim being measured.

In addition to the content-review panelists' ratings of the individual items, the panel can also be asked to judge how well the test's items represent the domain of content that *should* be assessed to determine whether a student is assigned to the after-school remediation extravaganza. Here is an example of how such a question for content-review panelists might be phrased.

An Illustrative Content-Coverage Question for Content-Review Panelists

First, try to identify mentally the full range of mathematics knowledge and/or skills you believe to be so important that, if they are not mastered, the student should be assigned to after-school remediation classes. Second, having mentally identified that domain of mathematics knowledge and/or skills, please estimate the percent of the domain represented by the set of test items you just reviewed. What percent is it?
_____ percent

If a content panel's review of a test's content coverage yields an average response to such a question of, say, 85 percent, that's not bad. If, however, the content-review panel's average response to the question about content coverage is only 45 percent, this indicates there is a solid chunk of important content not being measured by the test's items. For high-stakes tests, external reviewers' average responses to an item-by-item content question for all items and their average responses to a content-coverage question for the whole test constitute solid indicators of judgmentally derived evidence of validity. The more positive the evidence, the greater confidence one can have in making score-based inferences about a student's status with respect to the curricular aims being measured. Typically, summations of such judgments are placed in a validity report to accompany the test that's under scrutiny.

Although it would be possible for classroom teachers to go through these same content-review machinations for their own classroom assessments, few sane teachers would want to expend this much energy to review the content of a typical classroom test. Instead, a teacher might ask another teacher to look over a test's items and to render judgments akin to those asked of a content-review panel. Because it takes time to provide such judgments, however, a pair of teachers might trade the task of reviewing the content of each other's classroom assessments. ("You scratch my back/review my test, and I'll scratch/review yours.")

One of the significant dividends resulting from having a fellow teacher review the content of your classroom tests is that the *mere prospect* of having such a review take place will almost always lead to the proactive inclusion of more representative content coverage in your tests. The more carefully you consider your test's content coverage early on, the more likely it is that the test's content coverage will be appropriate.

In review, we have considered one kind of validity evidence—namely, content-related evidence of validity—that can be used to support the defensibility of score-based inferences about a student's status with respect to curricular aims. We've discussed this form of validity evidence in some detail because, as you will see, it is the most important form of validity evidence that class-room teachers need to be concerned with when they judge their own classroom assessment procedures.

Alignment

During the last decade or two, those who construct high-stakes accountability tests have been urged to make sure those assessments are in *alignment* with what-ever curricular aims are supposed to be measured by the tests under construction. It is not a silly notion. But it is an imprecise one.

What most people mean when they say they want tests to be aligned with curricular targets is that the tests should properly measure students' status with respect to those curricular targets. But "properly measure" is a fairly fuzzy con-cept. As one looks at the four sources of validity evidence we are dealing with here, it seems clear that the most appropriate form of alignment evidence is evi-dence of validity based on a test's content. Sometimes this test content is deter-mined based on scrutiny of the test itself, and sometimes those determining the degree of alignment will employ the sorts of test-content blueprints described in Chapter 2. Given the diversity of ways that different measurement specialists have attempted to analyze the nature of a test's alignment, we can understand why some commentators have opined that, "Assessment *alignment* is a nine-letter word that seems to function like a four-letter word!"

Thus, because federal assessment personnel have been calling for state accountability tests to be aligned with a state's content standards, a growth indus-try has emerged in recent years, especially since the enactments of NCLB and, more recently, ESSA. We have seen groups of assessment/curricular specialists spring up to independently determine whether a state's accountability tests are in alignment with that state's curricular aims. One of the most popular of the align-ment approaches being used these days is the judgmental procedure devised by Norman Webb of the University of Wisconsin. Briefly introduced in Chapter 2, Webb's method of determining alignment is centered on judgments being made about the following four questions (Webb, 2002).

- *Categorical concurrence.* Are identical or essentially equivalent categories employed for both curricular aims and assessments?
- *Depth-of-knowledge (DOK) consistency.* To what degree are the cognitive demands of curricular aims and assessments identical?
- *Range-of-knowledge correspondence.* Is the breadth of knowledge reflected in curricular aims and assessments the same?
- *Balance of representation.* To what degree are different curricular targets given equal emphasis on the assessments?

As you can see from Webb's four evaluative criteria, the emphasis of this approach parallels other, more traditional methods of ascertaining whether the content that's supposed to be assessed by a test has, indeed, been appropriately assessed. A number of modifications of Webb's general approach have been employed during the past few years, and it seems likely that we will see other approaches to the determination of a test's alignment with the curricular aims it assesses. At bottom, however, it is apparent that these alignment approaches are judgmentally rooted strategies for assembling evidence of validity based on test content.

Validity Evidence Based on Response Processes

An infrequently employed source of validity evidence for educational tests is *evidence based on response processes*. In attempting to measure students' status with respect to certain constructs, it is assumed that test takers engage in particular cognitive processes. For example, if a test is intended to measure students' logical reasoning abilities, it becomes important to know whether students are, in fact, relying on logical reasoning processes as they interact with the test.

Evidence based on response processes typically comes from analyses of individual test takers' responses during a test. For example, questions can be posed to test takers at the conclusion of a test asking for descriptions of the procedures a test taker employed during the test. More often than not, validation evidence from test takers' responses during the testing process will be used in connection with psychological assessments, rather than the somewhat more straightforward assessment of students' knowledge and skills.

A potentially useful setting in which validity evidence would be based on students' response processes can be seen when educators monitor the evolving nature of a sought-for skill such as students' prowess in written composition. By keeping track of the development of students' writing skills in the form of en route assessments of their written or electronic drafts, validity evidence can be assembled regarding how well students can write.

The 2014 *Standards* suggests that studies of response processes are not limited to test takers, but can also focus on observers or judges who have been charged with evaluating test takers' performances or products. Careful consideration of the 2014 *Standards* will reveal that the standards consist chiefly of sound recommendations and rarely set forth any "it must be done this way or else" proclamations.

As noted, even though this source of validity evidence has been identified as a legitimate contributor of evidence to support a validity argument, and teachers should probably know that studies of response processes can be germane for certain sorts of assessments, this particular source of validity evidence is rarely of interest to educators.

Validity Evidence Based on a Test's Internal Structure

For educators, another infrequently used source of validity evidence is the internal structure of a test. For example, let's say some test developers create an achievement test they attempted to make unidimensional. Such a test is intended to measure only one construct (such as a student's overall mathematical prowess). This test, then, ought to behave differently than a test that had been constructed specifically to measure several supposedly different dimensions, such as students' mastery of geometry, algebra, and basic computation.

This third source of validity evidence, of course, requires us to think more carefully about the "construct" supposedly being measured by a test. For many educational tests, the construct to be assessed is abundantly obvious. To illustrate, before the arrival of nifty computer programs that automatically identify one's misspelled words and, in most instances, instantly re-spell those words, most of the students in our school actually needed to *be able to spell*. The students were expected to be able to spell *on their own*, unabetted by electrical, digital, or extraterrestrial support. A teacher would typically choose a sample of words, for instance, 20 words randomly chosen from a district-identified set of 400 "slippery spelling" words, and then read the words aloud—one by one—so students could write on their test papers how each word was spelled. The construct being assessed by such spelling tests was, quite clearly, a student's spelling ability. To tie that to-be-assessed construct down more tightly, what was being measured was a student's ability to accurately spell the words on the 400-word "slippery spelling" list. A student's spelling performance on the 20-word sample was regarded as indicative of the student's ability to spell all 400 words. The construct being assessed so that educators could estimate students' mastery of the construct was gratifyingly straightforward.

Not all constructs that serve as the focus of educational assessments are as easy to isolate. For example, because of several recent federal initiatives, considerable attention has been given to ascertaining students' "college and career readiness"—that is, students' readiness to successfully tackle higher education or embark on a career. But when assessments are created to measure students' college and career readiness, what is the actual construct to be measured? Must that construct be an amalgam of both college readiness and career readiness, or should those two constructs be measured separately? The nature of the constructs to be measured by educational tests is always in the hands of the test developers.

Moreover, depending on the way the test developers decide to carve out their to-be-assessed construct, it may be obvious that if the construct carving has been done properly, we would expect certain sorts of statistical interactions among items representing the overall construct or certain of its subconstructs. This third source of validity evidence, then, can confirm or disconfirm that the test being considered does its measurement job (based on our understanding of the constructs involved, as well as on relevant previous research dealing with this topic) the test should be doing.

One of the more important validity issues addressable by evidence regarding how a test's items are functioning deals with the unidimensionality of the construct involved. This is a pivotal feature of most significant educational tests, and if you will think back to Chapter 3's treatment of internal-consistency reliability, you will see that we can pick up some useful insights about a test's internal structure simply by calculating one or more of the available internal-consistency reliability coefficients—for instance, Cronbach's *coefficient alpha*. Such internal-consistency coefficients, if positive and high, indicate that a test is measuring test takers' status with regard to a single construct. If the construct to be measured by the test is, in fact, unidimensional in nature, then this form of reliability evidence also can contribute to our understanding of whether we can arrive at valid interpretations from a test—that is, valid interpretations of a test taker's score for a specific purpose of the test being considered.

In carrying out efforts to secure this sort of validity evidence when judgments must be made by different raters regarding the caliber of a test taker's performance, it is frequently necessary to calculate the degree of **inter-rater reliability**. To do so, we simply verify the extent to which different raters concur in their evaluations of a student's performance (for example, a student's impromptu oral presentation). Clearly, the orientation of raters to the task at hand, coupled with their training and supervision, plays a prominent role in guaranteeing accuracy of the resultant qualitative estimates of students' performances. Estimates of inter-rater reliability are typically reported as correlation coefficients or simply percent of agreements.

As has been noted, however, this source of internal-structure validity evidence is not often relied on by those who develop or use educational tests. Such validity evidence is more apt to be used by those who create and use psychologically focused tests, where the nature of the constructs being measured is often more complex and multidimensional.

Validity Evidence Based on Relations to Other Variables

The final source of validity evidence identified in the 2014 *Standards* stems from the nature of relationships between students' scores on the test for which we are assembling validity-relevant evidence and those students' scores on other variables. This kind of validity evidence is often seen when educational tests are being evaluated—particularly for high-stakes tests such as we increasingly encounter in education. Consequently, teachers should become familiar with the ways that this kind of validation evidence is typically employed. We will now consider the two most common ways in which validation evidence is obtainable by seeing how the scores of test takers on a particular test are related to those individuals' status on other variables.

Test–Criterion Relationships

Whenever students' performances on a certain test are believed to be predictive of those students' status on some other relevant variable, a *test–criterion relationship* exists. In previous years, such a relationship supplied what was referred to as *criterion-related evidence of validity*. This source of validity evidence is collected only in situations where educators are using an assessment procedure to *predict* how well students will perform on some subsequent *criterion variable*.

The easiest way to understand what this kind of validity evidence looks like is to consider the most common educational setting in which it is collected—namely, the relationship between students' scores on (1) an aptitude test and (2) the grades those students subsequently earn. An *aptitude test*, as noted in Chapter 1, is an assessment device used in order to predict how well a student will perform academically at some later point. For example, many high school students complete a scholastic predictor test (such as the SAT or the ACT) when they're still in high school. The test is supposed to be predictive of how well those students are apt to perform in college. More specifically, students' scores on the predictor test are employed to forecast students' grade-point averages (GPAs) in college. It is assumed that those students who score well on the predictor test will earn higher GPAs in college than those students who score poorly on the aptitude test.

In Figure 4.3, we see the classic kind of relationship between a predictor test and the criterion it is supposed to predict. As you can see, a test is used to predict students' subsequent performance on a criterion. The criterion could be GPA, on-the-job proficiency rating, annual income, or some other performance variable in which we are interested. Most of the time in the field of education, we are concerned with a criterion that deals directly with educational matters. Thus, grades earned in later years are often employed as a criterion. Teachers could also be interested in such "citizenship" criteria as the number of times students vote after completing high school (a positive criterion) or the number of misdemeanors or felonies that are subsequently committed by students (a negative criterion).

Figure 4.3 The Typical Setting in Which Criterion-Related Evidence of Validity Is Sought

If we know a predictor test is working pretty well, we can use its results to help us make educational decisions about students. For example, if you discovered that one of your students, Cliff Carver, scored very poorly on a scholastic aptitude test while in high school, but Cliff's heart is set on attending college, you could devise a set of supplemental instructional activities so that he could try to acquire the needed academic skills and knowledge before he leaves high school. Test results, on predictor tests as well as on any educational assessment procedures, should always be used to make better educational decisions.

In some cases, however, psychometricians can't afford to wait the length of time that's needed between administration of the predictor test and the gathering of data regarding the criterion. For example, if the staff of a commercial testing company is developing a new academic aptitude test to predict high school students' GPAs at the end of college, the company's staff members might administer the new *high school* aptitude test to (much older) *college seniors* only a month or so before those seniors earn their baccalaureate degrees. The correlation between the aptitude test scores and the students' final college GPAs has been historically referred to as *concurrent* evidence of validity. Clearly, such evidence is less compelling than properly gathered *predictive* evidence of validity—that is, when a meaningful length of time has elapsed between the predictor test and the collection of the criterion data. So, for instance, if we were to ask high school students to complete an academic aptitude test as 11th-graders, and then wait for three years to collect evidence of their college grades, this would represent an instance of predictive criterion-relevant validity evidence.

What teachers need to realize about the accuracy of scholastic predictor tests such as the ones we've been considering is that those tests are far from perfect. Sometimes the criterion that's being predicted isn't all that reliable itself. (How accurate were *your* college grades?) For instance, the correlations between students' scores on academic aptitude tests and their subsequent grades rarely exceed .50. A correlation coefficient of .50 indicates that, although the test is surely to some degree predictive of how students will subsequently perform, there are many other factors (such as motivation, study habits, and interpersonal skills) that play a major role in the grades a student earns. In fact, the best predictor of students' future grades is not their scores on aptitude tests; it is their earlier grades. Previous grades more accurately reflect the full range of important grade-influencing factors, such as students' perseverance, that are not directly assessed via aptitude assessment devices.

Parent Talk

Mrs. Billings, the mother of one of your students, is this year's president of your school's parent-teacher organization (PTO). As a consequence of her office, she's been reading a variety of journal articles dealing with educational issues. After every PTO meeting, or so it seems to you, Mrs. Billings asks you to comment on one of the articles she's read. Tonight, she asks you to explain what is meant by the phrase *content standards* and to tell her how your classroom tests are related, if at all, to content standards. She says that the author of one article she read argued that "if teachers' tests didn't measure national content standards, the tests wouldn't be valid."

| *If I were you, here's how I'd respond to Mrs. Billings:*

"You've really identified an important topic for tonight, Mrs. Billings. Content standards are regarded by many of the country's educators as a key factor in how we organize our national education effort. Put simply, a *content standard* describes the knowledge or skill we want our students to master. You might think of a content standard as today's label for what used to be called an instructional objective. What's most imperative, of course, is that teachers focus their instructional efforts on *appropriate* content standards.

"As you may know, our state has already established a series of content standards at all grade levels in language arts, mathematics, social studies, and science. Each of these state-approved sets of

content standards is based, more or less, on a set of content standards originally developed by the national subject-matter association involved—for example, the National Council of Teachers of Mathematics. So, in a sense, teachers in our school can consider both the state-sanctioned standards as well as those devised by the national content associations. Most of our school's teachers have looked at both sets of content standards.

"Teachers look over these content standards when they engage in an activity we call *test sharing*. Each teacher has at least one other colleague look over all the teacher's major classroom assessments to make sure that most of the truly significant content standards have been addressed.

"Those teachers whose tests do not seem to address the content standards satisfactorily are encouraged to revise their tests so that the content standards are more suitably covered. It really seems to work well for us. We've used the system for a couple of years now, and the teachers uniformly think our assessment coverage of key skills and knowledge is far better."

| *Now, how would you respond to Mrs. Billings?*

Statistically, if you want to determine what proportion of students' performances on a criterion variable (such as college grades) is meaningfully related to students' scores on a predictor test (such as the ACT or the SAT), you must *square* the correlation coefficient between the predictor and criterion variables. Thus, if the coefficient is .50, simply square it—that is, multiply it times itself—and you end up with $.50 \times .50 = .25$. This signifies that about 25 percent of students' college grades can be explained by their scores on the aptitude test. Factors such as motivation and study habits account for the other 75 percent. Your students need to understand that when it comes to the predictive accuracy of students' scores on academic aptitude tests, *effort trumps test scores*. The more potently you can promote this simple but potent message to your students, the more likely it is that they will grasp the potential dividends of their own levels of effort.

Convergent and Discriminant Evidence

Another kind of empirical investigation providing evidence of validity is often referred to as a *related-measures study*. In such a study, we hypothesize that a given kind of relationship will be present between students' scores on the assessment device we're scrutinizing and their scores on a related (or unrelated) assessment device. To illustrate, if we churned out a brand-new test of students' ability to comprehend what they read, we could hypothesize that students' scores on the new reading test would be positively correlated with their scores on an already established and widely used reading achievement test. To the extent that our hypothesis is confirmed, we have assembled evidence of validity supporting the validity of our score-based interpretation (using the new test's results) about a student's reading skill.

When it is hypothesized that two sets of test scores *should* be related, and evidence is collected to show that positive relationship, this is referred to as *convergent evidence of validity*. For example, suppose you were a U.S. history teacher and you used a final exam to cover the period from the Civil War to the present. If another teacher of U.S. history in your school also had a final exam covering the same period, you'd predict that the students who scored well on

Peeves Make Poor Pets

Most people have at least one or two pet peeves. When it comes to educational assessment, a common Top-of-the-Charts Pet Peeve occurs when people use test results—without warrant— for a purpose other than what a test was originally created to accomplish. The "without warrant" is an important qualifier. That's because, if a test was initially built for Purpose 1 and has the validity evidence showing it can carry out that purpose properly, then if evidence indicates the test can also be used for Purpose 2, there is no problem with the test's accomplishing this second purpose. (It's like a 2-for-1 sale!) What ticks critics off, however, is when measurement folks build a test for one well-supported purpose, then cavalierly try to employ that test for a second, unsupported use.

That's what has been going on in the United States in recent years when we have seen hoards of policymakers call for the nation's teachers to be evaluated, as least in part, on the basis of their students' scores on achievement tests. Most of the achievement tests being trotted out for this teacher-evaluation mission were originally constructed to provide inferences about the degree of students' mastery regarding a large, often diverse, collection of curricular aims such as has been seen in the nation's annual accountability tests.

But when students' test scores are to be used to evaluate a teacher's *instructional quality*, then

there should be ample validity evidence on hand to show that students' test scores do, indeed, distinguish between effectively taught students and ineffectively taught students. Merely because a test yields a valid interpretation about a student's mastery of curricular aims does not indicate that the test automatically yields accurate interpretations about whether particular teachers are instructionally dazzling or instructionally dismal.

Nonetheless, the proponents of test-score–based teacher evaluation blithely assume that any old test will supply the evidence we can use to differentiate among teachers' instructional skills. This is truly a dumb assumption.

When you're thinking about which test to use for which function, remember that *usage governs validity*. That is, we need to assemble validity evidence to support *any* use of a test's results. When we employ students' test scores to evaluate teachers, and the tests we use have not been *demonstrated* to be capable of doing that evaluative job, then you can safely bet that poor inferences will be made regarding which teachers are winners and which teachers are losers. And when those mistakes about teachers' competence are made, so that weak teachers get tenure while strong teachers get bounced, guess who gets harmed most? That's right; it's the students.

We'll dig more deeply into test-based teacher evaluation in Chapter 15.

your final exam would also do well on your colleague's final exam. (Your dazzling students should dazzle on his exam and your clunky students should clunk on his exam.) If you went to the trouble of actually doing this (and, of course, why would you?), this would be a form of convergent validity evidence.

In contrast, suppose that as a test-crazed U.S. history teacher, you also tried to compare your students' final exam scores to their scores on a final exam in an algebra class. You'd predict a weaker relationship between your students' final exam scores in your history class and their final exam scores in the algebra class. This lower relationship is referred to as *discriminant evidence* of validity. It simply means that if your test is assessing what you think it is, then scores on your test ought to relate weakly to results of tests designed to measure other constructs. (This sort of test comparison, too, would be an unsound use of your time.)

If you can remember back—way, way back—to Figure 4.1 and its descriptions of the four kinds of validity evidence you're apt to encounter in a report regarding a test's quality, the fourth sort of evidence also identifies the relationship between a test's scores and both the foreseen and unforeseen consequences of using the test. In any serious attempt to ascertain the appropriateness of an educational test, it is important to consider the consequences of the test's use, and not only the consequences that were intended, such as being able to carry out certain sorts of mathematical procedures, but also those that were not intended, such a developing an antipathy toward math itself. If a teacher develops a new language arts exam that seems to do a terrific job of distinguishing students who need extra help from those who do not, but implementing the test's results also leads to an increase in language-rooted cliques and bullying, then this would be negative evidence counteracting the apparent positive ranking of students. Effects of testing, anticipated or unanticipated, are crucial commodities. They, too, must be built into a candid validity argument.

Sanctioned and Unsanctioned Labels for Validity Evidence

Validity is the linchpin of educational measurement. If teachers can't arrive at valid score-based interpretations about students, there's simply no reason to measure students in the first place. However, because validity is such a central notion in educational assessment, some folks have attached specialized meanings to it that, although helpful at some level, also may introduce confusion.

One of these is *face validity*, a notion that has been around for a number of decades. All that's meant by face validity is that the *appearance* of a test seems to coincide with the use to which the test is being put. To illustrate, if an assessment procedure is supposed to measure a student's actual ability to function collaboratively with a group of other students, then a true–false test that focused exclusively on abstract principles of group dynamics would not appear to be face valid. But appearance can be deceiving, as has been noted in a variety of ways, including the injunction to remember that we "can't judge a book by its cover."

Thus, even though an assessment procedure may *appear* to be consonant with the assessment procedure's mission, we must still assemble evidence that inclines us to put confidence in the score-based interpretation we arrive at by using the test for a particular purpose. If an assessment procedure has no face validity, we're less inclined to assume the assessment procedure is doing its job. Yet even in those circumstances, we still need to assemble one or more of the *Standards*-approved varieties of validity evidence to help us know how much confidence, if any, we can put in a score-based interpretation derived from using the assessment procedure.

Another more recently introduced variant of validity is something known as consequential validity. *Consequential validity* refers to whether the *uses* of test results are valid. If, for example, a test's results are inappropriately employed to deny students a reasonable expectation, such as progressing to the next grade level, the test may be said to be consequentially invalid because its results had been used improperly. Yet, because educators should obviously be attentive to the consequences of test use, the notion of consequential validity has been made superfluous because of the new *Standards'* stress on the validity of interpretations *for specific uses*. In other words, validity evidence is no longer to be collected to support just "any old interpretation." Now that interpretation must be focused on a particular, announced use of the test-based interpretation. In essence, framers of the new *Standards* have skillfully subsumed consequences into a more focused definition of assessment validity. Consequences must be heeded, of course, but they should be heeded in relation to a specified use of a test's results.

A final point is in order regarding the labels for validity evidence. No one expects classroom teachers to be psychometric whiz-bangs. Teachers should know enough about assessment so that they can do a solid instructional job. In terms of validity evidence and how it ought to be employed by teachers, this means that when it comes to assessment validity, you do not need to keep constantly *au courant*. (This is either a French phrase for "up-to-date" or a scone with especially small raisins.) However, even though you need not become a validity expert, you probably should know that because the 1999 *Standards* were the only game in town for about 15 years, some of the labels used in that document still linger today.

To illustrate, some of your colleagues or even some assessment specialist might still employ the following phrases to describe validity evidence: "content-related evidence of validity" and "criterion-related evidence of validity." We've already considered both of these under slightly different labels. The one type of validity evidence that, though it was widely used in years past, we have not considered is "construct-related evidence of validity." It was also sometimes called simply "construct validity." Those labels refer to a more comprehensive approach to collecting relevant evidence and building a validity argument that supports test-based interpretations regarding the construct that test developers are attempting to measure. Because of the more usage-emphasized manner in which the new *Standards* have attempted to lay out the validity landscape, there now seems to be no need for this traditional way of characterizing the accuracy with which we make score-based interpretations about test takers—interpretations *focused on particular uses*.

The Relationship Between Reliability and Validity

If convincing evidence is gathered that a test is permitting valid score-based interpretations for specific uses, we can be assured the test is also yielding reasonably reliable scores. In other words, valid score-based inferences almost certainly guarantee that consistent test results are present. The reverse, however, is not true. If a test yields reliable results, it may or may not yield valid score-based interpretations. A test *could* be measuring with remarkable consistency a construct the test developer never even contemplated measuring. For instance, although the test developer thought an assessment procedure was measuring students' punctuation skills, what was actually being measured might be students' general intellectual ability, which, not surprisingly, splashes over into how well students can punctuate. Inconsistent results invariably preclude the validity of score-based interpretations. Evidence of valid score-based interpretations almost certainly ensures that consistency of measurement is present.

What Do Classroom Teachers Really Need to Know About Validity?

Well, we've spent a fair number of words worrying about the validity of score-based inferences. How much, if anything, do classroom teachers really need to know about validity? Do classroom teachers need to collect validity evidence for their own tests? If so, what kind(s)?

As with reliability, a classroom teacher needs to understand what the essential nature of the most common kinds of validity evidence is, but classroom teachers don't need to embark on an evidence-gathering frenzy regarding validity. Clearly, if you're a teacher or a teacher in preparation, you'll be far too busy in your classroom trying keeping ahead of the students to spend much time assembling validity evidence. However, for your more important tests, you should probably devote at least some *attention* to validity evidence based on test content. Giving serious thought to the content of an assessment domain being represented by a test is a good first step. Having a colleague review your tests' content is also an effective way to help make sure that your classroom tests represent satisfactorily the content you're trying to promote, and that your score-based interpretations about your students' content-related status are not miles off the mark.

Regarding the other types of validity evidence, however, little more than a reasonable understanding of what those kinds of evidence are is needed. If you're ever asked to help scrutinize a high-stakes educational test, you'll want to know enough about such versions of validity evidence so that you're not intimidated when measurement specialists start reciting their "odes to validity."

Perhaps the most important thing classroom teachers need to understand about validity is that it does *not* reside in a test itself. Rather, it is a score-based interpretation that is either accurate or inaccurate. And because score-based interpretations reflect judgments made by people, some of those judgments will be in error. Validity is a far more elusive critter than is usually thought. Indeed, valid score-based interpretations in the field of education might properly be placed on our nation's endangered species list.

But What Does This Have to Do with Teaching?

Most teachers believe, mistakenly, that their classroom tests are pretty spiffy assessment instruments. Recently I asked five teachers whom I know, "Do you think your classroom tests are pretty spiffy assessment instruments?" Three of the five teachers said, "Yes." One said, "No." And one asked, "What does 'spiffy' mean?" (I counted this as a negative response.) Thus, based on my extensive opinion poll, I can support my contention that *most* teachers think their classroom tests are pretty good—that is, spiffy.

And that's where the concept of *validity* impinges on teaching. Many teachers, you see, believe their classroom assessments produce results that are rather accurate. Many teachers, in fact, think "their tests are valid." The idea that validity resides in tests themselves is a prevalent misconception among the nation's educators. And, unfortunately, when teachers think that their *tests* are valid, they begin to place unwarranted confidence in the scores their students attain on those "valid" tests—regardless of the nature of the decisions informed by a "valid" test's results.

What this chapter has been stressing, restressing, and re-restressing is the idea that validity applies to test-based interpretations, not to the tests themselves. Moreover, for teachers to be confident that their score-based inferences are valid, it's usually necessary to assemble some compelling evidence to support the accuracy of a teacher's score-based inferences. And because teaching decisions are often based on a teacher's estimate of students' current achievement levels, it is apparent that unwarranted confidence in those test-based estimates can sometimes lead to faulty interpretations and, as a result, to unsound instructional decisions.

Ideally, teachers will accept this text's central contention that validity of test-based inferences requires teachers to make a *judgment* about the accuracy of their own test-based inferences. Moreover, truly compelling data are needed for a teacher to be super-sure that test-based *judgments* about students' achievement levels are actually on target. Yet, because compelling data are rarely at hand, teachers are more likely to recognize that their instructional decisions must often be based on a fairly fragile assessment foundation.

In today's high-stakes environment, it is even more important that teachers regard validity as a judgment-derived commodity. For example, suppose your state's officially approved curriculum contains scads of content standards. Because *scads* signifies a large number (and is rarely encountered in its singular form, *scad*), your state clearly has a great many content standards to be taught—and tested. Now let's suppose your state's annual accountability tests are intended to assess students' mastery of those scads of content standards—in a few hours of testing. Well, if that's the situation, do you really think there is apt to be great accuracy in the following statement by an elected state official? "Mastery of our state's content standards can be determined on the basis of students' scores on our state's valid accountability tests." Even elected state officials, you see, can make mistakes in their judgment. For one thing, there are too many content standards for students' "mastery" to be determined. Second (and you know this by now), tests themselves aren't valid (or invalid).

Chapter Summary

This chapter attempted to promote not only an understanding of the nature of assessment validity, but also an appreciation on the part of the reader for the enormously important role that validity plays in educational assessment. Its content was meaningfully shaped by the publication in 2014 of the *Standards for Educational and Psychological Testing*. Because the periodically published *Standards* is developed under the aegis of the three national organizations most responsible for educational assessment, and because fully 15 years have elapsed since the previous publication of the *Standards*, it is almost certain that the 2014 guidelines will have a substantial impact on the way educational tests are developed, evaluated, and used.

The new *Standards*, far more explicitly than in any earlier version of this significant document, stress that validity consists of the "degree to which evidence and theory support the interpretations of test scores for proposed uses of tests" (AERA, 2014, p. 11). The new emphasis is on the need to collect validity evidence for any intended use of the tests—that is, for any usage-based interpretation of test takers' performances. Thus, if a test had been originally created to satisfy one purpose (such as supplying comparative score-interpretations of students' content mastery), and the test were to be used for another purpose, validity evidence should be collected and fashioned into separate arguments supporting the validity of score-based interpretations for both the original and the new use. Such evidence-laced arguments are typically presented then in some sort of technical report regarding a test's quality.

Four sources of validity evidence were described in the chapter. Two of those sources are encountered more frequently by educators and, therefore, were dealt with in greater detail. Those two validity sources were (1) evidence based on test content and (2) evidence based on relations with other variables. The kind of validity evidence most likely to be encountered by teachers involves test-based predictions of students' performances on a criterion variable (such as high school students' college grades). A second kind of relationship between students' test scores and other variables arises when evidence is collected so that those test scores can be correlated with both similar and dissimilar variables. As always, the quest on the part of test developers and test users is to devise a compelling argument attesting to the accuracy of score-based interpretations for particular test uses.

The relationship between validity evidence and reliability evidence was considered, as were certain unsanctioned labels for validity. It was suggested that, in general, more validity evidence is better than less, but that classroom teachers need to be realistic in deciding how much evidence of validity to secure for their own tests. A recommendation was given to have teachers become familiar with all forms of validity evidence, but to focus only on content-based evidence of validity for their own classroom assessment procedures. Most important, it was stressed that teachers must recognize validity as a judgmental inference about the interpretation of students' test performances—not an attribute of tests themselves.

MyLab Education Self-Check 4.1

MyLab Education Self-Check 4.2

MyLab Education Application Exercise 4.1: Validity Basics

MyLab Education Application Exercise 4.2: Sources of Validity

References

American Educational Research Association. (2014). *Standards for educational and psychological testing*. Washington, DC: Author.

Cizek, Gregory J., Kosh, Audra E., and Toutkoushian, Emily K. (2018). "Generalizing and evaluating validity evidence: The generalized assessment tool," *Journal of Educational Measurement*, 55, no. 4 (Winter): 477–512.

Haertel, E. (2013). "Getting the help we need," *Journal of Educational Measurement*, 50, no. 1 (Spring): 84–90.

Kane, M. (2013). "Validating the interpretations and uses of test scores," *Journal of Educational Measurement*, 50, no. 1 (Spring): 1–73.

Nichols, P. D., and Williams, N. (2009). "Consequences of test score use as validity evidence: Roles and responsibilities," *Educational Measurement: Issues and Practice*, 28, no. 1 (Spring): 3–9.

Popham, W. J. (1997). "Consequential validity: Right concern—wrong concept," *Educational Measurement: Issues and Practice*, 16, no. 2 (Summer): 9–13.

Webb, N. L. (2002). *Alignment study in language arts, mathematics, science, and social studies of state standards and assessment for four states*. Washington, DC: Council of Chief State School Officers.

A Testing Takeaway

Assessment Validity's *Two* Requisites*
W. James Popham, University of California, Los Angeles

Assessment validity is, hands down, the most important concept in educational testing. This is asserted in the most recent revision of the *Standards for Educational and Psychological Testing*, a significant collection of assessment guidelines issued by the three most prestigious national associations concerned with educational testing. As the revised standards put it, "validity is, therefore, the most fundamental consideration in developing and evaluating tests" (American Educational Research Association, 2014, p. 11).

What is this "most fundamental" concept in educational testing, and how do we determine whether it's present? First, a definition:

> Assessment validity is the degree to which an evidence-based argument supports the accuracy of a test's interpretations for a proposed use of the test's results.

As you can see, in testing, validity is focused on coming up with accurate interpretations. This is understandable, because the things educators are most concerned with, such as students' cognitive skills and bodies of knowledge, are invisible. We simply can't see what's going on inside students' minds. Accordingly, we use a student's *overt* responses to educational tests to help us arrive at interpretations regarding the student's *covert* skills and knowledge. Validity is, at bottom, an inference-making strategy for reaching conclusions about what we can't see.

Assessment validity, therefore, does not refer to test themselves. There is no such thing as "a valid test" or "an invalid test." Rather, what's valid or invalid is the *inference* about a student test taker that's based on the student's test performance. The danger with ascribing validity to a test itself is that once we regard a test as valid, we begin to believe this so-called "valid" test is suitable for all sorts of purposes, even some for which it isn't suitable at all.

Please note in the above definition that there are *two* requirements for assessment validity. When those who are developing or evaluating an educational test assemble evidence supporting assessment validity, *both* of these requirements must be addressed:

- *Interpretation Accuracy:* Evidence indicating that the score-based inferences about students' status are accurate
- *Usage Support:* Evidence indicating that a test's score-based inferences contribute to the proposed use of the test

The evidence to confirm an educational test's ability to provide accurate interpretations and support a test's intended use is typically presented in the form of a "validity argument." If this argument fails to supply convincing evidence regarding both interpretation accuracy *and* usage support, then employing the test will probably lead to unsound educational decisions and, consequently, miseducated children.

*From Chapter 4 of *Classroom Assessment: What Teachers Need to Know*, 9th Ed., by W. James Popham. Copyright 2020 by Pearson, which hereby grants permission for the reproduction and distribution of this *Testing Takeaway*, with proper attribution, for the intent of increasing assessment literacy. A digitally shareable version is available from www.pearsonmylabandmastering.com.

Chapter 5
Fairness

Chief Chapter Outcome

An understanding of the nature of assessment bias and the procedures by which it can be reduced in both large-scale tests and classroom assessments

5.1 Demonstrate conceptual knowledge of fairness and assessment bias by identifying biased assessment design.

5.2 Identify the educational needs of students with disabilities and English language learners in regards to the prevention of assessment bias and including federal protective legislation.

The last of the "big three" criteria for evaluating educational assessment devices is, in contrast to reliability and validity, a relatively new kid on the block. During the past couple of decades, educators have increasingly recognized that the tests they use are often biased against particular groups of students. As a consequence, students in those groups do not perform as well on a test, not because the students are less able but because there are features in the test that distort the nature of the students' performances. Even if you had never read a single word about educational measurement, you would quickly realize that such a test would be unfair. The third major factor to be used in judging the caliber of educational assessments is *fairness* and, as just pointed out, its arrival on the test-quality scene is far more recent than that of its time-honored evaluative cousins, reliability and validity.

Fairness in educational testing, however, has no single, technically sanctioned meaning. This is because the term *fairness* is used by educators—and noneducators alike—in different ways. For example, educators might regard fairness in testing as a desirable aspiration in general, and yet regard a particular testing program as flagrantly unfair. Authors of the 2014 *Standards for Educational and Psychological Testing* (American Educational Research Association, 2014) limit their focus to fairness related to the aspects of testing that are the responsibility of those who develop, use, and interpret the results of educational tests. Moreover, the *Standards* restrict its attention to those assessment considerations about which there is general professional and technical agreement. Accordingly, in the remainder of this chapter of *Classroom Assessment*, we'll be considering fairness in testing against a backdrop of what's recommended in the 2014 *Standards*.

More specifically, we'll first be looking at a potential source of unfairness that can arise when *assessment bias* is present in a test. Later, we'll consider the kinds of unfairness that can slither onto the scene when we try to assess students with disabilities or to measure the status of students whose first language is not English. Less than high-quality educational assessment of such students almost always leads to test-based interpretations—and subsequent interpretation-based educational decisions—that are far from fair.

At its most basic level, fairness in educational testing is a validity issue. As you saw in the previous chapter, validity refers to the accuracy of score-based interpretations about test takers (for intended uses of those scores). What happens to validity, however, if those interpretations are messed up because our tests contain serious assessment bias, or if we failed to accurately assess English-language learners or students with disabilities because of those students' atypicalities? Well, it is almost certain that the usage-focused interpretations we make based on students' test scores are going to be inaccurate—that is, invalid. Thus, in almost all situations, fairness in testing should be routinely regarded as a requisite precursor to assessment validity—in other words, function as a necessary—but not a sufficient—condition for assessment validity.

The Nature of Assessment Bias

Assessment bias refers to qualities of an assessment instrument that offend or unfairly penalize a group of students because of their gender, race, ethnicity, socioeconomic status, religion, or other such group-defining characteristics. Most teachers are sufficiently familiar with the idea of test bias these days that they recognize what's being talked about when someone says, "That test was biased." In this chapter, however, we'll take a deeper look at what test bias is—and what it isn't. Moreover, we'll consider some procedures that can help classroom teachers recognize whether bias is present in assessment procedures and, as a consequence, can help reduce or eradicate bias in teachers' own classroom tests. Finally, we'll tackle a particularly difficult issue—namely, how to reduce bias when assessing students with disabilities or students who are English language learners.

Because the other two criteria for evaluating educational tests—reliability and validity—are "good things," we're going to use the expression *absence-of-bias* to describe this evaluative criterion. When bias is absent in tests, this is also a "good thing." Before looking at procedures to promote the absence-of-bias in educational assessment procedures, let's first look more directly at what we're trying to eliminate. In other words, let's look at assessment bias itself.

As indicated earlier, assessment bias is present when there are elements in an assessment procedure that distort a student's performance merely because of the student's personal characteristics, such as gender, ethnicity, and so on. Most of the time, we think about distortions that tend to lower the scores of students because those students are members of certain subgroups. For example, suppose officials in State X installed a high-stakes mathematics test that must be passed before students receive an "honors" diploma. If the mathematics test contained many word problems based on certain competitive sports with which boys were more familiar than girls, then girls might perform less well on the test than boys. The lower performance by girls would not occur because girls were less skilled in mathematics, but because they were less familiar with the sports contexts in which the word problems were embedded. This mathematics test, therefore, appears to be biased against girls. On the other hand, it could also be said that the mathematics test is biased in favor of boys. In the case of assessment bias, what we're worried about is distortions of students' test performances—either unwarranted increases or unwarranted decreases.

Let's try another illustration. Suppose that a scholastic aptitude test featured test items based on five lengthy reading selections, two of which were based on content more likely to be known to members of a particular religious group. If, because of familiarity with the content of the two selections, members of that religious group outperformed others, this would be a distortion in their test performances. It would constitute an assessment bias in their favor.

If you think carefully about the issue we're considering, you'll realize that unfairness of testing and assessment bias interfere with the validity of the score-based inferences we draw from our assessment procedures. But because assessment bias constitutes such a distinctive threat to the validity of test-based interpretations, and a threat that can be directly addressed, it is usually regarded as a separate criterion when evaluating educational tests. To the extent that bias is present, for the groups of students against whom the test is biased, valid score-based interpretations are not apt to be forthcoming.

Let's look, now, at two forms of assessment bias—that is, two ways in which the test performances of individuals in particular groups can be distorted. It was noted earlier in the chapter that assessment bias is present when an educational assessment procedure either offends or unfairly penalizes students because of their membership in a gender, racial, ethnic, religious, or similar subgroup. We'll now consider both of these forms of assessment bias.

Offensiveness

An assessment procedure is biased if its content (for example, its items) is *offensive* to a subgroup of students. Such *offensiveness* often occurs when negative stereotypes of certain subgroup members are presented in a test. For instance, suppose that in all of an exam's items we saw males portrayed in high-paying and prestigious positions (e.g., attorneys and physicians), and we saw women portrayed in low-paying and less prestigious positions (e.g., housewives and clerks). Because at least some female students will, quite appropriately, be offended by this gender inequality, their resultant distress may lead to less than optimal performances on the exam and, as a consequence, to scores that do not accurately represent their capabilities. (Angry people aren't the best test takers.)

Other kinds of offensive content include slurs, blatant or implied, based on stereotypic negative attitudes about how members of certain ethnic or religious groups behave. This kind of offensive content, of course, can distract students in the offended group so that they end up focusing more on the offensiveness of a given item than on accurately displaying their own abilities on subsequent items.

Although most of the nation's major test-development agencies now employ item-writing and item-review procedures designed to eliminate such offensive content, one encounters far too many examples of offensive content in less carefully developed teacher-made tests. It is not that teachers deliberately set out to offend any of their students. Rather, many teachers have simply not thought seriously about whether the content of their classroom assessment procedures might cause distress for any of their students. Later in the chapter, we'll consider some practical ways of eradicating offensive content in teachers' classroom assessment procedures.

Unfair Penalization

A second factor contributing to assessment bias is content in a test that may cause *unfair penalization* for a student based on the student's ethnicity, gender, race, religion, and so on. Let's consider for a moment what an "unfair" penalty really is.

Unfair penalization arises when a student's test performance is distorted because of content that, although not offensive, disadvantages the student because of the student's group membership. The previously cited example about girls' unfamiliarity with certain competitive sports is an illustration of such an unfair penalty. As another example, suppose an assessment procedure includes content apt to be known only to children from affluent families. Let's say an assessment procedure is installed to see how well students can "collaboratively solve problems" in groups, and the assessment activity culminates when the teacher gives students a new problem to analyze collaboratively during a group discussion. If the content of the new problem deals with a series of locally presented operas and symphonies likely to have been attended only by those students whose parents can afford such performances' hefty ticket prices, then students from less affluent families will be unfairly penalized because there was probably much less dinner conversation about the unseen local operas and symphonies. Students from lower socioeconomic strata might perform less well on the "collaborative problem solving" assessment, not because they are less skilled at collaborative problem solving but because they are unfamiliar with the content of the particular assessment procedure being employed to gauge students' collaborative problem-solving skills.

Some penalties, of course, are as fair as they can be. If you're a classroom teacher who's generated a test on a unit you've been teaching, and some students perform poorly simply because they didn't pay attention in class or didn't do their homework assignments, then penalizing their lousy performance on your test is eminently fair. Their "penalty," in fact, simply reeks of righteousness. Poor performances on an assessment procedure do not necessarily mean that the resultant penalty to the student (such as a low grade) is unfair. Many of the students I taught in high school and college richly deserved the low grades I gave them.

Unfair penalization arises only when it is not the student's ability that leads to poor performance but, rather, the student's group membership. If, because of the student's gender, ethnicity, and so on, the content of the test distorts how the student would otherwise have performed, then a solid case of assessment bias is

Decision Time

Choose Your Language, Children!

Jaime Jemez teaches mathematics in Wilson Junior High School. He has done so for the past 10 years and is generally regarded as an excellent instructor. In the past few years, however, the student population at Wilson Junior High has been undergoing some dramatic shifts. Whereas there were relatively few Hispanic students in the past, almost 40 percent of the student population is now Hispanic. Moreover, almost half of those students arrived in the United States less than 2 years ago. Most of the newly arrived students in Jaime's classes came from Mexico and Central America.

Because English is a second language for most of these Hispanic students, and because many of the newly arrived students still have a difficult time with written English, Jaime has been wondering whether his mathematics examinations are biased against many of the Hispanic students in his classes. Because Jaime reads and writes Spanish fluently, he has been considering whether he should provide Spanish-language versions of his more important examinations. Although such a decision would result in some extra work for him, Jaime believes that language-choice tests would reduce the bias in his assessment procedures for students whose initial language was Spanish.

Jaime is also aware that the demographics of the district are still shifting and that an increasing number of Southeast Asian students are beginning to show up in his classes. He is afraid that if he starts providing Spanish-language versions of his tests, perhaps he will need to provide the tests in other languages as well. Regrettably, however, he is fluent only in Spanish and English.

If you were Jaime, what would your decision be?

at hand. As was true in the case of offensiveness of test content, we sometimes find classroom teachers who haven't thought carefully about whether their assessment procedures' content gives all students an equal chance to perform well. We'll soon consider some ways for classroom teachers to ferret out test content that might unfairly penalize certain of their students.

Disparate Impact and Assessment Bias

It is sometimes the case that when a statewide, high-stakes test is originally installed, it has disparate impacts on different ethnic groups. For example, African American students or Hispanic American students may perform less well than non-Hispanic White students. Does this *disparate impact* mean the test is biased? Not necessarily. However, if a test has a disparate impact on members of a specific racial, gender, or religious subgroup, this disparate impact certainly warrants further scrutiny to see whether the test is actually biased. *Disparate impact does not equal assessment bias.*

Let me tell you about an experience I had in the late 1970s that drove this point home so I never forgot it. I was working in a southern state to help its state officials develop a series of statewide tests that, ultimately, would be used to deny diplomas to students who failed to pass the 12th-grade level of the test. Having field-tested all of the potential items for the tests on several thousand children in the state, we had assembled a committee of 25 teachers from throughout the state, roughly half of whom were African American, to review the field-test results. The function of the committee was to see whether there were any items that should be discarded. For a number of the items, the African American children in the statewide tryout had performed significantly less well than the other children. Yet, almost any time it was proposed that such items be jettisoned because of such a disparate impact, it was the African American teachers who said, "Our children need to know what's in that item. It deals with important content. Don't you *dare* toss that item out!"

Those African American teachers were saying, in no uncertain terms, that African American children, just like non–African American children, *should* know what was being tested by those items, even if a disparate impact was currently present. The teachers wanted to make sure that if African American youngsters could not currently perform well enough on those items, the presence of the items in the test would allow such deficits to be identified and, as a consequence, to be remediated. The teachers wanted to make sure that *future* disparate impacts would be eliminated.

If an assessment procedure leads to a differential impact on a particular group of students, then it is imperative to discern whether the assessment procedure is biased. But if the assessment procedure does not offend or unfairly penalize any student subgroups, then the most likely explanation of disparate impact would be shortcomings in instruction given to the low-performing group. In other words, there's nothing wrong with the test, but there is something clearly wrong with the quality of instruction previously provided to the subgroup of students who scored poorly on the examination.

It is well known, of course, that genuine equality of education has not always been present in every locale. Thus, it should come as no surprise that some tests will, in particular settings, have a disparate impact on certain subgroups. But this does not necessarily indicate that the tests are biased. It may well be that the tests are helping identify prior inequities in instruction that, of course, should be ameliorated.

One of the most commonly encountered factors leading to students' lower than anticipated performance on an exam, particularly a high-stakes exam, is that students have not had an adequate *opportunity to learn*. Opportunity to learn describes the extent to which students have had exposure to the instruction or information that gives them a reasonable chance to master whatever knowledge or skills are being assessed by a test. Opportunity to learn simply captures the common-sense notion that if students have not been taught to do something that's to be tested, then those untaught students will surely not shine when the testing trumpet is blown.

A relatively recent illustration of a situation in which opportunity to learn was *not* present occurred when education officials in some states closed out the 2013–14 school year by administering newly developed assessments intended to measure students' mastery of a new, often unfamiliar set of curricular aims—namely, the *Common Core State Standards (CCSS)*. Yet, in at least certain of those states, most teachers had not received sufficient professional development dealing with the *CCSS*. Accordingly, many of those teachers were unable to teach about the new content standards with any instructional effectiveness. As a consequence, many of the state's students ended up not having been taught about the *CCSS* and, not surprisingly, scored poorly on the new tests. Did those lower-than-foreseen scores reflect the presence of assessment bias on the new *CCSS*-focused tests? Of course not. What was going on, quite obviously, was not assessment bias but, rather, a clear-cut case of students' trying to tackle a test's targeted content without having been given an opportunity to learn. Teachers must be wary of the opportunity-to-learn issue whenever substantially different content is being assessed by any tests linked to high-stakes decisions.

Let's conclude our consideration of assessment bias by dealing with two strategies for eliminating, or at least markedly reducing, the extent to which unsuitable content on assessment devices can distort certain students' scores. Such distortions, of course, erode the validity of the score-based interpretations educators arrive at when they use such assessment devices. And rotten interpretations regarding students' status, of course, usually lead to rotten decisions about those students.

Judgmental Approaches

One particularly useful way to identify any aspects of an assessment procedure that may be biased is to call on content-knowledgeable reviewers to *judgmentally scrutinize* the assessment procedure, item by item, to see whether any items offend or unfairly penalize certain subgroups of students. When any important, high-stakes test is developed these days, it is customary to have a bias review panel consider its items in order to isolate and discard any that seem likely to contribute to assessment bias. After seeing how such a procedure is implemented for high-stakes tests, we'll consider how classroom teachers can carry out the essential features of an analogous judgmental bias-detection review for their own assessment procedures.

Bias Review Panels

For high-stakes tests such as a state's accountability exams, a bias review panel of, say, 15 to 25 reviewers is typically assembled. Each of the reviewers should be conversant with the content of the test being reviewed. For example, if a sixth-grade language arts accountability test were under development, the bias review committee might be made up mostly of sixth-grade teachers, along with a few district-level language arts curriculum specialists or university professors. The panel should be composed exclusively, or almost exclusively, of individuals from the subgroups who might be adversely impacted by the test. In other words, if the test is to be administered to minority students who are Asian American, Native American, African American, and Hispanic American, there should be representatives of each of those groups on the panel. There should also be a mix of male and female panelists so that they can attend to possible gender bias in items.

After the bias review panel is assembled, its members should be provided with a thorough orientation regarding the overall meaning of fairness in testing and, more specifically, assessment bias—perhaps along the lines of the explanations presented earlier in this chapter. Ideally, panelists should be given some guided practice in reviewing actual assessment items—some of which have been deliberately designed to illustrate specific deficits—for instance, content that is offensive or content that unfairly penalizes certain subgroups. Discussions of such illustrative items usually help clarify panel members' understanding of assessment bias.

A Per-Item Absence-of-Bias Judgment

After the orientation, the bias review panelists should be asked to respond to a question such as the following for *each* of the test's items:

An Illustrative Absence-of-Bias Question for Bias Review Panelists

Might this item offend or unfairly penalize any group of students on the basis of personal characteristics, such as gender, ethnicity, religion, or race?

Panelists are to respond *yes* or *no* to each item using this question. Note that the illustrative question does not ask panelists to judge whether an item *would* offend or unfairly penalize. Rather, the question asks whether an item *might* offend or unfairly penalize. In other words, if there's a *chance* the item might be biased, then bias review panelists are to answer *yes* to the absence-of-bias question. Had the item-bias question used *would* instead of *might*, you can see that this would make it a less stringent form of per-item scrutiny.

The percentage of *no* judgments per item is then calculated so that an average per-item absence-of-bias index (for the whole panel) can be computed for each item and, thereafter, for the entire test. The greater the number of *no* judgments panelists supply, the less bias they think is present in the items. If the test is still under development, items that are judged to be biased by several panelists are generally discarded. Because panelists are usually encouraged to indicate (via a brief written comment) *why* an item appears to be biased, an item may be discarded because of a *single* panelist's judgment, if it is apparent the panelist spotted a bias-linked flaw that had been overlooked by other panelists.

An Overall Absence-of-Bias Judgment

Although having a bias review panel scrutinize the individual items in an assessment device is critical, there's always the chance that the *items in aggregate* may be biased, particularly with respect to the degree to which they might offend certain students. For instance, as the bias review panelists consider the individual items, they may find few problematic items. Yet, when considered as a collectivity, the items may prove to be offensive. Suppose, for example, that in an extensive series of mathematics word problems, the individuals depicted were almost always females. Although this gender disproportion was not apparent from panelists' reviews of individual items, it is apt to be discerned from panelists' responses to an overall absence-of-bias question such as the following:

An Illustrative Overall Absence-of-Bias Question for Bias Review Panelists

Considering all of the items in the assessment device you just reviewed, do the items, taken as a whole, offend or unfairly penalize any group of students on the basis of personal characteristics, such as gender, ethnicity, religion, or race?

Similar to the item-by-item judgments of panelists, the percent of *no* responses by panelists to this overall absence-of-bias question can provide a useful index of whether the assessment procedure is biased. As with the judgments of individual items, bias review panelists who respond *yes* to an overall absence-of-bias question are usually asked to indicate why. Typically, the deficits identified in response to this overall question can be corrected rather readily. For instance, in the previous example about too many females being described in the mathematics word problems, all that needs to be done is a bit of gender reassignment (verbally rather than surgically).

In review, then, judgmental scrutiny of an assessment procedure's items, separately or *in toto*, can prove effective in identifying items that contribute to assessment bias. Such items should be modified or eliminated.

Empirical Approaches

If a high-stakes educational test is to be administered to a large number of students, it is typically possible to gather tryout evidence regarding the performances of different groups of students on individual items, and then review any items for which there are substantial disparities between the performances of different groups. There are a number of different technical procedures for identifying items on which subgroups perform differently. Generally, these procedures are characterized as differential item functioning (DIF) procedures, because the analyses are used to identify items that function differently for one group (for example, girls) than for another (for example, boys). Numerous DIF analysis procedures are now available for use in detecting potentially biased items.

Even after an item has been identified as a differentially functioning item, this does not automatically mean the item is biased. Recalling our discussion of the difference between assessment bias and disparate impact, it is still necessary to scrutinize a differentially functioning item to see whether it is biased or, instead, is detecting the effects of prior instructional inadequacies experienced by a particular group of students—such as insufficient opportunity to learn. In most of today's large-scale test-development projects, even after all items have been subjected to the judgmental scrutiny of a bias review panel, items identified as functioning differentially are "flagged" for a second look by bias reviewers (for example, by an earlier bias review panel or by a different bias review panel). Those items that are, at this point, judgmentally identified as biased are typically excised from the test.

To reiterate, large numbers of students are required in order for empirical bias-reduction approaches to work. Several hundred responses per item for each subgroup under scrutiny are needed before a reasonably accurate estimate of an item's differential functioning can be made.

Bias Detection in the Classroom

If you're an experienced teacher, or are preparing to be a teacher, what can you do about assessment bias in your own classroom? I have a deceptively simple but, I believe, accurate answer to this question. The answer is: *Become sensitive to the existence of assessment bias and the need to eliminate it.*

Assessment bias can transform an otherwise fine educational test into one that falls short of what's needed for fairness in testing. Assessment bias really can be a serious shortcoming of your own tests. As indicated earlier, a test that's biased won't allow you to make valid inferences about your students' learning levels. And if your inferences are invalid, who cares whether you're making those inferences reliably? Absence-of-bias, in short, is significant stuff.

Okay, let's assume you've made a commitment to be sensitive to the possibility of bias in your own classroom assessments. How do you go about it? In general it is usually recommend that you always review your own assessments, insofar as possible, from the perspective of the students you have in your classes—students whose experiences will frequently be decisively different from your own. Even if you're an Hispanic American teacher, and you have a dozen Hispanic American students, this does *not* mean that their backgrounds parallel yours.

What you need to do is *think seriously* about the impact that differing experiential backgrounds will have on the way students respond to your classroom assessments. You'll obviously not always be able to "get inside the heads" of the many different students you have in class, but you can still give it a serious try.

My first teaching job was in a rural high school in an eastern Oregon town with a population of 1500 people. I had grown up in a fairly large city and had no knowledge about farming or ranching. To me, a "range" was a gas or electric kitchen appliance on which one cooked meals. In retrospect, I'm certain that many of my classroom test items contained "city" content that might have confused my students. I'll bet that many of my early test items unfairly penalized some of those boys and girls who had rarely, if ever, left their farms or ranches to visit more metropolitan areas. And, given the size of our tiny town, almost any place on earth was "more metropolitan." But, regrettably, assessment bias was something I simply didn't think about back then. I hope you will.

A similar "beware of differential affluence" problem lurks when teachers either purchase glitzy computer-controlled classroom assessments based or teachers insert computer gyrations into their own teacher-made tests. Fundamentally, computer-governed testing of any sort is always accompanied by a lurking potential for biased assessment. Let's concede that students from more affluent homes are likely to have cavorted with more sophisticated—and more costly—computers than students from less affluent homes. Ritzier and costlier computers can require more challenging per-item analyses than less costly computers. Thus, if a classroom test relies on esoteric computer machinations, we usually find that students who have been obliged to use less costly computers will be unfairly penalized by being asked to engage in digital dances with which they are unfamiliar.

Because some teachers are less familiar with some of the newer forms of assessments you'll be reading about in later chapters (particularly performance assessment, portfolio assessment, computer-controlled assessment, and a number of informal assessment procedures to be used as part of the formative-assessment process), those types of assessments contain serious potential for assessment bias. To illustrate, most performance assessments call for students to respond to a fairly elaborate task of some sort (such as researching a social issue and presenting an oral report to the class). Given that these tasks sometimes require students to draw heavily on their own experiences, it is imperative to select tasks that present the cherished "level playing field" to all students. You'd certainly not wish to use a performance assessment that gave an up-front advantage to students from more affluent families.

Then there's the problem of how to evaluate students' responses to performance assessments or how to judge the student-generated products in students' portfolios. All too often we see teachers evaluate students' responses on the basis of whether those responses displayed "good thinking ability." What those teachers are doing, unfortunately, is creating their own, off-the-cuff version of a group intelligence test—an assessment approach now generally repudiated. Students' responses to performance and portfolio assessments are too often judged on the

Parent Talk

Assume that you are White and were raised in a middle-class environment. During your fourth year of teaching, you've been transferred to an inner-city elementary school in which you teach a class of 27 fifth-graders, half of whom are African Americans. Suppose that Mrs. Johnson, a mother of one of your students, telephones you after school to complain about her son's test results in your class. Mrs. Johnson says, "George always got good grades until he came to your class. But on your tests, he always scores low. I think it's because your tests are biased against Black children!"

| *If I were you, here's how I'd respond to Mrs. Johnson:*

"First, Mrs. Johnson, I really appreciate your calling about George's progress. We both want the very best for him, and now that you've phoned, I hope we can work together in his best interest.

"About George's test performance, I realize he hasn't done all that well on most of the tests. But I'm afraid it isn't because of test bias. Because this is my first year in this school, and because about half of my fifth-graders are African American, I was really worried that, as a White person, I *might* be developing tests that were biased against some of my students.

"So, during my first week on the job, I asked Ms. Fleming—another fifth-grade teacher who's

African American—if she'd review my tests for possible bias. She agreed to do so, and she's been kind enough to review every single test item that I've used this year. I try to be careful myself about identifying biased items, and I'm getting pretty good at it, but Ms. Fleming helped me spot several items, particularly at the start of the year, that might have been biased against African American children. I removed or revised every one of those items.

"What I think is going on in George's case, Mrs. Johnson, is related to the instruction he's received in past years. I think George is a very bright child, but I know your family transferred to our district this year from another state. I really fear that where George went to school in the past, he may not have been provided with the building-block skills he needs for my class.

"What I'd like to do, if you're willing, is to set up a conference either here at school or in your home, if that's more convenient, to discuss the particular skills George is having difficulty with. I'm confident we can work out an instructional approach that, with your assistance, will help George acquire the skills he needs for our tests."

| *Now, how would you respond to Mrs. Johnson?*

basis of factors that are more background dependent than instructionally promotable. Assessment bias applies to *all* forms of testing, not merely to paper-and-pencil tests.

If you want to expunge bias from your own assessments, try to review *every* item in *every* assessment from the perspective of whether there is anything present in the item that might offend or unfairly penalize any of your students. If you ever find such potential bias in any of your items, then without delay patch them up or plow them under.

You'll probably never be able to remove *all* bias from your classroom assessments. Biased content has a nasty habit of slipping past even the most bias-conscious classroom teacher. But if you identify 100 teachers who are seriously sensitized to the possibility of assessment bias in their own tests and 100 teachers who've not thought much about assessment bias, there's no doubt regarding which 100 teachers will create less biased assessments. Such doubt-free judgment, of course, might be biased. But it isn't!

Assessing Students with Disabilities and English Language Learners

Assessment bias can blossom in often unforeseen ways when teachers attempt to assess two distinctive categories of children—namely, *students with disabilities* and students who are *English language learners*. In the past, because these two groups of students often received the bulk of their instruction from educational specialists rather than regular classroom teachers, many teachers gave scant attention to the testing of such students. However, largely due to the enactment of far-reaching federal laws, today's classroom teachers need to understand, at the very least, some fundamentals about how to assess children with disabilities, as well as English language learners. We'll briefly consider potential assessment bias as it relates to both of these types of students.

Children with Disabilities and Federal Law

Many teachers, when they hear the phrase *children with disabilities*, immediately think of children who, because they are mentally retarded, are euphemistically regarded as *special education* students. Such perceptions are way off the mark. Actually, only about 10 percent of children with disabilities are mentally retarded. Fully two thirds of children with disabilities either have specific learning disabilities—almost 80 percent of which arise from students' problems with reading—or impairments in speech or language. There are 13 categories of disability set forth in federal law, including such less-frequent disabilities as autism (2 percent of children with disabilities), emotional disturbance (8 percent), and hearing impairments (1 percent).

Federal law, you see, has triggered substantially reconceptualized views about how to teach and to test students with disabilities. The Education for All

Handicapped Children Act (Public Law 94-142) was enacted in 1975 because of (1) a growing recognition of the need to properly educate children who had disabilities and (2) a series of judicial rulings requiring states to provide a suitable education for students with disabilities if those states were providing one for students without disabilities. Usually referred to simply as "P.L. 94-142," this influential law supplied federal funding to states, but only if those states appropriately educated children with disabilities.

Public Law 94-142 also mandated the use of an *individualized education program (IEP)* for a student with disabilities. An IEP is the federally prescribed document developed by parents, teachers, and specialized services providers (such as an audiologist) describing how a particular child with disabilities should be educated. An IEP represents a per-child plan that spells out annual curricular aims for the child, indicates how the student's attainment of those goals will be determined, specifies whatever related services are needed by the child, and sets forth any adjustments or substitutions in the assessments to be used with the child. The architects of P.L. 94-142 believed it would encourage the education of many students with disabilities in regular classrooms to the greatest extent possible.

In 1997, P.L. 94-142 was reauthorized and, at the same time, labeled the Individuals with Disabilities Education Act (IDEA). That reauthorization called for states and districts to identify curricular expectations for special education students that were as consonant as possible with the curricular expectations that had been established *for all other students*. Under IDEA, all states and districts were required to include students with disabilities in their assessment programs—and to publicly report those test results. However, because IDEA of 1997 contained few negative consequences for noncompliance, most of the nation's educators simply failed to comply.

The special education landscape, however, was significantly altered when President George W. Bush affixed his signature to the No Child Left Behind Act (NCLB) in early 2002. Unlike IDEA of 1997, NCLB possessed significantly increased penalties for noncompliance. The act intended to improve the achievement levels of *all* students—including children with disabilities—and to do so in a way that such improvement would be *demonstrated* on state-chosen tests linked to each state's curricular aims. Students' test scores were to improve on a regular basis over a dozen years in order to reflect substantially improved student learning. Even though NCLB allowed states some flexibility in deciding how many more students must earn "proficient or higher" scores each year on that state's accountability tests, if a school failed to make adequate yearly progress (AYP) based on the state's 12-year improvement schedule, then the school was placed on a sanction-laden improvement track.

Importantly, NCLB required adequate yearly progress not only for students overall but also for subgroups reflecting race/ethnicity, the economically disadvantaged, students with limited English proficiency, and *students with disabilities*. Accordingly, if there were sufficient numbers of any of those subgroups in a school, and *one* of those subgroups failed to score high enough to make that subgroup's

AYP targets, then the whole school flopped on AYP. Obviously, the assessed performances of students with disabilities became far more significant to a school's educators than they were before the enactment of NCLB. As today's educators deal with the challenges of the 2015 Every Student Succeeds Act (ESSA), few of them look back at NCLB and regard it as a flaw-free, rousing success. Yet, still fewer educators fail to give credit to NCLB as the federal statute that obliged the nation's educators to look much harder at the caliber of education we provided to these special children.

In 2004, IDEA was reauthorized once again. At that juncture, however, there was already another significant federal statute on the books dealing with the assessment of students with disabilities—namely, NCLB. Federal lawmakers attempted to shape the reauthorized IDEA so it would be as consistent as possible with the assessment provisions of NCLB that had been enacted 2 years earlier. Even so, there were important procedural differences between IDEA and NCLB, though one could find few fundamental contradictions between those two laws. Remember that when P.L. 94-142 first scampered onto the scene, one of its most influential contributions was the IEP. Many teachers came to understand that an individualized education program was supposed to be just what it said it was—an *individualized* program for a particular student with disabilities. Thus, the push of IDEA has historically been directed toward an individualized approach to instruction and an individualized approach to assessing what a student has learned.

Instead of the more student-tailored approach embodied in IDEA, the accountability strategy embodied in NCLB and ESSA was a far more *group-based* (and *subgroup-based*) approach than the kid-by-kid orientation of IDEA. A key congressional committee put it well when it observed, "IDEA and NCLB work in concert to ensure that students with disabilities are included in assessment and accountability systems. While IDEA focuses on the needs of the individual child, NCLB focuses on ensuring improved academic achievement for *all* students."[1]

The most important thing teachers need to understand about the instruction and assessment of students with disabilities is that the education of all but a very small group of those children must be aimed at precisely *the same curricular targets* as the curricular targets teachers have for all other students. Both ESSA and IDEA required the *same* content standards for *all* children—with no exceptions! However, for students with the most severe cognitive disabilities, it is possible to use different definitions of achievement. Thus, this small group of students can use modified ways to display their performance related to the same content standards. These modifications take the form of ***alternate assessments***. Such alternate assessments were to be used with only that super-small percent of children who suffer from the most severe cognitive disabilities. In other words, whereas the academic content standards must stay the same for all students, the academic achievement standards (performance levels) can differ substantively for children who have the most severe cognitive disabilities.

Because IEPs are central to the assessment of many children with disabilities, we deal with the widespread misperception that IEPs are written documents allowing the parents and teachers of children with disabilities to do some serious bar-lowering, but to do so behind closed doors. Some general education teachers are not knowledgeable about the IEP process. To certain teachers, IEPs are born in clandestine meetings in which biased individuals simply soften expectations so that children with disabilities need not pursue the same curricular aims as those sought for all other children. Perhaps such perceptions were warranted earlier on, but IEP regulations have been seriously modified in recent years. If those who create today's IEPs deliberately aim at anything less than the same content standards being pursued by all students, such IEPs violate some big-stick federal statutes.

ACCOMMODATIONS

A prominent procedure to minimize assessment bias for students with disabilities is to employ *assessment accommodations*. An *accommodation* is a procedure or practice that permits students with disabilities to have equitable access to instruction and assessment. The mission of an assessment accommodation is to eliminate or reduce the inference-distorting effects of a student's disabilities. It is not the purpose of accommodations to lower the aspirations educators have for students with disabilities. Typically, but not always, the accommodations provided to a student in an assessment setting are similar to the ones used during instruction for that student.

Although accommodations are designed to enhance fairness by providing students with opportunities to circumvent their disabilities, there's a critical limitation on just how much fairness-induction can be provided. Here's the rub: An assessment accommodation must not fundamentally alter the nature of the skills or knowledge being assessed. This can be illustrated with respect to the skill of reading. Teachers clearly want children to learn to read—whether those children have disabilities or not. A teacher, however, can't simply look at a student and tell whether that student can read. That's because the ability to read is a *covert* skill. To determine a child's reading ability, teachers need to have a student engage in an *overt* act, such as silently reading a brief short story and then saying aloud—or in writing—what the story was about. A teacher then can, based on the child's *assessed* overt performance, arrive at an inference about the child's reading skills.

However, what if a teacher proposed to use an accommodation for a child with disabilities that called for a short story to be read aloud to the child? This would surely be a meaningful accommodation, and we can assume that the child would enjoy hearing a story read aloud. But suppose the child were then given a written or oral test about the content of the short story. Do you think the child's overt responses to that test would allow a teacher to arrive at a valid inference about the child's reading skills? Of course it wouldn't. Teachers who devise assessment accommodations for children with disabilities must be vigilant to avoid distorting the essential nature of the skills or knowledge being measured.

A cracking good analysis of the accommodations needed for the instruction and assessment of students with disabilities was published in 2005 by the Council of Chief State School Officers (CCSSO). If you wish to delve more deeply into the accommodation arena, that manual is highly recommended. That CCSSO manual is cited in the References at the close of this chapter (see Thompson et al., 2005). In that manual, there is a breakdown of the four common categories of accommodations typically considered for either assessment or instruction: presentation, response, setting, and timing and scheduling.

ACCESSIBILITY

During the past several decades, *accessibility* has become a key concept of increasing relevance for assessing students with disabilities—as well as for measuring students with limited English proficiency. Accessibility is intended to minimize assessment bias and, therefore, increase fairness. Accessibility refers to the notion that all test takers must have an unobstructed opportunity to demonstrate their status with respect to the construct(s) being measured by an educational test. If a student's access to the assessed construct(s) is impeded by skills and/or characteristics unrelated to what's being tested, this will limit the validity of score interpretations for particular uses. And those limitations in validity can affect both individuals and particular subgroups of test takers.

It is generally agreed that because 1997's Individuals with Disabilities Act (IDEA) called for students with disabilities to be given "access to the general curriculum," educators of such children became sensitized to the concept of accessibility. Although the term *access* has, in years past, not been used in this particular way, assessment specialists who work with special populations of students have concluded that the concept of accessibility captures a factor that, for many students, plays a prominent role in determining the fairness of testing.

What does it mean to test developers or to classroom teachers that students, whether those students have disabilities or are learning English, must have access to the construct(s) being assessed? Well, for developers of major external exams, such as a state's standardized accountability tests or a district's high school graduation test, it means that the test's developers must be continually on guard to make sure there are no features in a test's design that might preclude any students from having a chance to "show what they know"—that is, to demonstrate how they stack up against the construct(s) being measured. And for a teacher's classroom tests, it means the very same thing!

Put differently, both large-scale test developers and teachers who crank out their own tests must be constantly on guard to ensure that their assessments will provide total accessibility to each and every child. Given the wide range of student disabilities and the considerable variety of levels of students' English proficiency encountered in today's schools, this constant quest for accessibility often represents a genuine challenge for the test developers and teachers involved.

UNIVERSAL DESIGN

An increasingly applauded strategy for improving accessibility to educational tests is the process of **universal design**. Universal design describes an approach to the building of tests that *from the very outset* of the test-construction process attempts to maximize accessibility for *all* intended test takers. In years past, tests were first built, and then—often as an afterthought—the developers tried to make the tests accessible to more students. The motivations for those sorts of after-the-fact accessibility enhancements were, of course, commendable. But after-the-fact attempts to change an already completed assessment instrument are almost certain to be less effective than one might wish. Indeed, *accessibility* of a test's content to the test taker has become an increasingly important concern to members of the measurement community— and especially to measurement folks who are devising assessments for groups of special education learners.

When approaching test development from a universal-design perspective, however, the maximizing of accessibility governs the test developer's decisions from the get-go. Test items and tasks are designed with an overriding motive in mind: to minimize construct-irrelevant features that might reduce access for the *complete* array of potential test takers, not merely the typical test takers. Universal design constitutes an increasingly prevalent mind-set on the part of major test developers. It is a mind-set that classroom teachers can—and should—develop for themselves.

English Language Learners

And what about students whose first language is not English? In other words, how should classroom teachers assess such students? First off, we need to do a bit of term-defining, because there are a number of descriptive labels for such youngsters being used these days. **English language learners (ELLs)** represent a diverse, fast-growing student population in the United States and Canada. Included in the ELL group are (1) students whose first language is not English and know little, if any, English; (2) students who are beginning to learn English but could benefit from school instruction; and (3) students who are proficient in English but need additional assistance in academic or social contexts. English language learners also include language-minority students (also called linguistic-minority students) who use a language besides English in the home. The federal government sometimes uses the term *limited English proficient (LEP)* to describe ELL students. One also encounters the label *language learners*. Currently, most people, because they believe it more politically correct, describe those students as "English language learners," but it is equally accurate to employ the govern-mentally favored descriptor "limited English proficient." The ELL label will be employed from here on in this book.

It was indicated earlier that ESSA is the current reauthorization of a landmark federal 1965 law, the Elementary and Secondary Education Act (ESEA). So, if you are interested in the assessment requirements of the law insofar as ELLs are concerned, be sure to be attentive to any ESSA adjustments in the regulations for implementing the reauthorized federal statute. Until changes take place, however, two federal requirements spelled out the kinds of assessments to be used with language-minority students.

First, there is the requirement to determine the degree to which certain subgroups of students—specifically those subgroups identified in ESSA—are making adequate yearly progress. One of these groups consists of "students with limited English proficiency." If there are sufficient numbers of ELL students in a school (or in a district) to yield "statistically reliable information," then a designated proportion of those students must have earned proficient-or-above scores on a state's accountability tests. If enough students don't earn those scores, a school (or district) will be regarded as having failed to make its AYP targets.

Interestingly, because federal officials have allowed states some latitude in deciding on the minimum numbers of students (in a subgroup) needed in order to provide "statistically reliable information," there is considerable variation from state to state in these subgroup minimum numbers. You will easily recognize that if a state had set its minimum numbers fairly high, then fewer schools and districts would be regarded as having failed AYP. This is because low-performing students in a particular subgroup need not be counted in AYP calculations if there were too few students (that is, below state-set minima) in a particular subgroup. Conversely, a state whose subgroup minima had been set fairly low would find more of its schools or districts flopping on AYP because of one or more subgroups' shortcomings. Yet, because ESSA attempted to locate more of its high-stakes assessment decisions in states rather than in Washington, DC, this localization of such decision making has generally been approved.

Second, ESSA contains another assessment requirement related to ELL students. The law called for states to employ separate academic assessments of English language proficiency so that, on an annual basis, such tests can measure ELL students' skills in "oral language, reading, and writing." Because most states did not have such tests on hand (or, if they did, those tests usually measured beginning students' social English skills rather than the students' academic English skills), we have witnessed substantial test-development activity in individual states or, frequently, in test-development consortia involving several participating states.

The technical quality of these tests to assess students' English language proficiency, of course, will be the chief determinant regarding whether valid inferences can be made regarding ELL students' mastery of English. Clearly, considerable attention must be given to evaluating the caliber of this emerging collection of assessment instruments.

Lest you think that the assessment of ELL students, once addressed seriously because of federal requirements, is going to be easy to pull off, think again. Jamal Abedi, one of the nation's leading authorities on the assessment of ELL students, has reminded us of half a dozen issues that must be addressed if federal laws are going to accomplish for LEP students what those laws' architects intended (Abedi, 2004). He pointed to the following concerns:

1. *Inconsistency in ELL classification across and within states.* A variety of different classification criteria are used to identify ELL students among states and even within districts and schools in a state, thus affecting the accuracy of AYP reporting for ELL students.

2. *Sparse ELL populations.* In a large number of states and districts there are too few ELL students to permit meaningful analyses, thus distorting state and federal policy decisions in such settings.

3. *Subgroup instability.* Because a student's ELL status is not stable over time, a school's ELL population represents a moving, potentially unattainable target. To illustrate, if a given ELL student's mastery of English has improved sufficiently, that student is moved out of the ELL group, only to be replaced by a new student whose English proficiency is apt to be substantially lower. Therefore, even with superlative instruction, there is little chance of improving the AYP status of the ELL subgroup from year to year.

4. *Technical quality of AYP-determining assessment tools.* Because studies have shown that assessment instruments constructed for native English speakers have lower reliability and validity when used with ELL populations, results of such tests are likely to be misinterpreted when employed with ELL students.

5. *Lower baseline scores.* Because schools with large numbers of ELL students are likely to have lower baseline scores and thus may have improvement targets that will be unrealistically challenging, such schools may have difficulty in attaining state-set increments in students' achievement levels.

6. *Cut-scores for ELL students.* Unlike the previous version of ESEA, in which a student's weaker performance in one subject area could be compensated for by a higher performance in another subject (this is referred to as a *compensatory* model), federal statutes may require use of a *conjunctive* model in which students' performances in all assessed subject areas must be acceptable. Students' performances in mathematics are apt to be less dependent on language prowess than their performances in reading/language arts, where language demands are higher. This, then, renders the AYP expectations for schools with large ELL populations more challenging than those imposed on schools with fewer ELL students.

Even with all these issues that must be considered when assessing students in the accountability structure of federal assessment-related statutes, Abedi (2004) believes the isolation of subgroup performances is "a step in the right direction." He argued that state and federal officials appear to be addressing many of these issues at this time. Abedi regards this as necessary to resolve these problems if genuine fairness is to be attained in the assessment-based accountability focused on ELL students. And this quest means there needs to be some sensible judgments made by teachers. It is decisively *unsmart* to force a child who speaks and reads only Spanish to take an English-language test about mathematics and then, because the child's test score is low, to conclude that the child can't do math.

The issue of whether teachers should try to make available versions of their tests in non-English languages is, unfortunately, often decided on totally practical grounds. In many settings, teachers may find a dozen or more first languages spoken by their students. In some urban settings, more than 100 first languages other than English are found in a district's students. And if an attempt is made to create an alternate assessment only in the *most* common language a teacher's students possess, how fair is this to those students whose first languages aren't found in sufficient numbers to warrant the creation of a special test in their native language?

Assessment accommodations, in the form of giving language-minority students more time or the use of dictionaries, can, depending on students' levels of English mastery, often help deal with the measurement of such students. In recent years, several of the larger test-development groups, particularly the Smarter Balanced Assessment Consortium, have been experimenting with supplying cartoon-like, pictorial illustrations of the meaning of key words in some test items. If this more generic approach is successful, it would help address the myriad non-English languages that require language-specific dictionaries or glossaries. Results of early experiments with this sort of pictorial-definition approach are too fragmentary, however, for the immediate application of the approach.

It is difficult to attend any conference on educational assessment these days without finding a number of sessions devoted to the measurement of language-minority students or students with disabilities. Clearly, an effort is being made to assess these children in a fashion that is not biased against them. But, just as clearly, the problems of measuring such students with fairness, compassion, and accuracy are nontrivial.

The accurate assessment of students whose first language is not English will continue to pose a serious problem for the nation's teachers. To provide equivalent tests in English and all other first languages spoken by students represents an essentially impossible task. The policy issue now being hotly contested in the United States is whether to create equivalent tests for the most numerous of our schools' language-minority students.

Is Fairness a *Bona Fide* Member of Educational Testing's "Big Three"?

For roughly a century of serious-minded educational assessment, the roost was unarguably ruled by two powerful concepts, *validity* and *reliability*. But with the arrival of the 2014 AERA-APA-NCME *Standards*, educators were told to make room for a third make-a-difference assessment concept, *fairness*. This chapter has attempted to dig a bit into what's really going on when we set out to show that an educational test is fair.

But adding a new test-evaluative factor to a pair of traditional evaluative factors is easier to say than to do. This is because educators can find it tempting to endorse the importance of assessment fairness, but then go about their testing of students as usual. Advocacy of fairness might easily become little more than lip-service. Assessment specialists, as well as everyday teachers, may toss out a few sentences in support of assessment fairness but, when the testing rubber really hits the road, slip back into their adulation of *only* reliability and validity.

If you find yourself committed, at least in spirit, to the importance of educational assessment's fairness, how can you avoid treating test fairness in a tokenistic fashion? This should be, to you, an important question. Happily, the answer is a simple one. You can make fairness a *bona fide* member of educational measurement's "big three" by simply collecting and presenting relevant *evidence* of assessment fairness.

Think back, if you will, to this book's earlier treatments of both validity (Chapter 3) and reliability (Chapter 4). In both of those instances, the adequacy of assessment reliability and assessment validity was determined because of evidence. For validity, evidence related to the accuracy of score-based interpretations about test takers was called for. Although different intended uses of test results might call for different kinds of evidence, what was needed was a validity argument featuring *plentiful and potent evidence* that a test was apt to provide users with scores from which valid inferences could be made for specific purposes. Similarly, to calculate a test's reliability, once more we saw that reliability evidence of three sorts could be gathered so that judgments could be made about a test's ability to yield consistent scores. Thus, with regard to both of these two notions of a test's quality, the more solid evidence that's available to support either reliability or validity, the more likely it is that we will approve a test for a given measurement mission.

It is the same thing for fairness. Educators who want test fairness to play a prominent role in appraising the worth of an educational test must be able to present a compelling array of evidence (judgmental, empirical, or both) that a test is up to the measurement purpose it is supposed to accomplish. As this chapter indicated, either judgmental or empirical evidence can be collected that bears on the fairness of a specific educational assessment. But mere verbal support of assessment fairness without compelling evidence bearing on a specific test's fairness is likely to have little impact on judgments about the virtues of a given educational test.

Typically, educators will find today's large-scale standardized tests accompanied by increasing quantities of evidence regarding a specific test's fairness. For instance, you might encounter summaries of the per-item judgments rendered by a specially constituted bias review panel. Such summaries of judgmental evidence might be supplemented with analyses of the differing test performances of subgroups of student test takers. Similarly, when teachers try to collect evidence regarding their own classroom assessments, much less elaborate records can be made, such as a paragraph of two about whatever analyses were undertaken regarding validity, reliability, and fairness.

To illustrate, suppose you're a sixth-grade teacher who has asked a fifth-grade fellow teacher to review your midterm exam's items for any instances of subgroup-linked biases. Based on your colleague's report, you might simply summarize the percent of items thought to offend or unfairly penalize your sixth-grade students. Similar brief summaries of analyses dealing with reliability and validity could be summarized for the test you are evaluating. Such once-over-lightly analyses on your own classroom tests are likely to sensitize you to the strengths and weaknesses of the evaluative evidence supplied for larger, higher-stakes tests.

What Do Classroom Teachers Really Need to Know About Fairness?

Classroom teachers need to know that if assessment bias exists, then assessment fairness scampers out the door. Unfair bias in large-scale educational testing is less prevalent than it was a decade or two ago because many measurement specialists, after having been sensitized to the presence of assessment bias, now strive to eliminate such bias. However, for the kinds of teacher-developed assessment procedures seen in typical classrooms, systematic attention to bias eradication is much less common.

All classroom teachers need *routinely* to use fairness—and, in particular, absence-of-bias—as one of the evaluative criteria by which they judge their own assessments and those educational assessments developed by others. For instance, if you are ever called on to review the quality of a high-stakes test—such as a district-developed or district-adopted examination whose results will have a meaningful impact on students' lives—be sure that suitable absence-of-bias procedures, both judgmental and empirical, were employed during the examination's development.

But what about your own tests? How much effort should you devote to making sure that your tests are fair, and that they don't offend or unfairly penalize any of your students because of personal characteristics such as ethnicity or gender? A reasonable answer to that important query is that you really do need to devote attention to absence-of-bias for *all* your classroom assessment procedures. For the least significant of your assessment procedures, you can simply heighten your consciousness about bias eradication as you generate your test items or, having done so, as you review the completed test.

For more important examinations, try to enlist the assistance of a colleague to review your assessment instruments. If possible, attempt to secure the help of colleagues from the same subgroups as those represented among your students. For instance, if many of your students are Hispanics (and you aren't), then try to get a Hispanic colleague to look over your test's items to see whether there are any that might offend or unfairly penalize Hispanic students. When you enlist a colleague to help you review your tests for potential bias, try to carry out a mini-version of the bias review panel procedures described in this chapter. Briefly describe to your co-workers how you define assessment bias, give them a succinct orientation to the review task, and structure their reviews with absence-of-bias questions such as those illustrated earlier in the chapter.

But What Does This Have to Do with Teaching?

Decades ago I was asked to serve as an expert witness in a federal court case taking place in Florida. It was known as the *Debra P. v. Turlington* case, because Ralph Turlington was the Florida Commissioner of Education and Debra P. was one of nine African American children who were about to be denied high school diplomas because they had not passed a state-administered basic skills test. A class-action lawsuit had been brought against Florida to stop this test-based denial of diplomas.

When I was invited to serve as a witness for the state, I was initially pleased. After all, to be an "expert" witness in a federal court case sounded like a recipe for instant tenure. So my first inclination was to agree to serve as a witness. But then I learned that Florida's high school graduation test was having a substantially disparate impact on the state's African American children, far more of whom were going to be denied diplomas than their White counterparts. I pondered whether I wanted to support an assessment program that would surely penalize more minority than majority children.

So, before making up my mind about becoming a witness in the *Debra P.* case, I consulted a number of my African American friends at UCLA and in the Los Angeles Unified School District. "Should I," I asked, "take part in the support of a test that denies diplomas to so many African American youngsters?"

Well, *without exception*, my African American friends urged me to accept the Florida assignment. The essence of their argument was simple. What

was going on in Florida, they claimed, was the awarding of "counterfeit" diplomas to African American children. If so many African American youngsters were actually flopping on the state's basic skills test, then it was quite likely that those children did not possess the necessary basic skills. Yet, even without those basic skills, many of Florida's African American children had previously been receiving high school diplomas that allowed them to graduate *without* the skills they needed. My friends made it clear. As one put it, "Get your tail down to Tallahassee and support any test that shows many African American children are being instructionally short-changed. You can't fix something if you don't know it's broken."

And that's where bias detection comes in. If teachers can eliminate bias from their own assessments, then any gaps between the performance levels of minority and majority students can be attributed to instruction, not shortcomings in a test. Achievement gaps, properly identified, can then be ameliorated instructionally. If there's no recognition of a bona fide gap, then there's little reason for instructional alterations.

(As a postscript, the *Debra P.* case turned out to be an important precedent-setter. It was ruled that a state *can* deny a high school diploma on the basis of a basic skills test, but if the test covers content that students have not had an opportunity to learn, then this violates a student's—that is, a U.S. citizen's—constitutionally guaranteed property rights. I liked the ruling a lot.)

Most important, if you personally realize how repugnant all forms of assessment unfairness are, and how assessment bias can distort certain students' performances even if the bias was inadvertently introduced by the test's developer, you'll be far more likely to eliminate assessment bias in your own tests. In education, as in any other field, assessment bias should definitely be *absent*.

Assessment-related federal laws oblige today's teachers to rethink the ways they should test students with disabilities and ELL students. With few exceptions, children with disabilities are to be assessed (and instructed) in relation to the same curricular goals as all other children. This can often be accomplished through the use of accommodations—that is, alterations in presentations, responses, settings, and timing/scheduling. Assessment accommodations, however, must never alter the fundamental nature of the skill or knowledge being assessed. Assessment accommodations can also be used to reduce potential bias associated with the testing of ELL students. Given the enormous number of first languages other than English that are now found in the nation's schools, financial limitations tend to prevent the development of suitable assessments for many language-minority students.

Chapter Summary

This chapter on fairness in testing was, quite naturally, focused on how educators make their tests fair. Assessment bias was described as any element in an assessment procedure that offends or unfairly penalizes students because of personal characteristics, such as their gender or ethnicity. Assessment bias, when present, was seen to distort certain students' performances on educational tests and hence to reduce the validity of score-based interpretations about those students. The two chief contributors to assessment unfairness were identified as offensiveness and unfair penalization. The essential features of both of these factors were considered. An examination having a disparate impact on a particular subgroup is not necessarily biased, although such a differential impact certainly would warrant further scrutiny of the examination's content to discern whether assessment bias was actually present. In many instances, disparate impact of an examination simply indicates that certain groups of students have previously received inadequate instruction or an insufficient opportunity to learn.

Two procedures for identifying unfair—that is, biased—segments of educational assessment devices were described. A *judgmental* approach relies on the considered opinions of properly oriented bias reviewers. Judgmental approaches to bias detection can be formally employed with high-stakes tests or less formally used by classroom teachers. An *empirical* approach that relies chiefly on differential item functioning can also be used, although its application requires large numbers of students. It was recommended that classroom teachers be vigilant in the identification of bias, whether in their own tests or in the tests of others. For detecting bias in their own tests, classroom teachers were urged to adopt a judgmental review strategy consonant with the importance of the assessment procedures involved.

Issues associated with the assessment of ELL students or students with disabilities were identified near the chapter's conclusion. In many cases, assessment accommodations can yield more valid inferences about students who have disabilities or are less proficient in English. In other instances, alternate assessments need to be developed. Neither of these assessment modifications, however, is completely satisfactory in coping with this important assessment problem. Fairness, from an assessment perspective, currently appears to be much more difficult to attain in the case of students with disabilities and ELL students. Two relevant concepts, *accessibility* and *universal design*, hold promise for assessing such learners.

Finally, it was argued that to avoid having assessment fairness be regarded as a commendable but feckless notion, it is important for those creating tests (as well as those evaluating others' tests) to ensure that ample evidence bearing on test fairness accompanies educational tests, and even significant classroom assessments. Just as we need solid evidence to reach decisions about assessment reliability and validity, we need such evidence about an educational test's fairness.

MyLab Education Self-Check 5.1

MyLab Education Self-Check 5.2

MyLab Education Application Exercise 5.1: **Assessment Bias**

MyLab Education Application Exercise 5.2: **Understanding Disability Legislation and Protections**

References

Abedi, J. (2004). "The No Child Left Behind Act and English language learners: Assessment and accountability issues," *Educational Researcher, 33*, no. 1: 4–14.

Abedi, J. (2008). "Classification system for English language learners: Issues and recommendations," *Educational Measurement: Issues and Practice, 27*, no. 3 (Fall): 17–31.

American Educational Research Association. (2014). *Standards for educational and psychological testing.* Washington, DC: Author.

Pennock-Roman, M., and Rivera, C. (2011). "Mean effects of test accommodations for ELLs and non-ELLs: A meta-analysis of experimental studies," *Educational Measurement: Issues and Practice, 30*, no. 3 (Fall): 10–28.

Rose, M. (2013). "Being careful about character," *Phi Delta Kappan, 95*, no. 2 (October): 44–46.

Solano-Flores, G, Wang, C., Kachchaf, R., Soltero-Gonzalez, L., and Nguyen-Le, K. (2014). "Developing testing accommodations for English language-learners: Illustrations as visual supports for item accessibility," *Educational Assessment, 19*, no. 4: 267–283.

Thompson, S. J., et al. (2005, August). *Accommodations manual: How to select, administer, and evaluate use of accommodations for instruction and assessment of students with disabilities* (2nd ed.). Washington, DC: Council of Chief State School Officers.

Wolf, M. K., Farnsworth, T., and Herman, J. (2008). "Validity issues in assessing English language learners' language proficiency," *Educational Assessment, 13*, nos. 2–3: 80–107.

Endnote

1. U.S. Congressional Committee on Education and the Workforce. (2005, February 17). *IDEA Guide to Frequently Asked Questions* (p. 10). Washington, DC: Author.

Assessment Fairness: New Member of Testing's "Big Three"*

W. James Popham, University of California, Los Angeles

For well over 100 years, educational testing's two most important concepts were—without debate—*validity* and *reliability*. Assessment validity refers to the accuracy of score-based interpretations about test takers regarding a test's intended uses; assessment reliability represents the consistency with which an educational test measures whatever it is measuring.

But 15 years after its previous edition, a revised version of the *Standards for Educational and Psychological Testing* was published (AERA, 2014). Those guidelines changed the traditional notion of what's most important in educational assessment. The revised *Standards* are particularly influential because they often play a key role in the resolution of courtroom disputes about the uses of educational tests. In the 2014 *Standards* revision, *assessment fairness* not only received extensive coverage but was also placed atop a "most important three" pedestal along with validity and reliability. Persuasive evidence regarding *all three* of those concepts must now be routinely collected and presented when educational tests are developed or evaluated.

Whenever practicable, two kinds of evidence should be assembled to determine an educational test's fairness:

- *Judgmental Evidence.* One powerful form of evidence regarding an educational test's fairness consists of item-by-item judgments rigorously rendered by independent judges. Committees of "bias reviewers" typically provide per-item ratings according to whether an item might either offend or unfairly penalize any group of students because of such personal characteristics as race, gender, or religion.

- *Empirical Evidence.* If enough students have completed an educational test so that at least several hundred students have responded to every item, it is possible to analyze test takers' results to determine whether statistically significant differences exist among subgroup performances. If such differential item functioning (DIF) procedures reveal meaningful between-group differences in performance on any items, those items are then scrutinized more closely to detect and eliminate possible bias.

For significant high-stakes tests, both judgmental and empirical analyses are usually carried out to locate any biased items in a test. For special learners, such as students with physical or cognitive handicaps, a number of distinctive test adaptations are routinely employed to combat unfairness.

Most important, however, the isolation and elimination of test unfairness is no longer mere test-developer rhetoric. Since the publication of the 2014 revised assessment *Standards*, evidence of assessment fairness is every bit as important as the evidence provided for validity and reliability. Whenever you consider adopting an educational test, *demand* to see evidence of its fairness.

Chapter 6
Selected-Response Tests

Learning Outcomes

6.1 Using the "Five General Item-Writing Commandments" found in Chapter 6, identify and explain common characteristics of poorly constructed selected-response test items.

6.2 Differentiate between the four different varieties of selected-response test items (binary-choice items, multiple binary-choice items, multiple choice items, matching items) and be able to create an example of each.

∨ Chief Chapter Outcome

The ability to accurately employ professionally accepted item-writing guidelines, both general and item-type specific, when constructing selected-response items or evaluating those items constructed by others

In this and the following four chapters, you will learn how to construct almost a dozen different kinds of test items you might wish to use for your own classroom assessments. As suggested in the preceding chapters, you really need to choose item types that mesh properly with the inferences you want to make about students—and to be sure those inferences are directly linked to the educational decisions you need to make. Just as the child who's convinced that vanilla is ice cream's only flavor won't benefit from a 36-flavor ice cream emporium, the more item types you know about, the more appropriate your selection of item types will be. So in this chapter and the next four, you'll be learning about blackberry-ripple exams and mocha-mango assessment devices.

Realistically, what should you expect after wading through the exposition about item construction contained in the upcoming text? Unless you're a remarkably quick study, you'll probably finish this material and *not* be instantly transformed into a consummately skilled test constructor. It takes more than reading a brief explanation to turn someone into a capable item developer. But, just as the journey of a thousand miles begins with a single step, you'll have initiated a tentative trot toward the Test Construction Hall of Fame. You'll have learned the essentials of how to construct the most common kinds of classroom assessments.

What you'll need after you complete the upcoming study of test construction is tons of practice in churning out classroom assessment devices. And, if you remain in teaching for a while, such practice opportunities will surely come your way. Ideally, you'll be able to get some feedback about the quality of your classroom assessment procedures from a supervisor or colleague who is experienced and conversant with educational measurement. If a competent cohort critiques your test construction efforts, you'll profit by being able to make needed modifications in how you create your classroom assessment instruments.

Expanding Electronic Options

Once upon a time, when teachers churned out all their own classroom tests, about the only approach available was reliance on paper in order to present items that, back then, students responded to using pencils or pens. Oh, if you head back far enough in history, you might find Egyptian teachers relying on papyrus or pre-history teachers dishing up pop quizzes on tree bark.

But we have evolved (some more comfortably than others) into a technological age in which whole classrooms full of students possess laptop computers, electronic tablets, or super-smart cell phones that can be employed during instruction *and assessment*. Accordingly, because the availability of such electronically provided assessment options depends almost totally on what's available for use in a particular district or school, some of the test construction guidelines you will encounter here may need to be massaged because of electronic limitations in the way a test's items can be written. To illustrate, you'll learn how to create "matching" items for a classroom assessment. Well, one of the recommendations to teachers who use such items is that they put everything for a given item on a single page (of paper)—so that the students need not flip back and forth between pages when selecting their answers. But what if the electronic devices that a teacher's students have been given do not provide sufficient room to follow this all-on-one-page guideline?

Well, in that situation it makes sense for a teacher to arrive at the most reasonable/sensible solution possible. Thus, the test construction guidelines you'll encounter from here on in this text will be couched almost always in terms suitable for paper-presented tests. If you must create classroom assessments using electronic options that fail to permit implementation of the guidelines presented, just do the best job you can in adapting a guideline to the electronic possibilities at hand. Happily, the use of electronic hardware will typically expand, not truncate, your assessment options.

Ten (Divided by Two) Overall Item-Writing Commandments

As you can discern from its title, this text is going to describe how to construct selected-response sorts of test items. You'll learn how to create four different varieties of selected-response test items—namely, binary-choice items, multiple binary-choice items, multiple-choice items, and matching items. All four of these selected-response kinds of items can be used effectively by teachers to derive defensible inferences about students' cognitive status—that is, the knowledge and skills that teachers typically try to promote in their students.

But no matter whether you're developing selected-response or constructed-response test items, there are several general guidelines that, if adhered to, will lead to better assessment procedures. Because the original Ten Commandments were stated in fairly stern "Thou shall not" form, and have proved successful in shaping many folks' behavior, we will now dish out five general item-writing commandments structured along the same lines. Following these commandments won't get you into heaven, but it will make your assessment schemes slightly more divine. All five commandments are presented in a box. A subsequent discussion of each commandment will help you understand how to adhere to the five item-writing mandates being discussed. It will help if you refer to each of the following item-writing commandments (guidelines) before reading the discussion of that particular commandment. Surely, God would not be opposed to your doing just a bit of cribbing!

Five General Item-Writing Commandments

1. Thou shalt not provide opaque directions to students regarding how to respond.
2. Thou shalt not employ ambiguous statements in your assessment items.
3. Thou shalt not provide students with unintentional clues regarding appropriate responses.
4. Thou shalt not employ complex syntax in your assessment items.
5. Thou shalt not use vocabulary that is more advanced than required.

Opaque Directions

The first item-writing commandment deals with a topic most teachers haven't thought seriously about—the directions for their classroom tests. Teachers who have been laboring to create a collection of test items typically know the innards of those items very well. Thus, because of the teacher's intimate knowledge not only of the items but also of how students are supposed to deal with those items, it is often the case that only sketchy directions are provided to students regarding *how* to respond to a test's items. Yet, of course, unclear test-taking directions can result in confused test takers. And the responses of confused test takers don't lead to very accurate inferences about those test takers.

Flawed test directions are particularly problematic when students are being introduced to assessment formats with which they're not very familiar, such as the performance tests to be described in Chapter 8 or the multiple binary-choice tests to be discussed later in this chapter. It is useful to create directions for students early in the game when you're developing an assessment instrument. When generated as a last-minute afterthought, test directions typically turn out to be tawdry.

Ambiguous Statements

The second item-writing commandment deals with ambiguity. In all kinds of classroom assessments, ambiguous writing is to be avoided. If your students aren't really sure about what you mean in the tasks you present to them, the students are apt to misinterpret what you're saying and, as a consequence, come up with incorrect responses, even though they might really know how to respond correctly. For example, sentences in which pronouns are used can fail to make it clear to which individual or individuals a pronoun refers. Suppose that, in a true–false test item, you asked your students to indicate whether the following statement was true or false: "Leaders of developing nations have tended to distrust leaders of developed nations due to their imperialistic tendencies." Because it is unclear whether the pronoun *their* refers to the "leaders of developing nations" or to the "leaders of developed nations," and because the truth or falsity of the statement depends on the pronoun's referent, students are likely to be confused.

Because you will typically be writing your own assessment items, *you* will know what you mean. At least you ought to. However, try to slide yourself, at least figuratively, into the shoes of your students. Reread your assessment items from the perspective of the students, and then modify any statements apt to be even a mite ambiguous for those less well-informed students.

Unintended Clues

The third of our item-writing commandments calls for you to *intentionally* avoid something *unintentional*. (Well, nobody said that following commandments was going to be easy!) What this commandment is trying to sensitize you to is the tendency of test-development novices to inadvertently provide clues to students about appropriate responses. As a consequence, students come up with correct responses even if they don't possess the knowledge or skill being assessed.

For example, inexperienced item writers often tend to make the correct answer to multiple-choice items twice as long as the incorrect answers. Even clucko students will opt for the lengthy response; they get so many more words for their choice. As another example of how inexperienced item writers unintentionally dispense clues, absolute qualifiers such as *never* and *always* are sometimes used for the false items in a true–false test. Because even uninformed students know there are few absolutes in this world, they gleefully (and often unthinkingly) indicate such items are false. One of the most blatant examples of giving unintended clues occurs when writers of multiple-choice test items initiate those items with incomplete statements such as "The bird in the story was an . . . " and then offer answer options in which only the correct answer begins with a vowel. For instance, even though you had never read the story referred to in the previous incomplete statement, if you encountered the following four response options, it's almost certain that you'd know the correct answer: A. Falcon, B. Hawk, C. Robin, D. Owl. The article *an* gives the game away.

Unintended clues are seen more frequently with selected-response items than with constructed-response items, but even in supplying background information to students for complicated constructed-response items, the teacher must be wary of unintentionally pointing truly unknowledgeable students down the trail to the correct response.

Computer-Adaptive Assessment: Pros and Cons

Large-scale assessments, such as statewide accountability tests or nationally standardized achievement tests, are definitely different from the classroom tests that teachers might, during a dreary weekend, whip up for their students. Despite those differences, the assessment tactics used in large-scale tests should not be totally unknown to teachers. After all, parents of a teacher's students might occasionally toss out questions at a teacher about such tests, and what teacher wants to be seen, when it comes to educational testing, as a no-knowledge ninny?

One of the increasingly prevalent variations of standardized achievement testing encountered in our schools is known as *computer-adaptive assessment*. In some instances, computer-adaptive testing is employed as a state's annual, large-scale accountability assessment. In other instances, commercial vendors offer computer-adaptive tests to cover shorter segments of instruction, such as two or three months. School districts typically purchase such shorter-duration tests in an attempt to assist classroom teachers in adjusting their instructional activities to the progress of their students. In general, these more instructionally oriented tests are known as ***interim assessments***, and we will consider such assessments more deeply later (in Chapter 12). Given the near certainty that students in many states will be tested via computer-adaptive assessments, a brief description of this distinctive assessment approach is in order.

Not all assessments involving computers, however, are computer-adaptive. ***Computer-based assessments*** rely on computers to deliver test items to students. Moreover, students respond to these computer-transmitted items by using a computer. In many instances, immediate scoring of students' responses is possible. This form of computer-abetted assessment is becoming more and more popular as (1) schools acquire enough computers to make the approach practicable and (2) states and school districts secure sufficient "bandwidth" (whatever that is!) to transmit tests and receive students' responses electronically. Computer-based assessments, as you can see, rely on computers only as delivery and retrieval mechanisms. Computer-adaptive assessment is something quite different.

Here's a shorthand version of how ***computer-adaptive assessment*** is usually described. Notice, incidentally, the key term *adaptive* in its name. That word is your key to understanding how this approach to educational assessment is supposed to function. As a student takes this kind of test, the student is given items of known difficulty levels. Then, based on the student's responses to those initial items, an all-knowing computer supplies new items that are tailored in difficulty level on the basis of the student's previous answers. For instance, if a student is correctly answering the early items doled out by the computer, then the next items popping up on the screen will be more difficult ones. Conversely, if the student stumbles on the initially presented items, the computer will then cheerfully provide easier items to the student, and so on. In short, the computer's program constantly *adapts* to the student's responses by providing items better matched to the student's assessment-determined level of achievement.

Using this adaptive approach, a student's overall achievement regarding whatever the test is measuring can be determined with fewer items than would typically be required. This is because, in a typical test, many of the test's items might be too difficult or too easy for a given student. Accordingly, one of the advertised payoffs of computer-adaptive testing is that it saves testing time—that is, it saves those precious instructional minutes often snatched away from teachers because of externally imposed assessment obligations. And there it is, the promotional slogan for computer-adaptive testing: *More Accurate Measurement in Less Time!* What clear-thinking teacher does not get just a little misty eyed when contemplating the payoffs of computer-massaged testing?

But there are limitations of computer-adaptive testing that you need to recognize. The first of these limitations stems from the necessity for all the items in such assessments to be measuring a *single variable*, such as students' "mathematical mastery." Because many items are needed to make computer-adaptive assessment purr properly, and because the diverse difficulties of these items must *all* be linked to what's sometimes referred to as "a unidimensional trait" (for instance, a child's overall reading prowess), computer-adaptive assessment precludes the possibility of providing student-specific *diagnostic* data. Too few items dealing with a particular subskill or a body of enabling knowledge can be administered during a student's abbreviated testing time. In other words, whereas computer-adaptive assessment can supply teachers with an efficiently garnered *general fix* on a student's achievement of what's often a broadly conceptualized curricular aim, it won't reveal a student's specific strengths and weaknesses. Thus, from an instructional perspective, computer-adaptive assessment falls short of supplying the instructionally meaningful results most teachers need.

Second, as students wend their way merrily through a computer-adaptive test, depending on how they respond to certain items, different students frequently receive different items. The adjustments in the items that are dished up to a student depend on the student's computer-determined status regarding whatever unidimensional trait is being measured. Naturally, because of differences in students' mastery of this "big bopper" variable, different students receive different items thereafter. Consequently, a teacher's students no longer end up taking the *same* exam. The only meaningful way of comparing students' overall test performances, therefore, is by employing a scale that represents the unidimensional trait (such as a student's reading capabilities) being measured. We will consider such scale scores later, in Chapter 13. Yet, even before we do so, it should be apparent that when a teacher tries to explain to a parent why a parent's child tackled a test with a unique collection of items, the necessary explanation is a challenging one.

Finally, when most educators hear about computer-adaptive assessment and get a general sense of how it operates, they often assume that it does its digital magic in much the same way—from setting to setting. In other words, educators think the program governing the operation of computer-adaptive testing in State X is essentially identical to the way the computer-adaptive testing program operates in State Y. Not so! Teachers need to be aware that the oft-touted virtues of computer-adaptive testing are dependent on the *degree of adaptivity* embodied in the program employed to analyze the results. Many educators, once they grasp the central thrust of computer-adaptive testing, believe that after as student's response to *each* of a test's items, an adjustment is made in the upcoming test items. This, of course, would represent an optimal degree of adaptivity. But *item-adaptive* adjustments are not often employed in the real world because of such practical considerations as the costs involved.

Accordingly, most of today's computer-adaptive tests employ what is called a *cluster-adaptive* approach. One or more clusters of items, perhaps a half-dozen or so items per cluster, are used to make an adjustment in the upcoming items for a student. Such adjustments are based on the student's performance on the cluster of items. Clearly, the more clusters of items that are employed, the more tailored to a student's status will be the subsequent items. Thus, you should not assume that the computer-adaptive test being employed in your locale is based on an item-adaptive approach when, in fact,

it might be doing its adaptive magic based on only a single set of cluster-adaptive items. Computer adaptivity may be present, but it is a far cry from the conception of sustained adaptivity that most educators currently possess.

To sum up, then, computer-adaptive assessments can, indeed, provide educators with a pair of potent advantages—they deliver more accurate assessment and take less time. However, of necessity, any meaningful diagnostic dividends scurry out the window with such computer-adaptive testing, and even the advertised dividends of computer-adaptive testing tumble if cost-conscious versions of computer adaptivity are being employed. If computer-adaptive testing is going on in your locale, find out how it does its digital dance so that you can determine what instructional help, if any, this avant-garde version of educational assessment supplies to you. Few classroom teachers will attempt, on their own, to build computer-adaptive tests just for their own students. Classroom teachers are too smart—and have other things going on in their lives. Accordingly, teachers' knowledge about the general way in which computer-adaptive testing functions should position such teachers to better evaluate any district-selected or state-selected computer-adaptive assessments. Is a district-chosen computer-adaptive test that purports to be a boon to teachers' instructional decision making accompanied by *evidence* that it truly does so? Is a state-imposed computer-adaptive test that's intended to evaluate the state's schools accompanied by *evidence* that it does so accurately? In short, teachers should not assume that merely because an educational test is computer-adaptive, this guarantee that the test is reliable, valid, or fair for its intended uses. If you have *any* required test being used in your setting without enough evidence of its suitability for its intended purpose, you should consider registering your dismay over this educationally unsound practice. And this is true even for assessments cloaked in computer-adaptive attire.

Complex Syntax

Complex syntax, although it sounds something like an exotic surcharge on cigarettes and alcohol, is often encountered in the assessment items of neophyte item writers. Even though some teachers may regard themselves as

Steinbecks-in-hiding, an assessment instrument is no setting in which to wax eloquent. This fourth item-writing commandment directs you to avoid complicated sentence constructions and, instead, to use very simple sentences. Although esteemed writers such as Thomas Harding and James Joyce are known for their convoluted and clause-laden writing styles, they might have been mediocre item writers. Too many clauses, except at Christmas-time, mess up test items. (For readers needing a clue regarding the previous sentence's cryptic meaning, think of a red-garbed guy who brings presents.)

Difficult Vocabulary

Our fifth and final item-writing commandment is fairly straightforward. It indicates that when writing educational assessment items, *you should eschew obfuscative verbiage*. In other words—and almost *any* other words would be preferable—use vocabulary suitable for the students who'll be taking your tests. Assessment time is not the occasion for you to trot out your best collection of polysyllabic terms or to secure a series of thesaurus-induced thrills. The more advanced that the vocabulary level is in your assessment devices, the more likely you'll fail to get a good fix on your students' true status. They will have been laid low by the overblown vocabulary. In the case of the terminology to be used in classroom assessment instruments, simple wins.

In review, you've now seen five item-writing commandments that apply to any kind of classroom assessment device you develop. They certainly apply to tests containing selected-response items. And that's what we'll be looking at in the rest of the chapter. More specifically, you'll be encountering a series of item-writing guidelines to follow when constructing particular kinds of selected-response items. For convenience, we can refer to these guidelines linked to particular categories of items as "item-category guidelines" or "item-specific guidelines." These item-category guidelines are based either on empirical research evidence or on decades of teachers' experience in using such items. If you opt to use any of the item types to be described here in your own classroom tests, try to follow the guidelines for that kind of item. Your tests will typically turn out to be better than if you hadn't.

Here, and in several subsequent chapters, you'll be encountering sets of item-writing, item-revision, and response-scoring guidelines that you'll be encouraged to follow. Are the accompanying guidelines *identical* to the guidelines you're likely to find in other texts written about classroom assessment? No, they are not identical, but if you were to line up all of the texts ever written about classroom testing, you'd find that their recommendations regarding the care and feeding of items for classroom assessment were fundamentally similar.

In your perusal of selected-response options, when deciding what sorts of items to employ, this is a particularly good time to make sure that your items match the level of cognitive behavior that you want your students to display. As always, a student's performance on a batch of items can supply you with the evidence that's necessary to arrive at an inference regarding the student's status. If you are attempting to promote student's higher-order cognitive skills, then don't be satisfied with the sorts of selected-response items that do little more than tap into a student's memorized information.

Binary-Choice Items

A *binary-choice item* gives students only two options from which to select. The most common form of binary-choice item is the *true–false item*. Educators have been using true–false tests probably as far back as Socrates. (True or False: Plato was a type of serving-dish used by Greeks for special meals.) Other variations of binary-choice items are those in which students must choose between the pairs yes–no, right–wrong, correct–incorrect, fact–opinion, and so on.

The virtue of binary-choice items is they are typically so terse that students can respond to many items in a short time. Therefore, it is possible to cover a large amount of content in a brief assessment session. The greatest weakness of binary-choice items is that, because there are only two options, students have a 50–50 chance of guessing the correct answer even if they don't have the foggiest idea of what's correct. If a large number of binary-choice items are used, however, this weakness tends to evaporate. After all, although students might guess their way correctly through a few binary-choice items, they would need to be extraordinarily lucky to guess their way correctly through 30 such items.

Here are five item-category guidelines for writing binary-choice items. A brief discussion of each guideline is provided in the following paragraphs.

Item-Writing Guidelines for Binary-Choice Items

1. Phrase items so that a superficial analysis by the student suggests a wrong answer.
2. Rarely use negative statements, and never use double negatives.
3. Include only one concept in each statement.
4. Have an approximately equal number of items representing the two categories being tested.
5. Keep item length similar for both categories being tested.

Phrasing Items to Elicit Thoughtfulness

Typically, binary items are quite brief, but brevity need not reflect simplistic choices for students. In order to get the most payoff from binary-choice items, you'll want to phrase items so that students who approach the items superficially will answer them incorrectly. Thus, if you were creating the items for a true–false test, you would construct statements for your items that were not blatantly true or blatantly false. Blatancy in items rarely leads to accurate inferences about students. Beyond blatancy avoidance, however, you should phrase at least some of the items so that if students approach them unthinkingly, they'll choose false for a true statement, and vice versa. What you're trying to do is to get students to *think* about your test items and, thereby, give you a better idea about how much good thinking the students can do.

Minimizing Negatives

With binary-choice items, many students have a really difficult time responding to negatively phrased items. For instance, suppose that in a true–false test you were asked to decide about the truth or falsity of the following statement: "The League of Nations was not formed immediately after the conclusion of World War II." What the item is looking for as a correct answer to this statement is *true*, because the League of Nations was in existence prior to World War II. Yet, the existence of the word *not* in the item really will confuse some students. They'll be apt to answer *false* even if they know the League of Nations was functioning before World War II commenced.

Because seasoned teachers have churned out their share of true–false items over the years, most such teachers know all too well how tempting it is to simply insert a *not* into an otherwise true statement. But don't yield to the temptation. Only rarely succumb to the lure of the nagging negative in binary-choice items. Items containing double negatives or triple negatives (if you could contrive one) are obviously to be avoided.

Avoiding Double-Concept Items

The third guideline for binary-choice items directs you to focus on only a single concept in each item. If you are creating a statement for a right–wrong test, and you have created an item in which half of the statement is clearly right and the other half is clearly wrong, you make it mighty difficult for students to respond correctly. The presence of two concepts in a single item, even if both are right or both are wrong, tends to confuse students and, as a consequence, yields test results that are apt to produce inaccurate inferences about those students.

Balancing Response Categories

If you're devising a binary-choice test, try to keep somewhere near an equal number of items representing the two response categories. For example, if it's a true–false test, make sure you have similar proportions of true and false statements. It's not necessary to have exactly the same number of true and false items. The numbers of true and false items, however, should be roughly comparable. This fourth guideline is quite easy to follow if you simply keep it in mind when creating your binary-choice items.

Maintaining Item-Length Similarity

The fifth guideline is similar to the fourth because it encourages you to structure your items so there are no give-away clues associated with item length. If your two response categories are *accurate* and *inaccurate*, make sure the length of the accurate statements is approximately the same as the length of the inaccurate statements. When creating true–false tests, there is a tendency to toss in qualifying clauses for the true statements so that those statements, properly qualified, are truly true—but also long! As a result, there's a systematic pattern wherein long statements tend to be true and short statements tend to be false. As soon as students catch on to this pattern, they can answer items correctly without even referring to an item's contents.

In review, we've considered five item-writing guidelines for binary-choice items. If you follow those guidelines and keep your wits about you when creating binary-choice items, you'll often find this type of test will prove useful in the classroom. And that's true, not false.

Multiple Binary-Choice Items

A *multiple binary-choice item* is one in which a cluster of items is presented to students, requiring a binary response to each of the items in the cluster. Typically, but not always, the items are related to an initial statement or set of statements. Multiple binary-choice items are formatted so they look like traditional multiple-choice tests. In a multiple-choice test, the student must choose one answer from several options, but in the multiple binary-choice test, the student must make a response for each statement in the cluster. Figure 6.1 is an example of a multiple binary-choice item.

David Frisbie (1992) reviewed research on such items and concluded that multiple binary-choice items are (1) highly efficient for gathering student

---

Figure 6.1 An Illustrative Multiple True–False Item

• • • Suppose that a dozen of your students completed a 10-item multiple-choice test and earned the following numbers of correct scores:

5, 6, 7, 7, 7, 7, 8, 8, 8, 8, 9, 10

9. The median for your students' scores is 7.5. (True)

10. The mode for the set of scores is 8.0. (False)

11. The range of the students' scores is 5.0. (True)

12. The median is different than the mean. (False)

achievement data, (2) more reliable than other selected-response items, (3) able to measure the same skills and abilities as multiple-choice items dealing with comparable content, (4) a bit more difficult for students than multiple-choice tests, and (5) perceived by students as more difficult but more efficient than multiple-choice items. Frisbie believes that when teachers construct multiple binary-choice items, they must be attentive to all of the usual considerations in writing regular binary-choice items. However, he suggests the following two additional guidelines.

Item-Writing Guidelines for Multiple Binary-Choice Items

1. Separate item clusters vividly from one another.
2. Make certain that each item meshes well with the cluster's stimulus material.

Separating Clusters

Because many students are familiar with traditional multiple-choice items, and because each of those items is numbered, there is some danger that students may become confused by the absence of numbers where such numbers are ordinarily found. Thus, be sure to use some kind of formatting system to make it clear that a new cluster is commencing. In the illustrative item seen in Figure 6.1, notice that three dots (• • •) have been used to signify the beginning of a new cluster of items. You can use asterisks, lines, boxes, or some similar way of alerting students to the beginning of a new cluster.

Coordinating Items with Their Stem

In multiple-choice items, the first part of the item—the part preceding the response options—is called the *stem*. For multiple binary-choice items, we refer to the first part of the item cluster as the cluster's stem or stimulus material. The second item-writing guideline for this item type suggests that you make sure all items in a cluster are, in fact, linked in a meaningful way to the cluster's stem. If they're not, then you might as well use individual binary-choice items rather than multiple binary-choice items.

There's another compelling reason why you should consider adding multiple binary-choice items to your classroom assessment repertoire. Unlike traditional binary-choice items, for which it's likely students will need to rely on *memorized* information, that's rarely the case with multiple binary-choice items. It is rare, that is, *if* the stimulus materials contain content that's not been encountered previously by students. In other words, if the stem for a subset of multiple binary-choice items contains material that's new to the student, and if each binary-choice item depends directly on the previously unencountered content, it's dead certain the student will need to function above the mere recollection of knowledge, the lowest level of Bloom's cognitive taxonomy (Bloom et al., 1956). So, if you make certain that your stimulus material for multiple binary-choice items contains new content, those items will surely be more intellectually demanding than the run-of-the-memory true–false item.

In review, we've considered an item type that's not widely used but has some special virtues. The major advantage of multiple binary-choice items is that students can respond to two or three such items in the time it takes them to respond to a single multiple-choice item. Other things being equal, the more items students respond to, the more reliably we can gauge their abilities.

I must confess to a mild bias toward this oft-overlooked item type because for over 20 years I used such tests as the final examinations in an introductory educational measurement course I taught in the UCLA Graduate School of Education. I'd give my students 20 one- or two-paragraph descriptions of previously unencountered educational measurement situations and then follow up each description with five binary-choice items. In all, then, I ended up with a 100-item final exam that really seemed to sort out those students who knew their stuff from those who didn't. The five items in each cluster were simply statements to which students were to respond *accurate* or *inaccurate*. I could just as appropriately have asked for *true* or *false* responses, but I tried to add a touch of suave to my exams. After all, I was teaching in a *Graduate* School of Education. (In retrospect, my decision seems somewhat silly.) Nonetheless, I had pretty good luck with my 100-item final exams. I used 50-item versions for my midterm exams, and they worked well too. For certain kinds of purposes, I think you'll find multiple binary-choice items will prove useful.

Multiple-Choice Items

For a number of decades, the **multiple-choice test item** has dominated achievement testing in the United States and many other nations. Multiple-choice items can be used to measure a student's possession of knowledge or a student's ability to engage in higher levels of thinking. A strength of multiple-choice items is that they can contain several answers differing in their *relative* correctness. Thus, the student can be called on to make subtle distinctions among answer options, several of which may be somewhat correct. A weakness of multiple-choice items, as is the case with all selected-response items, is that students need only *recognize* a correct answer. Students need not *generate* a correct answer. Although a fair amount of criticism has been heaped on multiple-choice items, particularly in recent years, properly constructed multiple-choice items can tap a rich variety of student skills and knowledge, and thus they can be useful tools for classroom assessment.

The first part of a multiple-choice item, as noted earlier, is referred to as the item's *stem*. The potential answer options are described as *item alternatives*. Incorrect alternatives are typically referred to as *item distractors*. Two common ways of creating multiple-choice items are to use an item stem that is either (1) a direct question or (2) an incomplete statement. With younger students, the direct-question approach is preferable. Using either direct-question stems or incomplete-statement stems, a multiple-choice item can ask students to select either a correct answer or a best answer.

In Figure 6.2 there are examples of a direct-question item requesting a best-answer response (indicated by an asterisk) and an incomplete-statement item requesting a correct-answer response (also indicated by an asterisk). One frequently cited advantage of using a best-answer rather than a correct-answer to these sorts of items is that when students are faced with a set of best-answer choices, we can see whether they are able to make distinctions among subtle differences in a set of answers—all of which are technically "correct." Moreover, because best-answer items can require the student to do some serious thinking when choosing among a set of options, these sorts of items can clearly elicit higher-order cognitive thinking from students. And, of course, that's usually a good thing to do.

Let's turn now to a consideration of item-category guidelines for multiple-choice items. Because of the widespread use of multiple-choice items over the past half-century, experience has generated quite a few suggestions regarding how to create such items. Here, you'll find five of the more frequently cited item-specific recommendations for constructing multiple-choice items.

Figure 6.2 Illustrative Multiple-Choice Items

Direct-Question Form (best-answer version)

Which of the following modes of composition would be most effective in explaining to someone how a bill becomes a law in this nation?

    A. Narrative
* B. Expository
    C. Persuasive
    D. Descriptive

Incomplete-Statement Form (correct-answer version)

Mickey Mouse's nephews are named

    A. Huey, Dewey, and Louie.
    B. Mutt and Jeff.
    C. Larry, Moe, and Curly.
* D. Morty and Ferdie.

Item-Writing Guidelines for Multiple-Choice Items

1. The stem should consist of a self-contained question or problem.
2. Avoid negatively stated stems.
3. Do not let the length of alternatives supply unintended clues.
4. Randomly assign correct answers to alternative positions.
5. Never use "all-of-the-above" alternatives, but do use "none-of-the-above" alternatives to increase item difficulty.

Stem Stuffing

A properly constructed stem for a multiple-choice item will present a clearly described task to the student so the student can then get to work on figuring out which of the item's options is best (if it's a best-answer item) or is correct (if it's a correct-answer item). A poorly constructed stem for a multiple-choice item will force the student to read one or more of the alternatives in order to figure out what the item is getting at. In general, therefore, it's preferable to load as much of the item's content as possible into the stem. Lengthy stems and terse alternatives are, as a rule, much better than skimpy stems and long alternatives. You might try reading the stems of your multiple-choice items without any of the alternatives to see whether the stems (either direct questions or incomplete statements) make sense all by themselves.

Knocking Negatively Stated Stems

It has been alleged, particularly by overly cautious individuals, that "one robin does not spring make." Without debating the causal relationship between seasonal shifts and feathered flyers, in multiple-choice item writing we could say with confidence that "one negative in an item stem does not confusion unmake." Negatives are strange commodities. A single *not*, tossed casually into a test item, can make students crazy. Besides, because *not* is such a tiny word, and might be overlooked by students, a number of students (who didn't see the *not*) may be trying to ferret out the best alternative for a positively stated stem that, in reality, is negative.

For example, let's say you wanted to do a bit of probing of your students' knowledge of U.S. geography and phrased the stem of a multiple-choice item like this: "Which one of the following cities is located in a state west of the Mississippi River?" If your alternatives were: A. San Diego, B. Pittsburgh, C. Boston, and D. Atlanta, students would have little difficulty in knowing how to respond. Let's say, however, that you decided to add a dollop of difficulty by using the same alternatives but tossing in a *not*. Now your item's stem might read something like this: "Which one of the following cities is not located in a state east of the Mississippi River?" For this version of the item, the student who failed to spot the *not* (this, in psychometric circles, might be known as not-spotting) would be in big trouble.

By the way, note that in both stems, the student was asked to identify which *one* of the following answers was correct. If you leave the *one* out, a student might have interpreted the question to mean that there two or more cities were being sought.

If there is a compelling reason for using a negative in the stem of a multiple-choice item, be sure to highlight the negative with *italics*, **boldface** type, or underscoring so that students who are not natural not-spotters will have a fair chance to answer the item correctly.

Attending to Alternative Length

Novice item writers often fail to realize that the length of a multiple-choice item's alternatives can give away what the correct answer is. Let's say choices A, B, and C say blah, blah, blah, but choice D says blah, blah, blah, blah, blah, and blah. The crafty student will be inclined to opt for choice D not simply because one gets many more blahs for one's selection, but because the student will figure out the teacher has given so much attention to choice D that there must be something special about it.

Thus, when you're whipping up your alternatives for multiple-choice items, try either to keep all the alternatives about the same length or, if this isn't possible, to have at least two alternatives be of approximately equal length. For instance, if you were using four-alternative items, you might have two fairly short alternatives and two fairly long alternatives. What you want to avoid is having the correct alternative be one length (either short or long) while the distractors are all another length.

Incidentally, the number of alternatives is really up to you. Most frequently, we see multiple-choice items with four or five alternatives. Because students can guess correct answers more readily with fewer alternatives, three alternatives are not seen all that often, except with younger students. Having more than five alternatives puts a pretty heavy reading load on the student. Many teachers usually employ four alternatives in their own multiple-choice tests, but in a few instances, the nature of the test's content leads them to use three or five alternatives.

Assigning Correct Answer Positions

A fourth guideline for writing multiple-choice items is to make sure you scatter your correct answers among your alternatives so students don't "guess their way to high scores" simply by figuring out your favorite correct answer spot is, for instance, choice D or perhaps choice C. Many novice item writers are reluctant to put the correct answer in the choice-A position because they believe that gives away the correct answer too early. Yet the choice-A position deserves its share of correct answers too. Absence-of-bias should also apply to answer-choice options.

As a rule of thumb, if you have four-alternative items, try to assign *approximately* 25 percent of your correct answers to each of the four positions. But try to avoid *always* assigning exactly 25 percent of the correct answers to each position. Students can be remarkably cunning in detecting your cunningness. It may be necessary to do some last-minute shifting of answer positions in order to achieve what is closer to a random assignment of correct answers to the available positions. But always do a last-minute check on your multiple-choice tests to make sure you haven't accidentally allowed your correct answers to appear too often in a particular answer-choice position.

Dealing with "Of-the-Above" Alternatives

Sometimes a beginning item writer who's trying to come up with four (or five) reasonable alternatives will toss in a none-of-the-above or an all-of-the-above alternative simply as a "filler" alternative. But both of these options must be considered carefully.

The fifth guideline for this item type says quite clearly that you should never use the all-of-the-above alternative. Here's why. Let's say you're using a five-option type of multiple-choice item, and you want to set up the item so that the fifth option (choice E), "all of the above," would be correct. This indicates that the first four answers, choices A through D, must all be correct. The problem with such an item is that even a student who knows only that two of the first four alternatives are correct will be able to select the all-of-the-above response because if any two responses are correct, choice E is the only possible best answer. Even worse, some students will read only the first alternative, see that it is correct, mark choice A on their response sheet, and move on to the next test item without going over the full array of enticing alternatives for the item. For either of these reasons, you should never use an all-of-the-above alternative in your multiple-choice items.

What about the none-of-the-above alternative? The guideline indicates that it may be used when you wish to increase an item's difficulty. You should do so only when the presence of the none-of-the-above alternative will help you make the kind of test-based inference you want to make. To illustrate, let's say you want to find out how well your students can perform basic mathematical operations such as multiplying and dividing. Moreover, you want to be confident that your students can really perform the computations "in their heads," by using scratch paper, by employing an appropriate app with their cell phones or digital tablets, or—if permitted—by renting a mathematics consultant from a local rental agency. Now, if you use only four-alternative multiple-choice items, there's a real likelihood that certain students won't be able to perform the actual mathematical operations but may be able to select, by estimation, the answer that is most reasonable. After all, *one* of the four options *must* be correct. Yet, when you simply add the none-of-the-above option (as a fourth or fifth alternative), students can't be sure that the correct answer is silently sitting there among the item's alternatives. To determine whether the correct answer is *really* one of the alternatives for the item, students will be obliged to perform the required mathematical operation and come up with the actual answer. In essence, when the none-of-the-above option is added, the task presented to the student more closely approximates the task the teacher is interested in. A student's chance of guessing the correct answer to a multiple-choice item is markedly less likely when a none-of-the-above option shows up in the item.

Here's a little wrinkle on this guideline you might find useful. Be a bit careful about using a none-of-the-above option for a *best-answer* multiple-choice item. Care is warranted because there are wily students waiting out there who'll parade a series of answers for you that they regard as better than the one option you think is a winner. If you can cope with such carping, there's no problem. If you have a low carping-coping threshold, however, avoid none-of-the-above options for most—if not all—of your best-answer items.

If you opt for the use of multiple-choice items as part of your classroom-assessment repertoire, you might be prepared to respond to students' questions about *correction-for-guessing* scoring. Indeed, even if the teacher does not use any sort of correction-for-guessing when scoring students' choices, it is often the case that—because such scoring approaches are used with certain standardized tests—some students (or some parents) will raise questions about such scoring. The formula used on certain standardized tests to minimize guessing typically subtracts, from the number of correctly answered items, a fraction based on the number of items answered incorrectly, but *not* those items for which no response was given by the student.

For example, suppose that on a 50-item test composed of 4-option multiple-choice items, a student answered 42 items correctly, but also incorrectly answered 8 items. That student, instead of receiving a raw score of 42 items correct, would have 2 points subtracted—resulting in a score of 40 correct. It is assumed that, *by chance alone* on each of the 8 incorrectly answered items, taking one chance out of four would yield 2 correct answers (one out of the four options for the 8 items). If another student also answered 42 items correctly, but did not guess on any items—preferring instead to leave them blank—then that more cautious student would retain a score of 42 correct. Few teachers employ this sort of correction formula for their own classroom tests, but teachers should have at least a ball-park notion of what makes such formulae tick. (Please note the ritzy Latin plural just employed. Clearly, this is a classy book that you're reading.)

In review, we've sauntered through a cursory look at five guidelines for the creation of multiple-choice items. There are other, more subtle suggestions for creating such items, but if you combine these guidelines with the five general item-writing commandments presented earlier in the chapter, you'll have a good set of ground rules for devising decent multiple-choice items. As with all the item

Decision Time
Multiple-Guess Test Items?

For all six years that he has taught, Leroy Larson has worked with fifth-graders. Although Leroy enjoys all content areas, he takes special pride in his reading instruction, because he believes his students enter the sixth grade with dramatically improved comprehension capabilities. Leroy spends little time trying to promote his students' isolated reading skills but, instead, places great emphasis on having students "construct their own meanings" from what they have read.

All of Leroy's reading tests consist exclusively of four-option multiple-choice items. As Leroy puts it, "I can put together a heavy-duty multiple-choice item when I put my mind to it." Because he has put his mind to it many times during the past six years, Leroy is quite satisfied that his reading tests are as good as his reading instruction.

At the most recent open house night at his school, however, a group of five parents registered genuine unhappiness with the exclusive

multiple-choice makeup of Leroy's reading tests. The parents had obviously been comparing notes prior to the open house, and Mrs. Davies (the mother of one of Leroy's fifth-graders) acted as their spokesperson. In brief, Mrs. Davies argued that multiple-choice tests permitted even weak students to "guess their way to good scores." "After all," Mrs. Davies pointed out, "do you want to produce good readers or good guessers?"

Surprised and somewhat shaken by this incident, Leroy has been rethinking his approach to reading assessment. He concludes that he can (1) stick with his tests as they are, (2) add some short-answer or essay items to his tests, or (3) replace all of his multiple-choice items with open-ended items. As he considers these options, he realizes that he has given himself a multiple-choice decision!

If you were Leroy, what would your decision be?

types being described, there's no substitute for oodles of practice in item writing that's followed by collegial or supervisorial reviews of your item-writing efforts. It is said that Rome wasn't built in a day. Similarly, in order to become a capable constructor of multiple-choice items, you'll probably need to develop more than one such test—or even more than two.

Matching Items

A *matching item* consists of two parallel lists of words or phrases requiring the student to match entries on one list with appropriate entries on the second list. Entries in the list for which a match is sought are referred to as *premises*. Entries in the list from which selections are made are referred to as *responses*. Usually, students are directed to match entries from the two lists according to a specific kind of association described in the test directions. Figure 6.3 is an example of a matching item.

Notice that in Figure 6.3's illustrative matching item, both lists are *homogeneous*. All of the entries in the column at the left (the premises) are U.S. military

Figure 6.3 An Illustrative Matching Item

Directions: On the line to the left of each military conflict listed in Column A, write the letter of the U.S. president in Column B who was in office when that military conflict was concluded. Each name in Column B may be used no more than once.

Column A	*Column B*
_____ 1. World War I	A. Bush (the father)
_____ 2. World War II	B. Clinton
_____ 3. Korea	C. Eisenhower
_____ 4. Vietnam	D. Johnson
_____ 5. First Persian Gulf	E. Nixon
	F. Roosevelt
	G. Truman
	H. Wilson

conflicts, and all of the entries in the column at the right (the responses) are names of U.S. presidents. Homogeneity is an important attribute of properly constructed matching items.

An advantage of matching items is that their compact form takes up little space on a printed page or a computer screen, thus making it easy to tap a good deal of information efficiently. Matching items (presented on paper tests) can be easily scored by simply holding a correct-answer template next to the list of premises where students are to supply their selections from the list of responses. A disadvantage of matching items is that, like binary-choice items, they sometimes encourage students' memorization of low-level factual information that, in at least some instances, is of debatable utility. The illustrative matching item is a case in point. Although it's relatively easy to create matching items such as this, is it really important to know which U.S. chief executive was in office when a military conflict was concluded? That's the kind of issue you'll be facing when you decide what kinds of items to include in your classroom assessments.

Typically, matching items are used as *part* of a teacher's assessment arsenal. It's pretty difficult to imagine a major classroom examination consisting exclusively of matching items. Matching items don't work well when teachers are trying to assess relatively distinctive ideas, because matching items require pools of related entries to insert into the matching format.

Let's consider a half-dozen guidelines you should think about when creating matching items for your classroom assessment instruments. The guidelines are presented here.

Item-Writing Guidelines for Matching Items

1. Employ homogeneous lists.
2. Use relatively brief lists, placing the shorter words or phrases at the right.
3. Employ more responses than premises.
4. Order the responses logically.
5. Describe the basis for matching and the number of times responses may be used.
6. Place all premises and responses for an item on a single page (or screen).

Employing Homogeneous Entries

As noted earlier, each list in a matching item should consist of homogeneous entries. If you really can't create a homogeneous set of premises and a homogeneous set of responses, you shouldn't be mucking about with matching items.

Going for Relative Brevity

From the student's perspective, it's much easier to respond to matching items if the entries in both lists are relatively few in number. About 10 or so premises should be the upper limit for most matching items. The problem with longer lists is that students spend so much time trying to isolate the appropriate response for a given premise that they may forget what they're attempting to find. Very lengthy sets of premises or responses are almost certain to cause at least some students difficulty in responding because they lose track of what's being sought. It would be far better to take a lengthy matching item with 24 premises and split it into three 8-premise matching items.

In addition, to cut down on the reading requirements of matching items, be sure to place the list of shorter words or phrases at the right. In other words, make the briefer entries the responses. In this way, when students are scanning the response lists for a matching entry, they won't be obliged to read too many lengthy phrases or sentences.

Loading Up on Responses

A third guideline for the construction of matching items is to make sure there are at least a few extra responses. Otherwise, if the numbers of premises and responses are identical, the student who knows, say, 80 percent of the matches to the premises may be able to figure out the remaining matches by a process of elimination. A few extra responses reduce this likelihood substantially. Besides, these sorts of responses are inexpensive. Be a big spender!

Parent Talk

Assume that you've been using a fair number of multiple-choice items in your classroom examinations. Benito's parents, Mr. and Mrs. Olmedo, have set up a 15-minute conference with you during a Back-to-Classroom Night to talk about Benito's progress.

When they arrive, they soon get around to the topic in which they are most interested—namely, your multiple-choice test items. As Mr. Olmedo puts it, "We want our son to learn to use his mind, not his memory. Although my wife and I have little experience with multiple-choice tests because almost all of our school exams were of an essay nature, we believe multiple-choice tests measure only what Benito has memorized. He has a good memory, as you've probably found out, but we want more for him. Why are you using such low-level test items?"

If I were you, here's how I'd respond to Mr. Olmedo's question:

"I appreciate your coming in to talk about Benito's education and, in particular, the way he is being assessed. And I also realize that recently there has been a good deal of criticism of multiple-choice test items. More often than not, such criticism is altogether appropriate. In far too many cases, because multiple-choice items are easy to score, they're used to assess just about everything. And, all too often, those kinds of items do indeed ask students to do little more than display their memorization skills.

"But this doesn't need to be the case. Multiple-choice items, if they are carefully developed, can assess a wide variety of truly higher-order thinking skills. In our school, all teachers have taken part in a series of staff-development workshop sessions in which every teacher learned how to create *challenging* multiple-choice items that require students to display much more than memory." (At this point, you might whip out a few examples of demanding multiple-choice items used in your own tests and then go through them, from stem to alternatives, showing Mr. and Mrs. Olmedo what you meant. If you *don't* have any examples of such items from your tests, you might think seriously about the possible legitimacy of Benito's parents' criticism.)

"So, although there's nothing wrong with Benito's acquiring more memorized information, and a small number of my multiple-choice items actually do test for such knowledge, the vast majority of the multiple-choice items that Benito will take in my class call for him to employ that fine mind of his.

"That's what you two want. That's what I want."

Now, how would you respond to Mr. and Mrs. Olmedo's concerns?

Ordering Responses

So that you'll not provide unintended clues to students regarding which responses go with which premises, it's a good idea in matching items to order the responses in some sort of logical fashion—for example, alphabetical or chronological sequence. Notice that the names of the U.S. presidents are listed alphabetically in the illustrative matching item in Figure 6.3.

Describing the Task for Students

The fifth guideline for the construction of matching items suggests that the directions for an item should always make explicit the basis on which the matches are to be made and, at the same time, the number of times a response can be used. The more clearly students understand how they're supposed to respond, the more accurately they'll respond, and the more validly you'll be able to make score-based inferences about your students.

Same-Page Formatting

The final guideline for this item type suggests that you make sure all premises and responses for a matching item are on a single page or a solo electronic screen. Not only does this eliminate the necessity for massive (and potentially disruptive) page turning and discourage (quieter) screen trading by students, but it also decreases the likelihood that students will overlook correct answers merely because these answer choices were on the "other" page.

Matching items, if employed judiciously, can efficiently assess your students' knowledge. The need to employ homogeneous lists of related content tends to diminish the applicability of this type of selected-response item. Nonetheless, if you are dealing with content that can be addressed satisfactorily by such an approach, you'll find matching items a useful member of your repertoire of item types.

What Do Classroom Teachers Really Need to Know About Selected-Response Tests?

If you engage in any meaningful amount of assessment in your own classroom, it's quite likely you'll find that selected-response items will be useful. Selected-response items can typically be used to ascertain students' mastery of larger domains of content than is the case with constructed-response kinds of test items. Although it's often thought that selected-response items must measure only lower-order kinds of cognitive capabilities, inventive teachers can create selected-response options to elicit very high levels of cognitive skills from students.

As for the four types of items treated in this chapter, you really need to understand enough about each kind to help you decide whether one or more of those item types would be useful for a classroom assessment task you have in mind. If you do decide to use binary-choice, multiple binary-choice, multiple-choice, or matching items in your own tests, then you'll find that the sets of item-writing guidelines for each item type will come in handy.

In Chapter 12, you will learn how to employ selected-response items as part of the formative-assessment process. Rather than relying completely on paper-and-pencil versions of these items, you will see how to employ such items in a variety of less formal ways. Yet, in honesty, even if you adhere to the five general item-writing commandments discussed here, and to the set of guidelines for particular types of items, you'll still need practice in constructing selected-response items such as those considered here. As was suggested several times in the chapter, it is exceedingly helpful if you can find someone with measurement moxie, or at least an analytic mind, to review your test-development efforts. It's difficult in any realm to improve if you don't get feedback about the adequacy of your efforts. That's surely true with classroom assessment. Try to entice a colleague or supervisor to

But What Does This Have to Do with Teaching?

In this chapter, not only have you become acquainted with varied types of test items, but you have also learned how to construct them properly. Why, you might ask, does a classroom teacher need to possess such a resplendent repertoire of item types? After all, if a student knows that Abraham Lincoln was assassinated while attending a play, the student could satisfactorily display such knowledge in a variety of ways. A good old true–false item or a nifty multiple-choice item would surely do the necessary assessing.

Well, that's quite true. But what you need to recall, *from a teaching perspective*, is that students ought to master the skills and knowledge they're being taught so thoroughly that they can display such mastery in a good many ways, not just one. A cognitive skill that's been learned *well* by a student will be a cognitive skill that can be displayed in all sorts of ways, whether via selected-response items or constructed-response items.

And this is why, when you *teach* children, you really need to be promoting their generalizable mastery of whatever's being taught. Consistent with such a push for generalizable mastery, you will typically want to employ varied assessment approaches. If you gravitate toward only one or two item types (that is, if you become "Multiple-Choice Maria" or "True–False Fredrico"), then your students will tend to learn things only in a way that meshes with your favored item type.

Eons ago, when I was preparing to be a teacher, my teacher education professors advised me to employ different kinds of items "for variety's sake." Well, classroom teachers aren't putting on a fashion show. Variety for its own sake is psychometrically stupid. But using a variety of assessment approaches as a deliberate way of promoting and measuring students' *generalizable mastery* of what's been taught—this is psychometrically suave.

look over your selected-response items to see what needs to be strengthened. However, even without piles of practice, if you adhere to the item-writing guidelines provided here, your selected-response tests won't be all that shabby.

The most important thing to learn from this chapter is that there are four useful *selected*-response procedures for drawing valid inferences about your students' status. The more assessment options you have at your disposal, the more appropriately you'll be able to assess those students' status with respect to the variables in which you're interested.

Chapter Summary

The chapter began with a presentation of five item-writing commandments that pertain to both constructed-response and selected-response items. The five admonitions directed teachers to avoid unclear directions, ambiguous statements, unintentional clues, complex syntax, and hypersophisticated vocabulary.

Consideration was then given to the four most common kinds of selected-response test items: binary-choice items, multiple

binary-choice items, multiple-choice items, and matching items. For each of these four item types, after a brief description of the item type and its strengths and weaknesses, a set of item-writing guidelines was presented. These four sets of guidelines were presented on pages 162, 165, 168, and 174. Each guideline was briefly discussed. Readers were encouraged to consider the four item types when deciding on an answer to the how-to-assess-it question.

MyLab Education Self-Check 6.1

MyLab Education Self-Check 6.2

MyLab Education Application Exercise 6.1: Applying the Item-Writing Guidelines: Revising a Multiple Choice Item

MyLab Education Application Exercise 6.2: Applying the Item-Writing Guidelines: Evaluating True–False Items

References

Bloom, B. S., et al. (1956). *Taxonomy of educational objectives: Handbook I: Cognitive domain*. New York: David McKay.

Brookhart, S. M., and Nitko, A. J. (2014). *Educational assessment of students* (7th ed.). Boston: Pearson.

Frisbie, D. A. (1992). "The multiple true–false format: A status review," *Educational Measurement: Issues and Practice, 11*, no. 4 (Winter): 21–26.

Holler, E. W., Gareis, C. R., Martin, J., Clouser, A., and Miller, S. (2008). "Teacher-made assessments: Getting them right," *Principal Leadership, 9*, no. 1 (September): 60–64.

Waugh, C. K., and Gronlund, N. (2013). *Measurement and assessment in teaching* (10th ed.). Columbus, OH: Pearson.

A Testing Takeaway

Selected-Response Test Items: Making Them Glisten*

W. James Popham, University of California, Los Angeles

Today, educators agree that test items can reasonably be viewed as falling into two categories: selected-response items and constructed-response items. *Selected-response items* are those for which students must choose a correct answer from presented alternatives, such as in true–false items and multiple-choice items. *Constructed-response items*, in contrast, call for students to generate their own answers, such as when a test's items ask students to create short-answer or essay responses.

You'd think that by now we'd have hammered out a set of sure-fire rules for constructing truly terrific test items. However, advances in content knowledge invariably call for new items to cover this content, and specifics of the new content prevent us from coming up with sure-fire general rules for creating flawless new items. Item improvement, regrettably, is almost always needed.

The two basic strategies for improving test items are those relying on *empirical* and on *judgmental* procedures. *Empirical* item-improvement strategies are employed chiefly with large-scale standardized testing, where we can statistically analyze responses from thousands of students to detect deficient items. For teacher-made classroom tests, however, we lean heavily on *judgmental* scrutiny of test items that have already been constructed. Such judgmental reviews typically rely on seasoned item writers' guidelines to spot possible deficient items.

In almost any text used in graduate courses focused on educational testing, you'll find not only a set of general item-writing guidelines for any kind of selected-response items, but also a series of specific recommendations for writing different kinds of selected-response items. To illustrate, presented below are five item-writing guidelines for *multiple-choice items*, in which "stem" refers to the initial part of an item, and response options are called "alternatives."

- The stem should consist of a self-contained question or problem.
- Avoid negatively stated stems.
- Don't let the length of alternatives supply unintended clues.
- Randomly assign correct answers to alternative response positions.
- Use "None of the above" to increase item difficulty, but never use "All of the above."

For other types of selected-response items, such as matching items, additional guidelines have been assembled over the years. As indicated, such guidelines can be found in texts employed in graduate educational measurement courses. Those guidelines are quite similar.

If you are a teacher who builds your own classroom exams, consulting such texts has much to commend it. And if you are someone who wants to evaluate the quality of any test's selected-response items, those guidelines can be especially illuminating.

Chapter 7
Constructed-Response Tests

 ## Chief Chapter Outcome

A sufficient understanding of generally approved guidelines for creating constructed-response items, and scoring students' responses to them, so that errors in item-construction and response-scoring can be identified

You're going to learn about constructed-response tests in this chapter. To be truthful, you're going to learn about only two kinds of *paper-and-pencil* constructed-response items—namely, short-answer items and essay items (including students' written compositions). Although you probably know that "you can't tell a book by its cover," now you've discovered that a chapter's title doesn't always describe its contents accurately either. Fortunately, there are no state or federal "truth-in-titling" laws.

You might be wondering why your ordinarily honest, never-fib author has descended to this act of blatant mislabeling. Actually, it's just to keep your reading chores more manageable. Earlier, you learned that student-constructed responses can be obtained from a wide variety of item types. In this chapter, we'll be looking at two rather traditional forms of constructed-response items, both of them paper-and-pencil in nature. In the next chapter, the focus will be on *performance tests*, such as those that arise when we ask students to make oral presentations or supply comprehensive demonstrations of complex skills in class. After that, in Chapter 9, we'll be dealing with portfolio assessment and how portfolios are used for assessment purposes.

Actually, all three chapters could be lumped under the single description of *performance assessment* or *constructed-response measurement*. This is because anytime you assess your students by asking them to respond in other than a make-a-choice manner, the students are *constructing*; that is, they are *performing*. It's just that if all of this performance assessment stuff had been crammed into a single chapter, you'd have thought you were experiencing a season-long TV mini-series. Yes, it was an inherent concern for your well-being that led to a flagrant disregard for accuracy when titling this chapter.

The major payoff of all constructed-response items is they elicit student responses more closely approximating the kinds of behavior that students must display in real life. After students leave school, for example, the demands of daily living almost never require them to choose responses from four nicely arranged alternatives. And when was the last time, in normal conversation, you were obliged to render a flock of true–false judgments about a set of statements that were presented to you? Yet, you may well be asked to make a brief oral presentation to your fellow teachers or to a parent group, or you may be asked to write a brief report for the school newspaper about your students' field trip to City Hall. Constructed-response tasks unquestionably coincide more closely with customary nonacademic tasks than do selected-response tasks.

As a practical matter, if the nature of a selected-response task is sufficiently close to what might be garnered from a constructed-response item, then you may wish to consider a selected-response assessment tactic to be a reasonable surrogate for a constructed-response assessment tactic. Selected-response tests are clearly much more efficient to score. And, because almost all the teachers are busy folks, time-saving procedures are not to be scoffed at. Yet there will be situations wherein you'll want to make inferences about your students' status when selected-response tests just won't fill the bill. For instance, if you wish to know what kind of a cursive writer Jamal is, then you'll have to let Jamal write cursively. A true–false test about *i* dotting and *t* crossing just doesn't cut it.

Given the astonishing technological advances we see every other week, what today is typically a paper-and-pencil test is apt, perhaps by tomorrow or the following day, to be some sort of digitized assessment linked to an exotic outer-space satellite. It may become quite commonplace for teachers to develop computer-generated exams themselves. However, because such a digital-assessment derby does not yet surround us, in this chapter the guidelines and illustrations will tend to reflect what most teachers currently do: paper-and-pencil assessment. Happily, most of the guidelines you will encounter here apply with equal force to either paper-and-pencil or electronically dispensed assessments.

Short-Answer Items

The first kind of constructed-response item we'll look at is the ***short-answer item***. These types of items call for students to supply a word, a phrase, or a sentence in response to either a direct question or an incomplete statement. If an item asks students to come up with a fairly lengthy response, it is considered an essay item, not a short-answer item. If the item asks students to supply only a single word, then it's a *really* short-answer item.

Short-answer items are suitable for assessing relatively simple kinds of learning outcomes such as those focused on students' acquisition of knowledge. If crafted carefully, however, short-answer items can measure substantially more challenging kinds of learning outcomes. The major advantage of short-answer items is that students need to *produce* a correct answer, not merely recognize it from a set of selected-response options. The level of partial knowledge that might allow a student to respond correctly to a multiple-choice item won't be sufficient if the student is required to generate a correct answer to a short-answer item.

The major drawback with short-answer items, as is true with all constructed-response items, is that students' responses are difficult to score. The longer the responses sought, the tougher it is to score them accurately. And inaccurate scoring, as we saw in Chapter 3, leads to reduced reliability—which, in turn, reduces the validity of the test-based interpretations we make about students—which, in turn, reduces the quality of the decisions we base on those interpretations. Educational measurement is much like the rest of life—it's simply loaded with trade-offs. When classroom teachers choose constructed-response tests, they must be willing to trade some scoring accuracy (the kind of accuracy that comes with selected-response approaches) for greater congruence between constructed-response assessment strategies and the kinds of student behaviors about which inferences are to be made.

Here, you will find five straightforward item-writing guidelines for short-answer items. Please look them over, and then each guideline will be amplified by describing the essence of how it works.

Item-Writing Guidelines for Short-Answer Items

1. Usually employ direct questions rather than incomplete statements, particularly for young students.
2. Structure the item so that a response should be concise.
3. Place blanks in the margin for direct questions or near the end of incomplete statements.
4. For incomplete statements, use only one or, at most, two blanks.
5. Make sure blanks for all items are equal in length.

Using Direct Questions Rather than Incomplete Statements

For young children, the direct question is a far more familiar format than the incomplete statement. Accordingly, such students will be less confused if direct questions are employed. Another reason why short-answer items should employ a direct-question format is that the use of direct questions typically forces the item writer to phrase the item so that less ambiguity is present. With incomplete-statement formats, there's often too much temptation simply to delete words or phrases from statements the teacher finds in texts. To make sure there isn't more than one correct answer to a short-answer item, it is often helpful if the item writer first decides on the correct answer and then builds a question or incomplete statement designed to elicit a *unique* correct response from knowledgeable students.

Nurturing Concise Responses

Responses to short-answer items, as might be inferred from what they're called, should be *short*. Thus, no matter whether you're eliciting responses that are words, symbols, phrases, or numbers, try to structure the item so a brief response is clearly sought. Suppose you conjured up an incomplete statement item such as this: "An animal that walks on two feet is a _____." There are all sorts of answers a student might legitimately make to such an item. Moreover, some of those responses could be somewhat lengthy. Now note how a slight restructuring of the item constrains the student: "An animal that walks on two feet is technically classified as a _____." By the addition of the phrase "technically classified as," the item writer has restricted the appropriate responses to only one—namely, "biped." If your short-answer items are trying to elicit students' phrases or sentences, you may wish to place word limits on each, or at least to indicate, in the test's directions, that only a *short* one-sentence response is allowable for each item.

Always try to put yourself, mentally, inside the heads of your students and try to anticipate how they are apt to interpret an item. What this second guideline suggests is that you massage an item until it truly lives up to its name—that is, until it becomes a *bona fide* short-answer item.

Positioning Blanks

If you're using direct questions in your short-answer items, place the students' response areas for all items near the right-hand margin of the page, immediately after the item's questions. By doing so, you'll have all of a student's responses nicely lined up for scoring. If you're using incomplete statements, try to place the blank near the end of the statement, not near its beginning. A blank positioned too early in a sentence tends to perplex the students. For instance, notice how this too-early blank can lead to confusion: "The _____ is the governmental body that, based on the United States Constitution, must ratify all U.S. treaties with foreign nations." It would be better to use a direct question or to phrase the item as follows: "The governmental body that, based on the United States Constitution, must ratify all U.S. treaties with foreign nations is the _____."

Limiting Blanks

For incomplete-statement types of short-answer items, you should use only one or two blanks. Any more blanks and the item can be labeled a "Swiss-cheese item," or an item with holes galore. Here's a Swiss-cheese item to illustrate the confusion that a profusion of blanks can inflict on what is otherwise a decent short-answer item: "After a series of major conflicts with natural disasters, in the year _____, the explorers _____ and _____, accompanied by their _____, discovered _____." The student who could supply correct answers to such a flawed short-answer item should also be regarded as a truly successful explorer!

Inducing Linear Equality

Too often in short-answer items, a beginning item writer will give away the answer by varying the length of the answer blanks so that short lines are used when short answers are correct, and long lines are used when lengthier answers are correct. This practice tosses unintended clues to students, so it should be avoided. In the interest of linear egalitarianism, not to mention decent item writing, try to keep all blanks for short-answer items equal in length. Be sure, however, that the length of the answer spaces provided is sufficient for students' responses—in other words, not so skimpy that students have to cram in their answers in an illegible fashion.

Okay, let's review. Short-answer items are the most simple form of constructed-response items, but they can help teachers measure important skills and knowledge. Because such items seek students' constructed rather than selected responses, they can be employed to tap some genuinely higher-order skills. Although students' responses to short-answer items are more difficult to score than their answers to selected-response items, the scoring of such items isn't impossible. That's because short-answer items, by definition, should elicit only *short* answers.

Essay Items: Development

The essay item is surely the most commonly used form of constructed-response assessment item. Anytime teachers ask their students to churn out a paragraph or two on what the students know about Topic *X* or to compose an original composition describing their "Favorite Day," an **essay item** is being used. Essay items are particularly useful in gauging a student's ability to synthesize, evaluate, and compose. Such items have a wide variety of applications in most teachers' classrooms.

A special form of the essay item is the **writing sample**—when teachers ask students to generate a written composition in an attempt to measure students' composition skills. Because the procedures employed to construct items for such writing samples and, thereafter, for scoring students' compositions, are so similar to the procedures employed to create and score responses to any kind of essay item, we'll treat writing samples and other kinds of essay items all at one time at this point. You'll find it helpful, however, to remember that requiring students to generate a writing sample is, in reality, a widely used type of *performance test*. We'll dig more deeply into performance tests in the following chapter.

For assessing certain kinds of complex learning outcomes, the essay item is the hands-down winner. It clearly triumphs when you're trying to see how well students can create original compositions. Yet, there are a fair number of drawbacks associated with essay items, and if you're going to consider using such items in your own classroom, you ought to know the weaknesses as well as the strengths of this item type.

One difficulty with essay items is that they're harder to write—at least to write properly—than is generally thought. I must confess that as a first-year high school teacher, I sometimes conjured up essay items while walking to school and then slapped them up on the chalkboard so that I created almost instant essay exams. At the time, I thought my essay items were pretty good. Such is the pride of youth—and the consequence of naivete. I'm glad I have no record of those items. In retrospect, I must assume that they were pretty putrid. I now know that generating a really good essay item is a tough task—a task not accomplishable while strolling to school. You'll see this is true from the item-writing rules to be presented shortly. It takes time to create a solid essay item. You'll need to find time to construct suitable essay items for your own classroom assessments.

The most serious problem with essay items, however, is the difficulty that teachers have in reliably scoring students' responses. Let's say you use a six-item

Decision Time

Forests or Trees?

Allison Allen is a brand-new English teacher assigned to work with seventh-grade and eighth-grade students at Dubois Junior High School. Allison has taken part in a state-sponsored summer workshop that emphasizes "writing as a process." Coupled with what she learned while completing her teacher education program, Allison is confident that she can effectively employ techniques such as brainstorming, outlining, early drafts, peer critiquing, and multiple revisions. She assumes that her students will acquire not only competence in their composition capabilities but also confidence about possessing those capabilities. What Allison's preparation failed to address, however, was how to grade her students' compositions.

Two experienced English teachers at Dubois Junior High have gone out of their way to help Allison get through her first year as a teacher. Mrs. Miller and Ms. Stovall had both been quite helpful during the early weeks of the school year. However, when Allison asked them one day during lunch how she should judge the quality of her students' compositions, two decisively different messages were given.

Ms. Stovall strongly endorsed *holistic* grading of compositions—that is, a general appraisal of each composition as a whole. Although Ms. Stovall bases her holistic grading scheme on a set of explicit criteria, she believes a single "gestalt" grade should be given so that "one's vision of the forest is not obscured by tree-counting."

Arguing with equal vigor, Mrs. Miller urged Allison to adopt *analytic* appraisals of her students' compositions. "If you supply your students with a criterion-by-criterion judgment of their work," she contended, "each student will be able to know precisely what's good and what isn't." (It was evident during the fairly heated interchanges that Mrs. Miller and Ms. Stovall had disagreed about this topic in the past.) Mrs. Miller concluded her remarks by saying, "Forget about that forest-and-trees metaphor, Allison. What we're talking about here is clarity!"

If you were Allison, how would you decide to judge the quality of your students' compositions?

essay test to measure your students' ability to solve certain kinds of problems in social studies. Suppose that, by some stroke of measurement magic, all your students' responses could be transformed into typed manuscript form so you could not tell which response came from which student. Let's say you were asked to score the complete set of responses *twice*. What do you think is the likelihood your two sets of scores would be consistent? Well, experience suggests that most teachers aren't able to produce very consistent results when they score students' essay responses. The challenge in this instance, of course, is to *increase* the reliability of your scoring efforts so that you're not distorting the validity of the score-based inferences you want to make on the basis of your students' responses.

Although the potential of having computers gleefully and accurately score students' essays is often trotted out during discussions of essay scoring, for the present it seems that really particularized scoring of students' essay responses is somewhat in the future. Even though computer-based scoring programs can be taught to do some terrific scoring, the wide range of students' potential content typically limits computer-based scoring to judging only the most rudimentary sorts of good and bad moves by an essay writer. If the formidable obstacles to tailored computer scoring ever get wrestled to the mat, the classroom teachers will have access to a sanity-saving way of scoring students' essays. This is a scoring advance greatly to be sought.

Creating Essay Items

Because the scoring of essay responses (and students' compositions) is such an important topic, you'll soon be getting a set of guidelines on how to score responses to such items. The more complex the nature of students' constructed responses become, as you'll see in the next two chapters, the more attention you'll need to lavish on scoring. You can't score responses to items that you haven't written, however, so let's look now at five guidelines for the construction of essay items.

Item-Writing Guidelines for Essay Items

1. Convey to students a clear idea regarding the extensiveness of the response desired.
2. Construct items so the student's task is explicitly described.
3. Provide students with the approximate time to be expended on each item, as well as each item's value.
4. Do not employ optional items.
5. Precursively judge an item's quality by composing, mentally or in writing, a possible response.

Communicating the Extensiveness of Students' Responses Sought

It is sometimes thought that when teachers decide to use essay items, students have total freedom of response. On the contrary, teachers can structure essay items so that students produce (1) barely more than they would for a short-answer item or, in contrast, (2) extremely lengthy responses. The two types of essay items that reflect this distinction in the desired extensiveness of students' responses are described as restricted-response items and extended-response items.

A *restricted-response item* decisively limits the form and content of students' responses. For example, a restricted-response item in a health education class might ask students the following: "Describe the three most common ways in which HIV, the AIDS virus, is transmitted. Take no more than 25 words to describe each method of transmission." In this example, the number of HIV transmission methods was specified, as was the maximum length for each transmission method's description.

In contrast, an *extended-response item* provides students with far more latitude in responding. Here's an example of an extended-response item from a social studies class: "Identify the chief factors contributing to the U.S. government's financial deficit during the past two decades. Having identified those factors, decide which factors, if any, have been explicitly addressed by the U.S. legislative and/or executive branches of government in the last five years. Finally, critically evaluate the likelihood that any currently proposed remedies will bring about significant reductions in the U.S. national debt." A decent response to such an extended-response item not only should get high marks from the teacher but might also be the springboard for a student's successful career in politics.

One technique that teachers commonly use to limit students' responses is to provide a certain amount of space on the test paper, in their students' response booklets, or in the available response area on a computer screen. For instance, the teacher might direct students to "Use no more than two sheets (both sides) in your blue books to respond to each test item" or "Give your answer in the designated screen-space below." Although the space-limiting ploy is an easy one to implement, it really puts at a disadvantage those students who write in a large-letter, scrawling fashion. Whereas such large-letter students may only be able to cram a few paragraphs onto a page, those students who write in a small, scrunched-up style may be able to produce a short novella in the same space. Happily, when students respond to a computer-administered test "in the space provided," we can prohibit their shifting down to a tiny, tiny font that might allow them to yammer on endlessly.

This first guideline asks you to think carefully about whether the test-based inference that you wish to make about your students is best served by students' responses to (1) more essay items requiring shorter responses or (2) fewer essay items requiring extensive responses. Having made that decision, be sure to convey to make it clear to your students what degree of extensiveness you're looking for in their responses.

Describing Students' Tasks

Students will find it difficult to construct responses to tasks if they don't understand what the tasks are. Moreover, students' responses to badly understood tasks are almost certain to yield flawed inferences by teachers. The most important part of an essay item is, without question, the description of the *assessment task*. It is the task students respond to when they generate essays. Clearly, then, poorly described assessment tasks will yield many off-target responses that, had the student truly understood what was being sought, might have been more appropriate.

There are numerous labels used to represent the assessment task in an essay item. Sometimes it's simply called the *task*, the *charge*, or the *assignment*. In essay items that are aimed at eliciting student compositions, the assessment task is often referred to as a *prompt*. No matter how the assessment task is labeled, if you're a teacher who is using essay items, you must make sure the nature of the task is really set forth clearly for your students. Put yourself in the student's position and see whether, with the level of knowledge possessed by most of your students, the nature of the assessment task is apt to be understood.

To illustrate, if you wrote the following essay item, there's little doubt that your students' assessment task would have been badly described: "In 500 words or less, discuss democracy in Latin America." In contrast, notice in the following item how much more clearly the assessment task is set forth: "Describe how the checks and balances provisions in the U.S. Constitution were believed by the Constitution's framers to be a powerful means to preserve democracy (300–500 words)."

Providing Time-Limit and Item-Value Guidance

When teachers create an examination consisting of essay items, they often have an idea regarding which items will take more of the students' time. But students don't know what's in the teacher's head. As a consequence, some students will lavish loads of attention on items the teacher thought warranted only modest effort, and yet will devote little time to items the teacher thought deserved substantial attention. Similarly, sometimes teachers will want to weight certain items more heavily than others. Again, if students are unaware of which items count most, they may toss reams of rhetoric at the low-value items and end up without enough time to supply more than a trifling response to the high-value items.

To avoid these problems, there's quite a straightforward solution—namely, letting students in on the secret. If there are any differences among items in point value or in the time students should spend on them, simply provide this information in the directions or, perhaps parenthetically, at the beginning or end of each item. Students will appreciate such clarifications of your expectations.

Avoiding Optionality

It's fairly common practice among teachers who use essay examinations to provide students with a certain number of items and then let each student choose to answer fewer than the number of items presented. For example, the teacher might allow students to "choose any three of the five essay items presented." Students, of course, really enjoy such an assessment procedure because they can respond to items for which they're well prepared and avoid those items for which they're inadequately prepared. Yet, other than inducing student jubilation, this optional-items assessment scheme has little going for it.

When students select different items from a menu of possible items, they are actually responding to different examinations. As a consequence, it is impossible to judge their performances on some kind of common scale. Remember, as a classroom teacher you'll be trying to make better educational decisions about your students by relying on test-based interpretations regarding those students. It's tough enough to make a decent test-based interpretation when you have only one test to consider. It's far more difficult to make such interpretations when you are faced with a medley of different tests because you allowed your students to engage in a mix-and-match measurement procedure.

In most cases, teachers rely on an optional-items procedure with essay items when they're uncertain about the importance of the content measured by the items on their examinations. Such uncertainty gives rise to the use of optional items because the teacher is not clearheaded about the inferences (and resulting decisions) for which the examination's results will be used. If you spell out those inferences (and decisions) crisply, prior to the examination, you will generally find you'll have no need for optional-item selection in your essay examinations.

Previewing Students' Responses

After you've constructed an essay item for one of your classroom assessments, there's a quick way to get a preliminary fix on whether the item is a winner or a loser. Simply squeeze yourself, psychologically, into the head of one of your typical students, and then anticipate how such a student would respond to the item. If you have time and are inclined to do so, you could even try writing a response that the student might produce. More often than not, because you'll be too busy to conjure up such fictitious responses in written form, you might try to compose a mental response to the item on behalf of the typical student you've selected. An early mental run-through of how a student might respond to an item can often help you identify deficits in the item, because when you put yourself, even hypothetically, on the other side of the teacher's desk, you'll sometimes discover shortcomings in items that you otherwise wouldn't have identified. Too many times teachers assemble a platoon of essay questions, send those soldiers into battle on examination day, and only then discover that one or more of them are not adequately prepared for the task at hand. Mental previewing of likely student responses can help you detect such flaws while there's still time for repairs.

In review, we've looked at five guidelines for creating essay items. If you remember that all of these charming little collections of item-specific recommendations should be adhered to, *in addition to* the five general item-writing commandments set forth in Chapter 6 (see page 156), you'll probably be able to come up with a pretty fair set of essay items. Then, perish the thought, you'll have to score your students' responses to those items. That's what we'll be looking at next.

Essay Items: Scoring Students' Responses

Later in this text, you'll be looking at how to evaluate students' responses to performance assessments in Chapter 8 and how to judge students' portfolios in Chapter 9. In short, you'll be learning much more about how to evaluate your students' performances on constructed-response assessments. Thus here, to spread out the load a bit, we'll be looking only at how to score students' responses to essay items (including tests of students' composition skills). You'll find that many of the suggestions for scoring students' constructed responses you will encounter will also be applicable when you're trying to judge your students' essay responses. But just to keep matters simple, let's look now at recommendations for scoring responses to essay items.

Guidelines for Scoring Responses to Essay Items

1. Score responses holistically and/or analytically.
2. Prepare a tentative scoring key in advance of judging students' responses.
3. Make decisions regarding the importance of the mechanics of writing prior to scoring.
4. Score all responses to one item before scoring responses to the next item.
5. Insofar as possible, evaluate responses anonymously.

Choosing an Analytic and/or Holistic Scoring Approach

During the past several decades, the measurement of students' composition skills by having students generate actual writing samples has become widespread. As a consequence of all this attention to students' compositions, educators have become far more skilled in evaluating students' written compositions. Fortunately, classroom teachers can use many of the procedures that were identified and refined as educators scored thousands of students' compositions during statewide assessment extravaganzas.

A fair number of the lessons learned about scoring students' writing samples apply quite nicely to the scoring of responses to any kind of essay item. One of the most important of the scoring insights picked up from this large-scale scoring of students' compositions is that almost any type of student-constructed response can be scored either *holistically* or *analytically*. This is why the first of the five guidelines suggests that you make an early decision about whether you're going to score your students' responses to essay items using a holistic approach or an analytic approach or, perhaps, score them using a combination of the two scoring approaches. Let's look at how each of these two scoring strategies works.

A *holistic scoring* strategy, as its name suggests, focuses on the essay response (or written composition) as a whole. At one extreme of scoring rigor, the teacher can, in a somewhat unsystematic manner, supply a "general impression" overall grade to each student's response. Or, in a more systematic fashion, the teacher can isolate, in advance of scoring, those evaluative criteria that should be attended to in order to arrive at a single, overall score per essay. Generally, a score range of 4 to 6 points is used to evaluate each student's response. (Some scoring schemes have a few more points, some a few less.) A teacher, then, after considering whatever factors should be attended to in a given item, will give a score to each student's response. Here is a set of evaluative criteria that teachers might use in holistically scoring a student's written composition.

Illustrative Evaluative Criteria to Be Considered When Scoring Students' Essay Responses Holistically

For scoring a composition intended to reflect students' composition prowess:

- Organization
- Communicative Clarity
- Adaptation to Audience
- Word Choice
- Mechanics (spelling, capitalization, punctuation)

And now, here are four evaluative factors that a speech teacher might employ in holistically scoring a response to an essay item used in a debate class.

Potential Evaluative Criteria to Be Used When Scoring Students' Essay Responses in a Debate Class

For scoring a response to an essay item dealing with rebuttal preparation:

- Anticipation of Opponent's Positive Points
- Support for One's Own Points Attacked by Opponents
- Isolation of Suitably Compelling Examples
- Preparation of a "Spontaneous" Conclusion

When teachers score students' responses holistically, they do *not* dole out points-per-criterion for a student's response. Rather, the teacher keeps in mind evaluative criteria such as those set forth in the previous two boxes. The speech teacher, for instance, while looking at the student's essay response to a question about how someone should engage in effective rebuttal preparation, will not necessarily penalize a student who overlooks one of the four evaluative criteria. The response as a whole may lack one factor, yet otherwise represent a really terrific response. Evaluative criteria such as those illustrated here simply dance merrily in the teacher's head when the teacher scores students' essay responses holistically.

In contrast, an **analytic scoring** scheme strives to be a fine-grained, specific point-allocation approach. Suppose, for example, that instead of using a holistic method of scoring students' compositions, a teacher chose to employ an analytic method. Under those circumstances, a scoring guide such as the example in Figure 7.1 might be used by the teacher. Note that for each evaluative criterion in

---

Figure 7.1 An Illustrative Guide for Analytically Scoring a Student's Written Composition

Factor	Unacceptable (0 points)	Satisfactory (1 point)	Outstanding (2 points)
1. Organization	_____	✓	_____
2. Communicative Clarity	_____	_____	✓
3. Adaptation to Audience	_____	✓	_____
4. Word Choice	_____	_____	✓
5. Mechanics	_____	✓	_____

Total Score = __7__

the guide, the teacher must award 0, 1, or 2 points. The lowest overall score for a student's composition, therefore, would be 0, whereas the highest overall score for a student's composition would be 10 (that is, 2 points $\times$ 5 criteria).

The advantage of an analytic scoring system is it can help you identify the specific strengths and weaknesses of your students' performances and, therefore, allows you to communicate such diagnoses to your students in a pinpointed fashion. The downside of analytic scoring is that a teacher sometimes becomes so attentive to the subpoints in a scoring system that the forest (overall quality) almost literally can't be seen because of a focus on individual trees (the separate scoring criteria). In less metaphoric language, the teacher will miss the communication of the student's response "as a whole" because of paying excessive attention to a host of individual evaluative criteria.

A middle-of-the-road scoring approach can be seen when teachers initially grade all students' responses holistically and then return for an analytic scoring of only those responses that were judged, overall, to be unsatisfactory. After the analytic scoring of the unsatisfactory responses, the teacher then relays more fine-grained diagnostic information to those students whose unsatisfactory responses were analytically scored. The idea underlying this sort of hybrid approach is that the students who are most in need of fine-grained feedback are those who, on the basis of the holistic evaluation, are performing less well.

This initial guideline for scoring students' essay responses applies to the scoring of responses to all kinds of essay items. As always, your decision about whether to opt for holistic or analytic scoring should flow directly from your intended use of the test results. Putting it another way, your choice of scoring approach will depend on the educational decisions that are linked to the test's interpreted results. (Is this beginning to sound somewhat familiar?)

Devising a Tentative Scoring Key

No matter what sort of approach you opt for in scoring your students' essay responses, you'll find that it will be useful to develop a tentative scoring key for responses to each item *in advance* of actually scoring students' responses. Such tentative scoring schemes are almost certain to be revised based on your scoring of actual student papers, but that's to be anticipated. If you wait until you commence scoring your students' essay responses, there's too much likelihood you'll be unduly influenced by the responses of the first few students whose papers you grade. If those papers are atypical, the resultant scoring scheme is apt to be unsound. It is far better to think through, at least tentatively, what you really hope students will supply in their responses, and then modify the scoring key if unanticipated responses from students suggest that alterations are needed.

If you don't have a tentative scoring key in place, you are very likely to be influenced by such factors as a student's vocabulary or writing style, even though, in truth, such variables may be of little importance to you. Advance exploration of the evaluative criteria you intend to employ, either holistically or analytically, is a winning idea when scoring responses to essay items.

Let's take a look at what a tentative scoring key might look like if it were employed by a teacher in a U.S. history course. The skill being promoted by the teacher is a genuinely high-level one that's reflected in the following curricular aim:

> When presented with a description of a current real-world problem in the United States, the student will be able to (1) cite one or more significant events in American history that are particularly relevant to the presented problem's solution, (2) defend the relevance of the cited events, (3) propose a solution to the presented problem, and (4) use historical parallels from the cited events to support the proposed solution.

As indicated, this is no rinky-dink, low-level cognitive skill. It's way, way up there in its cognitive demands on students. Now, let's suppose our hypothetical history teacher routinely monitors students' progress related to this skill by having students respond to similar problems either orally or in writing. The teacher presents a real-world problem. The students, aloud or in an essay, try to come up with a suitable four-part response.

Figure 7.2 illustrates a tentative scoring key for evaluating students' oral or written responses to constructed-response items measuring their mastery of this

Figure 7.2 An Illustrative Tentative Scoring Key for a High-Level Cognitive Skill in History

Students' Subtasks	Tentative Point Allocation		
	Weak Response	*Acceptable Response*	*Strong Response*
1. Citation of Pertinent Historical Events	0 pts.	5 pts.	10 pts.
2. Defense of the Cited Historical Events	0 pts.	10 pts.	20 pts.
3. Proposed Solution to the Presented Problem	0 pts.	10 pts.	20 pts.
4. Historical Support of Proposed Solution	0 pts.	20 pts.	40 pts.

Total Points Possible = <u>90 pts.</u>

curricular aim. As you can discern, in this tentative scoring key, greater weight has been given to the fourth subtask—namely, the student's provision of historical parallels to support the student's proposed solution to the real-world problem the teacher proposed. Much less significance was given to the first subtask of citing pertinent historical events. This, remember, is a *tentative* scoring key. Perhaps, when the history teacher begins scoring students' responses, it will turn out that the first subtask is far more formidable than the teacher originally thought and the fourth subtask appears to be handled without much difficulty by students. At that point, based on the way students are actually responding, this hypothetical history teacher surely ought to do a bit of score-point juggling in the tentative scoring key before applying it in final form to the appraisal of students' responses.

Deciding Early About the Importance of Mechanics

Few things influence scorers of students' essay responses as much as the mechanics of writing employed in the response. If the student displays subpar spelling, chaotic capitalization, and pathetic punctuation, it's pretty tough for a scorer of the student's response to avoid being influenced adversely. In some instances, of course, mechanics of writing play a meaningful role in scoring students' performances. For instance, suppose you're scoring students' written responses to the task of writing an application letter for a position as a reporter for a local newspaper. In such an instance, it is clear that mechanics of writing would be pretty important when judging the students' responses. But in a chemistry class, perhaps the teacher cares less about such factors when scoring students' essay responses to a problem-solving task. The third guideline simply suggests that you make up your mind about this issue early in the process so that, if mechanics aren't very important to you, you don't let your students' writing mechanics subconsciously influence the way you score their responses.

Scoring One Item at a Time

If you're using an essay examination with more than one item, be sure to score all your students' responses to one item, then score all their responses to the next item, and so on. Do *not* score all responses of a given student and then go

Parent Talk

The mother of one of your students, Jill Jenkins, was elected to your district's school board 2 years ago. Accordingly, anytime Mrs. Jenkins wants to discuss Jill's education, you are understandably "all ears."

Mrs. Jenkins recently stopped by your classroom to say that three of her fellow board members have been complaining there are too many essay tests being given in the district. The three board members contend that such tests, because they must be scored "subjectively," are neither reliable nor valid.

Because many of the tests you give Jill and her classmates are essay tests, Mrs. Jenkins asks you whether the three board members are correct.

> *If I were you, here's how I'd respond to Jill's mom. (Oh yes, because Mrs. Jenkins is a board member, I'd simply ooze politeness and professionalism while I responded.)*

"Thanks for giving me an opportunity to comment on this issue, Mrs. Jenkins. As you've already guessed, I believe in the importance of constructed-response examinations such as essay tests. The real virtue of essay tests is that they call for students to *create* their responses, not merely *recognize* correct answers, as students must do with other types of tests, such as those featuring multiple-choice items.

"Your three school board colleagues are correct when they say it is more difficult to score constructed-response items consistently than it is to score selected-response items consistently. And that's a shortcoming of essay tests. But it's a

shortcoming that's more than compensated for by the far greater *authenticity* of the tasks presented to students in almost all constructed-response tests. When Jill writes essays during my major exams, this is much closer to what she'll be doing in later life than when she's asked to choose the best answer from four options. In real life, people aren't given four-choice options. Rather, they're required to *generate* a response reflecting their views. Essay tests give Jill and her classmates a chance to do just that.

"Now, let's talk briefly about consistency and validity. Actually, Mrs. Jenkins, it is important for tests to be scored consistently. We refer to the consistency with which a test is scored as its *reliability*. And if a test isn't reliable, then the interpretations about students we make based on test scores aren't likely to be valid. It's a technical point, Mrs. Jenkins, but it isn't a *test* that's valid or invalid; it's a score-based interpretation about a student's ability that may or may not be valid. As your board colleagues pointed out, some essay tests are not scored very reliably. But essay tests *can* be scored reliably and they *can* yield valid inferences about students.

"I hope my reactions have been helpful. I'll be happy to show you some of the actual essay exams I've used with Jill's class. And I'm sure the district superintendent, Dr. Stanley, can supply you with additional information."

> *Now, how would you respond to Mrs. Jenkins?*

on to the next student's paper. There is way too much danger that a student's responses to early items will unduly influence your scoring of the student's responses to later items. If you score all responses to item number 1 and then move on to the responses to item number 2, you can eliminate this tendency. In addition, the scoring will often go a bit quicker because you won't need to shift evaluative criteria between items. Adhering to this fourth guideline will invariably lead to more consistent scoring and, therefore, to more accurate response-based inferences about your students. There'll be more paper shuffling than you might prefer, but the increased accuracy of your scoring will be worth it. (Besides, you'll be getting a smidge of psychomotor exercise with all the paper shuffling.)

Striving for Anonymity

Because I've been a teacher, I know all too well how quickly teachers can identify their students' writing styles, particularly those students who have especially distinctive styles, such as the "scrawlers," the "petite letter-size crew," and those who dot their *i*'s with half-moons or cross their *t*'s with lightning bolts. Yet, insofar as you can, try not to know whose responses you're scoring. One simple way to help in that effort is to ask students to write their names on the reverse side of the last sheet of the examination in the response booklet. Try not to peek at the students' names until you've scored all of the exams.

I used such an approach for three decades of scoring graduate students' essay examinations at UCLA. It worked fairly well. Sometimes I was really surprised because students who had appeared to be knowledgeable during class discussions sometimes displayed just the opposite on my exams, while several Silent Sarahs and Quiet Quentins came up with really solid exam performances. I'm sure that had known whose papers I was grading, I would have been improperly influenced by my classroom-based perceptions of different students' abilities. I am not suggesting that you shouldn't use students' classroom discussions as part of your evaluation system. Rather, I'm advising you that classroom-based perceptions of students can sometimes cloud your scoring of essay responses. This is one strong reason for you to strive for anonymous scoring.

In review, we've considered five guidelines for scoring students' responses to essay examinations. If your classroom assessment procedures involve any essay items, you'll find these five practical guidelines will go a long way in helping you come up with consistent scores for your students' responses. And consistency, as you learned in Chapter 3, is something that makes psychometricians mildly euphoric.

In the next two chapters you'll learn about two less common forms of constructed-response items. You'll learn how to create and score performance assessments and how to use students' portfolios in classroom assessments. You'll find that what we've been dealing with here will serve as a useful springboard to the content of the next two chapters.

What Do Classroom Teachers Really Need to Know About Constructed-Response Tests?

At the close of a chapter dealing largely with the nuts and bolts of creating and scoring written constructed-response tests, you probably expect to be told you really need to internalize all those nifty little guidelines so that when you spin out your own short-answer and essay items, you'll elicit student responses you can score accurately. Well, that's not a terrible aspiration, but there's really a more important insight you need to walk away with after reading the chapter.

But What Does This Have to Do with Teaching?

A teacher wants students to learn the stuff that's being taught—to learn it well. And one of the best ways to see whether students have really acquired a cognitive skill or have truly soaked up scads of knowledge is to have them display what they've learned by *generating* answers to constructed-response tests. A student who has learned something well enough to toss it out from scratch, rather than choosing from presented options, clearly has learned it pretty darn well.

But, as this chapter has pointed out, the creation and scoring of first-rate constructed-response items, especially anything beyond short-answer items, require serious effort from a teacher. And if constructed-response items aren't first-rate, then they are not likely to help a teacher arrive at valid interpretations about students' knowledge and/or skills. Decent constructed-response tests take time to create and to score. And that's where this kind of classroom assessment runs smack into a teacher's instructional-planning requirements.

A classroom teacher should typically reserve constructed-response assessments for a modest number of really *significant* instructional outcomes. And, remember, a teacher's assessments should typically exemplify the outcomes the teacher wants most students to master. It's better to get students to master three to five really *high-level* cognitive skills, adroitly assessed by excellent constructed-response tests, than it is to have students master a litany of low-level—easy-come, easy-go—outcomes. In short, choose your constructed-response targets with care. Those choices will have curricular and instructional implications.

Putting it another way, if you, as a classroom teacher, want to determine whether your students have the skills and/or knowledge that can be best measured by short-answer or essay items, then you need to refresh your memory regarding how to avoid serious item construction or response scoring errors. A review of the guidelines presented on pages 182, 186, and 190 should give you the brushup you need. Don't assume you are obligated to use short-answer or essay items simply because you now know a bit more about how to crank them out. If you're interested in the extensiveness of your students' *knowledge* regarding Topic *Z*, it may be far more efficient to employ fairly low-level selected-response kinds of items. If, however, you really want to make inferences about your students' skills in being able to perform the kinds of tasks represented by excellent short-answer and essay items, then the guidelines provided in the chapter should be consulted.

That insight, not surprisingly, derives from the central purpose of classroom assessment—namely, to draw accurate inferences about students' status so you can make more appropriate educational decisions. What you really need to know about short-answer items and essay items is that you should use them as part of your classroom assessment procedures if you want to make the sorts of inferences about your students that those students' responses to such items would support.

Chapter Summary

After a guilt-induced apology for mislabeling this chapter, we started off with a description of short-answer items accompanied by a set of guidelines (page 182) regarding how to write short-answer items. Next, we took up essay items and indicated that, although students' written compositions constitute a particular kind of essay response, most of the recommendations for constructing essay items and for scoring students' responses were the same, whether measuring students' composition skills or skills in subject areas other than language arts. Guidelines were provided for writing essay items (page 186) and for scoring students' responses to essay items (page 190). The chapter concluded with the suggestion that much of the content to be treated in the following two chapters, because those chapters also focus on constructed-response assessment schemes, will also be related to the creation and scoring of short-answer and essay items.

MyLab Education Self-Check 7.1

MyLab Education Application Exercise 7.1: **Constructing Constructed Response Items**

References

Downing, S. M., and Haladyna, T. M. (Eds.). (2006). *Handbook of test development*. Mahwah, NJ: Erlbaum.

Humphry, S. M., and Heldsinger, S. A. (2014). "Common structural design features of rubrics may represent a threat to validity," *Educational Researcher*, 43, no. 5 (June/July): 253–263.

Miller, M. D., and Linn, R. (2012). *Measurement and assessment in teaching* (11th ed.). Columbus, OH: Pearson.

Nitko, A. J., and Brookhart, S. M. (2014). *Educational assessment of students* (7th ed.). Upper Saddle River, NJ: Prentice-Hall/Merrill Education.

Stiggins, R. J., and Chappuis, J. (2012). *An introduction to student-involved assessment FOR learning* (6th ed.). Upper Saddle River, NJ: Prentice-Hall.

Wiliam, D. (2014). "The right questions, the right way," *Educational Leadership, 71,* no. 6 (March): 16–19.

Evaluating Student-Constructed Responses Using Rubrics*

W. James Popham, University of California, Los Angeles

Two prominent categories of students' responses account for practically all items found in educational tests, namely, *selected-response items* and *constructed-response items*. Whereas selected-response items are particularly efficient to score, they sometimes constrain the originality of a test taker's response. In contrast, although constructed-response approaches such as essay and short-answer items provide test takers with ample opportunities to invoke their originality, the scoring of students' responses frequently represents a formidable challenge.

One strong argument in favor of constructed-response items is that the challenges they embody often coincide directly with what's required of people in the real world. Although a friend may often ask you to "explain your reasons" for supporting a politician's proposed policy changes, rarely does that friend solicit your opinion by providing you with four possible options from which you must choose one.

Given the potentially wide range of students' constructed responses, scoring those responses is a substantial task. If a satisfactory job of scoring students' responses to essay or short-answer items cannot be done, of course, it would be better never to employ such items in the first place.

For the last several decades, educators have evaluated the quality of students' constructed responses by employing a *rubric*. Such rubrics—that is, scoring guides—help identify whether a student's response is dazzling or dismal. A rubric that's employed to score students' responses has, at minimum, three features:

- *Evaluative criteria.* The factors used to judge the quality of a student's response
- *Descriptions of qualitative differences for all evaluative criteria.* Clearly spelled-out descriptions of qualitative distinctions for each criterion
- *Scoring approach to be used.* Whether the evaluative criteria are to be applied collectively (*holistically*) or on a criterion-by-criterion basis (*analytically*)

The virtue of a rubric is that it brings clarity to those who score a student's responses. But also, if provided to students early in the instructional process, rubrics can clarify what's expected. Yet not all rubrics are created equal. Here are two losers and one winner:

- *Task-specific rubric.* This loser focuses on responses to a single task, not on a skill.
- *Hypergeneral rubric.* Another loser, its meanings are murky because it lacks clarity.
- *Skill-focused rubric.* This winner addresses mastery of the skill sought, not of an item.

Thus, when working with rubrics, either to teach students or to score their work, always remember that even though many rubrics represent real contributors to the educational enterprise, some simply don't.

Chapter 8
Performance Assessment

Learning Outcomes

8.1 Identify the defining characteristics of performance tests, including effective scoring techniques.

⌄ Chief Chapter Outcome

A sufficiently broad understanding of performance assessment to distinguish between accurate and inaccurate statements regarding the nature of performance tests, the identification of tasks suitable for such tests, and the scoring of students' performances

During the early 1990s, a good many educational policymakers became enamored of *performance assessment*, which is an approach to measuring a student's status based on the way the student completes a specified task. Theoretically, of course, when the student chooses between *true* and *false* for a binary-choice item, the student is completing a task, although an obviously modest one. But the proponents of performance assessment have measurement schemes in mind that are meaningfully different from binary-choice and multiple-choice tests. Indeed, it was dissatisfaction with traditional paper-and-pencil tests that caused many educators to travel with enthusiasm down the performance-testing trail.

What Is a Performance Test?

Before digging into what makes performance tests tick and how you might use them in your own classroom, we'd best explore the chief attributes of such an assessment approach. Even though all educational tests require students to perform in some way, when most educators talk about performance tests, they are thinking about assessments in which the student is required to construct an original response. It may be useful for you to regard performance tests as an assessment task in which the students make products or engage in behaviors other than answering selected-response or constructed-response items. Often, an examiner (such as the teacher) *observes* the process of construction, in which case observation of the student's performance and judgment about the quality of that performance are required. Frequently, performance tests call for students to generate some sort of specified product whose quality can then be evaluated.

More than four decades ago, Fitzpatrick and Morrison (1971) observed that "there is no absolute distinction between performance tests and other classes of tests." They pointed out that the distinction between performance assessments and more conventional tests is chiefly the degree to which the examination simulates the criterion situation—that is, the extent to which the examination calls for student behaviors approximating those about which we wish to make inferences.

Suppose, for example, a teacher who had been instructing students in the process of collaborative problem solving wanted to see whether students had acquired this collaborative skill. The *inference* at issue centers on the extent to which each student has mastered the skill. The *educational decision* on the line might be whether particular students need additional instruction or, on the contrary, it's time to move on to other curricular aims. The teacher's real interest, then, is in how well students can work with other students to arrive collaboratively at solutions to problems. In Figure 8.1, you will see several assessment procedures that could be used to get a fix on a student's collaborative problem-solving skills. Note that the two selected-response assessment options (numbers 1 and 2) don't really ask students to construct anything. For the other three constructed-response assessment options (numbers 3, 4, and 5), however, there are clear differences in the degree to which

Figure 8.1 A Set of Assessment Options That Vary in the Degree to Which a Student's Task Approximates the Curricularly Targeted Behavior

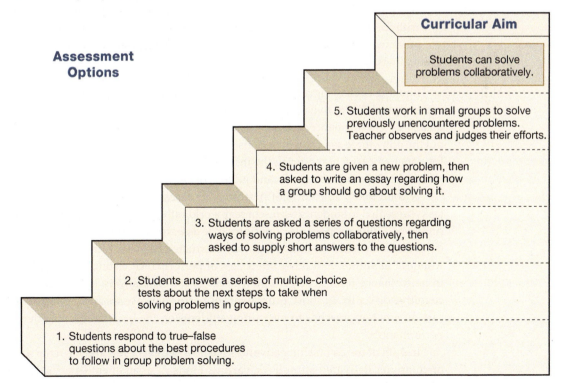

Curricular Aim

Students can solve problems collaboratively.

Assessment Options

5. Students work in small groups to solve previously unencountered problems. Teacher observes and judges their efforts.

4. Students are given a new problem, then asked to write an essay regarding how a group should go about solving it.

3. Students are asked a series of questions regarding ways of solving problems collaboratively, then asked to supply short answers to the questions.

2. Students answer a series of multiple-choice tests about the next steps to take when solving problems in groups.

1. Students respond to true–false questions about the best procedures to follow in group problem solving.

the task presented to the student coincides with the class of tasks called for by the teacher's curricular aim. Assessment Option 5, for example, is obviously the closest match to the behavior called for in the curricular aim. Yet Assessment Option 4 is surely more of a "performance test" than Assessment Option 1.

It should be apparent to you, then, that different educators will be using the phrase *performance assessment* to refer to very different kinds of assessment approaches. Many teachers, for example, are willing to consider short-answer and essay tests as a form of performance assessment. In other words, those teachers essentially equate performance assessment with any form of constructed-response assessment. Other teachers establish more stringent requirements for a measurement procedure to be accurately described as a performance assessment. For example, some performance-assessment proponents contend that genuine performance assessments must exhibit at least three features:

- *Multiple evaluative criteria.* The student's performance must be judged using more than one **evaluative criterion**. To illustrate, a student's ability to speak Spanish might be appraised on the basis of the student's accent, syntax, and vocabulary.

- *Prespecified quality standards.* Each of the evaluative criteria on which a student's performance is to be judged is clearly explicated in advance of judging the quality of the student's performance.

- *Judgmental appraisal.* Unlike the scoring of selected-response tests in which electronic computers and scanning machines can, once programmed, carry on without the need of humankind, genuine performance assessments depend on human judgments to determine how acceptable a student's performance really is.

Looking back to Figure 8.1, it is clear that if the foregoing three requirements were applied to the five assessment options, then Assessment Option 5 would qualify as a performance test, and Assessment Option 4 probably would as well, but the other three assessment options wouldn't qualify under a definition of performance assessment requiring the incorporation of multiple evaluative criteria, prespecified quality standards, and judgmental appraisals.

A good many advocates of performance assessment would prefer that the tasks presented to students represent real-world rather than school-world kinds of problems. Other proponents of performance assessment would be elated simply if more school-world measurement was constructed response rather than selected response in nature. Still other advocates of performance testing want the tasks in performance tests to be genuinely *demanding*—that is, way up the ladder of cognitive difficulty. In short, proponents of performance assessment often advocate different approaches to measuring students on the basis of those students' performances.

In light of the astonishing advances we now see every few weeks in the sorts of computer-delivered stimuli for various kinds of assessment—performance tests surely included—the potential nature of performance-test tasks seems practically unlimited. For example, the possibility of digitally simulating a variety of authentic performance-test tasks provides developers of performance tests with an ever-increasing range of powerful performance assessments placing students in a test-generated "virtual world."

You'll sometimes encounter educators who use other phrases to describe performance assessment. For example, they may use the label ***authentic assessment*** (because the assessment tasks more closely coincide with real-life, nonschool tasks) or the label *alternative assessment* (because such assessments constitute an alternative to traditional, paper-and-pencil tests). In the next chapter, we'll be considering *portfolio assessment*, which is a particular type of performance assessment and should not be considered a synonymous descriptor for the performance-assessment approach to educational measurement.

To splash a bit or reality juice on this chapter, it may be helpful for you to recognize a real-world fact about educational performance assessment. Here it goes: Although most educators regard performance testing as an effective way to measure students' mastery of important skills instead of using many traditional testing tactics, in recent years the financial demands of such testing have rendered them nonexistent or, at best, tokenistic, in many settings. Yes, as the chapter probes the innards of this sort of educational testing, you will discover that it embodies some serious advantages, particularly its contributions to instruction. Yet, you will also see that a full-fledged reliance on performance testing for many students, such as we see in states' annual accountability tests, often renders the widespread use of performance tests prohibitively expensive. More affordable, of course, is teachers' use of this potent assessment approach for their own classroom assessments.

We now turn to the twin issues that are at the heart of performance assessments: *selecting appropriate tasks* for students and, once the students have tackled those tasks, *judging the adequacy of students' responses.*

Identifying Suitable Tasks for Performance Assessment

Performance assessment typically requires students to respond to a small number of more significant tasks, rather than to a large number of less significant tasks. Thus, rather than answering 50 multiple-choice items on a conventional chemistry examination, students who are being assessed via performance tasks may find themselves asked to perform an actual experiment in their chemistry class and then prepare a written interpretation of the experiment's results, along with an analytic critique of the procedures they used. From the chemistry teacher's perspective, instead of seeing how students respond to the 50 "mini-tasks" represented in the multiple-choice test, an estimate of each student's status must be derived from the student's response to a single, complex task. Given the significance of each task used in a performance-testing approach to classroom assessment, it is apparent that great care must be taken in the selection of performance-assessment tasks. Generally speaking, classroom teachers will either have to (1) generate their own performance-test tasks or (2) select performance-test tasks from the increasing number of tasks currently available from educators elsewhere.

Inferences and Tasks

Consistent with the frequently asserted message of this text about classroom assessment, the chief determinants of how you assess your students are (1) the inference—that is, the interpretation—you want to make about those students

Decision Time
Grow, Plants, Grow!

Francine Floden is a third-year biology teacher in Kennedy High School. Because she has been convinced by several of her colleagues that traditional paper-and-pencil examinations fail to capture the richness of the scientific experience, Francine has decided to base most of her students' grades on a semester-long performance test. As Francine contemplates her new assessment plan, she decides that 90 percent of the students' grades will stem from the quality of their responses to the performance test's task; 10 percent of the grades will be linked to classroom participation and to a few short true–false quizzes administered throughout the semester.

The task embodied in Francine's performance test requires each student to design and conduct a 2-month experiment to study the growth of three identical plants under different conditions, and then prepare a formal scientific report describing the experiment. Although most of Francine's students carry out their experiments at home, several students use the shelves at the rear of the classroom for their experimental plants. A number of students vary the amount of light or the kind of light received by the different plants, but most students modify the

nutrients given to their plants. After a few weeks of the 2-month experimental period, all of Francine's students seem to be satisfactorily under way with their experiments.

Several of the more experienced teachers in the school, however, have expressed their reservations to Francine about what they regard as "overbooking on a single assessment experience." The teachers suggested to Francine that she will be unable to draw defensible inferences about her students' true mastery of biological skills and knowledge on the basis of a single performance test. They urged her to reduce dramatically the grading weight for the performance test so that, instead, additional grade-contributing exams can also be given to the students.

Other colleagues, however, believe Francine's performance-test approach is precisely what is needed in courses such as biology. They recommended that she "stay the course" and alter "not one whit" of her new assessment strategy. (Francine was obliged to look up the technical meaning of "whit.")

If you were Francine, what would your decision be?

and (2) the decision that will be based on the inference. For example, suppose you're a history teacher and you've spent a summer at a lakeside cabin meditating about curricular matters (which, in one lazy setting or another, is the public's perception of how most teachers spend their summer vacations). After three months of heavy curricular thought, you have concluded that what you really want to teach your students is to apply historical lessons of the past to the solution of current and future problems that, at least to some extent, parallel the problems of the past. You have decided to abandon your week-long, 1500-item true–false final examination, which your stronger students refer to as a "measurement marathon" and your weaker students refer to by using a rich, if earthy, vocabulary. Instead of using true–false items, you are now committed to a performance-assessment strategy, and you wish to select tasks for your performance tests. You want the performance test to help you infer how well your students can draw on the lessons of the past to illuminate their approach to current and/or future problems.

In Figure 8.2, you will see a graphical depiction of the relationships among (1) a teacher's key curricular aim, (2) the inference that the teacher wishes to draw about each student, and (3) the tasks for a performance test intended to secure data to support the inference that the teacher wants to make. As you will note, the teacher's curricular aim provides the source for the inference. The assessment tasks yield the evidence needed for the teacher to arrive at defensible inferences regarding the extent to which students can solve current or future problems using historical lessons. To the degree that students have mastered the curricular aim, the teachers will reach a decision about how much more instruction, if any, is needed.

The Generalizability Dilemma

One of the most serious difficulties with performance assessment is that, because students respond to fewer tasks than would be the case with conventional paper-and-pencil testing, it is often more difficult to generalize accurately about what

---

Figure 8.2 Relationships among a Teacher's Key Curricular Aim, the Assessment-Based Inference Derived from the Aim, and the Performance-Assessment Tasks Providing Evidence for the Inference skills and knowledge are possessed by the student. To illustrate, let's say you're trying to get a fix on your students' ability to multiply pairs of double-digit numbers. If, because of your instructional priorities, you can devote only a half-hour to assessment purposes, you could require the students to respond to 20 such multiplication problems in the 30 minutes available. (That's probably more problems than you'd need, but this example attempts to draw a vivid contrast for you.) From a student's responses to 20 multiplication problems, you can get a pretty fair idea about what kind of double-digit multiplier the student is. As a consequence of the student's performance on a *reasonable sample* of items representing the curricular aim, you can reasonably conclude that "Javier really knows how to multiply those sorts of problems," or "Fred really couldn't multiply double-digit multiplication problems if his life depended on it." It is because you have adequately sampled the kind of student performance (about which you wish to make an inference) that you can confidently make inferences about your students' abilities to solve similar sorts of multiplication problems.

With only a 30-minute assessment period available, however, if you moved to a more elaborate kind of performance test, you might only be able to have students respond to one big-bopper item. For example, if you presented a multiplication-focused mathematics problem involving the use of manipulatives, and wanted your students to derive an original solution and then describe it in writing, you'd be lucky if your students could finish the task in half an hour. Based on this single task, how confident would you be in making inferences about your students' abilities to perform comparable multiplication tasks?

And this, as you now see, is the rub with performance testing. Because students respond to fewer tasks, the teacher is put in a trickier spot when it comes to deriving accurate interpretations about students' abilities. If you use only one performance test, and a student does well on the test, does this mean the student *really* possesses the category of skills the test was designed to measure, or did the student just get lucky? On the other hand, if a student messes up on a single-performance test, does this signify that the student *really* doesn't possess the assessed skill, or was there a feature in this particular performance test that misled the student who, given other tasks, might have performed marvelously?

As a classroom teacher, you're faced with two horns of a classic measurement dilemma. Although performance tests often measure the kinds of student abilities you'd prefer to assess (because those abilities are in line with really worthwhile curricular aims), the inferences you make about students on the basis of their responses to performance tests must often be made with increased caution. As with many dilemmas, there may be no perfect way to resolve this dilemma. But there is, at least, a way of dealing with the dilemma as sensibly as you can. In this instance, the solution strategy is to devote great care to the selection of the tasks embodied in your performance tests. Among the most important considerations in selecting such tasks is to choose tasks that optimize the likelihood of accurately generalizing about your students' capabilities. If you really keep generalizability at the forefront of your thoughts when you select or construct performance-test tasks, you'll be able to make the strongest possible performance-based inferences about your students' capabilities.

Factors to Consider When Evaluating Performance-Test Tasks

We've now looked at what many measurement specialists regard as the most important factor you can consider when judging potential tasks for performance assessments—*generalizability*. Let's look at a set of seven such factors you might wish to consider, whether you select a performance-test task from existing tasks or create your own performance-test tasks anew.

Evaluative Criteria for Performance-Test Tasks

- *Generalizability.*   Is there a high likelihood that the students' performance on the task will generalize to comparable tasks?
- *Authenticity.*   Is the task similar to what students might encounter in the real world, as opposed to encountering it only in school?
- *Multiple foci.*   Does the task measure multiple instructional outcomes instead of only one?
- *Teachability.*   Is the task one that students can become more proficient in as a consequence of a teacher's instructional efforts?
- *Fairness.*   Is the task fair to all students—that is, does the task avoid bias based on such personal characteristics as students' gender, ethnicity, or socio-economic status?
- *Feasibility.*   Is the task realistically implementable in relation to its cost, space, time, and equipment requirements?
- *Scorability.*   Is the task likely to elicit student responses that can be reliably and accurately evaluated?

Whether you're developing your own tasks for performance tests or selecting such tasks from an existing collection, you may wish to apply some but not all the factors listed here. Some teachers try to apply all seven factors, although they occasionally dump the *authenticity* criterion or the *multiple foci* criterion. In some instances, for example, school tasks rather than real-world tasks might be suitable for the kinds of inferences a teacher wishes to reach, so the authenticity criterion may not be relevant. And even though it is economically advantageous to measure more than one outcome at one time, particularly considering the time and effort that goes into almost any performance test, there may be cases in which a single educational outcome is so important that it warrants a solo performance test. More often than not, though, a really good task for a performance test will satisfy most, if not all seven, of the evaluative criteria presented here.

Performance Tests and Teacher Time

Back in Chapter 1, you were promised that if you completed this text with a reasonable degree of attentiveness, you'd become a better teacher. Now, here comes another promise for you: This text promises to be *honest* about the measurement mysteries being dissected. And this brings us to an important consideration regarding performance testing. In brief, *it takes time*!

Think for a moment about the time that you, as the teacher, must devote to (1) the selection of suitable tasks, (2) the development of an appropriate scheme for scoring students' responses, and (3) the actual scoring of students' responses. Talk to any teacher who has already used many classroom performance tests, and you'll learn that it requires a ton of time to use performance assessment.

So here's one additional factor you should throw into your decision making about performance assessment. It is the *significance of the skill* you're using the performance test to assess. Because you'll almost certainly have time for only a handful of such performance tests in your teaching, make sure that every performance test you use is linked to a truly significant skill you're trying to have your students acquire. If performance assessments aren't based on genuinely demanding skills, you'll soon stop using them because, to be truthful, they'll be more trouble than they're worth.

The Role of Rubrics

Performance assessments invariably are based on constructed-response measurement procedures in which students generate rather than select their responses. Student-constructed responses must be scored, however, and it's clearly much tougher to score constructed responses than to score selected responses. The scoring of constructed responses centers on the *evaluative criteria* one calls on to determine the adequacy of students' responses. Let's turn our attention now to the evaluative criteria we use to decide whether students' responses to performance tests are splendid or shabby.

A *criterion*, according to most people's understanding, is a standard on which a decision or judgment can be based. In the case of scoring students' responses to a performance test's task, you're clearly trying to make a judgment regarding the adequacy of the student's constructed response. The specific criteria to be used in making that judgment will obviously influence the way you score a student's response. For instance, if you were scoring a student's written composition on the basis of organization, word choice, and communicative clarity, you might arrive at very different scores than if you had scored the composition on the basis of spelling, punctuation, and grammar. The evaluative criteria used when scoring students' responses to performance tests (or their responses to any kind of constructed-response item) really control the whole assessment game.

Referring to my previously mentioned compulsion to fall back on my 5 years of Latin studies in high school and college, I feel responsible for explaining that the Latin word *criterion* is singular and the Latin word *criteria* is plural. Unfortunately, so many of today's educators mix up these two terms that I don't even become distraught about it anymore. However, now that you know the difference, if you find any of your colleagues erroneously saying "the criteria is" or "the criterion were," you have permission to display an ever so subtle, yet altogether condescending, smirk.

The scoring procedures for judging students' responses to performance tests are usually referred to these days as *scoring rubrics* or, more simply, **rubrics**. A rubric that's used to score students' responses to a performance assessment has, at minimum, three important features:

- *Evaluative criteria.*   These are the factors to be used in determining the quality of a student's response.

- *Descriptions of qualitative differences for all evaluative criteria.*   For each evaluative criterion, a description must be supplied so that qualitative distinctions in students' responses can be made using the criterion.

- *An indication of whether a holistic or analytic scoring approach is to be used.*   The rubric must indicate whether the evaluative criteria are to be applied collectively in the form of *holistic* scoring, or on a criterion-by-criterion basis in the form of *analytic* scoring.

The identification of a rubric's evaluative criteria is probably the most important task for rubric developers. If you're creating a rubric for a performance test you wish to use in your own classroom, be careful not to come up with a lengthy laundry list of evaluative criteria that a student's response should satisfy. Many seasoned scorers of students' performance tests believe that when you isolate more than three or four evaluative criteria per rubric, you've identified too many. If you find yourself facing more than a few evaluative criteria, simply *rank all the criteria in order of importance,* and then chop off those listed lower than the very most important ones.

The next job you'll have is deciding how to *describe in words* what a student's response must be in order to be judged wonderful or woeful. The level of descriptive detail you apply needs to work *for you.* Remember, you're devising a scoring rubric for your own classroom, not for a statewide or national test. Reduce the aversiveness of the work by employing brief descriptors of quality differences that you can use when teaching and that, if you're instructionally astute, your students can use as well. However, because for instructional purposes you will invariably want your students to understand the meaning of each evaluative criterion and its worth, give some thought to how effectively your descriptions of evaluative criteria can be communicated to students.

Finally, you'll need to decide whether you'll make a single, overall judgment about a student's response by considering all of the rubric's evaluative criteria as an amalgam (holistic scoring) or, instead, award points to the response on a criterion-by-criterion basis (analytic scoring). The virtue of holistic scoring, of course, is it's quicker to do. The downside of holistic scoring is it fails to communicate to students, especially low-performing students, what their shortcomings are. Clearly, analytic scoring is more likely than holistic scoring to yield diagnostically pinpointed scoring and sensitive feedback. Some classroom teachers have attempted to garner the best of both worlds by scoring all responses holistically and then analytically rescoring (for feedback purposes) all of the responses made by low-performing students.

Because most performance assessments call for fairly complex responses from students, there will usually be more than one evaluative criterion employed to score students' responses. For each of the evaluative criteria chosen, a numerical scale is typically employed so that, for each criterion, a student's response might be assigned a specified number of points—for instance, 0 to 6 points. Usually, these scale points are accompanied by verbal descriptors; sometimes they aren't. For instance, in a 5-point scale, the following descriptors might be used: 5 = Exemplary, 4 = Superior, 3 = Satisfactory, 2 = Weak, 1 = Inadequate. If no verbal descriptors are used for each score point on the scale, a scheme such as the following might be employed:

In some cases, the scoring scale for each criterion is not numerical; that is, it consists only of verbal descriptors such as "exemplary," "adequate," and so on. Although such verbal scales can be useful with particular types of performance tests, their disadvantage is that scores from multiple criteria cannot be added together in order to produce a meaningful overall score.

The heart of the intellectual process in isolating suitable evaluative criteria is to get to the essence of what the most significant factors are that distinguish acceptable from unacceptable responses. In this instance, as in many others, less is more. A few truly important criteria are preferable to a ton of trifling criteria. Go for the big ones. If you need help in deciding which criteria to employ in conjunction with a particular performance test, don't be reluctant to ask colleagues to toss in their ideas regarding what *significant* factors to use (for a given performance test) in order to discriminate between super and subpar responses.

In this chapter you'll be presented with scoring rubrics that can serve as useful models for your own construction of such rubrics. In those illustrative scoring rubrics, you'll see that care has been taken to isolate a small number of *instructionally addressable* evaluative criteria. The greatest payoff from a well-formed scoring rubric is in its contribution to improved teaching.

To give you a better idea about the kinds of tasks that might be used in a performance test and the way you might score a student's responses, let's take a gander at illustrative tasks for a performance test. The tasks presented in Figure 8.3 are intended to assess students' mastery of an oral communication skill.

Figure 8.3 Task Description and Sample Tasks for a One-on-One Oral Communication Performance Assessment

> **An Oral Communication Performance Test**
>
> *Introduction*
>
> There are numerous kinds of speaking tasks students must perform in everyday life, both in school and out of school. This performance assessment focuses on some of these tasks—namely, describing objects, events, and experiences; explaining the steps in a sequence; providing information in an emergency; and persuading someone.
>
> In order to accomplish a speaking task, the speaker must formulate and transmit a message to a listener. This process involves deciding what needs to be said, organizing the message, adapting the message to the listener and situation, choosing language to convey the message and, finally, delivering the message. The effectiveness of the speaker may be rated in terms of how well the speaker meets the requirement of the task.
>
> *Sample Tasks*
>
> *Description Task:* Think about your favorite class or extracurricular activity in school. Describe to me everything you can about it so I will know a lot about it. (How about something like a school subject, a club, or a sports program?)
>
> *Emergency Task:* Imagine you are home alone and you smell smoke. You call the fire department and I answer your call. Talk to me as if you were talking on the telephone. Tell me everything I would need to know to get help to you. (Talk directly to me; begin by saying hello.)
>
> *Sequence Task:* Think about something you know how to cook. Explain to me, step by step, how to make it. (How about something like popcorn, a sandwich, or scrambled eggs?)
>
> *Persuasion Task:* Think about one change you would like to see made in your school, such as a change in rules or procedures. Imagine I am the principal of your school. Try to convince me the school should make this change. (How about something like a change in the rules about hall passes or the procedures for enrolling in courses?)
>
> *Source:* Based on assessment efforts of the Massachusetts Department of Education.

Rubrics: The Wretched and the Rapturous

Unfortunately, many educators believe a rubric is a rubric is a rubric. Not so. Rubrics differ dramatically in their instructional worth. We'll now consider two types of rubrics that are sordid and one type that's super.

Task-Specific Rubrics

Some rubrics are created so that their evaluative criteria are linked only to the particular task embodied in a specific performance test. These are called *task-specific rubrics*. Such a rubric does little to illuminate instructional decision making, because it implies that students' performances on the constructed-response test's specific task are what's important. They're not! What's important is the student's ability to perform well on the *class of tasks* that can be accomplished by using the skill being measured in the assessment. If students are taught to shine only on the single task represented in a performance test, but not on the full range of comparable tasks, students lose out. If students learn to become good problem solvers, they'll be able to solve all sorts of problems—not merely the single problem embodied in a particular performance test.

So, to provide helpful instructional illumination—that is, to assist the teacher's instructional decision making—a rubric's evaluative criteria dare not be task specific. Instead, those criteria must be rooted in the skill itself. This can be illustrated by your considering an evaluative criterion frequently employed in the rubrics used to judge students' written communication skills—namely, the evaluative criterion of *organization*. Presented here is a task-specific evaluative criterion that might be used in a scoring rubric to judge the quality of a student's response to the following task:

> "Compose a brief narrative essay, of 400 to 600 words, describing what happened during yesterday's class session when we were visited by the local firefighters who described a fire-exit escape plan for the home."
>
> **A task-specific evaluative criterion for judging the organization of students' narrative essays:** Superior essays will (1) commence with a recounting of the particular rationale for home fire-escape plans the local firefighters provided, then (2) follow up with a description of the six elements in home-safety plans in the order in which those elements were presented, and (3) conclude by citing at least three of the life–death safety statistics the firefighters provided at the close of their visit. Departures from these three organizational elements will result in lower evaluations of essays.

Suppose you're a teacher who has generated or been given this task-specific evaluative criterion. How would you organize your instruction? If you really tried to gain instructional guidance from this evaluative criterion, you'd be aiming your instruction directly at a particular task—in this case, a narrative account of the firefighters' visit to your class. You'd need to teach your students to commence their narrative essays with a rationale when, in fact, using a rationale for an introduction might be inappropriate for other sorts of narrative essays. Task-specific evaluative criteria do not help teachers plan instructional sequences that promote their students' abilities to *generalize* the skills they acquire. Task-specific criteria are just what they are touted to be—specific to one task.

During recent years, educators have seen a number of rubrics that classroom teachers have generated on their own. From an instructional perspective, most of these rubrics don't pass muster. Many of the rubrics are task specific. Such task-specific rubrics may make it easier to score students' constructed responses. Thus, for *scoring* purposes, the more specific evaluative rubrics are, the better. But task-specific rubrics do *not* provide teachers with the kinds of *instructional* insights that good rubrics should.

You'll not be surprised to learn that when the nation's large testing firms set out to score thousands of students' responses to performance tasks, they almost always employ task-specific rubrics. Such task-focused scoring keeps down costs. But regrettably, the results of such scoring supply teachers with few instructional insights.

Hypergeneral Rubrics

Another variety of scoring rubric that will *not* help teachers plan their instruction is referred to as a **hypergeneral rubric**. Such a rubric is one in which the evaluative criteria are described in exceedingly general and amorphous terms. The evaluative criteria are so loosely described that, in fact, teachers' instructional plans really aren't benefited. For example, using the previous example of a task calling for students to write a narrative essay, a hypergeneral evaluative criterion for organization might resemble the following one:

> **A hypergeneral evaluative criterion for judging the organization of students' narrative essays:** *Superior* essays are those in which the essay's content has been arranged in a genuinely excellent manner, whereas *inferior* essays are those displaying altogether inadequate organization. An *adequate* essay is one representing a lower organizational quality than a superior essay, but a higher organizational quality than an inferior essay.

You may think that you're being put on when you read the illustrative hypergeneral evaluative criterion just given. But you're not. Most seasoned teachers have seen many such hypergeneral scoring rubrics. These rubrics ostensibly clarify how teachers can score students' constructed responses, but really these vague rubrics do little more than loosely redefine such quality descriptors as *superior, proficient*, and *inadequate*. Hypergeneral rubrics often attempt to draw distinctions among students' performances no more clearly than among students' performances in earning grades of A through F. Hypergeneral rubrics provide teachers with no genuine benefits for their instructional planning, because such rubrics do not give the teacher meaningfully clarified descriptions of the criteria to be used in evaluating the quality of students' performances—and, of course, in promoting students' mastery of a rubric's evaluative criteria.

Robert Marzano, one of our field's most respected analysts of educational research, has taken a stance regarding scoring guides that seems to endorse the virtues of the kinds of hypergeneral rubrics currently being reviled here. Marzano (2008) has urged educators to develop rubrics for each curricular aim at each grade level using a generic rubric that can be "applied to all content areas" (pp. 10–11). However, for a rubric to be applicable to *all* content areas, it must obviously be so general and imprecise that much of its *instructional* meaning is likely to have been leached from the rubric.

The midpoint (anchor) of this sort of hypergeneral rubric calls for no major errors or omissions on the student's part regarding the simple or complex content and/or the procedures taught. If errors or omissions are present in either the content or the procedures taught, these deficits lead to lower evaluations of the student's performance. If the student displays "in-depth inferences and applications" that go beyond what was taught, then higher evaluations of the student's performance are given. Loosely translated, these generic rubrics tell teachers that a student's "no-mistakes" performance is okay, a "some-mistakes" performance is less acceptable, and a "better-than-no-mistakes" performance is really good.

When these very general rubrics are applied to the appraisal of students' mastery of given curricular goals, such rubrics' level of generality offers scant instructional clarity to teachers about what's important and what's not. I have enormous admiration for Bob Marzano's contributions through the years, and I count him as a friend. But in this instance, I fear my friend is pushing for a sort of far-too-general scoring guide that won't help teachers do a better instructional job.

Skill-Focused Rubrics

Well, because we have now denigrated task-specific rubrics and sneered at hyper-general rubrics, it's only fair to wheel out the type of rubric that helps score students' responses, yet can also illuminate a teacher's instructional planning. Such scoring guides can be described as *skill-focused rubrics* because they really are conceptualized around the skill that is (1) being measured by the constructed-response assessment and (2) being pursued instructionally by the teacher. Based on the views of numerous teachers who have used a variety of scoring rubrics, many teachers report that creating a skill-focused scoring rubric prior to their instructional planning nearly always helps them devise a more potent instructional sequence.

For an example of an evaluative criterion you'd encounter in a skill-focused rubric, look over the following illustrative criterion for evaluating the organization of a student's narrative essay:

> **A skill-focused evaluative criterion for judging the organization of students' narrative essays:** Two aspects of organization will be employed in the appraisal of students' narrative essays: *overall structure* and *sequence*. To earn maximum credit, an essay must embody an overall structure containing an introduction, a body, and a conclusion. The content of the body of the essay must be sequenced in a reasonable manner—for instance, in a chronological, logical, or order-of-importance sequence.

Now, when you consider this evaluative criterion from an instructional perspective, you'll realize that a teacher could sensibly direct instruction by (1) familiarizing students with the two aspects of the criterion—that is, overall structure and sequence; (2) helping students identify essays in which overall structure and sequence are, or are not, acceptable; and (3) supplying students with gobs of guided and independent practice in writing narrative essays that exhibit the desired overall structure and sequence. The better students become in employing this double-barreled criterion in their narrative essays, the better those students will be at responding to a task such as the illustrative one we just saw about the local firefighters' visit to the classroom. This skill-focused evaluative criterion for *organization*, in other words, can generalize to a wide variety of narrative-writing tasks, not just an essay about visiting fire-folk.

And even if teachers do not create their own rubrics—for instance, if rubrics are developed by a school district's curriculum or assessment specialists—those teachers who familiarize themselves with skill-focused rubrics in advance of instructional planning will usually plan better instruction than will teachers who aren't familiar with a skill-focused rubric's key features. Skill-focused rubrics make clear what a teacher should emphasize instructionally when the teacher attempts to promote students' mastery of the skill being measured. Remember, although students' acquisition of knowledge is an important curricular aspiration for teachers, assessment of students' knowledge can obviously be accomplished by procedures other than the use of performance tests.

Let's now identify five rules you are encouraged to follow if you're creating your own skill-focused scoring rubric—a rubric you should generate *before* you plan your instruction.

Rule 1: *Make sure the skill to be assessed is significant.* It takes time and trouble to generate skill-focused rubrics. It also takes time and trouble to score students' responses by using such rubrics. Make sure the skill being promoted instructionally, and scored via the rubric, is worth all this time and trouble. Skills that are scored with skill-focused rubrics should represent demanding accomplishments by students, not trifling ones.

Teachers should not be ashamed to be assessing their students with only a handful of performance tests, for example. It makes much more sense to measure a modest number of truly significant skills properly than to do a shoddy job in measuring a shopping-cart full of skills.

Rule 2: *Make certain that all the rubric's evaluative criteria can be addressed instructionally.* This second rule calls for you always to "keep your instructional wits about you" when generating a rubric. Most important, you must scrutinize every potential evaluative criterion in a rubric to make sure you can actually teach students to master it.

This doesn't oblige you to adhere to any particular instructional approach. Regardless of whether you are wedded to the virtues of direct instruction, indirect instruction, constructivism, or any other instructional strategy, what you must be certain of is that students can be *taught* to employ appropriately *every* evaluative criterion used in the rubric.

Rule 3: *Employ as few evaluative criteria as possible.* Because people who start thinking seriously about a skill will often begin to recognize a host of nuances associated with the skill, they sometimes feel compelled to set forth a veritable litany of evaluative criteria. But for instructional purposes, as for many other missions, *less* is more groovy than *more*. Try to focus your instructional attention on three or four evaluative criteria; you'll become overwhelmed if you try to promote students' mastery of a dozen evaluative criteria.

Rule 4: *Provide a succinct label for each evaluative criterion.* The instructional yield of a skill-focused rubric can be increased simply by giving each evaluative criterion a brief explanatory label. For instance, suppose you were trying to improve your students' oral presentation skills. You might employ a skill-focused rubric for oral communication containing four evaluative criteria—*delivery, organization, content,* and *language.* These one-word, easy-to-remember labels will help remind you *and your students* of what's truly important in judging mastery of the skill being assessed.

Rule 5: *Match the length of the rubric to your own tolerance for detail.* During educators' earliest experiences with scoring rubrics, those evaluative schemes were typically employed for use with high-stakes statewide or districtwide assessments. Such detailed rubrics were often intended to constrain scorers so their scores would be in agreement. But as years went by, most educators discovered that many classroom teachers consider fairly long, rather detailed rubrics to be altogether off-putting. Whereas those teachers might be willing to create and/or use a one-page rubric, they regarded a six-page rubric as repugnant. More recently, therefore, we encounter recommendations for much shorter rubrics—rubrics that rarely exceed one or two pages. In the generation of useful rubrics, brevity wins.

Of course, not all teachers are put off by very detailed rubrics. Some teachers, in fact, find that abbreviated rubrics just don't do an adequate job for them. Such detail-prone teachers would rather work with rubrics that specifically spell out just what's involved when differentiating between quality levels regarding each evaluative criterion. A reasonable conclusion, then, is that rubrics should be built to match the level-of-detail preferences of the teachers involved. Teachers who believe in brevity should create brief rubrics, and teachers who believe in detail should create lengthier rubrics. If school districts (or publishers) are supplying rubrics to teachers, ideally both a short and a long version will be provided. Let teachers decide on the level of detail that best meshes with their own tolerance or need for detail.

So far, skill-focused rubrics have been touted in this chapter as the most useful for promoting students' mastery of really high-level skills. Such advocacy has been present because of the considerable instruction contributions that can be made by skill-focused rubrics. But here's a requisite caution. If you are employing a rubric that incorporates multiple evaluative criteria, beware of the ever-present temptation to sum those separate per-criterion scores to come up with one, big "overall" score. Only if the several evaluative criteria, when squished together, make interpretive or instructional sense should such scrunching be undertaken.

But please do not feel obliged to carve out a skill-focused rubric every time you find yourself needing a rubric. There will be occasions when your instruction is not aimed at high-level cognitive skills, but you still want your students to achieve what's being sought of them. To illustrate, you might want to determine your students' mastery of a recently enacted federal law—a law that will have a significant impact on how American citizens elect their legislators. Well, suppose you decide to employ a constructed-response testing strategy for assessing your students' understanding of this particular law. More specifically, you want your students to write an original, explanatory essay describing how certain of the law's components might substantially influence U.S. elections. Because, to evaluate your students' essays, you'll need some sort of scoring guide to assist you, what sort of rubric should you choose? Well, in that sort of situation, it is perfectly acceptable to employ a task-specific rubric rather than a skill-focused rubric. If there is no powerful, widely applicable cognitive skill being taught (and assessed), then the scoring can properly be focused on the given task involved, rather than on a more generally usable skill.

To supply a close-to-home example, each of the chapters in *Classroom Assessment* contains a constructed-response Outcome Mastery at the end of each chapter. Readers are asked to score their own responses by considering (1) an illustrative response to the Outcome Mastery's task and (2) several suggested evaluative criteria that could be used in a rubric to score a reader's response to the chapter's task. If you consider those per-chapter evaluative criteria as components of a possible rubric, you will discern that they will lead to a task-specific rubric rather than a skill-focused one. What's being sought here is your mastery of particular content in each chapter. Particularistic curricular targets will almost always lead to the use of task-specific rather than skill-focused rubrics. It is okay if they do.

Ratings and Observations

Once you've selected your evaluative criteria, you need to apply them reliably to the judgment of students' responses. If the nature of the performance-test task calls for students to create some sort of *product*, such as a written report of an experiment carried out in a biology class, then at your leisure you can rate the product's quality in relation to the criteria you've identified as important. For example, if you had decided on three criteria to use in evaluating students' reports of biology experiments, and could award from 0 to 4 points for each criterion, then you could leisurely assign from 0 to 12 points for each written report. The more clearly you understand what each evaluative criterion is, and what it means to award different numbers of points on whatever scale you've selected, the more accurate your scores will be. Performance tests that yield student products are definitely easier to rate, because you can rate students' responses when you're in the mood.

It is often the case with performance tests, however, that the student's performance takes the form of some kind of *behavior*. With such performance tests, it will usually be necessary for you to observe the behavior as it takes place. To illustrate, suppose that you are an elementary school teacher whose fifth-grade students have been carrying out fairly elaborate social studies projects culminating in 15-minute oral reports to classmates. Unless you have the equipment to videotape your students' oral presentations, you'll have to observe the oral reports and make judgments about the quality of a student's performance as it occurs. As was true when scores were given to student products, in making evaluative judgments about students' behavior, you will apply whatever criteria you've chosen and assign what you consider to be the appropriate number of points on the scales you are using.

For some observations, you'll find it sensible to make instant, on-the-spot quality judgments. For instance, if you are judging students' social studies reports on the basis of (1) content, (2) organization, and (3) presentation, you might make observation-based judgments on each of those three criteria as soon as a report is finished. In other cases, your observations might incorporate a delayed evaluative approach. For instance, let's say that you are working with students in a speech class on the elimination of "filler words and sounds," two of the most prominent of which are starting a sentence with "Well" and interjecting frequent "uh"s into a presentation. In the nonevaluative phase of the observation, you could simply count the number of "well"s and "uh"s uttered by a student. Then, at a later time, you could decide on a point allocation for the criterion "avoids filler words and sounds." Putting it another way, systematic observations may be set up so you make immediate or delayed allocations of points for the evaluative criteria you've chosen. If the evaluative criteria involve qualitative factors that must be appraised more judgmentally, then on-the-spot evaluations and point assignments are typically the way to go. If the evaluative criteria involve more quantitative factors, then a "count now and judge later" approach usually works better.

Sources of Error in Scoring Student Performances

When scoring student performances, there are three common sources of error that can contribute to inaccurate inferences. First, there is the *scoring scale*. Second, there are the *scorers* themselves, who may bring a number of bothersome biases to the enterprise. Finally, there are errors in the *scoring procedure*—that is, the process by which the scorers employ the scoring scale.

Scoring-Instrument Flaws

The major defect with most scoring instruments is the lack of descriptive rigor with which the evaluative criteria to be used are described. Given this lack of rigor, ambiguity exists in the interpretations that scorers make about what the scoring criteria mean. This typically leads to a set of unreliable ratings. For example, if teachers are to rate students on the extent to which students are "controlling," some teachers may view this as a positive quality and some may view it as a negative quality. Clearly, an inadequately clarified scoring form can lead to all sorts of "noise" in the scores provided by teachers.

Procedural Flaws

Among common problems with scoring students' responses to performance tests, we usually encounter demands on teachers to rate too many qualities. Overwhelmed scorers are scorers rendered ineffectual. Teachers who opt for a large number of evaluative criteria are teachers who have made a decisively inept opt. Care should be taken that no more than three or four evaluative criteria are to be employed in evaluations of students' responses to your performance assessments. Generally speaking, the fewer the evaluative criteria used, the better.

Teachers' Personal-Bias Errors

If you recall Chapter 5's consideration of assessment bias, you'll remember that bias is clearly an undesirable commodity. Teachers, albeit unintentionally, are frequently biased in the way they score students' responses. Several kinds of personal-bias errors are often encountered when teachers score students' constructed responses. The first of these, known as *generosity error*, occurs when a teacher's bias leads to higher ratings than are warranted. Teachers with a proclivity toward generosity errors see good even where no good exists.

At the other extreme, some teachers display *severity errors*. A severity error, of course, is a tendency to underrate the quality of a student's work. When a pupil's product deserves a "good," a teacher suffering from this personal-bias error will award it only an "average" or even a "below average."

But What Does This Have to Do with Teaching?

Teachers are busy people. (This profound recognition will not come as a surprise to anyone who really knows what a teacher's life is like.) But busy people who survive in their task-buffeted lives will typically try to manage their multiple responsibilities efficiently. Busy people who are teachers, therefore, need to make sure they don't expend their finite reservoir of energy unwisely. And that's where caution needs to be exercised with respect to the use of performance tests. Performance testing, you see, can be so very *seductive*.

Because performance tests are typically focused on measuring a student's mastery of real-world, significant skills, such tests are appealing. If you're an English teacher, for example, wouldn't you rather determine whether your students possess composition skills by having them whip out actual "written-from-scratch" compositions than by having them spot punctuation problems in multiple-choice items? Of course you would.

But although the allure of performance assessment is considerable, you should never forget that *it takes time!* And the time-consumption requirements of performance testing can readily eat into a teacher's daily 24-hour allotment. It takes time for teachers to come up with defensible tasks for performance tests, time to devise suitable rubrics for scoring students' responses, and, thereafter, time to score those responses. Performance assessment takes time. But, of course, proper performance testing not only helps teachers aim their instruction in the right directions; it also allows students to recognize the skill(s) being promoted.

So, the trick is to select judiciously the cognitive skills you will measure via performance tests. Focus on a small number of truly significant skills. You'll be more likely to maintain your instructional sanity if you employ only a handful of high-level performance tests. Too many performance tests can quickly put a teacher over the edge.

Another sort of personal-bias error is known as *central-tendency error*. This describes a tendency for teachers to view everything as being "in the middle of the scale." Very high or very low ratings are avoided by people who exhibit central-tendency error. They prefer the warm fuzziness of the mean or the median. They tend to regard midpoint ratings as inoffensive, and they therefore dispense midpoint ratings almost thoughtlessly.

A particularly frequent error arises when a teacher's overall impression of a student influences how the teacher rates that student with respect to an individual criterion. This error is known as the **halo effect**. If a teacher has a favorable attitude toward a student, that student will receive a host of positive ratings (deserved or not) on a number of individual criteria. Similarly, if a teacher has an unfavorable attitude toward a student, the student will receive a pile of negative ratings on all sorts of separate criteria. One nifty way to dodge the halo effect, if the teacher can pull it off, is to score responses anonymously whenever this is a practical possibility.

One way to minimize the halo effect, at least a bit, is occasionally to reverse the order of the high and low positions on the scoring scale so the teacher cannot *unthinkingly* toss out a whole string of positives (or negatives). What you really need to do to avoid halo effect when you're scoring students' responses is to remember it's always lurking in the wings. Try to score a student's responses on each evaluative criterion by using that specific criterion, not a contaminated general impression of the student's ability.

Thinking back to Chapter 5 and its treatment of educational fairness, please recognize that in the scoring of students' responses to any sort of student-generated product or behavior, teachers are tromping around in terrain that's just brimming with the potential for unfairness. These are instances in which teachers need to be especially on guard against unconsciously bringing their personal biases into the scoring of students' responses. Fairness is one of educational testing's big three requisites (along with reliability and validity). When evaluating students' performances, unfairness can frequently flower. One of the most straightforward ways of spotting fairness-flaws in your teacher-made tests is to mentally plop yourself into the test-taking seats of students who, because they are different (according to the subgroup label they carry), might be offended or unfairly penalized by what's in your test. If you spot some potential problems, then do *something* that you think has a reasonable chance of fixing the problem. In short, put your unfairness-detection machinery into overdrive, and then follow up this unfairness-detection effort with your best effort to fix it.

What Do Classroom Teachers Really Need to Know About Performance Assessment?

Performance assessment has been around for a long, long while. Yet, in recent years, a growing number of educators have become strong supporters of this form of assessment because it (1) represents an alternative to traditional paper-and-pencil tests and (2) is often more authentic—that is, more reflective of tasks people routinely need to perform in the real world. One of the things you need to understand about performance assessment is that it differs from more conventional assessment chiefly in the degree to which the assessment task matches the skills and/or knowledge about which you wish to make inferences. Because performance tasks often coincide more closely with high-level cognitive skills than do paper-and-pencil tests, more accurate interpretations can often be derived about students. Another big plus for performance tests is that they establish assessment targets that, because such targets often influence the teacher's instruction, can have a positive impact on instructional activities.

You need to realize, however, that because performance tasks require a fair chunk of time from students, the teacher is often faced with making rather shaky generalizations on the basis of relatively few student performances. It's also important for you to recognize that the development of defensible performance tests is difficult cerebral work. It takes rigorous thinking to identify suitable tasks for performance tests and then to isolate appropriate evaluative criteria and spell out the scoring scale for each criterion. And, of course, once the test and its associated scoring procedures are in place, you still have to score students' performances—an operation that invariably takes much more time than is required to score a ream of answers to selected-response items.

The chapter's final admonitions regarding the biases that teachers bring to the scoring of students' responses to performance tests should serve as a reminder. If you employ performance tests frequently in your classrooms, you'll need to be careful at every step of the process—from the original conception and birthing of a performance test down to the bias-free scoring of students' responses.

Parent Talk

The vice president of your school's Parent Advisory Council has asked you to tell him why so many of your school's teachers are now assessing students with performance tests instead of the more traditional paper-and-pencil tests.

| *If I were you, here's how I'd respond:*

"The reason why most of us are increasingly relying on performance tests these days is that performance tests almost always measure higher-level student skills. With traditional tests, too many of our teachers found that they were inadvertently assessing only the students' abilities to memorize facts.

"In recent years, educators have become far more capable of devising really *demanding* performance tests that require students to display genuinely high-level intellectual skills—skills that are way, way beyond memorization. We've learned how to develop the tests *and* how to score students' responses using carefully developed scoring rules that we refer to as *rubrics*.

"Please stop by my classroom and I'll show you some examples of these demanding performance tests. We're asking more from our students, and we're getting it."

| *Now, how would you respond to the vice president of the Parent Advisory Council?*

Chapter Summary

Although this chapter dealt specifically with performance assessment, a number of the points made in the chapter apply with equal force to the scoring of any type of constructed-response items such as those used in essay tests or short-answer tests. After defining performance tests as a measurement procedure in which students create original responses to an assessment task, it was pointed out that performance tests differ from more conventional tests primarily in the degree to which the test situation approximates the real-life situation to which inferences are made.

The identification of suitable tasks for performance assessments was given considerable attention in the chapter because unsuitable tasks will surely lead to unsatisfactory performance assessments. Seven evaluative criteria were supplied for performance test tasks: (1) generalizability, (2) authenticity, (3) multiple foci, (4) teachability, (5) fairness, (6) feasibility, and (7) scorability. Particular emphasis was given to selecting tasks about which defensible inferences could be drawn regarding students' generalized abilities to perform comparable tasks.

The significance of the skill to be assessed via a performance task was stressed. Next, *evaluative criteria* were defined as the factors by which the acceptability of a student's performance is judged. The evaluative criteria constitute the most important features of a *rubric* that's employed to score student responses. The significance of selecting suitable evaluative criteria was emphasized. Once the criteria have been identified, a numerical scoring scale, usually consisting of from 3 to 6 score points, is devised for each evaluative criterion. The evaluative criteria are applied to student performances in the form of ratings (for student products) or observations (for student behaviors).

Distinctions were drawn among *task-specific*, *hypergeneral*, and *skill-focused rubrics*. Deficits in the former two types of rubrics render them less appropriate for supporting a teacher's classroom instructional effort. A skill-focused rubric, however, can markedly enhance a teacher's instruction.

MyLab Education **Self-Check 8.1**

MyLab Education **Application Exercise 8.1: Performance Assessments**

References

Boyd-Batstone, P. (2007). *Anecdotal records assessment: An observational tool with a standards-based focus.* Norwood, MA: Christopher-Gordon.

Fitzpatrick, R., and Morrison, E. J. (1971). "Performance and product evaluation." In E. L. Thorndike (Ed.), *Educational Measurement* (pp. 237–270). Washington, DC: American Council on Education.

Glickman-Bond, J., and Rose, K. (2006). *Creating and using rubrics in today's classrooms: A practical guide.* Norwood, MA: Christopher-Gordon.

Marzano, R. J. (2008). *Vision document.* Bloomington, IN: Marzano Research Laboratory.

Waugh, C. K., and Gronlund, N. (2013). *Measurement and assessment in teaching* (10th ed.). Columbus, OH: Pearson.

Wormeli, R. (2008, September). "Show what you know," *Principal Leadership, 9,* no. 1: 48–52.

A Testing Takeaway

Performance Tests: Tension in the Assessment World*

W. James Popham, University of California, Los Angeles

Educators test their students to determine what those students know and can do. This simplified depiction of educational assessment captures the rationale for teachers' testing of their students. But, as is the case with most simplifications, often lurking within such no-frills explanations are issues of considerable complexity. In educational testing, one of these rarely discussed complexities is the appropriate use of *performance testing*. Let's briefly consider it.

Even though all educational tests require students to "perform" in some way, most conventional test items ask students to respond (on paper or computer) to stimuli presented by others. In contrast, the essential element of a *performance test* is that the test taker is required to construct an original response—either as a *process* that can be evaluated as it takes place (for example, an impromptu speech) or as a *product* (for instance, a bookend made in woodshop) that's subsequently evaluated.

A performance test typically *simulates* the criterion situation; that is, it approximates the real-world setting to which students must apply a skill. More conventional assessment, such as paper-and-pencil tests and computer-administered exams, are clearly limited in the degree to which they can approximate lifelike demands for students' skills. Let's turn, however, to an emerging conflict about performance testing.

The most prominent reason for advocating more widespread performance testing is that whatever is tested in our schools will almost certainly end up being taught in our classrooms. If we can more frequently measure students' mastery of a wide range of real-world skills, such as composing persuasive essays or organizing a monthly budget, then more skills related to such performance tests will surely be taught.

During recent decades educators were sometimes asked to increase their performance testing, but currently such demands seem to have slackened. Whatever the instructional dividends of performance tests, *they are expensive to score*. The more elaborate the performance test, the more expensive it is to train and supervise scorers. Even though computers can be "trained" to provide accurate scores for uncomplicated performance tasks, for the foreseeable future we must rely mainly on costly human scorers.

Hence the positives and negatives of such assessments:

- *Pro:* Performance tests can simulate real-world demands for school-taught skills.
- *Con:* Employing performance tests is both costly and time-consuming.

Because better performance testing leads to better taught students, do what you can to support funding for the wider use of performance tests. It's an educationally sensible investment.

Chapter 9
Portfolio Assessment

	Chief Chapter Outcome

An understanding not only of the distinctive relationship between measurement and instruction inherent in portfolio assessment, but also of the essentials of a seven-step process teachers can use to install portfolio assessment

"Assessment should be a part of instruction, not apart from it" is a point of view most proponents of portfolio assessment would enthusiastically endorse. Portfolio assessment, a contemporary entry in the educational measurement derby, has captured the attention of many educators because it represents a clear alternative to more traditional forms of educational testing.

A *portfolio* is a systematic collection of one's work. In education, portfolios consist of systematic collections of students' work. Although the application of portfolios in education has been a relatively recent phenomenon, portfolios have been widely used in a number of other fields for many years. Portfolios, in fact, constitute the chief method by which certain professionals display their skills and accomplishments. For example, portfolios are traditionally used for this purpose by photographers, artists, journalists, models, architects, and so on. Although many educators tend to think of portfolios as collections of written works featuring "words on paper," today's explosion of technological devices makes it possible for students to assemble their work in a variety of electronically retained forms, rather than as a sheaf of hand-written papers in a manila folder. An important feature of portfolios is that they must be updated as a person's achievements and skills grow.

Portfolios have been warmly embraced, in particular, by many educators who regard traditional assessment with little enthusiasm. In Table 9.1, for example, a chart presented by Tierney, Carter, and Desai (1991) indicates what those three proponents of portfolios believe are the differences between *portfolio assessment* and assessment based on standardized testing.

One of the settings in which portfolio assessment has been used with success is in the measurement of students with severe disabilities. Such youngsters sometimes encounter insuperable difficulties in displaying their capabilities via more routine sorts of testing. The strength of portfolio assessment, as might be expected, also turns out to be its weakness. As you will see in this chapter, the use

Table 9.1 Differences in Assessment Outcomes between Portfolios and Standardized Testing Practices

Portfolio	Testing
Represents the range of reading and writing students are engaged in	Assesses students across a limited range of reading and writing assignments that may not match what students do
Engages students in assessing their progress and/or accomplishments and establishing ongoing learning goals	Mechanically scored or scored by teachers who have little input
Measures each student's achievement, while allowing for individual differences between students	Assesses all students on the same dimensions
Represents a collaborative approach to assessment	Assessment process is not collaborative
Has a goal of student self-assessment	Student self-assessment is not a goal
Addresses improvement, effort, and achievement	Addresses achievement only
Links assessment and teaching to learning	Separates learning, testing, and teaching

Source: Material from *Portfolio Assessment in the Reading-Writing Classroom*, by Robert J. Tierney, Mark A. Carter, and Laura E. Desai, published by Christopher-Gordon Publishers, Inc. © 1991, used with permission of the publisher.

of portfolios as a measurement method allows teachers to particularize assessment approaches for different students. Such particularization, although it may work well in the case of an individual student, leads to different collections of evidence from different students, thus making accurate comparisons of different students' work—or one student's work over time—somewhat difficult.

Classroom Portfolio Assessment Versus Large-Scale Portfolio Assessment

Classroom Applications

Most advocates of portfolio assessment believe the real payoffs for such assessment approaches lie in the individual teacher's classroom, because the relationship between instruction and assessment will be strengthened as a consequence of students' continuing accumulation of work products in their portfolios. Ideally, teachers who adopt portfolios in their classrooms will make the ongoing collection and appraisal of students' work a central focus of the instructional program, rather than a peripheral activity whereby students occasionally gather up their work to convince a teacher's supervisors or students' parents that good things have been going on in class.

Here's a description of how an elementary teacher might use portfolios to assess students' progress in social studies, language arts, and mathematics. The teacher, let's call him Phil Pholio, asks students to keep three portfolios, one in each of those three subject fields. In each portfolio, the students are to place their early and revised work products. The work products are always dated so that

Mr. Pholio, as well as the students themselves, can see what kinds of differences in quality take place over time. For example, if effective instruction is being provided, there should be discernible improvement in the caliber of students' written compositions, solutions to mathematics problems, and analyses of social issues.

Three or four times per semester, Mr. Pholio holds a 15- to 20-minute portfolio conference with each student about the three different portfolios. The other, nonconferencing students take part in small-group and independent learning activities while the portfolio conferences are conducted. During a conference, the participating student plays an active role in evaluating his or her own work. Toward the close of the school year, students select from their regular portfolios a series of work products that not only represent their best final versions, but also indicate how those final products were created. These selections are placed in a display portfolio featured at a spring open-school session designed for parents. Parents who visit the school are urged to take their children's display portfolios home. Mr. Pholio also sends portfolios home to parents who are unable to attend the open-school event.

There are, of course, many other ways to use portfolios effectively in a classroom. Phil Pholio, our phictitious (sic) teacher, employed a fairly common approach, but a variety of alternative procedures could also work quite nicely. The major consideration is that the teacher uses portfolio *assessment* as an integral aspect of the *instructional* process. Because portfolios can be tailored to a specific student's evolving growth, the ongoing diagnostic value of portfolios for teachers is immense.

Who Is Evaluating Whom?

Roger Farr, a leader in language arts instruction and assessment, contends that the real payoff from proper portfolio assessment is that students' *self-evaluation* capabilities are enhanced. Thus, during portfolio conferences the teacher encourages students to come up with personal appraisals of their own work. The conference, then, becomes far more than merely an opportunity for the teacher to dispense an "oral report card." On the contrary, students' self-evaluation skills are nurtured not only during portfolio conferences, but also throughout the entire school year. For this reason, Farr strongly prefers the term *working portfolios* to the term *showcase portfolios* because he believes self-evaluation is nurtured more readily in connection with ongoing reviews of products not intended to impress external viewers.

For self-evaluation purposes, it is particularly useful to be able to compare earlier work with later work. Fortunately, even if a teacher's instruction is downright abysmal, students grow older and, as a consequence of maturation, tend to get better at what they do in school. If a student is required to review three versions of her or his written composition (a first draft, a second draft, and a final draft), self-evaluation can be fostered by encouraging the student to make comparative judgments of the three compositions based on a rubric featuring appropriate evaluative criteria. As anyone who has done much writing knows, written efforts tend to get better with time and revision. Contrasting later versions with earlier versions can prove illuminating from an appraisal perspective and, because students' self-evaluation is so critical to their future growth, from an instructional perspective as well.

Large-Scale Applications

It is one thing to use portfolios for classroom assessment; it is quite another to use portfolios for large-scale assessment programs. Several states and large school districts have attempted to install portfolios as a central component of a large-scale accountability assessment program—that is, an evaluation approach in which students' performances serve as an indicator of an educational system's effectiveness. To date, the results of efforts to employ portfolios for accountability purposes have not been encouraging.

In large-scale applications of portfolio assessments for accountability purposes, students' portfolios are judged either by the students' regular teachers or by a cadre of specially trained scorers (often teachers) who carry out the bulk of scoring at a central site. The problem with specially trained scorers and central-site scoring is that it typically costs much more than can be afforded. Some states, therefore, have opted to have all portfolios scored by students' own teachers, who then relay such scores to the state department. The problem with having regular teachers score students' portfolios, however, is that such scoring tends to be too unreliable for use in accountability programs. Not only have teachers usually not been provided with thorough training about how to score portfolios, but there is also a tendency for teachers to be biased in favor of their own students. To cope with such problems, sometimes teachers in a school or district evaluate their students' portfolios, but then a random sample of those portfolios are scored by state officials as an "audit" of the local scoring's accuracy.

One of the most visible of the statewide efforts to use portfolios on every pupil has been a performance-assessment program in the state of Vermont. Because substantial national attention has been focused on the Vermont program, and because it has been evaluated independently, many policymakers in other states have drawn on the experiences encountered in the Vermont Portfolio Assessment Program. Unfortunately, independent evaluators of Vermont's statewide efforts to use portfolios found that there was considerable unreliability in the appraisals given to students' work. And, if you recall the importance of reliability as discussed in Chapter 3, you know that it's tough to draw valid inferences about students' achievements if the assessments of those achievements are not yielding consistent results.

But, of course, this is a book about classroom assessment, not large-scale assessment. It certainly hasn't been shown definitely that portfolios do *not* have a place in large-scale assessment. What has been shown, however, is that there are significant obstacles to be surmounted if portfolio assessment is going to make a meaningful contribution to large-scale educational accountability testing.

Decision Time

Does Self-Evaluation Equal Self-Grading?

After a midsummer, schoolwide 3-day workshop on the Instructional Payoffs of Classroom Portfolios, the faculty at Rhoda Street Elementary School have agreed to install student portfolios in all classrooms for one or more subject areas. Maria Martinez, an experienced third-grade teacher in the school, has decided to try out portfolios only in mathematics. She admits to her family (but not to her fellow teachers) that she's not certain she'll be able to use portfolios properly with her students.

Because she has attempted to follow the guidelines of the National Council of Teachers of Mathematics, Maria stresses mathematical problem solving and the integration of mathematical understanding with content from other disciplines. Accordingly, she asks her students to place in their mathematics portfolios versions of their attempts to solve quantitative problems drawn from other subjects. Maria poses these problems for her third-graders and then instructs them to prepare an initial solution strategy and to revise that solution at least twice. Students are directed to put all solutions (dated) in their portfolios.

Six weeks after the start of school, Maria sets up a series of 15-minute portfolio conferences with her students. During the 3 days on which the portfolio conferences are held, students who are not involved in a conference move through a series of learning stations in other subject areas, where they typically engage in a fair amount of peer critiquing of each other's responses to various kinds of practice exercises.

Having learned during the summer workshop that the promotion of students' self-evaluation is critical if students are to get the most from portfolios, Maria devotes the bulk of her 15-minute conferences to students' personal appraisals of their own work. Although Maria offers some of her own appraisals of most students' work, she typically allows the student's self-evaluation to override her own estimates of a student's ability to solve each problem.

Because it will soon be time to give students their 10-week grades, Maria doesn't know whether to base the grades on her own judgments or on the students' self-appraisals.

If you were Maria, what would you decide to do?

Key Ingredients in Classroom Portfolio Assessment

Although there are numerous ways to install and sustain portfolios in a classroom, you will find that the following seven-step sequence provides a reasonable template for getting under way with portfolio assessment. Taken together, these seven activities capture the key ingredients in classroom-based portfolio assessment.

1. *Make sure your students "own" their portfolios.* In order for portfolios to represent a student's evolving work accurately, and to foster the kind of self-evaluation so crucial if portfolios are to be truly educational, students must perceive portfolios to be collections of their own work, and not merely temporary receptacles for products that their teacher ultimately grades. You

will probably want to introduce the notion of portfolio assessment to your students (assuming portfolio assessment isn't already a schoolwide operation and your students aren't already familiar with the use of portfolios) by explaining the distinctive functions of portfolios in the classroom.

2. *Decide what kinds of work samples to collect.* Various kinds of work samples can be included in a portfolio. Obviously, such products will vary from subject to subject. In general, a substantial variety of work products is preferable to a limited range of work products. However, for portfolios organized around students' mastery of a particularly limited curricular aim, it may be preferable to include only a single kind of work product. Ideally, you and your students can collaboratively determine what goes in the portfolio.

3. *Collect and store work samples.* Students need to collect the designated work samples as they are created, place them in a suitable container (a folder or notebook, for example), and then store the container in a file cabinet, storage box, or some other safe location. You may need to work individually with your students to help them decide whether particular products should be placed in their portfolios. The actual organization of a portfolio's contents depends, of course, on the nature of the work samples being collected. For instance, today's rapidly evolving technology will surely present a range of new options for creating electronic, digital portfolios.

4. *Select criteria by which to evaluate portfolio work samples.* Working collaboratively with students, carve out a set of criteria by which you and your students can judge the quality of your students' portfolio products. Because of the likely diversity of products in different students' portfolios, the identification of evaluative criteria will not be a simple task. Yet, unless at least rudimentary evaluative criteria are isolated, the students will find it difficult to evaluate their own efforts and, thereafter, to strive for improvement. The criteria, once selected, should be described with the same sort of clarity we saw in Chapter 8 regarding how to employ a rubric's evaluative criteria when judging students' responses to performance test tasks.

5. *Require students to evaluate their own portfolio products continually.* Using the agreed-on evaluative criteria, be sure your students routinely appraise their own work. Students can be directed to evaluate their work products holistically, analytically, or using a combination of both approaches. Such self-evaluation can be made routine by requiring each student to complete brief evaluation slips on 3×5 cards on which they identify the major strengths and weaknesses of a given product and then suggest how the product could be improved. Be sure to have your students date such self-evaluation sheets so they can keep track of modifications in their self-evaluation skills. Each completed self-evaluation sheet should be stapled or paper-clipped to the work product being evaluated. For digital portfolios, of course, comparable electronic actions would be undertaken.

6. *Schedule and conduct portfolio conferences.*   Portfolio conferences take time. Yet these interchange sessions between teachers and students regarding students' work are really pivotal in making sure portfolio assessment fulfills its potential. The conference should not only evaluate your students' work products but should also help them improve their self-evaluation abilities. Try to hold as many of these conferences as you can. In order to make the conferences time efficient, be sure to have students prepare for the conferences so you can start right in on the topics of most concern to you and the student.

7. *Involve parents in the portfolio-assessment process.*   Early in the school year, make sure your students' parents understand the nature of the portfolio-assessment process that you've devised for your classroom. Insofar as is practical, encourage your students' parents/guardians periodically to review their children's work samples, as well as their children's self-evaluation of those work samples. The more active parents become in reviewing their children's work, the stronger the message will be to the child that the portfolio activity is really worthwhile. If you wish, you may have students select their best work for a showcase portfolio or, instead, you may simply use the students' working portfolios.

These seven steps reflect only the most important activities that teachers might engage in when creating assessment programs in their classrooms. There are obviously all sorts of variations and embellishments possible.

There's one situation in which heavy student involvement in the portfolio process may not make instructional sense. This occurs in the early grades when, in the teacher's judgment, those little tykes are not developmentally ready to take a meaningful hand in a full-blown portfolio self-evaluation extravaganza. Any sort of educational assessment ought to be *developmentally appropriate* for the students who are being assessed. Thus, for students who are in early primary grades, a teacher may sensibly decide to employ only *showcase* portfolios to display a child's accomplishments to the child and the child's parents. *Working* portfolios, simply bristling with student-evaluated products, can be left for later. This is, clearly, a teacher's call.

Purposeful Portfolios

There are numerous choice-points you'll encounter if you embark on a portfolio assessment approach in your own classroom. The first one ought to revolve around *purpose*. Why is it that you are contemplating a meaningful prance down the portfolio pathway?

Assessment specialists typically identify three chief purposes for portfolio assessment. The first of these is *documentation of student progress*, wherein the major function of the assembled work samples is to provide the student, the teacher, and the student's parents with evidence about the student's growth—or lack of it. Such *working* portfolios provide meaningful opportunities for self-evaluation by students.

Pointing out that students' achievement levels ought to influence teachers' instructional decisions, Anderson (2003) concludes that "the information should be collected as near to the decision as possible (e.g., final examinations are administered in close proximity to end-of-term grades). However, if decisions are to be based on learning, then a plan for information collection over time must be developed and implemented" (p. 44). The more current any documentation of students' progress is, the more accurate such documentation is apt to be.

From an *instructional* perspective, the really special advantage of portfolio assessment is that its recurrent assessment of the student's status with respect to mastery of one or more demanding skills provides both teachers and students with assessment-informed opportunities to make any needed adjustments in what they are currently doing. Later in Chapter 12, we will be considering the instructional dividends of the formative-assessment process. Because of its recurring assessment of students' evolving mastery of skills, portfolio assessment practically forces teachers to engage in a classroom instructional process closely resembling formative assessment.

A second purpose of portfolios is to provide an opportunity for *showcasing student accomplishments*. Stiggins (2007) describes portfolios that showcase students' best work as *celebration portfolios*, and he contends that celebration portfolios are especially appropriate for the early grades. In portfolios intended to showcase student accomplishments, students typically select their best work and reflect thoughtfully on its quality.

One teacher in the Midwest always makes sure students include the following elements in their showcase portfolios:

- A letter of introduction to portfolio reviewers
- A table of contents
- Identification of the skills or knowledge being demonstrated
- A representative sample of the student's best work
- Dates on all entries
- The evaluative criteria (or rubric) being used
- The student's self-reflection on all entries

Student self-reflections about the entries in portfolios is a pivotal ingredient in showcase portfolios. Some portfolio proponents contend that a portfolio's self-evaluation by the student helps the learner learn better and permits the reader of the portfolio to gain insights about how the learner learns.

A final purpose for portfolios is *evaluation of student status*—that is, the determination of whether students have met previously determined quality levels of performance. McMillan (2013) points out that when portfolios are used for this purpose, there must be greater standardization about what should be included in a portfolio and how the work samples should be appraised. Typically, teachers select the entries for this kind of portfolio, and considerable attention is given to scoring, so that any rubrics employed to score the portfolios will yield consistent results even if different scorers are involved. For portfolios being used to evaluate student status, there is usually less need for self-evaluation of entries—unless such self-evaluations are themselves being evaluated by others.

Well, we've peeked at three purposes underlying portfolio assessment. Can one portfolio perform all three functions? Many teachers who have used portfolios will supply a somewhat shaky *yes*. But if you were to ask those teachers whether one portfolio can perform all three functions *well*, you ought to get a rock-solid *no*. The three functions, though somewhat related—rather like second cousins—are fundamentally different.

That's why your very first decision, if you're going to install portfolios in your classroom, is to decide on the *primary purpose* of the portfolios. You can then determine what the portfolios should look like and how students should prepare them.

Scripture tells us that "no man can serve two masters." (The authors of that scriptural advice, clearly insensitive to gender equality, were not implying that females are more capable of double-master serving.) Similarly, one kind of portfolio cannot blithely satisfy multiple functions. Some classroom teachers rush into portfolio assessment because they've heard about all of the enthralling things that portfolios can do. But one kind of portfolio cannot easily fulfill all three functions. Pick your top-priority purpose and then build your portfolio assessment to satisfy this purpose.

Work-Sample Selection

For a teacher just joining the portfolio party, another key decision hinges on identifying the work samples to be put into the portfolios. All too often, teachers who are novices at portfolio assessment will fail to think divergently enough about the kinds of entries that should constitute a portfolio's chief contents.

But divergency is not necessarily a virtue when it comes to the determination of a portfolio's contents. You shouldn't search for varied kinds of work samples simply for the sake of variety. What's important is that the particular kinds of work samples to be included in the portfolio will allow you to derive valid inferences about the skills and/or knowledge you're trying to have your students master. It's far better to include a few kinds of *inference-illuminating* work samples than to include a galaxy of work samples, many of which do not contribute to your interpretations regarding students' knowledge or skills.

Remember, as you saw earlier in this text, that decent educational assessment requires that the assessment procedure being employed must exhibit validity, reliability, and fairness. The need to satisfy this trio of measurement criteria does not disappear into the ether when portfolio assessment is adopted. Yes, you still need evidence of valid assessment-based interpretations for the portfolio assessment's intended use. Yes, you still need evidence that your chosen assessment technique yields reliable scores. And yes, you still need evidence attesting to the fundamental fairness of your portfolio assessment.

One of the most common shortcomings of teachers who, for the first time, hop into the deep end of the portfolio-assessment pool is the tendency for teachers to let students' raw "smarts" or family affluence rule the day. That is, if the teacher has not done a crackerjack job in clarifying the evaluative criteria by which to evaluate students' efforts, then when portfolios are created and subsequently evaluated, students who inherited jolly good cerebral genes or whose families are more affluent will be seen to be the winners. Putting it differently, the danger is that students' portfolios will be evaluated dominantly by what students are bringing to the instructional situation, not by what they gain from it. To guard against this understandable bias—after all, what sensible teacher does not groove on good-looking and content-loaded portfolios—it is often useful for the teacher to adopt a mental trio of review "lenses" through which to consider a student's evolving and, finally, completed portfolio. As always, try to focus on all three of the sanctioned facets of educational testing: validity, reliability, and fairness. With this assessment trinity constantly in your mind, odds are that you can spot, and then jettison, instances of portfolio invalidity, unreliability, and unfairness.

Because of the atypicality of portfolio assessment, however, coming up with such evidence is often more challenging than when relying on more conventional sorts of tests. Challenging or not, however, the "big three" still apply to portfolio assessment with their customary force. For a portfolio assessment system to have the desired punch, it must be accompanied by meaningful evidence bearing on its validity, reliability, and fairness.

Appraising Portfolios

As indicated earlier in the chapter, students' portfolios are almost always evaluated by the use of a rubric. The most important ingredients of such a rubric are its evaluative criteria—that is, the factors to be used in determining the quality of a particular student's portfolio. If there's any sort of student self-evaluation to be done, and such self-evaluation is almost always desirable, then it is imperative that students have access to, and thoroughly understand, the rubric that will be used to evaluate their portfolios.

As you'll see when we treat formative assessment in Chapter 12, for certain applications of formative assessment, students must definitely understand the rubrics (and those rubrics' evaluative criteria). However, for *all* forms of portfolio assessment, students' familiarity with rubrics is imperative.

Here's one quick-and-dirty way to appraise any sort of portfolio assessments you might install in your classroom. Simply ask yourself whether your students' portfolios have substantially increased the accuracy of the inferences you make regarding your students' skills and knowledge. If your answer is *yes*, then portfolio assessment is a winner for you. If your answer is *no*, then pitch those portfolios without delay—or guilt. But wait! If your answer resembles "I'm not sure," then you really need to think this issue through rigorously and, quite possibly, collect more evidence bearing on the accuracy of portfolio-based inferences. Classroom assessment is supposed to contribute to more valid inferences from which better instructional decisions can be made. If your portfolio assessment program isn't *clearly* doing those things, you may need to make some serious changes in that program.

The Pros and Cons of Portfolio Assessment

You must keep in mind that portfolio assessment's greatest strength is that it can be tailored to the individual student's needs, interests, and abilities. Yet, portfolio assessment suffers from the drawback faced by all constructed-response measurement. Students' constructed responses are genuinely difficult to evaluate, particularly when those responses vary from student to student.

As was seen in Vermont's Portfolio Assessment Program, it is quite difficult to come up with consistent evaluations of different students' portfolios. Sometimes the scoring guides devised for use in evaluating portfolios are so terse and so general as to be almost useless. They're akin to Rorschach inkblots, in which different scorers see in the scoring guide what they want to see. In contrast, some scoring guides are so detailed and complicated that they simply overwhelm scorers. It is difficult to devise scoring guides that embody just the right level of specificity. Generally speaking, most teachers are so busy they don't have time to create elaborate scoring schemes. Accordingly, many teachers (and students) find themselves judging portfolios by using fairly loose evaluative criteria. Such criteria tend to be interpreted differently by different people.

Another problem with portfolio assessment is it takes time—loads of time—to carry out properly. Even if you're very efficient in reviewing your students' portfolios, you'll still have to devote many hours both in class (during portfolio conferences) and outside of class (if you also want to review your students' portfolios by yourself). Proponents of portfolios are convinced that the quality of portfolio assessment is worth the time such assessment takes. You at least need to be prepared for the required investment of time if you decide to undertake portfolio assessment. And teachers will definitely need to receive sufficient training to learn how to carry out portfolio assessment well. Any teachers who set out to do portfolio assessment by simply stuffing student stuff into containers built for stuff stuffing will end up wasting their time and their students' time. Meaningful professional development is a must whenever portfolio assessment is to work well. If several teachers in a school will be using portfolio assessment in their classes, this would be a marvelous opportunity to establish a *teacher learning community* in which, on a continuing basis during the year, portfolio-using teachers meet to share insights and work collaboratively on common problems.

But What Does This Have to Do with Teaching?

Portfolio assessment almost always fundamentally changes a teacher's approach to instruction. A nifty little selected-response test, or even a lengthy constructed-response exam, can usually be incorporated into a teacher's ongoing instructional program without significantly altering how the teacher goes about teaching. But that's not so with portfolio assessment. Once a teacher hops aboard the portfolio bus, there's a long and serious ride in the offing.

Portfolio assessment, if it's properly focused on helping children improve by evaluating their own work samples, becomes a continuing and *central* component of a teacher's instructional program. Work samples have to be chosen, scoring rubrics need to be developed, and students need to be taught how to use those rubrics to monitor the evolving quality of their efforts. Portfolio assessment, therefore, truly dominates most instructional programs in which it is employed.

The first thing you need to do is decide whether the knowledge and skills you are trying to have your students master (especially the skills) lend themselves to portfolio assessment.

Will there be student work samples that, because they permit you to make accurate interpretations about your students' evolving skill mastery, could provide the continuing focus for portfolio assessment?

Some content lends itself delightfully to portfolio assessment. Some doesn't. During my first year as a high school teacher, I taught two English courses and a speech class. Because my English courses focused on the promotion of students' composition skills, I think that a portfolio assessment might have worked well in either English course. My students and I could have monitored their improvements in being able to write.

But I don't think I could have used portfolios effectively in my speech class. At that time, television itself had just arrived on the West Coast, and videotaping was unknown. Accordingly, my speech students and I wouldn't have had anything to toss into their portfolios.

The first big question you need to ask yourself, when it comes to portfolio assessment, is quite simple: Is this powerful but time-consuming form of assessment suitable for what I'm trying to teach?

On the plus side, however, most teachers who have used portfolios agree that portfolio assessment provides a way of documenting and evaluating growth happening in a classroom in ways standardized or written tests cannot. Portfolios have the potential to create authentic portraits of what students learn. Stiggins (2007) contends that for portfolios to merge effectively with instruction, they must have a story to tell. Fortunately, this story can be made compatible with improved student learning.

If you speak with many of the teachers who use portfolio assessments, you'll often find that they are primarily enamored of two of its payoffs. They believe that the *self-evaluation* it fosters in students is truly important in guiding students' learning over time. They also think the *personal ownership* that students experience regarding their own work, and the progress they experience, makes the benefits of portfolio assessment outweigh its costs.

What Do Classroom Teachers Really Need to Know About Portfolio Assessment?

As noted at the beginning of this four-chapter excursion into item types, the more familiar you are with different kinds of test items, the more likely you will be to select an item type that best provides you with the information you need in order to draw suitable inferences about your students. Until recently, portfolios haven't been viewed as a viable assessment option by many teachers. These days, however, portfolio assessment clearly is a legitimate weapon in a teacher's assessment arsenal. And, as noted earlier in the chapter, portfolio assessment appears to be particularly applicable to the assessment of students with severe disabilities.

You need to realize that if portfolio assessment is going to constitute a helpful adjunct to your instructional program, portfolios will have to become a central, not a tangential, part of what goes on in your classroom. The primary premise in portfolio assessment is that a particularized collection of a student's *evolving* work will allow both the student and you to determine the student's progress. You can't gauge the student's progress if you don't have frequent evidence of the student's efforts.

It would be educationally unwise to select portfolio assessment as a one-time measurement approach to deal with a short-term instructional objective. Rather, it makes more sense to select some key curricular aim, such as the student's ability to write original compositions, and then monitor this aspect of the student's learning throughout the entire school year. It is also important to remember that although portfolio assessment may prove highly valuable for classroom instruction and measurement purposes, at this juncture there is insufficient evidence that it can be used appropriately for large-scale assessment.

A number of portfolio-assessment specialists believe that the most important dividend from portfolio assessment is the increased ability of students to evaluate their own work. If this becomes one of your goals in a portfolio-assessment approach, you must be certain to nurture such self-evaluation growth deliberately via portfolios, instead of simply using portfolios as convenient collections of work samples.

The seven key ingredients in portfolio assessment that were identified in the chapter represent only one way of installing this kind of assessment strategy. Variations of those seven suggested procedures are not only possible but also to be encouraged. The big thing to keep in mind is that portfolio assessment offers your students and you a way to particularize your evaluation of each student's growth over time. And, speaking of time, it's only appropriate to remind you that it takes substantially more time to use a portfolio-assessment approach properly than to score a zillion true–false tests. If you opt to try portfolio assessment, you'll have to see whether, *in your own instructional situation*, it yields sufficient educational benefits to be worth the investment you'll surely need to make in it.

Parent Talk

Suppose that Mr. and Mrs. Holmgren, parents of your student, Harry, stopped by your classroom during a back-to-school night to examine their son's portfolio. After spending almost 30 minutes going through the portfolio and skimming the portfolios of several other students, they speak to you—not with hostility, but with genuine confusion. Mrs. Holmgren sums up their concerns nicely with the following comments: "When we stopped by Mr. Bray's classroom earlier this evening to see how our daughter, Elissa, is doing, we encountered a series of extremely impressive portfolios. Elissa's was outstanding. To be honest, Harry's portfolio is a lot less polished. It seems that he's included everything he's done in your class, rough drafts as well as final products. Why is there this difference?"

If I were you, here's how I'd respond to Harry's parents:

"It's really good that you two could take the time to see how Harry and Elissa are doing. And I can understand why you're perplexed by the differences between Elissa's and Harry's portfolios. You see, there are *different* kinds of student portfolios, and different portfolios serve different purposes.

"In Mr. Bray's class, and I know this because we often exchange portfolio tips with one another during regular meetings of our teacher learning community, students prepare what are called *showcase* portfolios. In such portfolios, students pick their very best work to show Mr. Bray and their parents what they've learned. I think Mr. Bray actually sent his students' showcase portfolios home about a month ago so you could see how well Elissa is doing. For Mr. Bray and his students, the portfolios are collections of best work that, in a very real sense, celebrate students' achievements.

"In my class, however, students create *working* portfolios in which the real emphasis is on getting students to make progress and to evaluate this progress *on their own*. When you reviewed Harry's portfolio, did you see how each entry is dated and how he had prepared a brief self-reflection of each entry? I'm more interested in Harry's seeing the improvement he makes than in anyone seeing just polished final products. You, too, can see the striking progress he's made over the course of this school year.

"I'm not suggesting that my kind of portfolio is better than Mr. Bray's. Both have a role to play. Those roles, as I'm sure you'll see, are quite different."

Now, how would you respond to Mr. and Mrs. Holmgren?

Chapter Summary

After defining portfolios as systematic collections of students' work, contrasts were drawn between portfolio assessment and more conventional testing. It was suggested that portfolio assessment is far more appropriate for an individual teacher's classroom assessment than for large-scale accountability assessments.

An emphasis on self-assessment was suggested as being highly appropriate for portfolio assessment, particularly in view of the way portfolios can be tailored to an *individual* student's evolving progress. Seven steps were then suggested as key ingredients for classroom teachers to install and sustain portfolio assessment in their classroom: (1) establish student ownership, (2) decide what work samples to collect, (3) collect and score work samples, (4) select evaluative criteria, (5) require continual student self-evaluations, (6) schedule and conduct portfolio conferences, and (7) involve parents in the portfolio-assessment process.

Three different functions of portfolio assessment were identified—namely, documentation of student progress, showcasing of student accomplishments, and evaluation of student status.

Teachers were urged to select a primary purpose for portfolio assessment.

The chapter concluded with an identification of plusses and minuses of portfolio assessment. It was emphasized that portfolio assessment represents an important measurement strategy now available to today's classroom teachers.

MyLab Education Self-Check 9.1

MyLab Education Application Exercise 9.1: **Portfolio Assessments**

References

Anderson, L. W. (2003). *Classroom assessment: Enhancing the quality of teacher decision making.* Mahwah, NJ: Erlbaum.

Andrade, H. (2007/2008). "Self-assessment through rubrics," *Educational Leadership, 65,* no. 4 (December/January): 60–63.

McMillan, J. H. (2013). *Classroom assessment: Principles and practice for effective standards-based instruction* (6th ed.). Boston: Allyn and Bacon.

Miller, M. D., and Linn, R. (2012). *Measurement and assessment in teaching* (11th ed.). Columbus, OH: Pearson.

Stiggins, R. J. (2007). *Student-involved classroom assessment for learning* (5th ed.). Upper Saddle River, NJ: Prentice-Hall.

Stiggins, R. J., and Chappuis, J. (2011). *An introduction to student-involved classroom assessment for learning* (6th ed.). Boston: Pearson.

Tierney, R. J., Carter, M. A., and Desai, L. E. (1991). *Portfolio assessment in the reading-writing classroom.* Norwood, MA: Christopher-Gordon.

Portfolio Assessment: Finding a Sustainable Focus*

W. James Popham, University of California, Los Angeles

A portfolio is a systematic collection of one's work. In education, portfolios are systematic collections of a student's work products—and *portfolio assessment* is the appraisal of a students' evolving skills based on those collected products. Although a few states have attempted to use portfolio assessment in a statewide accountability system, the inability to arrive at sufficiently reliable scores for students' work products has led to portfolio assessment's being used almost exclusively at the classroom level.

Classroom portfolio assessment takes time and energy, both from the teacher and from the teacher's students. Everyone can get worn out making classroom portfolio assessment work. Yet classroom portfolio assessment can promote genuinely important learning outcomes for students. Accordingly, the challenge is to select a *sustainable* structure for classroom portfolio assessment.

Teachers who report the most success when employing portfolio assessment in their classrooms often focus their instructional efforts on enhancing their students' *self-evaluation* abilities. Depending on the skill(s) being promoted, a long-term collection of a student's evolving work products typically emerges—and those products can then be subjected to a *student's* use of whatever evaluative system has been adopted. Over time, then, and with suitable guidance from the teacher, students' self-evaluation skills are often seriously sharpened.

One of the most common targets for portfolio assessment is the improvement of students' composition skills. Although portfolio assessment can be used in many other content arenas, let's use composition as an example.

Early on, after the teacher explains the structure of the portfolio-evaluation system, the teacher describes the *rubric*—that is, the scoring guide to be employed in evaluating students' compositions. Scrutiny of the rubric allows students to become conversant with the criteria to be used as they *evaluate their own compositions*. Thereafter, at designated intervals, portfolio conferences are scheduled between each student and the teacher. These conferences are frequently led by students in evaluating their portfolio's work products.

Many teachers who employ this approach to portfolio assessment report meaningful success in promoting their students' self-evaluation skills. Yet some teachers who have attempted to use portfolio assessment have abandoned the process simply *because it takes too much time*. It is the teacher's challenge, then, to devise a way to assess portfolios that is truly sustainable, year after year, so the substantial dividends of portfolio assessment can be achieved while, at the same time, maintaining the teacher's sanity.

Chapter 10
Affective Assessment

Learning Outcomes

10.1 Determine the characteristics of affective assessment that result in teachers' ability to draw inferences about their students' affect.

⌄	Chief Chapter Outcome

An understanding of the potential instructional dividends of affective assessment and what's necessary for teachers to draw valid inferences about their students' affect—namely, the use of anonymity-cloaked self-report inventories leading to inferences about groups of students, not individuals

Affective variables, most educators concede, are important. Students' attitudes toward learning, for example, play a major role in how much learning those students subsequently pursue. The values students have regarding truthfulness and integrity shape their daily conduct. And students' self-esteem, of course, influences almost everything they do. There's little doubt that the affective status of students should concern all educators.

In truth, however, few classroom teachers give explicit attention to influencing their students' attitudes and values. Even fewer classroom teachers truly try to assess the affective status of their students. Certainly, a teacher may observe a student's sour demeanor and conclude that he's "out of sorts" or she's "a mite depressed," but how many times have you heard about a teacher who tried to gather *systematic* evidence regarding students' attitudes and interests? Unfortunately, systematic assessment of affect is quite uncommon.

This chapter will address the issue of affective assessment by providing you with general insights regarding the assessment of students' attitudes, interests, and values. Thereafter, the chapter will give you some practical, step-by-step procedures for gauging students' status regarding several educationally important affective variables.

Why Assess Affect?

One question you might be asking yourself is, why assess attitudes at all? Many teachers, particularly those who teach older students, believe that their only educational mission is to increase students' knowledge and skills. Affect, such teachers believe, simply doesn't fall into their proper sphere of influence. However, students who learn to perform mathematics like magicians, yet abhor mathematics, certainly aren't apt to apply the mathematics they've learned. Students who can compose outstanding essays, but believe they are "really rotten writers," typically won't spend much time eagerly churning out essays.

The Importance of Affect

I'd like to get my own bias regarding this issue out on the table so you don't think I'm trying to subliminally influence you. I believe affective variables are often more significant than cognitive variables. How many times, for example, have you seen people who weren't all that intellectually "gifted," yet still succeed because they were highly motivated and hard-working? Conversely, how many times have you seen truly able people simply veer away from challenges because they did not consider themselves worthy? Day in and day out, we see the enormous impact that people's affective status has on them. Affect is every bit as important as cognitive ability.

Have you ever seen a group of kindergarten students troop off to school loaded with enthusiasm and gumption, only to encounter those same students a few years later and see that a fair number were disenchanted with school and down on themselves? Well, I have. And what's going on with such children is surely taking place in the affective realm. When most kindergartners start school, they are excited about school and confident. However, after failing to be successful for a year or two, many of those formerly upbeat children carry around decisively lower self-concepts. They've tried and been found wanting. Such negative attitudes about self and school typically influence the entirety of a child's subsequent education. Yet, because few teachers try to assess their students' affective status, most teachers don't know what their students' attitudes, interests, and values really are. This situation needs to change.

Spurring Affectively Focused Instruction

Even if there were no such thing as externally imposed "educational accountability" whereby students' performances on high-stakes tests serve as indicators of educational effectiveness, what's on achievement tests would still influence the stuff teachers teach. When I was a high school teacher, I knew what kinds of items I had on my final exams. (That is, I knew in the second year of teaching, after I'd whipped out my first-year final exams only minutes before my students needed to take those exams.) Because I wanted my students to do well on my final exams, I made reasonably sure I spent at least some instructional time on the content covered by the final examinations.

It's the same with affective assessment. Let's say you've installed a straightforward pretest–posttest evaluation design to assess changes in your students' responses to an affective inventory regarding whether they are *interested* in the subject(s) you're teaching. Your recognition that there is to be a formal

Decision Time

Where Went Wonder?

Lance Larson has decided to try to get an accurate reading of his kindergarten students' attitudes toward school. Although he has worked with kindergartners for the past 4 years, only recently has Lance become convinced of the importance of student affect.

Because he is dealing with very young children, most of whom can't read when they arrive at Mission Elementary School, Lance uses an orally administered, anonymously completed inventory for which he reads a question aloud to the students and they are to respond by circling either a smiling face or a frowning face. Students respond to one question, and then another, after Lance tells them to "Answer next to the bird," "Answer by the star," and so on.

At the end of the first week of school, students' responses to Lance's inventory indicated that they really liked school. In fact, 100 percent of the children responded that they couldn't wait to find out what new things they would learn at school each day! However, 3 months later, a re-administration of the same inventory showed that students' attitudes toward school seemed to have taken a gnarly nosedive. Well over half of his kindergartners indicated that they no longer looked forward to coming to school. Almost 75 percent, in fact, indicated that they were often bored in class. Lance was alarmed.

If you were Lance, what would you decide to do?

pretest–posttest assessment of students' subject-matter interest will, as surely as school buses run late, influence you to provide instruction so your students become more positive about the subject(s) you're teaching.

In other words, the presence of affective postinstruction measurement will incline you to include affectively focused activities in your instruction. In a sense, you're saying to yourself—and anyone else you care to have understand your instructional planning—that affective outcomes are important enough for you to formally assess them. You can be assured that what's important enough to be assessed, even if it's measured in your classroom and nowhere else in the world, is likely to influence your instruction.

It has been said that *we measure what we treasure*. Well, if we really think affective outcomes are worth promoting, we darn well ought to measure them.

Monitoring Students' Status

In addition to serving as an end-of-instruction target, affective-assessment devices, if administered regularly, help teachers determine whether modifications in their instructional program are warranted. For example, let's say you're a physics teacher and you want to get a fix on how enthused your students are about continuing their study of physics when they are in college. Ideally, you'd like a fair number of your students to get mildly ecstatic over the raptures of future physics coursework. Suppose that each month you employ a brief self-report attitudinal inventory focused on the likelihood of students' pursuing future physics instruction. For illustrative purposes, let's assume that in September, 60 percent of your students registered an interest in taking college physics courses and that in October, about 65 percent indicated such an interest. In November, however, interest in future physics courses plummeted and only 25 percent of your students signified any interest in college physics. This is a clear message to you that something went on in late October or early November to really turn off your budding Nobel laureates. A review of your instructional program during that period and some serious effort on your part to generate more interest in postsecondary physics would seem warranted. As you can see, periodic monitoring of your students' affective status can help you determine what sorts of shifts in your instructional program might be needed.

In review, there are several reasons why classroom teachers should devote at least a segment of their assessment program to the measurement of students' affect. If you don't believe your students' attitudes, interests, and values are important, of course, you'll not agree. But if you do think student affect is significant, you'll want to learn what kinds of affective variables to assess and how to assess them. That's coming up shortly.

The Other Side of the Argument

Before turning to the nuts and bolts of affective assessment, it should be noted that not all citizens share my view regarding the importance of affective assessment and instruction. Particularly during the past decade or so, we have seen the emergence of vocal individuals who have taken strong positions against public schools' offering anything other than traditional academic (cognitive) education. Usually representing religious or conservative constituencies, these critics have argued that it is the job of the family and church to promote values in children and that any attempt by the schools to systematically modify students' attitudes or values should cease.

Most proponents of affectively focused instruction and assessment agree with these critics that if any attention to affective outcomes is to be given, it must be focused only on those affective consequences that would be close to universally approved. For example, the promotion of students' positive attitudes toward learning is an affective aspiration that almost everyone would support. Similarly, there are not many people who wouldn't want the schools to nurture students' self-esteem. Yet most citizens would hate to see public school educators dabbling with any controversial attitudes or values—those that a vast majority of parents wouldn't want their children to possess.

If you decide to devote some of your classroom assessment and instruction time to affective targets, you'll clearly need to consider carefully the legitimacy of the targets you select. And even if you do so, you should recognize that there will be some people who may disapprove of such affective education, regardless of the care with which you select your affective curricular aims. Thus, if you tread the affective trail, prepare yourself to defend the legitimacy of your curricular choices.

Which Affective Variables Should Be Assessed?

A Closer Look at Affect

Before discussing the sorts of variables that you, as a classroom teacher, might wish to assess, let's spend just a moment looking at the nature of *affect* itself. The reason why such affective variables as students' attitudes, interests, and values are important to us is that those variables typically influence students' future behavior. The chief reason why we want to promote positive attitudes toward learning is that students who have positive attitudes toward learning today will be inclined to pursue learning in the future.

The affective status of students lets us see how students are predisposed to behave subsequently. If we find that students believe healthy bodies are important, those students will be predisposed to maintain their own bodily health in the future. If we find that students have positive attitudes toward persons from other ethnic groups, then in the future such students will be predisposed to behave appropriately toward persons from other ethnic groups. As seen in Figure 10.1, current affective status predicts future behavior.

Do attitudes predict future behavior perfectly? Of course not. But suppose there are 100 third-graders who display very negative attitudes toward violence as a way of settling disputes, and there are 100 third-graders who believe violence is an altogether suitable way of resolving disputes. In the future, there will probably be fewer violent dispute-resolution behaviors from the first group of 100 third-graders than from the second. Affective assessment, therefore, allows teachers to get a far better fix on the future behavioral dispositions of their students than they could achieve without affective assessment. That's why affective assessment is so important.

As you know, schools have historically focused on cognitive variables. And that's probably the way it's always going to be. Thus, if you are interested in giving some attention to affect in your own classroom, you'll need to select your affective foci judiciously. That's what we'll deal with next. We'll look at attitudes first and then consider interests and values.

Figure 10.1 The Relationship between Current Affect and Future Behavior Wherein an Individual's Affective Status Predicts That Individual's Future Behavior

Potential Attitudinal Targets

There are all sorts of possible attitudinal targets for a teacher's instruction. Here are a few of the attitudes most commonly endorsed by teachers as reasonable attitudinal targets:

- *Positive attitudes toward learning.*   Students should regard the act of learning positively. Students who are positive today about learning will tend to be tomorrow's learners.

- *Positive attitudes toward self.*   Self-esteem is the attitude on which most people's personal worlds turn. Although children's self-esteem is probably influenced more by parents and nonschool events than by teachers, what happens in the classroom can have a significant impact on children's self-esteem.

- *Positive attitudes toward self as a learner.*   Self-esteem as a learner is an affective variable over which educators have substantial influence. If students believe they are capable of learning, they typically tend to learn.

- *Appropriate attitudes toward those who differ from us.*   The more tolerant and accepting students are toward members of other ethnic, gender, national, racial, or religious groups, the more likely those students will behave properly toward such individuals in the future.

There are numerous other subject-specific kinds of attitudes that teachers will want to foster. For example, many teachers who deal with language arts will want to enhance students' heightened confidence as writers—that is, students' more positive attitudes toward their own composition capabilities. Science teachers will want to foster their students' curiosity. Health education teachers will wish to promote students' accurate perceptions of their vulnerability to health risks such as sexually transmitted diseases. Depending on your own instructional responsibilities, you'll discover there are usually several attitudinal assessment contenders you'll want to consider.

Potential Interest Targets

Students' interests represent another set of potential targets. Clearly, if you're a high school chemistry teacher, you'd like at least some of your students to develop an interest in chemistry. Similarly, teachers of U.S. government would prefer that their students become interested in governmental affairs rather than regarding such topics as repugnant. Here, then, are a few illustrations of the kinds of interest targets teachers might consider for possible assessment:

- *Subject-related interests.*   Students should regard the subject matter taught (for example, mathematics) as more interesting at the end of instruction than they did when instruction began. At the very least, students should be no less interested in the subject being taught as a consequence of the teacher's instruction.

- *Interest in reading.* Because of the enormous impact that students' reading prowess has on their subsequent lives, we'd like students to be interested in reading and, indeed, to enjoy it. Children who read because of their interest will—almost whether they want to or not—become good readers.

- *Interest in emerging technology.* As the world becomes increasingly dependent on technological advances, students who are interested in these sorts of technological improvements are more apt to learn about computers and, as a consequence, be able to utilize such technological tools.

To get a fix on possible interest-focused affective targets that might be suitable for assessment in your particular teaching situation, simply give a good, hard think to the things you'd like to see your students, as a consequence of what goes on in your classroom, become more interested in. It's just that straightforward.

Potential Value Targets

There are all sorts of values to which people subscribe that the schools should have nothing to do with. Most educators agree that political values and religious values, for example, should not be dealt with instructionally in the schools. Whether students turn out to be liberals or conservatives is really none of a teacher's business. And, historically, there's been a long tradition in the United States of separating church and state. Teachers, therefore, certainly shouldn't be advocating acceptance of particular religions or rejection of others. Well, then, what sorts of values are sufficiently meritorious and noncontroversial that they could serve as targets for classroom attention? Here are a few to consider:

- *Honesty.* Students should learn to value honesty in their dealings with others.

- *Integrity.* Students should firmly adhere to their own code of values—for example, moral or artistic values.

- *Justice.* Students should subscribe to the view that all citizens should be the recipients of equal justice from governmental law enforcement agencies.

- *Freedom.* Students should believe that democratic nations must provide the maximum level of freedom to their citizens.

Although these kinds of values may seem to be little more than lofty, flag-waving endorsements of goodness, you may still wish to consider them and similar values for potential affective assessment in your own classroom. If there really are significant values you would like your students to embrace, and if those values fall properly in the sphere of what schools should be about, then the possibility of including such values in a classroom assessment program may have real appeal for you.

Don't try to assess too many affective variables. You'd be surprised how quickly you can become overwhelmed with the time required to gather affectively oriented data, and the time needed to make sense of the data you collect. This is another "less is more" setting in which you should try to get a fix on only a few of the affective dimensions you regard as most important for your students.

Here's an issue you'll need to consider if you decide to assess your students' affect with regard to one or more of the sorts of variables just described. Put simply, it calls for an answer to the following question: Should you let your students know—early on—what affective targets you have selected for them? When we think about *cognitive* curricular aims, it is universally agreed that there is a positive impact on learning when—early on—the teacher informs students about the nature of the intended learning outcomes. However, with regard to *affective* curricular aims, the picture is less clear. If students know, in advance, what kinds of affective variables are being sought, will this knowledge have a positive or a negative impact on students' acquisition of the affect being sought? The answer to this question almost always depends on the particular affective aim being fostered and on the students involved. Each teacher must answer this question for each affective target being sought.

How Should Affect Be Assessed in Classrooms?

The assessment of affect can be carried out at varying levels of complexity and sophistication. To illustrate, in psychological experiments designed to get a fix on children's honesty, researchers have utilized trained accomplices who contrive elaborate situations in which a child can or cannot cheat; then the researchers observe the child's behavior through one-way mirrors in order to draw inferences about the child's tendencies to be honest or dishonest in situations where the attractiveness of the temptations vary. As you know, few teachers have the time or inclination to engage in very elaborate assessment of their students' affective status, although one suspects that those teachers would know how to use one-way mirrors advantageously.

As a practical matter, the classroom assessment of student affect must be relatively easy to pull off, or it simply isn't going to happen. Teachers are often too busy to carry out the galaxy of responsibilities they already face each day. Accordingly, this chapter will set out for you a single, readily accomplishable procedure to assess your students' attitudes and values. If you wish to consider more elaborate and time-demanding ways of measuring your students' affect, there are several excellent volumes cited in the References section at the end of this chapter. Those by Anderson and Bourke (2000) and by Webb and colleagues (1981) are particularly thought-provoking.

Self-Report Assessment

You can get a decent fix on students' affective status by asking them to complete *self-report inventories*. If you set up the assessment situation so students can respond in a truly anonymous fashion, the data derived from self-report instruments can really be useful to you. Just as importantly, the use of straightforward self-report devices won't be so onerous that you become disenchanted with such measurement. Anderson and Bourke (2000) provide a compelling argument in favor of self-report affective measurement by educators.

Likert Inventories

Because of its ready applicability to a variety of affective-assessment targets, the approach to attitudinal measurement introduced many years ago by Rensis Likert (1903–1981) is the most widely used today (Likert, 1932). You've probably responded to *Likert inventories* many times in your life. They consist of a series of statements in response to which you register your agreement or disagreement. For example, you are given a statement such as "Reading this text about classroom assessment represents the flat-out, finest professional experience of my career." You then choose from a set of options to decide whether you agree or disagree with the statement. The usual options, at least for adults, are *strongly agree, agree, uncertain, disagree,* and *strongly disagree.* (Surely you would have opted for the *strongly agree* response to the previous illustrative statement about this text's impact on you.)

Clearly, depending on the age of the students you're teaching, you'll need to make adjustments in the statements used and in the number and/or phrasing of the response options. For example, with very young children you might need to use brief statements containing very simple words. You might even have to read the statements aloud. Older students might be able to handle the five-choice agreement scale just described, but for younger students you'll most likely want to drop down to three response options (for instance, *agree, don't know,* and *disagree*) or even two response options (perhaps *yes* and *no*). You'll be the best judge of the language level to be used with the students you teach. In general, err in the direction of less-demanding rather than more-demanding language. Incidentally, you could probably win a few faculty-lounge trivia contests by quizzing your colleagues about Likert's first name. Face it, Rensis is not a widely used moniker!

The essence of this sort of measurement, of course, boils down to the way students who complete an inventory respond to a collection of negative and positive statements about the same affective variable. This being so, the statements in any affective inventory must be created with considerable care. To illustrate, you should never be so positive or so negative that no student will ever agree (or disagree) with a statement. Take a look at the two statements about school given here and then decide which statement would elicit a greater *range* of agreement in students' responses.

- *Every day in every way, school is always the most enjoyable part of my day.*   (Strongly Agree, Agree, Not Sure, Disagree, Strongly Disagree)
- *Even though I occasionally find school disagreeable, most of the time I enjoy it.*   (Strongly Agree, Agree, Not Sure, Disagree, Strongly Disagree)

The initial statement is so "goody-goody" that few students are apt to agree with it. In contrast, the second statement has enough qualifiers ("occasionally" and "most of the time") so that there will most likely be students who will agree with it and also students who will disagree with it. You need to be certain your inventory's statements are constructed so that they are neither *too* positive nor *too* negative.

Even though Likert-type inventories have been around for more than three-quarters of a century (Likert, 1932), traditional Likert-type scales are rarely recommended these days to assess students' affect. As you now see, a Likert inventory is focused on a *single* affective variable. Thus, Likert inventories require a substantial amount of inventory-development energy from the teacher, and most teachers are interested in several, rather than only one, affective variable. Accordingly, teachers usually want to employ assessment devices that can simultaneously get at several affective variables, not just one. Let's consider how to build the kind of affective inventory that will have the most utility for you in your own classroom. As you will see, the assessment strategy being used in this procedure is essentially the same as the one used in a traditional Likert-like inventory, but it is focused on more than a solitary affective variable.

Multifocus Affective Inventories

A *multifocus affective inventory* is an assessment device that attempts to collect information about several affective dispositions of students at the same time. Such inventories must, therefore, reduce the number of statements (items) dealing with a particular affective variable. So, whereas a traditional Likert inventory might devote 10–20 items to a single affective dimension, a multifocus affective inventory might contain items measuring only 5 or 6 affective dimensions and yet assess each one of those with just a few items.

The trade-off is obvious. Will two items dealing with, for example, a student's "interest in science" yield inferences as accurate as a 10-item inventory devoted only to that same affective dimension? Of course not. The key question, however, is the following: For whatever assessment purpose is at hand, does a teacher really *require* 10 items on an inventory in order to arrive at a sufficiently valid inference regarding a classroom full of students' interest in history? Typically, the answer is no.

Remember, all educational measurement devices are much less precise than educators and non-educators alike typically think. Affective assessment is no exception. This issue boils down to the following question: If you're trying to get a fix on the affective status of an entire class of students, what's the minimum number of items (statements) you'll be willing to rely on? Having dealt with this issue in my own classes more than a few times, for me the answer turns out to be *two*. That's right; I think I can garner sufficient insights from my students' responses to two affect-related items—one stated positively and one stated negatively—to come up with an actionable inference about my students' affect.

If you regard two items per affective focus as too skimpy, then you might bump that number up to four items per affective focus. Doing so, of course, will either (1) reduce the number of affective dimensions you can address in an inventory or (2) make your inventory so long that students, having seen the numerous upcoming responses they must supply, will race rapidly through such a lengthy inventory and, thereby, reduce the thoughtfulness of their responses to all of the inventory's items. You'll get a better idea about how to create a multifocus affective inventory if you're supplied with a step-by-step construction procedure—along with an illustrative inventory of this type.

Building a Multifocus Affective Inventory

Here, then, is a five-step process for creating multifocus affective inventories suitable for classroom use.

1. *Select the affective variables to measure.*   In recognition that you will be devoting only a small number of items to each affective variable you choose, you'll need to identify the educationally significant attitudes, interests, or values about which you will ask students to respond.

2. *Determine how many items to allocate to each affective variable.* You must include an equal number of positive *and* negative statements for each affective variable you choose. For openers, start with a minimum of two items per variable. Then, if you decide you need to add more items per variable, increase the number of items in multiples of two. For instance, with two items per affective variable, you would use one positively phrased statement and one negatively phrased statement. For four items per affective variable, you would use two positive statements and two negative statements. In a given affective inventory, incidentally, there is no need to devote an identical number of items to each affective variable being assessed. So you might attempt to measure several variables with two items per variable but allocate four items to other variables being measured in the same inventory. The choice regarding numbers of items you'll need hinges on your judgment regarding the minimum number of items necessary to yield reasonably accurate inferences about a student group's affective status with respect to a specific affective variable.

3. *Create a series of positive and negative statements related to each affective variable.* The statements in a multifocus affective inventory are similar to those used in Likert-type inventories. Yet, because you are attempting to gauge your students' affective dispositions with only a few items, even greater care should be taken to craft the statements so they are apt to elicit differential responses from students. All of these statements (items) should be scattered randomly throughout the inventory—that is, they should not be placed in any sort of identifiable groups related to a particular affective dimension.

4. *Determine the number and phrasing of students' response options.* At this point you need to determine whether you'll use three, four, or five response options for students to register agreement or disagreement with the inventory's statements. You'll also need to decide whether you're using the traditional Likert responses (such as "strongly agree") or some sort of alternative responses (such as "true for me").

5. *Create clear directions for the inventory and an appropriate presentation format.* Directions for affective inventories should be given more attention than is usually allotted by those who develop typical classroom achievement tests. Students are often unfamiliar with these sorts of affective assessment devices and, therefore, need to understand what they're being asked to do. Be certain to include (a) lucid directions about how to respond; (b) at least one sample item; (c) a request for students to supply anonymous, honest responses; and (d) a reminder that there are no right or wrong answers to the inventory's items.

Please refer to the illustrative multifocus affective inventory presented in Figure 10.2. This inventory was developed for use with students in grades 4 through 6 and was intended to allow teachers to get a fix on students' sentiments regarding three subject areas (science, mathematics, and social studies), as well as three important skills students need to acquire (reading, writing, and making oral presentations). In addition, the inventory seeks students' responses regarding school in general. In all, then, the inventory in Figure 10.2 tries to tap seven affective variables by using two items per variable.

Figure 10.2 An Illustrative Multifocus Affective Inventory for Students in Grades 4–6

SCHOOL AND ME

Directions: Please indicate how much the statements in this inventory are true for you. Some of the statements are positive and some are negative. Decide whether each statement is true *for you*. There are no right or wrong answers, so answer honestly. Do not write your name on the inventory. Only make X marks.

Here is a sample:

Response (one per statement)

	True for me.	Not true for me.	I'm not sure.
I like to go to the movies.	☒	☐	☐

When you are finished, a student will collect your inventory and place it and all other completed inventories in a sealed envelope that will be taken by the student directly to the principal's office. Thank you for your help.

Response (one per statement)

Statements	True for me.	Not true for me.	I'm not sure.
1. In general, I like school a lot.	☐	☐	☐
2. I like to learn about scientific things.	☐	☐	☐
3. I can write good reports and stories.	☐	☐	☐
4. I don't like to read.	☐	☐	☐
5. I don't like to speak in front of the class.	☐	☐	☐
6. I think that doing mathematics is fun.	☐	☐	☐
7. I like when we learn about social studies.	☐	☐	☐
8. I don't want to grow up to be a scientist.	☐	☐	☐
9. I really don't like to write very much.	☐	☐	☐
10. I like to read books when I have the time.	☐	☐	☐
11. I usually enjoy speaking in front of other students.	☐	☐	☐
12. I don't like to do mathematics problems.	☐	☐	☐
13. When we do social studies in school, I don't like it.	☐	☐	☐
14. Overall, I don't enjoy school very much.	☐	☐	☐

Spend just a few moments looking at the items in the Figure 10.2 inventory. Note, for instance, that each positively phrased statement regarding a particular variable is balanced by a counterpart statement that's phrased negatively. To illustrate, Statement 5 is a negative statement about giving oral reports, but Statement 11 is a positive statement regarding that same skill. Note also that the two statements for each variable *need not* be mirror-image contradictions, such as "I like school" versus "I don't like school."

Multifocus affective inventories are scored in the same way Likert inventories are scored: Points are awarded for students' agreement with positive statements and also for students' disagreement with negative statements. For example, let's say there were five level-of-agreement options available, ranging from strong agreement to strong disagreement in an inventory using only two items per affected variable. You would assign a maximum of five points per item (for strong agreement with a positive item or strong disagreement with a negative item) and a minimum of one point per item (for strong agreement with a negative item or strong disagreement with a positive item). Thus, focusing on a pair of items dealing with, for instance, students' interest in science, the scores on this two-item pair could range from a high of 10 to a low of 2.

Perhaps you are uncomfortable about arriving at inferences for an entire class of students based on only two items. But the purpose of this sort of assessment is to give *you* insights regarding your students' affect. If the inference you come up with based on only a pair of items is way out of whack with your own best judgment about your students' affective learnings, then treat the two-item data with a slug of suspicion. *You* are always the decision maker in your class. Insights based even on two-item inventories—administered to a whole group of students—will often prove useful to you.

The Importance of Genuine Anonymity

For you to draw accurate inferences about your students' affective status based on their responses to self-report inventories, it is clearly necessary for students to *respond truthfully* to your affective inventories. Unfortunately, many students tend to provide what are referred to as **socially desirable responses** to affective self-report devices. In other words, many students are inclined to respond in the way they think society (in this case, you) wants them to respond. Students are particularly apt to provide socially desirable responses if they believe the teacher can trace their responses. Consequently, to increase the likelihood that students will respond honestly to your affective inventories, it is imperative that you not only make all students' responses anonymous but also employ as many procedures as are practicable to ensure that most students regard their responses as truly untraceable.

Among the more simple but effective *anonymity-enhancement procedures* you might want to consider are these:

1. *Directions.* Make sure the directions for your affective inventories stress the importance of honest answers and that students are *not* to put their names on their inventories.

2. *Response restrictions.* Set up your inventories so that the *only* form of student response is to be check marks, circling of preferred answers, or the like. Because students believe the teacher may figure out who supplied which inventory by recognizing students' handwriting, don't allow any handwriting whatsoever on affective inventories. If you are desperate to give students an opportunity to supply written comments, then provide your students with totally separate forms on which they can make written comments—also anonymous.

3. *Collection.* Install a procedure whereby students deposit their completed inventories in a collection box, or have a student (not one thought to be your "pet" student) collect the completed inventories. Announce *before* students start to fill out the inventories that one of these collection methods will be employed.

As you can see, you must try to make sure your students really don't think there's any way to trace their responses back to them. Even these precautions don't guarantee that students will respond truthfully. However, well-conceived anonymity-enhancement techniques increase the odds that students will respond honestly.

In recent years, we have often seen attempts made to secure students' responses to affectively oriented inventories via anonymous, computer-collected online inventories. Such inventories, given the magic of computers, can be truly anonymous—that is, a student's responses cannot be traced back to the student. What is worrisome, however, is whether students who fill out a computer-delivered inventory *believe* their responses are truly anonymous. The more likely it is that students regard their electronic responses as traceable back to them, the greater will be the social desirability of their answers.

When to Assess Affect

When should classroom teachers assess their students' affective status? Well, for openers, it seems important to set up at least a preinstruction and a postinstruction measure of students' attitudes, interests, and/or values. Thus, for elementary teachers teaching students in self-contained classrooms, an affective assessment at the start of the school year and another at its close will allow teachers to discern any meaningful changes in students' affect. Ideally, however, teachers can engage in occasional "affective dip-sticking" to monitor students' affect. For example, every couple of months, a teacher might measure

Parent Talk

"You're messing with my child's head," was the first comment you heard from Mrs. Jillian, Paul's mother, when she telephoned you at school during your after-school planning period. Mrs. Jillian then continued by saying she had heard from Paul that you were getting students to fill out "attitude tests" that try to find out "whether kids have the right attitudes." Mrs. Jillian concluded by asking, "How dare you delve into Paul's values and attitudes! Isn't this something his dad and I should be influencing?"

If I were you, here's how I'd respond to Mrs. Jillian:

"I agree completely with you, Mrs. Jillian, about whose right it is to influence Paul's values and attitudes. That responsibility is yours and Mr. Jillian's. But I have a hunch you may not have a clear picture of what I'm trying to do in Paul's class. Let me explain.

"As you may know, children at Paul's age often lose interest in certain subjects, especially mathematics and science. What I've been trying to do is determine ways I can help improve or sustain my students' interest in science and mathematics. I've been administering *anonymous* attitude inventories related to math and science on a pretest and posttest basis—that is, in the fall and in the spring. But I'm not using the results of those anonymous inventories to influence the attitudes or values of Paul or any other child. What I'm trying to do is figure out how my own teaching can engender more interest, from the entire class, in science and mathematics.

"I would *never* try to influence a value or attitude that falls within your family's purview. But I'm sure you'd like Paul, and the other students in his class, to regard science and mathematics positively, not negatively. Whether the children eventually pursue careers related to science or mathematics will, of course, be up to them and their families."

Now, how would you respond to Mrs. Jillian?

students' self-esteem as learners as well as their attitudes toward learning. If these occasional assessments suggest that inappropriate affective changes are occurring, the teacher may wish to modify affect-related aspects of the instructional program.

In the next section of the chapter, you'll discover that you can often *sample* your students' affective status rather than measuring all students' affective status. Thus, some of the suggested affective dip-sticking might be carried out with only a portion of your students.

What Kinds of Inferences Are at Stake in Affective Assessment?

When teachers use cognitively oriented tests, they typically make inferences—that is, interpretations about individual students. If, for instance, Harvey Haley earns a high score on a mathematics test, the teacher makes an inference about Harvey's possession of certain mathematics skills and knowledge. Teachers need to make inferences about individual students in order to make decisions about how to provide suitable instruction for those students.

Teachers also aggregate students' individual scores on achievement tests to arrive at group-focused inferences. For example, if most students in a history class performed poorly on a start-of-the-term achievement pretest, yet most students earned top scores on a comparable posttest administered near the term's conclusion, the teacher would conclude that the students, as a group, had learned substantially more about history.

It's different with affect. Whereas cognitive tests (and, in most cases, psychomotor tests) are measures of students' *optimum performance*, affective inventories strive to measure students' *typical performance*. Remember that when students complete most affective devices, those results don't count toward the students' grades, so self-report assessment offers students a wonderful opportunity to distort their responses. Thus, there's a strong likelihood that at least some students won't respond honestly. Consequently, inferences about the affective status of *individual* students (based on a student's responses to an affective inventory) are risky.

Besides, instructional decisions about individual students based on affective-assessment devices are rare. If Harry Helms knows history well, but happens to hate it, few teachers will give Harry a low grade in history based on his disdain for "dead folks' foolishness."

In contrast, however, teachers often make *instructional* decisions about what goes on in class based on aggregated affective data. Assuming there will be a small number of students who supply inaccurate responses, it is still reasonable to assume that the total collectivity of students' responses will permit meaningful *group-focused inferences*. And those are the kinds of inferences you should be making when you use affective-assessment instruments. Because affective inventories must be administered anonymously, you've surely recognized that getting a fix on a particular student's affective status is literally impossible. Anonymity is, after all, anonymity.

However, there's another good reason for arriving at only group-focused affective inferences. Even if you were to use all sorts of anonymity-enhancement procedures when you administer any affective inventory, some students will *still* not respond honestly. Certain students will be fearful of offending you in any way, even though shrouded by the shield of anonymity, and thus will respond more positively than they would if they were being completely truthful. Interestingly, however, there are also some students who will use their anonymity cloaks as an opportunity to "get even" with you for your real or imagined shortcomings. Such students will then toss more negativity your way than they really feel. Will these too-positive and too-negative responses cancel each other out perfectly? Of course not. But they will do at least *some* canceling out and, as a consequence, should allow you to put greater confidence in your students' *average* response as a reflection of the entire group's affective status.

Affective assessment devices are simply too crude to permit individual-focused inferences. However, you ought to be able to make some very solid

But What Does This Have to Do with Teaching?

Few teachers don't believe, at some level, that student affect is important. Most teachers realize that if students learn to detest schooling, it's unlikely those students will wind up near the top of any academic sweepstakes. Most chemistry teachers want their students to groove on chemistry. Most math teachers want their students to get mildly ecstatic over the theorem formulated at the Pythagorean School of Mathematics some 2500 years ago. Yet, although most teachers recognize that students' interests, attitudes, and values are important, few teachers deliberately strive to promote appropriate affect in their students.

One of the reasons for this neglect of affect is that students' affective dispositions often get lost in the curricular roads that today's teachers must travel. There are simply *so much* knowledge and so many skills that society wants today's students to master. And the current accountability pressures for teachers to boost students' test scores have made it even less likely that teachers will have time to promote positive student affect. It's easy to see how affect gets overlooked, even by teachers who recognize its importance. And this is when affective assessment arrives to save the day. Even if a teacher uses only one self-report inventory at the start of a term, and another at its conclusion, the very *presence* of this assessment instrument will almost certainly incline the teacher to think about the degree to which any classroom activities are being directed toward the promotion of appropriate affective outcomes.

Affective assessment instruments, even a 10-item self-report inventory, will sensitize the teacher to affect's importance. And such sensitized teachers will typically devote at least *some* effort to promoting the kinds of student attitudes, interests, and values that—far more, perhaps, than the cognitive content we cram into their heads—will surely influence their lives.

judgments about how your students, as a group, are affectively disposed. This is why, in some cases, you can collect affective data from only, say, half of your class yet still make a fairly accurate inference about the group based on responses from that 50-percent sample. Sample-based, en route affective assessment of your students, especially as a way of coming up with dip-stick inferences about that group of students, really works quite well.

What Do Classroom Teachers Really Need to Know About Affective Assessment?

The most important thing you need to know about affective assessment is that if you don't measure your students' affective status in a systematic fashion, you're far less likely to emphasize affect *instructionally*. Moreover, without systematic affective assessment, you're not apt to have a very decent fix on the affective consequences, possibly unintentional, that you're having on your students.

If you do decide to engage in some affective measurement in your own classes, you'll be much better off if you rely on straightforward self-report instruments (Likert-like inventories or multifocus affective inventories) rather than trying to employ some exotic affective-measurement strategies that are time-consuming and yield interpretations of arguable validity. You also need to know that affective-assessment devices are too imprecise to allow you to make inferences about individual students. Group-focused inferences are as far as you should go in the affective realm.

There's one other thing teachers ought to recognize about the assessment of affect—namely, that most teachers do not possess even a foggy notion about how to promote affect *instructionally*. If teachers actually decide to measure important student affect, they'll typically need some solid professional-development support to learn how to *modify* students' attitudes, values, and interests. There are a number of instructional techniques for doing so, but most teachers are unaware of those affective-focused instructional procedures. Here's where a ***professional learning community***—that is, a group of educators who meet periodically to deal with topics such as "affective instructional techniques"—would be especially useful.

Looking back, then, at the description of affective assessment as it might be carried out by a typical classroom teacher, it is possible to isolate three key features that can lead toward more valid interpretations of students' affective status. Those three features are reliance on (1) *self-report inventories* to be completed by students under conditions of (2) *actual and perceived anonymity* leading to (3) *group-focused inferences* rather than individual inferences about students' current affective status. If teachers can satisfy all three of these procedural requirements, then the resultant inferences about students' affect will have greater likelihood of being valid. Given the impact that assessing students' affect is likely to have on what and how a teacher teaches, the instructional dividends of affective assessment were underscored. The chapter concluded with a reminder that the validity of inferences drawn from affective assessment depends directly on a teacher's forming group-focused inferences about students' affect using self-report inventories to which students respond with real *and* perceived anonymity.

Chapter Summary

This chapter began with an unabashed endorsement of the instructional importance of affect and, as a consequence, the importance of assessing students' affective status. It was suggested that the use of affective assessment in classrooms would incline teachers to address affective goals instructionally. It was also argued that if teachers monitor their students' affective status, instructional modifications can be made whenever inappropriate or insufficient affective shifts in students are occurring. Affective variables were described as important predictors of individuals' future behaviors because people's affective status reveals their behavioral predispositions. It was also pointed

out, however, that there are vocal groups whose members oppose instructional attention to affect.

Regarding the kinds of affective variables to assess in one's classroom, a series of potential attitudinal, interest, and value foci were presented. Teachers were urged to select only a few highly meaningful affective variables, rather than so many as to overwhelm students.

Self-report assessment procedures were suggested as the most practical way to gather affective data in classrooms. Multifocus affective inventories were recommended over Likert inventories on the practical ground that Likert inventories assess only a single affective dimension. Teachers are usually interested in more than one affective variable. A five-step process for constructing multifocus affective inventories was described. Anonymity was identified as an indispensable component of appropriate affective assessment. Several anonymity-enhancement procedures were presented. It was also suggested that affective assessments be made prior to and at the conclusion of instruction, as well as in the form of occasional affective "dip-sticking."

The nature of assessment-based affective inferences was also explored. It was argued the imprecision of affective assessment devices should incline teachers to make group-focused inferences rather than inferences about individual students.

References

Anderson, L. W., and Bourke, S. F. (2000). *Assessing affective characteristics in the schools* (2nd ed.). Mahwah, NJ: Erlbaum.

Aschbacher, P. R., Ing, M., and Tsai, S. M. (2013). "Boosting student interest in science," *Phi Delta Kappan, 95*, no. 2 (October): 47–51.

Chamberlin, S. A. (2010). "A review of instruments created to assess affect in mathematics," *Journal of Mathematics Education, 3*, no. 1 (June): 167–182.

Likert, R. (1932). "A technique for the measurement of attitudes," *Archives of Psychology, 140*: 1–55.

Preble, B., and Taylor, L. (2008/2009). "School climate through students' eyes," *Educational leadership, 66*, no. 4 (December/January): 35–40.

Webb, E. J., Campbell, D. T., Schwartz, R. D., Sechreat, L., and Grove, J. B. (1981). *Nonreactive measures in the social sciences* (2nd ed.). Boston: Houghton Mifflin.

Weissberg, R. P., and Cascarino, J. (2013). "Academic learning + social-emotional learning = national priority," *Phi Delta Kappan, 95*, no. 2 (October): 8–13.

Assessing Students' Affect—Because Dispositions Shape Conduct*

W. James Popham, University of California, Los Angeles

Historically, our schools have focused their instructional efforts on promoting students' cognitive outcomes, such as the mastery of intellectual skills or bodies of knowledge. Regrettably, little attention has been given to students' acquisition of appropriate attitudes, interests, or values. Yet these *affective* variables play a powerful role in students' school success and, later, in their life success. Many educators believe that, in the long term, the affective consequences of schooling are more important for students than cognitively focused learning.

The reason why affective variables are so significant is that they predispose students to act in certain ways. Students who become genuinely interested in science during high school chemistry courses often maintain such interests for years. And a child who learns to truly love reading in elementary school will frequently become a life-long reader.

Why is it, then, that we see so little affectively focused instruction in our schools? Well, one reason is that educators must be wary of influencing values or attitudes that are clearly the province of the home—not the school. Educators should promote only those affective dimensions that are universally, or almost universally, approved.

A second obstacle to affectively oriented instruction is that many educators are unfamiliar with how to effectively measure students' affect. Teachers who are considering assessing their students' affect should definitely learn about the basic nuts and bolts of such assessment. Here are three overriding ground rules governing the assessment of students' affect:

- *Assess regularly.* Because affective dispositions acquired in school can profoundly influence students' success in school and far beyond, a small number of key affective variables should be regularly assessed—and then addressed instructionally.

- *Use anonymously completed self-report inventories.* When students respond to an affective inventory's items, anonymity enhances the honesty of responses. Thus, complete real and perceived anonymity are absolute musts.

- *Make group-focused, not individual-student, inferences.* Valid group-focused inferences about a student group's affective status can be invaluable to teachers in choosing affect-related instructional activities. Inferences about an individual student's affect, however, are not apt to be valid.

Teachers, individually or in concert with colleagues, should learn more about the measurement of students' affect, as well as how to defensibly promote students' affective dispositions. Then, having selected such targets as promoting positive attitudes toward the importance of student effort, or negative attitudes regarding bullying, teachers should cautiously move forward in determining students' affect, influencing such affect, and then evaluating the success of those instructional efforts.

Chapter 11

Improving Teacher-Developed Assessments

<table>
<tr><td>

Chief Chapter Outcome

</td><td>

Learning Outcomes

11.1 Apply judgmental-based test-improvement procedures in order to improve teacher-developed assessments.

11.2 Apply empirical-based test-improvement procedures in order to improve teacher-developed assessments.

</td></tr>
</table>

Sufficient comprehension of both judgmental and empirical test-improvement procedures so that accurate decisions can be made about the way teachers are employing these two test-improvement strategies

If you've ever visited the manuscript room of the British Museum, you'll recall seeing handwritten manuscripts authored by some of the superstars of English literature. It's a moving experience. Delightfully, the museum presents not only the final versions of famed works by such authors as Milton and Keats, but also the early drafts of those works. It is somewhat surprising and genuinely encouraging to learn that even those giants of literature didn't get it right the first time. They had to cross out words, delete sentences, and transpose phrases. Many of the museum's early drafts are genuinely messy, reflecting all sorts of rethinking on the part of the author. Well, if the titans of English literature had to revise their early drafts, is it at all surprising that teachers usually need to spruce up their classroom assessments?

This chapter is designed to provide you with several procedures by which you can improve the assessment instruments you develop. It's a near certainty that if you use the chapter's recommended procedures, your tests will get better. (But they probably won't make it to the British Museum—unless you carry them in when visiting.)

Two general improvement strategies are described in this chapter. First, you'll learn about *judgmental item-improvement* procedures, in which the chief means of sharpening your tests is human judgment—your own and that of others. Second, you'll be considering *empirical item-improvement* procedures based on students' responses to your assessment procedures. Ideally, if time permits and your motivation abounds, you can use both forms of test-improvement procedures for your own classroom assessment devices.

But, here's a heads-up regarding the upcoming *empirical* item-repair procedures. What you'll recognize when you get into that section is that there are *numbers* in it. (There's even a formula or two.) When encountering this material, perhaps you'll conclude that you've been tricked—lulled into a sense of nonnumeric complacency for 10 chapters and then blindsided with a quagmire of quantitative esoterica. But that's not so. Don't be intimidated by quantitative stuff in the last half of the chapter. It truly constitutes a fairly Mickey Mouse level of number nudging. Just take it slow and easy. You'll survive surprisingly well. It's a promise.

Judgmentally Based Improvement Procedures

Human judgment, although it sometimes gets us in trouble, is a remarkably useful tool. Judgmental approaches to test improvement can be carried out quite systematically or, in contrast, rather informally. Judgmental assessment-improvement strategies differ chiefly in who is supplying the judgments. There are three sources of test-improvement judgments you should consider—those supplied by (1) yourself, (2) your colleagues, and (3) your students. We'll consider each of these potential judgment sources separately.

Judging Your Own Assessment Instruments

Let's suppose you've created a 70-item combination short-answer and multiple-choice examination for a U.S. government class and, having administered it, you want to improve the examination for your next year's class. We'll assume that during item development you did a reasonable amount of in-process sharpening up of the items so that they constituted what, at the time, was your best effort. Now, however, you have an opportunity to revisit the examination to see whether its 70 items are all that marvelous. It's a good thing to do.

Let's consider other kinds of assessments—and particularly the directions for them. Suppose you have devised what you think are pretty decent directions for your students to follow when preparing portfolios or when responding to tasks in a performance test. Even if you regard those directions as suitable, it's always helpful to review such directions after a time to see whether you can now detect shortcomings that, when you originally prepared the set of directions, escaped your attention.

As you probably know from other kinds of writing, when you return to one of your written efforts after it has had time to "cool off," you're likely to spot deficits that, in the heat of the original writing, weren't apparent to you. However, beyond a fairly casual second look, you will typically be able to improve your assessment procedures even more if you approach this test-improvement task systematically.

To illustrate, you could use specific review criteria when you judge your earlier assessment efforts. If a test item or a set of directions falls short on any criterion, you should obviously do some modifying. Presented here are five review criteria that you might wish to consider if you set out systematically to improve your classroom assessment procedures.

- *Adherence to item-specific guidelines and general item-writing commandments.* When you appraise your assessment procedures, it will be useful to review briefly the general item-writing commandments supplied earlier (in Chapter 6) as well as the particular item-writing guidelines provided for the specific kind of item(s) you've developed. If you now see violations of the principles set forth in either of those two sets of directives, fix the flaws.

- *Contribution to score-based inference.* Recall that the real reason why teachers assess students is in order to arrive at score-based interpretations about the status of students. Therefore, it will be helpful for you to reconsider each aspect of a previously developed assessment procedure to see whether it does, in fact, really contribute to the kind of inference you wish to draw about your students.

- *Accuracy of content.* There's always the possibility that previously accurate content has now been superseded or contradicted by more recent content. Make sure that the content you included earlier in the assessment instrument is still accurate and that your answer key is still correct.

- *Absence of content lacunae.* This review criterion gives me a chance to use one of my favorite words, the plural form of *lacuna*, which, incidentally, means "gap." Although *gaps* would have done the job in this instance, you'll admit that *gaps* look somewhat tawdry when stacked up against *lacunae*. (This, of course, is a norm-referenced contrast.) Hindsight is a nifty form of vision. Thus, when you take a second look at the content coverage represented in your assessment instrument, you may discover that you originally overlooked some important content. This review criterion is clearly related to an earlier review criterion regarding the assessment's contribution to the score-based inference that you want to make. Any meaningful lacunae in content will obviously reduce the accuracy of your inference.

- *Fairness.* Although you should clearly have tried to eradicate any bias in your assessment instruments when you originally developed them, there's always the chance that you overlooked something. Undertake another bias review just to make certain you've been as attentive to bias elimination as you possibly can be.

I can personally attest to a case of bias blindness when I authored a textbook on educational evaluation in the 1970s. Recognizing that a number of women at the time were beginning to take offense at authors' use of masculine pronouns when referring to unnamed individuals (for example, "The student lost *his* lunch"), I had assiduously written the textbook so that all my illustrative make-believe people were plural. I never had to use *his* or *her* because I could always use *their*. After churning out the last chapter, I was smugly proud of my pluralization prowess. Yet, having been so attentive to a pronoun issue that might offend some women, I blithely included a cartoon in the book that showed scantily clad females cavorting before male members of a school board. Talk about dumb! If only I'd taken a serious second look at the book before it hit the presses, I might have spotted my insensitive error. As it was, because the cartoon appeared in all copies of the first edition (not the second!), I received more than a few heated, and richly deserved, complaints from readers—both male and female!

I am not suggesting that you fill out an elaborate rating form for each of these five review criteria—with each criterion requiring a numerical rating. Rather, I recommend that you seriously think about these five criteria before you tackle any judgmental review of a previously developed assessment instrument.

This chapter dealing with the improvement of teacher-made classroom tests has a clear mission, and it's probably a good idea to remind you of the nature of that mission. Remember how, earlier in this book, the three most important concepts of educational measurement were fawned over at length. Yes, *validity, reliability*, and *fairness* were applauded so relentlessly that you might have suspected they were being groomed for some sort of sainthood. Well, the "big three" are, indeed, important assessment concepts, and by improving the classroom assessments you've churned out, you're surely hoping to improve one or more of those three concepts in your very own tests. Remember, the stronger that your teacher-made tests are, the more defensible will be the test-based interpretations you make about the unseen, covert status of your students. Often, a little tightening up of just a few items from your tests can lead to meaningfully better interpretations and, thereafter, better educated students.

Collegial Judgments

If you are working with a colleague whose judgment you trust, it's often helpful to ask this person to review your assessment procedures. To get the most mileage out of such a review, you'll probably need to provide your coworker with at least a brief description of review criteria such as the five previously cited ones—that is, (1) adherence to item-specific guidelines and general item-writing commandments, (2) contribution to score-based inference, (3) accuracy of content, (4) absence of content gaps or lacunae, and (5) fairness. You will need to describe to your colleague the key inference(s) you intend to base on the assessment procedure. It will also be useful to your colleague if you identify the decisions that will, thereafter, be influenced by your inferences about students.

Collegial judgments are particularly helpful to teachers who employ many performance tests or who use portfolio assessments. Most of the empirically based improvement procedures you'll be learning about later in this chapter are intended to be used with more traditional sorts of items such as those found in multiple-choice exams. For portfolio assessment and performance tests, judgmental approaches will often prove more useful.

Remember, if *you* are the creator of the portfolio assessment or performance tests you're setting out to improve, you're apt to be biased in their favor. After all, parents almost always adore their progeny. What you need is a good, hard, *nonpartisan* review of what you've been up to assessment-wise.

To do a thorough job of helping you review your assessment approaches, of course, your colleague will need to put in some time. In fairness, you'll probably feel obliged to toss in a *quid pro quo* or two whereby you return the favor by reviewing your colleague's tests (or by resolving a pivotal personal crisis in your colleague's private life). If your school district is large enough, you might also have access to some central-office supervisorial personnel who know something about assessment. Here's a nifty opportunity to let them earn their salaries—get one of those district supervisors to review your assessment procedures. It is often asserted that another pair of eyes can help improve almost any written document. This doesn't necessarily mean the other pair of eyes see accurately while yours are in need of contact lenses. You should listen to what other reviewers say, but you should be guided by your own judgments about the virtues of their suggestions.

Student Judgments

When teachers set out to improve assessment procedures, a rich source of data is often overlooked because teachers typically fail to secure advice from their students. Yet, because students have experienced test items in a most meaningful context, akin to the way a potential executionee experiences a firing squad, student judgments can provide teachers with useful insights. Student reactions can help you spot shortcomings in particular items and in other features of your assessment procedures, such as a test's directions or the time you've allowed for completing the test.

The kinds of data secured from students will vary, depending on the type of assessment procedure being used, but questions such as those on the item-improvement questionnaire in Figure 11.1 can profitably be given to students after they have completed an assessment procedure. Although the illustrative

---

Figure 11.1 An Illustrative Item-Improvement Questionnaire for Students

Item-Improvement Questionnaire for Students

1. If any of the items seemed confusing, which ones were they?
2. Did any items have more than one correct answer? If so, which ones?
3. Did any items have no correct answers? If so, which ones?
4. Were there words in any items that confused you? If so, which ones?
5. Were the directions for the test, or for particular subsections, unclear? If so, which ones?

questionnaire in Figure 11.1 is intended for use with a selected-response type of test, only minor revisions would be needed to make it suitable for a constructed-response test, a performance test, or a portfolio assessment system.

It is important to let students finish a test prior to their engaging in such a judgmental exercise. If students are asked to *simultaneously* play the roles of test takers and test improvers, they'll probably botch up both tasks. No student should be expected to perform two such functions, at least not at the same time.

Simply give students the test as usual, collect their answer sheets or test booklets, and provide them with new, blank test booklets. *Then* distribute a questionnaire asking students to supply per-item reactions. In other words, ask students to play examinees and item reviewers, but to play these roles consecutively, not simultaneously.

Now, how do you treat students' reactions to test items? Let's say you're a classroom teacher and a few students come up with a violent castigation of one of your favorite items. Do you automatically buckle by scrapping or revising the item? Of course not; teachers are made of sterner stuff. Perhaps the students were miffed about the item because they didn't know how to answer it. One of the best ways for students to escape responsibility for a dismal test performance is to assail the test itself. Teachers should anticipate a certain amount of carping from low-scoring students or those questing for "perfection only" in their responses.

Yet, allowing for a reasonable degree of complaining, student reactions can sometimes provide useful insights for teachers. A student-castigated item may, indeed, deserve castigation. To overlook students as a source of judgmental test-improvement information, for both selected-response and constructed-response items, would clearly be an error.

To review, then, judgmentally based test-improvement procedures can rely on the judgments supplied by you, your colleagues, or your students. In the final analysis, you will be the one who decides whether to modify your assessment procedures. Nonetheless, it is typically helpful to have others react to your tests.

Empirically Based Improvement Procedures

In addition to judgmentally based methods of improving your assessment procedures, there are improvement approaches based on the empirical data students supply when they respond to the assessment instruments you've developed. Let's turn, then, to the use of student-response data in the improvement of assessment procedures. A variety of empirical item-improvement techniques have been well honed over the years. We will consider the more traditional item-analysis procedures first, turning later to a few more recent wrinkles for using student data to improve a teacher's classroom assessments.

Most of the procedures employed to improve classroom assessments on the basis of students' responses to those assessments rely on numbers. Clearly, there are some readers of this text (*you* may be one) who are definitely put off by numbers. It has been said, typically with feigned sincerity, that there is a secret cult among teachers and prospective teachers who have taken a "tremble pledge"—a vow to tremble when encountering any numerical value larger than a single digit (a number larger than 9). If you are one of these mathphobics, please stay calm because the numbers you'll be encountering in this and later chapters will really be Simple Simon stuff. Tremble not. It'll be pain free. Just work through the easy examples and you'll survive with surprising ease.

Difficulty Indices

One useful index of an item's quality is its *difficulty*. The most commonly employed item-difficulty index, often referred to simply as a *p value*, is calculated as follows:

$$\text{Difficulty } p = \frac{R}{T}$$

where R = the number of students responding correctly (right) to an item
T = the total number of students responding to the item

To illustrate, if 50 students answered an item, and only 37 of them answered it correctly, then the *p* value representing the item's difficulty would be

$$\text{Difficulty } p = \frac{37}{50} = .74$$

It should be clear that such *p* value can range from 0 to 1.00, with higher *p* values indicating items that more students answered correctly. For example, a *p* value of .98 would signify an item answered correctly by almost all students. Similarly, an item with a *p* value of .15 would be one that most students (85 percent) missed.

The *p* value of an item should always be viewed in relationship to the probability of the student's getting the correct response purely by guessing. For example, if a binary-choice item is involved, then *on the basis of chance alone,* students should be able to answer the item correctly half of the time, and thus the item would have a *p* value of .50. On a four-option multiple-choice test, a .25 *p* value by chance alone would be expected.

Educators sometimes err by referring to items with high *p* values (for instance, *p* values of .80 and above) as "easy" items, while items with low *p* values (of, say, .20 and below) are described as "difficult" items. Those descriptions may or may not be accurate. Even though we typically refer to an item's *p* value as its *difficulty* index, the actual difficulty of an item is tied to the instructional program surrounding it. If students are especially well taught, they may perform excellently on a complex item that, by anyone's estimate, is a tough one. Does the resulting *p* value of .95 indicate that the item is easy? No. The item's complicated content may just have been taught effectively. For example, almost all students in a pre-med course for prospective physicians might correctly answer a technical item about the central nervous system that almost all "people off the street" would answer incorrectly. A *p* value of .96 based on the pre-med students' performances would not render the item intrinsically easy.

What is a suitable *p* value for a test item? Well, as is so often the answer in educational measurement whenever crystal-clear questions are posed, *it depends*. For instance, sometimes teachers want to include in one of their tests a wide range of items with decidedly different difficulty levels—as an attempt to differentiate among the full range of their students' mastery of a given body of knowledge. In other instances, the teacher may wish to delete items that are answered incorrectly by too many students or answers indicating that an item's content is too difficult or, perish the possibility, items whose content has not been well taught! Accordingly, *p* values provide a useful indication of the proportion of students who flew or flopped on a given item, but the varying contexts of educational assessment require teachers to arrive at judgments regarding a given item. That is, is it too tough, is it too easy, or did it hit the Goldilocks' magic 'just right" mark?

Item-Discrimination Indices

For tests designed to yield norm-referenced inferences, one of the most powerful indicators of an item's quality is the *item-discrimination index*. In brief, an item-discrimination index typically tells us how frequently an item is answered correctly by those who perform well on the total test. Fundamentally, an item-discrimination index reflects the relationship between students' responses for the total test and their responses to a particular test item. One approach to computing an item-discrimination statistic is to calculate a correlation coefficient between students' total test scores and their performances on a particular item.

We should pause for just a moment to forestall potential confusion that might arise when the term "discrimination" is applied to two very different sorts of assessment activities. In just a moment, you will be learning that in the empirical improvement of a teacher's test items, it is often the case that discrimination is something positive—a quality much to be sought. Yet, when you grappled in Chapter 5 with the nuances of assessment bias, you saw that when items discriminate against subgroups of students, such discrimination renders the item unfair enough to warrant the its being bounced from the test. As you tangle with subsequent paragraphs in this section, remember that there is nothing inherently evil about an *item* that discriminates. Imagine, for example, that you had just finished a spectacular two-week teaching unit dealing with a set of conventions regarding comma usage. Your test items covering those two weeks of pedagogical bliss should most definitely *discriminate* between those students who learned what you were teaching and those students who apparently took a two-week cognitive vacation during your dazzling unit called *Caring for One's Commas.*

A *positively discriminating item* is one that is answered correctly more often by those who score well on the total test than by those who score poorly on the total test. A *negatively discriminating item* is answered correctly more often by those who score poorly on the total test than by those who score well on the total test. A *nondiscriminating item* is one for which there's no appreciable difference between the correct-response proportions of those who score well and those who score poorly on the total test. This set of relationships is summarized in the following chart. (Remember that < and > signify *less than* and *more than,* respectively.)

Type of Item	Proportion of Correct Responses on Total Test
Positive Discriminator	High Scorers > Low Scorers
Negative Discriminator	High Scorers < Low Scorers
Nondiscriminator	High Scorers = Low Scorers

In general, teachers would like to discover that their items are positive discriminators, because a positively discriminating item tends to be answered correctly by the most knowledgeable students (those who scored high on the total test) and incorrectly by the least knowledgeable students (those who scored low on the total test). Negatively discriminating items indicate something is awry, because the item tends to be missed more often by the most knowledgeable students and answered correctly more frequently by the least knowledgeable students.

Now, how do you go about computing an item's discrimination index? Increasingly, these days, teachers can send off a batch of machine-scorable answer sheets (for selected-response items) to a district-operated assessment center where electronic machines have been programmed to spit out p values and item-discrimination indices. Happily, a number of easy-to-use computer programs are now available to teachers for such analyses. Teachers can also carry out such analyses themselves. The following four steps can be employed for the analysis of classroom assessment procedures:

1. *Order the test papers from high to low by total score.* Place the paper having the highest total score on top, and continue with the next highest total score sequentially until the paper with the lowest score is placed on the bottom.

2. *Divide the papers into a high group and a low group, with the same number of papers in each group.* Split the groups into upper and lower halves. If there is an odd number of papers, simply set aside one of the middle papers. If there are several papers with identical scores at the middle of the distribution, then randomly assign them to the high or low distributions so that there is the same number of papers in both groups. The use of 50-percent groups has the advantage of providing enough papers to permit reliable estimates of upper- and lower-group performances.

3. *Calculate a p value for the high group and a p value for the low group.* Determine the number of students in the high group who answered the item correctly, and then divide this number by the number of students in the high group. This provides you with p_h. Repeat the process for the low group to obtain p_l.

4. *Subtract p_l from p_h to obtain each item's discrimination index (D).* In essence, then, $D = p_h - p_l$.

Suppose you are in the midst of conducting an item analysis of your midterm examination items. Let's say you split the papers for your class of 30 youngsters into two equal upper-half and lower-half papers. All 15 students in the high group answered item 42 correctly, but only 5 of the 15 students in the low group answered it correctly. The item discrimination index for item 42, therefore, would be $1.00 - .33 = .67$.

Now, how large should an item's discrimination index be in order for you to consider the item acceptable? Ebel and Frisbie (1991) offer the experience-based guidelines in Table 11.1 for indicating the quality of items to be used for making norm-referenced interpretations. If you consider their guidelines as approximations, not absolute standards, they'll usually help you decide whether your items are discriminating satisfactorily.

An item's ability to discriminate is highly related to its overall difficulty index. For example, an item answered correctly by all students has a total p value of 1.00. For that item, p_h and p_l are also 1.00. Thus, the item's discrimination index is zero $(1.00 - 1.00 = 0)$. A similar result would be obtained for items in which the overall p value was zero—that is, for items no student had answered correctly.

Table 11.1 Guidelines for Evaluating the Discriminating Efficiency of Items

Discrimination Index	Item Evaluation
.40 and above	Very good items
.30–.39	Reasonably good items, but possibly subject to improvement
.20–.29	Marginal items, usually needing improvement
.19 and below	Poor items, to be rejected or improved by revision

Source: Ebel, R.L. and Frisbie, D.A. (1991). *Essentials of Educational Measurement* (5th ed.). Englewood Cliffs, NJ: Prentice Hall.

With items that have very high or very low p values, it is thus less likely substantial discrimination indices can be obtained. Later in the chapter you will see that this situation has prompted proponents of criterion-referenced interpretations of tests (who often hope almost all postinstruction responses from students will be correct) to search for alternative ways to calculate indices of item quality.

In looking back at the use of item-discrimination indices to improve a test's items, it is important to understand that these indices, as their name signifies, were designed to *discriminate*. That is, such indices have been employed to help spot items that do a good job in contributing sufficient variation to students' total-test scores so that those total-test scores can be accurately compared with one another. Educators in the United States have been using most educational tests to do this sort of discriminating between high scorers and low scorers for almost a century. To make the kind of norm-referenced, comparative interpretations that have historically been the chief function of U.S. educational testing, we needed to refine a set of test-improvement procedures suitable for sharpening the accuracy of our comparative interpretations of scores. Item-discrimination indices help us to locate the optimal items for contrasting students' test performances.

But although it is certainly appropriate to employ educational tests in an effort to come up with norm-referenced interpretations of students' performances, there are educational settings in which a test's comparative function should be overshadowed by its instructional mission. In those more instructionally oriented settings, traditional item-discrimination indices may be quite *inappropriate*. To illustrate, suppose a mathematics teacher decides to get her students to become skilled in the use of a really demanding mathematical procedure. (We can call it Procedure X.) Well, when the teacher gave her students a test containing Procedure X items early in the year, students' performances on the items were rather scattered, and the resulting item-discrimination indices for all the Procedure X items looked quite acceptable— between .30 and .60. However, at the end of the school year, after an awesomely wonderful instructional job by our plucky math teacher, almost every student answered almost every Procedure X item correctly. The p value for every one

Decision Time

To Catch a Culprit: Teacher or Test?

Susan Stevens teaches sixth-grade social studies in Exeter Middle School. During the seven years she has taught at Exeter, Susan has always spent considerable time in developing what she refers to as "credible classroom assessments." She really has put in more than her share of weekends working to create crackerjack examinations.

This last spring, however, Susan completed an extension course on educational testing. In the course, she learned how to compute discrimination analyses of her test items. As a consequence, Susan has been subjecting all of her examinations to such analyses this year.

On one of her examinations containing mostly selected-response items, Susan discovered to her dismay that 4 of the test's 30 items turned out to have negative discriminators. In other words, students who performed well on the total test answered the 4 items incorrectly more often than students who didn't do so well on the total test. To her surprise, all 4 negatively discriminating items dealt with the same topic—that is, relationships among the legislative, judicial, and executive branches of the U.S. government.

Susan's first thought was to chuck the 4 items because they were clearly defective. As she considered the problem, however, another possibility occurred to her. Because all 4 items were based on the same instructional content, perhaps she had confused the stronger students with her explanations.

If you were Susan and wanted to get to the bottom of this issue so you could decide whether to overhaul the items or the instruction, how would you proceed?

of those items was .95 or above! As a consequence of this almost nonexistent variation in her students' Procedure X item performances, those items produced particularly low item-discrimination indices—much lower than those regarded as acceptable. Were those Procedure X items flawed? Do they need to be revised or replaced? Of course not! The "culprit" in this caper is simply the teacher's excellent instruction. When almost all students score perfectly on a related set of test items because their teacher has done a spectacular instructional job teaching whatever those items measure, does this make the items unacceptable? Obviously not.

Item-discrimination indices, therefore, are often quite inappropriate for evaluating the quality of items in teacher-made tests if those tests are being employed chiefly for instructional purposes. Be wary of unthinkingly submitting your classroom assessments to a medley of traditional item-improvement procedures—empirical or judgmental—that do not mesh with the purpose for which the test was created. For norm-referenced measurement missions, item-discrimination indices have much to recommend them; for criterion-referenced assessment, the results of item-discrimination procedures are often misleading.

Table 11.2 A Typical Distractor-Analysis Table

Item No. 28	Alternatives				
$(p = .50, D = -.33)$	A	B*	C	D	Omit
Upper 15 students	2	5	0	8	0
Lower 15 students	4	10	0	0	1

Distractor Analyses

For a selected-response item that, perhaps on the basis of its p value or its discrimination index, appears to be in need of revision, it is necessary to look deeper. In the case of multiple-choice items, we can gain further insight by carrying out a *distractor analysis*, in which we see how the high and low groups are responding to the item's distractors.

Presented in Table 11.2 is the information typically used when conducting a distractor analysis. Note that the asterisk in Table 11.2 indicates that choice B is the correct answer to the item. For the item in the table, the difficulty index (p) was .50 and the discrimination index (D) was $-.33$. An inspection of the distractors reveals that something in alternative D seems to be enticing the students in the high group to choose it. Indeed, while over half of the high group opted for choice D, not a single student in the low group went for choice D. Alternative D needs to be reviewed carefully.

Also note that alternative C is doing nothing at all for the item. No students at all selected choice C. In addition to revising choice D, therefore, choice C might be made a bit more appealing. It is possible, of course, particularly if this is a best-answer type of multiple-choice item, that alternative B, the correct answer, needs a bit of massaging as well. For multiple-choice items in particular, but also for matching items, a more intensive analysis of student responses to individual distractors can frequently be illuminating. In the same vein, careful scrutiny of students' responses to essay and short-answer items can typically supply useful insights for revision purposes.

Item Analysis for Criterion-Referenced Measurement

When teachers use tests intended to yield criterion-referenced interpretations, they typically want most students to score well on those tests after instruction has occurred. In such instances, because postinstruction p values may approach 1.0, traditional item-analysis approaches often yield low discrimination indices. Accordingly, several alternative approaches to item analysis for criterion-referenced measurement have been devised in recent years.

Parent Talk

Suppose a parent of one of your students called you this morning, before school, to complain about his son's poor performance on your classroom tests. He concludes his grousing by asking you, "Just how sure are you that the fault is in Tony and not in your tests?"

| *If I were you, here's how I'd respond to the parent:*

"I'm glad you called about your son's test results because I'm sure we both want what's best for Tony, and I want to be sure I'm making the instructional decisions that will be best for him.

"The way I use my classroom tests is to try to arrive at the most accurate conclusion I can about how well my students have mastered the skills

and knowledge I'm trying to teach them. It's very important, then, that the conclusions I reach about students' skill levels are valid. So every year I devote systematic attention to the improvement of each of my major exams. You'll remember that it was on the last two of these exams that Tony scored so badly.

"What I'd like to do is show you the exams I've been giving my students and the data I use each year to improve those exams. Why don't we set up an after-school or, if necessary, an evening appointment for you and your wife to look over my classroom assessments and the evidence I've been compiling over the years to make sure my tests help me make valid inferences about what Tony and the rest of my students are learning?"

| *Now, how would you respond to this parent?*

Two general item-analysis schemes have been employed thus far, depending on the kinds of student groups available. Both of these item-analysis schemes are roughly comparable to the item-discrimination indices used with tests that yield norm-referenced inferences. The first approach involves administration of the test to *the same group of students* prior to and following instruction. A disadvantage of this approach is that the teacher must wait for instruction to be completed before securing the item-analysis data. Another problem is that the pretest may be *reactive*, in the sense that its administration sensitizes students to certain items such that their posttest performance is actually a function of the instruction *plus* the pretest's administration.

Using the strategy of testing the same groups of students prior to and after instruction, we can employ an item-discrimination index calculated as follows:

$$D_{ppd} = p_{post} - p_{pre}$$

where p_{post} = proportion of students answering the item correctly on posttest
p_{pre} = proportion of students answering the item correctly on pretest

The value of D_{ppd} (discrimination based on the pretest–posttest difference) can range from -1.00 to $+1.00$, with high positive values indicating that an item is sensitive to instruction.

For example, if 41 percent of the students answered item 27 correctly in the pretest, and 84 percent answered it correctly on the posttest, then item 27's D_{ppd} would be .84 − .41 = .43. A high positive value would indicate that the item is sensitive to the instructional program you've provided to your students. Items with low or negative D_{ppd} values would be earmarked for further analysis, because such items are not behaving the way one would expect them to behave if instruction were effective. (It is always possible, particularly if many items fail to reflect large posttest-minus-pretest differences, that the instruction being provided was not so very wonderful.)

The second approach to item analysis for criterion-referenced measurement is to locate two *different groups of students*, one of which has already been instructed and one of which has not. By comparing the performances on items of instructed and uninstructed students, you can pick up some useful clues regarding item quality. This approach has the advantage of avoiding the delay associated with pretesting and posttesting the same group of students, and it also avoids the possibility of a reactive pretest. Its drawback, however, is that you must rely on human judgment in the selection of the "instructed" and "uninstructed" groups. The two groups should be fairly identical in all other relevant respects (for example, in intellectual ability) but different with respect to whether or not they have been instructed. The isolation of two such groups sounds easier than it usually is. Your best bet would be to prevail on a fellow teacher whose students are studying different topics than yours.

If you use two groups—that is, an instructed group and an uninstructed group—one of the more straightforward item-discrimination indices is D_{uigd} (discrimination based on uninstructed versus instructed group differences). This index is calculated as follows:

$$D_{uigd} = p_i - p_u$$

where p_i = proportion of instructed students answering an item correctly
   p_u = proportion of uninstructed students answering an item correctly

The D_{uigd} index can also range in value from −1.00 to +1.00. To illustrate its computation, if an instructed group of students scored 91 percent correct on a particular item, while the same item was answered correctly by only 55 percent of an uninstructed group, then D_{uigd} would be .91 − .55 = .36. Interpretations of D_{uigd} are similar to those used with D_{ppd}.

As suggested earlier, clearly there are advantages associated with using both judgmental and empirical approaches to improving your classroom assessment procedures. Practically speaking, classroom teachers have only so much energy to expend. If you can spare a bit of your allotted energy to spiff up your assessment instruments, you'll usually see meaningful differences in the quality of those instruments.

But What Does This Have to Do with Teaching?

Because of the demands on most teachers' time, the typical teacher really doesn't have time to engage in unbridled test polishing. So, as a practical matter, very few teachers spend *any* time trying to improve their classroom assessments. It is all too understandable.

But there are two approaches to item improvement described in this chapter, one of which, a judgmentally based strategy, doesn't burn up much time at all. It's a judgmental approach to item improvement that represents a realistic item-improvement model for most classroom teachers.

Whereas teachers should understand the basics of how a test can be made better by using empirical data based on students' responses, they'll rarely be inclined to use such data-based strategies for improving items unless a test is thought to be a super-important one.

During the 29 years that I taught courses in the UCLA Graduate School of Education, the *only* tests that I ever subjected to empirical item-improvement analyses were my midterm and final exams in courses I taught year after year. Oh, to be sure, I applied judgmental improvement techniques to most of my other tests, but the only tests I did a full-throttle, data-based improvement job on were the one or two most important tests for an oft-taught course.

My fear is that the apparent complexity of empirical item-improvement efforts might even dissuade you from routinely employing *judgmental* item-improvement procedures. Don't let it. Even if you *never* use students' data to sharpen your classroom tests, those tests will almost surely still need sharpening. Judgmental approaches will help do the job.

What Do Classroom Teachers Really Need to Know About Improving Their Assessments?

You ought to know that teacher-made tests can be improved as a consequence of judgmental and/or empirical improvement procedures. Judgmental approaches work well with either selected-response or constructed-response test items. Empirical item-improvements have been used chiefly with selected-response tests and hence are more readily employed with such test items. You should realize that most of the more widely used indices of item quality, such as discrimination indices, are intended for use with test items in norm-referenced assessment approaches, and such indices may have less applicability to your tests if you employ criterion-referenced measurement strategies. You must also understand that because educators have far less experience in using (and improving) performance assessments and portfolio assessments, there isn't really a delightful set of improvement procedures available for those assessment strategies—other than good, solid judgment.

One issue not addressed in detail revolves around the question, How do you fix a guilty item? Clearly, because the range of what's potentially rancid about items can be wide indeed, it would be foolish to toss out a list of "Do this when an item is flawed." Flawed items can vary immensely, and so can the context of the settings in which they are used.

For example, one of the frequent floppers in a teacher-made test arises when a teacher employs a pronoun in an item that, because of the way the item is phrased, defies a student's ability to discern to whom the offending pronoun refers. Consider the following true–false item, and then indicate whether—even if a student has clearly understood the meaning of a teacher-selected essay—the italicized statement reeks of truth or falsity: TRUE OR FALSE: *In the essay you just read, Felipe's treatment of Jorge, because of his underlying timidity, resulted in silence.* Now, if Felipe and Jorge were *both* described in the essay as timid, then because of the item's *faulty pronoun referent*, the student can't tell which of the lads remained silent. Thus, an editing fix is clearly in order such as TRUE OR FALSE: *In the essay you just read, Jorge's underlying timidity led to his silence.* Similarly, if teachers are constantly attentive to potential shortcomings in their tests' items, then they'll be more likely to spot some loser items in need of first aid.

Your first analysis of what might be done to improve an item will often be your best bet. It is also possible to enlist the aid of a colleague to help you figure out what might be wrong with an item and how best to obliterate that deficit. The chief thing you have going for you is that you definitely believe that there is something decidedly tawdry about the item, and this is where you use your wits to dispel some of that!

Chapter Summary

This chapter focused on two strategies for improving assessment procedures. It was suggested that, with adequate time and motivation, teachers can use judgmental and/or empirical methods of improving their assessments.

Judgmentally based improvement procedures were described for use by teachers, teachers' colleagues, and students. Five review criteria for evaluating assessment procedures were presented for use by teachers and their colleagues: (1) adherence to item-specific guidelines and general item-writing commandments, (2) contribution to score-based inferences, (3) accuracy of content, (4) absence of gaps in content coverage, and (5) fairness. A set of possible questions to ask *students* about test items was also provided.

Two empirical item-improvement indices described in the chapter were p values and item-discrimination indices. A step-by-step procedure for determining item-discrimination values was described. Designed chiefly for use with norm-referenced measurement, item-discrimination indices do not function well when large numbers of students respond correctly (or incorrectly) to the items involved. Distractor analyses have proven highly useful in the improvement of multiple-choice items because the effectiveness of each item's alternatives can be studied. Finally, two indices of item quality for criterion-referenced measurement were described. Although roughly comparable to the kind of item-discrimination indices widely used with norm-referenced measurement, the two indices for criterion-referenced assessment can be used in settings where many effectively taught students perform well on examinations.

MyLab Education **Self-Check 11.1**

MyLab Education **Self-Check 11.2**

MyLab Education **Application Exercise 11.1: Improving Teacher-Based Assessments**

References

Downing, Steven M., and Haladyna, T. M. (Eds.). (2006). *Handbook of test development.* Mahwah, NJ: Erlbaum.

Ebel, R. L., and Frisbie, D. A. (1991). *Essentials of educational measurement* (5th ed.). Englewood Cliffs, NJ: Prentice-Hall.

Miller, M. D., and Linn, R. (2012). *Measurement and assessment in teaching* (11th ed.). Columbus, OH: Pearson.

Thorndike, Robert M., and Thorndike-Christ, T. (2010). *Measurement and evaluation in psychology and education* (8th ed.). Boston: Allyn and Bacon.

Waugh, C. K., and Gronlund, N. (2012). *Measurement and assessment in teaching* (11th ed.). Columbus, OH: Pearson.

Improving Teachers' Test Items: The Oft-Misunderstood p Value*

W. James Popham, University of California, Los Angeles

Perhaps the most frequent empirical indicator of an item's performance is the p value. Frequently referred to as an item's "difficulty," a p value simply indicates what percent of the students who responded to an item answered it correctly. Thus, if an item were answered correctly by 82 percent of test takers, then this item would have a p value of .82.

Where many educators get in trouble, however, is when they think of items with a high p value as "easy" and of items with a low p value as "hard." Yet, an item with a low p value of, say, .30, might be associated with a topic that hasn't been taught yet or was taught less than wonderfully. It is more sensible to consider an item's p value *only* in the context of previous instruction regarding the item's content. We want well-taught students earning gobs of high p values on intrinsically challenging items.

Teachers who construct their own classroom tests typically do so with the best of intentions. Indeed, most teachers aspire to create assessments containing only fabulous, flaw-free items. But, of course, despite such laudable aspirations, some teacher-made tests include items with serious shortcomings. Defective items, obviously, reduce a test's ability to provide an accurate estimate of a test taker's status regarding whatever's being assessed—with a resultant distortion in score-based interpretations regarding what a test taker knows and can do.

Fortunately, through the years, assessment specialists have devised a winning two-part strategy to improve test items—a strategy that can be successfully employed with both teacher-made items and items in the standardized tests administered to thousands of students. The strategy's two item-improvement components are *judgmental* and *empirical*.

Judgmental item-improvement calls for items to be reviewed, one item at a time, according to a set of evaluative guidelines painstakingly generated over the years regarding how best to construct specific sorts of items such as short-answer questions. Items that don't adhere to those guidelines can be improved.

Empirical item-improvement is based on the way a test's items function when they are used in an actual examination. Statistical analyses of the items provide such evidence as whether certain items seem to be performing too differently than other items intended to measure the same skill or body of knowledge. Clearly, the more students who complete a test, the more confidence we have in such analyses.

Understandably, classroom teachers use judgmental improvement techniques. In contrast, builders of large-scale tests lean more heavily, but not exclusively, on empirical item improvement.

Chapter 12
Formative Assessment

Learning Outcomes

12.1 Distinguish the characteristics of formative assessment and identify their proper and improper implementation.

Chief Chapter Outcome

An understanding of research-ratified formative assessment's essence sufficient for identifying teachers' proper and improper implementations of the formative-assessment process

Suppose there were a really convincing collection of research evidence showing that a particular *assessment-based* instructional strategy helped students learn more and learn it better. Suppose, further, that because this assessment-based instructional strategy helped students learn more and learn it better, teachers who used this research-supported strategy became demonstrably more successful.

Because both of those two suppositions are stone-cold true, wouldn't it seem that most of today's teachers would be using this assessment-based instructional strategy in their classrooms? Yet, currently, most teachers aren't. In this chapter, you'll discover why.

Assessment That Transforms Teaching

The assessment-based instructional strategy to be treated in this chapter is *formative assessment*, and you'll learn what it is and what it isn't. You'll also learn why, when abundant evidence is at hand indicating that formative assessment works—and works well—this potent process is not more widely employed by teachers. As you read further in the chapter, see whether you can figure out—on your own—why far fewer teachers are currently employing formative assessment than one might think. That's right, think of the chapter as a condensed mystery novel in which your task is to understand what formative assessment is, discover how it can improve a teacher's effectiveness, and then come up with an accurate answer to the following question: *Why is formative assessment, a research-ratified instructional strategy, not more widely used in our schools?*

Early on, however, I want to get my personal preference out there in plain view so you can interpret my chapter-chatter more accurately. I am a definite believer in formative assessment. I think research evidence aplenty exists showing us that formative assessment helps kids learn better. Based on this belief, I want to see formative assessment used more extensively in our schools. As you continue to read, whether you are an experienced teacher or a teacher in preparation, you'll sometimes find me touting the merits of formative assessment. This is because I think formative assessment constitutes a potent process that *all* educators should be advocating.

What Is Formative Assessment?

Let's look at the definition of formative assessment and then poke briefly into this definition's key elements:

> Formative assessment is a planned process in which assessment-elicited evidence of students' status is used by teachers to adjust their ongoing instructional procedures, or by students to adjust their current learning tactics.

A process, not a test. Perhaps what's most important in this definition is that formative assessment is a process rather than a test. Moreover, it is a *planned* process. So, during a teachers' lounge conversation, if one of your colleagues were to describe a particular test as "a formative test," you now know that, according to the previous definition, your colleague would be mistaken. Formative assessment is not a test but, instead, a carefully conceived process wherein the results of assessments are used by teachers or students to improve what they are doing. The process of collecting such assessment-based evidence, and then using this evidence to make any needed adjustments, is at the very heart of the formative-assessment process. If you prefer, you can accurately think of formative assessment as an *instructional strategy*. It's a strategy for using assessment-elicited evidence to enhance teachers' instruction and to improve students' learning. It is, most definitely, not a particular type of test.

As you will soon see, thoughtful planning needs to take place early in the formative-assessment process—a process that is definitely not a spur-of-the-moment undertaking. Teachers, of course, make on-the-spot changes all the time. For example, in the midst of what a teacher believes will be a lucid explanation of a particular concept, if the teacher sees that most students look totally confused, the teacher might sensibly make an instant decision to start the explanation over again, trying thereby to improve its clarity. Spontaneous instructional changes of this sort are fine, and they'll often improve instruction. Such on-the-spot instructional changes should be encouraged. *They just aren't formative assessment.* Formative assessment is a process requiring some serious up-front thinking by teachers if it is going to work as well as the research evidence says it can work.

TERMINOLOGICAL LINEAGE

The "formative" part of the formative-assessment label traces its ancestry to a distinction first drawn by Scriven (1967) over half a century ago. Scriven's separation of formative and summative functions, however, was related to educational *evaluation*, not to assessment. As you will see, the gist of that evaluation-related distinction has been retained when today's educators contrast formative and summative *assessment*. Scriven argued that *summative evaluation* took place when educators appraised the worth of a fully mature, completed instructional program such as a published collection of self-study history booklets. In contrast, *formative evaluation* occurred when educators appraised the worth of a yet malleable instructional program—for example, a set of instructional materials still in the tryout-and-revision stage of development. Summative evaluation is employed to inform *go/no-go decisions* about a program, whereas formative evaluation is used to make *improvement decisions* regarding a program. These evaluation-related meanings of the adjectives *formative* and *summative* have carried over to today when those two labels are applied to the use of educational assessments.

Summative assessment takes place when educators collect test-based evidence to inform decisions about instructional activities already completed, such as when statewide accountability tests are administered each spring to determine the instructional effectiveness of a state's schools during the soon-to-be-completed school year. As another example of summative assessment, think of the final examination a teacher administers to her students, one key purpose of that exam being to help the teacher assign an appropriate grade to her students based on how much those students have learned during a semester or school year. The decision riding on results of the student's performance on the final exam is not an instructional-improvement decision but, rather, a decision about what grades the teacher should dole out to her students.

In contrast to summative assessment, formative assessment focuses on improving the way teachers are teaching something and the way students are learning something. Formative assessment has a "make-better" measurement mission, whereas summative assessment tries to answer the oft-voiced "instructional-quality" question.

Although a given test may be employed in connection with a summative-assessment function, it is possible (if the test is properly crafted) for this very same test also to be used as part of the formative-assessment process. In other words, *tests*, all by themselves, are neither formative nor summative. It is the *use* to which a given test's results are put that makes the assessment a part of the formative-assessment process or, instead, finds it contributing to a summative-assessment decision. Of course, if educators specifically build a test to fulfill a specific function, such as the improvement of a teacher's instruction, then the test will more likely be suited for a formative-measurement mission than for a summative-measurement purpose. You'll soon see examples of how to build tests so that they contribute optimally to the formative-assessment process.

ASSESSMENT-BASED EVIDENCE

Getting back to the definition of formative assessment, a central feature of the formative-assessment process is the collection of *evidence* from students via some sort of assessment procedure. This evidence-gathering activity need not rely on formal exams such as paper-and-pencil tests or, these days, computer-presented tests. Although time-honored test tactics are typically time-honored because, over time, they have worked well enough to be retained, you will soon be seeing several more innovative ways of collecting evidence regarding students' mastery of certain skills or knowledge. The assessment-elicited evidence referred to in the definition of formative assessment can be obtained by a wide variety of assessment ploys, not merely traditional assessment procedures.

ADJUSTMENTS

If you take a careful look at the definition of formative assessment, you'll see that the evidence elicited by assessment procedures is used either by *teachers* to adjust their ongoing *instruction*, or by *students* to adjust their current *learning tactics* (the procedures students are using in an attempt to learn what they are supposed to be learning). Formative assessment, therefore, is a process involving teachers and/or students—not merely teachers. Instructional adjustments are made by teachers regarding their ongoing—that is, *current*—instruction, not instruction aimed at a subsequent group of students. Similarly, the adjustments by students in how they're trying to learn something are those adjustments that are made with respect to their current learning tactics, not those learning tactics to be used in next year's or later classes. Formative assessment, although planned in advance, is a "right now" process focused on shaping up what's currently being taught and learned.

It is not a silly idea, of course, for teachers to assess their current students at the close of instruction to see how well those students have learned, and then for those teachers to make changes in next year's or next term's instruction. No, making such changes represents instructional savvy. Indeed, the label often used these days to characterize educators' use of test results and other information in their decision making is ***data-driven education***. Although it is not equivalent to the formative-assessment process, data-driven education clearly focuses on decision makers' utilization of relevant evidence—including, of course, students' test performances. Assessing the impact of this year's instruction on students in order to make improvement-focused adjustments in next year's instruction is a smart way for teachers to operate. But those make-better adjustments, if they do not center on a teacher's *current* collection of students, are not part of the formative-assessment process.

A DISTINCTIVE WAY OF THINKING ABOUT INSTRUCTION

Definitions, even carefully crafted ones, often can't capture the richness of what's being defined. As you look again at the definition of formative assessment, what may not come through is that the formative-assessment process represents a decidedly *distinctive* instructional strategy, a strategy in which teachers and students routinely employ assessments to come up with the evidence to let them know whether adjustments are called for in what's going on in class. Formative assessment is, at bottom, a strategy in which the most important decisions about instruction or learning are based on students' current *assessed* achievement status.

If you, as a teacher-in-training or an experienced teacher, decide to employ formative assessment in your own classes, it is almost certain that you'll end up thinking about instruction in a manner profoundly different from the way most teachers have traditionally conceived of teaching. Formative assessment can, indeed, transform the way a teacher teaches.

Is Formative Assessment the Same as "Assessment *for* Learning"?

In the past several years, some educators have become excited about the potential instructional dividends of swapping a three-letter preposition for a two-letter preposition. You probably recognize that it's difficult to imagine any sort of preposition-exchanging generating even a tiny bit of educational excitement but, surprisingly, it has.

What I am referring to is the notion of assessment *for* learning that's being recommended, instead of the more traditional way of thinking about assessment—namely, assessment *of* learning. You see, when most educators thought about assessment in years past, those educators saw assessment chiefly as a way of figuring out how much their students have learned. Clearly, the time-honored way of regarding testing was to conceive of it as assessment *of* learning. But, increasingly, we find prominent instructional specialists arguing that if teachers are ever to get the most instructional mileage out of their classroom testing, then the way to regard such testing is to view it as a vehicle to enhance instructional effectiveness or, with only a simple preposition-flip, to view it as assessment *for* learning.

Incidentally, assessment *for* learning is not supposed to replace all instances of assessment *of* learning. There are many situations in education when we really do want to find out what kids know and what they don't know. That's assessment *of* learning, and it's not a bad thing. However, there should be many more occasions when assessment *for* learning should dominate an instructional scene. But before getting into some of the ways in which assessment *for* learning can be installed in a teacher's classroom, let's clarify where this feisty little phrase came from in the first place.

In the United States, the expression "assessment *for* learning" is often mistakenly attributed to Richard Stiggins (2007) or to Paul Black and Dylan Wiliam (1998a), even though all three of these individuals always deny paternity regarding their fathering of the phrase. Because Dylan Wiliam is an able colleague and a good friend, and because he is associated with the Assessment Reform Group in England, where many people think the phrase emerged, I asked Dylan if he would be willing to sleuth out the origin of assessment *for* learning. (Sherlock Holmes, after all, was British.) Dylan agreed, and what he came up with you'll find in the following paragraph.

The earliest use of the phrase "assessment for learning" appears to have been in a paper presented by a Brit, Mary James (1992), at a New Orleans conference of the Association for Supervision and Curriculum Development.

Three years later, the phrase was used by Ruth Sutton of England as the title of a book she wrote (Sutton, 1995). However, the first explicit contrast of assessment *for* learning with assessment *of* learning seems to have occurred in the third edition of a book by Gipps and Stobart (1997) where their first chapter is titled "Assessment of Learning" and their second chapter is titled "Assessment for Learning." This prepositional distinction was brought to a wider audience two years later by England's Assessment Reform Group in a guide for policymakers (Broadfoot et al., 1999).

So, thanks to Dylan's dogged Sherlocking, we now have an idea where this fine formulation came from. It is apparent that most, if not all, of the early thinking on this issue came to the United States from Great Britain. Thus, in addition to the debt we owe the Brits for tea, scones, and the Beatles, we now have something in the assessment realm for which we should be grateful.

For all practical purposes, the phrases *formative assessment* and *assessment for learning* can be seen as essentially interchangeable. However, not everyone who employs either one of these two descriptors always does so properly. As you'll see in a moment, the research evidence supporting the use of formative assessment is compelling. But that evidence does not support *any old* approach that someone decides to label as formative assessment, assessment for learning, or my Aunt Agnes's way of teaching and testing.

Regrettably, we now find test publishers hawking all sorts of assessment products using the label "formative assessment." Lorrie Shepard, a leading U.S. assessment expert, has become particularly vexed with what she regards as test vendors' corruption, for marketing purposes, of an otherwise powerful assessment concept. As Shepard (2006) points out,

> The research-based concept of formative assessment, closely grounded in classroom instructional processes, has been taken over (hijacked) by commercial test publishers and used instead to refer to formal testing systems called benchmark or interim assessment systems. (p. 5)

What Formative Assessment Isn't

As you look back at the definition of formative assessment, you can discern that some applications of educational assessment would obviously not satisfy the definition's requirements. For instance, when annual accountability tests are administered at the close of a school year to evaluate a state's schools, this would clearly not be an instance of formative assessment.

And you've already learned that a test itself is not formative assessment. Tests are used to collect information that can lead teachers or students to adjust what they are currently doing. But tests, all by themselves, are not formative assessment.

You've also seen that formative assessment is a *planned* process, not a collection of off-the-cuff alterations in what's going on in class. Although teachers make instant, unplanned changes in their instructional activities, such changes do not make what's going on formative assessment. Careful thought must be given to what sorts of changes might be made, what sorts of evidence might be collected related to those changes, and what kinds of assessment devices might be used to secure this evidence. Don't let a colleague tell you, "I already use formative assessment because I can tell from my students' comments and their facial expressions whether I need to make any instructional adjustments." Such adjustments, though frequently informative to a teacher, simply aren't formative assessment.

Moreover, as you saw earlier from Shepard's comment, formative assessment is most definitely *not* what commercial companies happen to call their products. As she noted, some vendors are now peddling assessment materials they describe by using labels such as *interim assessments* and *benchmark assessments*. Other vendors are calling the very same types of tests "formative." Commercial companies, of course, can call their products pretty much what they want to—barring violations of registered trademarks. But just because a commercial product is *called* formative assessment by vendors, or even by a group of well-intentioned educators who have built their own test, this mislabeling does not make that product automatically mesh with the kind of empirical research evidence undergirding the success of the formative-assessment process.

When does a teacher use formative assessment? Is it a once-in-a-while activity or an every-single-minute activity? Well, different educators may have different answers to such questions, but most teachers will use the formative-assessment process selectively. To be blunt, properly conceived formative assessment demands a heap of hard thinking on the teacher's part, not to mention the necessary collection of assessment evidence from students. Formative assessment has the clear potential to prove burdensome to teachers and, therefore, to dissuade them from using it. But, as you'll soon see, formative assessment helps students learn. If it's not used, then students will be instructionally short-changed. Accordingly, teachers should use formative assessment judiciously—not constantly—as they promote students' mastery of truly significant curricular aims.

What this judicious use of formative assessment means, in practice, is that teachers will typically be using the formative-assessment process as they pursue students' attainment of really challenging outcomes. Such outcomes, because they tend to be dependent on higher-order cognitive competencies, typically take some time to teach, perhaps several weeks or even a full semester or school year. It just doesn't make much sense for teachers to direct the powerful formative-assessment process at a student's mastery of, say, a set of memorized information that can be taught successfully in a couple of days. This is not a knock on the importance of students' acquisition of knowledge. Possession of knowledge is a tremendous accomplishment for a student. But more often than not, one's knowledge is then employed in the application of higher-order cognitive skills. Because such skills take a hefty hunk of time to teach, formative assessment often works best when it is employed by teachers as they promote their students' mastery of these really significant curricular aims.

Research Supporting Formative Assessment

Certain actions should be taken whether or not there is research evidence supporting those actions. A mother should protect her child even if she has not read a definitive research-rooted article in *Pediatrics* that attests to the wisdom of a particular maternal protective action. Similarly, we hold the door open for an overloaded supermarket shopper because it's the proper thing to do—despite our not having reviewed empirical evidence supporting the positive consequences of such door-opening behavior. Common sense, not research evidence, often inclines people to do the right thing.

Let's think for a moment about formative assessment, an approach to instructional decision making in which a teacher uses along-the-way assessment evidence from students as a guide to whether any instructional adjustments are needed. Formative assessment is an instructional strategy that, on the face of it, makes a sack full of sense. Because teachers are human beings, and human beings often make mistakes, formative assessment simply asks a teacher to monitor students' progress to see whether the teacher's instructional decisions were good ones. Thus, if instructional changes are needed, those changes can be made. Teachers invariably try to "get it right the first time." But, of course, many times an original instructional design will be substantially less than perfect. By monitoring students' status to see how the instruction is working, less-than-wonderful instruction can be altered so it becomes more wonderful. Similarly, if students are given evidence regarding their own progress in learning whatever they're supposed to be learning, then those students can determine whether their learning tactics need to be adjusted. In almost any sort of instructional setting, formative assessment would make sense even if not one dollop of empirical research were at hand to support its effectiveness.

But such research has, in fact, been carried out. It's much more than a dollop, and it's quite persuasive. So, in addition to a common-sense rationale supporting formative assessment as a classroom instructional strategy, teachers now have ample empirical evidence on hand to confirm the commonsensical.

The Black and Wiliam Research Review

Paul Black and Dylan Wiliam are two British researchers who, in 1998, published a remarkably influential review of almost 10 years' worth of empirical research dealing with classroom assessment (Black and Wiliam, 1998a). "Assessment and Classroom Learning," their rather technical review, appeared in the March 1998 issue of the journal *Assessment in Education* and, frankly, attracted only modest attention among U.S. educators. However, in October of the same year, these two authors published a follow-up article in the more widely read *Phi Delta Kappan* (Black and Wiliam, 1998b) not only summarizing their earlier review of research evidence but also describing policy implications of that evidence. In contrast to the March article's almost nonexistent impact on the thinking of American educators, the October essay in the *Kappan* garnered considerable attention. It was Black and Wiliam's March review of classroom assessment research, however, that provided the chief empirical underpinnings of today's formative assessment. As a consequence, let's first look at what these two British researchers concluded from their analyses.

The following quotation is, for all current teachers and all prospective teachers, worth at least two or three readings:

> The research reported here shows conclusively that formative assessment does improve learning. (Black and Wiliam, 1998a, p. 61)

Are those learning improvements something substantial or something trifling? Well, Black and Wiliam (1998a) concluded that the student gains in learning triggered by formative assessment were "amongst the largest ever reported for educational interventions" (p. 61)! Let's look at this last conclusion for a moment. First off, we need to take seriously any assertion containing the term *amongst*. (Even in print, British people seem so convincingly credible.) But, more important, please note that formative assessment, when used by teachers in their classrooms, is capable of causing student gains as great as any ever reported for educational interventions. We are not talking here about tiny improvements in kid learning. No, on the contrary, these are whopping gains that formative assessment can bring about in students' achievement.

One conclusion reached by Black and Wiliam that makes their work especially relevant to teachers' day-to-day instruction is their finding that formative assessment is truly robust. In other words, if formative assessment is installed by teachers, *it is nearly certain to work.* As Black and Wiliam observe, "Significant gains can be achieved by many different routes, and initiatives here are not likely to fail through neglect of delicate and subtle features" (1998a, p. 61). In their review, Black and Wiliam supply numerous examples of research investigations in which it is apparent that formative assessment makes a meaningful contribution to students' learning. Sometimes the studies being reviewed focused on teachers' adjustments of their instruction; sometimes the reviewed reports dealt with students' adjustments of their own learning tactics. As Black and Wiliam observe,

> [T]he consistent feature across the variety of these examples is that they all show that attention to formative assessment can lead to significant learning gains. Although there is no guarantee that it will do so irrespective of the context and the particular approach adopted, we have not come across any report of negative effects following . . . an enhancement of formative practice. (1998a, p. 17)

But even though there was some interest in the 1998 *Kappan* summary of the March 1998 research review, it was not until the enactment of No Child Left Behind (NCLB) that U.S. educators turned their attention seriously to the instructional recommendations provided by these two British scholars. This was because NCLB's 2002 enactment called for U.S. educators to boost students' scores on accountability tests substantially, moving toward a point where, in 2014, all students in U.S. public schools would achieve "proficient or better" scores on NCLB-required state exams. Faced with this nontrivial challenge, many American educators recalled the 1998 *Kappan* article, which had pointed out that formative assessment could boost students' achievement—not just a little, but a lot!

Well, it did not require a huge inferential leap for numerous U.S. educators to conclude that if students' in-classroom learning could be improved by formative assessment, why would not those same improvements splash over onto students' performances on NCLB accountability tests? And this ushered in what soon became a sometimes frenzied advocacy of formative assessment by many educational leaders. Formative assessment was being touted as an NCLB salvation strategy. Numerous educational administrators really believed that if they could only get enough of their teachers to use formative assessment ("whatever 'formative assessment' is"), then students' scores on NCLB tests would go up sufficiently for educators to dodge NCLB failure.

Wrapping up this quick look at the empirical evidence underlying formative assessment, it is difficult to consider the Black and Wiliam synthesis of classroom assessment research without concluding that the formative-assessment process represents a particularly potent way for assessment to bolster the caliber of teachers' instruction. More recently, Wiliam reported that "Five reviews of the research in this area synthesized a total of more than 4000 research studies undertaken during the last 40 years. The conclusion was clear: When implemented well, formative assessment can effectively double the speed of student learning" (Wiliam, 2007–2008). Let's now look at the fundamental framework around which this speed-doubling assessment-rooted instructional process can be carried out.

Learning Progressions as Frameworks

We can begin by turning to what some readers might regard as a topic more suited for a book about instruction than a book about assessment. But don't forget that the text you're currently reading is about *classroom* assessment, and the major activity that goes on in classrooms is *instruction*. Indeed, it is because formative assessment is an assessment-based way of making a teacher's *instruction* better that you'll find the upcoming topics particularly pertinent to what might go on in your own classroom.

What Is a Learning Progression?

You've seen that formative assessment is basically a process in which assessment evidence is used by teachers or students to adjust what they are doing. Well, when is this assessment evidence to be collected? Clearly, teachers can't be collecting assessment evidence from kids every few minutes. After all, the really big job facing teachers is to *teach* students, not *test* students. At what points, then, during an instructional sequence should students be assessed so that teachers (or the students themselves) can decide whether adjustments are in order? The answer to this significant question revolves around teachers' reliance on a *learning progression*. Here's what a learning progression is:

> A learning progression is a sequenced set of building blocks—that is, subskills or bodies of enabling knowledge—that it is thought students must master in the course of mastering a more remote, target curricular aim.

In plain language, a learning progression is an ordered sequence of the stuff a student must learn so as to achieve a significant curricular outcome. Because the construction of a learning progression requires an expenditure of time and energy from a teacher, the "significant curricular outcome" being sought will typically deal with students' mastery of a high-level cognitive skill, the kind of skill that is apt to take a meaningful amount of time to teach. Examples of such skills include a student's ability to (1) design a defensible scientific investigation, (2) write a powerful persuasive essay, or (3) select and compute the most effective statistical indicators to accurately represent a set of empirical data. Thus, the use of learning progressions and, in truth, the use of the formative-assessment process itself, is often focused on the pursuit of significant curricular aims.

Let's briefly consider the key components of the preceding definition of a learning progression. First off, the purpose of a learning progression is to identify what students need to master on their way to mastering a more remote, *target curricular aim*. This aim, as already noted, is usually a higher-order cognitive skill. So that students can master such a target curricular aim, they will almost always first need to master one or more lesser curricular aims. These lesser aims are called *building blocks*, and they consist of either *bodies of enabling knowledge* or *cognitive subskills*.

To illustrate, if the target curricular aim being sought were for students to be able to write a clear expository (explanatory) essay, then one building block might be for the student to know (that is, to have memorized) the important mechanical conventions of spelling, punctuation, and grammar. Knowing and adhering to those conventions, the student is likely to write a clearer essay than one laden with errors in spelling, punctuation, and grammar. Thus, the student's knowledge of mechanical conventions would be one *enabling knowledge* building block in a learning progression that's aimed at the student's skill in writing expository essays.

Another building block in this instance might be a *cognitive subskill*. Such a subskill might be the student's ability to effectively organize the information to be presented in an expository essay so that the essay's readers would most readily understand what was being explained. The appropriate organization of an essay's content, then, might be a second building block for this learning progression.

One of the most common mistakes teachers make in developing a learning progression is to include too many building blocks. That's right, the more conversant a teacher becomes with the subskills and knowledge a student must possess to master a target curricular aim, the greater the teacher's tendency to toss in more and more building blocks. This is surely understandable, for the more we know about something, the more attentive we become to its nuances. Yet, as you will soon see, students' mastery of *each* building block in a learning progression must be assessed. With too many building blocks in a learning progression, this assessment obligation often gets out of hand. It makes more sense to focus on a modest number of building blocks that are *truly* requisite for a student's mastery of the target curricular aim than to focus on a larger number of building blocks that are *arguably* requisite. In learning progressions, as in many realms of life, less is most definitely more.

Finally, the building blocks in a learning progression should be sequenced in the order in which it is believed students can most effectively master those building blocks on their way to mastering the target curricular aim. This sequence of building blocks is the one that the persons who are developing a learning progression believe is the most sensible. Although there are several intuitively reasonable guidelines for this sequencing of building blocks, such as "transmit knowledge before asking students to apply such knowledge," the actual sequence of building blocks in a learning progression is up to the persons who are building the progression. Here's where a teacher's pedagogical prowess comes into play, for a teacher must determine the *optimal* order in which students should try to master knowledge and subskills along the way to mastery.

Figure 12.1 shows one way in which a learning progression can be represented graphically. Note that, in this instance, the target curricular aim is represented by a rectangle, the two bodies of enabling knowledge are signified by squares, and the solo requisite subskill is depicted by a circle. If you generate your own learning progressions, of course, you can employ any symbols that suit you. Learning progressions can be displayed horizontally as well as vertically. Again, graphical representations are up to those who are trying to represent the learning progression. But most educators report that having access to some sort of graphical depiction of a learning progression helps them more easily grasp the relationships among the progression's building blocks and its target curricular aim.

Recalling that formative assessment rests on the use of assessment-elicited evidence by teachers (or students) to make adjustment decisions, when teachers identify the key building blocks that they believe their students must master en

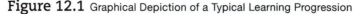

Figure 12.1 Graphical Depiction of a Typical Learning Progression

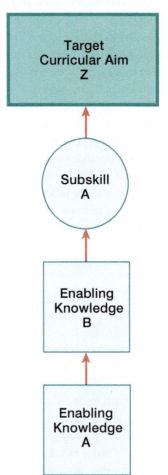

route to the attainment of a target curricular aim, those teachers have thereby determined *when to assess* their students. If every building block is regarded as genuinely *requisite* for the student's advancement toward mastery of a curricular aim, then it is apparent that a teacher will need to see whether each building block has, in fact, been mastered. The formative-assessment process revolves around assessments and the adjustment decisions associated with every building block in a learning progression. Clearly, this is why learning progressions are regarded as the guiding framework for formative assessment.

Teachers should know, however, that a learning progression is *not* unerringly accurate. In few instances are we are able to send learning progressions through the tryout-and-revision cycles that would empirically confirm their accuracy. Rather, learning progressions usually represent the best estimate that educators can make about what things students must master on their way to mastery of a significant curricular aim—and about what constitutes a sensible instructional sequence for those things. Most learning progressions undergo a good many modifications as they are developed and as they are used. Finally, a particular learning progression is unlikely to work well for all students. Some students learn in different, seemingly mysterious ways. A learning progression that might function marvelously for most students will often flop for a few. For those few students, meaningful modifications in "their" learning progression will be needed.

Building a Learning Progression

How does a teacher, or a group of teachers, build a learning progression? In a moment, you will be presented with a four-step process that you might try when doing so. But if you do, then you'll need to invoke not only your emerging measurement moxie, but also your teaching talents. This is because the decisions made regarding the creation of a formative assessment's learning progression will usually determine the success or failure of a given application of the formative-assessment process. More specifically, because a learning progression's building blocks are the things that *must* be learned by students, then near the close of instruction *for each building block*, students' status regarding the building block *must* be assessed. This means that the grain size of the target curricular aim, as well as the grain size of the learning progression's building blocks, should be "just right." The term *grain size* refers to the scope of a curricular aim or building block. Large grain-size building blocks are broader and take more time to teach. Large grain-size building blocks sometimes subsume smaller chunks of knowledge or lesser subskills.

Because too many building blocks can clutter up the formative-assessment process so that it becomes too time-consuming to use, the builders of learning progressions must strive to identify fairly large grain-size building blocks so that a learning progression doesn't contain more building blocks than the teacher has the energy to consider. At the same time, those larger grain-size building blocks should not contain such a heterogeneous bundle of skills and knowledge that what's in a building block is too scattered to be approached instructionally. Yes, the builders of learning progressions need to know not only their testing basics, but also their teaching basics.

Here, then, are four steps you might consider following in the creation of a learning progression to serve as the formative-assessment framework for a fairly significant target curricular aim—typically a powerful cognitive skill that your students are supposed to master.

Step 1: *Acquire a thorough understanding of the target curricular aim.* Don't even think about building a learning progression unless you first arrive at a fuzz-free fix on the nature of the target curricular aim itself. You can't come up with appropriate building blocks unless you completely comprehend the essence of the outcome being sought. One of the best ways to understand the nature of that target curricular aim is to become familiar with the *assessment* procedure (or procedures) to be employed in measuring students' mastery of the aim. If you are the person who will build this assessment procedure (or have already built it), then you surely have a good idea what the target curricular aim is. If, however, others have built the end-of-instruction assessment(s), be sure you understand it (them) completely. Tests "operationalize" curricular aims—that is, tests constitute the operations that students must display in order to show us the degree to which they've mastered a curricular aim.

Step 2: *Identify all requisite precursory subskills and bodies of enabling knowledge.* This second step is really the toughest of our four-step process. In this second step, you need to think through what students really must know and be able to do if they are going to be successful in mastering the target curricular aim. The most influential word in this second step is *requisite.* This second step is an effort to isolate all "must-know" subskills and knowledge. This second step is not a time to identify "nice-to-know" subskills and knowledge. To keep the number of building blocks manageable, it is sometimes necessary for several lesser subskills or bodies of enabling knowledge to be coalesced into larger, yet teachable grain sizes. But the focus in this second step must be the isolation of what is truly *necessary* for students to have mastered on their way to mastery of the target curricular aim.

Step 3: *Determine the measurability of each preliminarily identified building block.* So far, you will have identified—in Step 2—the building blocks you deem to be necessary precursors to a student's mastery of the target curricular aim. In this third step, you must make certain that you can realistically collect evidence regarding students' mastery of each building block. The heart of the formative-assessment process is to find out how students are progressing with respect to each building block, and this means measuring students' status regarding *all* the building blocks in the learning progression. Although the assessments of students' building-block status must be carefully conceived, those assessments need not be formal, elaborate, "big deal" tests. Frequently, for example, teachers can get a sufficiently accurate fix (for making adjustment decisions) by using mini-quizzes of only a few binary-choice items or, perhaps, by employing a short-answer essay item. But, if you can't—in a practical manner—assess students' mastery of each building block, then you ought to dump the unmeasurable ones.

Step 4: *Arrange all the building blocks in an instructionally sensible sequence.* This final step calls for you to think through what sort of sequence makes the most sense from an instructional perspective and then place the learning progression's building blocks in that order. As noted before, teachers rarely have time to try these sequences out to make sure a given sequence is working properly, and it is often necessary to rearrange the sequences after the learning progression has been used a time or two. However, this is the point at which a teacher's instructional acumen is needed. Simply sequence the learning progression's building blocks in the order in which a teacher should most effectively tackle them.

Because formative assessment is a planned process in which students are periodically assessed and, if necessary, adjustments are made, the importance of learning progressions cannot be overestimated. If you decide to employ formative assessment in your own classes, any time that you devote to generating a defensible learning progression for your most significant curricular aims will be time well spent.

In certain other nations—for instance, Australia and New Zealand—educators often think of learning progressions as much more elongated sequences of students' likely learning chains. For example, a group of educators might describe a step-by-step progression of skills and knowledge that a student would typically acquire, over the course of several years, en route to a sophisticated mastery of a given subject. Such long-term views of learning progressions can be useful to teachers, particularly in devising the kinds of shorter-duration learning progressions described in this chapter.

Formative Assessment: A Means-Ends Game

So far, in this chapter's look at formative assessment, we've considered what formative assessment is, its research base, and the role of learning progressions as frameworks for formative assessment. Happily, during the past decade, a host of different measurement and/or instructional specialists have written an array of readable and practical step-by-step approaches to the planning and delivery of first-rate formative assessment. These books are cited in the references section at the close of this chapter. They offer you a considerable range of strategies and tactics for thinking about and implementing the formative-assessment process.

One of the most encouraging conclusions emerging from Black and Wiliam's (1998a) influential review of classroom assessment studies is that the formative-assessment process is remarkably robust. That is, a teacher who uses it is likely to boost students' learning, irrespective of the way in which the teacher employs formative assessment. As long as the teacher focuses on the collection of assessment evidence from students so that, based on such evidence, either the teacher or the teacher's students can make decisions about adjusting what they're doing, then the odds are that formative assessment will work.

Perhaps we should not be surprised that evidence galore now exists undergirding the effectiveness of the formative-assessment process. After all, what is formative assessment other than the instantiation of means-ends thinking? In truth, means-ends thinking (or, if you prefer, ends-means thinking) has surely been around ever since humans first trod the earth. It has been around because it works. Formative assessment is merely means-ends thinking in action.

In traditional means-ends strategies unrelated to education, someone—or some group—identifies an outcome to be sought—for instance, reduction in the temperature of the water in a lake with much tourist traffic where, in recent years, many of the lake's animals and fish have perished because of atypically high lake temperatures. Okay, there's the *end* of our brief illustration—*cooling the lake water's temperature*. Now, the question is what means we should use to successfully achieve our cool-the-lake end. Well, one approach might be to divert several cold-water mountain streams into the lake via water pipes 1 yard in diameter. At a substantial cost, two small streams are then diverted so that much of their water enters the lake—with the obvious intention of lowering the lake's temperature. After one year of implementing this tactic, the lake's temperature shows a substantial decrease. The desired end was achieved by using the means that had been chosen for that purpose.

But not all means-ends forays end so smilingly. Suppose, for example, that despite the water diversion scheme described previously, no meaningful lowering of the lake's temperature was seen. The chosen means did not lead to the end that had been sought. Those in charge of the project would then select another tactic (that is, a different means), still hoping to achieve a bit of lake cooling. And again, subsequently determining the temperature of the lake would be the best way to find out whether the new set of means was more successful than those previously tried, but unsuccessful, means. Just as in lake cooling, we carry out similar means-ends approaches, often subconsciously, in our everyday lives because ends-means thinking works. Why wouldn't we apply this approach to assessment?

And this is precisely the reason why the formative-assessment process has been shown to be so potent in our schools. After having identified an important curricular goal to be promoted for a group of students—that is, an educational end—teachers then consider how best to instruct their students so that the target goal will be achieved. Along the way, as the instruction is taking place, teachers collect assessment-elicited evidence from students to determine the degree to which what's going on instructionally is working. If evidence from en route assessments indicates that students are learning what they are supposed to be learning, then no major alterations in instruction are needed. However, if the results of en route assessments (the tests linked to building blocks) indicate that inadequate progress is occurring in students' learning, then it seems patently appropriate for the teacher to install serious adjustments in the previously selected instructional means. Application of a means-ends strategy has indicated that the chosen means were not getting the instructional job done. It is clearly time for teachers and/or students to make adjustments in the means being implemented.

Why the Delay?

At the beginning of this chapter, you were asked to figure out why formative assessment, an assessment-based instructional strategy boasting all sorts of research support, is not more widely used in our schools. Now it's time to come up with an answer to that question. Why do *you* think we don't currently see formative assessment flourishing in most of the nation's classrooms?

There is no right answer to this important question, but we can identify at least three reasons why we seem to be dawdling in the implementation of formative assessment. Let's see how these answers mesh with those you may have come up with on your own as you were reading the chapter.

One deterrent to our greater use of formative assessment is educators' *considerable misunderstanding about the nature of formative assessment*. Large numbers of educators think of formative assessment as a test, not a process. It's tough to get substantial benefits in kid learning if teachers think some sort of magic-bullet test is going to help them transform a faulty instructional sequence into a terrific one. Another form of misunderstanding occurs when educators believe formative assessment is intended to help only *teachers* adjust what they are up to, not to help *students* alter their learning tactics as well. The Black and Wiliam research review (1998a) makes it clear that if students are actively involved in the learning process, and are given the assessment data to manage their own learning tactics, those students will display achievements superior to those displayed by students who are not involved in the learning process and do not monitor their own ongoing progress. A misunderstood formative-assessment process is unlikely to be widely adopted, because those educational leaders who are encouraging teachers to employ formative assessment will end up advocating with imprecision that which they themselves do not understand.

Parent Talk

Suppose one of your better students, Mary Ruth Green, brings in a note from her parents, expressing concern that your classes seem to be organized to "teach to the test, not educate students." Mr. and Mrs. Green ask you to call them at home so that, using their speaker phone, they can both discuss this concern with you.

> If I were you, here's what I'd say on the phone to Mary Ruth's parents:

"Thanks for raising this issue. It's an important concern, and because we all want what's best for Mary Ruth, I'm pleased to be able to explain how we're using tests in my class.

"Actually, I do use tests to influence my instruction. But the tests really only *represent* the skills and knowledge I'm trying to get Mary Ruth and her classmates to learn. I use the tests to help me plan my instruction and to make an interpretation about whether students are mastering what the test represents. In this way, I'll know whether more instruction is needed on particular topics.

"Please be assured that I am definitely not teaching to particular test items. All of the items on my tests, in fact, have never been seen before by the students. But those items do reflect the knowledge and skills my class is supposed to promote for students.

"Remember also that half of Mary Ruth's grade is based on the portfolio-assessment system we use. I think the portfolio work samples, when blended with the test results, give me an even better picture of my students' progress."

> Now, how would you respond to Mr. and Mrs. Green?

Nor do most of the nation's assessment companies help out in this regard. Many, but certainly not all, testing vendors have developed their own for-purchase assessment products that they promote as the way to boost students' scores on high-stakes accountability tests. Such companies have little interest in helping teachers understand that, according to the research evidence now at our disposal, it is formative assessment *as an evidence-informed, classroom monitoring/ adjustment process* that has been shown to be effective—not a collection of pre-fabricated, off-the-shelf assessment systems labeled as *formative*. Thus, some self-interested assessment firms are contributing directly to misunderstandings about formative assessment on the part of educators.

A second roadblock to educators' greater use of formative assessment is the inherent difficulty of getting people to change their ways. Most of today's educators have been educating students for more than a few minutes. And during the years that those educators have been doing their jobs, they have adopted certain instructional behaviors that, in their estimation, work! Almost all teachers think what they're doing helps their students. Otherwise, most teachers would not be doing those things. Now, because of most teachers' firm beliefs that what they have been doing will benefit students, you can see how difficult it is to get those teachers to adopt something fundamentally different. So, another factor slowing down teachers' acceptance of a research-supported classroom strategy that works is, simply, human beings' reluctance to abandon their established behaviors.

Finally, despite the fact that formative assessment can improve students' achievement, and improve it dramatically, this improved achievement may not show up on many external accountability tests. In Chapter 15 you will learn why this is so. But in a nutshell preview of that chapter's message, certain kinds of external accountability tests are basically unable to accurately measure the quality of instruction students receive. Insofar as this is true, teachers who might be doing a crackerjack instructional job by using formative assessment may discover that, despite what their *classroom* tests demonstrate is considerable improvement in their students' achievement, those improvements simply don't show up on the high-stakes tests being used in that locale to evaluate schools. Disillusioned with such results, some teachers understandably back away from using what seems to be an ineffectual formative-assessment process. After you read Chapter 15, you will see why this is so.

These, then, are three reasons why formative assessment is not more widely employed in our schools: (1) misunderstandings about formative assessment, (2) teachers' tendencies to resist altering their current conduct, and (3) the failure of many external accountability tests to accurately mirror the improvements occurring in the classrooms of teachers who use formative assessment. You may, of course, arrive at other reasons why we are not currently surrounded by swarms of teachers who rely on formative assessment to deliver the best possible instruction to their students.

Whatever obstacles exist to the greater use of formative assessment, we need to overcome those impediments. We must do whatever is necessary so that formative assessment will be used far more widely in our nation's classrooms. Formative assessment works, and it works to help students learn. Accordingly, we need much more of it.

What Do Classroom Teachers Really Need to Know About Formative Assessment?

What a teacher really needs to know about formative assessment depends almost completely on what the teacher intends to do with formative assessment. If teachers don't plan to use formative assessment in their own classrooms, then there's much less that such teachers must know about it. A "non-user" teacher, however, should still know what formative assessment is—and what it isn't. It's especially important these days, even for non-using teachers, to understand the essential means-ends nature of formative assessment. This is because, as a member of a school's faculty, such teachers can help forestall their colleagues' sometimes unthinking adoption of commercial products that, though praised by those products' publishers, have essentially no evidence to support their use. If a non-user teacher has a general understanding of what the research basis underlying formative assessment actually is, then research-free claims of effectiveness for commercial products can be contrasted with the kind of substantial empirical evidence that has now shown that classroom assessment, if used formatively, can benefit students. Summing up, even teachers who don't intend to use formative assessment should know what it is, what it isn't, and the nature of its research support.

On the other hand, if a teacher intends to actually use formative assessment, then what that teacher needs to know is substantially greater. For openers, a would-be user of formative assessment must obviously understand what formative assessment is and what it isn't. Any prospective user of formative assessment must surely grasp the means-ends nature of formative assessment as a process in which assessment-elicited evidence allows teachers to adjust their instruction and enables students to adjust their learning tactics—if such adjustments are warranted.

Teachers who intend to use formative assessment must be thoroughly conversant with the structure of learning progressions, and with the role those progressions play in the formative-assessment process. Unless a teacher is fortunate enough to stumble onto an already-developed learning progression for the same target curricular aim a teacher has chosen, then the teacher should be able to build a brand-new learning progression from scratch.

But What Does This Have to Do with Teaching?

Formative assessment is not the same thing as teaching. Rather, formative assessment is an assessment-rooted process capable of making teaching better. It may be useful for educators to think of formative assessment as a *companion activity* whose one and only *raison d'être* is to improve the quality of teaching. It does so by providing the assessment-based evidence that informs selected instructional decisions a teacher should make.

Accordingly, formative assessment must be a *classroom-based* process. Formative assessment doesn't take place in a principal's office or at a school district's central offices. Formative assessment occurs in a particular classroom taught by a particular teacher, and it is based on assessment evidence collected from that teacher's current students. To the extent that anyone tries to make formative assessment an activity occurring outside what goes on in a given teacher's classroom, those efforts really cannot be supported by the existing research base that so strongly undergirds the use of classroom-based formative assessment.

Teaching consists of the instructional activities a teacher chooses to employ, and those activities are chosen because of conscious decisions made by the teacher. One category of such instructional decisions can be accurately characterized as *adjustment decisions*—that is, decisions regarding whether preplanned instruction should be adjusted by a teacher and, if so, in what ways. Well, those adjustment decisions are precisely the ones that the formative-assessment process is intended to inform. If formative assessment is employed properly, teachers' adjustment decisions will be better, and as a consequence, kids will be better educated.

What does formative assessment have to do with teaching? *Everything!*

Chapter Summary

Formative assessment was defined, at the beginning of this chapter, as a planned process in which assessment-elicited evidence of students' status is used by teachers to adjust their ongoing instructional procedures, or by students to adjust their current learning tactics. Because a teacher's understanding of this conception of formative assessment is essential, considerable attention was given to describing the key components of the definition.

The second emphasis of the chapter was on the research evidence underlying the formative-assessment process. The Black and Wiliam (1998a) review of almost a decade's worth of classroom assessment investigations currently supplies the bulk of evidence usually called on to support the effectiveness of formative assessment. Based on 250 solid studies drawn from almost 700 such studies, Black and Wiliam concluded that the empirical evidence they studied "shows conclusively that formative assessment does improve learning." Moreover, the improvements in students' learning attributed to formative assessment were among the largest ever reported for educational interventions. Finally, Black and Wiliam pointed out that the formative-assessment process is so robust that it can be employed by teachers in diverse ways, yet still work well. In the years following the 1998 review by Black and Wiliam, additional scientific evidence has only buttressed their findings.

Considerable attention was given in the chapter to learning progressions—the sequenced sets of building blocks students must master en route to mastering a more remote, target curricular aim. The building blocks in a learning progression are either (1) bodies of enabling knowledge or (2) cognitive subskills. Learning progressions function as the frameworks for the formative-assessment process because assessments of students' building-block mastery supply the evidence on the basis of which teachers (or students) to decide whether to make adjustments. Suggestions were provided on how to build a learning progression for a selected curricular aim.

The chapter concluded with some speculation regarding why it is that this research-supported, assessment-rooted process is not more widely used by teachers. Possible explanation for the reluctance of many teachers to adopt formative assessment include (1) educators' misunderstandings about formative assessment, (2) teachers' natural hesitation to alter their current behaviors, and (3) the inability of many accountability tests to accurately measure classroom improvements attributable to formative assessment.

MyLab Education **Self-Check 12.1**

MyLab Education Application Exercise 12.1: **Analyzing Formative Assessment Part 1**

MyLab Education Application Exercise 12.1: **Analyzing Formative Assessment Part 2**

References

Black, P., and Wiliam, D. (1998a). "Assessment and classroom learning," *Assessment in Education: Principles, Policy and Practice, 5*, no. 1: 7–73.

Black, P., and Wiliam, D. (1998b). "Inside the black box: Raising standards through classroom assessment," *Phi Delta Kappan, 80*, no. 2: 139–148.

Broadfoot, P. M., Daugherty, R., Gardner, J., Gipp, C. V., Harlen, W., James, M., and Stobart, G. (1999). *Assessment for learning: the Beyond black box.* Cambridge, UK: University of Cambridge School of Education.

Brookhart, S. M. (2013). "Develop a student-centered mind-set for formative assessment," *Voices from the Middle, 21*, no. 2 (December): 21–25.

Crooks, T. (1988). "The impact of classroom evaluation practices on students," *Review of Educational Research, 58*, no. 4: 438–481.

Duckor, B. (2014). "Formative assessment in seven good moves," *Educational Leadership, 71*, no. 6 (March): 28–33.

Fisher, D., and Frey, N. (2015). *Checking for understanding* (2nd ed.). Alexandria, VA: ASCD.

Gipps, C. V., and Stobart, G. (1997). *Assessment: A teacher's guide to the issues* (3rd ed.). London, UK: Hodder and Stroughton.

Heritage, M. (2010). *Formative assessment: Making it happen in the classroom.* Thousand Oaks, CA: Corwin.

Kingston, N., and Nash, B. (2011). "Formative assessment: A meta-analysis and a call for research," *Educational Measurement: Issues and Practice, 30*, no. 4 (Winter): 28–37.

James, M. (1992). *Assessment for learning.* Paper presented at the Annual Conference of the Association for Supervision and Curriculum Development.

Leahy, S., Thompson, C. L. M., and Wiliam, D. (2005). "Classroom assessment—Minute by minute, day by day," *Educational Leadership, 63*, no. 3 (November): 18–24.

Masters, G., and Forster, M. (1996). *Progress maps.* Melbourne: Australian Council for Educational Research.

Natriello, G. (1987). "The impact of evaluation processes on students," *Educational Psychologist*, 22, no. 2: 155–175.

Popham, W. J. (2008). *Transformative assessment*. Alexandria, VA: ASCD.

Popham, W. J. (2011). *Transformative assessment in action*. Alexandria, VA: ASCD.

Scriven, M. (1967). "The methodology of evaluation." In R. W. Tyler, R. M. Gagne, and M. Scriven (Eds.), *Perspectives of curriculum evaluation*, Volume I (pp. 39–83). Chicago: Rand McNally.

Shepard, L. (2006). *Can benchmark assessments be formative? Distinguishing formative assessment from formative program evaluation*. A presentation during the National Large-Scale Assessment Conference, Council of Chief State School Officers, San Francisco, CA.

Stiggins, R. J. (2007). *Student-involved classroom assessment for learning* (5th ed.). Upper Saddle River, NJ: Prentice-Hall.

Stiggins, R., and Popham, W. J. (2008). *Assessing students' affect related to assessment for learning*. Washington, DC: The Council of Chief State School Officers.

Sutton, R. (1995). *Assessment for learning*. Salford, UK: RS Publications.

Tomlinson, C. A. (2014). "The bridge between today's lesson and tomorrow's," *Educational Leadership*, 71, no. 6 (March): 10–15.

Wiliam, D. (2007/2008). "Changing classroom practices," *Educational Leadership*, 65, no. 4 (December–January): 36–42.

Wiliam, D. (2011). *Embedded formative assessment*. Bloomington, IN: Solution Tree.

Formative Assessment: A Process, Not a Test*

W. James Popham, University of California, Los Angeles

It was back in 1998 that American educators first heard about *formative assessment*, roughly three years before enactment of the No Child Left Behind Act (NCLB). Two British researchers, Paul Black and Dylan Wiliam, had just published a substantial review covering 10 years of research on classroom assessment. On the basis of their review of more than 250 solid studies, they concluded, "The research reported here shows conclusively that formative assessment does improve learning." Thus, when NCLB arrived with its pressures to improve students' performances on states' accountability tests, numerous U.S. educators turned to formative assessment as a score-raising strategy.

What is "formative assessment"? Here's one definition that's reasonably representative of current definitions: *Formative assessment is a planned process in which assessment-elicited evidence of students' status is used by teachers to adjust their ongoing instructional procedures, or by students to adjust their current learning tactics.*

Drawing on 4000 investigations during the last 40 years, Dylan Wiliam has observed that, when appropriately implemented, formative assessment can effectively *double* the speed of student learning.

A useful way to think about formative assessment is that it constitutes a version of the "means-ends thinking" that humans have employed for millennia. *Through formative assessment, we can evaluate the means we're using to reach curricular ends and, importantly, can adjust those means if they're not achieving the desired ends.* Indeed, some believe it is the ends-means nature of formative assessment that makes it so successful.

Formative assessment is a *process—not a test*. The process calls for the careful collection of assessment information from students so that, if needed, adjustments in instruction can be made by teachers, or learning tactics can be adjusted by students.

Typically, first-time users of formative assessment attempt to make this ends-means process more complicated than it needs to be. As a consequence, many overly zealous teachers abandon this potent, assessment-supported instructional process. It is far better to employ the formative-assessment process selectively, and keep using it, than to plunge feverishly into an elaborate use of formative assessment for a short while, only to abandon it from exhaustion. Remember:

- Formative assessment's effectiveness is backed up by a host of supportive research.

- Formative assessment is used far less frequently than it ought to be.

- When the formative-assessment process is not routinely used, students are the losers.

Accordingly, if you have an opportunity to implement formative assessment yourself, or to support others' implementation of formative assessment, *do it*. Students will benefit.

Chapter 13
Making Sense Out of Standardized Test Scores

Chief Chapter Outcome

A sufficient knowledge of standardized educational testing's fundamentals so that, when an issue related to such testing is encountered, or when a basic question about standardized testing is asked, appropriate responses can be supplied

Classroom teachers need to be able to interpret the results not only of their own assessment procedures, but also of the various kinds of standardized tests that are frequently administered to students. Teachers should to be able to interpret such test results so they can base classroom instructional decisions on those results. Teachers also should be able to respond accurately when students' parents raise such questions as, "What does my child's grade-equivalent score of 7.4 really mean?" or "When my child's achievement test results are at the 97th percentile, is that three percentiles from the top or from the bottom?"

This chapter focuses on the task of making sense out of students' performances on standardized achievement and aptitude tests. One of the kinds of tests under consideration will be the achievement tests (for instance, in mathematics or reading) developed and distributed by commercial testing companies. Achievement tests are also developed and administered by state departments of education as a part of annual statewide accountability assessments in such subjects as social studies, sciences, mathematics, reading, and writing. These state tests often employ reporting procedures akin to those used with commercially distributed standardized achievement tests.

And, in spite of an earnest attempt to avoid numbers much larger than 9 in this chapter, you'll encounter a few that are, indeed, larger. Don't be dismayed. Simply go through the examples, one step at a time, and you'll emerge a finer human being. The numbers in this chapter will be easier to deal with than they look at first glance.

Learning Outcomes

13.1 Describe and apply the fundamental characteristics of standardized testing.

13.2 Describe the contributions and characteristics of instructionally diagnostic tests.

These days, standardized tests (especially standardized *achievement* tests) are often misused. In Chapter 15 you'll learn why it is unwise to try to evaluate educators' effectiveness based on students' scores on many such tests. Nonetheless, standardized tests *do* have an important, educationally useful role to play. This chapter focuses on the appropriate uses of standardized tests.

The chapter will conclude with a consideration of two aptitude tests that have a whopping impact on students' lives. You'll be looking at the two examinations that often function as determiners of a student's continued education. That's right, we'll be dealing with the two most widely used college entrance exams: the SAT and the ACT.

If you're a current or would-be secondary school teacher, you'll immediately recognize the need for you to know about the SAT and the ACT. After all, many of your students will soon be taking one or both of these tests. But if you're an elementary school teacher, or are preparing to be one, you might be thinking, "What do college entrance exams have to do with me?" Well, all teachers—elementary and secondary—ought to understand at least the most significant facts about these two examinations. Indeed, even teachers of primary-grade kids will find parents asking questions such as, "How can we get our child really ready for those important college entrance tests when the time comes?" Every teacher should be familiar with any truly significant information associated with the teaching profession. Thus, because most students and their parents will, at some point, want to know more about college entrance exams, it seems that every single teacher—and even married ones!—should know the basic SAT and ACT facts you'll learn about in this chapter.

Standardized Tests

A *standardized test* is a test that is designed to yield either norm-referenced or criterion-referenced inferences and that is administered, scored, and interpreted in a standard, predetermined manner. Almost all *nationally* standardized tests are distributed by commercial testing firms. Most such firms are for-profit corporations, although there are a few not-for-profit measurement organizations, such as the Educational Testing Service (ETS), that distribute nationally standardized tests. Almost all nationally standardized tests, whether they're focused on the measurement of students' aptitude or of their achievement, are chiefly intended to provide norm-referenced interpretations.

Standardized achievement tests have also been developed in a number of states under the auspices of state departments of education. In some instances, these state-chosen standardized tests may have been acquired from a confederation of states, for instance, the states affiliated with the Smarter Balanced Assessment Consortium (SBAC)—or even from smaller consortia of only a few collaborating states. These statewide tests (clearly intended to be administered, scored, and interpreted in a standard, predetermined fashion) have usually been installed to satisfy a legislative mandate that establishes an educational account-ability program of some sort. In certain instances, important decisions about individual students are made on the basis of a student's test performance. In many states, for example, if a student does not pass a prescribed statewide basic-skills examination by the end of high school, the student is not awarded a state-sanctioned diploma—even though the student has satisfied all other curricular requirements. In other instances, although no contingencies for individual students depend on how a student performed on a test, the results of student tests are publicized by the media on a district-by-district or school-by-school basis. The test results thus serve as an indicator of local educators' effectiveness, at least in the perception of many citizens. These state-sired standardized *achievement* tests are generally intended to yield criterion-referenced interpretations. Educational *aptitude* tests are rarely, if ever, developed by state departments of education.

Although standardized tests have traditionally consisted almost exclusively of selected-response items, in recent years the developers of standardized tests have attempted to incorporate a certain number of constructed-response items in their tests. Standardized tests, because they are intended for widespread use, are developed with far more care (and cost) than is possible in an individual teacher's classroom. Even so, the fundamentals of test development that you've learned about in earlier chapters are routinely employed when standardized tests are developed. In other words, the people who create the items for such tests attempt to adhere to the same kinds of item-writing and item-improvement precepts that you've learned about. The writers of multiple-choice items for standardized tests worry, just as you should, about inadvertently supplying students with clues that

Decision Time

Which Test to Believe

Each spring in the Big Valley Unified School District, students in grades 5, 8, 10, and 12 complete nationally standardized achievement tests in reading and mathematics, as well as a nationally standardized test described by its publishers as "a test of the student's cognitive aptitude." Because William White teaches eighth-grade students in his English classes, he is given the task of answering any questions raised by his eighth-graders' parents about the test results.

He is faced with one fairly persistent question from most parents, particularly those parents whose children scored higher on the aptitude test than on the achievement test. For example, Mr. and Mrs. Wilkins (Wanda's parents) put the question like this: "If Wanda scored at the 90th percentile on the aptitude test and only at the 65th percentile on the achievement test, does that mean she's not logging enough study time? Putting it another way," they continued, "should we really believe the aptitude test's results or the achievement test's results? Which is Wanda's 'true' test performance?"

If you were William and had to decide how to answer the questions posed by Wanda's parents, what would your answer be?

give away the correct answer. The writers of short-answer items for standardized tests try to avoid, just as you should, the inclusion of ambiguous language anywhere in their items.

There are, of course, substantial differences in the level of effort associated with the construction of standardized tests and the construction of classroom tests. A commercial testing agency may assign a flotilla of item writers and a fleet of item editors to a new test-development project, whereas teachers are fortunate if they have a part-time aide or, possibly, a malleable spouse to proofread teacher-made tests to detect typographical errors.

Group-Focused Test Interpretation

Although the bulk of this chapter will be devoted to a consideration of score-reporting mechanisms used to describe an individual student's performance, you'll sometimes find you need to describe the performance of your students as a group. To do so, you'll typically compute some index of the group of scores' *central tendency*, such as when you determine the group's **mean** or **median** performance. For example, you might calculate the *mean raw score* or the *median raw score* for your students. A **raw score** is simply the number of items that a student has answered correctly. The *mean*, as you probably know, is the arithmetic average of a set of scores. For example, the mean of the scores 10, 10, 9, 8, 7, 6, 3, 3, and 2 is 6.4 (found by summing the nine scores and then dividing that sum by 9). The *median* is the midpoint of a set of scores. For the nine scores in the previous example, the median is 7 because this score divides the group into two equal parts. Means and medians are useful ways to describe the point at which the scores in a set of scores are centered.

In addition to describing the central tendency of a set of scores (via the mean and/or median), it is also helpful to describe the *variability* of the scores—that is, how spread out the scores are. One simple measure of the variability of a set of students' scores is the **range**. The range is calculated by simply subtracting the lowest student's score from the highest student's score. To illustrate, suppose the highest test score by students in your class was 49 correct out of 50, earned by Hortense (she always tops your tests; it is surprising she missed one item). Suppose further that the lowest score of 14 correct was, as usual, earned by Ed. The range of this set of scores would be 35—that is, Hortense's 49 minus Ed's 14.

Because only two scores influence the range, it is less frequently used as an index of test-score variability than is the standard deviation. A **standard deviation** is a kind of average. More accurately, it's the average difference between the individual scores in a group of scores and the mean of that set of scores. The larger the size of the standard deviation, the more spread out are the scores in the **distribution**. (That's a posh term to describe a set of scores.) Here is the formula for computing a standard deviation for a set of scores:

$$\text{Standard Deviation } (\{S.D.\}) = \sqrt{\frac{\Sigma(X - M)^2}{N}}$$

where $\Sigma(X - M)^2$ = the sum of the squared raw scores (X) − the mean (M)

N = the number of scores in the distribution

Here's a step-by-step description of how you compute a standard deviation using this formula. First, compute the mean of the set of scores. Second, subtract the mean from each score in the distribution. (Roughly half of the resulting values, called *deviation score*, will have positive values, and roughly half will have negative values.) Third, square each of these deviation scores. This will make them all positive. Fourth, add the squared deviation scores together. Fifth, divide the resulting sum by the number of scores in the distribution. Sixth, and last, take the square root of the results of the division you did in the fifth step. The square root that you get is the standard deviation. Not too tough, right?

To illustrate the point that larger standard deviations represent more spread in a distribution of scores than smaller standard deviations, compare the two fictitious sets of scores on a 10-item short-answer test presented in Figure 13.1. Both sets of scores have a mean of 5.0. The distribution of scores at the left is much more homogeneous (less spread out) than the distribution of scores at the right. Note that the standard deviation for the more homogeneous scores is only 1.1, whereas the standard deviation for the more heterogeneous scores is 3.2. The larger the standard deviation, therefore, the more distant, on average, will be the distribution's scores from the distribution's mean.

You may have occasions to describe the scores of an entire group of the students you teach. Those descriptions might portray your students' performances on standardized tests or on teacher-made tests. If you get at all comfortable with means and standard deviations, those two indices usually provide a better picture of a score distribution than do the median and range. But if you think means and standard deviations are statistical gibberish, then go for the median (midpoints are easy to identify) and range (ranges require only competence in subtraction). With group-based interpretations out of the way, let's turn now to interpreting individual students' scores from the kinds of standardized tests commonly used in education.

Figure 13.1 Two Fictitious Sets of Tests Scored with Equal Means but Different Standard Deviations

More Homogeneous Scores:	*More Heterogeneous Scores:*
3, 4, 4, 5, 5, 5, 5, 6, 6, 7	0, 1, 2, 4, 5, 5, 6, 8, 9, 10
Mean = 5.0	*Mean* = 5.0
$S.D. = \sqrt{\dfrac{12}{10}} = 1.1$	$S.D. = \sqrt{\dfrac{102}{10}} = 3.2$

Individual Student Test Interpretation

Two overriding frameworks are generally used to interpret students' test scores. Test scores are interpreted in *absolute* or *relative* terms. When we interpret a student's test score *absolutely*, we infer from the score what it is that the student can or cannot do. For example, based on a student's performance on test items dealing with mathematics computation skills, we make an inference about the degree to which the student has mastered the array of computation skills represented by the test items. The teacher may even boil the interpretation down to a dichotomy—namely, whether the student should be classified as having mastered or as not having mastered the skill or knowledge being assessed. A mastery-versus-nonmastery interpretation represents an *absolute* interpretation of a student's test score. Classroom teachers often use this absolute interpretive approach when creating tests to assess a student's knowledge or skills based on a particular unit of study.

When we interpret a student's test score *relatively*, we infer from the score how the student stacks up against other students who are currently taking the test or who have already taken the test. For example, when we say that Johnny's test score is "above average" or "below average," we are making a relative test interpretation because we use the average performance of other students to make sense of Johnny's test score.

As pointed out earlier, this chapter focuses on how teachers and parents can interpret scores on standardized tests. Because almost all standardized test scores require relative interpretations, the three interpretive schemes to be considered in the chapter are all relative score-interpretation schemes. The vast majority of standardized tests, whether achievement tests or aptitude tests, provide relative interpretations. Accordingly, teachers need to be especially knowledgeable about relative score-interpretation schemes.

Percentiles

The first interpretive scheme we'll consider, and by all odds the most commonly used one, is based on **percentiles**, or as they are sometimes called, *percentile ranks*. Percentiles are used most frequently in describing standardized test scores, because percentiles are readily understandable to most people.

A percentile compares a student's score with those of other students in a *norm group*. A student's percentile indicates the percent of students in the norm group that the student outperformed. A percentile of 60, for example, indicates that the student performed better than 60 percent of the students in the norm group.

Let's spend a moment describing what a norm group is. As indicated, a percentile compares a student's score with scores earned by those in a norm group. This comparison with the norm group is based on the performances of a group of individuals who have already been administered a given examination. For instance, before developers of a new standardized test publish their test, they usually administer the test to a large number of students who then become the norm group for the test. Typically, different norm groups of students are assembled for all the grade levels for which percentile interpretations are made.

Figure 13.2 shows a graphical depiction of a set of 3000 students' scores such as might have been gathered during the norming of a nationally standardized achievement test. Remember, we refer to such students as the norm group. The area under the curved line represents the number of students who earned scores at that point on the baseline. You'll notice that for a typical norm group's performance, most students score in the middle, and only a few students earn very high or very low scores.

In fact, *if* the distribution of test scores in the norm group is *perfectly* normal, then, as you see in Figure 13.3, over two-thirds of the scores (represented by the

Figure 13.2 A Typical Norm Group

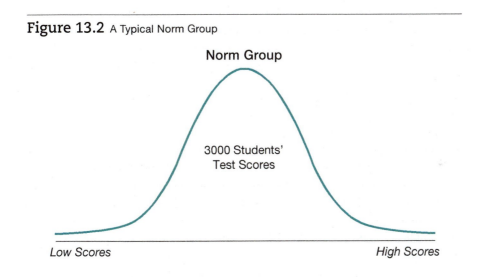

Norm Group

3000 Students'
Test Scores

Low Scores   *High Scores*

Figure 13.3 A Normally Distributed Set of Norm-Group Scores

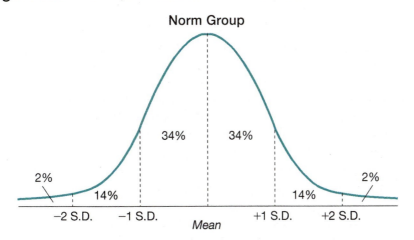

Norm Group

34%   34%

2%   2%

14%   14%

−2 S.D.   −1 S.D.   +1 S.D.   +2 S.D.
Mean

area under the curved line) will be located relatively close to the center of the distribution—that is, plus or minus 1 standard deviation (S.D.) from the mean.

Not all norm groups are national norm groups. Sometimes test publishers, at the request of local school officials, develop local norms. These local norms can be either state norms or school-district norms. Comparisons of students on the basis of local norms are sometimes seen as being more meaningful than comparisons based on national norms. Indeed, if the educators in a relatively large school district wished to compare students' test scores within their district, then it would not take a ton of energy to compute tables of district-level norms and distribute them to district educators. In other words, when reasonably large numbers of students are involved, norm groups can be constructed in almost any setting.

In many instances, local norms are different from national norms because the students in a particular locality are not representative of the nation's children as a whole. If there is a difference between local and national norms, then there will be a difference in a student's percentile scores. A student's raw score—that is, the number of test items answered correctly—might be equal to the 50th percentile based on *national* norms, but be equal to the 75th percentile based on *local* norms. This kind of situation would occur if the students in the local group hadn't performed as well as students in the nation at large. National and local norms provide decisively different frameworks for interpreting standardized test results. When reporting test scores to parents, make sure you communicate clearly whether a child's percentiles are based on national or local norms.

It's also true that some norm groups have been more carefully constituted than others. For example, certain national norm groups are more representative of the nation's population than are other national norm groups. There are often large differences in the representativeness of norm groups based on such variables as gender, ethnicity, geographic region, and socioeconomic status of the students in the groups. In addition, many standardized tests are re-normed only every 5 to 10 years. It is important to make sure that the normative information on which percentiles are based is both representative and current.

Grade-Equivalent Scores

Let's turn from percentiles to look at *grade equivalents*, or as they're often called, *grade-equivalent scores*. Grade-equivalent scores constitute another effort to provide a relative interpretation of standardized test scores. A *grade equivalent* is an indicator of a student's test performance based on grade levels and months of the school year. The purpose of grade equivalents is to transform scores on standardized tests into an index reflecting a student's grade-level progress in school. A grade-equivalent score is a *developmental* score in the sense that it represents a continuous range of grade levels.

Let's look at a grade-equivalent score of 4.5:

A Grade-Equivalent Score
Grade → 4.5 ← Month of School Year

The score consists of the grade, a decimal point, and a number representing months. The number to the left of the decimal point represents the grade level—in this example, the fourth grade. The number to the right of the decimal point represents the month of the school year—in this example, the fifth month of the school year.

Some test publishers, using statistical schemes, convert raw scores on standardized tests to grade-equivalent scores. These grade-equivalent scores often appear on students' score reports. Grade-equivalent scores are most appropriate for basic skills areas, such as reading and mathematics, where it can be assumed that the degree of instructional emphasis given to the subject is rather uniform from grade to grade.

The appeal of grade-equivalent scores is that they appear to be readily interpretable to both teachers and parents. However, many teachers and parents actually have an incorrect understanding of what grade-equivalent scores signify. To see why these scores are misunderstood, it's necessary to understand a bit about where they come from in the first place.

To determine the grade-equivalent scores that will be hooked up with particular raw scores, test developers typically administer the same test to students in several grade levels and then establish a trend line reflecting the raw-score increases at each grade level. Typically, the test developers then *estimate*, at other points along this trend line, what the grade equivalent for any raw score would be.

Let's illustrate this important point. In Figure 13.4, you will see the respective performances of students at three grade levels. The same 80-item test has been given to students at all three grade levels: grades 4, 5, and 6. A trend line is then established from the three grades where the test was actually administered. The result of that estimation procedure is seen in Figure 13.5.

Figure 13.4 Student Performances at Three Grade Levels

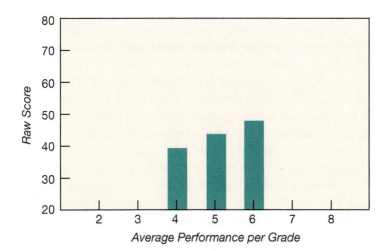

Figure 13.5 A Trend Line Used to Estimate Average Performance of Students at Nontested Grades

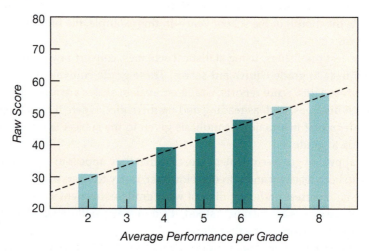

In order for these estimated grade-equivalent scores to be accurate, several assumptions must be made. First, it must be assumed that the subject area tested is emphasized equally at each grade level. It must also be assumed that students' mastery of the tested content increases at a reasonably constant rate at each grade level over an extended period of time. The assumption that the mastery of the test's content increases consistently over time is particularly difficult to support in subject areas other than reading and mathematics. And even in those two bread-and-butter subjects, students' grade-to-grade consistency of increased content mastery is definitely debatable.

The implied precision associated with a grade-equivalent score of 6.2, therefore, is difficult to defend. A 6.2 grade-equivalent score suggests a degree of accuracy that's simply not warranted. An unskilled interpreter of the results of a standardized achievement test may think a 6.2 grade-equivalent score indicates the student's raw score represents a performance equal to that of a sixth-grade pupil in the second month of the sixth-grade year. Remember, most grade-equivalent scores are created on the basis of estimation, not real test-score data. Because substantial sampling and estimation errors are apt to be present, grade-equivalent scores should always be taken with several grains of salt.

Now that you understand grade-equivalent scores to be, at best, rough estimates, let's return to the misinterpretations that teachers and parents often make regarding grade-equivalent scores. Let's say a third-grade student makes a grade-equivalent score of 5.5 in reading. What does this grade-equivalent score mean? Here's a wrong answer: "The student can do fifth-grade work." Here's a *really* wrong answer: "The student should be promoted to the fifth grade." The right answer, of course, is that the third-grader understands those reading skills that the test covers about as well as an average fifth-grader does at midyear.

A grade-equivalent score should be viewed as the point where a student currently is along a developmental continuum, not as the grade level in which the student should be placed.

If standardized tests are used in your school district, and if those tests yield grade-equivalent scores, it is important to provide parents with an accurate picture of what a grade-equivalent score means. Parents who have not been given an accurate description of such scores frequently think a high grade-equivalent score means their child is capable of doing work at the grade level specified. Some parents even use high grade-equivalent scores as a basis for arguing that their child should be advanced to a higher grade. Because many parents misunderstand what a grade-equivalent score means, some parents may have an inflated estimate of their child's level of achievement. The high frequency of parental (and teacher) misinterpretations is the reason why some districts have, as a matter of policy, eliminated grade-equivalent scores when reporting standardized test results.

Remember, if a fourth-grade student gets a grade-equivalent score of 7.5 in mathematics, it is *not* accurate to say the fourth-grader is doing well in seventh-grade mathematics. It is more appropriate to say that a grade-equivalent score of 7.5 is an estimate of how an average seventh-grader might have performed *on the fourth-grader's mathematics test*. Obtaining a 7.5 grade-equivalent score doesn't mean the fourth-grader has any of the mathematics skills taught in the fifth, sixth, or seventh grade, because those mathematics skills were probably not even measured on the fourth-grade test.

But what happens when grade-equivalent scores are *below* the actual grade level tested? Let's say a fifth-grader earns a mathematics grade-equivalent score of 2.5. It doesn't make much sense to say the fifth-grader is doing fifth-grade mathematics work as well as a second-grader, because second-graders obviously aren't given fifth-grade mathematics work. About the best you can say is that, in mathematics achievement, the fifth-grader appears to be lagging several years behind grade level.

Given the shortcomings of grade-equivalent scores, most measurement specialists are delighted that the use of these scores is diminishing.

Scale Scores

Let's move, now, to the last of our three score-interpretation schemes: *scale scores*. A scale score constitutes yet another way to give relative meaning to a student's performances on standardized tests. Scale scores are being employed with increasing frequency these days to report the results of national and state-level standardized programs.

Although scale scores are sometimes not used in reporting standardized test results to parents, scale-score reporting systems are often employed in describing group test performances at the state, district, and school levels. Because of the statistical properties of scale scores, they can be used to permit longitudinal tracking of students' progress. Scale scores can also be used to make direct comparisons among classes, schools, or school districts. The statistical advantages of scale scores are considerable. Thus, we see scale-score reporting systems used with more frequency in recent years. As a consequence, you need to become familiar with the main features of scale scores, because such scores are likely to be used when you receive reports of your students' performances on standardized tests—particularly those performances earned on important, high-stakes tests.

A *scale* used for reporting test scores typically consists of numbers assigned to students on the basis of their test performances. Higher numbers (higher scale scores) reflect superior levels of achievement or ability. Thus, such a scale might be composed of a set of raw scores where each additional test item that is correctly answered yields 1 more point on the raw-score scale. Raw scores, all by themselves, however, are difficult to interpret. A student's score on a raw-score scale provides no idea of the student's *relative* performance. Therefore, measurement specialists have devised different sorts of scales for test-interpretation purposes.

Scale scores are *converted raw scores* that use a new, arbitrarily chosen scale to represent levels of achievement or ability. Shortly, you'll be given some examples to help you understand what is meant by converting scores from one scale to another. In essence, a scale-score system is created by devising a brand-new numerical scale that's often very unlike the original raw-score scale. Students' raw scores are then converted to this brand-new scale so that, when score interpretations are to be made, those interpretations rely on the converted scores based on the new scale. Such converted scores are called *scale scores*.

For example, in Figure 13.6, you see a range of raw-score points from 0 to 40 for a 40-item test. Below the raw-score scale, you see a new, converted scale ranging from 500 to 900. For a number of reasons, to be described shortly, it is sometimes preferable to use a scale-score reporting scheme rather than a raw-score reporting scheme. Thus, a student who achieved a raw score of 30 items correct might be assigned a scale score of 800, as shown in Figure 13.7.

One of the reasons why scale scores have become popular in recent years is the necessity to develop several equidifficult forms of the same test. For example, a basic-skills test must sometimes be passed before high school diplomas are awarded to students. Those students who initially fail the test are typically given other opportunities to pass it. The different forms of the test used for such retake purposes should, for the sake of fairness, represent assessment challenges for students that are equivalent to those represented by the initial form of the test. However, because it is next to impossible to create test forms that are absolutely identical, scale scores can be used to help solve the problem. Scores on two test forms of differing difficulty levels can be statistically adjusted so that, when placed on a converted-score scale, the new scale scores represent students' performances as if the two test forms had been completely equidifficult.

Most of the more popular types of scale-score systems are based on what statisticians refer to as *item response theory*, or IRT. These types of scale-score reporting systems are distinctively different from raw-score reporting systems, because IRT scale-score schemes take into consideration the difficulty and other technical properties of every single item on the test. Thus, some test publishers

Figure 13.6 A Raw-Score Scale and a Converted-Score Scale

Raw-Score Scale

| 0 | 10 | 20 | 30 | 40 |

Converted-Score Scale

| 500 | 600 | 700 | 800 | 900 |

Figure 13.7 An Illustration of a Raw-Score Conversion to a Scale Score

Raw-Score Scale

| 0 | 10 | 20 | × 30 | 40 |

Converted-Score Scale

| 500 | 600 | 700 | × 800 | 900 |

have produced IRT-based scale scores for their tests ranging from 0 to 1000 across an entire K–12 grade range. For each grade level, there is a different average scale score. For example, the average scale score for third-graders might be 585, and the average scale score for the tenth-graders might be 714.

These IRT-based scale scores can, when constructed with care, yield useful interpretations if one can link them to some notion of relative performance such as percentiles. If average scale scores are provided at different grade levels, this also can aid in the interpretation of scale scores. Without such interpretation crutches regarding a scale score's *relative* meaning, however, scale scores cannot be meaningfully interpreted by either educators or parents.

Item response theory scales are often employed by psychometricians to devise a *vertical scale* that will allow students' test performances to be tracked across a number of grade levels. Clearly, especially in an accountability context where educators are often eager to show students' growth from year to year, such vertical scales have a special appeal. But they also have a serious drawback. In order for a vertical scale to do its job across many grade levels, the test items being used must correlate well with a *single* trait—for instance, a unitary trait such as "students' mathematical comprehension." It is this global unitary trait that permits a vertical scale to do its job properly. However, because the test's items must be linked to the unitary trait on which the vertical scale is based, those items are unable to yield meaningful diagnostic information to teachers about students' differing mathematics skills and knowledge. Legitimate diagnosticity must often be jettisoned if a test's developers are preoccupied with making all their items hook into the unitary trait chosen for their test's vertical scale.

So, if officials in your school or district are considering adoption of a standardized test whose chief virtue is that it supplies a meaningful vertical scale for cross-grade comparisons of students' scores, then don't be fooled, even if the test is accompanied by marketing assertions about the test's diagnostic dividends. The vertical scale has been achieved by undermining the sort of diagnostic evidence that teachers need for sensible instructional decision making.

Errors are often made in interpreting scale scores because teachers assume all scale scores are somehow similar. For example, when the SAT was initially administered over 80 years ago, the mean scale score on the verbal section of the Scholastic Assessment Test was 500. This does not signify that the mean score on that test today is 500 or that other tests using scale scores will always have mean scores of 500. Scale-score systems can be constructed so that the mean score is 50, 75, 600, 700, 1000, or any number the scale's constructor has in mind.

One kind of scale score you may encounter when you work with your students' scores on standardized tests is the **normal curve equivalent**. A normal curve equivalent, usually referred to as an NCE, represents an attempt to use a student's raw score to arrive at a percentile for a raw score *as if* the distribution of scores on the test had been a perfectly symmetrical, bell-shaped normal curve. So one of your students might get an NCE score indicating that the student was performing at or near the top of a norm group's performance. Sometimes, unfortunately, neither the norm group's

---

Figure 13.8 Stanine Units Represented in Approximate Percentages of the Normal Curve

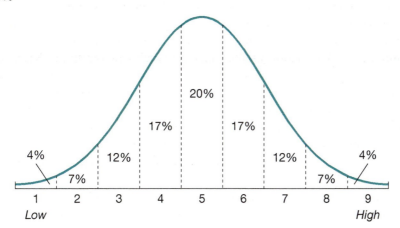

performance nor that of subsequent test takers is distributed in a normal fashion, so the meaningfulness of the student's NCE simply evaporates. Normal curve equivalents were originally created in an effort to amalgamate students' performances from *different* standardized tests, perhaps none of which yielded normal distributions. As might be suspected, NCEs failed to solve this problem satisfactorily.

A final kind of scale score you should know about is called a *stanine*. Stanines are somewhat like normal curve equivalents in the sense that they assume a normal distribution for a set of scores. And this assumption, as you just read, runs counter to reality. But, as you'll soon see, a stanine score is a more gross score, so it can more easily tolerate a score distribution's departure from a normal shape.

A stanine scale divides a score distribution into nine segments that, although they are equal along the baseline of a set of scores (actually one-half standard deviation in distance), contain differing proportions of the distribution's scores. As you can see in Figure 13.8, the fifth stanine is at the center of a score distribution and contains about 20 percent of the scores. A ninth-stanine score, however, contains only about 4 percent of the scores.

One advantage of stanines is that they are *approximate* scale scores, and their very inexact nature conveys more clearly to everyone that educational measurement is not a superprecise assessment enterprise. As with most hierarchical classification systems, of course, a student may be *almost* at the next higher (or lower) stanine, and yet may miss out by only a point or two. Such is the imprecision of measurement, even if you're using a deliberately approximation-engendering scoring system.

Contrasting Common Interpretive Options

We've now considered several types of score-interpretation schemes, the most frequently used of these being percentiles, grade-equivalent scores, and scale scores. (Stanines and NCEs tend to be used less frequently.) It's time to review and summarize what's really important about the three most popular ways of making sense out of standardized test scores.

We first considered percentiles. A *percentile* indicates a student's standing in relationship to that of a norm group. If a student's test score is equal to the 25th percentile, the student's performance exceeds the performances of 25 percent of the individuals in the norm group. One advantage of percentiles is that they're easy to interpret. And, for the most part, people's interpretations of percentiles are accurate. A disadvantage of percentiles is that the defensibility of the interpretation is totally dependent on the nature of the normative data on which the percentiles are based. Unrepresentative or out-of-date norm data yield inaccurate percentile interpretations. As pointed out earlier, because percentile interpretations are so widely used, it's imperative for teachers to be knowledgeable about such interpretations.

Percentiles

Advantage: readily interpretable
Disadvantage: dependent on quality of norm group

Next, we considered grade-equivalent scores. A *grade equivalent* indicates the nature of a student's test performance in terms of grade levels and months. Thus, a grade equivalent of 3.7 indicates that the student's test score was estimated to be the same as the average performance of a third-grader during the seventh month of the school year. One advantage of grade-equivalent scores is that, because they are based on grade levels and months of the school year, they can be readily communicated to parents. A significant disadvantage associated with grade-equivalent scores, however, is that they're frequently misinterpreted.

Grade Equivalents

Advantage: readily communicable
Disadvantage: often misinterpreted

Finally, scale scores were described. *Scale scores* are interpreted according to a converted numerical scale that allows us to transform raw scores into more statistically useful scale-score units. A student who gets a raw score of 35 correct out of 50 items, for example, might end up with a converted scale score of 620.

An advantage of scale scores is they can be used to create statistically adjusted equidifficult test forms. Scale-score schemes based on *item response theory (IRT)* do this by weighting individual test items differently based on an item's difficulty and other technical properties in relation to those same properties for all of a test's items. A disadvantage of scale-score reporting schemes is that, with the possible exception of stanines, they're almost impossible to interpret all by themselves. Unless we mentally link scale scores to percentiles or average grade-level scale scores, such scores are essentially uninterpretable.

Scale Scores

Advantage: useful in equalizing difficulties of different test forms
Disadvantage: not easily interpretable

It should be clear to you that each of these three score-interpretation schemes has some potential virtues as well as some potential vices. You probably realize that, even if you understand the general nature of each of these three interpretation schemes, it may be necessary to secure additional technical information to interpret each reporting scheme with confidence. Such information is usually found in the technical manuals that accompany standardized tests. For example, what was the nature of the norm group on which a test's percentiles were based? What sort of mathematical operations were used in generating a scale-score reporting scheme? Is a score distribution sufficiently normal to warrant the use of NCEs? To interpret a particular standardized test's results sensibly, teachers sometimes need to do a bit of homework themselves regarding the innards of the reporting scheme being used.

The Instructional Yield from Standardized Achievement Tests

Nationally standardized achievement tests, as noted previously, are developed and sold by commercial testing companies. The more tests those companies sell, the more money those companies make. Accordingly, the representatives of commercial testing companies usually suggest that their standardized achievement tests will not only yield valid norm-referenced interpretations about the students who take the tests but will also provide classroom teachers with a galaxy of useful information for instructional decision making. In my experience, the *instructional* payoffs of standardized achievement tests are more illusory than real. More often than not, claims for the instructional dividends of such achievement tests reflect the zeal of a testing firm's sales force, not how teachers can actually use the results of standardized tests for instructional purposes.

Instructionally Diagnostic Tests

Diagnostic test is a label more often uttered than understood. Yes, although the phrase pops up in educators' conversations every few days, it is a safe bet that most of those who use this phrase have only a murky understanding of what constitutes a genuine diagnostic test. Yet, because today's teachers are increasingly buffeted by commercial vendors trying to peddle their "instructionally powerful" diagnostic tests, teachers ought to understand whether vendors' claims are legitimate.

Generally, of course, diagnostic tests are thought to be good things. Most people regard such tests as useful measurement tools—often associated with medical applications, for example, when physicians employ diagnostic tests to pinpoint a patient's illness. A diagnostic test, according to most dictionaries, is "concerned with identification of the nature of illness or other problems" (Frank R. Abate, Elizabeth Jewel, *The New Oxford American Dictionary*, Oxford University Press, 2001). When diagnostic testing occurs in the field of education, we see such tests used for purposes of either *classification* or *instruction*.

Classification-focused diagnostic tests are often employed by educators who are working with atypical students—that is, with students who are particularly gifted or students who have pronounced disabilities. Such tests allow educators to identify with greater accuracy the exact nature of a student's exceptionality—so that the student can then be classified in a specific category.

Instruction-oriented diagnostic tests are used when teachers attempt to provide particularized instruction for individual students so the teacher's upcoming instructional activities will better mesh with the precise learning needs of different students. The following analysis will be devoted exclusively to *instructionally diagnostic tests*.

What Is an Instructionally Diagnostic Test?

Because the mission of an instructionally diagnostic test is to help teachers do an effective instructional job with their students, we need to identify how using such a test would enlighten a teacher's instructional decisions—for example, such decisions as *when* to give or withhold additional or different instruction from *which* students. Appropriately matching instruction, both its quantity and its type, with students' current needs constitutes a particularly important element of effective teaching. An instructionally diagnostic test, if properly fashioned, permits teachers to identify those students who need more or less instruction, and, if the diagnostic test is shrewdly constructed, such a test might even help teachers determine what kinds of instruction are likely to succeed with those students.

Here, then, is a definition of an instructionally diagnostic test:

> An instructionally diagnostic test is an assessment instrument whose use permits teachers to draw accurate inferences about individual test takers' strengths and/or weaknesses with respect to two or more skills or bodies of knowledge— thereby permitting teachers to take more effective next-step instructional actions.

Several components of this definition can influence the development of instructionally diagnostic tests and, thus, warrant elaboration.

SOLO-STUDENT INFERENCES

Let's begin with the idea that, based on students' performances on an instructionally diagnostic test, a teacher will be able to draw more valid (or, if you prefer, more accurate) inferences about an *individual* student's status. Putting it differently, a good instructionally diagnostic test will help a teacher get a more exact fix on what each of the teacher's students currently knows or is able to do. Clearly, if a teacher chooses to aggregate the individual test results of multiple students in order to make subgroup-focused inferences, or even inferences focused on the whole class, this is altogether appropriate. However, the preceding definition specifies that an honest-to-goodness instructionally diagnostic test must be capable of yielding valid inferences about the status of individual test takers.

STRENGTHS AND/OR WEAKNESSES

Some words (e.g., *however*) or phrases (e.g., *of course*) and some abbreviations (e.g., *e.g.*) are seen so often in our everyday reading that we tend to pay little attention to them. One important example of this sort familiarity occurs with the oft-encountered, paired conjunctions *and/or*. In the definition given for an instructionally diagnostic test, however, the *and/or* has an important role to play. It signifies that a student's performance on an instructionally diagnostic test can provide results permitting a teacher to draw inferences *exclusively* about the particular student's strengths, *exclusively* about the particular student's weaknesses, or about *both* the strengths and weaknesses of the particular student. Although, in most settings, teachers are likely to be more interested either in students' strengths or in their weaknesses, the proposed definition of instructionally diagnostic tests makes it clear that this *and/or* should be taken seriously.

TWO OR MORE SKILLS OR BODIES OF KNOWLEDGE

The strengths and/or weaknesses addressed in an instructionally diagnostic test must be *at least two*. This is where the diagnosticity of such tests gallops onstage. If a test only helps teachers establish a student's status with respect to *one* cognitive skill that's been tested, or if it identifies the student's mastery level regarding of only *one* body of knowledge, such information might obviously be useful to a teacher. For example, if a fifth-grade teacher uses a teacher-made or commercial test to measure students' status regarding a single high-level skill in mathematics, results from the test could reveal which students have, and which have not, mastered the specific math skill being assessed. This is definitely useful information. The teacher can rely on it to make better current or future instructional decisions. But a single-focus test is not instructionally diagnostic. It's not a *bad* test; it's just not instructionally diagnostic.

NEXT-STEP INSTRUCTIONAL ACTIONS

The final requisite feature of the much-discussed definition stems from the fundamental orientation of an instructionally diagnostic test—namely, *instruction*.

The definition indicates that, based on the results of such tests, teachers can make next-step instructional decisions, such as what to teach tomorrow or how to teach something next week. Moreover, those next-step instructional decisions are apt to be more effective than would have been the case had a teacher's decisions not been abetted by information about students' current status.

What this definitional requirement calls for, in plain language, are test results that can be readily translated into sound next-step pedagogical moves by a teacher. To supply such data, an instructionally diagnostic test must provide its results in an *actionable* grain size—that is, at a level of generality addressable by routine teacher-chosen instructional actions. Accordingly, if the reports from a supposedly diagnostic test are provided at such a broad grain size that the only reasonable action implication is for the teacher to "make students smarter," this test would be a diagnostic flop.

How Good Is an Instructionally Diagnostic Test?

Once tests have been identified as instructionally diagnostic, they are still apt to differ in their quality, sometimes substantially. The following evaluative criteria can be employed to help determine an instructionally diagnostic test's merits. A brief description will now be presented of each of the following attributes of an instructionally diagnostic test's quality: (1) curricular alignment, (2) sufficiency of items, (3) item quality, and (4) ease of usage.

Many commercial vendors currently realize that, "There's gold in them thar schools." Some of this "gold" can be seen when districts, and even schools within those districts, plunk down big hunks of their school budgets to purchase instructionally useful tests, particularly instructionally diagnostic tests touted to boost students' achievement. For this reason, teachers really ought to be a position to offer educational officials advice regarding the wisdom or spending big bucks on those assessment devices being marketed as "instructionally diagnostic tests." Some of these diagnostic tests will be terrific, some will be terrible. You need to know what to look for when appraising such assessments. The following evaluative factors should, hopefully, be of assistance when you review the virtues of an instructionally diagnostic test.

CURRICULAR ALIGNMENT
The overriding purpose of educational tests is to collect students' responses in such a way that we can use students' *overt* responses to test questions to arrive at valid inferences about students' *covert* status with respect to such variables as students' knowledge or their cognitive skills. Ideally, we would like instructionally diagnostic tests to measure lofty curricular aims such as students' attainment of truly high-level cognitive skills or their possession of genuinely significant bodies of knowledge. But the grandeur of the curricular aims that a test sets out to measure is often determined not by the test-makers but, rather, by higher-level educational authorities.

Thus, if the developers of an instructionally diagnostic test have been directed by their superiors to create a test assessing students' mastery of trivial outcomes, and the resultant test performs this measurement job quite successfully, it seems unfair to downgrade the test itself because of the paltry curricular dictates over which the test's developers had no control.

The most important judgment to be made when evaluating a test on the basis of this first evaluative criterion (curricular alignment) hinges on the answer to a question such as: "Will students' responses to items in this test provide evidence permitting valid inferences to be drawn about a test-taker's status with respect to each body of knowledge and/or skill being assessed?"

Ideally, because the of match between the curricular aims being assessed and the test's items being used to measure students' mastery of those aims is so important, evaluators of diagnostic tests should look for compiled judgmental evidence, perhaps supplied by a specially convened content-review committee regarding the degree to which the items employed do, indeed, elicit scores that reflect students' mastery levels.

SUFFICIENCY OF ITEMS

This second evaluative criterion for appraising an instructionally diagnostic test is easy to understand, but difficult to formally operationalize. Put simply, a decent instructionally diagnostic test needs to contain enough items dealing with each of the skills and/or bodies of knowledge being measured so that, when we see a student's responses to those items, we can identify—with reasonable confidence—how well a student has achieved each of the assessment's targets.

This is an easily understood feature of diagnostic testing because most of us realize intuitively that we will usually get a more accurate fix on students' mastery levels if we ask those students to respond to more items rather than fewer items. And here, of course, is where sensible, experienced educators can differ. Depending on the nature of the curricular targets being measured by an instructionally diagnostic test, seasoned educators might understandably have different opinions about the number of items needed. For larger grain-size curricular targets, more items would typically be needed than for smaller grain-size curricular targets. What's being sought from students is not *certainty* about mastery of what's being measured in a test. No, to reach *absolute* certainty, then we might well be required to measure students' mastery of the complete universe of items that could conceivably be generated to measure students' mastery. Such exhaustive testing would constitute an inefficient use of both students' and teachers' time.

ITEM QUALITY

With few exceptions, educational tests are made up of individual items. Occasionally, of course, we encounter one-item tests such a when we ask students to provide a writing sample by composing a single, original essay. But most tests, and especially those tests intended to supply instructionally diagnostic information, contain multiple items. If a test's items are good ones, the test is obviously apt to be better than a test composed of shoddy items. This is true whether the test is supposed to serve a classification function, an instructional function, or some other function completely. Better items make better tests.

You have already seen in earlier chapters a flock of guidelines regarding how to generate high-quality items for educational tests. Those guidelines surely apply to the items used in instructionally diagnostic tests.

EASE OF USAGE

Testing takes time. Teaching takes time. Most teachers, therefore, have very little discretionary time to spend on anything else—including diagnostic testing. Accordingly, an effective instructionally diagnostic test, if it is going to be employed by many teachers, must be genuinely easy to use. If an instructionally diagnostic test is difficult to use—or time-consuming to use—its easiness evaporates.

If, for example, scoring of students' responses must be carried out by the teacher personally, then such scoring should require minimal time and very little effort. These days, of course, because of advances in technology, much scoring is done electronically. But if hassles arise when using a test, and most certainly when scoring a test, these hassles will diminish the test's use.

Then there are the *results* of the test—that is, the numbers or the words that help teachers (and, if the teacher wishes, can help students as well) determine what a student's strengths and weaknesses actually are. Some time ago, one of our nation's leading test-development agencies published a test that it argued was instructionally helpful to teachers. The test's results, however, were reported exclusively on an *item-by-item* basis, thus requiring the teacher to consider the test's results only one item at a time. Absurd!

What the ease-of-usage evaluative criterion addresses, of course, is the inherent *practicality* of the test, meaning its administration, its scoring, its interpretation, and the *instructional actionability* of its results. And this is when a "satisfactory" diagnostic test can, if carefully conceptualized, become truly "stellar." A diagnostic test that's super will have carved up the content and subskills it measures in suitable grain sizes so that teachers and students can tackle greater mastery of diagnosed shortcomings directly. The more instructionally addressable are the "chunks" in which the test's results are reported. the easier it will be for teachers or students to directly ameliorate diagnosed weaknesses.

By employing these four evaluative criteria to judge tests that have been identified as instructionally diagnostic assessments, it is possible to make at least rudimentary qualitative distinctions among such tests.

Looking back, then, at instructionally diagnostic tests, today's teachers will be urged by commercial testing firms to "buy our nifty diagnostic tests." Well, as you will see, some of those allegedly diagnostic tests really are nifty-free. Because *bona fide* diagnostic tests can be remarkably useful to teachers, if you ever have the opportunity to influence a decision regarding the potential purchase of commercially created diagnostic tests, be sure you review the potential acquisitions with considerable care. Not all so-called instructionally diagnostic tests really are.

Yet, teachers would be foolish to believe that most standardized tests will provide the most appropriate results from which both teachers and students can arrive at interpretations regarding their next-step moves. Remember, in almost all

But What Does This Have to Do with Teaching?

Depending on the grade levels at which elementary school teachers teach, or the different subjects that secondary school teachers teach, many teachers these days find their attention focused on their students' scores on standardized achievement tests. That's because students' scores on such tests are increasingly used as an indicator of educators' instructional success. So, if you're a teacher whose state (or school district) requires that standardized achievement tests be administered at the end of school for a grade level you teach, you can be assured that plenty of attention will be paid to your students' standardized test performances. In Chapter 15 you'll learn why this practice is flat-out wrong when inappropriate standardized tests are employed.

But even if you're a teacher whose students are at grade levels or in classes where standardized tests don't play a major role, you still need to become familiar with the way teachers and parents should interpret such test performances. And that's because, as a professional, a teacher is supposed to know such things. Parents will sometimes ask

you what is meant by a percentile or an NCE. You definitely don't want to blubber forth, "Beats me!"

And, of course, if your students *are* assessed with a standardized achievement test, such as statewide accountability exams, you'll want to be able to interpret what the students' scores signify. One reason is that such scores may help you instructionally. Suppose, for example, it is the first week of school and you're reviewing your new fifth-grade students' end-of-year *fourth*-grade test performances. You discover that Martha Childs earned a 94th percentile in mathematics, but only a 43rd percentile in reading. This information should give you some insight into how you'll approach Martha instructionally.

And if Billy Jenkins's fourth-grade test scores gave him a seventh stanine in language arts, but a first stanine in math, perhaps you should not ask Billy to keep track of your students' lunch money.

The better fix you get on your students' relative achievement levels, the more appropriately you can teach them. Proper interpretations of standardized test scores will often help you do so.

instances, the major standardized achievement tests that are used in our schools, whether those tests be state or national, were created by psychometric specialists who know oodles about test building but very little about using test results instructionally. Are standardized achievement tests better than no tests at all? Of course they are. But teachers need to be significantly wary regarding the instructionally useful insights provided by many of the nation's standardized achievement tests.

If you wish to get a quick fix on the instructional virtues of a standardized achievement test, here's the most direct way to do it: Simply *find out how the test's results are reported.* This lets you know immediately whether the test's reported results are being doled out at a grain size that has a decent chance of being accurate, yet it can also help teachers know what next-step instructional actions to take. If the results are reported at too large a grain size, such as the test taker "can read" or "can't read," then what's a teacher to do with such an undifferentiated lump of truth? At the other extreme, if the grain size is so small that the teacher becomes overwhelmed with a plethora of tiny status reports about each student, then this too constitutes a dysfunctional reporting structure. To spot a standardized test's instructional utility, simply scurry to see how its results are reported.

The SAT and the ACT: Three-Letter, High-Import Exams

Each year, millions of students put their futures on the line when they sit down to take the SAT and ACT exams, the nation's college entrance tests. Because not only students, but also students' parents, are understandably apprehensive about one or both of these college admission tests, teachers at all grade levels are apt to be questioned about the SAT or the ACT. Therefore, in the next few paragraphs you'll be receiving general descriptions of the nature of both exams, how they came into existence, and what their scale scores look like. This treatment of the two tests will conclude with a candid look at the accuracy with which those tests predict a high school student's academic success in college.

The significance of the SAT and ACT was decisively ratcheted up by the enactment of ESSA in December 2015. In this law, the successor to NCLB, it was stipulated that if states wished to employ nationally recognized tests (such as the ACT or SAT) as the assessments they employ to carry out annual accountability determinations, they could do so. Even though neither of these quasi-aptitude tests had been designed for school evaluation, and they were not accompanied by evidence supporting their suitability for this measurement mission, a handful of states have already opted to have their high school students complete one of the two tests for accountability purposes. Surely, then, if you happen to be teaching in a state whose officials have opted to use the SAT or ACT to satisfy EESA, you will want to learn more about your state-chosen high school assessment. Tests that, prior to EESA, were merely high-stakes tests, have become "high-as-the-sky"-stakes tests.

The SAT

First administered in 1926, the SAT was initially called the *Scholastic Aptitude Test*, and its function was to assist admissions officials in a group of elite Northeastern universities to determine which applicants should be admitted. The original name of the test really reveals what the test's developers were up to—namely, they wanted their tests to measure the largely inborn academic *aptitudes* of high school students. Because, much later, the idea of a test's measuring innate, genetically determined aptitudes became unappetizing to many educators, the Scholastic Aptitude Test became known only as the SAT. (One wonders whether the developers of the SAT took their cues from the purveyors of Kentucky Fried Chicken who, recognizing the public's concern about the health risks of fried foods, truncated their famous spelled-out label into KFC. It is, of course, difficult to become genuinely negative toward any three-letter label—with the possible exception of the IRS.)

The SAT was originally conceived of as a group-administrable intelligence test designed to compare test takers according to their inherited verbal, quantitative,

Parent Talk

Suppose that one of your students' parents, Mr. Lopez, visits your classroom during a back-to-school evening and raises a series of questions about his daughter, Concepción. Most prominently, Mr. Lopez is concerned with Concepción's scores on the nationally standardized achievement tests administered each spring in your district's schools. Mr. Lopez is troubled by spring-to-spring changes in Concepción's percentiles. As he says, "For the last three springs, her percentile scores in language arts have been the 74th, the 83rd, and the 71st. What's going on here? Is she learning, and then unlearning? What accounts for the differences?"

If I were you, here's how I'd respond to Mr. Lopez:

"You are certainly wise to look into what appears to be inconsistent measurement on Concepción's standardized achievement tests. But what you need to understand, Mr. Lopez, is that these sorts of tests, even though they are nationally standardized, developed by reputable testing firms, and widely used, *are not all that precise* in how they measure students. Many parents, of course, recognize that their children's test scores are often reported numerically in the form of national percentiles. But this does *not* mean that a given child's national percentile is unerringly accurate.

"The kinds of year-to-year shifting you've seen in Concepción's language arts percentiles is quite normal because a given year's test result is not unerringly accurate. Assessment specialists even admit the *anticipated* amount of flip-flop in students' scores when they talk about each test's 'standard error of measurement.' It's something like the sampling errors we hear about for national surveys—you know, 'plus or minus so many percentage points.' Well, measurement error is akin to sampling error. And let me assure you that Concepción's future test scores will, quite predictably, vary from spring to spring.

"What we do see in her language arts performances over the last three years is a consistently high (indeed, well above average) achievement level. When her performance is compared to that of a representative, nationally normed sample, Concepción is doing very well, indeed."

Now, how would you respond to Mr. Lopez?

and spatial aptitudes. For many years, the SAT functioned in precisely that way, although during recent years we have seen less attention given to the *inherited* nature of what's being assessed.

The current SAT, introduced in 2016, takes 3-4 hours to complete (depending on whether the student completes an optional essay exam. Scores on the SAT range from 400 to 1600, combining results from two 800-point sections, (1) Mathematics and (2) Critical Reading and Writing. Scores are reported in 10-point increments for each of the two sections. Over the years, the specific makeup of the SAT has been periodically modified, so if teachers and students wish to remain abreast of the latest configurations of this exam, they should consult the SAT website.

Although a 2005 addition of an essay-writing task to the SAT attracted substantial media attention, students' scores on the optional essay section do not contribute heavily to their overall SAT scores—or even to their scores on the Writing section.

The test is still owned by the College Board, the group that originally created the test, but since 1947 the SAT has been developed and administered for the College Board by the Educational Testing Service (ETS). Both organizations are not-for-profit entities. A less demanding version of the test, referred to most often as the PSAT, is administered once each year in October—typically to high school students during their sophomore or junior year. The College Board also offers *Readi Step*, a standardized test for middle school students. This 2-hour test, consisting exclusively of multiple-choice items, assesses students' achievement in reading, writing, and mathematics during fall and spring testing windows. The SAT itself is administered throughout the nation on seven preannounced occasions during the year and four times annually outside the United States.

Historically, the SAT was originally designed *not* to be aligned with high school curricula, but in 2016, David Coleman, College Board president since 2012, announced his intention to make the test's content more closely aligned with what students learned in high school. Commencing with the 2015–16 school year, the College Board announced that it would be teaming with the Khan Academy, a free online education site, to provide free-of-charge SAT preparation for prospective test takers.

More than 1.7 million high school graduates from the class of 2017 completed the SAT, both in the United States and abroad. Given the huge number of students sitting for the SAT, it should not surprise you to learn that, in recent years, numerous security violations have been reported in connection with the SAT's multiple administrations. Although security breaches certainly occur in the United States, substantial security violations have been reported abroad. To illustrate, since October 2014, the College Board has been required to delay issuing scores in Asia six times and has canceled an exam in two locations there (Reuters, 2016).

Because of the personal college-admission significance to so many young boys and girls, as well as their parents, teachers should be aware of the lengths to which some individuals will go to come up with shining scores. Although, in years past, most educators presumed that super-significant examinations such as college admission tests were essentially tamper-proof, this is simply not the case. An individual teacher can do little to forestall such security violations, of course, because test-administration operations are typically in the hands of test-company personnel. Yet, to regard high-stakes college admission tests as invulnerable to the threat of sophisticated cheating would be naïve.

The ACT

For the past several decades, the SAT was typically used more often by students living in coastal states, whereas the ACT was completed more frequent in the Midwest and South. However, in recent years we have seen increasing numbers of high school graduates on the East and West coasts completing the ACT. Often, of course—and depending on the affluence of the test taker's family—students complete both the SAT and the ACT. We now turn to this somewhat more recent addition to the college admissions test options, the ACT.

Although both the SAT and the ACT are typically characterized as *aptitude* exams because they are employed in an attempt to predict a high school student's subsequent academic performance in college, the ACT's lineage makes it a decisively different kind of "aptitude" test than the SAT. Following World War II, and the subsequent enactment of the G.I. Bill of Rights (a federal law providing college tuition for returning military personnel), many more American men and women wanted to secure a college education. There was therefore a substantially increased need for college entrance exams.

At the University of Iowa, a gifted professor named E. F. Lindquist believed the that SAT, given its ancestry as an aptitude test designed for students attending elite colleges, was not a suitable exam for many of these post-WWII college applicants. Thus, in 1959, Lindquist and his colleagues established the American College Testing Program as a not-for-profit testing company; later, in 1996, its official name was changed to ACT.

From the very outset, the ACT was intended to be an unabashed *achievement* test. Architects of the ACT certainly wanted their new test to be predictive of a high school student's academic success in college, but they conceived of their new test chiefly as a measure of a student's "educational development."

The ACT is made up of separate tests in essentially the same four content areas it initially assessed: English, mathematics, reading, and science. An optional writing test is now available, in which the student has 30 minutes to write an essay supporting one of two positions presented in a writing "prompt," or a task. Like the SAT, the ACT takes between 3 and 4 hours to complete.

Developers of the ACT routinely solicit content suggestions, in each of the content areas tested, from large samples of secondary teachers and curriculum coordinators, as well as from college professors in the four core subject areas. Secondary-school educators are asked to identify the skills and content that students in their school or district have an option to learn by the end of their junior year in high school. College professors are asked what skills or knowledge acquired at the secondary-school level are essential for students to be academically successful during their first year of college. Based on a combination of what's taught in secondary schools and what's considered requisite for first-year success in college, items are then developed for the ACT.

Every ACT item is multiple-choice in nature, and a student gets one point for every correct answer, with no subtraction of points (or partial points) for a wrong answer. Number-correct scores are then converted to a new 1- to 36-point scale (all scores being reported as integers). For each of the separate tests from which an overall (composite) score is derived representing an *average* of the four separate-tests' 1 to 36 points is computed (unlike the SAT, where scores from its three sections are added together). The optional writing test, equivalent to the SAT's essay test, is scored on the basis of a 2- to 12-point scale using the judgments of two scorers, who can each award from 1 to 6 points to a student's essay.

As with the SAT, there are variations of the ACT available to be used with younger students. EXPLORE is aimed at eighth- and ninth-grade students, and PLAN is available for tenth-graders. More information about these three tests is available on the ACT website.

Predictive Accuracy—And Its Implications

Because of the important decisions linked to secondary students' scores on the SAT and the ACT, test-preparation options abound for each test. These test-prep possibilities range from low-cost printed and online Internet materials all the way up to very pricy in-person preparation classes and tutorials. Although there are exceptions, the more money that's spent on a preparation activity for either of these two tests, the more effective such preparation is apt to be. This is a troubling reality, of course, because children from more affluent families have greater access to the most costly preparation options, so they tend to score better than their less affluent classmates who can't afford high-cost preparation alternatives.

But, as important as it is, let's put test-prep bias aside for a moment. There is one overridingly important realization all teachers must arrive at regarding the predictive accuracy of the SAT and the ACT. Here it is, all gussied up in italics:

> Only about 25 percent of academic success in college is associated with a high school student's performance on the SAT or ACT.

To calculate how well a high school student's scores on a college entrance test accurately predict his or her academic success in college, a correlation is computed between high school students' scores on the SAT (or the ACT) and their subsequent college grades—for instance, their first-year college grade-point averages. With few exceptions, the resulting correlation coefficients turn out to be approximately .50. A predictive coefficient of .50 is statistically significant and certainly reflects a *bona fide* relationship between students' scores on college entrance tests and their subsequent college grades.

However, to determine the *practical meaningfulness* of that relationship, what we must do is *square* the .50 coefficient so that it becomes .25 (.50 × .50 = .25). This tells us that 25 percent of students' college grades can be linked to their performances on college admission tests. In other words, fully 75 percent of a student's college grades are due to factors *other* than students' scores on the SAT or the ACT. Such factors would include a student's motivation, study habits, and other variables over which a student has substantial control.

Even if you are a numerical ninny, you'll realize that a student's college grades are three times more dependent on nontest factors than they are on test factors—that is, 75 percent (test-unrelated) versus 25 percent (test-related). And yet we find hoards of students who earn only "so-so scores" on the SAT or the ACT simply writing themselves off as "not smart enough" to succeed in college. College success, and success in life, is unarguably dependent on much more than a test score. Unfortunately, because the nation's educators are often unfamiliar with the predictive *imprecision* of college entrance tests, they don't do enough to dissuade students from prematurely foreclosing their college aspirations.

Over the years, a student's SAT or ACT scores have become, to many, and to students themselves, an unalterable definition of one's ability. That's simply not true. And teachers need not only to know it, but also to make sure their students (and their students' parents) know it too.

The SAT and the ACT help college officials distinguish among applicants in the common fixed-quota setting where there are more applicants for admission to a college than there are openings at that college. But the *general* predictive power of the SAT and the ACT doesn't transform those exams into definitively accurate assessment tools for any *particular* student. Teachers at all levels need to help students recognize what the SAT and the ACT exams can do—and what they can't.

Moreover, as indicated earlier, the SAT and ACT have now received federal approval, via 2015's ESSA, for use as part of a state's educational accountability program. Although neither of these tests was developed to function in evaluating the quality of a state's schools, some states will soon be using them for that purpose. We must be attentive to the success with which the ACT and SAT fulfill their new measurement mission—particularly in states where the ACT or SAT has hopped to the top of the accountability testing mountain.

What Do Classroom Teachers Really Need to Know About Interpreting Standardized Test Scores?

Because the results of standardized tests are almost certain to come into your professional life, you need to have some understanding of how to interpret those results. The most common ways of describing a set of scores is to provide an index of the score distribution's central tendency (usually the mean or median) and an index of the score distribution's variability (usually the standard deviation or the range). There will probably be instances in which you must either describe the performances of your students in this manner or interpret these descriptions of the performances of other groups of students (such as all students in your school or your district).

To make accurate interpretations of standardized test scores for your own students, and to help parents understand how to make sense of their child's standardized test scores, you need to comprehend the basic meaning of percentiles, grade-equivalent scores, and scale scores. You also ought to understand the major advantage and disadvantage of each of those three score-interpretation schemes. You'll then be in a position to help parents make sense of their children's performances on standardized tests.

Two of the more influential tests many students will ever take are the SAT and the ACT, the most widely used college entrance tests. Classroom teachers need to know that, because of their differing lineages, the SAT and the ACT represent somewhat overlapping but fundamentally different assessment strategies. Whereas the SAT's focus is more heavily on assessing students' academic aptitudes, the ACT's focus is on measuring the kinds of skills and knowledge that, having been previously learned, are necessary in college. Although both tests are predictive of a student's college grades, only about 25 percent of students' college grades are associated with students' SAT or ACT scores. Finally, because both tests must make certain that the performances of test takers are spread out enough so that fine-grained comparisons among students can be made, we will continue to see the inclusion of test items that spread out students' scores. Whether those difference-producing test items will be aligned with what's taught in a state's schools remains to be seen.

Chapter Summary

Standardized tests were defined as assessment instruments administered, scored, and interpreted in a standard, predetermined manner. Standardized tests are used to assess students' achievement and aptitude. Tests of student achievement are developed by large testing companies, as well as by state departments of education (usually to satisfy a legislatively imposed educational accountability requirement). Although most standardized tests feature the use of selected-response items, many developers of such tests attempt to incorporate modest numbers of constructed-response items in their assessment devices.

We saw that a distribution of test scores can be described using two indices of central tendency—the mean and the median—as well as two indices of variability—the range and the standard deviation.

Several ways of interpreting the results of standardized tests were discussed: percentiles, grade-equivalent scores, scale scores, stanines, and normal curve equivalents (NCEs). The nature of each of these interpretation procedures,

as well as the strengths and weaknesses of the three most popular interpretation procedures, were described.

The contribution of instructionally diagnostic tests was described. Factors to consider were presented to help teachers determine whether a test so marketed is indeed instructionally diagnostic, and if so, how to gauge its quality.

The SAT and the ACT are, by far, America's most widely used college entrance tests. Because of its history, the SAT (originally known as the Scholastic Aptitude Test) aims to assess students' academic aptitudes—for example, a student's innate verbal, quantitative, and spatial aptitudes. The ACT attempts to function as an achievement test that, although it is predictive of students' college success, measures high school students' mastery of the skills and knowledge needed in college. Although predictive criterion-related validity coefficients of approximately .50 indicate that students' SAT and ACT scores are certainly correlated with students' college grades, fully 75 percent of a student's academic success in college is linked to factors *other* than scores on either of these two tests.

MyLab Education Self-Check 13.1

MyLab Education Self-Check 13.2

MyLab Education Application Exercise 13.1: Fundamental Characteristics of Standardized Testing

References

Miller, M. D., and Linn, R. (2012). *Measurement and assessment in teaching* (11th ed.). Columbus, OH: Pearson.

Nitko, A. J., and Brookhart, S. M. (2014). *Educational assessment of students* (7th ed.). Boston: Pearson.

Phelps, R. P. (Ed.). (2005). *Defending standardized testing*. Mahwah, NJ: Erlbaum.

Reuters. (2016). "'Massive' breach exposes hundreds of questions for upcoming SAT exams." Reuters. Retrieved 20 July 2017 from https://www.reuters.com/investigates/special-report/college-sat-security/

Tankersley, K. (2007). *Tests that teach: Using standardized tests to improve instruction.* Alexandria, VA: Association for Supervision and Curriculum Development.

Waugh, C. K., and Gronlund, N. (2012). *Assessment of student achievement* (11th ed.). Columbus, OH: Pearson.

A Testing Takeaway

Score Reporting: Where Recipients Must Rule*

W. James Popham, University of California, Los Angeles

If anyone wants to get a good idea of what a standardized educational test is measuring, one of the best ways to do so is to consult the score report describing students' test performances. In many instances, different versions of these reports are created for different recipients. Such audience-tailored score reports might be designed for teachers, for students' parents, and for educational policymakers such as school boards and state legislators.

But no matter who the recipients for a standardized test's score report are, one essential attribute of such reports is that they should be *easy to comprehend*. If the users of a score report can't readily make sense of the report's information, then why test students at all?

A second essential feature of a standardized test's score report is *actionability*. We shouldn't be testing students merely because the results are "interesting." Instead, a standardized test's score report should help inform decisions about what should come next educationally.

Accordingly, even though standardized educational tests can be employed for several important uses—such as *evaluation* of instructional quality, improvement of *instruction*, and *prediction* of test takers' future success—those tests' score reports should all embody the following two attributes:

- *Clarity*. Descriptions of students' results should be easily understood. Whether a standardized test's score report is provided for a single student, a school-full of students, or an entire state's students, recipients of that report must be able, without difficulty, to quickly grasp what's being reported.

- *Actionability*. Having become aware of what's being reported, the recipients of a standardized test's score report must then be able to use those reported results to select the actions for students to take next.

These two requirements will vary depending on the intended purpose of a standardized test. For example, if a standardized test's results are intended to help teachers improve their instruction, then results should be reported at "grain sizes" judged to be optimal for teachers' instructional planning. Test results aimed at modifying a state's major curricular emphases should be reported at much broader grain sizes.

The most important realization in judging the quality of a standardized test's score report is that it's less important to satisfy the preferences of the measurement folks who design the report than to satisfy the needs of users of the score reports. If a standardized test's score report fails to satisfy report users, recipients of the report should band together and raise such a ruckus that the report will be improved.

Chapter 14

Appropriate and Inappropriate Test-Preparation Practices

Chief Chapter Outcome

An understanding of two test-preparation guidelines intended to help teachers distinguish between test-preparation practices that are appropriate and those that are inappropriate

Learning Outcomes

14.1 Apply the professional ethics guideline and the educational defensibility guideline provided in this chapter to distinguish between appropriate and inappropriate test practices.

This chapter deals with an important assessment-related issue that never seriously troubled teachers a few decades ago. Unfortunately, it is a problem that today's classroom teachers must confront seriously. Faced with growing pressures to increase students' scores on achievement tests (pressures that have been ratcheted up dramatically because of today's accountability demands and, in a number of settings, teacher-evaluation requirements), some teachers have responded by engaging in test-preparation practices that are highly questionable. In recent years, for example, reports have been issued describing teachers and administrators who deliberately coached students with actual copies of a supposedly "secure" examination. There are even reports of educators' erasing students' incorrect answers, then substituting correct answers in their place. Teachers caught cheating on high-stakes tests have lost both their teaching licenses and their jobs. Rather than a few isolated instances, such violations of test security have become, sadly, quite common.

High-Stakes Assessment Arrives

The preoccupation with student test scores as the definitive indicator of educational effectiveness first surfaced in the 1980s. Although attention had been given to the quality of student test performances prior to that decade, it was in the 1980s that attentiveness to student test performance became pervasive. In large measure, the focus on pupils' test scores stemmed from increasing incredulity on the part of citizens about whether public education was performing properly. Taxpayers, and their elected representatives, registered serious doubts that educational tax dollars were being well spent. Spawned by such doubts, the era of educational accountability became a reality in the 1980s, when state after state enacted laws requiring students to be assessed by annually administered achievement tests. Students' performances on such tests were used not only to determine the quality of statewide schooling but also (because of the widespread practice of publishing such test scores in local newspapers) to mirror the effectiveness of individual school districts and schools.

In every sense of the expression, these legislatively mandated achievement tests were *high-stakes tests* because there were significant contingencies associated with the tests' results. Those contingencies were experienced either by the students who took the tests or by the educators who administered the tests. To students, the tests were significant because test scores were often linked to high school graduation or to grade-level promotion. To educators, because of the way in which test results were publicized by the local media, high test scores were viewed as indicating an effective instructional program, and of course, low test scores were seen to indicate the opposite. Because of these contingencies, teachers and administrators found themselves frequently called on to raise test scores. Candid educators will agree that pressures to boost students' test scores are still widespread.

When NCLB was enacted in 2002, high-stakes testing in America became the law of the land. Not surprisingly, a good many educators regarded federal accountability with both fear and loathing. Some protesters came up with a variety of arguments and slogans against such testing. My favorite was "High stakes are for tomatoes!" But protesters notwithstanding, the enactment of NCLB elevated our test-related stakes to previously unforeseen heights. When NCLB was replaced by ESSA in 2015, test-based accountability did not evaporate in U.S. schools. Indeed, even though ESSA's accountability requirements provided greater flexibility in the way states chose to implement their accountability preferences, and the NCLB-demand for student's scores to display "Adequate Yearly Progress" were abandoned, most state officials still did what they could to improve students' scores on their annual accountability examinations. As a result, in almost all the nation's school districts, there is still pressure on teachers to improve students' test performances. In schools or districts where year-to-year scores go up, teachers are thought to be effective. In schools or districts where no improvement is seen, or—even worse—where test scores go down, teachers are often regarded as ineffectual. Is it any wonder that some teachers, eager to boost their students' scores, engage in test-preparation practices that might be a bit dodgy?

Discussions with classroom teachers regarding what sorts of test-preparation practices they view as appropriate and what sorts they see as inappropriate have led to one inescapable conclusion: Most teachers have not devoted serious thought to the appropriateness of their test-preparation practices. Given the relatively recent arrival of high-stakes testing in education, it is not surprising that scant attention has been given to the appropriateness of various

Decision Time

Was It Really Wrong?

Judy Jameson is a 10th-grade history teacher in Grant High School. All 10th-graders are given state-wide language arts and mathematics tests that they must pass if they are to receive a state-sanctioned diploma from the district.

The test administration takes place during a 2-day period in the school cafetorium and is supervised by Grant High teachers. During those 2 days, on three occasions Judy overheard Mr. Pelkins respond to students who raised their hands for clarification. Mr. Pelkins did not merely clarify; he *literally*

told the student what the correct answer was to the test item. After some subtle inquiries, Judy learned that all of the students whom Mr. Pelkins had helped were currently in his 10th-grade general mathematics class.

Judy is now trying to decide whether she should do anything about Mr. Pelkins's conduct and, if so, what?

If you were Judy, what would your decision be?

---

test-preparation practices. Yet, because no decrease in the pressure on educators to promote higher test scores seems likely, it is apparent that teachers need to consider seriously what sorts of test-preparation practices are, indeed, appropriate.

Assessment Results as Inference Illuminators

Before addressing topics related to test preparation, it is important to remember the function of educational achievement tests. An educational achievement test is employed in order to make a valid inference about a student's status with respect to the knowledge and/or skills in the curricular aim the test represents. Ideally, of course, an achievement test will sample whatever is in the curricular aim representatively, so the level of a student's performance on the achievement test will serve as a reasonably accurate reflection of the student's status with respect to the curricular aim. The nature of this relationship is illustrated in Figure 14.1 where it is indicated that a student who answered correctly

---

Figure 14.1 The Inference-Illuminating Relationship between a Test and the Curricular Aim It Represents

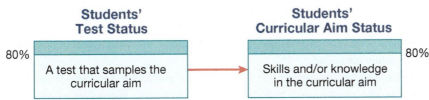

80 percent of the items in an achievement test would be expected to have mastered about 80 percent of the content in the curricular aim (and its knowledge and/or skills) that the test was measuring. The relationship between a student's test performance and the student's mastery of the curricular aim represented by the achievement test is a key factor in establishing the appropriateness of test-preparation practices.

Two Evaluative Guidelines

Two guidelines can be employed by teachers who wish to ascertain whether given test-preparation practices are appropriate. Taken together, the two guidelines provide teachers with advice regarding the suitability of particular test-preparation activities. Here, then, is the first guideline—the *professional ethics guideline*.

Professional Ethics

No test-preparation practice should violate the ethical norms of the education profession.

This first guideline obliges teachers to avoid any unethical test-preparation practice. Ethical behaviors, of course, are rooted not only in fundamental morality, but also in the nature of a particular profession. For example, physicians should be governed by general ethical principles dealing with honesty and respect for other people's property, as well as by the ethical principles that have evolved specifically for the medical profession. Similarly, teachers should not engage in test-preparation practices that involve violations of general ethical canons dealing with theft, cheating, lying, and so on. In addition, however, teachers must take seriously the ethical obligations arising because teachers have agreed to serve *in loco parentis*. Teachers who serve "in place of the parent" take on an ethical responsibility to serve as models of appropriate behavior for children.

When teachers engage in test-preparation practices that, if brought to the public's attention, would discredit the education profession, such practices should be considered professionally unethical. This is because, in the long term, such practices erode public confidence in our schools and, as a result, diminish taxpayers' financial support for the schools. Consequently, this erosion of public support renders the education profession less effective and, as a result, leaves children less appropriately educated.

Thus, according to the professional ethics guideline, teachers should not engage in test-preparation practices that involve such behaviors as violating state-imposed security procedures regarding high-stakes tests. A growing number of states have enacted serious and widely promulgated regulations stipulating that teachers who breach state test-security procedures will have their credentials revoked. Accordingly, teachers should not engage in test-preparation practices that are unethical because there are potential personal repercussions (for example, loss of credentials) or professional repercussions (for example, reduced citizen confidence in public schooling). Most important, teachers should avoid unethical test-preparation practices because such practices are *wrong*.

Let's look, then, at the second of our two guidelines—the *educational defensibility guideline*.

Educational Defensibility

No test-preparation practice should increase students' test scores without simultaneously increasing students' mastery of the curricular aim tested.

This second standard emphasizes the importance of engaging in instructional practices that are in the best educational interests of students. Teachers should not, for example, artificially increase students' scores on a test while neglecting to increase students' mastery of the knowledge and/or skills that the test is supposed to reflect.

An appropriate (ethical) test-preparation practice not only raises students' prepreparation-to-postpreparation performance on a test; it also raises students' prepreparation-to-postpreparation mastery of the curricular aim being tested. This situation is illustrated in Figure 14.2, where you can see that a 20 percent prepreparation-to-postpreparation jump in students' mastery was seen both on the test and on the curricular aim it represents.

Figure 14.2 Appropriate Test Preparation Based on the Guideline of Educational Defensibility

Conversely, an inappropriate test-preparation practice raises students' pre-preparation-to-postpreparation performance on the test, but not students' mastery of the curricular aim itself. This situation is illustrated in Figure 14.3 where students' test performances increase, but their mastery of the curricular aim doesn't.

The result of such inappropriate test-preparation practices is that a deceptive picture of students' achievement is created. The test results no longer serve as an accurate indicator of students' status with respect to a curricular aim. As a consequence, students who in reality have not mastered a curricular aim's content may fail to receive appropriate instruction regarding such content. The students will

Figure 14.3 Inappropriate Test Preparation Based on the Guideline of Educational Defensibility have been instructionally short-changed because inappropriate test-preparation practices led to an inflated estimate of their content mastery. Such test-preparation practices, because they lead to invalid interpretations of scores and rob students of needed instruction, are educationally indefensible.

Five Test-Preparation Practices

We can now turn to a consideration of five common test-preparation practices. These five practices are not exhaustive in the sense that there are no other conceivable test-preparation procedures. The five practices do, however, capture most of the important test-preparation options available to teachers. Some of these involve special instruction rather than regular classroom instruction. *Special instruction* consists of extra preparation sessions, during or outside class, devoted exclusively to the readying of students for tests. In contrast, *regular classroom instruction*, although its focus may be relevant to the content represented by a test, occurs as part of the teacher's ongoing instructional program. The five test-preparation practices follow.

1. *Previous-form preparation* provides special instruction and practice based directly on students' use of a previous form of the actual test. For example, if the currently published form of a nationally standardized achievement test is being used on a statewide basis as part of a state's accountability system, the teacher gives students guided or independent practice with earlier versions of the same test, which are no longer being published.

2. *Current-form preparation* provides special instruction and practice based directly on students' use of the form of the test currently being employed. For example, the teacher gives students guided or independent practice with actual items copied from a state-developed high school graduation test that is currently being used.

3. *Generalized test-taking preparation* provides special instruction covering test-taking skills for dealing with a variety of achievement-test formats. For example, the teacher shows students how to make calculated guesses for certain types of items or how to allocate test-taking time judiciously. (If you ask almost any search engine to locate test-taking tips on the Internet, you can incorporate any that you regard as worthwhile. It turns out that there may be more test-taking tips on the Internet than there are tests in our schools.)

4. *Same-format preparation* provides regular classroom instruction dealing directly with the content covered on the test, but it employs only practice items that embody the same format as items actually used on the test. For example, if a mathematics achievement test includes addition problems formatted only in vertical columns, the teacher provides practice with addition problems formatted solely in this manner. Some teachers create "clone" items for same-format preparation activities—such items being almost mirror

images of a test's actual items. For many of these "clone" items, the practice items are essentially indistinguishable from the actual items.

5. *Varied-format preparation* provides regular classroom instruction dealing directly with the content covered on the test, but it employs practice items representing a variety of test-item formats. For example, if the achievement test uses subtraction problems formatted only in vertical columns, the teacher provides practice with problems formatted in vertical columns, in horizontal rows, and in story form.

Applying the Two Guidelines

When these five test-preparation practices are scrutinized according to the guidelines of professional ethics and educational defensibility, only two practices turn out to be appropriate.

Previous-form preparation violates the educational defensibility guideline because students' test scores are apt to be boosted via such special preparation sessions without concomitant rises in students' mastery of the curricular aim being tested. In addition, because in the public's view this kind of test-preparation practice may be seen as an improper instance of coaching students *merely* for test-score gains, it may be viewed by some as professionally unethical. Previous-form preparation, therefore, is inappropriate. (This same judgment would apply to the use of commercial test-preparation materials based chiefly on specially created "parallel" forms of a currently used test.)

Current-form preparation clearly loses out on both guidelines. Not only is it educationally indefensible, but such preparation also constitutes an outright example of cheating. Current forms of the test must be stolen or surreptitiously copied in order to be used in such potentially improper score-boosting special sessions. Teachers who are caught readying their students via current-form preparation should, in fact, be caught.

Generalized test-taking preparation turns out to be an appropriate form of test preparation, because such special instruction on how to take tests is, characteristically, rather brief and not seriously deflective of a student's ongoing education. More important, because such test-taking preparation readies students to cope with a number of different sorts of tests, students will be less apt to be intimidated by a previously unencountered type of test item. In a very real sense, therefore, generalized test-taking preparation sessions allow students' test performances to be more accurately reflective of their true state of knowledge and/or skill. Such preparation, *if not excessively lengthy*, is clearly appropriate.

Same-format preparation, although it may be ethical, is not educationally defensible. If students in their regular classroom instruction are allowed to deal *only* with the explicit item format used on a test, then those students will be far less likely to generalize what they have learned. Test scores may rise, but mastery of comparable content is not apt to rise. Although many administrators may, because

Table 14.1 Per-Guideline Indicator of the Appropriateness of Five Test-Preparation Practices

	Guideline Satisfied?	
Test-Preparation Practice	Professional Ethics	Educational Defensibility
Previous Form	No	No
Current Form	No	No
Generalized Test-Taking	Yes	Yes
Same Format	Yes	No
Varied Format	Yes	Yes

of powerful pressures to boost scores, endorse this form of test-preparation practice, it should be resisted because it is educationally unsound. The more "clone" items there are in a set of practice items, the more inappropriate such test-preparation activities are.

Varied-format preparation, in contrast, satisfies both of our two evaluative guidelines. Students during their regular classroom instruction are given practice not only with content as it is conceptualized on the test but also with content conceptualized in other ways. Rises in test scores will, in general, be accompanied by rises in mastery of the curricular aim being tested because such preparation fosters students' generalized mastery of the content.

Of the five test-preparation variants, then, only varied-format preparation and generalized test-taking preparation satisfy both evaluative guidelines. This can be seen in Table 14.1.

Parent Talk

Mrs. Stern is the mother of Sara, one of your most talented students. Mrs. Stern, it is rumored, will be running for election to your district's school board in the fall. Accordingly, whenever Mrs. Stern raises questions about Sara's education, you always try to be especially responsive. You are no dummy.

When Sara arrived at school this morning, she gave you a brief note from her mother. The note said, "Why is so much time spent in our school, and in your class, 'teaching to the test' this year? Shouldn't our children be learning more than what's on a test?"

If I were you, here's how I'd respond to Mrs. Stern in person or with a note (if in person, I might reply on bended knee):

"You're right on target to be raising this issue, Mrs. Stern, but I want you to understand an important difference between 'teaching to the test' in the sense of teaching students to do well on particular test items, and 'teaching to the test' in the sense of teaching students to master the skills and/or knowledge represented by the test.

"What I do in my class is the latter, and that's also what most of my colleagues do. In other words, we teach directly toward the important skills and knowledge that our tests measure. Those are the key kinds of skills and the significant bodies of knowledge that you and I both want Sara to acquire. But the classroom assessments that we use will only sample a student's mastery of such knowledge or skills. In fact, when you hear people talk about 'test validity,' they are referring to the accuracy of a score-based interpretation about students' mastery of the *full range of skills and knowledge being represented by the test*, not merely students' mastery of a particular set of test items.

"So it would be instructionally unwise for us to teach toward particular test items. We want Sara and her classmates to master skills and knowledge so that our students can apply what they've learned in many settings, not merely on a specific test.

"Putting it simply, we do not teach toward a set of test items, but we do teach toward the skills and knowledge that our tests represent."

Now, how would you respond to Mrs. Stern?

What About "Teaching to the Test"?

If you get into any sort of meaningful discussion of test preparation, it's almost certain that someone will soon use the expression "teaching to the test." This someone should not be you! Here's why.

There are two decisively different meanings that people may have in mind when they use the phrase *teaching to the test*. First, they may mean that a teacher is directing instruction toward the knowledge, skills, or affective variables represented by the test. Another way to put this same meaning of "teaching to the test" is that teachers are aiming their instruction so that students achieve the curricular aim sampled by the actual test. This is good instruction. However, other people may use "teaching to the test" to describe teachers who are directing their instruction specifically toward the actual items on the test itself. This is bad instruction.

So, when someone uses the expression "teaching to the test," we can't tell whether they're talking about something swell or something sordid. Conversations about test preparation in which this ambiguous expression is tossed around mindlessly will, almost certainly, end up being mindless conversations.

As a consequence, you should *never use this ambiguous expression* yourself. Rather, say either "teaching to the test's items" or "teaching to the curricular aim represented by the test." To emphasize the importance of this advice, it has been summarized in this box:

    NEVER, NEVER SAY: "Teaching to the test"
SAY:
    "Teaching to the test's items"

(or)
SAY:
    "Teaching to the curricular aim represented by the test"

If you should momentarily forget this fine advice and find yourself blurting out the foul phrase that's just been castigated, or if you are forced with pepper-spray to say it aloud, try to quickly follow up by indicating which meaning of the expression you intended. By and large, however, you'll be better off if you expunge the phrase completely from your potential utterances.

If a *friend* uses the phrase, you might gently and supportively seek clarification about which of the two meanings is intended. If an *enemy* uses the phrase, however, you might display to that vile perpetrator a brow-furrowed sneer— while issuing snarling sounds of serious disdain—thereby signifying total repudiation of this "teaching to the test" utterance.

One way of thinking about how teachers ought to prepare their students for important assessments is presented in Figure 14.4. As you can see, a teacher's instruction should be directed toward the body of knowledge and/or skills (or even affect) represented by the test, but not toward the specific set of items doing the representing.

And this way of thinking about test preparation brings us to an important point for teachers to understand. You can direct your instruction toward the knowledge and/or skills represented by a high-stakes test only if there is a suitable description of the assessed curricular aim available. You can't expect a teacher to teach toward a curricular aim if no clear description of that aim has been provided.

Unfortunately, many of the nation's teachers continue to experience pressure to raise their students' scores on high-stakes test that are unaccompanied by instructionally actionable descriptions of what those tests actually measure. And without such descriptions, it is far from surprising that many pressured teachers have succumbed to the lure of item-focused teaching.

If you spend a meaningful chunk of time reviewing the descriptions of assessed behaviors provided by publishers of all the nation's standardized achievement tests, you'll find that, from a teacher's perspective, the descriptions of these tests' curricular targets fall way short of what teachers need. Oh,

---

Figure 14.4 Appropriate and Inappropriate Directions for a Teacher's Instruction

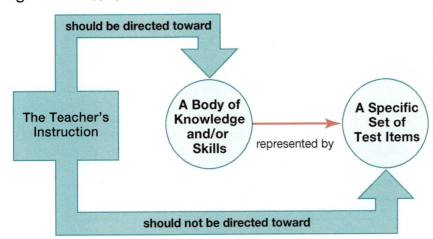

of course there are some loose descriptions of objectives or content assessed, but those descriptions just aren't sufficient for a teacher who is planning day-to-day instruction.

The point is this: If the high-stakes test on which you're asked to boost students' scores is not accompanied by descriptions of what the test's items *represent*, then you should let the world know you're being put in an untenable instructional position. Teachers should not be forced to play the score-boosting game if they are obliged to use rules that make it certain the teacher will lose. And there's no way to satisfy this chapter's two test-preparation guidelines if a curricular aim's description (suitable for instructional action) has not been supplied.

One of the important reasons why today's teachers need their test-influenced instruction to be rip-roaringly effective is that inherent in teaching what's tested is the seductive temptation to teach *only* what's to be tested. Accordingly, if a teacher is not alert, curricular reductionism creeps into the classroom. As suggested way back in Chapter 2, in far too many settings, teachers are being asked to teach and test way too much in the available instructional time. Although the architects of

But What Does This Have to Do with Teaching?

Today's teachers find themselves in a terrible bind, Their competence is often being judged on the basis of students' scores on high-stakes tests. And, as a consequence, teachers frequently find themselves pressured by their principals to improve students' scores on the locally anointed high-stakes tests. But many heavily pressured teachers fail to recognize that their principal is often being squeezed just as hard to make sure a school's test scores take a giant jump.

As you'll learn in the next chapter, evaluating a school's staff on the basis of students' scores on certain kinds of standardized tests is fundamentally wrong. Yet this recognition, all by itself, doesn't make the score-boosting pressure on teachers or administrators evaporate.

As a teacher or a prospective teacher, you really must comprehend the nature of the two test-preparation guidelines offered in this chapter, and you need to understand (from Chapter 15) why it is that some standardized achievement tests measure the socioeconomic makeup of a school's student body, not how well the school's teachers are teaching.

At that point, instead of assuming a school's principal is the "heavy" in this score-boosting frenzy, you need to recognize that school principals are, themselves, under substantial pressure to elevate their school's test scores. Accordingly, by the time you wrap up this book, you'll know (1) how to and how not to prepare students for high-stakes tests and (2) what kinds of high-stakes tests give educators—that is, teachers *and* principals—a chance to succeed.

Therefore, why not collaborate *with* your school's principal to explain ways of responding to extant test pressures with test-preparation practices that help, not harm, children. What you need to do, frankly, is put the stuff you've already learned in Chapter 12 (about formative assessment) and this chapter (about test preparation) together with what you will learn in Chapter 15. Then, working collaboratively with your school's administrator(s), figure out a strategy to make accurate evaluative judgments while, at the same time, benefiting kids.

state curricular aims understandably want their state's students to learn just about *everything*, as a practical matter, this is not possible. Too much to teach translates into, at best, only superficial mastery of vast content domains by students. Teachers need to efficiently (that is, successfully) teach students to master the highest-priority skills and knowledge that they should be mastering. A teacher's skillfully targeted instructional program, relying on only appropriate preparation strategies such as the two identified in this chapter, will give teachers their best chance to teach well those high-priority things that students should learn.

What Do Classroom Teachers Really Need to Know About Test-Preparation Practices?

As a classroom teacher, you may find that your own test-preparation practices do not coincide perfectly with one of the five practices described in this chapter. However, you'll probably discover that if you are preparing your students specifically for some sort of high-stakes test, your approach will be reasonably close to one of the five practices. More important than the five preparation practices, of course, are the two evaluative guidelines. You should review with care your own preparation activities linked to high-stakes tests. The two evaluative guidelines provided here—professional ethics and educational defensibility—should prove useful in such a review.

Chapter Summary

This chapter dealt with an important assessment-related issue: how teachers should prepare their students for significant tests. After a recounting of why classroom teachers are under substantial pressure to boost their students' test scores, two evaluative guidelines were supplied by which to judge test-preparation practices. The two guidelines were (1) *professional ethics*, which indicates that no test-preparation practice should violate the ethical norms of the education profession, and (2) *educational defensibility*, which indicates that no test-preparation practice should increase students' test scores without simultaneously increasing students' mastery of the curricular aim tested. Five test-preparation variants were then described: (1) previous-form preparation, (2) current-form preparation, (3) generalized test-taking preparation, (4) same-format preparation, and (5) varied-format preparation. Having applied the two evaluative guidelines to the five test-preparation practices, we concluded that only two practices satisfy both guidelines: generalized test-taking preparation (if brief) and varied-format preparation. Readers were urged to eschew the phrase *teaching to the test*. The chapter concluded with a discussion of the necessity for the creators of high-stakes tests to supply curricular aim descriptions from which sound instructional decisions can be made.

MyLab Education **Self-Check 14.1**

MyLab Education **Application Exercise 14.1:** Applying the Two Test-Preparation Guidelines

References

Cannell, J. J. (1989). *How public educators cheat on standardized achievement tests.* Albuquerque, NM: Friends for Education.

Hardison, C. M., and Sackett, P. R. (2008). "Use of writing samples on standardized tests: Susceptibility to rule-based coaching and the resulting effects on score improvement," *Applied Measurement in Education, 21,* no. 3 (July–September): 227–252.

Harris, P., Smith, B. M., and Harris, J. (2011). *The myths of standardized tests: Why they don't tell you what you think they do.* Lanham, MD: Rowman & Littlefield.

Lai, E. R., and Waltman, K. (2008). "Test preparation: Examining teacher perceptions and practices," *Educational Measurement: Issues and Practice, 27,* no. 2 (Summer): 28–45.

Mehrens, W. A., and Kaminski, J. (1989). "Methods for improving standardized test scores: Fruitful, fruitless, or fraudulent?" *Educational Measurement: Issues and Practice, 8,* no. 1: 14–22.

Sacks, P. (1999). *Standardized minds: The high price of America's testing culture and what we can do to change it.* Cambridge, MA: Perseus Books.

"Teaching to the Test" or "Teaching What's to Be Tested"*

W. James Popham, University of California, Los Angeles

Today's teachers are coping with relentless pressure to boost their students' test scores—particularly on "high-stakes" tests such as the annual statewide accountability assessments now commonly used throughout the United States. Many citizens assume that high scores on these tests indicate properly educated children, but low scores reveal the opposite. Thus, if significant standardized tests reveal little or no improvement by students or, worse, if those test scores show lower performances, a public outcry soon follows.

It is understandable, then, when teachers sometimes pay more attention to improving their students' scores on standardized tests than to promoting genuine learning on the part of those students. Everyone wants to succeed in their work, and if the effectiveness of teachers is to be judged according to students' test scores, some teachers may begin "teaching to the test." Perhaps they should; perhaps they shouldn't. As you'll soon see, *it depends* on the kind of test-teaching involved.

It turns out that there are two distinctive meanings associated with the idea of *teaching to the test*. One of those meanings is positive; one is negative. Let's see which is which.

- *Positively "teaching to the test"* occurs when a teacher tries to improve students' mastery of the knowledge or skills that are *represented* by a test's items—rather than merely helping students answer more items correctly.

- *Negatively "teaching to the test"* takes place when a teacher only tries to help students answer more test items correctly—rather than promoting students' mastery of the knowledge or skills that those items represent.

Fortunately, if teachers adhere to the following two test-preparation commandments, it is nearly certain that any test preparation being provided will be appropriate:

- *Educational Defensibility:* No test-preparation practice should increase students' test scores without simultaneously increasing students' mastery of the knowledge or skills tested. If *only* test scores rise, without a corresponding increase in students' mastery of what's being tested, then the test preparation is clearly inappropriate.

- *Professional Ethics:* No test-preparation practice should violate the ethical norms of the education profession. If it is found that teachers are negatively teaching to the test, then public opinion of the teaching profession will become more negative, often with adverse long-term consequences.

What's most important is that teachers, whether inexperienced or experienced, devote some serious think-time to this issue. If a teacher adheres to the two test-preparation commandments above, while *positively* teaching to the test, then what's going on is simply good instruction.

Chapter 15
The Evaluation of Instruction

Learning Outcomes

15.1 Describe characteristics of test-elicited evidence of instructional quality as they pertain to the evaluation of schools and teachers.

Chief Chapter Outcome

An understanding of the potential contributions and limitations of test-elicited evidence of instructional quality sufficient for the identification of likely shortcomings in such evidence or in its use for the evaluation of schools or teachers

Most teachers, at the conclusion of a set of instructional activities—whether those activities consume an hour, a week, or an entire school year—do not systematically try to determine how successful their instruction actually was. But they should. In this chapter, then, we'll consider ways in which teachers can tell whether their just-completed instruction was great or grimy. It's really a rather straightforward task, yet not without some significant sand traps to avoid.

Because the chapter after this one deals with the appraisal of students, let's make sure we are using two key labels accurately. In casual conversation, you'll often find educators using the terms *evaluation* and *grading* interchangeably, but these two words really stand for distinctively different education-related activities.

There was a time when educators really didn't distinguish between *evaluation* of students and *grading* of students, but those days have passed. Because program evaluation has now become such a prominent part of educational practice, when most educators encounter the term *evaluation* these days, they think about the evaluation of an educational program, such as a school district's newly installed cooperative learning scheme.

When classroom teachers engage in **evaluation**, those teachers are typically arriving at conclusions about the quality of their own instructional efforts. In this sense, therefore, you should think about evaluation as "program evaluation." Because the "program" under consideration in most classrooms is the instructional program provided to students by the teacher, the term *evaluation* will be used in this chapter to signify the attempt on the part of teachers to determine how well they're doing instructionally. The evaluation of instruction, then, can sometimes be loosely equated with "teacher evaluation," because when teachers evaluate their instructional endeavors, they're really evaluating the quality of the instructional program they put together, as well as the way they delivered that program. The focus of *evaluation* in this chapter, therefore, is on teachers' evaluation of their instruction.

In contrast, the focus of **grading** is on *students*. When a teacher grades a student, the teacher is assigning some kind of symbol (we'll discuss several options in the next chapter), such as letter grades of A, B, C, D, or F, that signify "how well the student has done." Although in most classrooms there's surely a relationship between the quality of the teacher's instructional program and the grades that students receive, those two notions are really independent. For example, Mrs. Bevins, a third-grade teacher, could evaluate her own language arts program very negatively because her instruction seemed to confuse many students. Nevertheless, Mrs. Bevins would still award grades of A to numerous students who, despite the confusing language arts instruction they were receiving, seemed effortlessly to grasp the language arts concepts being considered.

Although you're witnessing an attempt to draw a nice, crisp distinction between *evaluation* as the appraisal of an instructional activity and *grading* as the appraisal of a student's performance, don't be surprised if you encounter colleagues who don't slice their appraisal cake in the same way. Some educators refer to the grading of students as the "evaluation" of students. Other educators talk about "grading" the quality of instruction. So prepare yourself for some semantic stumbling when you discuss these concepts with others.

Two types of evaluation have a bearing on teachers' appraisals of their instructional efforts. *Teachers' self-evaluation* is the personal appraisal of the teacher's instructional program for purposes of improving the program. For example, suppose you're teaching a 3-week social studies unit on international cooperation to a class of fifth-graders for the first time. You want to improve the unit so that the next time you offer it, your teaching will be more effective. That's a task for self-evaluation, and students' assessment results will surely help you. *External teacher evaluation*, in contrast, is often not focused on improvement. This kind of evaluation frequently refers to appraisals of teachers' competencies in order to make significant decisions about those teachers, such as (1) whether their contracts should be renewed or (2) whether they should be awarded tenure. When teachers are evaluated externally, they're almost always evaluated by an administrator or supervisor.

External evaluations of teachers are typically divided into two categories: summative teacher evaluations and formative teacher evaluations. **Summative teacher evaluations** focus on the sorts of high-stakes personnel decisions mentioned in the previous paragraph. **Formative teacher evaluations**, often made by teachers in collaboration with a supervisor or school-site administrator, are intended to help teachers improve their instructional effectiveness. The distinction between these two versions of teacher evaluation is of considerable significance to all educators because, depending on whether federal or state advocacy of formative or summative evaluation is in the ascendency at that moment, profoundly different approaches to teacher evaluation will be endorsed locally. To illustrate, you might find yourself teaching in a school where the evaluation of teachers emphasizes a "let's improve" orientation, or you might end up teaching in a school where there is great pressure to "locate any teacher losers." Clearly, the atmosphere in those two settings can be staggeringly different. The current national orientation to teacher evaluation is strikingly different than it was just a few years ago. More about this shift in the nation's teacher evaluation mood later in the chapter.

A Focus on Consequences

You can't tell how well teachers teach by watching them do it. Instead, to determine the effectiveness of a teacher's instruction, we need to focus on the *effects* a teacher's instruction has on students. There are precious few exceptions to this "focus on consequences" strategy for the evaluation of instruction. To illustrate one such exception, on the ineffective end of the quality scale, this would occur if we were to observe a teacher engaging in a series of badly explained, mind-numbing, and off-target activities—all of which were taking place in the midst of loud talking, misbehaving, and clearly out-of-control students. Anyone walking into such a cacophonous classroom would instantly be able to conclude, with good reason, that some seriously shabby instruction was taking place. At the other end of the quality yardstick—the cool end—we might observe a teacher who is carrying out a galaxy of diverse, research-supported instructional practices in a classroom where well-behaved students are clearly engaged in what is taking place and, when asked by the teacher, actively participate in a series of cleverly devised learning activities. This second "does it all perfectly" teacher is likely to be regarded as successful based on just about any evaluative factors we might choose when judging instructional quality. But, with the possible exception of such spectacularly wonderful or spectacularly woeful teachers, we really can't tell by *watching* how successful a teacher is. The vast majority of teachers are neither phenomenally fabulous nor flat-out flops; they're somewhere in the middle. Accordingly, in almost all instances we really need to evaluate a teacher's instruction according to its *consequences*—that is, by determining its effect on students' learning.

To properly evaluate a teacher's instruction, we should employ a rather traditional ends–means model. Using such a time-honored paradigm, the curricular aims sought by a teacher represent the teacher's intended *ends*, whereas what the teacher does in an effort to achieve those ends constitutes the teacher's instructional *means*. When we assess students at the close of an instructional sequence, therefore, we are usually attempting to determine whether the teacher's instructional means have, indeed, promoted students' attainment of the curricular ends being sought by the teacher.

For years, empirical evidence has shown conclusively that there is no "one best way" to teach something. The instructional procedures used marvelously by a particular teacher in a particular setting with a particular set of students might turn out to be thoroughly ineffectual in the hands of another teacher in a different setting with a dissimilar set of students. Put simply, for almost all teachers, the only way to evaluate instruction accurately is to determine what happens to students as a consequence of the teacher's instruction. And this is where assessment evidence comes bounding onto the scene, for *it is only by using assessment evidence that we can tell whether what was taught has actually been learned.* Assessment evidence, therefore, helps us arrive at accurate evaluations of a teacher's success, whether this evidence is used as part of a teacher's own self-evaluation or in connection with an externally imposed evaluation of teachers. Remember, we use educational assessments to garner the evidence that allows us to derive inferences about students' unseen knowledge and skills. Here's where all the attention to collecting purpose-specific validity evidence enters the picture. If the evidence is intended to be used for the evaluation of teachers—either formative or summative—then we need to know for sure whether the test-produced evidence permits accurate interpretations that contribute to this evaluative mission.

If a teacher's instructional success is going to be evaluated on the basis of students' learning, then what evidence of students' learning ought to be employed to arrive at such an evaluation? Well, there are two prominent kinds of assessment evidence that should, if at all possible, be included in any sort of instructional-evaluation sweepstakes. First off, evidence of students' learning that is collected via *classroom assessments* is clearly one source of assessment data to be considered. Second, if a teacher's students are required to complete one or more *external accountability tests*, then students' performances on such tests—if those tests are appropriate for this function—should definitely be used in the evaluation of instruction.

In a moment, we'll look at ways of collecting both of these kinds of evidence, but please realize that not all results of classroom assessments *or* accountability tests should be treated equally. In earlier chapters you tussled with a number of test-development and test-refinement ideas that, clearly, bear on the quality of the data collected by the use of teacher-made classroom assessments. Obviously, there are profound differences in the persuasiveness of students' test results depending on the caliber of the tests themselves. For instance, let's assume that a teacher's classroom tests assess students' mastery of a set of several genuinely high-level cognitive skills, and those tests do so by using a collection of items that assiduously follow all of the item guidelines given earlier in this text. Students' performances on such a well-built test ought to play a prominent role in the evaluation of instructional activities. On the other hand, let's assume that a teacher's classroom test not only measures a collection of trifling curricular aims, but does so with items that reek of wretchedness. In short, this second fictional test measures unimportant stuff and measures it badly. Clearly, students' performances on this second test should be given little if any importance when evaluating a teacher's instruction.

A second source of assessment evidence that we should employ to evaluate instructional quality occurs when external achievement tests are used as part of a governmentally required accountability program. Obviously, a teacher has far less influence over the makeup of such tests—in contrast to the teacher's own classroom assessments. But external accountability tests, such as the annual exams administered in accord with a statutorily required accountability program, also vary dramatically in quality. As you will see later in this chapter, many of the accountability tests now being used in the United States are seriously flawed from an evaluative perspective, and thus should not be employed to evaluate instructional quality. So, just as we saw with the evidence collected by teacher-made tests, the appropriateness of evidence provided by external accountability tests also can vary considerably. It is a mistake to automatically regard external accountability tests as trustworthy merely because they take more time to create and are more expensive to develop than teacher-made tests. For purposes of evaluating instructional quality, you should definitely know that some standardized tests stink.

Okay, so when we set out to evaluate instructional quality, two potentially useful kinds of evidence to be considered are students' performances on (1) classroom assessments and (2) external accountability tests. As already noted, because both of these two categories of tests can vary in their quality, caution is clearly warranted when using students' performances on either type of test.

But there's one additional factor to consider when teachers evaluate their instruction, and it's an important one that should be considered every time an instructional evaluation takes place. That additional factor consists of the *unintended side effects of instruction*. With test results, whether from classroom assessments or external accountability exams, teachers have at least a general idea of what's to be assessed; hence they can usually engage in instructional activities aimed at improving students' test performances. But what happens if, although the teacher has not planned on it, some significant side effects on the teacher's students occur as a consequence of instruction? Shouldn't these side effects be taken into consideration in the evaluation of instruction? You bet they should.

To illustrate, let's say a middle school mathematics teacher has done a simply spectacular job in getting her students to perform well on a series of exams she personally constructed, and she's even seen dramatic increases in her students' performances on the state's annual mathematics assessments. So, clearly, students' scores have soared on both kinds of assessments that we have been considering as potential evidence for the evaluation of instruction. Unfortunately, what also happened in this teacher's math classes is that almost all of the students acquired seriously negative attitudes toward math, some of the students claiming privately that they "would never, *ever* take another math class voluntarily." So, despite the teacher's test-based evidence of success—seen on both classroom tests and statewide accountability tests—a serious side effect seems to have soured this teacher's instructional soufflé. If a math teacher's instruction makes students abhor mathematics, then this constitutes a significant side effect to be taken into consideration when evaluating the teacher. Unanticipated side effects, both negative and positive, should *always* be considered when evaluating instructional quality.

But how, you might be asking, does a teacher identify the side effects of a completed instructional sequence? Well, that task is a truly tough one. As a teacher, what you most need to do is *be on the lookout for any consequences of instruction that you had not foreseen.* You might, as you near the close of an instructional sequence, ask a colleague to help you think about such a question. You might also try to poll your students with anonymous self-report inventories akin to those you learned about in Chapter 10. But the chief thing is for you to be *looking for* such unanticipated side effects, and you should never regard a set of instructional activities as having been properly evaluated without raising the possibility that some unforeseen positive or negative effects might have taken place because of the instruction.

The evidence a teacher uses regarding unforeseen side effects might be collected by fairly traditional data-gathering approaches, or more innovative assessment ploys could be used. And in some cases, side effects will be found without any reliance at all on assessment devices. For example, let's think of a sixth-grade teacher whose hyperdemanding and stressful style, when used with recently arrived immigrant children, apparently leads to massive dropouts on the part of those children. (Fully half of those children have already left school during the current school year.) The evidence of such an adverse side effect might not be collected by using any sort of typical or even innovative assessment tactics. Instead, the school's attendance office might be the source of such information. For identifying side effects, all legitimate sources of information are fair game.

Summarizing, then, to evaluate the quality of your instruction, I encourage you to structure your evaluative strategy around the following three factors:

1. Assessment evidence collected via classroom assessments
2. Assessment evidence collected via accountability tests
3. Evidence pertaining to any positive or negative side effects

As noted before, the quality of the assessment devices used is critical when we set out to appraise instructional quality. Good assessments—ones that measure worthwhile things—typically provide good evaluative evidence. The opposite is also true. In earlier chapters, we've already looked at how teachers can devise appropriate classroom assessments. In the remainder of this chapter, we will be giving serious consideration to external accountability tests, because those kinds of tests are often used to supply the dominant evidence regarding most teachers' instructional success. But before leaving the evidence available from classroom assessments, let's take a brief look at *how* a teacher can use classroom assessments to collect evaluative evidence regarding the teacher's instructional success.

Classroom Assessment Evidence

Most teachers realize that if they collect assessment evidence from their students only *after* instruction is over, they won't be able to determine the effectiveness of the instruction they're trying to evaluate. After all, students might have known already—before any instruction took place—what the teacher was setting out to teach. Thus, whether evidence is being collected for teachers' self-evaluation or for external teacher evaluation, some sort of *pretest versus posttest* data-gathering model is usually employed. Let's consider two such models, both of which can make contributions to teachers' efforts to evaluate the quality of their instruction.

Pretests Versus Posttests

Whether for self-evaluation or external evaluation, the classic pretest–posttest model presented in Figure 15.1 will prove serviceable for gauging instructional impact. If you assess your students prior to teaching them, and then assess your students after you've taught them, any difference between their pretest and post-test performances ought to be chiefly attributable to what went on in between—your teaching.

Certain problems are associated with the classic pretest–posttest scheme for discerning instructional impact, of course, but as a general paradigm for figuring out whether your instruction is making any dents in your students, the approach represented in Figure 15.1 isn't all that bad. One of the difficulties with the pre-test–posttest model that you may need to watch out for is the possibility that the pretest will be *reactive*; that is, it will sensitize your students to "what's impor-tant" so they behave atypically when being taught about what was on the pretest. In other words, the effects measured by the posttest will really be a function of your instruction *plus* the pretest. However, if the posttest results for Topic X truly turn out to be what you want when you use a reactive pretest, then you might decide to toss in a pretest every time you teach Topic X.

For purposes of external evaluation, such as when you are being evaluated by school district officials for purposes of continued employment, there's a genu-inely tricky problem to consider, and this is the extent to which pretest-to-posttest assessment results for students will be influenced by the caliber of the students that you happen to be teaching. If you're teaching a ninth-grade geography class and have been blessed with a group of bright, motivated, and well-informed students, it is certain that the pretest-to-posttest gains you obtain will be quite different from the gains you might see if you were teaching a collection of dull, unmotivated students whose conception of geography stopped at the boundaries of the schoolyard.

It is imperative, however, that those who use student-assessment data for purposes of external teacher evaluation do so in the context of the situation in

Figure 15.1 A Classic Pretest versus Posttest Model for Determining Instructional Impact which the teacher teaches—the most important feature of which is the specific students being taught. For your own self-evaluation purposes, there's somewhat less need to get caught up with the "dissimilar students" problem. After all, you'll know your own students and will be able to judge whether you have a group of fast-thinking wizards whose pretest-to-posttest gains will be astounding or a group of slow-thinking students whose progress will be substantially less electrifying.

To the extent that you're using gain scores (that is, posttest-minus-pretest scores), you should be aware of another technical problem likely to get in your way. If your students did *very* well on the pretest, it will be more difficult for them to show gains than it would have been if they had scored low prior to instruction. When students score very high on tests, they tend to "top out" because of what is called a *ceiling effect*. Also, if your students score quite poorly on a pretest, they'll be likely to score higher on the posttest *by chance alone*. (If you want to intimidate your colleagues during faculty meetings, this is called a ***regression effect***, wherein extremely low-scoring (or high-scoring) students tend to regress toward the mean when retested. By casually asserting that your "students' progress, of course, might be attributable to a regression effect," you'll surely awe a few of your fellow teachers.)

There's another potential way of dealing with the difficulties of a simple pretest-versus-posttest evaluation design, and that's to use different but *equidifficult* tests. The only problem with this solution is that it's almost impossible for busy classroom teachers to create two truly equidifficult forms of a test. So, if the form used as a posttest is easier than its pretest counterpart, the teacher's instruction might look terrific, but students' high posttest performances could be caused chiefly by the softer posttest. Or, worse, if the posttest form is tons tougher than the pretest form, then a pretest-to-posttest comparison might suggest that the impact of the teacher's instruction has been to make students "unlearn" what they knew when they took the pretest. Sadly, two test forms, even if they are intended to be equidifficult, won't save the day.

The Split-and-Switch Design

There is a simple modification of the classic pretest–posttest design that can work wonders for you if you have a reasonably large class of, say, 25 or more students. It's called the ***split-and-switch design***, and here's how it works.

First, you need two forms of the test you're going to use as a pretest and as a posttest. The two forms ought to be *somewhat similar* in degree of difficulty, but they need not be equidifficult or super close to it. Let's call the two forms Test 1 and Test 2.

Second, you *split* your class into two roughly equal *half-class* groups, perhaps by counting half-way down your class roster so all students whose last names start with the letters A through L end up in Half-Class A, and all students whose last names start with the letters M through Z are in Half-Class B.

Next, you administer one of the two forms to each half-class, but you ask students *not* to date their test forms. Ideally, in fact, students should write their names only on the *back* of their completed tests. You should then *code* the two sets of pretests (Test 1 and Test 2) so you can tell they are pretests. You can even use the pretest to help you plan your instruction. But you should not score, or write on, the pretests (on the actual test forms) at this time.

Then you should instruct all your students for as long as you have allowed for the instruction. Suppose, for example, you were trying to teach your students how to write an effective narrative essay. This might take several months or even a full school year. Let's say, however, that you devote one full semester to the teaching of this skill.

At the end of instruction, you then *switch* your two half-classes so that if Half-Class A took Test 1 as a pretest, it now takes Test 2 as a posttest. Similarly, if Half-Class B received Test 2 as a pretest, at the end of instruction it will receive Test 1 as a posttest.

You then *code* the posttests so *you* can distinguish them, after consulting the codes, from the pretests. You next *mix* together all the copies of Test 1 (both pretests and posttests). You do the same with Test 2.

Then you, colleagues, or even parents judge the quality of the mixed-together Test 1s. That is, the tests are subjected to **blind scoring**. The same is then done for the mixed-together Test 2s. *After* all scoring has been done, the codes are consulted so that the blind-scored papers can be separated into pretests and posttests.

This data-gathering model is called a *split-and-switch design*, and it provides you with *two* indications of whether your instruction promoted learning improvements: the pretest-to-posttest changes for Test 1 and those for Test 2.

Because the pretest and posttest comparisons are made using the *very same test*, there is clearly no problem caused by differential test difficulty. Moreover, because your students will not have previously seen the posttest they receive, the reactive impact of the pretesting is minimized.

In essence, you have taken two 50 percent samples of your class, at both pretest time and posttest time, to help you determine whether students have made the progress you wish. The split-and-switch design, of course, becomes less accurate as class sizes get smaller, but it does help you dodge some of the more troublesome aspects of the simple pretest versus posttest data-gathering model. The evidence that this atypical data-gathering design provides can be particularly compelling if you secure *nonpartisans* (such as parents) to supply the blind scoring.

The split-and-switch design is depicted graphically in Figure 15.2. If you are not sure yet how it is supposed to function, please carefully consider the Figure 15.2 diagram until you understand what happens when. Note that the appropriate comparisons, and there will be *two*, are signified by the colored, double-headed arrows.

Figure 15.2 A Split-and-Switch Data-Gathering Design

Half-Class A
completes
Test 1.

Instruction

Half-Class A
completes
Test 2.

Half-Class B
completes
Test 2.

Half-Class B
completes
Test 1.

←——→ = Appropriate comparisons

Teachers can use pretest results to guide their instructional decision making. And they can use posttest results to assign grades (remembering to make allowances for test forms of differing difficulties). But, of course, no permanent marks should be made on any tests until after they've been mixed together and blind-scored.

Decision Time

To Buttress or Not to Buttress?

Madeline teaches fifth-graders in an inner-city school. In recent years, her school's students have performed poorly on the state's annual account-ability tests. Madeline's principal, Mr. Jenkins, is convinced that the state accountability test is little more than a measure of students' socioeconomic status, and that students' scores on the test don't accurately reflect the instructional success of his school's teachers.

Accordingly, Mr. Jenkins recently issued an invitation to all the school's teachers to evaluate their ability to promote their students' mastery of a high-level cognitive skill in any subject area by collecting pretest-to-posttest evidence regarding whether their instruction was, in fact, successful. The purpose of this activity is to supply evidence to buttress stu-dents' scores on the annual accountability test—and to "show the community that our teachers are doing a good job." Mr. Jenkins asks all volunteers to pur-sue a cognitive skill requiring students to generate their own responses on the pretests and posttests. The instruction should take at least 2 months to complete, and the collected pretests and post-tests should be coded and then mixed together so scorers could not tell whether a student's response was written prior to or following instruction. The test responses would be blind-scored by parent volunteers, then separated into pretest and posttest groups after the blind scoring had been completed. Mr. Jenkins plans to summarize the results from all participating teachers, prepare a brief report, and then send that report to all of the school's parents.

Madeline realizes that if the pretest-to-posttest results are positive, this would surely have a posi-tive impact on parents' perceptions of the faculty's effectiveness. However, if the results are not posi-tive, then this evidence would confirm the view, based on the annual state tests, that the school's staff is not very effective. She must let Mr. Jenkins know by the end of the week whether she will be a volunteer in this proposed activity.

If you were Madeline, what would your decision be?

The split-and-switch design should be used for determining students' achievement of only a relatively small number of particularly significant cognitive outcomes—for instance, a handful of curricular aims calling for students' attainment of truly high-level cognitive skills. If this data-gathering design is overused, students will soon realize that their future "posttest" will be the "pretest" taken by half of their classmates prior to instruction. As a consequence of this realization, some students will start asking classmates what they remembered about the "other pretest." However, for measuring students' mastery of a few genuinely significant curricular outcomes, especially when nonpartisan scorers have been employed to judge students' constructed responses, this data-gathering design can provide powerful evaluative data that will be seen as credible even when used as part of an external evaluation of a teacher's effectiveness.

What to Assess

Whether you use your students' assessment results yourself for the self-evaluation of your teaching or, in contrast, supply those results to others who will use such evidence for an external evaluation, you still must decide what to assess. Think back, if you can remember that long ago, to Chapter 2's discussion of what to assess. Remember that the key factor governing what you should assess in your classroom is always the educational decision(s) you need to make. For purposes of your self-evaluation, you'll have to think through for yourself what kinds of evidence you'll need in order to tinker with or to fundamentally overhaul your instructional activities. Surely, it would seem, you'll want to know how well your students have learned the most important things that they were supposed to learn.

You should also seriously consider the assessment of students' *affect*. Affective assessment is of little utility for decisions about individual students because, as seen in Chapter 10, such measurement is too imprecise for defensible inferences about particular students. However, for judging the effectiveness of your instructional efforts, group-based inferences about students' pretest-to-posttest shifts in affect are useful. The split-and-switch design, because it minimizes pretest reactivity, works wonderfully when affective data are being gathered for evaluative purposes.

If a classroom teacher is stuck with a small class (tough luck!), so small that a split-and-switch design wouldn't work, then the straight-out pretest–posttest model, with all of its warts, is usually recommended. You can still use blind scoring of coded pretests and posttests after having mixed them together. And you can also round up one or more nonpartisan scorers. Such pretest-to-posttest evidence is surely way better than none.

In sum, students' performances on classroom assessments are clearly important when teachers evaluate themselves or when others evaluate teachers. Although there are several important sources of evidence to be used in appraising a teacher's instructional efforts, what happens to students as a direct consequence of instruction is, unarguably, the most significant source of evidence.

Evidence from External Accountability Tests

"If we're going to evaluate teachers, why don't we simply do so by seeing what their students have learned—as shown by those students' scores on significant achievement tests?" This statement, or statements similar to it, can often be heard these days as part of a chorus of demands for teachers to be evaluated chiefly on the basis of their students' test scores. And the test scores referred to in these entreaties for test-determined teacher evaluation are, almost always, the scores earned by students on externally imposed, standardized accountability tests—not scores on teachers' home-grown classroom tests. This is because most proponents of such an approach to teacher evaluation fear that *teacher-made* classroom tests, if employed to evaluate teachers, will often be softened by teachers themselves in a self-serving manner so that many teachers will appear to be more effective than, in fact, they truly are.

Thus, in recent years we have seen some critics clamor mightily for **test-based teacher evaluation**—that is, teacher appraisals in which the dominant (but not the only) determiner of a teacher's quality is the performance of that teacher's students on an externally imposed standardized achievement test. Typically, the tests selected for this purpose are the annual accountability tests that have been administered each year for many years in all of our 50 states. Those state-level accountability tests were required by federal law, especially by recent reauthorizations of the Elementary and Secondary Education Act of 1965. To appraise the teachers in a particular state's schools, these annual accountability tests were often the only available standardized test that seemed suitable for this sort of evaluative task.

About a decade ago, federal education officials believed that they were going to be able to foster the generation of a series of essentially identical annual achievement tests to be used by states chiefly for summative evaluation purposes, and that those tests would measure essentially all students' mastery of nearly identical curricular aims (namely, Common Core State Standards). Approximately 350 million federal dollars supported the test-building efforts of the Partnership for the Assessment of Readiness for College and Careers (PARCC) and the Smarter Balanced Assessment Consortium (SBAC). Those tests were to be up and running by the 2014–15 school year. Obviously, having two sets of tests measure all U.S. students' levels of mastering identical content standards would simplify enormously the collection of students' scores for purposes of evaluation. Moreover, in the early days of developing the SBAC and PARRC tests, leaders of both of those assessment consortia contended that they would be able to devise statistical procedures suitable for sensibly comparing students' performances on the two consortium-built tests. Soon after the test-development efforts of PARRC and SBAC had been initiated, officials from almost all the nation's states signed on with one or both of the assessment consortia.

At the same time that the two consortia's test-development activities were under way, a related pair of federal teacher evaluation initiatives were afoot. In 2009 the Race to the Top Program, and in 2011 the ESEA Flexibility Program, functioned as powerful catalysts for states to overhaul their often dated teacher evaluation systems. One of those programs, Race to the Top, provided substantial fiscal incentives for those states awarded federal grants from a program funded at $4.35 billion. The other program, the one focused on ESEA flexibility, permitted states to secure a waiver that exempted a state from satisfying certain conditions of the No Child Left Behind Act (NCLB). The Race to the Top Program, therefore, employed a "carrot," while the ESEA Flexibility Program relied on a "stick." To qualify for *either* of these programs, a state's educational officials were required to install a teacher evaluation system in which teachers must be evaluated using multiple sources of evidence. In that array of evidence, federal officials insisted that student growth must be "a significant factor." These federal initiatives—both of which emphasized summative teacher evaluation more heavily than formative teacher evaluation—sparked what most observers regarded as an unprecedented new look at how the nation should evaluate its teachers. Clearly, test-based teacher evaluation satisfies the requirement that student growth will be a significant factor in the appraisal of teachers. Other evidence of a teacher's instructional quality can, of course, be appropriately included in a sensible teacher-appraisal program. For example, systematic classroom observations of a teacher in action, as well as students' anonymous ratings of teachers, can both make contributions to the accurate evaluation of a teacher's skill. This issue is treated more extensively elsewhere (Popham, 2013a).

So here were the nation's educational leaders, as the presidency of Barack Obama was nearing its final years, having been urged to adopt a pair of suitable-for-all accountability tests built by the SBAC and PARRC consortia and, thereafter, to apply those test results as part of a more stringent summative teacher evaluation. These two developments, clearly, could have an impact on the kinds of classroom assessments that the nation's teachers would soon be using—and on the ways in which those tests would be employed. Here's a highlights-only version of what happened to this formidable federal vision.

First off, although a whopping majority of our 50 states initially intended to use the accountability tests developed by SBAC and PARRC, as time went by, more and more states hopped off the national consortium assessment locomotive. Although roughly a dozen states actively participate in the governance of that consortium and still use SBAC tests for annual accountability testing, the PARRC tests have been abandoned by all but a handful of states. The reasons for this dramatic change in the utilization of federally underwritten accountability tests are myriad, but one hoped-for plan flopped—that is, the possibility of sensibly comparing students' performances between the two consortia. Indeed, because of state variations in the administration of the consortia tests, even within-consortium state-to-state comparisons of students' performance became perilous. More and more states, as indicated way back in Chapter 1, decided to go it alone by hiring an external test-development contractor to create, administer, and score their annual accountability tests.

Second, let's turn to the hefty federal push for more rigorous summative teacher evaluations heavily determined by students' performances on states' annual accountability tests. With the conclusion of President Obama's administration, what had been an emphasis on summative evaluation soon morphed into a decidedly formative orientation. Realistically, the defensible evaluation of teachers is a nontrivial undertaking, and the demands of formative teacher evaluation are candidly less severe than the demands linked to the summative appraisal of a teacher's effectiveness. (After all, when jobs and effectiveness bonuses are on the line, intensified evaluative care must be taken.) We should not be surprised by these developments, of course, but from your perspective, it is imperative for you try to get a good handle on what the current appraisal of teachers is like in your state *and* your school district. An efficient and accurate system for supplying teachers and their administrators with formatively focused evaluative evidence can make a genuine contribution to students' educations. On the other hand, a shabbily implemented "pretend" summative evaluation of teachers is typically a noncontributing time-waster. Find out what the lay of the land is with respect to your local teacher evaluation—especially the formative versus summative orientation—and then try to determine what sorts of approaches make the most sense in your situation.

Harking back to the collection of suitable evaluative evidence, the following is a helpful four-point logic chain underlying an argument in favor of test-based teacher evaluation featuring external achievement tests:

- *Point 1.*   Teachers should be evaluated carefully so that (a) effective teachers can be rewarded and (b) ineffective teachers can either be helped to improve or, if improvement does not transpire, be fired.

- *Point 2.*   In evaluating a teacher's success, the most important factor must be the depth, breadth, and quality of students' learning that takes place because of instruction provided by the teacher.

- *Point 3.*   The depth, breadth, and quality of student learning will best be represented by students' performances on carefully created, externally determined, and properly administered achievement tests.

- *Point 4.*   Therefore, the scores of a teacher's students on externally administered exams, such as a state's annual accountability tests, should be the dominant determiner of a given teacher's evaluated success.

If the foregoing logic chain is to be implemented properly, however, a pivotal requirement is that the tests on which such a teacher evaluation system is based must be unarguably suitable for this significant evaluative task. In other words, in order for Point 3 to be satisfied, the "carefully created, externally determined, and properly administered" tests must be capable of accurately differentiating between well-taught and badly taught students. When such exams are "carefully created," those who are developing the exams must do their best to make sure the exams can correctly detect the depth, breadth, and quality of student learning. This is easier to say than it is to do. What is imperative, if test-based teacher evaluation is going to work properly, is that the tests that are used be sensitive to the *quality of instruction* provided by the specific teacher who is being evaluated.

Comparative Estimates of Progress: Student Growth Percentiles

In 2002, when the No Child Left Behind Act first frolicked into American educators' lives, we learned that our schools would soon be seen as unsuccessful unless ever-increasing proportions of students' annual test scores represented "adequate yearly progress" (AYP). The term AYP was defined as the percent of students—overall, as well as for students in NCLB-designated subgroups—who were test-classified as "proficient" or "advanced."

But, because NCLB's minimum proportions of AYP proficient-and-above students were federally regulated, and those proportions became more and more stringent as time went by, many school leaders began to chaff under these required AYP minima. Such educators were dismayed because, although their students may have been displaying substantial improvements in how well they were learning, those increases might not be sufficient to push a school's students over the AYP-required proportions of students who needed to score at proficient or advanced levels on a state's annual accountability tests.

Accordingly, a widespread clamor from the field was heard for schools to be evaluated, at least in part, according to *how much growth* a school's students had displayed—even though this growth might not be enough to reach a given year's AYP targets. For several years, therefore, various approaches to the determination of a school's test-based growth were introduced. Of these, the most widely accepted model has been the system devised by Betebenner (2007). Betebenner's analytic model, first used in Colorado and referred to by some as the "Colorado Growth Model," is predicated on a particular numerical quantity representing an individual student's comparative progress in one school year. This quantity, the heart of his approach, is called a *student growth percentile*.

Student growth percentiles are straightforward to understand, and here's how they work. First off, students who scored at a given point on the *previous* end-of-school-year accountability test (Year 1) are identified. Let's say we're looking at students who earned a scale score of 214 when 300 scale-score points are available. Then, in the next year (Year 2), using those same students (Year 1's 214-scorers), we employ their Year 2 scores to compute how much gain (that is, growth) each student made from the first year to the second year. The amount of gain students made from Year 1 to Year 2, however, is *not* reported according to how many scale-score points those students advanced (or retreated) but, instead, is reported as a student growth percentile. On such a percentile scale, students at the 95th percentile have made as much growth as 95 percent of students in the state whose Year 1 scores were 214. Similarly, students at the 40th growth percentile have made as much growth as 40 percent of the state's students who had a Year 1 score of 214.

Student growth percentiles, however, are calculated for students with Year 1 scores at *all* points on the score scale. Thus, there is a set of student growth percentiles computed for students with a Year 1 score of 212, another set of student growth percentiles for students with Year 1 scores of 213, and so on—across all Year 1 scores at which students have scored in sufficient numbers to calculate student growth percentiles.

We can calculate a particular teacher's *average* student growth percentile (Betebenner recommends that we use the median, rather than the mean, as this average) based on the performances of that teacher's students on the Year 2 accountability test. But because a given teacher's students will have earned Year 1 scores all over the lot, we base a specific teacher's median student growth percentile on the complete collection of student growth percentiles earned by all the teacher's students. Similarly, such an amalgam median growth percentile could be calculated for all students in an entire school or for the students at a particular grade in that school. The interpretation most often made when a school's (or a teacher's) average student growth percentile is above the 50th percentile is that the school (or the teacher) promoted better-than-average growth among students. Conversely, an average student growth percentile below the 50th percentile would indicate that whatever growth had been promoted among students, it was below average.

Statistical adjustments can be made in this approach to compensate for the real-world problem that some teachers (and some schools) end up serving very high-achieving students who actually have little room to grow on tests. This is because they are already bumping up against a ceiling effect due to a test's limited difficulty. At the other end of the achievement spectrum, teachers (and schools) dealing with very low-achieving students are working with students who have much more room to grow—because they have scored so dismally on the previous year's tests. Thus, in a sense it may sometimes be "statistically easier" for teachers who instruct particularly low-achieving students to demonstrate that their students have grown during a school year.

If you've never encountered the concept of student growth percentiles, it may take you a bit of time to grasp how they work. Fortunately, these quantities are relatively easy to explain to parents and policymakers. As a way of representing how well a teacher's students perform in a given school year—relative to other students who entered the school year with comparable achievement levels—student growth percentiles, when abetted by an example or two, are intuitively comprehensible to most people.

To the extent that the architects of an accountability program wish to incorporate a legitimate representation of the degree to which students have grown in their mastery of what was to be learned, Betebenner's approach incorporating student growth percentiles is definitely worth considering.

Instructional Sensitivity

Children learn, thank goodness. But this learning takes place both inside a school and outside of it. Students learn at home from interactions with family members. Students learn at the park or at a shopping mall. Students learn from watching television programs, even reality television shows. Students learn darn near everywhere. And aren't we happy that they do! But when we tie the evaluation of a teacher to students' performances on tests supposedly measuring what students *have learned in school*, we must be reasonably certain that the tests being employed do, in fact, measure what a particular teacher has taught those students. In other words, we need to make certain that any test used to evaluate a teacher's competence can accurately gauge the teacher's students' mastery of what has been taught. We need, in fact, to ascertain the ***instructional sensitivity*** of a test. Here's what this concept, a remarkably important one when we set out to evaluate teachers or schools, involves:

> Instructional sensitivity is the degree to which students' performances on a test accurately reflect the quality of instruction specifically provided to promote students' mastery of what is being assessed.

Notice in the definition of instructional sensitivity that the focus is on *instructional quality*—that is, the caliber of instruction that's directed toward students' achievement of whatever is being measured by a test. An instructionally sensitive test, therefore, would be one that can accurately distinguish between effectively taught and ineffectively taught students. Instructional sensitivity of a test, however, is not an either/or variable. A test need not be *completely* insensitive or *completely* sensitive to instruction. Tests can vary in the degree to which, based on students' performances, they can properly distinguish between students who have been taught splendidly and those who have been taught shabbily.

The push for test-based teacher evaluation comes from a variety of quarters, but sometimes even the most ardent advocates of this evaluative strategy fail to recognize a potential problem with this approach—namely, that if the tests being used for such evaluations do *not* do a good job in distinguishing between successfully and unsuccessfully taught students, then test-based teacher evaluation simply can't work. To illustrate, suppose that a state's education officials have created brand new accountability tests for the specific purpose of evaluating teachers' skills. More specifically, the new tests are to be used so see how well individual teachers have done in promoting their students' mathematics and reading achievements. Further, suppose that the new tests were built by following fairly traditional test-construction practices, and that students' performances on the newly developed accountability tests turn out, therefore, to be closely linked to the socioeconomic status (SES) of students' families. In other words, when the tests are administered, students from more affluent families almost invariably outperform students from less affluent families—*no matter how effectively all of those students have been taught.* In other words, SES invariably trumps teachers' skills because of the SES-linked nature of the test. Given those circumstances, genuinely skilled teachers in schools serving low-SES kids would often be regarded as ineffective (because of their students' weak performances on the new SES-linked accountability tests), while genuinely weak teachers in schools serving high-SES kids would be seen as effective (because of their students' strong performances on the new SES-linked accountability tests).

In such a fictitious scenario, inaccurate decisions would often be made about many teachers' skills, and the ultimate losers in such a situation would be the students themselves. Truly strong teachers might be bounced out of the profession, and truly weak teachers might be retained or even applauded. It is to prevent these sorts of errors, and their subsequent impact on students' educations, that any tests used in test-based teacher evaluation should be accompanied by compelling evidence they are, in truth, instructionally sensitive. (And by the way, in many states during recent years, this "fictitious scenario" is not fictitious at all.)

The Genesis of Instructional Insensitivity

How do educational achievement tests, especially those that are carefully developed by reputable test-development organizations, become instructionally insensitive? Is this some sort of plot, perpetrated by assessment companies, to subvert the test-based evaluation of the nation's schools and teachers? No, there's no discernible malevolence on the part of those who crank out the standardized achievement tests we have historically used in our schools. Rather, the cause underlying today's instructionally insensitive tests flows from a traditional, long-standing perspective from which U.S. psychometricians have viewed the tests they have built and polished.

The traditional mission of U.S. educational achievement tests, you see, has been to produce results leading to accurate score-based *comparisons* among test takers. Indeed, almost a century of large-scale educational testing in the United States has revolved around the creation of comparative score-interpretations. And, giving credit where it is due, educational psychometricians have become darn good at providing such comparative score-interpretations. We can usually do a pretty decent job of determining that Conchita's reading scores put her at the 84th percentile whereas Althea's reading scores are only at the 63rd percentile. Conceding that educational tests scores are not as precisely accurate as most people think, it is frequently useful to educators to find out how students compare to one another.

Much of the impetus for the generation of comparative score-interpretations can be traced back to World War I (not World War II), when the United States, having become involved in an unprecedented world conflict, found itself in need of a way to identify young men who would be successful in the Army's officer-training programs. Army officials approached the American Psychological

Association (APA) for assistance in developing a suitable screening tool, and soon a committee of APA appointees met at Vineland Training School in Vineland, New Jersey, to develop the *Army Alpha*, a group-administrable intelligence test that presented verbal and quantitative problems to examinees in an attempt to get a fix on new Army recruits' intellectual aptitudes. The *Alpha* was administered to about 1,750,000 Army recruits during World War I, and it was regarded as a major success because it allowed test takers' to be *compared*. The highest-scoring recruits were placed in officer-training programs, and their success in those programs substantially exceeded the success rates of pre-*Alpha* placement efforts. The *Army Alpha* was most certainly an *aptitude test*, for its intent was to locate those Army recruits who had the most cognitive aptitude to succeed in the Army's officer-training programs. Interestingly, however, the comparative assessment strategy employed in the *Alpha*'s aptitude test soon became the prototype for a range of educational assessments—not all of which were focused on the measurement of test takers' aptitudes.

For example, as soon as World War I was over, several assessment firms in the United States began to create educational *achievement* tests using the psychometric approach embodied in the *Alpha*. To illustrate, the *Stanford Achievement Tests*, a widely used set of nationally standardized achievement tests that have been revised almost a dozen times, were first published in 1923, shortly after the close of World War I. And, although the Stanford Achievement Tests were *achievement* rather than *aptitude* tests, they nevertheless hewed closely to the comparison-oriented mission of the *Army Alpha*. Indeed, for almost 100 years, the psychometric community in the United States has been committed to the creation of tests intended to yield comparative score-interpretations for test takers.

One key tenet of assessments intended to yield comparative score-interpretations is that they produce sufficient **score spread**—that is, differences among test-takers' total scores—so that those scores can be meaningfully contrasted with scores earned by other test takers. For example, other things being equal, for tests intended to provide comparative score-interpretations, it would be better to have a test's items answered correctly by roughly half of the test takers than for items to be answered correctly by 100 percent of the test takers or answered incorrectly by 100 percent of the test takers. Items answered by all or none of those taking a test make no contribution whatsoever to creating the kind of score spread that contributes to accurate, fine-grained comparisons of test takers' scores.

Over the years, traditional psychometricans have frequently enhanced an educational test's score spread by linking its items to socioeconomic status or linking its items to students' inherited academic aptitudes. Both SES and inherited academic aptitude tend to be nicely spread-out variables, and they're also variables that are not readily altered. Thus, if an item on an educational test can be linked to either SES or inherited academic aptitude, then this item is likely to produce the kind of score spread that brings joy to a traditional psychometrician's heart. Let' look briefly at both of these kinds of items.

SES-LINKED ITEMS

A particularly troubling kind of item on standardized achievement tests chiefly assesses what students have learned outside of school. Unfortunately, you'll find more of these items on standardized achievement tests than you'd expect. If children come from affluent families, then those children are more apt to succeed on certain items contained in standardized achievement tests than will other children whose environments don't mesh as well with what the items measure. The item in Figure 15.3 will illustrate what's being assessed by a number of the items on standardized achievement tests.

This fourth-grade reading item asks students to tell from context what the meaning of a multiple-meaning word is. There is no problem with the skill measured by this item as a skill that children should acquire. But there is a big problem with the item itself.

Notice that the fourth-grader's task is to figure out how the word *field* is being used in the item's boxed sentence. And, of course, answer Option C is correct. But please recognize that parents who are physicians, attorneys, or journalists do, indeed, have a *field*. If a child's parents, however, work in a car wash or as a cashier in a convenience store, the child's parents will rarely, if ever, refer to their *field* of employment.

Those parents have *jobs*. Clearly, kids from affluent families in which one or more parents are professionals will be more likely to do well on Figure 15.3's reading item than kids whose parents are employed in menial jobs. This item is clearly linked to children's socioeconomic status.

Suppose you're a teacher at a school in which most students come from a genuinely low socioeconomic environment. How are your students likely to perform on a standardized achievement test if a substantial number of the test's items are linked to the affluence of your students' backgrounds? In other words, how

---

Figure 15.3 A Fourth-Grade Reading Item

> My uncle's *field* is computer programming.

■ Look at the sentences below. In which sentence does the word *field* mean the same as it does in the boxed sentence above?

   A. The softball pitcher knew how to *field* her position.

   B. They prepared the *field* by spraying and plowing it.

   C. I know the *field* I plan to enter when I finish college.

   D. The doctor used a wall chart to examine my *field* of vision.

will your students do if many of the test's items are SES-influenced? That's right, your students are not apt to earn very high scores. Does this mean your school's teachers are doing a poor instructional job? Of course not.

Conversely, let's imagine you're a teacher in an affluent school whose students tend to be the offspring of upper-SES, well-educated parents. Each spring, your students' scores on standardized achievement tests are dazzlingly high. Does this mean your school's teachers are doing a superb instructional job? Of course not.

One of the chief reasons why children's SES is so highly correlated with standardized test scores is that there are often many items on standardized achievement tests that are actually focused on assessing knowledge and skills learned *outside* of school. Most of such knowledge and skills are more likely to be learned in higher-SES settings than in lower-SES settings.

Again, you might ask, "Why would developers of nationally standardized achievement tests place such items on their tests?" As usual, the answer is consistent with the dominant measurement mission of those tests—namely, *to spread out students' test scores* so that accurate and fine-grained comparative (norm-referenced) interpretations can be made. Because there is substantial variation in children's socioeconomic strata, and because this variation doesn't evaporate overnight, items reflecting such variation are efficient in producing the traditional psychometrician's much-cherished spread in test scores.

ITEMS LINKED TO INHERITED ACADEMIC APTITUDES

We turn now to another kind of item favored by traditional psychometricians in their quest for sufficient score spread in their tests—that is, items linked to the *inherited* academic aptitudes of students. That's right, items hooked up to how lucky a student happened to be from birth.

Most of us wish that all children were born with identical intellectual abilities, but they aren't. Some kids were luckier at gene-pool time. Some children, from birth, will find it easier to mess around with mathematics than will others. If children came into the world having inherited identical academic aptitudes, teachers' pedagogical problems would be far less challenging.

Current thinking among many leading educators suggests that there are various forms of intelligence, not just one (Gardner, 1994). A child who is born with less aptitude for dealing with quantitative or verbal tasks, therefore, might possess greater "interpersonal" or "intrapersonal" intelligence, but these two abilities are not tested by conventional achievement tests. For the kinds of items most commonly found on nationally standardized achievement tests, children differ in their innate aptitudes, especially their verbal, quantitative, and spatial aptitudes. And some items on nationally standardized achievement tests are linked directly to such *inherited* academic aptitudes.

Consider, for example, the social studies item in Figure 15.4. This item attempts to measure a sixth-grader's ability to "figure out" what the right answer

Figure 15.4 Sixth-Grade Standardized Achievement Test Item in Social Studies

- If a person truly wants to conserve natural resources, one good way to do so is to:

    A. leave the radio turned on even if no one is listening to it.

    B. wash tiny loads instead of large loads in an automatic dishwashing machine.

    C. write on both sides of a piece of paper.

    D. discard used magazines in the trash.

is. The item probably does not measure well what's taught in school. The item—at least in part—measures what students come to school with, not what they learn there.

In Figure 15.4, look carefully at the four answer options. Read each option and see whether it might be correct. A verbally advantaged student, we can surmise, can figure out that Choices A, B, and D really would not "conserve natural resources" particularly well; hence, Choice C turns out to be the winning option. Verbally adept kids will have a better time with this item than their less verbal classmates.

You'll find many such "native smarts" items in any of today's nationally standardized achievement tests. The items that are particularly galling are the ones that measure a child's inborn spatial aptitude. To illustrate, one math item in a current fourth-grade standardized achievement test presents four letters to students (such as "F, L, R, and B"), then asks, Which letter, "when bent in half," will have two equal parts? The answer, in case you weren't born with adequate spatial aptitude, is the B. But what sort of a silly skill is involved in mental letter-bending? Yet many standardized achievement tests contain items that tap the spatial-visualization aptitudes children have obviously inherited.

But why, you might be thinking, do developers of nationally standardized tests include such items on their tests? The answer is really quite simple. Remember, these sorts of items, because they are based on nicely spread-out innate academic aptitudes not readily modifiable in school, do a terrific job in spreading out test takers' scores. The quest for score spread, coupled with the limitation of having only a few items to use in assessing students, makes such items alluringly appealing to those who construct traditional standardized achievement tests.

And yet, items that primarily measure differences in students' inborn academic verbal, quantitative, and spatial aptitudes obviously do not contribute to valid inferences about "how well children have been taught." Would we like all children to do well on such "inherited aptitudes" items? Of course, we would. But to use such items to arrive at a judgment about a teacher's instructional effectiveness or a school's educational success is absurd.

Parent Talk

Suppose you're a teacher in a large suburban high school whose students score consistently high on almost any kind of statewide or national test they're obliged to take. Indeed, anyone who knows much about your state's schools would be surprised if your school did not score among the top schools on any standardized achievement test. Nonetheless, at a recent Back-to-School Night, one of your students' parents, Mr. Chan, corners you with a barrage of questions about the meaning of these test results. He prefaces his questions with an indication that he is pleased with his daughter's test scores, but then he says, "Okay, I know our school serves super-affluent families, and I know students' test scores are always high, but I also know that there is some seriously shabby teaching going on here. When my daughter Lee has her girlfriends come to our place for

sleep-overs, they level with Lee's mom and me. They often tell us about really boring classes they have had to sit through. How can the school's test scores be so darn high, and yet this sort of poor teaching takes place?"

If I were you, here's how I'd respond to Mr. Chan:

"Well, for openers, Mr. Chan, I'd have to say that I've definitely not heard reports of the sort of weak teaching Lee's friends have described to you. I'm sure that in a school as large as ours, not all teachers are wonderful, but let's assume—just for the sake of discussion—that some less-than-lustrous teaching is going on in the school. What you want to know is how our school's high test scores can be produced by weak teaching.

"Here's how that sort of thing can happen. First off, you need to know that almost all standardized achievement tests are developed in a very traditional way. That is, those tests are intended to provide *comparative* interpretations of different test takers' scores so that the students can be compared with one another. To produce the range of different scores needed for such comparisons, many of the items on these tests are closely linked to students' socioeconomic status—in other words, their SES. As you probably know, SES is a variable that's well spread out, and it really doesn't change very rapidly. Kids who come from more affluent families will tend to answer SES-linked items correctly, while kids from less affluent families will tend to miss those same items. This gives a school such as ours a tremendous edge when it comes to such tests. Our school's students are likely to score well on SES-linked items no matter how well or how badly they have been taught. That's just what happens.

"If there are many SES-linked items on a standardized achievement test, you can bet that our school's students will always shine. Personally, what I find myself worrying about is how the teachers who teach low-SES kids feel about this. I myself might have ended up in a school where I was teaching students from disadvantaged backgrounds. Remember, Lee attends a school where, to the outside world, teaching seems to be wonderful. But in a low-SES school, students' scores on SES-linked items are, with few exceptions, destined to be low. It's really not fair."

❚ *Now, how would you respond to Lee's father?*

Avoidance of Instructionally Insensitive Items

It is easy to forget that most educational tests are nothing more than a collectivity of items to which students must respond. If the items are good, the test will be good; but if the items are bad, then the test itself will be similarly bad. So, when we are trying to create an instructionally sensitive accountability test, we must be inordinately attentive to the items themselves. If teachers have effectively taught students to master a curricular aim that's being measured by a collection of, say, 6 to 12 items, will the bulk of those items be answered correctly by the teacher's students? And what about a teacher whose instruction is focused on the same curricular aim but produced a less-than-effective instructional effort? For those same 6 to 12 items, to support our claim of having an instructionally sensitive test, what we need to see is that most of the teachers' students come up with incorrect answers.

One way to discern how many instructionally insensitive items there are on an accountability test is to have a group of properly oriented reviewers—usually experienced teachers—consider each item on the test, one at a time, and then respond to a review question such as the following:

> Attention reviewers: Please note the specific curricular aim which, according to the test's developers, this item is assessing, and only then answer this question: *If a teacher has provided reasonably effective instruction to promote students' mastery of the specific curricular aim being assessed, is it likely that the bulk of the teacher's students will answer this item correctly?* (Choose one: YES, NO, NOT SURE).

The nature of the orientation provided for any instructional-sensitivity reviewers should focus on the kinds of factors that might render an item instructionally insensitive. Reviewers must be completely conversant with such factors.

For example, consider the following six qualities of an item that might cause the item to be instructionally insensitive:

1. *Alignment leniency.* If an item has been too leniently judged to be in alignment with the curricular aim it ostensibly assesses, that alignment is questionable. Teachers will be trying to get their students to master a specified curricular aim, but the test's items will be measuring something else.

2. *Excessive easiness.* If an item is so very easy that completely untaught students would answer it correctly, then the item is apt to be measuring students' achievement of something other than what the teacher was trying to teach.

3. *Excessive difficulty.* If an item is so very difficult that even marvelously taught students might not answer it correctly, then the item can't distinguish between well-taught and poorly taught students.

4. *Item flaws.* If an item has serious deficits such as ambiguities or garbled syntax, these flaws will prevent well-taught students from answering it correctly, thereby making it impossible for the item to accurately distinguish between well-taught and poorly taught students.

5. *Links to socioeconomic status.* If an item gives a meaningful advantage to students from higher-SES families, then the item will tend to measure what students bring to school, rather than how well they are taught once they get there.

6. *Link to academic aptitude.* If an item gives a meaningful advantage to students who possess greater inherited quantitative, verbal, or spatial aptitudes, then the item will tend to measure what students arrive with at school, instead of how well they are taught.

By establishing item-review committees to scrutinize all items under development, much as is currently done by bias-review committees, it would be possible to identify items that might be instructionally insensitive on the basis of one or more of the factors just listed. If, after further analysis, there is a reasonable chance that an item might be insensitive to the accurate detection of instructional quality, then it can be modified or jettisoned from the test before being used. Will we ever completely excise all instructionally insensitive items from our accountability tests? Probably not. However, we need to make sure that the proportion of instructionally insensitive items on any accountability tests—tests presumed to accurately measure the quality of educators' instructional efforts—will be small indeed. Although instructional-sensitivity judgmental reviews of items headed for large-scale accountability tests are common, such reviews are rarely seen with teacher-made tests.

In addition to the use of judgmentally based procedures for identifying instructionally insensitive items, empirically based procedures are also available for this purpose. By identifying two groups of "outlier" teachers who have, based on several years' worth of previous instruction, been extraordinarily successful and extraordinarily unsuccessful, respectively, in promoting students' growth, any unpredictable per-item performances by students taught by those two outlier groups can help spot items likely to be instructionally insensitive. Such empirical approaches to the detection of instructionally insensitive items, however, require very large samples of students, as well as accessible test-score records for several years—and a heap of statistical gyrations. Those sorts of empirical studies of instructionally insensitive items, therefore, would need to be undertaken at the state level or by very large school districts.

Determining Students' Progress: With Value-Added Models

As part of attempts to isolate the instructional success of particular teachers, or particular schools, considerable attention has been given to an approach known as a *value-added model (VAM)*. This approach represents a statistical strategy aimed at isolating the cause of students' progress—or lack of such progress. The VAM procedures employ students' prior achievement and/or background characteristics as statistical controls to help isolate the effects on student achievement of specific teachers, schools, or school districts. Often relying on exotic statistical gyrations, VAMs try to contrast the effects on students' test scores of (1) *school-unrelated variables* such as family or friends and (2) the *instructional impact* of a given school or teacher.

The very name given to this statistical strategy usually evokes a positive response from people who are interested in getting a fix on the effectiveness of teachers or schools. After all, when we refer to a "value-added" contribution to students' achievement, we typically think of increases in students' learning attributable to educators *above and beyond what might have taken place simply because students grew older*. Accordingly, the "value-added" label generates a fair amount of support—sometimes unthinking support—from educational policymakers and the public in general. Anything that is "value-added" sounds so darn good. But is this widespread support warranted?

The most widely known VAM is the Tennessee Value-Added Assessment System (TVAAS) devised by William Sanders. However, because the statistical machinery of TVAAS is proprietary, and unavailable to public scrutiny, many proponents of VAMs have sought to employ other VAM approaches. Basically, all of these procedures require data tracking students' academic growth across several years, usually in different subjects, to estimate the contributions that teachers have made to this growth.

Increasing numbers of technical reviewers of value-added procedures, however, have identified several serious methodological problems when such strategies are employed to identify teachers' contributions to students' achievement. To illustrate, a significant shortcoming with these approaches is that VAMs produce a statistically massaged *estimate* of a teacher's relative contribution to a particular student's learning. Making causal attributions for these estimates is most defensible when teachers are randomly assigned to classes and when students are randomly assigned to teachers. As we know, however, randomized assignment of teachers and students is rarely encountered in most school districts. Parents frequently influence the schools their children attend, and beyond that, parents often have a serious say in the teachers to whom their children are assigned. The less random the undergirding of VAM procedures, the less credible will be the causal inferences about teachers' impact that we can base on these approaches.

Moreover, students' academic progress is influenced by a substantial array of variables beyond a teacher's control—for instance, the physical condition of a school, the instructional resources at hand, the quality of a school's administrators, a district's instructional policies, and the degree of parental encouragement of their children's learning. Because these variables often vary systematically across a district's schools, they can substantially erode the accuracy of VAM conclusions.

Another serious shortcoming of most VAMs is that their use is frequently advocated *irrespective* of the suitability of the achievement tests to be used in the analysis. Earlier in this chapter, instructionally *insensitive* achievement tests were described. Such tests often contain numerous items linked closely to students' socioeconomic status (SES). These items tend to be answered correctly more often by students from affluent families than by students from impoverished families. Well, if the results of achievement tests being employed in a VAM are highly correlated with test takers' SES, all the statistical high-jinks in the world will be unable to transform SES-governed test results into data that accurately gauge teachers' instructional effectiveness. Such tests may permit students' scores to be compared—as is the measurement mission of traditional achievement tests. But such tests—even when all their causality implications have been statistically squeezed out of them—can't tell us which teachers are effective.

A final shortcoming of value-added models is that it is nearly impossible to explain to normal human beings how VAMs work. The statistical operations associated with these value-added strategies are often so esoteric that their opacity defies description.

In a highly readable introduction to the topic of VAMs, Braun (2005) concludes that "VAM results should *not* be used as the sole or principal basis for making consequential decisions about teachers" (p. 4). He argues that too many mistakes will be made when VAM approaches use the kinds of data typically available from school districts. Value-added models, although enticingly labeled and enthusiastically touted by their devotees, are regarded by most nonpartisans as inappropriate for evaluating the quality of educators' endeavors.

What's a Teacher to Do?

Those who evaluate teachers need to make up their own minds about the degree to which students' test performances should figure in the appraisal of a teacher. Most teacher evaluation authorities believe it is foolish for teachers to be evaluated without at least some consideration of the assessed display of students' learning. However, the *degree of emphasis* to be placed on students' test performances should be linked directly to the caliber of the tests being employed to provide such evidence. If an external accountability test, for instance, measures students' mastery of important skills and knowledge that have been approved by relevant policymakers (such as a state board of education), and the test is demonstrably sensitive to instruction, then we can argue that the results of such a test should play a prominent role in the evaluation of teachers. If no evidence exists that the tests being employed to evaluate teachers are instructionally sensitive, then we should assume that the tests are instructionally *insensitive* and should therefore play a minimal, if any, role in the evaluation of teachers' effectiveness.

This assumption applies not only to the major, externally administered assessments that are used to appraise teachers and schools but also to teacher-made tests that, for teachers whose students are not tested by large-scale assessments, might be created by individual teachers or by groups of teachers. Putting it simply, if policymakers have mandated that students' test performances are to play a key role in the evaluation of teachers, then it may be necessary for teachers to rely on teacher-made tests to supply the needed assessment evidence. Yet, for test-based teacher evaluation to function properly, so that evaluation errors are minimized, even teacher-made tests should be fashioned in such a way that they are as instructionally sensitive as possible.

Remember, although the assessments being touted for use in test-based teacher evaluation are almost invariably some form of "achievement test," do not succumb to the widespread misconception that what's measured by such achievement tests represents what's been taught in schools. It is certainly possible that achievement tests do, in fact, assess what students have been taught by their teachers. But it is also possible, especially if the tests have been built by measurement traditionalists, that the tests being employed actually measure what students have brought to school, not what they've learned once they arrived.

Even the staunchest advocates of test-based teacher evaluation typically recommend that factors other than students' test scores play a role in the appraisal of a teacher. For example, evidence based on observations of teachers' classroom activities, students' anonymous appraisals of their teachers, or administrative ratings frequently are mentioned as additional evidence to consider when appraising a teacher. But you're reading a text about classroom assessment, and whether the assessments administered in a classroom are teacher-generated instruments or externally created assessments, how much weight to give students' test performances should be heavily dependent on the energy expended in rendering the tests involved as instructionally sensitive as possible.

If the skills you choose (1) measure really important cognitive outcomes, (2) are seen by parents and policymakers as genuinely significant, and (3) can be promoted instructionally by competent teachers, then the assembly of a set of pretest-to-posttest evidence showing substantial student growth in such skills can be truly persuasive. Earlier in this chapter you saw how a split-and-switch design (with blind scoring of students' responses by nonpartisan raters) can be employed to collect compelling evidence of a teacher's instructional effectiveness. Use of pretest-to-posttest designs to gauge your own instructional success makes much more sense than succumbing to the senselessness of measuring your teaching prowess with the wrong kinds of tests.

Right Task, Wrong Tools

Teachers should surely be held accountable. The teaching of a nation's children is too important to be left unmonitored. But to evaluate educational quality by using unsound assessment instruments is a subversion of good sense. Although teachers need to produce accurate evidence regarding their effectiveness, instructionally insensitive accountability tests are the wrong tools for this important task.

When students' test performances are being used to evaluate schools or teachers, what's needed is *evidence* supporting the appropriateness of such an evaluative measurement mission. And this is why the 2014 AERA-APA-NCME standards present—as the *overarching* standard for validity—a call for the clear explication of each of a test's intended uses, as well as "appropriate validity evidence in support of each intended interpretation" (American Educational Research Association, 2014, p. 23). Evidence regarding the suitability of a test *to perform an educational evaluation function* must, of necessity, attest to the instructional sensitivity of that test.

If inappropriate standardized tests are chosen by a state's officials to satisfy the provisions of federal accountability laws, you can bet that a good many public schools are going to be labeled as failing when, in fact, those schools are doing a good instructional job. Equally disturbing, many schools will appear to be doing a stellar job based on their students' test scores, but those high scores will be chiefly attributable to the composition of the advantaged students who make up such schools' student bodies. In contrast, instructionally *sensitive* accountability tests are the right kinds of assessments to use when evaluating schools. Teachers should, solo or in collaboration, use whatever influence they can to ensure that the proper kinds of accountability tests are used with their students.

What Do Classroom Teachers Really Need to Know About Assessment-Based Evaluation of Teaching?

You must realize that when you use students' test results as indicators of your own instructional prowess, a major determiner of how well your students perform will be the particular students with whom you're working. Even using a straightforward pretest–posttest evaluation approach doesn't circumvent the problem created by the dissimilarity of different teachers' students. For purposes of teachers' self-evaluation, especially of the formative sort, disparities in students'

But What Does This Have to Do with Teaching?

It is inconceivable that an entire profession would allow its members to be judged using the wrong measuring tools. Yet, in education, this is precisely what is going on. And some teachers, largely because they do *not* understand why certain kinds of accountability tests ought not be used to evaluate schooling, compliantly accept this profound misuse of educational tests. Such teachers may have an intuitive idea that students' scores on some accountability tests don't provide a clear picture of instructional quality, but they can't tell you why.

If, as a teacher, you don't help people understand why it is that particular sorts of accountability tests should not be used to judge instructional effectiveness, then you probably deserve what you'll get—thoroughly inaccurate judgments about your skill. But you're not the only one who gets hurt because of this glaring miscarriage of measurement-based justice. Your students will get hurt too. And *that's* why you need first to understand the ins and outs of this important issue, and then to let others know about the misuse of certain kinds of tests to judge educational quality.

Who are those "others" whom you need to acquaint with this issue? Well, start off with your colleagues. Few teachers or administrators really understand, at a meaningful level, why some accountability tests aren't the answer for judging schools. Then there are parents who need to understand. And, of course, there are educational policymakers. They definitely need to learn what constitutes solid evidence of instructional quality and what evidence ought never to be used.

In short, if you don't want your own teaching to be appraised using the wrong microscope, then outfit yourself in evangelical garb and start doing a bit of educative gospel-spreading!

---

entry behaviors don't pose all that much of a problem. However, for purposes of external teacher evaluation, particularly *summative* teacher evaluation, disparities in the abilities and motivation levels of different teachers' students should induce caution in the evaluative use of students' test results. Judgments about the caliber of growth attained by a given teacher must be made in the context of the instructional situation in which the teacher is functioning. A useful way of collecting evidence regarding a teacher's instructional effectiveness is the split-and-switch design.

Perhaps one of the most important understandings you should carry from this chapter is the recognition that certain kinds of accountability tests—instructionally insensitive ones—should not be employed to evaluate a teacher's instructional effectiveness. You need to understand *why* such tests are inappropriate for this purpose. And once you recognize why the evidence derived from the wrong kinds of accountability tests is unsuitable for the evaluation of a school staff's quality, then you should see that other evidence, more defensible and more credible, needs to be collected by educators. The public has a right to see how well their tax-supported schools are doing. The public doesn't have the right to do so by using the wrong evidence. *Instructionally sensitive accountability tests, in concert with teacher-made assessments,* could provide accurate evidence of teachers' success.

Chapter Summary

This chapter argued that the most defensible way to evaluate instruction, whether such evaluations are to be used for a teacher's self-evaluation or for external teacher evaluations, is to focus on the consequence of instruction—that is, the impact of instruction on students. Three sources of evaluative evidence were considered: (1) students' performances on classroom assessments, (2) students' performances on accountability tests, and (3) evidence regarding unanticipated effects of instruction. For the two test-elicited forms of evidence, the caliber of the tests themselves must be considered when deciding how much weight to give certain kinds of assessment evidence.

For the collection of classroom assessment evidence, two forms of a pretest-to-posttest data-gathering design were described: (1) a basic pretest–posttest design and (2) the split-and-switch design. Instructional sensitivity was described as the degree to which students' performances on a test accurately reflect the quality of instruction specifically provided to promote students' mastery of what is being assessed. When evaluating the quality of instruction, educators should rely exclusively on instructionally sensitive tests. For the identification of unanticipated side effects of instruction, teachers were encouraged to be constantly attentive to the possibility of such unforeseen effects.

Educators were urged to learn more about both the appropriateness and the inappropriateness of various kinds of evidence regarding instructional quality, and then to share their conclusions with concerned constituencies.

MyLab Education Self-Check 15.1

MyLab Education Application Exercise 15.1: **Instructional Effectiveness**

References

American Educational Research Association. (2014). *Standards for educational and psychological testing*. Washington, DC: Author.

Betebenner, D. W. (2007). *A primer on student growth percentiles*. Dover, NH: National Center for the Improvement of Educational Assessment.

Braun, H. I. (2005). *Using student progress to evaluate teachers: A primer on value-added models*. Princeton, NJ: Educational Testing Service.

D'Agostino, J. V., Welsh, M. E., and Corson, N. M. (2007). "Instructional sensitivity of a state's standards-based assessment." *Educational Assessment, 12,* no. 1: 1–22.

Gardner, H. (1994). "Multiple intelligences: The theory in practice." *Teacher's College Record, 95,* no. 4: 576–583.

Grossman, P., Cohen, J., Ronfeldt, M., and Brown, L. (2014). "The test matters: The relationship between classroom observation scores and teacher value added on multiple types of assessment," *Educational Researcher, 43,* no. 6 (August/September): 293–303.

Jennings, J. L., and Bearak, J. M. (2014). "'Teaching to the test' in the NCLB era: How test predictability affects our understanding of student performance," *Educational Researcher, 43,* no. 8 (November): 381–389.

Jones, N. D., Buzick, H. M., and Turkan, S. (2013). "Including students with disabilities and English learners in measures of educator effectiveness," *Educational Researcher, 42,* no. 4 (May): 234–241.

Marzano, R. J. (2013). "How to show student learning," *Educational Leadership, 71,* no. 2 (October): 82–83.

Master, B. (2014). "Staffing for success: Linking teacher evaluation and school personnel management in practice," *Educational Evaluation and Policy Analysis, 36,* no. 2 (June): 207–227.

Nichols, S. L., and Berliner, D. C. (2008). "Why has high-stakes testing so easily slipped into contemporary American life?" *Phi Delta Kappan, 89,* no. 9 (May): 672–676.

Popham, W. J. (2009). *Unlearned lessons: Six stumbling blocks to our schools' success.* Cambridge, MA: Harvard Education Press.

Popham, W. J. (2010). *Everything school leaders need to know about assessment.* Thousand Oaks, CA: Corwin.

Popham, W. J. (2013a). *Evaluating America's teachers: Mission possible?* Thousand Oaks, CA: Corwin.

Popham, W. J. (2013b). "Tough teacher evaluation and formative assessment: Oil and water?" *Voices from the Middle, 21,* no. 2 (December): 10–14.

Popham, W. J., and DeSander, M. (2014). "Will the courts save teachers?" *Educational Leadership, 71,* no. 5 (February): 55–59.

Popham, W. J. (2014). "The right test for the wrong reason," *Phi Delta Kappan, 96,* no. 1 (September): 46–52.

A Testing Takeaway

Instructional Sensitivity: A Key Factor in Teacher Evaluation*

W. James Popham, University of California, Los Angeles

Teacher evaluation comes in two varieties, both of which make a difference. *Summative* teacher evaluation is typically carried out by external agencies such as a school district or state department of education. It focuses on such high-stakes personnel decisions as the awarding of tenure and employment termination. *Formative* teacher evaluation is undertaken by an individual teacher—often in collaboration with a supervisor or school-site administrator. It is aimed at improving a teacher's instructional effectiveness.

Governmental preference influences whether summative or formative teacher evaluation is emphasized at any given time. For example, during President Obama's administration, American educators were urged to stress rigorous summative teacher evaluation. More recently, U.S. teachers have been asked to emphasize formatively oriented teacher evaluation.

But whether a given teacher evaluation program is more formative or more summative, students' test performances invariably play a pivotal role in the evaluation process. It is this inclusion of students' test performances in the evaluation of teachers that requires us to understand the concept of *instructional sensitivity*. Accordingly, its definition follows.

> Instructional sensitivity is the degree to which students' performances on a test accurately reflect the quality of instruction specifically provided to promote students' mastery of what is being assessed.

When evaluating teachers, *only* students' performances on instructionally sensitive tests should be used as evidence. This means that anyone involved in appraising a teacher's success—either formatively or summatively—should understand the factors capable of diminishing a test's instructional sensitivity. Systematic judgmental scrutiny of a test by using those factors can reveal whether students' test results should be used in the evaluation of teachers—and, if so, how much evaluative weight those test scores should be accorded.

A test will be instructionally *insensitive* if too many of its items are (1) linked to a student's socioeconomic status, (2) correlated with a student's inherited academic aptitude, (3) so difficult that few correct answers are made, (4) so easy that nearly all students answer correctly, or (5) too leniently judged as adequately aligned to the curricular aim being measured so that off-target instruction is likely. Students' scores on instructionally insensitive tests often tell us what students brought to school, not what they learned there.

If there is no compelling *evidence* that a test is instructionally sensitive—that is, can accurately distinguish between well taught and badly taught students—then such a test should *not* be employed to evaluate teachers.

Chapter 16
Assessment-Based Grading

Chief Chapter Outcome

Learning Outcomes

16.1 Describe and apply the characteristics of goal-attainment grading.

A sufficient familiarity with goal-attainment grading to be able not only to describe its key steps, but also to identify when teachers are or are not employing goal-attainment practices in their grading determinations

Teachers give grades. One supposes that when the original blueprints for "teacher" were drawn, there must have been a mandatory grade-giving component included somewhere. Other than tradition, however, why is it that teachers dispense grades to students so regularly?

The answer's fairly simple. A teacher needs to let students know (1) how well they're doing at the moment, as when a teacher assigns grades for various assignments during the course of the school year; and (2) how well they've done overall, as when a teacher dishes out end-of-year grades. For teachers to find out how well they've *taught*, as we saw in the previous chapter, the level of students' achievement must be determined. For students to find out how well they've *learned*, the extent of their achievement must also be determined.

Although, as you'll soon see, there are a number of factors that teachers sometimes consider when grading students—other than simply how well those students performed on classroom assessments—there's little argument that a *major* consideration in the grade a student receives should be the quality of the student's assessment performances. In this final chapter, we'll be looking at different ways in which those assessment results can be incorporated into students' grades.

The Purpose of Grading

How teachers grade their students stems chiefly from what those teachers believe the purpose (or purposes) of grading should be. I know that, as a beginning high school teacher, my understanding of the potential purposes of grading was almost nonexistent. Oh, sure, I knew that good grades should be given to students who performed well on my tests, and that students who performed poorly on those tests should end up with low grades. After all, teachers who—as students themselves—have gone through years of schooling, surely recognize that students' test performances and students' grades are closely linked. But is that all there is to it? In truth, when I began teaching, I simply had not devoted any thought, *none at all*, to how I was going to grade my students. In retrospect, I'm certain that, as a novice teacher, I made a number of bone-headed grading mistakes.

The mission of this final chapter in *Classroom Assessment* is to encourage you to give some serious think-time to the topic of grading. In almost every school setting, teachers will need to grade their students. And although teachers will probably never acquire a precise, zero-errors grading strategy, teachers can at least come up with a defensible way of thinking about this important task. Such defensibility begins with a teacher's understanding the purpose of grading.

Susan Brookhart (2009), who writes often and well about grading, contends that the primary purpose of grading, whether for individual assignments or report cards, should be to communicate with students and parents about students' achievement of curricular aims. At first glance, this sensible statement might appear to be little more than the sort of educational platitude that teachers routinely encounter. It isn't. Indeed, if you agree with what Brookhart thinks the purpose of grading should be—namely, *communicating information to both students and their parents about students' goal attainment*—then this stance will profoundly influence how you grade your own students.

Brookhart's conception of grading identifies not only *who* are the targets of the information that's being communicated (in this instance, students and parents) but also *what* is being communicated (in this instance, students' goal-attainment status). You'll find most educators agree that the target audiences of grading should be students and their parents. Where more disagreement bubbles up, however, is with what's being communicated to those audiences. Brookhart's exclusive focus is on *goal attainment*. But some educators want grades not only to communicate students' goal attainment, but also to incorporate evaluations of students' effort, attendance, attitudes, classroom behavior, and so on. Clearly, if teachers are grading students only on the basis of students' goal attainment, those teachers will arrive at substantially different grades than will teachers who try to incorporate such factors as students' attitudes and effort into their grading.

As Brookhart (2009) points out, "In a perfect world, there would be no need for the kinds of grades we use in school today" (p. 4). She would prefer replacing grades on individual assignments with discussions about strengths and weaknesses—based on a student's progress toward goal attainment—and these discussions would take place among students themselves, as well as between the student and the teacher. The focus would be on how to improve. There would be no "failures," because students would continue with additional tasks and assignments until a curricular aim had been achieved. All performances would be seen as capable of being improved. As she points out, however, "The demands of schooling as we know it have kept us from reaching that utopia" (Brookhart, 2009, p. 4).

Yet, even in such a utopian educational world, the focus of all these improvement-oriented evaluative discussions among teachers and students would revolve around the level of students' goal attainment. Thus, whether you are a seasoned teacher or a teacher-in-training, an early decision you must make is precisely *what it is* that you want to be communicating to your students and to their parents.

Okay, what about teachers giving grades—at least in part—on the basis of their students' effort, attitudes, levels of class participation, behavior, attendance, tardiness, and punctuality in assignment submission? Should factors such as these play *any* role in the awarding of grades? Well, Ken O'Connor thinks not.

O'Connor is another colleague who has devoted much of his career to helping teachers decide how best to award grades to their students. "For grades to have real meaning," wrote O'Connor, "they must be relatively pure measures of each student's achievement of the learning goals"(O'Connor, 2009, p. 90). He, too, advocates that teachers relate their grading procedures to learning goals. In fact, he recommends that when officially sanctioned content standards exist, as is true now in almost all jurisdictions, students' achievement of those standards should be the *only* determiner of students' grades. O'Connor would definitely supply students and their parents with information about such factors as class participation and punctuality in assignment submission, but this would be done separately. (We'll look at techniques for doing so later in the chapter.)

I must confess that the laser-like focus on using students' attainment of curricular aims as an exclusive grading criterion, the stance taken by both O'Connor and Brookhart, was surely not the way I approached grading when I was a neophyte teacher. I sometimes gave certain underachieving students grades higher than they had earned because I thought it might boost them into an "I can do it" mood. I also graded some students according to what I believed were the levels of effort they were giving to their studies. I graded hard-working, albeit low-performing, students generously, while also grading lazy, yet high-performing, students harshly. And I used the lure of high grades as a motivation ploy—that is, as a way of getting students to study harder. In hindsight, my grading practices would have been condemned by my friends Sue Brookhart and Ken O'Connor. They would have been right. My grading practices were an ill-conceived mess.

When I became a college professor, students' achievement seemed to be the only thing my fellow professors deemed worth grading, so I nestled into a comfortable, achievement-dominated approach to grading. But this professorial grading stance was not dictated by careful thought on my part. Rather, it was a knee-jerk acceptance of my peers' expectations.

So, with the hope that my now-confessed grading sins will ultimately be forgiven, I want to go on record as saying that the central grading position taken by O'Connor, Brookhart, and those who share their views is the one I recommend to you with enthusiasm. I now believe that truly defensible grading requires the teacher to make students' achievement of clearly understood curricular aims the solitary consideration in determining the grades to be communicated to students and parents. For report-card grading, this typically means the teacher will be relying on assessment-based evidence concerning students' status regarding the curricular aims themselves. For assignment grading, or for grading en route assessments, the teacher must decide what contribution those assignments and en route assessments will make to students' mastery of the target curricular aims. Certain en route tests, for example, may deal with knowledge or subskills deemed more significant than others to students' mastering the target curricular aims. The more significant tests (or assignments) would obviously carry more grading weight than the less significant ones.

Not all curricular aims, of course, are created equal. Many teachers simultaneously promote their students' attainment of several curricular aims, and some curricular aims are more important than others. It is perfectly acceptable, therefore, for a teacher to assign more significance to some curricular aims than to others. If teachers try to make their grading decisions transparent rather than cloud-cloaked, a teacher can announce in advance which curricular aims, if any, are regarded as more significant than others. The same sort of thinking would apply to the assignment of grades for en route tests or for grades given to students' assignments. Those aimed at more important curricular aims would be assigned more grade-determining import than those aimed at less significant curricular aims.

To review, then, when arriving at a sensible stance regarding grading, teachers must first make up their minds about what the fundamental purpose of grading is. Teachers should adopt a position that grading can be regarded as a communication activity aimed at students and their parents, and that this activity should be based exclusively on a student's status with respect to the mastery of curricular aims. In many settings, however, a teacher has little choice about which curricular aims should be regarded as important—because governmental or policymaking groups will have already made those curricular decisions. Thus, in those settings, teachers will characteristically endorse students' attainment of officially sanctioned curricular aims. Accordingly, what's communicated to students and parents will be a student's status regarding each of these official curricular goals—perhaps called "standards," "learning outcomes," "content standards," or some synonymous descriptor. I recommend, therefore, that without reservation you adopt a grading strategy based only on students' goal attainment.

How Does Goal-Attainment Grading Take Place?

Let's assume that you see a mite of merit in the idea of linking students' grades to their progress in mastering curricular aims. How, precisely, would a teacher go about using this approach? Let's take a look at a few nuts and bolts of such a goal-attainment grading strategy.

We can safely presume that teachers will want their grading approaches to be as transparent as is practical. Some teachers, of course, might prefer to keep their grading practices under wraps. Most such teachers, of course, are reluctant to bring their grading practices into the sunlight chiefly out of fear that those practices would be found wanting. This is all too understandable. My early grading practices were so deplorable that the only way I could have defended them was by hiring fully armed mercenaries. But if one accepts the view that the grading of students is a less than completely scientific enterprise, and that mistakes will inevitably be made, then letting the world know what went into one's grading decisions seems so much more responsible than trying to camouflage what transpired while grades were being determined.

Step 1: *Clarifying curricular aims.*   The first step in any grade-giving approach that's wedded to students' attainment of curricular aims is to make certain that all participants in the grading game understand the nature of the curricular aims involved. What this means, in practice, is that teachers must provide *understandable* renditions of all curricular aims to those involved—specifically, to students and parents. Sometimes those understandable versions of curricular aims will employ identical language for both students and parents. In most instances, after students have entered middle school, any statements of curricular aims thought suitable for students will probably also be suitable for their parents. But for younger children, especially those in primary grades, separate "kid-friendly" versions of curricular aims are usually needed in addition to the descriptions of curricular aims provided for parents.

These statements of curricular aims are often more readily understood when accompanied by illustrative test items. It helps both students and parents to see sample items that might be used to assess a student's mastery of a specified curricular aim. Care must be taken, however, to indicate that these sample items do not exhaust the assessment techniques that might be employed to measure students' mastery. The accompanying items should be identified as "illustrative, but not exhaustive" examples of how students might be asked to display mastery of a given curricular aim. We want our students to master a curricular aim so they possess a truly generalizable mastery of this aim, not merely one way of displaying such mastery. Genuine mastery of a curricular aim signifies that a student can display this mastery in a variety of ways, not in just one or two.

To truly understand the nature of a curricular aim, it is often necessary for us to know the nature of the criteria by which a student's mastery of the aim will be determined. Such criteria are the factors to be used in determining the student's level of aim mastery. For instance, when judging the quality of a student's ability to write expository essays, the scoring guide/rubric that's employed for this purpose might isolate judgmental criteria such as the quality of an essay's (1) organization, (2) content, and (3) avoidance of mistakes involving the mechanics of writing. When the absence of such criteria would appreciably reduce someone's understanding of what mastery of a curricular aim really means, then the teacher must identify and, if necessary, explain what those criteria are.

Both for both the improvement of instruction and for the clarification of a grading process, it is almost always helpful to supply students with examples of acceptable and unacceptable responses to assessments or to assignments. When students are just starting to learn about something (such as when they're just beginning to acquire mastery of a sophisticated new skill), it typically makes sense to provide exemplars at the extreme ends of the quality continuum. Once more using our example of an expository essay, a teacher could pass out a truly terrific expository essay, as well as one that was sublimely shabby. Ideally, both examples would be actual responses made by previous students. Later, when students become more conversant with the nature of the curricular aim being sought, exemplars exhibiting more fine-grained differences in quality could be distributed. The idea here, of course, is to help students understand what is being sought and how students' mastery of it will be appraised.

Step 2: *Choosing goal-attainment evidence.* After identifying and describing the curricular aims (goals) on which grades are to be based, the teacher then decides what *evidence* will be used to help arrive at a determination of the student's progress toward mastery of each curricular aim being sought. It is altogether appropriate to let parents, as well as students, know what's coming in the way of evidence-eliciting assessment approaches. Well-described goals communicate effectively to students and parents. Well-described goals along with well-described assessments communicate quite effectively to students and parents.

Most of today's teachers, when they were students themselves, saw their teachers typically rely on important exams to assign grades. To illustrate, a final-exam grade counted more toward an end-of-course grade than did a grade on a midterm exam or grades on weekly quizzes. The final exam was, in other words, the test that made the most difference in the grade a student received. It is the assumption in such instances, and this is often a warranted assumption, that the more significant the exam, the more influential should be its contribution to a teacher's judgment about a student's mastery of curricular aims. In many instances, this may be true. But sometimes it isn't.

When reviewing the alternative assessment options for grading or, more generally, for the evidence-gathering ploys that might play a role in a teacher's grading strategy, it will be useful for you to remind yourself about the wide range of students' learning styles that are apt to be represented in almost all your classes. These various styles affect your students' abilities to demonstrate their learning achievements. The greater variety of assessment options you provide for your students, the more likely it is that you will land on an accurate interpretation of what a given student truly knows and can do. After snaring that valid interpretation, grade giving—especially goal-attainment grade giving—becomes much less foreboding.

Step 3: *Weighting goal-attainment evidence.* The third step in goal-attainment grading calls for the teacher to judge whatever assessment evidence is available regarding students' goal-attainment status. Here's what's typically going on when a teacher arrives at a judgment about a student's mastery of a specific curricular aim. First off, the teacher decides what evidence might be germane to a "goal-mastery" decision. Perhaps there are two homework assignments that the teacher's students were obliged to complete, as well as one classroom quiz, and also about 40 percent of the specific items on the midterm exam most related to the goal(s) being considered. Well, when the teacher looks at those four chunks of evidence, it is up to the teacher to decide which evidence will best support an interpretation about a student's mastery of this particular aim. It may well be that the two homework assignments actually give the teacher a better idea about the student's goal-mastery status than the evidence provided by either the classroom quiz or the items on the midterm exam. What the teacher must do, then, is decide how much weight to give each source of evidence, and be prepared to let any concerned individuals know about the nature of those weighting decisions. Again, transparency is the motive here. If grades are to be awarded on the basis of the degree to which a student has mastered a curricular aim, then a teacher should make clear (1) the evidence being relied on when the teacher makes those inferences about mastery and (2) the importance that the teacher assigns to this evidence.

In earlier editions of this book, I advocated assigning more grading weight on the basis of the type of assessment involved, with final exams and midterm exams trumping en route quizzes and homework assignments. I hope I was assuming that those exams would supply the most useful evidence in helping teachers arrive at inferences about students' goal attainment. But for the record, if you have adopted the grading posture recommended so far in this chapter, it may well be that your most significant evidence in support of an inference about students' goal attainment might come from "lesser" exams. All you need to do is decide how much significance to assign to different sources of evidence, and then let the world know—preferably in advance—what your interpretation-informed weighting decisions were.

Step 4: *Arriving at a final goal-attainment grade.* Let's assume there are several curricular aims being pursued, and there are several sources of assessment evidence at hand related to each of those aims. This is when the teacher focuses on the overall status of a student with regard to the attainment of the complete array of goals. More-important goals will count more than less-important goals. More-significant assessment evidence of goal attainment will be counted more heavily than less-significant assessment evidence of goal attainment. Clearly, arriving at a reasonably coalesced conclusion with so many things to keep track of is not a task for the dull-witted. But in the final analysis, that's what grading boils down to. And, at least with the overriding grading consideration being a student's attainment of goals, a teacher is at least playing an understandable grade-giving game.

Elementary school teachers, of course, often are concerned about grading considerations that are of less interest to teachers in middle schools or high schools. For instance, first-grade teachers may think a significant *educational* aim in their classrooms is to have children develop self-control in a social setting. For example, a 7-year-old boy who pounds on male or female classmates during recess would not be behaving in an appropriate manner, nor would a 7-year-old girl who pounds on male or female classmates during recess. (A teacher afflicted with many such students might, to capitalize on students' interests, consider establishing a "cooperative pounding group.")

As students become older, a teacher's grading scheme might be based on typical academic criteria. Teachers who work with younger children will often need to describe—and weigh—a much more developmentally appropriate set of factors. The essentials of such teachers' grading practices are identical to the approach used in later grades. But elementary teachers need to think through what they regard as relevant curricular aims, describe them, and then weigh their contribution to a child's grade.

Grade-Giving Specifics

When teachers award grades, there are several options available to them. For final, end-of-term, or end-of-year grades, it is necessary to adhere to whatever grade-descriptor system has been adopted by the district. Thus, if the district's policy is to use grades of A, B, C, D, and F, then the district's teachers must use those grades even if, during the course of the year, the teachers employed a different grade-descriptor scheme in class. Although many school districts, or schools within those districts, have grading policies that are quite general, some grading policies are particularly restrictive—setting forth specific limits on the percentages of particular grades that can be awarded by teachers.

Generally speaking, there are three major options available to teachers when they describe how well a student has performed. Teachers can use (1) letter grades, (2) numerical grades, or (3) verbal descriptors. Most of us are familiar with *letter grades*, because such grades have been widely used for a long, long time. A grade of A is yummy and a grade of F is crummy. In some districts, teachers are also allowed to add pluses or minuses to letter grades, thus transforming a grading scale that has 5 points (A, B, C, D, and F) to one that theoretically has 15. We can assume that a grade of F– reflects genuinely abysmal rock-bottom performance. A *numerical grading system* is usually organized around some chosen number of points such as 100, 50, or 10. Students are then given a number of points on each classroom assessment so that when they see their grade for the assessment, they realize they have earned, for example, "7 points out of a possible 10." *Verbal descriptors* are used instead of numerical or letter grades when teachers rely exclusively on phrases such as "excellent," "satisfactory," and "needs improvement." The number of such phrases used—that is, the number of possible verbal-descriptor grades that might be employed—is up to the teacher. If verbal-descriptor grades are used throughout an entire district, the choice of verbal descriptors is typically determined by district officials.

One increasingly common form of a verbal-descriptor grade is the *achievement-level* classification system used to describe performance on the National Assessment of Educational Progress (NAEP). When NAEP tests are administered, students' performances are classified as Advanced, Proficient, Basic, or Below Basic. (Although "Below Basic" is not an official NAEP-designated reporting category, it is typically employed so that students' totals add up to 100 percent!) This four-category achievement-level classification model has become widely used across the United States. Because the NCLB Act called for states to use at least three of these descriptive labels (that is, *Basic, Proficient*, and *Advanced*), many states simply adopted the NAEP four-category model. Thus, the use of the NAEP achievement-level labels is clearly a prominent variation of verbal-descriptor grades used in the United States. A number of districts have tried to devise *standards-based report cards* wherein the quality of each student's mastery of each content standard (curricular aim) is described. In many instances, the level of detail being used in such reporting systems has proven overwhelming to students, their parents, and more than a few teachers.

These standards-based report cards, a fundamentally sensible approach—especially given the increasingly widespread advocacy of basing grades dominantly on the basis of students' attainment of curricular aims (content standards)—is dependent on the *artistry* of those who crafted the content standards in the first place. If the grain size (breadth) of the content standards is too small, then teachers end up being obliged to evaluate students' status with respect to an overwhelming litany of such standards. The teachers might know what each content standard means, but there are simply too darn many of them! As a result, teachers tend to give less than careful attention to the whole array of standards, and both students and their parents become overwhelmed. In contrast, if the grain size of the standards is too large, then what the content standards truly mean sometimes vanishes into too-general verbiage. That's why it truly takes verbal artistry for those who craft standards-based report cards to arrive at versions that make those report cards educationally useful. I have seen many examples of standards-based report cards, all of them well-intentioned. I have seen few examples of standards-based report cards that I regarded as educationally useful.

The only sensible way to wrestle with the grain-size dilemma when relying on standards-based report cards is to *prioritize, prioritize,* and, for good measure, *prioritize.* If standards-based report cards can be structured around a manageable number of understandable curricular aims, then the standards set forth in such report cards can be crafted at a suitable grain size so this grading strategy pays off for both teachers and students. If grading is seen as a way of communicating about a student's level of goal attainment, then it is difficult to conceive of an approach to report-card grading that is not chiefly dependent on the quality of the content standards involved.

In contrast to more traditional letter grades, or even some of the alternative grading descriptors considered earlier, teachers should recall the dividends of *descriptive feedback* presented in Chapter 12's treatment of formative assessment. Descriptive feedback is rooted in a three-step operation in which the teacher lets the student know (1) what the curricular aim is—or what are the building blocks leading to master of the aim, (2) where the student is in relation to that aim's attainment, and (3) what the student should do to reduce the gap between the student's current status and desired status. Insofar as possible, teachers should try not to dispense grades that have few implications for students' learning. Instead, teachers should replace those grades with descriptive feedback whose function is to guide students toward the achievement of the curricular aims that, if the teacher adopts a goal-attainment approach to grading, will ultimately determine the student's grade.

Evaluative Options

Let's look at three common grade-giving approaches. Each of these approaches can be used not only for end-of-term or end-of-year grades but also for grading the classroom assessment performances and assignments of students during the school year. In other words, these grading approaches can be applied whether you are assigning Johnny an end-of-term grade in your science class or grading his 2-week experiment dealing with "Psychological Depression in Earthworms."

You're probably already familiar with the three grading approaches to be described, because when you were a student, you most likely encountered them all:

- *Absolute grading.* In absolute grading, a grade is given based on a teacher's idea of what level of student performances is truly necessary to earn—for instance, an A. Thus, if an English teacher has established an absolute level of proficiency needed for an A grade, and in a given class no student performs at the A-level of proficiency, then no student will get an A. Conversely, if the teacher's absolute grading standards were such that all students had performed beyond the A-level requirements, then the teacher would shower all these students with A grades. An absolute system of grading has much in common with a criterion-referenced approach to assessment. If the teacher has adopted a goals-attainment approach to grading, then an absolute implementation of this strategy would revolve around a teacher's judgment about the levels of goal attainment needed for all grades that were to be awarded.

The major argument in favor of an absolute approach to grading is that there are, indeed, legitimate levels of expectation for students that, although judgmentally devised by teachers, must be satisfied in order for specific grades to be awarded. And, of course, it is always the case that people form their absolute expectations based on seeing how folks usually perform. Thus, there's a sense in which *absolutes flow from relatives*.

- *Relative grading.* In relative grading, a grade is given based on how students perform in relation to one another. Thus, for any group of students, there will always be the *best* and the *worst* performances. Those students who outperform their classmates will get high grades irrespective of the absolute caliber of the students' performances. Conversely, because some students will always score relatively worse than their classmates, such low scorers will receive low grades no matter what. This system of grading is somewhat analogous to a norm-referenced approach to assessment.

As noted earlier, there is a sense in which even a teacher's *absolute* expectations regarding the level of performance needed to achieve an A, B, C, D, or F are derived from years of working with students and discerning how well similar students are usually capable of performing. But a relative grading system uses the students *in a given class* as the normative group and does not take into consideration all the students whom the teacher has taught in the past.

The chief argument in favor of a relative system of grading is that because the quality of the teacher's instructional efforts may vary, and the composition of a given group of students may vary, some type of class-specific grading is warranted. Teachers who use a relative-grading approach tend to appreciate its flexibility because their grading expectations change from class to class.

- *Aptitude-based grading.* In aptitude-based grading, a grade is given to each student based on how well the student performs in relation to that student's academic potential. To illustrate, if a particularly bright student outperformed all other students in the class, but still performed well below what the teacher believed the student was capable of, the student might be given a B, not an A. In order to grade on aptitude, of course, the teacher needs to have an idea of what students' academic potentials really are. To estimate each student's academic aptitude, teachers either need to rely on the student's prior performance on some sort of academic aptitude test or, instead, must form their own judgments about the student's academic potential. Tests of academic aptitude are being administered less frequently these days, so in order to use an aptitude-based grading approach, teachers will generally need to arrive at their own estimate of a student's potential.

  The main argument in favor of aptitude-based grading is that it tends to "level the playing field" by grading students according to their innate gifts and, thereby, encourages students to fulfill their potential. A problem with this grading approach, as you might guess, is the difficulty of deciding on just what each student's academic potential really is.

As indicated earlier, any of these three grading approaches can be used to assign grades for individual efforts of students (such as their performances on a short essay examination) or to arrive at a student's total-year grade. For instance, thinking back to Chapter 9's treatment of portfolio assessment, it would be possible to use any of the three grading approaches to arrive at students' portfolio grades—grades dispensed in letter, numerical, or verbal form.

What About Effort?

Students' effort is, educationally, so profoundly important. If a teacher can engender in students the inclination to expend effort in their school and nonschool endeavors, those students will be well served in the future. Students who believe the level of their effort will make the most difference in their success will be more likely to succeed than their classmates who rely on luck or on inherited smarts to carry them through life.

Okay, if students' effort is so significant, why shouldn't we take it into consideration when we grade students? In other words, why shouldn't we give higher grades to kids who put out the effort—regardless of their assessed levels of achievement? Regrettably, as Wormeli points out, "We don't have a commonly accepted, legally justifiable, non-subjective method for measuring how hard or sincerely someone is working" (2006, p. 108). This single sentence, sadly, torpedoes any hope of a worthwhile "effort-grading" approach. Even if, as a teacher, you would desperately like to incorporate effort into your grading approach, *you*

Decision Time

Should Level of Effort Be Rewarded?

Karl Kramer teaches second-graders at Twelfth Street Elementary School. He's been doing so for 6 years. During the past year, however, Karl has seriously been reconsidering his whole approach to grading. This reconsideration was stimulated by three students who in the past would have been placed in some form of special needs program, but now have been included in Karl's second-grade class.

Although the three students, Marie, Floyd, and James, are having difficulty with much of the content treated in class, all three are obviously trying hard to succeed. In fact, if Karl were to grade on effort alone, the three students would probably get the highest grades in class.

In the past, Karl has given no credit for student effort when grades were awarded. Now, however, he finds that he's rethinking that decision.

❚ *If you were Karl, what would you do?*

can't get an accurate fix on your students' effort levels. Although you might identify anecdotal evidence that seemingly tells you how hard a student is trying, such evidence can be misinterpreted. And such evidence *is* misinterpreted—way too often. We simply don't have an effort-determining measuring stick on which we can rely.

Let's suppose a teacher (we'll call him Elmer) cares so much about incorporating effort into students' grades that he goes totally overboard to try to accurately identify a student's level of effort. Indeed, in this fictional fantasy, Elmer even rents a set of pricey lie-detection equipment and hires an expensive lie-detector technician to operate it. Okay, say Elmer and the technician are in the teachers' lounge, interviewing students one at a time to reach a conclusion about each student's level of effort. What scale will Elmer employ to represent students' effort levels? Will the scale range from 10 for "Loads of Effort" to a 1 for "Little Effort"? And what about the personal judgments of our truth-telling students when they try to identify their own levels of effort? Is a self-identified effort level of 9 by Sally Lou the same as a self-identified effort level of 9 by Billy Bob? When we are dealing with such a covert, person-specific variable, even completely honest respondents can't help us arrive at an unerring fix on students' levels of effort. Effort levels are decidedly squishy. Effort is almost as elusive as it is important.

Accordingly, teachers who try to incorporate effort into their students' grades are usually fooling themselves. They simply can't arrive at an accurate identification regarding a student's effort associated with a given assignment or a particular assessment.

What About Those Important Intangibles?

Suppose that a teacher accepts the central grading guideline that's been endorsed in this chapter—namely, that students' grades should be based only on the degree to which a student has achieved the curricular aims set forth for the student. What about the many variables other than goal attainment that most teachers regard as important? If those are significant education-related variables, shouldn't teachers find a way to let students and their parents know how a student is doing with respect to, for instance, *social skills* (such as showing respect for classmates and adults) and *study skills* (such as working independently)? The answer is definitely *yes*. But the way to communicate such information is not by trying to piggy-back it onto a goal-attainment grade. Rather, the solution is to employ report cards embodying what O'Connor (2009, p. 238) calls "expanded format reporting," in which teachers render judgments about what I'll call *evaluative factors*.

These evaluative factors are the educationally relevant variables that educators believe students and those students' parents should know about. For instance, we know that "effort" is a potent consideration in the way a student prospers—not only in school but also after schooling is over. Yet, there's no way of accurately measuring an individual student's effort level. Nonetheless, if a report card clearly indicates that a teacher's estimate of a student's level of effort is just that, *a judgment-based estimate*, then both students and parents may benefit from those estimates.

As a practical matter, of course, individual teachers cannot craft their own report cards, so what's on a report card is typically decided at a district, state, or provincial level. Typically, an expanded-format report card lists a series of evaluative factors and then provides an interpretation key so that a teacher can indicate whether—for each listed evaluative factor—a student should be rated, for example, "Excellent, Good, Satisfactory, or Needs Improvement."

Ideally, the report card itself, or an accompanying letter, will provide an explanation regarding the judgmental nature of the teacher's estimates regarding each evaluative factor that's included in an expanded-format report card. Such "disclaimer" explanations can play a powerful role in educating both parents and students about the difference between a teacher's *evidence-based* grades focused on a student's goal attainment and the teacher's *judgmental estimates* about a student's status a student's status with respect to an other important evaluative factors."

In Figure 16.1 you will find an example of an expanded-format report card in which, at the right, you see a list of the five curricular aims (called goals in this instance) and a place where, at the close of every quarter, a student's status with respect to each goal is to be given a "mastery-status grade" by the teacher—namely, *Complete Goal Mastery (CGM), Developing Goal Mastery (DGM)*, and *Inadequate Goal Mastery (IGM)*. A total-course grade is supplied at the bottom of each quarter. (In this example, the total-course grade would be based on a teacher's judgment about the student's composite goal mastery.) On the right of Figure 16.1's report card, you will see two sets of evaluative factors (Social Skills and Study Skills), each of which is given a mark by the teacher on the basis of the teacher's judgmental estimate of whether the student's effort to improve has been *Consistent* (3 points), *Inconsistent* (2 points), or *Minimal* (1 point).

As you consider the report card presented in Figure 16.1, you will realize that the mastery-status grades or, indeed, the overall course grade itself, is going

Figure 16.1 An Illustrative Expanded-Format Report Card

Student's Name: _____

Goal Mastery

Interpretation Key: The letters below indicate a student's assessment-based mastery of each goal. Goal descriptions were distributed at the beginning of school. The *overall grade* (A, B, C, D, F) represents a student's overall goal mastery.

Mastery Status Grade:

CGM = *Complete Goal Mastery*

DGM = *Developing Goal Mastery*

IGM = *Inadequate Goal Mastery*

Evaluative Factors

Interpretation Key: For the factors listed to the right, you will find a teacher's *judgmental estimate* of the student's effort to improve.

3 = *Consistent*

2 = *Inconsistent*

1 = *Minimal*

Curriculum Goals

	Q1	Q2	Q3	Q4
Goal 1				
Goal 2				
Goal 3				
Goal 4				
Goal 5				
Overall Grade				

Social Skills Factors

	Q1	Q2	Q3	Q4
Respects classmates				
Follows rules				
Is self-disciplined				

Study Skills Factors

	Q1	Q2	Q3	Q4
Stays on task				
Organizes work				
Uses time well				
Employs technology				

to make no sense if the persons on the receiving end of such a report card do not understand the nature of the five goals on which the course grades will depend. This information (distributed at the beginning of the school year in this illustration) needs to be written in language readily understandable to both students and parents. Providing an additional description of those goals whenever report cards are issued is usually a smart move.

Again, recognizing that not all of a district's teachers are apt to have a hand in carving out the specifics of how a district's report cards are constructed, there may be some occasions when you might actually have an opportunity to register your personal preferences regarding the structure of district report cards. If you do have a chance to toss your ideas into such a mix, please remember that in the reporting of students' grades, a profound truth is that "less is more." Too many grading dimensions incline both students and parents to become so swamped with information that they end up paying only superficial attention to any of those dimensions. And, of course, if there are too many grading tasks for teachers to undertake, they will typically end up racing through the "grading agony" as quickly as they can—often thoughtlessly. Really influential report cards are crafted in such a way that the number of judgments a teacher must make is intellectually manageable. This will lead to a modest, understandable interpretation task for both students and their parents. This will also lead to teachers' more thoughtful decisions regarding students' grades.

Electronic Record Keeping

Although many seasoned teachers have traditionally kept records of their students' accomplishments by making handwritten entries in a gradebook, the dramatic increase in the use of teacher-friendly computers promises to alter that practice. As more and more youthful, computer-canny teachers enter the field of education, we will surely see marked expansion in the use of computer-based records regarding students' performances.

A number of readily usable programs to help teachers keep track of their students' performances now exist, and more will surely be available in years to come. The mission of these electronic grading programs is to simplify the teacher's tasks, so even a rudimentary notion of how to use a computer will save teachers tons of record-keeping time. Some observers of America's classrooms predict that within a decade or so, teachers' entering grades by hand in a traditional gradebook will be quite rare.

Student-Involved Grading Conferences

One useful alternative to the exclusive reliance on traditional report cards is the use of grading conferences. Grading conferences, when first introduced, usually involved only teachers and students' parents. Increasingly, however, students themselves are playing a role. There is, of course, a considerable range in the level of involvement for students in such grading conferences. This range starts off with

Parent Talk

Imagine that one of your students' parents, Mrs. Aquino, wants to discuss her daughter's grade in your class. Specifically, she wants to know, "What goes into Maria's grade?"

| *If I were you, here's how I'd respond to Mrs. Aquino:*

"I'm delighted you want to look into how Maria is graded in my class. What I'd like you to do is look over the classroom information system I've been able to get up and running this year on my lap-top computer. Why don't you come to my class before or after school and I'll show you how I arrive at each of the components contributing to Maria's grade. I'll also show you how I've tried to weight the grade-determination importance of certain tests and other assignments that Maria and her classmates complete. I am especially concerned

about the progress Maria is making toward the nine state-set curricular aims that are to be achieved by students this year.

"What you need to understand, Mrs. Aquino, is that any grade given to any student is almost always a teacher judgment based on an amalgam of different sorts of evidence. And, to be honest, because teachers' judgments are involved, and teachers are altogether human, there will invariably be some teacher errors in grading.

"But I assure you, the other teachers in our school and I are trying to do the fairest and most accurate job we can when we grade our students. Why don't you visit and we can review what goes into Maria's grade?"

| *Now, how would you respond to Mrs. Aquino's concerns?*

---

the student being present but not taking any part—other than being a listener—in the conference. At a greater level of involvement, the student participates actively in the conference. At the most substantial level of involvement, the student actually *leads* the grading conference. Clearly, for most variations of student-involved grading conferences, students will need to be carefully prepared by their teachers so that the resulting conferences will be maximally productive. (The vast majority of students possess no experience in grading themselves, and definitely no experience in supplying *goal-attainment* grades for themselves.) Remember, if the grading conference is based on a goal-attainment conception of grading, then all three parties in the conference (student, teacher, and one or both parents) will need to consider the *evidence* regarding a student's level of goal mastery. And that, of course, is where assessment provides the key information around which the grading conference is structured.

Let's recall that the basic purpose of grading is for teachers to communicate to students and parents the degree to which a student is making progress toward the goals this student is supposed to master. To the degree that a teacher accepts this conception of grading, then when students understand the chief thrust of the grading process—by being actively involved in that process—this provides those students with information they need not only to evaluate their own achievements but, just as important, to monitor their ongoing progress toward goal attainment. Student-involved grading conferences can be a powerful *instructionally* relevant way of grading students so that they and their parents comprehend, if they are the recipients of descriptive feedback, where students currently are and what students need to do in order to achieve complete goal mastery.

Grading's Inherent Imprecision

Wouldn't it be nice if teachers never made mistakes when they graded students? But, as you probably know all too well from having been the recipient of too-low or too-high grades during your own years as a student, teachers do make grading errors. Certainly, teachers don't want to make mistakes in the grades they give to their students. However, grading is a judgment-based enterprise in which flawed decisions will surely be made.

Fortunately, in the long haul, such errors tend to balance one another out. You may recall from Chapter 8 that there are three kinds of rater bias—namely, generosity bias, severity bias, and central-tendency bias. It is true that many teachers are biased in one of these three ways when they grade their students. Thus, over the years, a given student will probably be on the receiving end of some undeserved high grades and some unwarranted low grades. What you need to remember is that if you do the best job you can in dispensing grades to your students—that is, if you assign grades carefully and with the kind of deliberateness suggested in this chapter—you'll have done your grading as well as you can. Human judgment, as potent as it is, is not flawless. And it certainly isn't flawless when it comes to grading students.

And because this text deals with classroom assessment, we dare not bid adieu to grading without reminding ourselves that the quality of the grades you dole out will almost always depend on the quality of the assessment instruments you rely on to collect evidence regarding your students. Students' performances on high-caliber assessments can turn into on-the-money, educationally useful grades. Students' performances on low-quality assessments almost certainly will lead to grades of which you will be less than proud. And in education, as in most fields, the prospect of upcoming shame can be genuinely motivating. Accordingly, test well!

What Do Classroom Teachers Really Need to Know About Assessment-Based Grading of Students?

It should now be apparent to you that adoption of a goal-attainment approach to grading makes solid educational sense, and that separating grading from a teacher's judgments about other evaluative factors is the way to proceed. First off,

But What Does This Have to Do with Teaching?

The purpose of teaching is to bring about worthwhile changes in boys and girls. Most of these changes focus on students' acquisition of knowledge and skills. In truth, the very act of teaching can be seen as the use of the instructional means that a teacher uses in order to promote students' attainment of worthwhile ends—namely, curricular aims. If this is to be the teacher's chief aspiration—to have students master the curricular aims set forth for those students—why not evaluate students according to precisely the same framework? To the extent that both the teacher and the teacher's students are using the same targets to orient their activities, and to judge the success of those activities, then the resulting synergy from having both teacher and students pursuing identical aspirations will surely prove educationally beneficial. Goal-attainment grading pushes students to attain the very same goals the teacher wants those students to attain. Instruction will follow aspiration. Learning, too, will follow aspiration. Evaluative structures alter conduct. Why not alter students' conduct in a manner that leads to a greater likelihood of their attaining educational goals?

Grading based on students' goal attainment, therefore, is an approach that makes sense from both an evaluative perspective and an instructional perspective. Regarding those other important factors that teachers would like to communicate, adoption of expanded-format reporting seems to be the way to go, as long as the evaluative factors don't overwhelm. Remember, the converse of "less is more" embodies every bit as much truth—namely, "more is less." An expanded-format report card, where students are graded in terms of their goal attainment, yet where a modest number of evaluative factors other than goal attainment are also included, seems to represent the most sensible way to proceed.

there will be greater clarity about grades on the part of teachers who base their grades on students' attainment of well-described goals. Students and parents will better understand the resultant grades than they would understand such traditional grading approaches as simply comparing the relative achievement levels of the students in a particular classroom.

But just as important as the communication dividends derived from goal-attainment grading is the manner in which such an approach meshes with the way teachers should approach their *instructional* tasks. Let's face it, the chief reason why teachers teach kids is to help those kids acquire skills and knowledge. The skills and knowledge to be promoted by teachers are called *standards, goals,* or some similar label. Those are the *ends* of a teacher's instruction, and teaching constitutes the *means* by which the teacher promotes students' mastery of those curricular ends. Indeed, as you saw in the previous chapter, the quality of a teacher's instructional efforts should be evaluated predominantly according to whether the teacher has promoted students' attainment of curricular goals. So, from an instructional perspective focused on students' goal attainment, why not devise a student-appraisal system that meshes perfectly with the fundamental reason why teachers teach?

Chapter Summary

Conceding that the grading of students is a process fraught with imprecision, this chapter argued that the most defensible system of grading is one rooted in teachers' judgments about the degree to which students have mastered the curricular aims a teacher is promoting for those students. The guiding premise of the chapter was that the purpose of grading is for teachers to communicate with students and their parents about the degree to which students are attaining (or have attained) the goals those students are supposed to achieve. Thus, a goal-attainment approach to grading was advocated.

Four steps for teachers when implementing a goal-attainment approach to grading were presented: (1) clarifying curricular aims, (2) choosing goal-attainment evidence, (3) weighting goal-attainment evidence, and (4) arriving at a final goal-attainment grade.

Regarding the incorporation of factors *other* than assessment-based evidence of a student's goal attainment, it was suggested that an expanded-format type of report card be employed to allow the teacher to provide judgmental estimates regarding the student's status with respect to these educationally relevant variables. However, it was stressed that the *grades* awarded by teachers should be based exclusively on assessment-obtained evidence of goal attainment. As always, in the awarding of grades based on identified evaluative factors, less is so meaningfully more than more.

MyLab Education Self-Check 16.1

MyLab Education Application Exercise 16.1: Goal-Attainment Grading

References

Brookhart, S. M. (2009). *Grading* (2nd ed.). New York: Merrill.

Brookhart, S. M. (2011). *Grading and learning: Practices that support student achievement.* Bloomington, IN: Solution Tree.

Guskey, T. R. (Ed.). (2008). *Practical solutions for serious problems in standards-based grading.* Thousand Oaks, CA: Corwin.

Guskey, T. R. (2015). *Challenging the conventions of grading and reporting.* Bloomington, IN: Solution Tree.

O'Connor, K. (2009). *How to grade for learning: Linking grades to standards* (3rd ed.). Thousand Oaks, CA: Corwin.

O'Connor, K. (2011). *A repair kit for grading: 15 fixes for broken grades* (2nd ed.). Boston: Pearson.

Pattison, E., Grodsky, E., and Muller, C. (2013). "Is the sky falling? Grade inflation and the signaling power of grades," *Educational Researcher*, 42, no. 5 (June/July): 259–265.

Sadler, P. M., and Good, E. (2006). "The impact of self- and peer-grading on student learning," *Educational Assessment*, 11, no. 1: 1–32.

Townsley, M. (2013/2014). "Redesigning grading, districtwide," *Educational Leadership*, 71, no. 4 (December/January): 56–61.

Welsh, M. E., D'Agostino, J. V., and Kaniskan, B. (2013). "Grading as a reform effort: Do standards-based grades converge with test scores?" *Educational Measurement: Issues and Practice*, 32, no. 2 (Summer): 26–36.

Wormeli, R. (2006). *Fair isn't always equal: Assessment and grading in the differentiated classroom.* Portland, ME: Stenhouse.

Wormeli, R. (2011). "Effective grading in standards-based schools," *Educational Leadership*, 69, no. 3 (November): 40–44.

Goal-Attainment Grading in Four Not-So-Easy Steps*

W. James Popham, University of California, Los Angeles

One of the most vexing of the many tasks that teachers face each year is giving grades to their students. If you've never personally dispensed grades to students, it may seem like a wonderful opportunity to righteously reward the reward-worthy, while dispensing lower grades to students whose performances warrant them. Any experienced teach will tell you, however, that giving grades is far from fun.

What you'll typically hear from seasoned teachers are complaints about the judgmentally based imprecision of grading. Yes, grading invariably calls for teachers to rely on their personal judgments to arrive at students' grades—and some of those judgments are almost certain to be flawed.

In recent years, most educational leaders have agreed that the most defensible strategy to grade students is *goal-attainment grading*. Goal-attainment grading appears to be the approach most consonant with *improved student learning*. Following, then, is a super-scrunched, four-step description of goal-attainment grading.

- *Step 1: Clarify curricular goals.* Because goal-attainment grading depends on evidence-based judgments about the degree to which a student has achieved a specified goal, it is obvious that great precision is required in describing the nature of the curricular goal(s) being sought. It is often helpful to supply "illustrative but not exhaustive" examples of the kinds of test items that might be employed to measure the attainment of each goal.

- *Step 2: Choose goal-attainment evidence.* It is quite appropriate to describe to students—and to their parents—the assessment approach employed in determining students' goal mastery. The tests themselves need not be provided, but crisp descriptions of eligible testing tactics can help everyone understand what's expected of students.

- *Step 3: Weight the goal-attainment evidence.* This third step of goal-attainment grading is often messier than anticipated. Typically, there will be more than one kind of evidence contributing to a judgment regarding how well a given goal has been achieved. Nonetheless, a teacher must make the most defensible weighting judgments possible.

- *Step 4: Arrive at a final grade.* Given the likelihood that more than one goal is being pursued, and that more than one sort of evidence per goal is at hand, this final grade-awarding decision is surely not fool's play. Yet it clearly must be done.

Although the approach is challenging, when teachers adopt goal attainment as the overriding consideration in the dispensing of grades, those teachers are at least playing a comprehensible grade-giving game that's focused on what we want for our students.

Glossary

absence-of-bias   The degree to which an assessment instrument is free of qualities that offend or unfairly penalize test takers because of those test takers' personal characteristics such as race, gender, socioeconomic status, or religion.

accessibility   The extent to which students are readily able to display their abilities with respect to what is being assessed, such as a student's mastery of a cognitive skill or a body of knowledge.

achievement tests   A measurement of the knowledge and/or skills a student possesses. Although often thought to assess what a student has *achieved* in school, some commercially published achievement tests contain many items measuring a student's out-of-school learning or the students' inherited academic aptitudes.

affective assessment   A measurement of a student's attitudes, interests, and/or values.

alignment   The substantive agreement between two or more of the following: curriculum, instruction, and assessment.

alternate assessments   Meaningfully different tests intended for students with disabilities so that more valid inferences can be made about the students than would be possible if the original test were used (even with assessment accommodations).

alternate-form reliability   The consistency of measured results yielded by different forms of the same test.

analytic scoring   A method of scoring a student's constructed responses involving the application of multiple evaluative criteria, one criterion at a time. After the evaluative criteria have been employed separately, there may be an aggregation of these separate judgments into a final, overall evaluation.

anonymity-enhancement procedures   The steps a teacher takes so that a student accurately perceives that his or her responses to self-report affective assessment inventories are truly untraceable.

aptitude tests   A measurement device intended to predict a student's likelihood of success in some future setting, often an academic one. Although formerly referred to as *intelligence tests*, and thought to assess a person's innate potential, aptitude tests often contain a number of the same sorts of items one finds in achievement tests.

assessment   A formal attempt to determine a student's status with respect to an educational variable of interest. Synonyms: *measurement, test.*

assessment accommodations   The techniques used when assessing a student with disabilities or a language-minority student in order to secure more valid inferences about such a student's knowledge and skills. Typical accommodations include allowing increased time to complete a test or, perhaps, presenting a test's items in a manner more suitable, given the student's limitations.

assessment bias   If an assessment instrument offends or unfairly penalizes a student because of personal characteristics—such as race, gender, ethnicity, or socioeconomic status—the instrument is biased against that student.

assessment literacy   An individual's understandings of the fundamental assessment concepts and procedures deemed likely to influence educational decisions.

assessment task   The part of an essay item or performance test that describes what it is the student should do to complete the assessment.

authentic assessment   A performance assessment in which the student's tasks resemble real-life tasks.

benchmark assessments   Also referred to as interim assessments, tests administered periodically during a school year, perhaps three or four times, typically covering segments of the skills and/or knowledge measured by more comprehensive summatively focused tests.

binary-choice item   A test item requiring a student to select one of two presented options.

blind scoring   When a student's tests are judged without the judges' knowing whether a test was completed as a pretest or as a posttest.

classification consistency   A representation of the proportion of students who are placed in the same classification category on two testing occasions or by using two forms of the same test.

cognitive assessment   Measurement of a student's knowledge and/or intellectual skills.

cognitive demand   The essence of the intellectual operation(s) a student must carry out in order to respond successfully to a test's items or tasks.

***Common Core State Standards* (CCSS)**   These are curricular goals developed as targets for the nation's instructional programs. The reading and mathematics curricular aims created for the *Common Core State Standards* were originally accepted as official curricular aspirations by many of the 50 U.S. states.

Although authorities in some states have retained these previously adopted curricular aims, other states have relabeled them or made minor modifications of the original CCSS curricular goals. These shifts occurred because of antipathy toward content standards that were increasingly seen as federally inspired.

computer-adaptive assessment Computer-adjusted presentation of test items to students so that, depending on students' responses to previous items on the test, new items can be chosen that mesh most appropriately with a student's demonstrated level of achievement.

computer-based assessment The use of computers not only to present assessment tasks to students but also when those students respond to such items via computers.

construct-irrelevant variance Factors that are unrelated to the construct being measured but nonetheless diminish the accuracy of assessment.

construct-related evidence of validity Empirical evidence that (1) supports the posited existence of a hypothetical construct and (2) indicates that an assessment device does, in fact, measure that construct.

constructed responses A student's answers to assessment tasks, such as essay items, that require a response to be generated by the student "from scratch."

content-related evidence of validity Evidence indicating that an assessment instrument suitably reflects the content domain it is supposed to represent.

content standards The knowledge and skills that a student is supposed to learn.

content underrepresentation An instance when the content being assessed (for example, a collection of curricular aims) has not been satisfactorily addressed by the items constituting a test.

convergent evidence of validity When students' performances on a test are positively related to their performances on other tests intended to measure the same variable or, perhaps, similar variables.

correlation coefficient A numerical index reflecting the nature and strength of the relationship between two variables—for example, between students' scores on two different kinds of tests. The strongest positive relationship is signified by a correlation coefficient (r) of $+1.00$; the strongest negative relationship is signified when r equals -1.00. An r of 0.0 indicates no relationship between the two variables under analysis.

criterion A variable deemed to be of such significance that it is regarded as the most prominent variable involved, as, for example, when a predictor test measures students' aptitude levels to predict a criterion such as students' college grades.

criterion-referenced measurement An approach to assessment in which a student's test performance is interpreted according to how much of a defined assessment domain the student has mastered.

criterion-related evidence of validity Evidence demonstrating the systematic relationship of test scores on a predictor test to a predicted criterion variable.

criterion variable An external variable that serves as the to-be-predicted target for a predictor exam, such as an aptitude test.

curricular aim A skill, body of knowledge, or affective outcome that teachers intend their students to acquire.

curriculum The set of educational aims—for instance, goals or objectives—that teachers wish their students to achieve.

data-driven education A popular descriptor for an educational orientation in which all or most key decisions are made in light of data—that is, evidence—much of it being students' scores on tests of some type. Although similar in meaning to "measurement-driven education," data-driven education typically relies on a wider array of data than students' test scores.

Depth of Knowledge The level of cognitive demand that students must meet to master a given curricular aim or to respond successfully to a test item. A lower Depth of Knowledge (DOK) might call for mere memorization, but a higher DOK could require students to employ evaluation or synthesis.

descriptive feedback Information that is communicated to students about their performances and is intended to help students determine how to narrow the gap between their current achievement and the achievement embodied in the curricular aim(s) they are pursuing. Descriptive feedback moves beyond mere comparative reporting so that the specific quality of the student's test performance is delineated.

disparate impact If test scores of different groups (for example, different ethnic or religious groups) are decidedly different, this is described as an assessment procedure having a disparate impact on test takers.

distractor analysis Scrutiny of a student's empirical performances on the different answer options contained in multiple-choice and matching items.

distribution A term used to describe a set of test scores, such as when one says, "The final exam score distribution from the students in Ms. Hill's class was very homogeneous."

educational accountability The imposition of required evidence, usually a student's test scores, as a way of holding educators responsible for the quality of schooling.

educational defensibility guideline A guideline for test preparation stipulating that no test-preparation practice should increase a student's test scores without simultaneously increasing her or his mastery of the assessment domain represented by the test.

empirical item improvement Improvement in an item's quality based on a student's performance on the item.

English language learners (ELLs) A diverse group of students whose first language is not English. Such students are referred to often as limited English proficient (LEP) students and, sometimes, simply as language learners.

essay item A test item eliciting a response of one or more paragraphs from a student.

evaluation An appraisal of the worth of an educational program or, in the case of classroom teachers, either the effectiveness of an instructional activity or the competence of the teacher.

evaluative criterion A factor with which, along with other such factors, we judge the quality of a student's performance.

evidence based on response processes Validity evidence that generally comes from analyses of individual test takers' responses, such as when students, after having been tested, are questioned about their thought processes during an examination.

evidence of validity based on test content Formerly referred to as *content validity* or *content-related validity*, this validity evidence stems from a formal scrutiny of the content assessed by a test's items or the procedures employed to choose that content.

extended-response item An essay item that gives a student few constraints about how he or she is to respond, especially with respect to the length of his or her responses.

fairness The validity of test-score interpretations and uses for students from all relevant subgroups. Fairness is present when assessments are developed, administered, scored, and reported in ways that are evenhanded for all students.

formative assessment A planned process in which assessment-elicited evidence of students' status is used by teachers to adjust their ongoing instructional procedures or by students to adjust their current learning tactics.

formative teacher evaluation The appraisal of a teacher's instructional performance with the exclusive purpose of improving the teacher's performance, rather than supporting such summative decisions as tenure denial, reward recognition, or job termination.

grade-equivalent scores An often misinterpreted estimated score based on the grade level and months of the school year represented by a student's test performance.

grading An assignment of a quality-designating label (numerical or verbal) to describe the caliber of a student's work.

grain size The breadth of a curricular aim, ranging from small-grain-size to large-grain-size aims. Typically, the breadth of a curricular aim—that is, its grain size—is directly linked to the amount of instructional time it is thought will be required for students to master the curricular aim.

halo effect The error of allowing a test scorer's overall impression of a student to influence any criterion-by-criterion evaluations of the student's response to a test.

high-stakes test An assessment with consequences that have important implications either for students (such as grade-to-grade promotion) or for educators (such as when schools are qualitatively ranked on the basis of students' test scores).

holistic scoring The method of scoring a student's constructed responses that calls for the synthesized application of multiple evaluative criteria—that is, simultaneously using several distinguishable factors to arrive at an overall judgment about the quality of a student's response.

hypergeneral rubrics Scoring guides wherein the evaluative criteria are described in excessively general—hence, dysfunctional—terms.

individualized education program (IEP) A federally required document describing the specifics of how a child with disabilities is to be educated.

instruction The activities carried out by teachers with their students that are intended to help students achieve teachers' curricular aims.

instructional sensitivity The degree to which students' performances on a test accurately reflect the quality of instruction specifically provided to promote students' mastery of what is being assessed.

interim assessments Tests administered periodically during a school year, perhaps three or four times, typically covering segments of the skills and/or knowledge measured by more comprehensive, summatively focused tests. Sometimes used for predicting students' scores on subsequent high-stakes tests, a number of commercially available interim tests purport to be useful as instructionally diagnostic tools.

internal consistency reliability The degree to which a test's items are functioning in a similar (that is, homogeneous) fashion.

Inter-rater reliability The calculated level of agreement between two or more *independent* judges in their appraisal of students' performances on an assessment task requiring a solo student's response—such as when separate judges rate the quality of individual students' written essays or oral presentations.

item alternatives The answer options used in a multiple-choice test item.

item-discrimination index   A numerical indicator contrasting, on a particular test item, the proportion of high total-test performers and the proportion of low total-test performers.

item distractors   The wrong-answer options in multiple-choice items.

item response theory (IRT)   This scale-score approach to reporting a student's test performances takes into consideration not only a student's raw score but also other factors, such as item difficulty, the guessability of items, and so on. The computation of IRT scale scores requires considerable computer-based statistical analysis.

judgmental item improvement   Ranging from an individual teacher's judgmental improvement-focused scrutiny of her or his own test items all the way to elaborate and systematic reviews of the items in important tests. The level of scrutiny employed can be quite casual or very elaborate, employing sophisticated evaluative procedures.

learning progression   A sequenced set of building blocks—that is, subskills or bodies of enabling knowledge—that it is thought students must master en route to mastering a more remote target curricular aim.

Likert inventories   Affective assessment devices organized around a respondent's self-reported degree of agreement with a series of presented statements.

limited English proficient (LEP)   A label, often used in governmental publications, referring to students whose first language is not English. These students are frequently described as English language learners, ELL students, or language learners.

matching item   A test-item format that requires students to associate items, as directed, from two different lists.

mean   The arithmetic average of a set of scores.

measurement   A formal attempt to determine a student's status with respect to an educational variable of interest. Synonyms: *assessment, test.*

measurement-driven instruction   An approach to educational reform in which the installation of high-stakes assessments is intended to influence teachers to teach toward the knowledge and skills that those assessments purport to measure.

median   The midpoint in a set of scores when the scores are ranked from lowest to highest.

multiple binary-choice item   A binary-choice item that, along with other binary-choice items, is based on a single, usually somewhat lengthy set of stimulus material.

multiple-choice test item   A test item requiring a student to choose a response from three or more presented options.

normal curve equivalent   Often referred to as an NCE, a normal curve equivalent is a scale score representing a raw score's relative position in a distribution of scores that is assumed to be normally distributed. The meaningfulness of this scale-score approach, of course, depends on the degree to which the score distribution involved is, in fact, normal.

norm-referenced measurement   An approach to assessment in which a student's test performance is interpreted relatively—that is, according to how the student's performance compares with that of other test takers.

offensiveness   A test is offensive when it contains elements that would insult any particular group of test takers on the basis of their personal characteristics, such as religion or race.

opportunity to learn   Because several important court cases indicate that if a test's consequences are significant for the test taker, then that test taker must have been given an instructional program constituting a reasonable opportunity for the student to learn what is being tested. This test-relevant instruction is often described as opportunity to learn.

p value   An indicator of an item's difficulty based on the percent of students who answer the item correctly. Thus, an item answered correctly by 67 percent of students would have a p value of .67.

percentiles   An interpretive scoring system based on the percent of students in the norm group outperformed by a given student. For example, a student whose raw score exceeded the performance of 84 percent of the norm-group students would have earned an 84th percentile score.

performance assessment   A form of testing in which a student is given a task, typically a demanding one, and then asked to respond to the task orally, in writing, or by constructing a product.

performance standard   The level of proficiency at which content standards should be mastered.

portfolio assessment   An assessment approach centered on the systematic appraisal of a student's collected work samples.

preassessment   A pretest given prior to instruction, typically to (1) determine a student's entry skills and knowledge or (2) employ as part of a pretest–posttest collection of evidence regarding instructional quality.

premises   In an item on a matching test, the elements listed on the left for which a match is sought from a list of responses on the right.

professional ethics guideline   A guideline for test preparation stipulating that no test-preparation practice should violate the ethical norms of the education profession.

professional learning community   A group of educators who meet periodically, over an extended period of time, to enhance their competencies related to one or more particular topics.

prompt The assessment task, typically for a writing sample, that indicates what the focus of a student's composition should be.

psychomotor assessment Measurement of a student's small-muscle or large-muscle skills.

quartile One of three points in a distribution of test scores dividing those test scores into four groups. Those three points are the 25th percentile, the 50th percentile, and the 75th percentile. Quartiles are often mistakenly referred to as representing a quarter of a set of test scores (e.g., "He scored in the top quartile" (*sic*), quartiles refer to points, not to proportions of a test-score distribution.

range An infrequently used measure of a score distribution's variability that is calculated simply by subtracting the value of the lowest test score from the value of the highest test score.

raw score The number of items, without any sort of numerical transformation, answered correctly by a student.

reactive The often confounding effect of early assessment on a student's subsequent learning, most vividly seen in the impact caused by preassessment of an affective variable, wherein the student is unduly sensitized to the affective variable with which a teacher is concerned.

regression effect A well-known statistical phenomenon in which extremely high scorers or extremely low scorers will, when retested, tend to earn scores closer to the mean of the score distribution.

reliability The consistency of results produced by measurement devices.

reliability coefficient The numerical indicator of whatever type of reliability evidence has been assembled to represent the consistency with which a test measures—most commonly presented as a correlation coefficient in which higher, positive coefficients represent greater measurement consistency.

reliability/precision The degree to which scores of a particular group of test takers are consistent over repeated administrations of a test, thereby leading to the inference that scores for an individual test taker are similarly dependable and consistent.

response In general, a student's answer to an assessment task (or test item). For matching items, responses are the listed elements (on the right) from which selections are made to match premises (on the left).

restricted-response item An essay item that markedly limits the form and content of a student's response to the item.

rubric A scoring guide employed to evaluate the quality of a student's responses to performance tests, a student's portfolio, or any kind of student-generated response.

scale scores Converted raw scores that employ a new, arbitrarily chosen scale to represent a student's performance. A considerable number of scale scores are used in education. (See *normal curve equivalent, stanine*.)

score spread The degree to which a set of test scores is dispersed (that is, spread out).

selected responses A student's answers to test items that present options from which the student must choose—for instance, multiple-choice or binary-choice items.

self-report inventories An assessment tool, often completed anonymously, wherein a student's responses reveal his or her values, behaviors, attitudes, and so on.

short-answer item A test item eliciting a brief response, usually a word or phrase, from a student.

showcase portfolios Collections of a student's "best work"—that is, the work samples deemed to be of the highest quality. Such portfolios are typically used for celebrating students' accomplishments with parents, policymakers, and so on.

skill-focused rubrics Scoring guides whose evaluative criteria are applicable for judging a student's responses to any suitable skill-measuring task.

socially desirable responses Responses of a student that do not represent the student's actual sentiments but, instead, reflect how the student believes he or she *should* respond.

split-and-switch design A data-gathering design in which a class is split into two halves, each half taking a different pretest. Then, after instruction, the tests are switched so that students take the other test form. Two comparisons are then made between students' pretest and posttest performances on the same test form.

stability reliability The consistency of assessment results over time. Synonym: *test–retest reliability*.

standard deviation A statistical index revealing the degree to which the scores in a group of scores are spread out from the group's mean score; larger standard deviations reflect more score spread than smaller standard deviations.

standard error of measurement An estimate of the consistency of an individual's test performance(s) represented by an index of how likely it is that another test performance (on an equidifficult test) would yield a comparable score.

standardized test Any test that is administered, scored, and interpreted in a standard, predetermined manner.

stanine A scale score based on the division of test scores into nine units of one-half standard deviation distances (on the score distribution's baseline). The highest stanine, number 9, contains about 4 percent of the scores—as does the lowest stanine, number 1. The middle stanine, number 5, contains about 20 percent of the scores if the distribution is fairly normal in shape.

stem   The initial part of a multiple-choice item—that is, the stimulus to which one of the multiple-choice options serves as the best response.

student growth percentile   A norm-referenced representation of students' relative changes in test performances during a single school year—such changes being represented on the current test by percentile comparisons of all students who had scored identically on the prior year's test. The growth of a given teacher's students would therefore be determined by an average of those growth percentiles based on different starting points.

summative assessment   When tests are used to make final judgments about students or about the quality of a teacher's instruction.

summative teacher evaluation   Appraisal of the quality of a teacher's instruction not to improve it but, rather, to support more high-stakes decisions, such as the teacher's job status or compensation.

task-specific rubrics   Scoring guides whose evaluative criteria deal only with scoring a student's responses to a particular task, not to the full range of tasks that might represent the skill being measured.

teaching to the test   A teacher's directing of instruction toward the assessment domain represented by the test *or* toward the specific items that make up the actual test. Because of this dual meaning, and the confusion apt to result from its use, the expression should be avoided or immediately defined.

test   A formal attempt to determine a student's status with respect to an educational variable of interest. Synonyms: *assessment, measurement.*

test-based teacher evaluation   Teacher appraisals in which the dominant determiner of a teacher's quality is the performance of a particular teacher's students on an externally imposed standardized achievement test.

test–criterion relationship   The relationship that emerges when validity evidence regarding a predictor test, such as an aptitude exam, is collected with respect to the empirical relationship between scores on the predictor test and the student's status on a criterion variable, such as the student's subsequent grades.

test–retest reliability   Often referred to as *stability reliability*, evidence of a test's consistency of measurement that is collected by testing a group of students and then re-administering that test to the same group of students at a later time.

true–false item   A common binary-choice item in which a student's two options regarding the accuracy of a presented statement are *true* and *false*.

unfair penalization   A test item unfairly penalizes test takers when there are elements in the item that would disadvantage a group because of its members' personal characteristics, such as gender or ethnicity.

universal design   A "from-the-get-go" approach to assessment development that strives to maximize the accessibility of a test for all those who are intended to take the test.

validity   The degree to which evidence supports the accuracy of test-based inferences (interpretations) about students for a test's specific purpose.

validity argument   A justification of the degree to which accumulated evidence and theory support the proposed inferences (interpretations) about a student's test performances.

value-added model (VAM)   A statistical procedure intended to employ students' prior achievement and/or background characteristics as statistical controls to estimate the effects on student achievement of specific teachers, schools, or school districts.

working portfolios   Ongoing collections of a student's work samples focused chiefly on the improvement, over time, in a student's self-evaluated skills.

writing sample   A student-generated composition intended to allow inferences about a student's writing abilities.

Index

A

Abedi, Jamal, 145–146
Absence-of-bias, 128, 134–135, 137, 149
Absolute grading, 398–399
Accessibility, 143, 144
Accommodations, 142–143
Accountability. *See* High-stakes test
Accuracy of content, 267
Achieve, 55
Achievement tests, 19, 22, 28, 43, 73, 114. *See also* Consequences; Standardized tests; Test preparation
  evaluation, teacher, 358–361
  formative assessment, 303
  high-stakes test, 63–64
  influence on instruction, 245, 255, 260, 287
  internal consistency reliability evidence, 84–86
  labels, 397
  measurement errors, 90
  No Child Left Behind (NCLB), 293
  test-retest correlation, 76, 79
  validity based on internal structure, 114, 119, 123
ACT, 310, 334–337
Actionability, 340
Adequate yearly progress (AYP), 140–141, 370
  English language learners (ELLs), 144
Adoption rate, formative assessment, 301–303
Advanced, 397
AERA. *See* American Educational Research Association
AERA-APA-NCME standards, 384
Affective assessment, 41
  anonymity, importance of, 257–258
  attitudinal targets, 249
  behavior, predicting, 248
  in classrooms, 252
  conduct and dispositions, 264
  detractors, 247
  focusing instruction, 245–246
  importance, 244–245
  inferences, 260–261
  interest targets, 249–250
  Likert inventories, 252–253
  multifocus affective inventories, 254–257
  parents, 259
  self-report, 252–259
  students' status, 246–247
  teacher assessment, 360–361
  teachers' need to know, 261–262
  timing, 258–259
  value targets, 250–251
Alignment, 57–58, 334
Alignment leniency, 380
Alternate assessment, 205
Alternate-form reliability, 78, 82–84, 86, 87
Alternative length multiple-choice items, 169
Ambiguity
  constructed-response questions, 182–183
  selected-response tests, 157
American Association for the Advancement of Science, 55
American Educational Research Association (AERA), 9, 75
American Psychological Association (APA), 9, 75, 373–374
Analytic scoring, 211–212
Analytic writing appraisals, 185, 191–193
Anonymity-enhancement procedures
  importance in affective assessment, 257–258
  in scoring essay responses, 197
Answer positions, 169–170
APA. *See* American Psychological Association
Aptitude, 28, 376–377, 380
  grading based on, 400
  tests, 28
Army Alpha, 374
Army testing, 373–374
Artistry, content standards, 397–398

Assessment
  affective, 41
  clarifying curriculum, 65–66
  clarifying instructional intentions, 22–24
  classroom, standards-based, 41–43
  classroom instruments, creating, 25–26
  cognitive, 41
  curricular aims, 36–40
  decision-driven, 35–36
  definition of, 12
  evaluating teachers, 20–22
  fairness and, 127
  federal mandates, 2–9
  grades, assigning, 17–18
  influencing public perceptions, 19–20
  instructional decision making, 28–30
  instructional effectiveness, evaluating own, 18–19
  instructional inertia, 68–69
  instruction and, 63–65
  interpreting standardized test results, 26, 28
  items, 66–68
  for learning, 288–289
  literacy, 27
  non-state tests, 58–60
  norm-referenced versus criterion-referenced, 43–45
  psychomotor, 41
  reliability, 74–79
  responses, selected and constructed, 46–47
  reviewing with colleagues, 61
  science, 55–56
  Standards for Educational and Psychological Testing, 9–10
  state accountability tests, 56–58
  states' official curricular aims, 47–54
  student progress, monitoring, 15–17, 29

Assessment (*Continued*)
  student status, determining, 14–15
  teachers' need to know about, 1–2, 14–30
  testing versus, 10–13
  validity, primary importance of, 97
  what to assess, 34–35
Assessment accommodations, 142–143
Assessment-based grading. *See* Grading
Assessment bias. *See* Fairness
Assessment blueprints, 60–61
Assessment literacy, 27
Assessment task, 188, 205–210
Attitudinal targets, 249
Australia, 299
Authentic assessment, 205
AYP. *See* Adequate yearly progress

B
Backlash against Common Core, 57
Balance of representation, 112
Basic, 397
Behavior, predicting, 248
Behavioral objectives, 38
Behaviors, 46
Benchmark assessments, 290
Betebenner, D. W., 370–371
Bias review panels, 134
Bill and Melinda Gates Foundation, 7
Binary-choice items, 162–164
Black, Paul, 16–17, 288, 292–294, 300, 301
Blanks
  limiting in constructed-response tests, 183–184
  positioning in constructed-response tests, 183
Blind scoring, 364
Bloom, B. S., 41
Blueprints, 60–61
Bodies of enabling knowledge, 295, 327
Braun, H. I., 382
Brevity, 174
Broadfoot, P. M., 289
Brookhart, Susan, 390–392
Bush, George W., 3

C
California Achievement Tests, 43
Carter, Mark A., 227
Categorical concurrence, 112
CCSS. *See* Common Core State Standards

CCSSO. *See* Council of Chief State School Officers
Celebration portfolios, 234
Center on Education Policy, 54
Central tendency, 312
Central-tendency error, 222
CGM. *See* Complete Goal Mastery
Chappuis, J., 17
Chronological age, 28
Classification, 326
Classification-consistency approach to reliability, 80–82
Classroom assessment
  affective assessment, 252
  evidence, 359, 361–366
  instruments, creating, 25–26
  portfolio assessment, 228–229
  standards-based, 41–43
  state-approved testing and, 9
Clues, unintended, 157
Clusters
  mathematics standards, 52
  multiple binary choice tests, 165
Cognitive assessment, 41
Cognitive demand, 60
Cognitive subskills, 295
Coleman, David, 334
Colleagues, 61
Collection, 258
College Board, 334
College placement exams, 30, 332–337
Collegial judgments, 268–269
Colorado Growth Model, 370–371
Common Core State Standards (CCSS), 5, 7–9
  assessments, 133
  curricular aims, 48–51
  English Language arts, 51–52
  mathematics, 52–54
  teacher accountability tests, 367
Complete Goal Mastery (CGM), 402
Complex syntax, 160–161
Computer-adaptive assessment, 158–160
Computer-based assessment, 11–12
Computer usage, 137
  electronic record keeping for grades, 404
  grade record keeping, 404
  selected-response tests, 155
  selected-response tests, adaptive assessment, 158–160
  testing with constructed-response items, 181
Concise responses, 183

Conduct, 264
Conferences
  parent (*See* Parents)
  portfolio assessment, 233
  students, 404–406
Consequences
  diploma denial, 23, 132
  evaluation, teacher, 358–361
  high-stakes testing, 63–64, 128–129
Consequential validity, 121
Consistency. *See* Reliability
Constructed responses, 179
Constructed-response tests, 180–181
  blanks, 183–184
  concise responses, 183
  direct questions, 182–183
  essay items, creating, 184–190
  essay items, scoring, 190–197
  evaluating with rubrics, 201
  linear equality, 184
  options, 189
  previewing responses, 189–190
  short-answer items, 181–184
  teachers, importance to, 198–199
  time-limit and item-value guidance, 188–189
Construct-irrelevant variance, 100–101
Construct-related evidence of validity, 121
Content standards, 36–37, 42, 105–106, 267
Content underrepresentation, 100
Convergent evidence of validity, 119
Coordinating items with stem, 165–166
Correlation coefficient
  alternate-form consistency, 83
  aptitude test scores, 117, 118, 336
  item-discrimination statistic, 273
  reliability and, 78–79, 94
Council of Chief State School Officers (CCSSO), 5, 49
  children with disabilities, 143
Covert skills and knowledge, 126
Criterion-referenced measurement
  item analysis, 277–279
  judging tests, 69–70
  norm-referenced assessment versus, 43–45
Criterion-related evidence of validity, 116, 121
Criterion variable, 116
Cronbach, Lee J., 86, 115

Cronbach's *coefficient alpha*, 86, 115
Current-form test preparation, 347, 348
Curricular aim, 98
  artistry of creators, 397–398
  assessment, 36–40, 203
  defined, 37
  report cards, 392, 393–394, 410
  student status and responses to performance assessment, 207
  teacher assessment, 359
  from testing, 99, 106
  test preparation, 345–346
Curriculum, 37
  clarifying for assessment, 65–66
  diagnostic tests and, 328–329, 334
Curriculum and Evaluation Standards for School Mathematics, 42

D

Data-driven education, 287
Data literacy, 27
Daugherty, R., 289
Decision-driven assessment, 35–36
Decision time
  biology assessment, 206–207
  buttressing accountability tests, 365
  developmentally appropriate instruction, 21
  effort, rewarding, 401
  group-influenced grading, 101–102
  holistic versus analytic writing appraisals, 185
  kindergartners' attitudes, 246
  multiple-guess test items, 172
  on-demand assessment, 38
  self-evaluation in portfolio assessment, 231
  Spanish-language testing, 131
  standardized tests, choosing, 311
  surprise quizzes, reliability of, 81
  teaching or the test, 276
Degree of emphasis, 383
Depth of Knowledge (DOK) categories, Webb's, 60–61, 112
Desai, Laura E., 227
Descriptions, 175
Descriptive feedback, 398
Descriptive rigor, 221
Developing Goal Mastery (DGM), 402

Developmentally appropriate instruction, 21
DGM. *See* Developing Goal Mastery
Dichotomous items, 86
DIF. *See* Differential item functioning procedures
Differential affluence, 137–138
Differential item functioning (DIF) procedures, 136, 153
Difficult vocabulary, 161–162
Difficulty, 380
Difficulty indices, 271–272
Digital assessments, 181
Diploma denial, 23, 128–129, 132
Directions
  anonymity in affective assessment, 258
  selected-response tests, 156–157
Direct questions, 182–183
Discriminating items, 273
Disparate impact, 131–133, 136, 150–151
Disposition, 264
Distractor analyses, 277
Distribution, 312
Documentation of student progress, 234
DOK. *See* Depth of Knowledge categories, Webb's
Domains, 52
Double-concept items, 163

E

Easiness, 380
Ebel, R. L., 274–275
Educational accountability, 63
Educational defensibility, 345–347
Educational standards movement, 41–42
Educational Testing Service (ETS), 310, 334
Education for All Handicapped Children Act (P.L. 94-142), 139–141
Effectiveness, instructional, 18–19
Effort, student, 400–401
Electronic devices. *See* Computer usage
Elementary and Secondary Education Act (ESEA) of 1965, 2–3, 144, 367
Elementary school grading priorities, 396
Empirical evidence, 153

Empirical item-improvement strategies, 179
Empirically based improvement procedures, 270–277, 283
Employment
  pretest/posttest scheme, 362
  summative assessment, 369
English language arts, 51–52
English language learners (ELLs), 144–145
ESEA. *See* Elementary and Secondary Education Act of 1965
ESSA. *See* Every Student Succeeds Act
Essay items
  creating for constructed-response tests, 184–190
  scoring in constructed-response tests, 190–197
ETS. *See* Educational Testing Service
Evaluating
  constructed-response tests with rubrics, 201
  grading, 402–404
  performance assessment, 204
  portfolios, 237
Evaluation, teacher, 20–22, 119, 357
  classroom assessment evidence, 361–366
  consequences, 358–361
  external accountability tests, 367–382
  grading versus, 356–357
  instructional insensitivity, 373–381
  instructional sensitivity, 372–373, 388
  parents, 378–379
  pretests versus posttests, 362–363
  split-and-switch design, 363–366
  student affect, 366
  student growth percentiles, 370–371
  student test performance, 382–384
  teachers', 357
  teachers' need to know, 384–385
  value-added models (VAM) for student progress, 381–382
Every Student Succeeds Act (ESSA), 3–5
  alignment issues, 112
  English language learners (ELLs), 144–145

Every Student Succeeds
Act (*Continued*)
high-stakes testing, 342
significance of SAT and ACT, 332
special education, 141
Evidence
assessment fairness, 153
based on response processes, 113
of effectiveness, 64
formative assessment, 286–287
grading students, 405–406
validity, 102–105
validity based on relations to
other variables, 115–118
of validity based on test content,
105–113
validity based on test's internal
structure, 114–115
Excellent, 397
Extended-response item, 187
External accountability tests,
367–382
External reviews, 109–112

F

Face validity, 120–121
Fairness, 127–128, 267
assessment bias, 128–131
children with disabilities,
139–144
classroom bias detection,
136–139
disparate impact, 131–133
empirical approaches, 136
English language learners
(ELLs), 144–147
evidence, 153
as important evaluative factor,
147–149
judgmental approaches, 133–136
scoring, 222–223
teachers' need to know about,
149–151
Farr, Roger, 229
Federal law. *See* Elementary
and Secondary Education
Act (ESEA) of 1965; Every
Student Succeeds Act (ESSA);
No Child Left Behind Act
(NCLB)
assessment, 2–9
Education for All Handicapped
Children Act (P.L. 94-142),
139–141
Individuals with Disabilities
Education Act (IDEA), 140, 143

Fitzpatrick, R., 203
Focusing instruction, affective
assessment, 245–246
Formative assessment, 16, 284–285
adjustments, 287
adoption, slow rate of, 301–303
assessment for learning versus,
288–289
evidence, 286–287
instruction, thinking about,
287–288
learning progressions, 294–299
as means-ends game, 299–301
origins of term, 285–286
parents, 302
as process, 285, 289–290, 308
research, 291–294
of teachers, 388
teachers' need to know about,
303–304
Formative teacher evaluations, 357
Freedom, 250
Frisbie, D. A., 274–275

G

Gaps, content, 267
Gardner, H., 376
Gardner, J., 289
Generalizability dilemma, 207–209
Generalized test-taking
preparation, 347, 348
Gipps, C. V., 289
Glaser, Robert, 45
Goal-attainment
choosing evidence, 394–395, 410
grade, setting, 395–396
steps for grading, 392–396, 410
students' choices, 405
weighting evidence, 395, 410
Go/no go decisions, 286
Grade-equivalent scores, 316–320,
324
Grading
absolute, 398–399
aptitude-based, 400
assigning, 17–18
electronic record keeping, 404
versus evaluation, teacher,
356–357
evaluative factors, 402–404
goal-attainment, steps of,
392–396, 410
imprecision, 406
letter grades, 396–397
numerical grades, 397
parents, talking with, 405

purpose of, 389–396
relative, 399–400
social skills, 402
standards-based report cards,
397–398
student effort, 400–401
student-involved conferences,
404–406
study skills, 402
teachers' need to know, 406–407
Grain size, 40, 297
Grants, 21
Great Britain, 288–289
Group-focused inferences, 260
Group-focused interpretation,
standardized test scores,
312–313
Group-influenced grading, 101–102

H

Halo effect, 222
Harrison, C., 16–17
High school grading priorities, 396
High-stakes test, 22–23
educational accountability, 63–64
preparation, 341–343
Holistic scoring, 211–212
Holistic versus analytic writing
appraisals
choosing, 191–193
decision time, 185
Homogeneous matching items,
172–174
Honesty, 250
Hypergeneral rubric, 201, 215–216

I

IEA. *See* International Association
for the Evaluation of
Educational Achievement
Improvement, in formative
assessment, 286
Inadequate Goal Mastery (IGM),
402
Incomplete statements, 182–183
Individual interpretation
diagnostic tests, 327
standardized test scores,
314–325, 340
Individualized education program
(IEP), 140–142
Individuals with Disabilities
Education Act (IDEA), 140,
143
Inertia, assessment, 69
Inference, 98

Informal appraisals, 12–13
Informational text, 51
Inherited aptitudes, 376–377
In loco parentis, 344
Instruction, 37
  affective assessment focusing, 245–246
  assessment, 28–30
  and assessment, 63–65
  diagnostic tests, 327–328
  effectiveness, evaluating, 18–19
  formative assessment, 287–288
  intentions, clarifying through assessment, 22–24
  standards and goals, 407
Instructional goals, 36–37
Instructional inertia, 68–69
Instructional insensitivity, 373–381
Instructionally diagnostic tests, 326–331
Instructional payoff, 325
Instructional sensitivity, 372–373, 388
Integrity, 250
Intelligence quotient (IQ), 28
Interest targets, 249–250
Interim assessments, 290
Internal consistency reliability evidence, 78, 84–88, 86
Internal structure, 104
International Association for the Evaluation of Educational Achievement (IEA), 59
Interpretation, of test results, 98
Inter-rater reliability, 115
Iowa Tests of Basic Skills, 43
IRT. *See* Item response theory
Item alternatives, 167–171, 175, 179
Item analysis
  criterion-referenced measurement, 277–279
  reviewing your own assessment procedures, 269
  student questionnaire, 269–270
Item difficulty (*p* value), 283
  distractor analysis, 277
  misunderstandings, 283
  teacher-developed assessments, 274, 283
Item-discrimination indices, 272–276
Item distractors, 167, 169, 277
Item flaws, 380
Item-length similarity, maintaining, 164

Item response theory (IRT), 84, 321–322, 325
Items
  assessment, 66–68
  selected-response tests, writing, 155–162
  sufficiency in diagnostic tests, 329
Item-value guidance, 188–189

J
James, Mary, 288–289
Johnson, Lyndon B., 2
Judgment
  assessment fairness, 153
  report cards, 402
  test validity and, 123
Judgmental appraisal, 204
Judgmental item improvement, 265–270
Justice, 250

K
Kennedy, Robert F., 3
Kuder-Richardson procedures (K-R formulae), 86

L
Labels, 120–121
Lacuna, 267
Language, 51
Large-scale accountability programs, 230
Learning, assessment for, 288–289
Learning outcomes, 36–37
Learning progressions, 294–299
Lee, C., 16–17
Letter grades, 396–397
Likert, Rensis, 252–253
Likert inventories, 252–253
Limited English proficient (LEP), 144
Lindquist, E. F., 335
Linear equality, 184
Literacy, 27, 51
Literature, 51

M
Marshall, B., 16–17
Marzano, Robert, 215–216
Mastery-status grade, 402–403
Matching items, 172–176
McMillan, J. H., 235
Mean scores, 312
Measurement
  assessment versus, 13
  measurability, 39
Measurement-driven instruction, 64

Mechanics, 195–196
Median scores, 312
Middle school grading priorities, 396
Morrison, E. J., 203
Motivation, grades and, 391
Multifocus affective inventories, 254–257
Multiple binary-choice items, 164–166
Multiple-choice items, 166–172, 179

N
National Academy of Science, 56
National Assessment of Educational Progress (NAEP), 58–60, 397
National Council of Teachers of Mathematics (NCTM), 42
National Council on Measurement in Education (NCME), 9, 75
National Governors Association (NGA), 5
National Research Council, 55
National Science Teachers Association, 55
NCE. *See* Normal curve equivalent
Needs improvement, 397
Negatively discriminating item, 273
Negatives, minimizing, 163
New Zealand, 299
Next Generation Science Standards (NGSS), 55–56
No Child Left Behind Act (NCLB), 3–4
  adequate yearly progress (AYP), 370
  alignment issues, 127
  descriptive labels in grading, 397
  formative assessment, interest in, 293, 308
  grants, 21
  high-stakes testing, 342
  special education, 140–141
Nondiscriminating item, 273
Non-state assessment tests, 58–60
Normal curve equivalent (NCE), 322–323
Norm-referenced assessment, 43–45
Numerical grades, 397

O
Obama, Barack, 3
Observations, 219–220
O'Connor, Ken, 391, 402
Offensiveness, as assessment bias, 129–130

"Of-the-above" alternatives, 170–172
Opportunity to learn, 133
Oral communication performance test, 213
Organization for Economic Cooperation and Development (OECD), 59
Overall absence-of-bias judgment, 135–136
Overt responses to tests, 126

P
Paper-and-pencil tests. *See* Constructed-response tests
Paper testing, 11
PARCC. *See* Partnership for the Assessment of Readiness for College and Careers
Parents
    affective assessment, 259
    assessment, explaining, 29–30
    assessment bias, 138
    content standards, 117–118
    curricular aims, 393
    educational standards, 48
    essay tests, 196
    evaluation, teacher, 378–379
    formative assessment, 302
    grading, elements, 405
    multiple-choice items, 175
    performance assessment, 224
    portfolio assessment, 233, 241
    reliability of standardized test, 85–86
    standardized test scores, 311, 319, 333
    teacher-developed assessments, 278
    test preparation practices, 349–350
Partnership for the Assessment of Readiness for College and Careers (PARCC), 8, 367, 368
Pellegrino, James, 56
Percentiles, 314–316, 324
Performance assessment, 67, 202–205. *See also* Constructed-response test
    appropriate use of, 226
    generalizability dilemma, 207–209
    parent talk, 224
    ratings and observations, 219–220
    rubrics, hypergeneral, 215–216

rubrics, role of, 210–213
rubrics, skill-focused, 216–219
rubrics, task-specific, 214–215
scoring errors, sources of, 220–223
tasks, 209
tasks, identifying, 205–210
teachers' need to know about, 223
teacher time, 210
Performance standard, 42
Per-item absence-of-bias judgment, 134–135
Personal-bias errors, 221–222
Pet peeves, 119
PIRLS (Progress in International Reading Literacy Study), 59
PISA (Programme for International Student Assessment), 59
Polytomous items, 86
Popham, W. James, 45, 73, 96, 126, 153, 179, 201, 226, 243, 264, 283, 308, 340, 355, 388, 410
Portfolio assessment, 66, 205, 227–228
    appraisal, 237
    classroom applications, 228–229
    key elements, 231–234
    large-scale accountability programs, 230
    parent talk, 241
    pros and cons, 237–239
    purposeful portfolios, 234–235
    self-evaluation, 229–230, 231
    versus standardized testing, 228
    sustainable focus, finding, 243
    teachers' need to know about, 240
    work-sample selection, 236
Positively discriminating item, 273
Posttests versus pretests, 362–363
Practice standards, in mathematics, 52–53
Preassessment, 15
Precision
    alternate-form evidence, 82–84, 87
    defined, 76
    importance to teachers, 91–93, 96
    internal consistency evidence, 84–88
    overview, 74–79
    standard error of measurement (SEM), 88–91
    test-retest evidence, 80–82, 87
Premises, 172

Previewing responses, 189–190
Previous-form test preparation, 347, 348
Prioritizing, 43, 73
    standards-based report cards, 398
Procedural flaws, 221
Products, 46
Professional ethics guideline, 344–345
Professional judgment, reliability coefficient, 79
Professional learning community, 262
Proficient, 397
Progress, monitoring, 15–17, 29
Prompt, 188
Psychometricians, 374
Psychomotor assessment, 41
Public perceptions, 19–20
Purposeful portfolios, 234–235
P value (item difficulty)
    distractor analysis, 277
    misunderstandings, 283
    teacher-developed assessments, 274, 283

Q
Quality standards
    items in diagnostic tests, 329–330
    prespecified, in performance assessment, 204
Quartile, 415

R
Race to the Top Program, 21, 368
Range-of-knowledge correspondence, 112
Range of students' scores, 312
Ratings, 219–220
Raw score, 171
    grade-equivalent, 316–318
    groups, 312–313
    scales, 320–322, 324
Reactive, 279, 362, 364
Reading, 51, 250
Readi Step, 334
Regression effect, 363
Related-measures study, 118–119
Relations to other variables, 104
Relative grading, 399–400
Reliability, 74–75
    alternate-form evidence, 82–84, 87
    defined, 76
    on essay tests, 196
    importance to teachers, 91–93, 96

internal consistency evidence, 84–88
overview, 74–79
standard error of measurement (SEM), 88–91
test-retest evidence, 80–82, 87
and validity, 122
Reliability coefficient, 76
Research, 291–294
Response categories, balancing, 163
Response processes, 104
Response restrictions, 258
Responses, 172
  assessment, 46–47
  extra, 174
  ordering, 175
  previewing in constructed-response tests, 189–190
Restricted-response item, 187
Rubrics
  evaluating constructed-response tests with, 201
  hypergeneral, performance assessment and, 215–216
  portfolio assessment, 243
  role in performance assessment, 210–213
  skill-focused and performance assessment, 216–219
  task-specific in performance assessment, 214–215

S

Same-format test preparation, 347–349
Same-page formatting, 176
Sanders, William, 381
SAT, 310, 332–334
Satisfactory, 397
SBAC. *See* Smarter Balanced Assessment Consortium
Scale scores, 320–325
Scholastic predictor tests, 116–117, 129
Science assessment, 55–56
Score spread, 374, 377
Scoring
  ease, 330–331
  errors, 220–223
  essay items in constructed-response tests, 190–197
  inferences, 267
  Likert inventories, 253
  multifocus affective inventories, 257
  short-answer items, 182

Scoring rubrics. *See* Rubrics
Scriven, M., 285–286
Selected-response tests, 154–155, 179
  ambiguous statements, 157
  binary-choice items, 162–164
  complex syntax, 160–161
  computer-adaptive assessment, 158–160
  coordinating items with stem, 165–166
  defined, 179
  difficult vocabulary, 161–162
  directions, opaque, 156–157
  double-concept items, avoiding, 163
  electronic options, 155
  item-length similarity, maintaining, 164
  items, rules for writing, 155–162
  matching items, 172–176
  multiple binary-choice items, 164–166
  multiple-choice items, 166–172
  negatives, minimizing, 163
  response categories, balancing, 163
  separating clusters, 165
  teachers' need to know, 176–177
  thoughtfulness, eliciting, 162–163
  unintended clues, 157
Self-evaluation, portfolio, 229–230, 231, 232
Self-report inventories, 252–262, 361
SEM. *See* Standard error of measurement
Separating clusters, 165
SES. *See* Socioeconomic status
Shepard, L., 289
Short-answer items, 181–184
Showcase portfolios, 229, 241
Showcasing student accomplishments, 234
Skill-focused rubric, 201, 216–219
Skills, 327
Smarter Balanced Assessment Consortium (SBAC), 8, 310, 367, 368
Socially desirable responses, 257
Social skills grading, 402
Socioeconomic status (SES)
  insensitive achievement tests, 382
  instructional sensitivity, 372–373

items learned outside school, 375
links, 380
test score spread, 374, 376, 378–379
Spanish-language testing, 131
Spatial aptitude, 377
Speaking and listening, 51
Specialists, subject-matter, 42–43
Split-and-switch design, 363–366
Squishy, 58
Stability reliability, 80
Standard deviation, 312–313
Standard error of measurement (SEM), 88–91
Standardized achievement tests, 45
Standardized tests, 310–312
  portfolio assessment versus, 228
  scores, assessing (*See* Standardized test scores)
Standardized test scores
  ACT, 334–337
  college placement exams, 332–337
  grade-equivalent scores, 316–320, 324
  group-focused interpretation, 312–313
  individual interpretation, 314–325, 340
  instructionally diagnostic tests, 326–331
  instructional payoff, 325
  interpreting, 26, 28
  labels, 397
  parents, 311, 319, 333
  percentiles, 314–316, 324
  SAT, 332–334
  scale scores, 320–325
  teachers' need to know about, 309–310, 337–338
Standards, 42
  report cards, 397–398
  science, 52
Standards for Educational and Psychological Testing, 9–10, 75–77, 80
  fairness, 127, 147
  old terms, resilience of, 121
  response processes, 113
  validity, 98–99, 104
Stanford Achievement Tests, 374
Stanine, 323
States
  assessment, 56–58
  Common Core adoption and assessment, 8–9

States (*Continued*)
  official curricular aims, 47–54
  state-wide testing, 310–311
  teacher accountability testing, 368–369
Stem
  coordinating items with, 165–166
  defined, 179
  negatively stated, 168–169
  stuffing, 168
Stiggins, Richard, 17, 234, 239, 288
Stobart, G., 289
Strengths, 327
Student progress
  assessments, monitoring, 15–17, 29
  value-added models (VAM) for, 381–382
Students
  affect, 366 (*See also* Affective assessment)
  assessment literacy, 27
  attitudes, 36
  in conferences, 404–406
  effort, 400–401
  formative assessment and, 287
  growth percentile, 370–371
  judgments, 269–270
  "ownership" of portfolios, 231–232
  status, 14–15, 343–344
  test performance, 382–384
Study skills, 402
Subject interest, 249
Summative assessment, 286
Summative teacher evaluations, 357, 369
Sutton, Ruth, 289
Synthesis and Evaluation, 61

T
Target curricular aim, 295
Tasks, identifying, 205–210
Task-specific rubric, 201, 214–215
Taxonomy of Educational Objectives, 41, 60
Teacher-developed assessments
  collegial judgments, 268–269
  difficulty indices, 271–272
  distractor analyses, 277
  empirically based improvement procedures, 270–277, 283
  improving, 265–266
  item analysis, criterion-referenced measurement, 277–279
  item-discrimination indices, 272–276

  judging your own instruments, 266–268
  judgmental item improvement, 283
  parents, talking with, 278
  p value (item difficulty), 283
  student judgments, 269–270
  teachers' need to know, 280–281
Teacher evaluation. *See* Evaluation, teacher
Teachers
  to constructed-response tests, 198–199
  formative assessment and, 287
  performance assessment, 210
  personal-bias errors, 221–222
  time, performance tests and, 210
Teachers' need to know
  about formative assessment, 303–304
  affective assessment, 261–262
  evaluation, teacher, 384–385
  grading, 406–407
  performance assessment, 223
  portfolio assessment, 240
  reliability/precision, 91–93, 96
  selected-response tests, 176–177
  standardized test scores, 309–310, 337–338
  teacher-developed assessments, 280–281
  test preparation, 352–353
  for validity, 97–101, 122–123
Teaching to the test, 350–352, 355
Technology, interest in, 250
Tennessee Value-Added Assessment System (TVAAS), 381
Tentative scoring key, 193–195
Test-based inference, 47
Test-based teacher evaluation, 367
Test blueprint. *See* Assessment blueprint
Test content validity, 104
Test–criterion relationship, 116–118
Test preparation, 341
  current-form preparation, 347, 348
  educational defensibility, 345–347
  generalized test-taking preparation, 347, 348
  high-stakes assessment, 341–343
  parents, 349–350
  previous-form preparation, 347, 348
  professional ethics, 344–345

  same-format preparation, 347–349
  students' status, 343–344
  teachers' need to know about, 352–353
  teaching to the test, 350–352, 355
  varied-format preparation, 348, 349
Test-retest reliability, 78, 80–82, 86, 87
Tests
  assessment versus, 10–13
  external accountability, 367–382
  formative assessment, 303
  formative assessment versus, 285
Test-score-based teacher evaluation, 119
Thoughtfulness, eliciting selected-response tests, 162–163
Tierney, Robert J., 227
Time
  limit on constructed-response tests, 188–189
  teachers', performance tests and, 210
Timing affective assessment, 258–259
TIMSS (Trends in International Mathematics and Science Study), 59
Title I, 3
True–false item, 162, 179, 181
  length similarity, 164
  multiple, 166
  negatives, minimizing, 163
  sample flawed, 281
TVAAS. *See* Tennessee Value-Added Assessment System
Typical performance, in affective assessment, 260

U
Unfair penalization, 130–131
Unintended clues, 157
Unintended side effects of instruction, 360–361
Unitary measurability, 39
Universal design, 144
U.S. Department of Education, 4

V
Validity
  alignment, 112–113
  convergent and discriminant evidence, 118–120
  evidence, 102–105

evidence based on relations to other variables, 115–118
evidence based on response processes, 113
evidence based on test content, 105–113
evidence based on test's internal structure, 114–115
external reviews, 109–112
importance of, 97–101
reliability and, 122
requisites, 126
sanctioned and unsanctioned labels, 120–121

teachers' need for, 97–101, 122–123
Validity argument, 103
Value-added model (VAM), 381–382
Value targets, 250–251
Variables, 12
Varied-format test preparation, 348, 349
Verbal descriptors, in grading, 397
Vermont Portfolio Assessment Program, 230, 237
Versus evaluation, teacher, 356–357
Vertical scale, 322

W
Weaknesses, of diagnostic tests, 327
Webb, Norman, 60–61, 112–113
Wiliam, Dylan, 16–17, 288, 292–294, 300, 301, 308
Working portfolios, 229
Work-sample selection for portfolios, 232, 236
World War I, 374
Wormeli, R., 400
Writing, 51, 195–196
analytic versus holistic appraisals, 185
Writing sample, 184